High-Powered Investing

ALL-IN-ONE

FOR DUMMIES®

A Wiley Brand

2nd Edition

by Jason W. Best; Amine Bouchentouf;
Zak Cassady-Dorion; Brian Dolan;
Joe Duarte, MD; Janet Haley;
Faleel Jamaldeen, DBA; Ann C. Logue, MBA;
Paul Mladjenovic; Sherwood Neiss; Optionetics;
Kerry Pechter; Barbara Rockefeller;
Peter J. Sander, MBA; and Russell Wild, MBA

FOR DUMMIES®
A Wiley Brand

High-Powered Investing All-in-One For Dummies,® 2nd Edition

Published by:
John Wiley & Sons, Inc.,
111 River Street,
Hoboken, NJ 07030-5774,
www.wiley.com

For general information on our other products and services, please contact our Customer Care Department within the U.S. at 877-762-2974, outside the U.S. at 317-572-3993, or fax 317-572-4002. For technical support, please visit www.wiley.com/techsupport.

Wiley publishes in a variety of print and electronic formats and by print-on-demand. Some material included with standard print versions of this book may not be included in e-books or in print-on-demand. If this book refers to media such as a CD or DVD that is not included in the version you purchased, you may download this material at http://booksupport.wiley.com. For more information about Wiley products, visit www.wiley.com.

Library of Congress Control Number: 2013952424

ISBN 978-1-118-72467-4 (pbk); ISBN 978-1-118-75599-0 (ebk); ISBN 978-1-118-75613-3 (ebk)

Manufactured in the United States of America

10 9 8 7 6 5 4 3 2 1

Contents at a Glance

Table of Contents

Book IX: Crowdfund Investing 573

Introduction

● ●

Many investors are perfectly satisfied with the more traditional invest-ing opportunities: They build solid portfolios containing individual stocks and bonds, mutual and exchange-traded funds, and so forth, and are generally content to let investment counselors manage their accounts. Other investors, however, prefer to take a more active role: Perhaps they want to manage their accounts themselves or broaden their investment horizons (and increase their potential returns) by delving into more volatile markets.

As an investor, you can be as aggressive as your personality and bank account allow. To be successful, however, you need more than the right atti-tude or a boatload of cash. You need information, and that's what this book tries to give you. *High-Powered Investing All-in-One For Dummies,* 2nd edition, is a book written specifically for experienced investors who want to pursue and manage more aggressive investment vehicles.

About This Book

The key to successfully expanding your investment opportunities is, of course, information. This book introduces you to high-powered investing techniques and options you can pursue as you expand your portfolio — all in plain English. Whether you're just beginning to explore more advanced investing or have been dabbling in it for a while but need strategies to increase your success, this book can give you the information you want. For example, you can find

- ✔ **What your high-powered investing or trading options are:** A whole series of investment opportunities go beyond the traditional stocks and bonds. You can trade commodities, foreign currencies, and futures and options, all of which require a more hands-on approach. If you're well-heeled, you may decide that hedge funds — private investment partnerships — are the way to go. You can find information on all these vehicles in this book.

- ✔ **Keys to being a successful trader:** Investing and trading are vastly dif-ferent. With the former, you buy and hold with the expectation that your returns will increase over time as the value of the security goes up. With the latter, your success depends on how accurately you're able to read the market and how quickly you can react to fluctuations. Nearly all the higher-end investment options covered in this book — currencies, commodities, futures, and options — rely to a greater or lesser extent on these trading skills.

✔ **How to value a business or spot pricing trends:** One key to being a successful investor is knowing how to get the information you need to make good — and timely — decisions. When the value of the underlying security is important, you need to know how to evaluate it. When being able to recognize market trends is the key to success, you have to know how to forecast them.

This updated edition of *High-Powered Investing All-in-One For Dummies* gives you the information and answers you need to incorporate these investing strategies and options into your own personal investing style. Even if you don't adopt most of the principles and techniques described in this book, your awareness of them will make you a better investor.

Unless you're going to become a professional trader (rather than simply an empowered personal investor), you probably don't need to know everything in this book. You can bypass paragraphs with a Technical Stuff icon, which highlights esoteric details that not everyone has the stomach or time for, and sidebars, for those dizzyingly technical explanations that go on for more than a paragraph (and don't they usually?). Neither are vital to your ability to ramp up your investing strategy.

Within this book, you may also note that some web addresses break across two lines of text. If you're reading this book in print and want to visit one of these web pages, simply key in the web address exactly as it's noted in the text, pretending as though the line break doesn't exist. If you're reading this as an e-book, you have it easy — just click the web address to be taken directly to the web page.

Foolish Assumptions

Aggressive or high-end investing options aren't an ideal fit (or a good option) for everyone, and *High-Powered Investing All-in-One For Dummies, 2nd Edition*, was written with a particular reader in mind. Here's what we assume about you:

✔ You're fairly familiar with basic investments and have some experience in the world of investing. You know what the markets are, for example, and have already bought and sold some securities.

✔ You want to expand your investment options to include more than the traditional stocks and bonds.

✔ You want to become a more active trader and make money more consistently by letting your profits run and cutting your losses short.

✔ You have enough investment capital that you can safely invest in more volatile markets or participate in a hedge fund.

✔ You understand basic market forecasting strategies but want to know more about how to use technical analysis to anticipate and react to trends.

Icons Used in This Book

You'll see several icons scattered around the margins of the text. Here's the function of each:

This icon notes something you should keep in mind about the topic at hand. It may refer to something covered elsewhere in the book, or it may highlight something you need to know for future investing decisions.

Tip information tells you how to invest a little better, a little smarter, a little more efficiently. The information can help you ask better questions or make smarter moves with your money.

Plenty of things in the world of investing can cause you to make expensive mistakes. These points help you avoid big problems.

Here's where you'll find interesting but nonessential information. Whether this icon highlights background info, investment theories, or trivia, it's all skippable. Read it or pass it up as you like.

Beyond the Book

In addition to the material in the print or e-book you're reading right now, this product also comes with additional information you can access on the web. Check out the free Cheat Sheet at www.dummies.com/cheatsheet/highpoweredinvestingaio for information on important financial ratios, essential economic reports, and financial risk variables known as the Greeks.

Head to www.dummies.com/extras/highpoweredinvestingaio to find secrets that successful investors and traders use, tactics to help you align your investment portfolio with your values, strategies that let you take advantage of emerging markets and new technologies, tips that help you avoid costly mistakes, and more.

Where to Go from Here

Where you go from here depends entirely on you. If you're a start-at-the-beginning-and-read-through-to-the-end type of person, by all means, feel free to do just that. But you may find that picking and choosing topics of interest is more suited to your style. Fortunately, you can find what you're looking for in a number of ways. You can use the Table of Contents to find general discussions or the index to find specific topics. Or if you prefer, you can simply thumb through the pages and alight on whatever topic catches your eye. The bottom line? Use this book however you need to. If you're just beginning your foray into more advanced investing, however, you may want to begin with Book I, which contains basic information.

Book I
Getting Started with High-Powered Investing

getting started with

high-powered

investing

Chapter 1

What Every Investor Should Know

*I*f you're inclined to invest in the markets or engage in trading, you should be familiar with a few fundamentals, such as the different types of investments and investment strategies, what the risks are, who brokers are and what they do, and the indexes and exchanges you'll trade on.

Taking a Glance at Investment Options and Strategies

As an investor, you have a variety of options and strategies to choose from. The best choice for you depends on your financial goals, your investment preferences, and your tolerance for risk. Some tactics are suitable for all investors; others are geared more toward the experienced investor.

Surveying traditional investment vehicles

The investment vehicles mentioned in this section are those that, by and large, any investor — big or small, novice or experienced — can take advantage of. You may have some of these in your portfolio already. With these investments, you put your money down and hold on. Although you want to make changes as necessary to protect your investment, these types of investments can add ballast to more aggressive investment strategies (like trading and hedging; see the next section):

✔ **Stocks:** With stocks, you're buying ownership in a corporation (or company). If the corporation profits, you profit as well. Typically, investors buy stocks and hold them for a long time, making decisions along the way about reallocating investment capital as financial needs change, selling underperformers, and so on. For details on stock investing, head to Chapter 2 in Book I.

✔ **Bonds:** To raise money, governments, government agencies, municipalities, and corporations can sell bonds. When you buy a bond, you're essentially lending money to this entity for the promise of repayment in addition to a specified annual return. Although some entities are more reliable than others (the federal government isn't as likely as a company that's facing hard financial times to go bankrupt and renege on its obligations), bonds generally offer stability and predictability well beyond that of most other investments. To find out more about bonds, go to Book I, Chapter 2.

✔ **Mutual funds:** Simply put, a mutual fund is an investment company. Investors put money into that company, and an investment manager buys securities on behalf of all the investors. Those securities may include various types of stocks, various types of bonds, or both. If you invest in mutual funds, you have thousands of options to choose from, each representing a different mixture of securities. For all the details on mutual funds, see Chapter 3 of Book I.

✔ **Exchange-traded funds:** An exchange-traded fund (ETF) is basically a cross between an index mutual fund and a stock. Among the characteristics that make ETFs so compelling is the fact that they're cheap. Many ETFs carry total management expenses under 0.2 percent a year. Some of the larger ETFs carry management fees as low as 0.07 percent a year. The average mutual fund, in contrast, charges 1.3 percent a year. ETFs are also tax-smart. Because of the way they're structured, the taxes you pay on any growth are minimal. Chapter 3 of Book I gives an overview of ETFs.

✔ **Annuities:** Annuities are investments with money-back guarantees: You invest a certain amount of money for a promise that you'll get your money back, with interest, after (or over) a certain time period. The insurance company issuing the annuity is the one making the money-back guarantee, and the exact nature of the guarantee varies with the type of annuity. Also keep in mind that the guarantee is only as strong as the insurance company backing it. Book I, Chapter 4, has the details.

Considering high-end investment or speculation vehicles

Some higher-end investments aren't much different than traditional investments: You invest your money in stocks, bonds, mutual funds, or ETFs and make all the same decisions that an average investor does. The difference is the amount of capital in play (typically a lot) or the risk exposure (typically high). Other high-end investments are almost completely different beasts. You're not so much investing (buying and holding on) as you are *trading* or *speculating* — assuming a financial risk with the hope of profiting from market fluctuations. The following list outlines the not-so-traditional high-end investment vehicles you can find out about in this book:

- **Futures and options:** Although by nature they're complex financial instruments, futures and options provide you with leverage and risk management opportunities that your average financial instruments don't offer. If you can harness the power of these instruments, you can dramatically increase your leverage — and performance — in the markets. Book II explains investing in futures and options.

- **Commodities:** Commodities are the raw materials humans use to create a livable world: the agricultural products, mineral ores, and energy sources that are the essential building blocks of the global economy. The commodities markets are broad and deep, presenting both challenges and opportunities for experienced investors. Turn to Book III for details on trading commodities.

A lot of folks equate (incorrectly) commodities exclusively with the futures markets. Undoubtedly, the two are inextricably linked: The futures markets offer a way for commercial users to hedge against commodity price risks and a means for investors and traders to profit from this price risk. But equity markets are also deeply involved in commodities, as are a number of investment vehicles, such as master limited partnerships (MLPs), exchange-traded funds (ETFs), and commodity mutual funds.

- **Foreign currency trading:** When you get involved in foreign currency trading (sometimes called *forex* trading), you're essentially speculating on the value of one currency versus another. You "buy" a currency just as you'd buy any other financial security in the hope that it will make a profitable return. But the value of your security is particularly volatile because of the many factors that can affect a currency's value and the amazingly quick time frame in which these values can change. Nevertheless, if you're an active trader looking for alternatives to stocks or futures, the forex market is hard to beat. Find out more in Book IV.

Trading foreign currencies is a challenging and potentially profitable opportunity *for educated and experienced investors.* The leveraged nature of forex trading means that any market movement has an equally proportional effect on your deposited funds; this may work against you as well as for you.

- **Hedge funds:** Hedge funds are private partnerships that pursue high returns through multiple strategies and with relatively little regulation. Through hedge funds, you can net some high returns for your portfolio — if you don't mind the risk and have *a lot* of money to invest. Because of the risk and the investment criteria, hedge funds aren't open to most investors. To find out more about hedge funds, head to Book V.

✔ **Emerging markets:** A full 43 percent of the world's wealth is in nations that are emerging out of poverty and onto the world's financial and trade markets. Most of the world's people are in such countries as well — some 5.5 billion live in emerging, frontier, or pre-emerging markets. These markets are where the growth opportunities are now. The world's developing nations are growing faster than the developed ones. That faster growth can lead to higher profits than you may get from similar investments in the established markets found in North America, Western Europe, Australia, and Japan. Head to Book VI for details.

Investigating investment strategies

Regardless of what investment vehicle you choose — whether traditional, high-end, or a combination — you want to invest smart. And that means making good decisions about where to put your money and when to make a trade. The strategy you use depends on the particular investment vehicle. Sometimes, the dividing line between success and failure is knowing the value of the business or company you're putting your money in. Other times, the key component is recognizing a trend — what the market is doing or getting ready to do — so you can beat the crowd. The following list explains:

✔ **Value investing:** In value investing the key question is "What is something *really* worth?" You can round up all the buildings, trucks, pallet jacks, and PCs that a company owns, assign a value to each, and add it all up, but that still doesn't tell you what's really important about the business. What you want is a way to evaluate a business's intrinsic value. Value investing is about figuring out the intrinsic value of a business so that you can recognize when a business is undervalued: That's where the potential is. Book VII has the details.

✔ **Socially responsible investing:** Many people seek to align their investment options with their value systems and principles. Although your investment options are largely the same as any other investor's, you consider more than your returns when choosing which companies to invest in. You also pay attention to a company's culture, its products, and the impact it has in the larger community. Go to Book VIII to find out more.

✔ **Crowdfund investing:** In crowdfund investing, start-up businesses use social media sites like Facebook, Twitter, and LinkedIn to connect with and attract vast numbers of investors. Each of these investors then contributes a small portion of the investment capital the company needs. Because of the high failure rate of new businesses and to protect unsophisticated investors who may underestimate the risk, regulations limit who can invest via crowdfunding and how much they can contribute. For details on crowdfunding, head to Book IX.

✔ **Technical analysis:** Technical analysis (sometimes called *charting, market timing,* and *trend-following*) is the study of how securities prices behave and how to exploit that information to make money. With technical analysis, your goal is to identify price trends for a certain time period and/or forecast the price of a security in order to buy and sell that security to make a cash profit. Technical analysis is ideal for *traders* (those who want to make profits from trading), not *investors* (those who view securities as savings vehicles). You can find the details in Book X.

Managing Investment Risks

Investors face many risks. The most obvious is financial risk. Companies go bankrupt, trading decisions go south, the best laid investment plans go awry, and you can end up losing your money — all or some of it, whether the economy is strong or weak.

As an investor you also face

✔ *Interest rate risk,* the impact that rising or falling interest rates have on your investments

✔ *Market risk,* the impact that the laws of supply and demand and the market's mood (bullish or bearish) have on your investments

✔ *Inflation risk,* also referred to as *purchasing power risk,* which impacts how much you can buy for your money

✔ The risks associated with political and governmental policies that influence the financial stability of companies, the value of commodities, the value of currencies — you name it

✔ *Emotional risks,* namely fear and greed, which have sidetracked many investors

In addition to all these risks, your investments have tax implications, affecting how much of your money you get to keep.

Despite this rather lengthy list of all the ways your investments can be at risk, the good news is that you can take steps to minimize risk:

✔ **Diversify:** *Diversification* lets you reduce risk by spreading your money across different investments. It's a fancy way of saying, "Don't put all your eggs in one basket." To properly diversify your investments:

• Put your money in a variety of investment vehicles rather than in just one.

What exactly does the SEC do?

The role of the Securities and Exchange Commission (SEC) is to protect investors from fraud and other unlawful activity designed to fleece them. Created during the early 1930s to crack down on abuses that led to the Great Depression, the SEC continues to be the most important watchdog of the investment industry. Go to www.sec.gov to access the SEC resources for both novice and experienced investors. Find out about its free publications, services, and resources before you invest. If you've already been victimized by unscrupulous operators, call the SEC for assistance.

- Spread the wealth among different asset classes, investing in both large cap and small cap, for example.
- Don't put all your money in one industry. If a problem hits an entire industry, you'll get hurt.

✔ **Research your investment:** Research all aspects of the investment you're about to undertake — before you undertake it — including anything that could affect the industry in general and your specific investments or trades in particular.

Many investors jump in on hype; they hear a certain thing mentioned in the press, and they leap in just because everyone else is. Acting on impulse is one of the most detrimental habits you can develop as an investor or a trader. Before you put your money in anything, find out as much as possible about this potential investment.

✔ **Practice:** Before you actually put money in any type of new investment or make your first trade, make a few dry runs: Pick a few stocks that you think will increase in value and then track them for a while to see how they perform. Watch a few trades online and see how the process works. Create a few technical charts and see how accurately you're able to identify trends.

Going for Brokers

Many investment options require that you negotiate your trades or buy and sell through a broker. Brokers can be organizations (Charles Schwab, Merrill Lynch, E*TRADE, and so on) and individuals. Although the primary task of brokers is to act as the intermediary, some brokers also provide advisory services and offer limited banking services, like interest-bearing accounts and check writing.

Brokers make their money through various fees, including the following:

Book I

Getting
Started
with High-
Powered
Investing

- ✔ **Brokerage commissions:** These are fees for buying and/or selling stocks and other securities.

- ✔ **Margin interest charges:** This is interest charged to investors for borrowing against their brokerage account for investment purposes.

- ✔ **Service charges:** These are charges for performing administrative tasks and other functions. For example, brokers charge fees to investors for individual retirement accounts (IRAs) and for mailing stocks in certificate form.

Any broker you deal with should be registered with the Financial Industry Regulatory Authority (FINRA) and the Securities and Exchange Commission (SEC), or, if applicable, with the security division in your state. In addition, to protect your money after you've deposited it into a brokerage account, that broker should be a member of Securities Investor Protection Corporation (SIPC). To find out whether the broker is registered with these organizations, contact FINRA (`www.finra.org`), the SEC (`www.sec.gov`), and SIPC (`www.sipc.org`).

The following sections distinguish between the two main types of brokers and give you the scoop on several different brokerage accounts.

Distinguishing between full-service and discount brokers

Brokers fall into two basic categories: full-service and discount. The type you choose really depends on what type of investor you are. Full-service brokers are suitable for investors who need some guidance, while discount brokers are better for those who are sufficiently confident and knowledgeable about investing to manage with minimal help. The next sections have the details.

Before choosing a broker, analyze your personal investing style. After you know yourself and the way you invest, you can find the kind of broker that fits your needs. Keep the following points in mind:

- ✔ Match your investment style with a brokerage firm that charges the least amount of money for the services you're likely to use most frequently.

- ✔ Compare all the costs of buying, selling, and holding stocks and other securities through a broker. Don't compare only commissions. Compare other costs, too, such as margin interest and other service charges.

✔ Use broker comparison services available in financial publications such as *SmartMoney* and *Barron's*. You can also get a free report on the broker from FINRA by calling 800-289-9999 or visiting its website at `www.finra.org` (click on BrokerCheck). The report can indicate whether any complaints or penalties have been filed against that brokerage firm or the individual broker.

Full-service brokers

Full-service brokers provide as many services as possible for investors who open accounts with them. When you open an account at a brokerage firm, a representative is assigned to your account. This representative is usually called an *account executive,* a *registered rep,* or a *financial consultant* by the brokerage firm. This person usually has a securities license and is knowledgeable about stocks in particular and investing in general.

Your account executive is responsible for assisting you, answering questions about your account and the securities in your portfolio, and transacting your buy and sell orders. Full-service brokers can do these things for you:

✔ **Offer guidance and advice:** The greatest distinction between full-service brokers and discount brokers is the personal attention you receive from your account rep. You disclose information about your finances and financial goals, and the rep makes recommendations about stocks and funds that are suitable for you.

Brokers are salespeople. No matter how well they treat you, they're still compensated based on their ability to produce revenue for the brokerage firm. (In other words, they're paid to sell you things.)

✔ **Provide access to research:** Full-service brokers can give you access to their investment research department, which can give you in-depth information and analysis on a particular company.

✔ **Make investment decisions on your behalf:** Full-service brokers can actually make decisions for your account with your authorization.

Letting others make financial decisions for you is always dicey — especially when they're using *your* money. If they make poor investment choices that lose you money, you may not have any recourse. More egregious is a practice called *churning:* buying and selling securities for the sole purpose of generating commissions. Be sure to require the broker to explain his choices to you.

Discount brokers

Perhaps you don't need any hand-holding from a broker. You know what you want, and you can make your own investment decisions. All you want is someone to transact your buy/sell orders. In that case, go with a discount broker. Discount brokers, as the name implies, are cheaper to engage than

Book I

Getting
Started
with High-
Powered
Investing

full-service brokers. They don't offer advice or premium services, though — just the basics required to perform your transactions.

For a while, the regular investor had two types of discount brokers to choose from: conventional discount brokers and Internet discount brokers. The two are basically the same now, so the differences are hardly worth mentioning. Through industry consolidation, most of the conventional discount brokers today have fully featured websites, while Internet brokers have adapted to adding more telephone and face-to-face services.

Charles Schwab (www.schwab.com) and TD Ameritrade (www.tdameritrade.com) are examples of conventional discount brokers that have adapted well to the Internet era. Internet brokers such as E*TRADE (www.etrade.com), TradeKing (www.tradeking.com), and Scottrade.com (www.scottrade.com) have added more conventional services.

Discount brokers offer a couple of advantages over full-service brokers, including the following:

- **Lower cost:** This lower cost is usually the result of lower commissions.

- **Access to information:** Established discount brokers offer extensive educational materials at their offices or on their websites.

Before choosing a discount broker, make sure you understand all possible fees you may be charged. (Many discount brokers charge extra for services that you may think are included.)

Picking among types of brokerage accounts

Most brokerage firms offer investors several different types of accounts, each serving a different purpose. The three most common are cash accounts, option accounts, and margin accounts. The basic difference boils down to how particular brokers view your creditworthiness when it comes to buying and selling securities. If your credit isn't great, your only choice is a cash account. If your credit is good, you can open either a cash account or a margin account. Here are the details:

- **Cash accounts (also referred to as *Type 1* accounts):** You deposit a sum of money with the new account application to begin trading. The amount of your initial deposit varies from broker to broker, usually between $500 and $10,000. With a cash account, your money has to be deposited in the account before the closing (or *settlement*) date for any trade you make.

If you have cash in a brokerage account (keep in mind that all accounts are brokerage accounts, and "cash" and "margin" are simply types of brokerage accounts), see whether the broker will pay you interest on it and how much. Some offer a service in which uninvested money earns money-market rates.

✔ **Margin accounts (also called *Type 2* accounts):** A margin account has all the benefits of a cash account plus the ability of buying on margin (that is, borrowing money against the securities in the account to buy more stock). A margin account is also necessary if you plan on doing short selling.

✔ **Option accounts (also referred to as *Type 3* accounts):** This type of account gives you all the capabilities of a margin account plus the ability to trade stock and index options. To open an options account, the broker usually asks you to sign a statement that you are knowledgeable about options and are familiar with the risks associated with them.

Looking at Indexes and Exchanges

Indexes can be useful, general gauges of stock market activity. They give investors a basic idea of how well (or how poorly) the overall market is doing. *Exchanges* — the places (physical or electronic) where the buying and selling actually take place — are important too. The following sections give you the lowdown on both.

Indexes: Tracking the market

Indexes, which measure and report changes in the value of a selected group of securities, give investors an instant snapshot of how well the market is doing. Through them, you can quickly compare the performance of your portfolio with the rest of the market. If the Dow goes up 10 percent in a year and your portfolio, which holds securities of similar risk to the Dow, shows a cumulative gain of 12 percent, you know that you're doing well.

Indexes are *weighted;* that is, their calculations take into account the relative importance of the items being evaluated. There are several kinds of indexes:

✔ **Price-weighted index:** This index tracks changes based on the change in the individual stock's price per share. If Stock A is worth $20 per share and Stock B is worth $40 per share, the stock at $40 is allocated a greater proportion of the index than the one at $20.

Book I

Getting
Started
with High-
Powered
Investing

✔ **Market value–weighted index:** This index tracks the proportion of a stock based on its market capitalization (or market value). Say that in your portfolio the $20 stock (Stock A) has 10 million shares and the $40 stock (Stock B) has only 1 million shares. Stock A's market cap is $200 million, while Stock B's market cap is $40 million. In a market value–weighted index, Stock A represents a much larger percentage of the index's value because of its much larger market cap.

✔ **Composite index:** This type of index is a combination of several indexes. An example is the New York Stock Exchange (NYSE) Composite, which tracks the entire exchange by combining all the stocks and indexes that are included in it.

The following sections give you the scoop on several major indexes.

Dow Jones Industrial Average

The Dow Jones Industrial Average (DJIA or, more commonly, *the Dow*) tracks a basket of 30 of the largest and most influential public companies in the stock market. Because the Dow tracks only 30 companies, it doesn't communicate the true pulse of the market. Nor is the Dow a pure gauge of industrial activity because it also includes a hodgepodge of nonindustrial issues such as JPMorgan Chase and Citigroup (banks), Home Depot (retailing), and Microsoft (software). For more information, visit www.djindexes.com.

Serious investors are better served by looking at broad-based indexes, such as the S&P 500 and the Wilshire 5000, and industry or sector indexes, which better gauge the growth (or lack thereof) of specific industries and sectors.

Standard & Poor's 500

The Standard & Poor's 500 (S&P 500) is an index that tracks the 500 largest publicly traded companies and is more representative of the overall market's performance than the Dow. The S&P 500 includes companies that are widely held and widely followed. The companies are also leaders in a variety of industries, including energy, technology, healthcare, and finance. It's a market value–weighted index. For more information, visit www.standardand poors.com.

Despite the fact that it tracks 500 companies, the top 50 companies encompass 50 percent of the index's market value. That is, those 50 companies have a greater influence on the S&P 500 index's price movement than any other segment of companies. For that reason, the index may not offer an accurate representation of the general market.

NASDAQ-100

NASDAQ-100 is the top 100 stocks (based on market value) traded on the NASDAQ exchange. This index is for investors who want to concentrate on the largest companies, which tend to be especially weighted in technology issues. NASDAQ-100 is a favorite index among day-traders — much more so than the S&P 500 or the Dow — because it tends to be much more volatile.

Russell 1000, 2000, and 3000

The Russell 3000 index includes the 3,000 largest publicly traded companies (nearly 98 percent of publicly traded stocks) and includes many mid-cap and small-cap stocks. Most companies covered in the Russell 3000 have an average market value of a billion dollars or less.

The Russell 2000 contains the smallest 2,000 companies from the Russell 3000, while the Russell 1000 contains the largest 1,000 companies. The Russell indexes do not cover *micro-cap* stocks (companies with a market capitalization under $250 million). For more information, visit www.russell.com.

Dow Jones Wilshire 5000

The Wilshire 5000, which is often referred to as the *Wilshire Total Market Index,* is probably the largest stock index in the world, covering more than 7,500 stocks. The advantage of the Wilshire 5000 is that it's very comprehensive, covering nearly the entire market and including all the stocks that are on the major stock exchanges (NYSE, AMEX, and the largest issues on NASDAQ), which by default also includes all the stocks covered by the S&P 500. The Wilshire 5000 is a market value–weighted index. For more information, visit www.wilshire.com.

Morgan Stanley Capital International

With indexes of all kinds — stocks, bonds, hedge funds, and U.S. and international securities — Morgan Stanley Capital International (MSCI), although not quite a household name, has been gaining ground as the indexer of choice for many exchange-traded fund (ETF) providers. MSCI indexes are the backbone of Barclays iShares individual-country ETFs. For more information, visit www.msci.com.

International indexes

The whole world is a vast marketplace that interacts with and exerts tremendous influence on individual national economies and markets. Here are some of the more widely followed international indexes:

- ✓ **Nikkei (Japan):** Japan's version of the Dow. If you're invested in Japanese stocks or in stocks that do business with Japan, you can bet that you want to know what's up with the Nikkei.

Book I

Getting
Started
with High-
Powered
Investing

✔ **FTSE 100 (Great Britain):** Usually referred to as the *footsie,* this is a market value–weighted index of the top 100 public companies in the United Kingdom.

✔ **CAC 40 (France):** This index tracks the 40 largest public stocks, based on market value, that trade on the Paris stock exchange.

✔ **DAX (Germany):** This index tracks the 30 largest and most active stocks that trade on the Frankfurt Stock Exchange.

You can track these international indexes (among others) at major financial websites, such as www.bloomberg.com and www.marketwatch.com.

Exchanges: Securities marketplaces

Stock exchanges are organized marketplaces for the buying and selling of stocks and other securities. The main exchanges for most stock investors are the following:

✔ **New York Stock Exchange (NYSE):** The NYSE lists nearly 2,800 securities and trades about 1.5 billion shares a day. Many of the member companies are among the largest in the United States. All together, NYSE companies represent over three-quarters of the total market capitalization in the nation. Trading occurs on the floor of the exchange with specialists and floor traders running the show. The website for the New York Stock Exchange is www.nyse.com.

✔ **NASDAQ:** The NASDAQ lists over 3,200 securities and trades about 2 billion shares a day. (The acronym NASDAQ stands for National Association of Securities Dealers Automated Quotation system.) To be listed on the NASDAQ stock exchange, a company must meet certain financial and liquidity standards. NASDAQ's website is www.nasdaq.com.

Stocks that don't meet the minimum NASDAQ listing requirements are traded as over-the-counter or bulletin-board stocks (OTCBB). The OTCBB is a regulated quotation service that displays real-time quotes, last-sale prices, and volume information for the stocks traded OTCBB. These stocks are generally more difficult to buy and sell. See www.otcbb.com for more information.

✔ **Electronic communications networks (ECNs):** ECNs enable buyers and sellers to meet electronically to execute trades. The trades are entered into the ECN systems by market makers at one of the exchanges or by an OTC market maker. Transactions are completed without a broker-dealer, saving users the cost of commissions normally charged for more traditional forms of trading. More than a dozen ECNs operate in the U.S. securities markets, including Archipelago Exchange, Brut, Instinet, Island, and SelectNet.

ECNs are accessed through a custom terminal or directly via the Internet. Orders are posted by the ECN for subscribers to view. The ECN then matches orders for execution. In most cases, buyers and sellers maintain their anonymity and do not list identifiable information in their buy or sell orders.

Chapter 2

Playing the Market: Stocks and Bonds

In This Chapter

▶ Making sense of stocks and stock tables

▶ Investing in stocks for growth or income

▶ Understanding bond ratings, maturity levels, and yields

▶ Selecting the right types of bonds for your investment needs

Stocks and bonds are two of the most traditional investment vehicles — and many Americans are familiar with them. But just because they're familiar doesn't mean you don't have to make an effort to understand them. Successfully investing in stocks and bonds requires a realistic approach and quite a bit of know-how. This chapter gives you an overview.

Starting with Stock Basics

Stocks represent ownership in companies, and stock markets are the places — either online (think NASDAQ) or in real, brick-and-mortar buildings (think the New York Stock Exchange) — where stocks are bought and sold. When you buy stock in a company, you get electronic confirmation of the trade, rather than a physical certificate, to prove how many shares you own.

The stock tables in major business publications, such as the *Wall Street Journal* and *Investor's Business Daily,* are loaded with information that can help you become a savvy investor. You can use this information not only to select promising investment opportunities but also to monitor your stocks' performance. Table 2-1 shows a sample stock table for you to refer to as you read the list that follows. Each item gives you some clues about the current state of affairs for a particular company.

Table 2-1		A Sample Stock Table						
52-Wk High	52-Wk Low	Name (Symbol)	Div	Vol	Yld	P/E	Day Last	Net Chg
21.50	8.00	SkyHighCorp (SHC)		3,143		76	21.25	+0.25
47.00	31/75	LowDownInc (LDI)	2.35	2,735	5.7	18	41.00	–0.50
25.00	21.00	ValueNowInc (VNI)	1.00	1,894	4.5	12	22.00	+0.10
83.00	33.00	DoinBadlyCorp (DBC)		7,601			33.50	–0.75

Here's what each column means:

✔ **52-week high:** The highest price that particular stock has reached in the most recent 52-week period. This info lets you gauge where the stock is now versus where it has been recently.

✔ **52-week low:** The lowest price that particular stock has reached in the most recent 52-week period. This info lets you analyze stocks over a period of time.

✔ **Name and symbol:** The company name (usually abbreviated) and the stock symbol assigned to it.

✔ **Dividend:** Dividends are payments made to stockholders. The amount shown is the annual dividend quoted as if you owned one share of that stock.

✔ **Volume:** How many shares of that particular stock were traded that day.

Trading volume that's far in excess (either positively or negatively) of the stock's normal range is a sign that something is going on with that stock.

✔ **Yield:** What percentage that particular dividend is of the stock price. Yield changes daily as the stock price changes, and it's always reported as if you're buying the stock that day.

✔ **P/E:** The ratio between the price of the stock and the company's earnings. It's frequently used to determine whether a stock is a good value. Value investors (see Book VII) find P/E ratios to be essential to analyzing a stock as a potential investment.

In the P/E ratios reported in stock tables, *price* refers to the cost of a single share of stock. *Earnings* refers to the company's reported earnings as of the most recent four quarters.

✔ **Day last:** How trading ended for a particular stock on the day represented by the table. Some newspapers report the high and low for that day in addition to the stock's ending price.

> ✔ **Net change:** The stock price at the close of the day represented by the table compared with its price at the close of the prior day's trading.

Book I

Getting
Started
with High-
Powered
Investing

Stocking Up

Certain types of stocks tend to be riskier than others. As a rule, those that carry more risk also tend to carry more potential for growth. In the following sections, you discover growth stocks, which fall into the higher risk/return category, and income stocks, which tend to involve lower risk, lower return, and a different set of pros and cons than growth stocks.

Choosing growth stocks

A stock is considered a *growth stock* when its earnings grow at an above-average rate relative to the market and do so with some consistency. To qualify as a growth stock, earnings must outpace the S&P 500's average consistently over time. If a company has earnings growth of 15 percent per year over three years or more and the industry's average growth rate over the same time frame is 10 percent, then this stock qualifies as a growth stock. The following sections explain how to analyze growth stocks and describe small caps (a type of growth stock).

Analyzing growth stocks

Although comparison is a valuable tool for evaluating a stock's potential, don't pick growth stocks on the basis of comparison alone. Also scrutinize the stock to make sure that it has other things going for it to improve your chance of success, as the following list explains:

> ✔ **Checking out a company's fundamentals:** In the context of investing, the word *fundamentals* refers to the company's financial condition and related data as represented by the company's balance sheet, income statement, cash flow, and other operational data, along with external factors such as the company's market position, industry, and economic prospects. Essentially, the fundamentals should indicate to you that the company is in strong financial condition: It has consistently solid earnings, low debt, and a commanding position in the marketplace.

> ✔ **Deciding whether a company is a good value:** A value-oriented approach to growth serves you best. Whereas *growth stocks* perform better than their peers in categories such as sales and earnings, *value stocks* are stocks that are priced lower than the value of the company and its assets. You can identify a value stock by analyzing the company's fundamentals and looking at some key financial ratios, such as the price-to-earnings ratio. If the stock's price is lower than the company's fundamentals indicate it should be (in other words, it's undervalued), then it's

a good buy — a bargain — and the stock is considered a great value. For more on value investing, see Book VII.

✔ **Looking for leaders and megatrends:** A *megatrend* is a major development that will have huge implications for most (if not all) of society for a long time to come. A good example of a megatrend is the aging of Americans. Federal government studies indicate that senior citizens will be the fastest-growing segment of the U.S. population during the next 20 years. How does the stock investor take advantage of a megatrend? By identifying a company that's poised to address the opportunities that such trends reveal. A strong company in a growing industry is a common recipe for success. The key question you should ask: What's the current megatrend, and how does the company you're investigating fit into it?

✔ **Considering a company with a strong niche:** Companies that have established a strong niche are consistently profitable. Look for a company with one or more of the following characteristics:

- **A strong brand:** Companies that have a positive, familiar identity — such as Coca-Cola and Microsoft — occupy a niche that keeps customers loyal. Other companies have to struggle to overcome that loyalty if they want a share of the market.

- **High barriers to entry:** United Parcel Service and FedEx have set up tremendous distribution and delivery networks that competitors can't easily duplicate. High barriers to entry offer an important edge to established companies.

- **Research & development (R&D):** Companies such as Pfizer and Merck spend a lot of money researching and developing new pharmaceutical products. This investment becomes a new product with millions of consumers who become loyal purchasers, so the company's going to grow.

✔ **Noticing who's buying and/or recommending the stock:** You can invest in a great company and still see its stock go nowhere. Why? Because what makes the stock go up is high demand, or having more buyers than sellers of the stock. If you pick a stock for all the right reasons and the market notices the stock as well, that attention will cause the stock price to climb. The things to watch for include the following:

- **Institutional buying:** Are mutual funds and pension plans buying up the stock you're looking at? This type of buying power exerts tremendous upward pressure on the stock's price.

- **Analysts' attention:** Are analysts talking about the stock on the financial shows? A single recommendation by an influential analyst can be enough to send a stock skyward.

- **Newsletter recommendations:** If influential newsletters, which are usually published by independent researchers, are touting your choice, that praise is good for your stock.

- **Consumer publications:** Publications such as *Consumer Reports* regularly look at products and services and rate them for consumer satisfaction. Having its offerings well received by consumers is a strong positive for the company. This kind of attention ultimately has a positive effect on that company's stock.

Exploring small caps

Small cap (or *small capitalization*) refers to the company's market size. Small-cap stocks are stocks from companies that have market capitalization (the number of shares outstanding multiplied by the price per share) of under $1 billion. Investors may face more risk with small caps, but they also have the chance for greater gains.

Out of all the types of stocks, small-cap stocks continue to exhibit the greatest amount of growth. In the same way that a tree planted last year has more opportunity for growth than a mature, 100-year-old redwood, small caps have greater growth potential than established large-cap stocks. Of course, a small cap won't exhibit spectacular growth just because it's small. It will grow when it does the right things, such as increasing sales and earnings by producing goods and services that customers want. As you consider small caps, keep these things in mind:

- **Understand your investment style.** Small-cap stocks may have more potential rewards, but they also carry more risk. No investor should devote a large portion of his capital to small-cap stocks. If you're considering retirement money, you're better off investing in large-cap stocks (which offer steady appreciation with greater safety), investment-grade bonds (covered in the later section "Getting Your Bond Basics"), exchange-traded funds (see Chapter 3 in Book I), and/or mutual funds (also discussed in Chapter 3 in Book I).

- **Check with the SEC.** Get the financial reports that the company must file with the U.S. Securities and Exchange Commission (SEC). These reports offer more complete information on the company's activities and finances. Go to the SEC website at www.sec.gov and check its massive database of company filings at EDGAR (Electronic Data Gathering, Analysis, and Retrieval system). Also check to see whether any complaints have been filed against the company.

- **Make sure it's making money.** Make sure that the company is established (being in business for at least three years is a good minimum) and that it's profitable. These rules are especially important for investors in small-cap stocks. Plenty of start-up ventures lose money initially and hope to make a fortune down the road. You may say, "But shouldn't I jump in now in anticipation of future profits?" You may get lucky, but understand that when you invest in small-cap stocks, you're speculating.

✔ **Check other sources.** See whether brokers and independent research services, such as Value Line, follow the stock. If two or more different sources like the stock, it's worth further investigation.

Investing for income

When you invest for income, you're investing in stocks that you hope will provide you with regular money payments (dividends). Income stocks may not offer stellar growth, but they're good for a steady infusion of money. They're the least volatile of all stocks. They can be appropriate for many investors, but they're especially well suited for the following individuals:

✔ **Conservative and novice investors:** Conservative investors like to see a slow-but-steady approach to growing their money while getting regular dividend checks. Novice investors who want to start slowly also benefit from income stocks.

✔ **Retirees:** Growth investing is best suited for long-term needs, whereas income investing is best suited to current needs. Retirees may want some growth in their portfolios, but they're more concerned with regular income that can keep pace with inflation.

✔ **Dividend reinvestment plan (DRIP) investors:** A DRIP is a program that a company may offer to allow investors to accumulate more shares of its stock without paying commissions. For those who like to compound their money with DRIPs, income stocks are perfect.

If you have a low tolerance for risk or if your investment goal is anything less than long term, income stocks are your best bet. The following sections explain how to analyze income stocks and describe different types of income stocks.

Analyzing income stocks

When you gain income from stocks, you usually do so in the form of dividends. A *dividend* is nothing more than money paid out to the owner of a stock. A good income stock is a stock that has a higher-than-average dividend (typically 4 percent or higher) and is purchased primarily for income — not for spectacular growth potential. Here are some things to know about income stocks:

✔ **A dividend is quoted as an annual number but is usually paid on a quarterly, pro-rata basis.** If a stock is paying a dividend of $4, for example, and you have 200 shares, you'll be paid $800 every year (if the dividend doesn't change during that period), or $200 per quarter.

✔ **Dividend rates are not guaranteed; they can go up or down or, in some extreme cases, the dividend can be discontinued.** Fortunately, most companies that issue dividends continue them indefinitely and actually increase dividend payments from time to time. Historically, dividend increases have equaled or exceeded the rate of inflation.

✔ **The main thing to look for in choosing income stocks is yield.** *Yield* is the percentage rate of return paid on a stock in the form of dividends. Looking at a stock's dividend yield is the quickest way to find out how much money you'll earn from a particular income stock versus other dividend-paying stocks (or even other investments, such as a bank account). Dividend yield is calculated in the following way:

$$\text{dividend yield} = \text{annual dividend income per share} \div \text{current stock price per share}$$

When you see a stock listed in the financial pages, the dividend yield is provided along with the stock's price and annual dividend (refer to Table 2-1 for examples). The dividend yield in the financial pages is always calculated as if you bought the stock on that given day.

Based on supply and demand, stock prices change every day (almost every minute!) that the market's open. When the stock price changes, the yield changes as well. Monitor the company's progress for as long as its stock is in your portfolio. Use resources such as www.bloomberg.com and www.marketwatch.com to track your stock and to monitor how well that particular company is continuing to perform.

✔ **If you're concerned about the safety of your dividend income, regularly watch the payout ratio.** The *payout ratio* is simply a way to figure out what percentage of the company's earnings are being paid out in the form of dividends. The maximum acceptable payout ratio should be 80 percent, and a good range is 50 to 70 percent. A payout ratio of 60 percent or lower is considered very safe (the lower the percentage, the safer the dividend).

✔ **Pay attention to a company's bond rating.** The bond rating offers insight into the company's financial strength. Standard & Poor's (S&P) is the major independent rating agency that looks into bond issuers. The highest rating issued by S&P is AAA. The grades AAA, AA, and A are considered *investment grade,* or of high quality. Bs and Cs indicate a poor grade, while anything lower than that is considered very risky (these bonds are referred to as *junk bonds*).

Look at income stocks in the same way that you do growth stocks when assessing the financial strength of a company. Getting a nice dividend can come to a screeching halt if the company can't afford to pay dividends anymore. If your budget depends on dividend income, monitoring the company's financial strength is that much more important.

Looking at typical income stocks

Income stocks tend to be in established industries with established cash flows and less emphasis on financing or creating new products and services. When you're ready to start your search for a great, high-dividend income stock, start looking at utilities and real estate trusts — two established industries with proven track records — as well as royalty trusts (the new kid on the block):

- ✔ **Utilities:** Utilities generate a large cash flow, which includes money from income (sales of products and/or services) and other items (the selling of equipment, for example). This cash flow is needed to cover things such as expenses, including dividends. Utilities are considered the most common type of income stocks, and many investors have at least one in their portfolios.

- ✔ **Real estate investment trusts (REITs):** A REIT is an investment that has the elements of both a stock and a *mutual fund* (a pool of money received from investors that's managed by an investment company; see Book I, Chapter 3 for details).

  - A REIT is like a stock in that it's a company whose stock is publicly traded on the major stock exchanges, and it has the usual features that you expect from a stock — it can be bought and sold easily through a broker, income is given to investors as dividends, and so on.

  - A REIT resembles a mutual fund in that it doesn't make its money selling goods and services; it makes its money by buying, selling, and managing an investment portfolio — in the case of a REIT, the portfolio is full of real-estate investments. It generates revenue from rents and property leases as any landlord would. In addition, some REITs own mortgages, and they gain income from the interest.

- ✔ **Royalty trusts:** *Royalty trusts* are companies that hold assets such as oil-rich and/or natural gas–rich land and generate high fees from companies that seek access to these properties for exploration. The fees paid to the royalty trusts are then disbursed as high dividends to their shareholders. During early 2013, royalty trusts sported yields in the 7 to 12 percent range, which is very enticing given how low the yields have been in this decade for other investments such as bank accounts and bonds.

Although energy has been a hot field in recent years and royalty trusts have done well, keep in mind that their payout ratios are very high (often in the 90 to 100 percent range), so dividends will suffer should their cash flow shrink. (Payout ratios are covered in the preceding section.)

Getting Your Bond Basics

Book I

Getting
Started
with High-
Powered
Investing

Bonds are basically IOUs. When you buy a bond, you're lending your money to Uncle Sam, General Electric, Procter & Gamble, the city in which you live — whatever entity issues the bonds — and that entity promises to pay you a certain rate of interest in exchange for borrowing your money.

By and large, bonds' most salient characteristic — and the one thing that most, but not all bonds share — is a certain stability and steadiness well above and beyond that of most other investments. Because you are, in most cases, receiving a steady stream of income, and because you expect to get your principal back in one piece, bonds tend to be more conservative investments than, say, stocks, commodities, or collectibles.

Some key things to know about bonds:

- ✔ **Face amount:** A bond is always issued with a certain *face amount* (also called the *principal* or the *par value* of the bond). Most often, bonds are issued with face amounts of $1,000.

- ✔ **Secondary market value:** After a bond is issued, it may sell on the secondary market for more or less than its face amount. If it sells for more than its face amount, the bond is said to sell at a *premium*. If it sells for less than its face amount, the bond is said to sell at a *discount*. Many factors determine the price of a bond in the secondary market.

- ✔ **Interest rate and repayment at maturity:** Every bond pays a certain rate of interest, and typically (but not always) that rate is fixed over the life of the bond (that's why some people call bonds *fixed-income* securities). The life of the bond is known as the bond's *maturity*. The rate of interest is a percentage of the face amount and is typically paid out twice a year. For example, if a corporation or government issues a $1,000 bond paying 6 percent, that corporation or government promises to fork over to the bondholder $60 a year — or, in most cases, $30 twice a year. Then, when the bond matures, the corporation or government gives the bondholder the original $1,000 back.

- ✔ **Buying and selling methods:** In some cases, you can buy a bond directly from the issuer and sell it back directly to the issuer, but in most cases, bonds are bought and sold through a brokerage house or a bank, which charges a fee for this service. For information on brokers, refer to Chapter 1 of Book I.

The following sections describe bond maturity choices, investment-grade versus junk-grade bonds, individual bonds versus bond funds, types of yield, and total return.

Maturity choices

Almost all bonds these days are issued with maturities of up to 30 years. Any bond with a maturity of less than 5 years is called a *short bond*. Bonds with maturities of 5 to 12 years are called *intermediate bonds*. Bonds with maturities of 12 years or more are called *long bonds*.

In general, the longer the maturity, the greater the interest rate paid. That's because bond buyers generally demand more compensation the longer they agree to tie up their money. The difference between the rates you can get on short bonds versus intermediate bonds versus long bonds is known as the *yield curve*. *Yield* simply refers to the annual interest rate.

Investment-grade or junk bonds

When choosing a bond, you may think that the bonds that offer the best interest rates are the best investments. But that's not necessarily the case. When you fork over your money to buy a bond, your principal is guaranteed only by the issuer of the bond, which means that it's only as solid as the issuer itself.

Bond issuers with the shakiest reputations pay higher interest rates. Because the U.S. government, which has the power to levy taxes and print money, is not going bankrupt any time soon, U.S. Treasury bonds, which are thought to carry minimal risk of default, tend to pay relatively modest interest rates. Corporations and municipalities that issue bonds pay higher interest rates because of the greater risk of default. How much higher the interest rate is depends on the stability of the issuing entity. (You can read more about the ratings of the different type of bonds in the later section "Exploring Your Bond Options.")

Bonds that carry a relatively high risk of default are commonly called *high-yield* or *junk* bonds. Bonds issued by solid companies and governments that carry very little risk of default are commonly referred to as *investment-grade* bonds.

Individual bonds versus bond funds

One of the big questions about bond investing is whether to invest in individual bonds or bond funds. Here's a very broad overview of the pros and cons of owning individual bonds versus bond funds:

Book I

Getting
Started
with High-
Powered
Investing

✔ **Individual bonds:** Individual bonds offer you the opportunity to really fine-tune a fixed-income portfolio. With individual bonds, you can choose exactly what you want in terms of bond quality, maturity, and taxability. For larger investors — especially those doing their homework — investing in individual bonds may also be more economical than investing in a bond fund. That's especially true for those investors who are up on the latest advances in bond buying and selling.

✔ **Bond funds:** Investors now have a choice of more than 5,000 bond mutual funds or exchange-traded funds. Both represent baskets of securities (usually stocks, bonds, or both) and allow for instant and easy portfolio diversification. Yet all have the same basic drawback: management expenses and a certain degree of unpredictability above and beyond individual bonds. Even so, some make for very good potential investments, particularly for people with modest portfolios.

Consider buying *index funds* — mutual funds or exchange-traded funds that seek to provide exposure to an entire asset class (such as bonds or stocks) with very little trading and very low expenses. Such funds are the way to go for most investors to get the bond exposure they need. Chapter 3 in Book I has the scoop on mutual funds and exchange-traded funds.

Various types of yield

Yield is what you want in a bond. It's income and contributes to return, but it can also be confusing. People (and that includes overly eager bond salespeople) often use the term incorrectly. Understand what kind of yield is being promised on a bond or bond fund, and know what it really means.

Coupon yield

The coupon yield, or the coupon rate, is part of the bond offering. A $1,000 bond with a coupon yield of 4 percent pays $40 a year. A $1,000 bond with a coupon yield of 6 percent pays $60 a year. Usually, the $40 or $60 or whatever is split in half and paid out twice a year on an individual bond.

Bond funds don't really have coupon yields, although they have an average coupon yield for all the bonds in the pool. That average tells you something, for sure, but you need to keep in mind that a bond fund may start the year and end the year with a completely different set of bonds — and a completely different average coupon yield.

Current yield

Current yield is derived by taking the bond's coupon yield and dividing it by the bond's current price. Suppose you have a $1,000 face-value bond with a coupon rate of 5 percent, which equates to $50 a year in your pocket. If the bond sells today for 98 (meaning that it's selling at a discount for $980), the current yield is $50 divided by $980, which equals 5.10 percent. If that same bond rises in price to a premium of 103 (meaning it's selling for $1,030), the current yield is $50 divided by $1,030, or 4.85 percent.

The current yield is a sort of snapshot that gives you a very rough (and possibly entirely inaccurate) estimate of the return you can expect on that bond over the coming months. If you take today's current yield (translated into nickels and dimes) and multiply that amount by 30, you may think that gives you a good estimate of how much income your bond will generate in the next month, but that's not the case. The current yield changes too quickly for that kind of prediction to hold true.

Unscrupulous bond brokers have been known to tout current yield, and only current yield, when selling especially premium-priced bonds. The current yield may look great, but you'll take a hit when the bond matures by collecting less in principal than you paid for the bond. Your yield-to-maturity, which matters more than current yield (read about it in the next section), may, in fact, stink.

Yield-to-maturity

A much more accurate measure of return, although still far from perfect, is the *yield-to-maturity*. Yield-to-maturity factors in not only the coupon rate and the price you paid for the bond, but also how far you have to go to get your principal back and how much that principal will be.

Yield-to-maturity calculations make a big assumption that may or may not prove true: They assume that as you collect your interest payments every six months, you reinvest them at the same interest rate you're getting on the bond. You can calculate the yield-to-maturity in three ways:

- ✔ **By hand:** You can use a terribly long formula with all kinds of horrible Greek symbols and lots of multiplication and division, if you're so inclined.

- ✔ **With a hand-held calculator:** You can use a financial calculator if you have one (thank heaven for modern technology!).

- ✔ **With an online calculator:** You can go to any number of online calculators. (Try putting "yield-to-maturity calculator" in your favorite search engine.) Consider the calculator on MoneyChimp.com, a great financial website that features all sorts of cool calculators. Then just put in the par (face) value of the bond (almost always $1,000), the price you're considering paying for the bond, the number of years to maturity, and the coupon rate, and press "calculate."

Yield-to-call

If you buy a *callable* bond, the company or municipality that issues your bond can ask for it back, at a specific price, long before the bond matures. Premium bonds, because they carry higher-than-average coupon yields, are often called. What that means is that your yield-to-maturity is pretty much a moot point. What you're likely to see in the way of yield is *yield-to-call.* It's figured the same way that you figure yield-to-maturity (use `MoneyChimp.com` if you don't have a financial calculator), but the end result — your actual return — may be considerably lower.

Keep in mind that bonds are generally called when market interest rates have fallen. In that case, not only is the yield on the bond you're holding diminished, but your opportunity to invest your money in anything paying as high an interest rate has passed. From a bondholder's perspective, calls are not pretty, which is why callable bonds must pay higher rates of interest to find any buyers.

Certain hungry bond brokers may "forget" to mention yield-to-call and instead quote you only current yield or yield-to-maturity numbers. In such cases, you may pay the broker a big cut to get the bond, hold it for a short period, and then have to render it to the bond issuer, actually earning yourself a *negative* total return. Ouch. Fortunately, regulatory authorities have gotten somewhat tougher, and such forgetfulness on the part of brokers is less common, but it still happens.

Worst-case basis yield

Usually a callable bond doesn't have one possible call date, but several. *Worst-case basis yield* (or *yield-to-worst-call*) looks at all possible yields and tells you what your yield would be if the company or municipality decided to call your bond at the worst possible time.

Callable bonds involve considerably more risk than noncallable bonds. If interest rates drop, your bond will likely be called. Not only will your yield on the existing bond drop from what you expected, but you'll also be unable to reinvest your money for a like rate of return. If interest rates have risen, the company probably won't call your bond, but you'll be stuck with an asset that, should you try to sell it, will have lost principle. (Bond prices always drop when interest rates rise.)

The 30-day SEC yield

Because yield can be measured in so many ways, and because bond mutual funds were once notorious for manipulating yield figures, the SEC requires that all bond funds report yield in the same manner. The 30-day SEC yield, which attempts to consolidate the yield-to-maturity of all the bonds in the portfolio, exists so the mutual-fund bond shopper can have some measure with which to comparison shop. It isn't a perfect measure, in large part because the bonds in your bond fund today may not be the same bonds in your bond fund three weeks from now. Nonetheless, the 30-day SEC yield can be helpful in choosing the right funds.

Total return — what matters most!

Total return is the entire pot of money you wind up with after the investment period has come and gone. In the case of bonds or bond funds, that includes both interest and any changes in the value of your original principal. Ignoring for the moment the risk of default (and losing all your principal), here are other ways in which your principal can shrink or grow:

✔ **Figuring in capital gains and losses:** In the case of a bond fund, your principal is represented by a certain number of shares in the fund multiplied by the share price of the fund. As bond prices go up and down (usually in response to prevailing interest rates), so, too, does the share price of the bond fund. Because of bond volatility, the share price of a bond fund may go up and down quite a bit, especially if the bond fund is holding long-term bonds, and doubly-especially if those long-term bonds are of questionable quality (junk bonds).

In the case of individual bonds, your principal should come back to you whole — but only if you hold the bond to maturity or if the bond is called. If you choose to sell the bond before maturity, you wind up with whatever market price you can get for the bond at that point.

✔ **Factoring in reinvestment rates of return:** Total return of a bond can come from three sources: interest on the bond, any possible capital gains (or losses), and whatever rate of return (if any) you get when you reinvest the money coming to you every six months. Believe it or not, on a very long-term bond, the last factor — your so-called *reinvestment rate* — is probably the most important of the three because of the amazing power of compound interest.

The only kind of bond where the reinvestment rate is not a factor is a *zero-coupon* bond, or a bond where your only interest payment comes at the very end when the bond matures. In the case of zero-coupon bonds, there is no compounding. The coupon rate of the bond is your actual rate of return, not accounting for inflation or taxes.

✔ **Allowing for inflation adjustments:** Your truest total rate of return needs to account for inflation. To get a very rough estimate of your total real return after accounting for inflation, simply take the nominal rate of return (perhaps 5 or 6 percent) and subtract the annual rate of inflation (which has been about 3 percent in recent years).

Book I

Getting
Started
with High-
Powered
Investing

✔ **Weighing pretax versus post-tax:** For most bonds, the interest payments are taxed as regular income, and any rise in the value of the principal, if the bond is sold (and sometimes even if it isn't), is taxed as capital gain. For most people these days, long-term capital gains (more than one year) on bond principal are taxed at 15 percent. Any appreciated fixed-income asset bought and sold within a year is taxed at your ordinary income-tax rate.

Here are two exceptions:

- **Tax-free municipal bonds** where there's neither a capital gain nor a capital loss, nor is the bondholder subject to any alternative minimum tax

- **Bonds held in a tax-advantaged account,** such as an IRA or a 529 college savings plan

Exploring Your Bond Options

Every year, millions — yes, literally millions — of bonds are issued by thousands of different governments, government agencies, municipalities, financial institutions, and corporations. The following sections give an overview of things to consider about each major kind of bond.

"Risk-free" investing: U.S Treasury bonds

The U.S. Treasury issues umpteen different kinds of debt securities. *Savings bonds,* which can be purchased for small amounts and come in certificate form, are one kind. In fact, when investment people speak of *Treasuries,* they usually aren't talking about savings bonds. Rather, they're talking about larger-denomination bonds, formerly known as *Treasury bills, Treasury notes,* and *Treasury bonds,* that are issued only in electronic (sometimes called *book-entry*) form.

All U.S. Treasury debt securities, whether a $50 savings bond or a $1,000 Treasury note, share four things in common:

✔ **Safety:** Every bond, an IOU of sorts from Uncle Sam, is backed by the "full faith and credit" of the United States government and, therefore, is considered by most investors to be the safest bet around.

- ✔ **Relatively low interest:** Because it is assumed that any principal you invest is absolutely safe, Treasury bonds, of whatever kind, tend to pay relatively modest rates of interest — lower than other comparable bonds, such as corporate bonds, that may put your principal at some risk.

- ✔ **Subjection to risk:** True, the United States government is very unlikely to go bankrupt anytime soon, but Treasury bonds are nonetheless still subject to other risks inherent in the bond market. Prices on Treasury bonds, especially those with long-term maturities, can swoop up and down in response to such things as prevailing interest rates and investor confidence in the economy.

- ✔ **Freedom from state and local taxes:** All interest on U.S. government bonds is off-limits to state and local tax authorities (just as the interest on most municipal bonds is off-limits to the Internal Revenue Service). But you do pay federal tax.

Beyond these four similarities, the differences among the U.S. government debt securities in the following sections are many and, in some cases, like night and day.

Savings bonds for beginning investors

Until recently, U.S. savings bonds made for popular gifts in part because they were sold in pretty certificate form. On January 1, 2012, however, they became electronic entities, just like other Treasury securities. You may now buy your electronic savings bonds straight from the official Treasury website at www.treasurydirect.gov. And if you still want to present the bond as a gift, the website allows you to print a gift certificate, which you can present in lieu of the once keepsake-quality, elaborately designed bond.

Savings bonds are a natural for small investors because you can get started with as little as $25. Beyond that, you don't need to pick a specific denomination. If you want to invest, say, $43.45, go for it, or if you want to invest $312.56, that's fine, too. Any amount over $25 but under $10,000 (per individual, per year) is accepted.

Aside from the ability to invest a small amount, savings bonds are unique among Treasury debt securities in that they're strictly non-marketable. When you buy a U.S. savings bond, you put either your own name and Social Security number on the bond or the name and Social Security number of someone you're gifting it to. The only person entitled to receive interest from that bond is the one whose name appears on the bond. The bond itself can't be sold to another buyer. This limitation is in stark contrast to Treasury bills and bonds that can, and often do, pass hands more often than poker chips.

Among savings bonds, two kinds are sold today:

Book I

Getting
Started
with High-
Powered
Investing

- ✔ **EE bonds:** EE bonds are the most traditional kind of savings bond. Series EE bonds carry a face value of twice what you purchase them for. They're *accrual bonds,* which means that they accrue interest as the years roll on even though you aren't seeing any cash. You can pay taxes on that interest as it accrues, but in most cases deferring taxes until you decide to redeem the bond makes more sense. Uncle Sam allows you to do that. If you use your savings bonds to fund an education, the interest may be tax-free.

  EE bonds are nonredeemable for the first year you own them, and if you hold them fewer than five years, you surrender three months of interest. Any individual can buy up to $10,000 in EE savings bonds a year. Interest compounds twice a year for 30 years. Be aware, however, that the interest rate is fixed for the life of the savings bond. Therefore, EE bonds are less attractive in low-interest-rate environments.

- ✔ **I bonds:** I bonds are built to buttress inflation. The I Series bonds offer a fixed rate of return plus an adjustment for rising prices. Every May 1 and November 1, the Treasury announces both the fixed rate for all new I bonds and the inflation adjustment for all new and existing I bonds. After you buy an I bond, the fixed rate is yours for the life of the bond. The inflation rate adjusts every six months. You collect all your interest only after cashing in the bond. (Interest accounted for via this method is called *accrual* interest.)

  The rules and parameters for I bonds are pretty much the same as they are for EEs: You have to hold them a year, and if you sell within five years, you pay a penalty. The number of I bonds you can invest in is limited to $10,000 a year, per person. And in certain circumstances, the proceeds may become tax-free if used for education expenses.

If you plan to hold I bonds as a long-term investment (longer than a year or two), you should be more concerned with the fixed rate, which will be in effect throughout the life of the bond, than the inflation adjustment, which will vary.

Treasury bills, notes, and bonds for more serious investing

About 99 percent of the approximately $16 trillion in outstanding Treasury debt is made up not of savings bonds but of *marketable* (tradable) securities known as bills, notes, and bonds. This "bills, notes, and bonds" stuff can be a little confusing because technically they're all bonds:

- ✔ They're all backed by the full faith and credit of the U.S. government.

- ✔ They're all issued electronically.

✔ They can all be purchased either directly from the Treasury, through a broker, or in fund form.

✔ They can all trade like hotcakes.

The major difference among them is the time you need to wait to collect your principal:

✔ **Treasury bills** have maturities of a year or less.

✔ **Treasury notes** are issued with maturities from two to ten years.

✔ **Treasury bonds** are long-term investments that have maturities of 10 to 30 years from their issue date.

The bills carry denominations of $100 but are sold on the open market at a discount from their face value. You get the full amount when the bill matures. The notes and bonds, on the other hand, are sold at their face value, have a fixed interest rate, and kick off interest payments once every six months. The minimum denomination for all three is $1,000.

Keep in mind that you don't have to hold any of these securities (bills, notes, or bonds) till maturity. You can, in fact, cash out at any point. The longer until the maturity of the bond, however, the more its price can fluctuate and, therefore, the more you risk losing money.

Treasury Inflation-Protected Securities (TIPS)

Like the I bonds described in the earlier section "Savings bonds for beginning investors," Treasury Inflation-Protected Securities (TIPS) receive both interest and a twice-yearly kickoff of principal for inflation. As with interest on other Treasury securities, interest on TIPS is free from state and local income taxes. Federal income tax, however, must be coughed up each year on both the interest payments and the growth in principal.

TIPS are transferable. You can buy TIPS directly from the Treasury or through a broker. They are currently being issued with terms of 5, 10, and 30 years, although plenty of 20-year-term TIPS are in circulation. The minimum investment is $100.

One of the sweet things about TIPS is that if inflation goes on a rampage, your principal moves north right along with it. If *deflation,* a lowering of prices, occurs (which it hasn't since the 1930s), you won't get any inflation adjustment, but you won't get a deflation adjustment, either. You'll get back at least the face value of the bond.

TIPS sound great, and in many ways they are. But be aware that the coupon rate on TIPS varies with market conditions and tends to be minimal — perhaps a couple of percentage points or less. If inflation is calmer than expected moving into the future, you can almost certainly do better with traditional Treasuries. If inflation turns out to be higher than expected, your TIPS will be the stars of your fixed-income portfolio.

Industrial returns: Corporate bonds

When it comes to adding stability to a portfolio — the number-one reason that bonds belong in your portfolio — Treasuries (covered earlier in this chapter) are one option; investment-grade (high-quality) corporate bonds are another. To put it bluntly, corporate bonds can be something of a pain in the pants, especially when compared to Treasury bonds. Here's what you need to worry about when investing in corporate bonds:

- **The solidity of the company issuing the bond:** If the company goes down, you may lose some or all of your money. Even if the company doesn't go down but merely limps, you can lose money.

- **Callability:** The issuing company may call in your bonds and spit your money back in your face at some inopportune moment (such as when prevailing interest rates have just taken a tumble).

- **Liquidity:** Will someone be there to offer you a fair price if and when you need to sell? Will selling the bond require paying some broker a big, fat markup?

- **Economic upheaval:** In tough economic times when companies are closing their doors (and the stocks in your portfolio are plummeting), your bonds may decide to join in the unhappy nosedive, en masse. Generally, corporate bonds tend to outperform Treasuries when the economy is good and underperform when the economy lags.

Nevertheless, by including both Treasuries *and* corporate bonds in your portfolio you get the best of both worlds. The key is knowing which corporate bonds to consider and which ones to steer clear of. The following sections outline the issues you need to think about when investing in corporate bonds.

Giving credit ratings their due

The largest determinant of the risk and return you take on a bond is the fiscal muscle of the company behind the bond. That fiscal muscle is measured by a company's credit ratings. The most common ratings come from Moody's and Standard & Poor's, but other rating services, such as Fitch Ratings, DBRS, and A.M. Best, exist.

The highest ratings — Moody's Aaa and Standard & Poor's AAA — are the safest of the safe among corporate bonds, and those ratings are given to few corporations. If you lend money to one of these stellar companies, you should expect in return a rate of interest only modestly higher than that of Treasuries (even though S&P in 2011 downgraded Treasuries to a "mere" AA rating). As you progress from these five-star companies down the ladder, you can expect higher rates of interest to compensate you for your added risk. Table 2-2 shows how Moody's, Standard & Poor's, and Fitch define corporate bond credit quality ratings.

Table 2-2	Corporate Bond Credit Quality Ratings		
Credit Risk	*Moody's*	*Standard & Poor's*	*Fitch*
Investment grade			
Tip-top quality	Aaa	AAA	AAA
Premium quality	Aa	AA	AA
Near-premium quality	A	A	A
Take-home-to-Mom quality	Baa	BBB	BBB
Not investment grade			
Borderline ugly	Ba	BB	BB
Ugly	B	B	B
Definitely don't-take-home-to-Mom quality	Caa	CCC	CCC
You'll be extremely lucky to get your money back	Ca	CC	CC
Interest payments have halted or bankruptcy is in process	C	D	C
Already in default	C	D	D

One risk inherent to corporate bonds is that they may be downgraded, even if they never default. Say a bond is rated A by Moody's. If Moody's gets moody and later rates that bond a Baa, the market will respond unfavorably. Chances are, in such a case, that the value of your bond will drop. Of course, the opposite is true, as well. If you buy a Baa bond and it suddenly becomes an A bond, you'll be sitting pretty. If you want to hold your bond to maturity, such downgrades and upgrades don't matter much. But should you decide to sell your bond, they can matter very much.

It's a very good idea to diversify your bonds not only by company but also by industry. If a major upheaval occurs in, say, the utility industry, the rate of both downgrades and defaults is sure to rise. In such a case, you're better off not having all utility bonds.

Going for high-yield bonds (or not)

No distinct line separates investment-grade and high-yield bonds, sometimes known as *junk* bonds. But generally, if a bond receives a rating less than a Baa from Moody's or a BBB from Standard & Poor's, the market considers it high yield.

The old adage that risk equals return is clear as day in the world of bonds. High-yield bonds offer greater yield than investment-grade bonds, and they're more volatile. But they're also one other thing: much more correlated to the stock market. In fact, Treasuries and investment-grade corporate bonds aren't correlated to the stock market at all. So if bonds are going to serve as ballast for your portfolio, which is what they do best, why would you want high-yield bonds? You probably wouldn't, regardless of whether good times or bad times are coming.

If you want junk bonds in your portfolio, take a serious look at foreign high-yield bonds, especially the bonds of emerging-market nations, which can make a lot of sense. That's because they have less correlation to the ups and downs on Wall Street than do U.S. junk bonds. Head to Book VI for information on emerging markets.

Calculating callability

If you own a callable bond, chances are it'll be called at the worst moment — just as interest rates are falling and the value of your bonds is on the rise. And that can make a huge difference in the profitability of your investment. Because calls aren't fun, callable bonds must pay higher rates of interest.

If you're inclined to go for that extra juice that comes with a callable bond, fine, but do so with the assumption that your callable bond will be called. With that in mind, ask the broker to tell you how much (after taking his markup into consideration) your yield will be between today and the call date. Consider that a worst-case yield. (It's often referred to as *yield-to-worst-call,* sometimes abbreviated YTW; see the earlier section "Various types of yield" for more details.) Consider it the yield you'll get. And compare that to the yield you'd get on other comparable bonds. If you choose the callable bond and it winds up not being called, hey, that's gravy.

To encourage you to place your order to buy, some squirrelly bond brokers will assure you that a certain callable bond is unlikely to be called. They may be right in some cases, but you should never bank on such promises.

Considering convertibility

Some corporate bond issuers sell bonds that can be converted into a fixed number of shares of common stock. With a convertible bond, a lender (bondholder) can become a part owner (stockholder) of the company by converting the bond into company stock. Having this option is desirable, so convertible bonds generally pay lower interest rates than do similar bonds that are not convertible.

If the stock performs poorly, no conversion occurs. You're stuck with your bond's lower return (lower than what a nonconvertible corporate bond would get). If the stock performs well, conversion does occur, and you win, so to speak.

Perhaps the most important investment decision you can make is how to divide your portfolio between stocks and bonds. With convertibles, whatever careful allotment you come up with can change overnight. Your bonds suddenly become stocks. You're rewarded for making a good investment, but just as soon as you receive that reward, your portfolio becomes riskier. It's the old trade-off in action.

One relative newcomer to the world of corporate bonds is the *reverse convertible security,* sometimes referred to as a *revertible* or a *revertible note.* A reverse convertible converts to a stock automatically if a certain company stock tumbles below a certain point by a certain date. Why would anyone want such a thing? Because the bond pays a thrillingly high interest rate, but only for a year or so. That's the hook. The catch is that the company paying the high interest rate is in dire trouble. If it goes under, you could lose a bundle.

Lots of protection: Agency bonds

Agency bonds are issued by governmental agencies or quasi-governmental agencies, like the Federal Farm Credit Banks (FFCB), the Federal Home Loan Mortgage Corporation (FHLMC), the General Services Administration (GSA), the Small Business Administration (SBA), the Tennessee Valley Authority (TVA), and the U.S. Agency for International Development (USAID). The following sections list types of agencies and provide important details on agency bonds.

Types of agencies

The first thing to know about these (and the many other) government agencies is that they fit under two large umbrellas:

- **Real U.S. federal agencies:** The agencies in this category are an actual part of the government. Such official agencies include the General Services Administration, the Government National Mortgage Association, and the Small Business Administration. Bonds issued by this group carry the full faith and credit of the U.S. government. As such, the difference in yield between these bonds and Treasuries (covered earlier in this chapter) is almost immeasurable.

✓ **Government-sponsored enterprises (GSEs):** These agencies aren't quite parts of the government. Instead, they're corporations that are created by Congress to work for the common good but are then set out more or less on their own. Because this second group is much larger than the first — both in terms of the number of agencies and the value of the bonds it issues — when investment experts speak of *agency bonds,* they're almost always talking about the bonds of the GSEs.

Many GSEs are publicly held, issuing stock on the major exchanges. Bonds issued by these groups carry an implicit guarantee that the U.S. government will bail them out in times of trouble. The yield difference between Treasuries and the faux-agency bonds is typically within half a percentage point, if even that much. Such pseudo-agencies include the Federal Home Loan Mortgage Corporation and the Federal National Mortgage Association.

After finding themselves in hot water during the subprime mortgage crisis, the two largest of the GSEs — Freddie Mac and Fannie Mae — are currently in *receivership.* What this means is that they've more or less been taken over by the federal government. For the moment, they are, in effect, more like real federal agencies than GSEs. For the time being, bonds from these agencies no longer carry the implicit guarantee; they now carry an explicit guarantee. Their future remains uncertain.

Things to know about agency bonds

Here are some things to know about agency bonds:

✓ With all agency bonds, you pay a markup when you buy and sell, which you don't with Treasuries if you buy them directly from the government. If you're not careful, that markup could easily eat up your first several months of earnings.

✓ Most agency bonds pay a fixed rate of interest twice a year. About 25 percent of them are callable. The other 75 percent are noncallable bonds (sometimes referred to as *bullet* bonds).

✓ Investing in individual agency bonds is not an activity for poor people. Although you may be able to get into the game for as little as $1,000, bond brokers typically mark up such small transactions to the point that they simply don't make sense. Don't even look at individual agency bonds unless you have at least $50,000 to invest in a pop. Otherwise, you should be looking at bond funds or individual Treasuries that you can buy without paying any markup whatsoever.

✓ The taxes you pay on agency bonds vary. Interest from bonds issued by Freddie Mac and Fannie Mae, for example, is fully taxable. The interest on most other agency bonds — including the king of agency bonds, the Federal Home Loan Banks — is exempt from state and local tax.

(Almost) tax-free havens: Municipal bonds

Any government, local agency, nonprofit, or what-have-you that is deemed to serve the public good, with a blessing from the SEC and the IRS (and sometimes voters), may have the honor of issuing a municipal bond, or *muni*. Therefore, issuers of municipal bonds include municipalities (cities, towns, and counties, for example), public and certain private universities, airports, not-for-profit hospitals, public power plants, water and sewer administrations, various and sundry nonprofit organizations, bridge and tunnel authorities, housing authorities, and an occasional research foundation. The following sections give you the full scoop on municipal bonds.

Comparing and contrasting munis with other bonds

Like most bonds, munis come with differing maturities. Some mature in a year or less, others in 20 or 30 years. Unlike most bonds, munis tend to be issued in minimal denominations of $5,000 and multiples of $5,000 (not a minimum of $1,000 and multiples of $1,000, like corporate bonds and Treasuries).

Like many corporate bonds, but unlike Treasuries, many municipal bonds are callable. Like other bonds, the interest rate on munis is generally fixed, but the price of the bond can go up and down; unless you hold your bond to maturity, you may or may not get your principal returned whole. If the maturity is many years off, the price of the bond can go up and down considerably.

Although the tax-exempt status of munis is unquestionably their most notable and easily recognizable characteristic (more on that in the next section), municipal bonds also offer a fair degree of diversification, even from other bonds. Because they're the only kind of bond more popular with households than with institutions, the muni market is swayed more by public demand than the markets for other bonds. For example, when the stock market tanks and individual investors get butterflies in their stomachs, they tend to sell out of their stock holdings (often a mistake) and load up on what they see as less risky investments, such as munis. When the demand for munis goes up, it tends to drive prices higher. Popular demand or lack of demand for munis typically affects their prices more than it does the price of corporate bonds and Treasuries. Those taxable bonds, in contrast, tend to be more interest-rate sensitive than munis.

Consulting the taxman

Municipal bonds offer tax-exempt features. Here's the scoop:

- ✔ *National munis* are exempt from federal tax but aren't necessarily exempt from state income tax. (Some states tax bond coupon payments and others don't.)

- ✔ *State munis,* if purchased by residents of the same state, are typically exempt from state tax, if there is one. Some, but not all, state munis are also exempt from all local taxes.

- ✔ Munis that are exempt from both federal and state tax are called *double-tax-free* bonds. Those exempt from federal, state, and local tax are often referred to as *triple-tax-free* bonds.

- ✔ Munis from Puerto Rico and Guam are free from federal and state tax, regardless of where you live.

Taxable municipal bonds exist on the market because the federal government doesn't give a break to the financing of certain activities — like funding a new hockey stadium or re-funding a municipality's ailing pension plan — that it perceives as not offering significant benefit to the public. Build America Bonds (BABs) are a special category of taxable muni. Issued in 2009 and 2010 to revive the sagging economy, they allow local governments to raise capital and the Treasury subsidizes 35 percent of the municipality's interest costs. Most of these bonds carry top ratings but tend to be especially volatile because of their lengthy maturity dates (sometimes as high as 30 years).

Enjoying low risk

Municipal bonds come in two varieties:

- ✔ *General obligation bonds* are secured by the full faith and credit of the issuer and are typically supported by that issuer's power to tax the heck out of the citizenry, if necessary.

- ✔ *Revenue bonds'* interest and principal are secured only by the revenue derived from a specific project. If the project goes bust, so does the bond.

By and large, municipal bonds are very safe animals — at least those rated by the major rating agencies (such as Moody's), which are the vast majority of munis. In addition, some municipal bonds come insured; you can't lose your principal unless the issuer *and* its insurance company go under, which is very unlikely! And even if the insurance company were to fail, the general feeling among industry insiders is that most states would be very, very reluctant to allow one of their cities to default on a general obligation bond.

Rating munis

Like the corporations that issue corporate bonds, the entities (cities, hospitals, universities, and so on) that issue municipal bonds are of varying economic strength — although the degree of variance isn't nearly as large as it is in the corporate world. Municipal bonds, like corporate bonds, are rated by the major bond-rating agencies, using the same system as that used for corporate bonds. Refer to Table 2-2 to see the rating scale.

Choosing from a vast array of possibilities

You definitely want munis that are rated. I suggest going with the top-rated munis: Moody's Aa or higher. The lower-rated munis may give you a wee bit of extra yield but probably aren't worth the added risk.

Keep in mind that a lower-rated bond can be more volatile than a high-rated bond. Default isn't the only risk. If you suddenly need to cash out the muni part of your portfolio, and high-yield munis are in the tank, you may not have access to much cash.

If you're looking for even more safety in a muni than a top-rated general obligation bond, you can try to find a *pre-refunded* municipal bond. For this type of muni, the municipality puts money aside into an escrow account to ensure payment to bondholders. Keep in mind, though, that great safety means low yields.

You also want to choose a municipal bond that carries a maturity you can live with. If the bond is callable, well, is that something you can live with and be happy with?

Of great importance in choosing munis are tax benefits. Do you want a muni that's merely free from federal tax, or do you want a muni that's double- or triple-tax-free? (Note that some Build America Bonds are entirely taxable.) To decide, consult your tax advisor before laying out any big money on munis. The tax rules are complicated and forever changing.

Municipal bonds, like any tax-free investment, make the most sense in a taxable account. If you're looking to fill your IRA with fixed-income investments, don't look at munis. Taxable bonds provide greater return, and if the taxes can be postponed (as in an IRA) or avoided (as in a Roth IRA), then taxable bonds are almost always the way to go.

Chapter 3

Getting to Know Mutual Funds and ETFs

In This Chapter

▶ Sorting through mutual funds

▶ Considering some of your ETF choices

Making money trading single stocks is really hard for an individual investor. To reduce portfolio risk, you should hold about 30 different stocks, and it takes a lot of money and time to accumulate that many. You could buy individual bonds, as well, but minimum prices start at $1,000, making it costly to build a diversified portfolio of those. What if you don't have a lot of money to get started? What if you don't have a lot of time to spend analyzing securities and making trades? What if there were easier ways to invest? Well, there is an easier way: mutual funds.

Another option is *exchange-traded funds* (ETFs). In a world of very pricey investment products and very lucratively paid investment-product salespeople, ETFs are the ultimate killjoys. ETFs allow people of average means investment opportunities that don't involve shelling out fat commissions or paying layers of ongoing, unnecessary fees. And they've saved investors oodles and oodles in taxes.

In this chapter, you discover what you need to know to get started making money with these popular, powerful investment vehicles.

Going Over Mutual Fund Basics

Mutual funds are simply investment companies. They contract with an investment manager who takes the money of all the fund investors and buys securities on their behalf. Because thousands of different shareholders in the fund pool their money together, the investment manager can buy a diverse portfolio of securities. And because managing money is her full-time job, she can do lots of research that may help her to choose securities that collectively will beat the market. Alternatively, she may decide to simply invest in the market, or a big slice of it, and not pick securities. Such funds, which tend to be the least expensive, are known as *index* funds (they're discussed in the section "Stock funds").

The following sections describe open- versus closed-end funds, list a variety of mutual funds to consider, discuss sales charges, and provide pointers for being a wise mutual fund investor.

Comparing open- and closed-end funds

Each of the thousands of mutual funds falls into two main categories: open-end and closed-end. Which type you choose affects your rights, your costs of buying and selling, and your potential profit, so you want to know the difference.

- **Open-end funds:** With open-end mutual funds, you buy and sell shares directly from the fund, and the fund company continually issues and redeems new shares. This means that there's always a market for the fund shares. If the fund doesn't have enough cash to meet its redemptions, the portfolio manager — the person who invests the money — sells some of the securities to raise the funds. Most mutual funds sold in the U.S. are open-end funds.

  In an open-end fund, the share value is its *net asset value* (NAV), which is the total value of all the securities in the fund divided by the total number of shares that the fund has issued. Shares never trade for more or less than the NAV. An additional sales charge, called a *load,* may be assessed (see the later section "Loading up: Sales charges" for more detail).

- **Closed-end funds:** Closed-end funds don't buy and sell shares continuously. Instead, the fund organizers collect money from investors all at one time and then do an initial public offering of stock (just like a regular company would). The fund's portfolio managers invest the money, and investors who want to buy or sell shares in the fund do so through the exchange, trading the closed-end fund shares just as they would the shares of any other public company. Closed-end funds are relatively rare.

  Now, if markets were truly efficient, a closed-end fund's share price would be its net asset value (NAV), yet closed-end funds rarely trade at NAV. Instead, they usually trade at a discount. Some investors like to buy closed-end funds just for the bargain. They wait until the share price is well below the NAV; then they swoop in. In some cases, closed-end fund shareholders have forced the fund managers to either disband the fund or convert it to an open-ended fund in order to eliminate the discount.

Meeting myriad types of mutual funds

Book I

Getting
Started
with High-
Powered
Investing

Mutual fund managers don't just invest willy-nilly. Instead, they invest your money in specific types of securities to meet a specific investment objective, which is described in the fund's prospectus. (Closed-end funds issue a prospectus when they're organized; after that, they must file annual reports with the SEC.)

The investment objective gives you a sense of the fund's expected return — and the expected amount of risk that the fund will take. That information helps you make decisions about whether the fund is right for you. Because the prospectus also tells you about the fund's investments, you can get a sense of how the fund works with other investments you have.

The following sections describe the most common types of mutual funds: stock, bond, total return, and money market.

Stock funds

Stock funds, also called *equity funds,* invest in shares of stock of different companies. Stock funds make it easy for investors to get exposure to a wide range of companies, helping them get better long-term performance than they can probably get on their own. Stock funds are usually designed to generate capital gains, which mean that they try to make profits by buying the stock at one price and selling it at a higher one.

Stock funds fall into many different styles, because the fund managers usually concentrate on specific market sectors or types of stocks. Following are some that you may come across:

- **Growth funds:** Growth funds invest in companies that are developing new products and new markets, that have good control over their expenses, and that are expected to grow their profits faster than the average company trading in the stock market. Investors choose growth funds when they're looking to get a high return on their money, especially if they're saving their money for a long time, as for retirement.

  Some growth fund managers specialize in small, medium, or large companies. In general, small company stocks offer greater long-term returns (with greater risk), while larger company stocks have lower returns and lower risk.

- **Value funds:** Value funds want to buy companies when they're cheap and then collect the profits when the business is sold or when it improves. Value investors have to be patient, because it can take a while for the rest of the market to see that these stocks are underpriced. But if and when that happens, the value fund will be sitting pretty.

- ✔ **Index funds:** Market returns are measured by indexes — such as the S&P 500 or the Dow Jones Industrial Average — which track a large number of stocks and are designed to demonstrate the performance of an entire market or a segment of a market. An index fund is designed to mimic the performance of one of the indexes, performing no better and no worse. The fund manager buys all the securities in the index in proportion to their size in the index, using futures (contracts designed to generate the same return as the index) to help if buying the right securities on any given day is difficult. The fund manager also handles purchases and redemptions. (See Chapter 1 of Book I for more details on indexes.)

  Most investors find that index funds are an easy, low-cost way to match market performance. These funds are popular with novice investors who are uncertain about making choices among all the funds out there, as well as with experienced investors who appreciate the inexpensive way to match market performance.

- ✔ **Sector (or specialty) funds:** Specialty funds invest in specific industries, to the exclusion of all others. The fund managers tend to know what's happening in their sectors inside and out. The downside is that these funds offer less diversification; if technology stocks are out of favor, your technology fund probably isn't doing very well, even if the rest of the stock market is going gangbusters.

- ✔ **International funds:** Many great investment opportunities can be found outside of the United States, making international funds appealing. Some of these funds specialize in a specific region, like Europe, or in specific types of markets, such as developing economies. International funds give you exposure to returns available in other countries, and you don't have to learn a new language, figure out the currency issues, or master different accounting systems — the international fund manager does that for you. A variant, the global fund, invests anywhere in the world, at home or abroad.

Bond funds

For less risk than the stock market in exchange for a more predictable return, a bond fund may be right for you. Bonds are essentially loans in which the issuing company, government, or agency is borrowing money from the bond investor. In exchange, the investor receives a regular interest payment. (Chapter 2 in Book I has much more detail about bonds.)

Bond funds pool money from many investors to buy a diversified portfolio of bonds, often with different maturities and interest rates. Read on for descriptions of some of the most common types of bond funds:

- ✔ **U.S. government bond funds:** Some U.S. government bond funds invest in all sorts of securities issued by the government and its agencies, while others specialize. Most government issues are known as *Treasuries,* and Treasury is often shortened to *T. T bonds* are those that mature in ten years or more. *T notes* mature in less than ten years but more than one year. Treasuries that mature in less than one year are known as *T bills.*

In addition to Treasuries, the U.S. government backs bonds issued by entities that are affiliated with the government. These are known as *agency securities,* and they're often issued by such mortgage guarantee agencies as Fannie Mae, Freddie Mac, and Ginnie Mae.

✔ **Corporate bond funds:** Corporations borrow money, often by issuing bonds, to build new factories, make acquisitions, or simply finance continuing operations. Corporate bonds have some risk because the company can go bankrupt and not pay back the money that it borrowed. Some funds invest only in higher-quality bonds, whereas others look for opportunities among less credit-worthy bond offerings (known as *junk bonds* or *high-yield bonds*), trading higher risk for higher interest rates.

✔ **Municipal bond funds:** Many state and local governments need to raise money and do so through bonds. Because of the tax advantages associated with municipal bonds, they're of most interest to individual investors in a high tax bracket looking for high current income. They're not appropriate for retirement or college savings accounts because those accounts usually have their own tax advantages.

✔ **International bond funds:** Companies and governments around the world need to borrow money, and international bond funds are happy to loan it to them. Investors may find better returns and increased diversification benefits from international bond funds, especially if exchange rates happen to move in favorable ways. Some international bond funds organize themselves around a currency or region, buying both corporate and government bonds from the area. Others invest only in corporate bonds or only in government bonds.

Many international investments offer great returns in the foreign currency that may disappear when converted back to U.S. dollars. Many fund managers use hedging techniques to reduce this risk, but exchange rate risk can have a real effect on your return — positive or negative.

Total return funds

Most stock fund managers look to get capital gains and stock dividends, while bond fund managers try to generate interest income. But suppose you want an investment that offers both income and appreciation? That's the goal of a total return fund, also called a *balanced fund.* These funds invest in a mix of stocks and bonds to get a better return than is available with most bond funds, with less risk than with most stock funds.

Many fund companies offer a type of total return fund called a *target-date fund.* It's designed for investors who are saving money for retirement or other long-term goals. The fund managers adjust the investment strategy over time, generally investing in riskier investments in the earlier years and more conservative ones as the fund gets closer to the target date.

Money-market funds

Are you looking for a safe investment that pays a higher return than you can get from a bank CD or savings account? You may want to consider a money-market mutual fund. These funds invest in such short-term investments as one-month jumbo bank CDs, Treasury bills, and corporate overnight securities, which are one-day loans to companies that may have a temporary mismatch between when their bills are due and when their customers pay them. The short time frame means that the risk is very low, so money-market funds effectively function like cash. In fact, many mutual fund management companies allow their money-market fund customers to write checks on their accounts.

A money-market mutual fund is not federally insured, so your investment is not guaranteed. That being said, the risk is extremely low, and money-market investors have rarely lost money. The funds are managed to maintain a net asset value of $1.00 per share; some fund management companies have added their own money to poorly performing funds in order to avoid "breaking the buck."

Loading up: Sales charges

A *load* is a sales charge, and many mutual funds have them. Sometimes this charge compensates a broker or financial planner for helping you manage your money, and other times it's just pure profit to the fund company for services that they need to provide anyway. Because loads reduce the amount of money that you invest, they affect your total investment return. The following sections describe the different types of loads you're likely to encounter.

If you're getting good advice from a broker or a financial planner before you buy the fund, it may be worth your while to pay a load. If you're making the entire investment decision yourself, you should seek funds that don't have loads. Why compensate someone else for the work you've done?

No-load funds

A no-load fund is a fund with no sales charge. With a no-load fund, you may buy and sell shares directly from the fund company or from a brokerage house. You make the decisions and take the responsibility for your choices. In exchange for investigating the fund yourself, you save the sales fee.

If you buy a mutual fund in your 401(k) or other employer retirement plan, you probably won't pay a load, no matter how the fund is sold to other types of accounts. You may pay a 12b-1 fee, though, which is similar to a load and is described in an upcoming section.

Front-end load funds

With a front-end load fund, the investor pays a sales charge at the time the investment is made. If you're buying a mutual fund through a broker or financial planner, you'll almost definitely pay a front-end load. And that may not be the only load you pay.

Some good funds carry high front-end loads because they're sold through brokers and financial planners. However, the fund companies may also allow customers of discount brokerage firms to buy these funds directly at a lower, or even no, sales charge. One such operation is the Charles Schwab Mutual Fund OneSource (www.schwab.com). If you like to make your own decisions, consider buying funds that way.

Most load funds have breakpoints, which means that the percentage of the sales charge goes down as you invest more money. For example, the load may be 4 percent of the first $1,000 invested, 3 percent of the second $1,000, and 1 percent on amounts over $2,000. Some unscrupulous advisors have been known to charge the highest load on the entire investment. Check to make sure this doesn't happen to you.

Back-end load funds

Some funds levy a sales charge when you take money out of the fund, enabling you to put all your money to work up-front and possibly making the back-end load fund cheaper for you than a front-end load.

In some cases, the load is charged only if the money is in the fund for a short period of time, in which case it's known as a *contingent deferred sales charge.* This contingent load compensates the fund company for the up-front costs of opening the account, and it discourages fund investors from trading in and out of their accounts. (And that's as it should be, because mutual funds aren't really appropriate for traders with short time horizons.) After the customer has proven that he's a long-term investor, no sales charge is levied on redemption.

12b-1 fees

Most funds charge 12b-1 fees. These fees are usually small — maybe 0.25 percent per year — but they come out of your investment performance. They compensate the fund company for its ongoing marketing costs. If you work with a financial advisor, part of the 12b-1 fee goes toward paying an ongoing commission for keeping you up-to-date on the fund.

In 1980, the SEC decided to allow mutual fund companies to charge an ongoing sales charge. The paragraph of the law is Rule 12b-1, and hence the fees are known as 12b-1 fees. And doesn't that sound nicer than "license to print money"?

Some funds charge very high 12b-1 fees — as much as 1 percent. It's difficult to generate enough performance to offset that amount, especially in a low-risk, low-return investment like a bond fund. In very few cases is a 1 percent 12b-1 fee worth the money.

Being a savvy mutual fund investor

Mutual fund investing is one of the easiest ways for an individual investor to set up a cost-effective, diversified portfolio that helps generate returns to meet long-term financial goals. Although getting started in mutual funds may be easier than getting started in other types of financial vehicles, you should still do some work to make sure that the fund you invest in is right for you right now. You also want to understand the effects of fees and the rights you may have. All the fun stuff is in the fine print.

Doing the research

Before you buy a mutual fund, do some up-front research on the fund, its investment style, and its historical performance to make sure it fits your risk and return objectives.

Different research services, magazines, and newspapers evaluate mutual funds and offer information on news and trends that affect mutual fund investors. Here are a few of the many that you should check out:

- ✔ **The *Wall Street Journal:*** No newspaper covers U.S. finance as thoroughly as the *Wall Street Journal* (www.wsj.com).
- ✔ **Morningstar:** Morningstar is an investment research company that makes its data available to investors at its website, www.morningstar.com.
- ✔ **Lipper:** Although its services are primarily for fund companies rather than individual investors, Lipper (www.lipperweb.com) has news and performance information that you may find useful.

The goal of investing is to buy low and sell high. Unfortunately, many mutual fund investors get this all wrong: they *chase return.* They buy the fund that was last year's top-performer in the top-performing sector, hoping that the performance will continue; inevitably, they buy at a very high price and watch the fund go down. When evaluating performance, look for a fund and fund manager who offer consistent performance relative to their sector, not relative to the market as a whole. Sometimes, the right fund to buy is one that performed poorly last year.

Reading the prospectus

Under Federal law, anyone soliciting your money for a mutual fund must give you a *prospectus,* which is a legal document describing how the fund will invest its money, listing all the fees, and laying out any rights you may have. Your financial advisor gives you a prospectus when making fund recommendations, and fund companies that sell shares directly to investors put the prospectus on their website.

Although you should read the whole thing, pay particular attention to two sections: the fees and the share classes:

- **Fees:** All mutual funds charge fees, but some charge higher fees than others. You need to know what they are to see whether you're getting your money's worth. These fees fall into several categories:

  - **Management fees:** Management fees go to the investment advisor to cover the costs of research services and the salaries of the investment analysts and portfolio managers who work on the fund. In general, these fees are higher for actively managed stock funds and lower for bond funds and index funds.

  - **Loads and 12b-1 fees:** These fees, described earlier in this chapter, compensate the fund and the brokers and financial planners who recommend it for their sales and advisory services.

  - **Other expenses:** These include legal costs, auditing fees, and fees paid to fund directors, and they're usually quite low.

  When these costs are added together, you end up with the *expense ratio,* which is the total percentage of the fund that is charged to expenses each year. Expenses come off the top to reduce your performance, so in general, the lower the expense ratio, the better for you. However, some funds perform well enough to justify a high expense ratio, so be sure to consider the expense ratio along with the performance.

- **Share classes:** Many mutual fund companies divide their portfolio into different classes of shares. Every investor buys into the same underlying investments, but holders of different share classes are charged different fees and may have different rights for reinvestment and redemption. For example, investors who buy shares directly from the fund buy one class of shares, those who work with a financial planner buy a different class, and those who are buying shares through a qualified retirement plan at work buy yet another class. When you read the prospectus, make sure you check the expenses and features for the share class that applies to you.

Making the investment

So how do you actually make an investment in a mutual fund? Well, if you're buying shares from the fund company directly, you fill out a paper form and mail in a check, or you fill out an online form and transfer money from your bank account. If you buy from a broker or financial planner, the process is similar, but you may be transferring money from your brokerage account or writing the check to the planning firm.

After you make that initial investment, you may want to consider adding more money to the fund. You can do this by simply writing another check or making another transfer from your bank account. Or you can set up an automatic investment program whereby the fund company takes a set amount of money from your bank account every month. That way, you never even consider spending the money.

Handling the taxes

Mutual funds themselves are exempt from paying federal taxes. But there's a catch: The funds push the tax obligations on to you. Now, if your mutual fund investment is part of such qualified retirement plans as IRAs or 401(k)s, you won't have to pay taxes on the fund until you withdraw the money, if you even have to then. Many qualified college savings plans that use mutual funds have similar tax benefits, so investigate those before you open the account.

If your mutual fund investment is not part of a retirement or college account, you'll probably have to pay taxes on the fund's income and capital gains. If you do, in January the mutual fund company will send you a year-end tax form that tells you the fund's dividends and its capital gains distributions. If the fund had any of these, you need to put those amounts on your own tax return and pay the taxes accordingly.

When you cash in shares in the fund, you'll trigger another tax event, which is the capital gain. In general, the *capital gain* is the profit you made on your investment (the change between the net asset value when you bought the fund and the net asset value when you sold the fund times the number of shares you owned), and your fund company will probably send you a form before your tax return is due telling you how much of a gain you have. (You may also have a capital loss, in which case, you'll likely qualify for a tax write-off.)

The ABCs of ETFs

Just as a deed shows that you have ownership of a house, and a share of common stock certifies ownership in a company, a share of an exchange-traded fund (ETF) represents ownership (most typically) in a basket of company stocks or bonds.

Mutual funds, covered in the first part of this chapter, also represent baskets of stocks or bonds, but ETFs offer quite a few advantages that mutual funds don't. Table 3-1 compares ETFs and mutual funds (with stocks thrown in for good measure), and the following sections explain the key differences — and advantages — in more detail.

Table 3-1   ETFs Versus Mutual Funds Versus Individual Stocks

	ETFs	Mutual Funds	Individual Stocks
Priced, bought, and sold throughout the day?	Yes	No	Yes
Offer some investment diversification?	Yes	Yes	No
Is there a minimum investment?	No	Yes	No
Purchased through a broker or online brokerage?	Yes	Sometimes	Usually
Do you pay a fee or commission to make a trade?	Usually	Sometimes	Yes
Can you buy/sell options?	Sometimes	No	Sometimes
Indexed (passively managed)?	Usually	Not usually	No
Can you make money or lose money?	Yes	Yes	You bet

Looking at the positives and negatives

On the plus side, ETFs have ultra-low management expenses, super tax efficiency, transparency, and a lot of fancy trading opportunities, such as shorting, if you're so inclined. Here are the details:

✔ **Lower fees:** In the world of mutual funds, the average management fee at present, according to Morningstar, is 1.3 percent (of the account balance) annually. That may not sound like a lot of money, but it's a very substantial sum. In the world of ETFs, the expenses are much, much lower, averaging 0.4 percent, and many of the more traditional domestic indexed ETFs cost no more than 0.2 percent a year in management fees. A handful are under 0.1 percent.

✔ **Lower capital gains taxes:** With mutual funds, the fund itself may enjoy a capital gain by selling off an appreciated stock, but you pay the capital gains tax regardless of whether you sell your fund shares and regardless of whether the share price of the mutual fund has increased or decreased since the time you bought it. Because ETFs are index-based, there is generally little turnover to create capital gains. To boot, ETFs are structured in a way that insulates shareholders from having to pay capital gains tax, as mutual fund shareholders must often do, when other shareholders cash in their chips.

✔ **What you see is what you get:** A key to building a successful portfolio is diversification. You can't diversify optimally unless you know exactly what's in your portfolio. With a mutual fund, you often have little idea of what stocks (if any) the fund manager is holding at a particular moment in time. When you buy an ETF, you get complete transparency. You know exactly what you're buying. No matter what the ETF, you can see on the prospectus or on the ETF provider's website (or on any number of independent financial websites) a complete picture of the ETF's holdings.

✔ **Index advantage:** Index funds, which buy and hold a fixed collection of stocks or bonds, consistently outperform actively managed funds over the long term.

Okay, so what about the negatives? Here are some other facts about ETFs that you should consider before parting with your precious dollars:

✔ **You pay commissions whenever you buy and sell:** You have to pay a commission every time you buy and sell an ETF. Here's the good news: Trading commissions for stocks and ETFs (the commission is the same for both) have been dropping. What once would have cost you a bundle, now — if you trade online, which you definitely should — is really pin money, perhaps as low as $4 a trade. However, you can't simply ignore trading commissions. They aren't always that low, and even $4 a pop can add up.

✔ **You may be tempted to trade on impulse:** The fact that ETFs can be traded throughout the day like stocks makes them, unlike mutual funds, fair game for day-traders and institutional wheeler-dealers. For the rest of us common folk, not much about the way that ETFs are bought and sold makes them especially valuable. Indeed, the ability to trade throughout the day may make you more apt to do so, perhaps selling or buying on impulse, which (although it can get your endorphins pumping) generally isn't the most profitable investing strategy.

Getting in on the action

Buying ETFs isn't all that difficult. You find a brokerage house (or supplier), open an account, and place an order, either by phone or online. The following sections have the details.

Choosing a brokerage house

You — you personally — can't just buy a share of an ETF as you would buy, say, a negligee. You need someone to actually buy and hold it for you. That someone is a broker, sometimes referred to as a *brokerage house* or a *broker-dealer.* Here are some things you want from any broker who's going to be holding your ETFs:

- ✔ Reasonable prices

- ✔ Freebies, including free trades on certain ETFs

- ✔ Good service and good advice

- ✔ A user-friendly website (or, if you like doing business with real human beings, a service center near you)

- ✔ Incentives for opening an account, which can run the gamut from a certain number of free trades to laptop computers

- ✔ Financial strength

The following list gives an overview of some of the major brokerage houses and a brief look at their pricing. Before choosing, always look at the entire brokerage package, which includes not only the price of trades but total account fees.

- ✔ **The Vanguard Group:** At Vanguard, the trading commissions are middle-of-the-road, and the service is middle-of-the-road (better than that if you have big bucks with the company). What really shines about Vanguard is its broad array of top-rate index mutual funds and ETFs. If you want to hold index mutual funds alongside your ETFs, Vanguard is a logical place to hold them because you can buy and sell Vanguard funds, provided you don't do it often, at no charge. Vanguard is owned "mutually" by its shareholders, unlike, say, Fidelity, which is privately owned, or just about all the other brokerage houses, which are publicly owned. The mutual ownership means that investors are shareholders in the company, and that means the Vanguard elite, although well paid, for sure, have an obligation to serve your best interests. You can find Vanguard at www.vanguard.com or 877-662-7447.

- ✔ **Fidelity Investments:** Fidelity has great service, and the price of trades is competitive. Fidelity also has some excellent low-cost index funds of its own, which you may want to keep alongside your ETF portfolio. And the Fidelity website has some really good tools — some of the best available — for analyzing your portfolio and researching new investments. You can find Fidelity at www.fidelity.com or call 800-343-3548.

- ✔ **Charles Schwab:** Schwab offers a lineup of 15 low-cost, sensible ETFs of its own creation, and they trade free if you open an account with this brokerage. All other ETFs cost $10 per online trade. The staff is friendly and knowledgeable. Go to www.schwab.com or call 866-855-9102.

✔ **T. Rowe Price:** This Baltimore-based shop has several claims to fame, including its bend-over-backward friendliness to small investors and its plethora of really fine financial tools, especially for retirement planning, available to all customers at no cost. The price of trading is a wee bit higher than average. At the time of this writing, T. Rowe Price was gearing up to launch its own lineup of ETFs, which, rumor has it, will all be actively managed. The service is excellent (reps tend to be very chummy). Go to www.troweprice.com or call 800-225-5132.

✔ **TD Ameritrade:** The trading prices at TD are just about middle-of-the-pack, and the service is reputedly quite high. The website has a very clean and crisp feel to it. On the downside (in my opinion, of course), the TD culture and many of the articles on the website promote frequent trading, as opposed to, say, Vanguard, where the culture is decidedly more buy-and-hold. In 2010, the firm acquired online futures brokerage *thinkorswim.* Find TD at www.tdameritrade.com or call 800-454-9272.

✔ **Other major brokerage houses:** Here are a few more to consider:

- **E*TRADE:** Phone 800-387-2331; website www.etrade.com.

- **TIAA-CREF:** Phone 800-842-2755; website www.tiaa-cref.org.

- **Folio Investing:** Phone 888-973-7890; website www.folio investing.com.

- **TradeKing:** Phone 877-495-5464; website www.tradeking.com.

- **ShareBuilder:** Phone 800-747-2537; website www.sharebuilder.com

Opening an account

When you open an account with a brokerage house. you'll be asked a zillion questions related to the following:

✔ **Retirement or non-retirement account:** If you want a retirement account, you need to specify what kind (IRA? Roth IRA? SEP?).

✔ **Margin account or cash account:** A *margin* account is somewhat similar to a checking account with overdraw protection. It means that you can borrow from the account or make purchases of securities (such as ETFs, but generally not mutual funds) without actually having any cash to pay for them on the spot. Cool, huh? Unless you have a gambling addiction, go with margin. You never know when you may need a quick and potentially tax-deductible loan. But, before you blithely begin to buy on margin, read the next paragraph for dire warnings!

Margin buying is very dangerous business. The stock market is risky enough. Don't ever compound that risk by borrowing money to invest. You may wind up losing not only your nest egg but your home. In addition, the brokerage house can usually change the rate of interest you're paying without notice, and if your investments dip below a certain percentage of your margin loan, the brokerage house can sell your stocks and bonds from right under you. Buy on margin only with great caution.

✔ **Beneficiaries and titling (or registration):** Be certain that who you name is who you want to receive your money if you die. Beneficiary designations supercede your will. In other words, if your will says that all your ETFs go to your spouse, and your beneficiary designation on your account names someone else, your spouse loses; all the ETFs in your account will go to someone else.

✔ **Your employment, your wealth, and your risk tolerance:** Don't sweat these topics! Federal securities regulations require brokerage houses to know something about their clients, but honestly, no one is ever likely to look at the personal section of the forms.

Placing an order to buy

ETFs are usually traded just as stocks are traded. Same commissions. Mostly the same rules. Same hours (generally 9:30 a.m. to 4:00 p.m., Manhattan Island time). Through your brokerage house, you can buy 1, 2, or 10,000 shares.

Most brokerage houses give you a choice: Call in your order or do it yourself online. Calling is typically much more expensive; place all your orders online. If you need help, a representative of the brokerage house will walk you through the process step-by-step — at no expense to you.

Managing risk with ETFs

Asking how risky, or how lucrative, ETFs are is like trying to judge a soup knowing nothing about the soup itself except that it's served in a blue china bowl. The bowl — or the ETF — doesn't create the risk; what's inside it does. Thus stock and real estate ETFs tend to be more volatile than bond ETFs. Short-term bond ETFs are less volatile than long-term bond ETFs. Small-stock ETFs are more volatile than large-stock ETFs. And international ETFs often see more volatility than U.S. ETFs.

To minimize risk and maximize return, diversify. Include both stocks and bonds and both domestic and international holdings in your portfolio. You also need to diversify the domestic stock part of a portfolio, and that part's a bit trickier because not even the experts agree on how to accomplish that. Two competing methods predominate, and either is fine (as is a mixture of both for those with good-sized portfolios):

✔ Divide the portfolio into domestic and foreign, and then into different styles: large cap, small cap, mid cap, value, and growth.

✔ Allocate percentages of the portfolio to various industry sectors: healthcare, utilities, energy, financials, and so on.

Exploring ETF options

To help you wade through the myriad ETF choices, the following sections introduce a few that may be worth a look, divided according to style or type of ETF.

Today, all competent investment pros develop their portfolios with at least some consideration given to the cap size and growth or value orientation of their stock holdings. *Capitalization* or *cap* refers to the combined value of all shares of a company's stock. The following divisions are generally accepted:

- ✔ **Large caps:** Companies with over $5 billion in capitalization
- ✔ **Mid caps:** Companies with $1 billion to $5 billion in capitalization
- ✔ **Small caps:** Companies with $250 million to $1 billion in capitalization

Anything from $50 million to $250 million would usually be deemed a *micro cap.* And your local pizza shop, if it were to go public, might be called a *nano cap.* There are no nano-cap ETFs. For all the other categories, you can find ETFs to your heart's content.

All the expense ratios, average cap sizes, price/earnings ratios, and top five holdings listed here (and elsewhere) are subject to change. Before making a purchase, be sure to get the most recent data.

Blended options for large-cap exposure

Among the *blended* (large-cap value and growth) options for smaller portfolios ($10,000 to $20,000), consider the ETFs listed in Table 3-2.

Table 3-2	Blended Options for Large-Cap Exposure				
ETF	*Indexed To*	*Expense Ratio*	*Avg. Cap Size*	*P/E Ratio*	*Top Holdings*
Vanguard Large-Cap ETF (VV)	CRSP U.S. Large-Cap Value Index	0.10%	$50.6 billion	15.6	Exxon Mobil, Johnson & Johson, Chevron, GE, Pfizer
Vanguard Mega-Cap ETF (MGC)	CRSP U.S. Mega-Cap Index	0.12%	$75.6 billion	18.6	Exxon Mobil, Apple, Chevron, GE, IBM

ETF	Indexed To	Expense Ratio	Avg. Cap Size	P/E Ratio	Top Holdings
Schwab U.S. Large-Cap ETF (SCHX)	Dow Jones U.S. Large-Cap Total Stock Market Index	0.04%	$50.3 billion	16.8	Apple, Exxon Mobil, GE, Microsoft, Johnson & Johnson
iShares Russell 1000 ETF (IWB)	Russell 1000	0.15%	$45.9 billion	22.0	Exxon Mobil, Apple, Microsoft, GE, Chevron

Strictly large growth

For large growth and large growth alone (complimented by large value, of course) — a position for people with adequate assets ($20,000+) — the four options listed in Table 3-3 all provide good exposure to the asset class at a very reasonable cost.

Table 3-3	Options for Large Growth				
ETF	Indexed To	Expense Ratio	Avg. Cap Size	P/E Ratio	Top Holdings
Vanguard Growth ETF (VUG)	CRSP U.S. Large-Cap Growth Index	0.10%	$45.3 billion	16	Apple, IBM, Google, Coca-Cola, Philip Morris International
Vanguard Mega-Cap Growth ETF (MGK)	CRSP U.S. Mega-Cap Growth Index	0.12%	$67.2 billion	15	Apple, IBM, Google, Coca-Cola, Philip Morris International
iShares Morningstar Large Growth Index ETF (JKE)	Morningstar Large Growth Index	0.25%	$81 billion	18	Apple, IBM, Coca-Cola, Google, Philip Morris International

(continued)

Table 3-3 *(continued)*

ETF	Indexed To	Expense Ratio	Avg. Cap Size	P/E Ratio	Top Holdings
Schwab U.S. Large-Cap Growth ETF (SCHG)	Dow Jones U.S. Large-Cap Growth Total Stock Market Index	0.07%	$45.2 billion	16	Apple, Berkshire Hathaway, Google, Microsoft, Johnson & Johnson

Large value stock best buys

In the past 77 years, large value stocks have enjoyed an annualized growth rate of 11.4 percent, versus 9.5 percent for large growth stocks — with roughly the same volatility. Thanks to ETFs, such as those listed in Table 3-4, investing in value has never been easier.

Table 3-4 — Large Value Stocks

ETF	Indexed To	Expense Ratio	Avg. Cap Size	P/E Ratio	Top Holdings
Vanguard Large-Cap ETF (VTV)	CRSP U.S. Large-Cap Value Index	0.10%	$50.6 billion	15.6	Exxon Mobil, Johnson & Johson, Chevron, GE, Pfizer
Vanguard Mega-Cap Value Index ETF (MGV)	CRSP U.S. Mega-Cap Value Index	0.12%	$78 billion	12	Exxon Mobil, Chevron, GE, Johnson & Johnson, Pfizer
iShares Russell 1000 Value Index ETF (IWD)	Russell 1000 Index	0.20%	$43.4 billion	13	Exxon Mobil, GE, Chevron, JPMorgan Chase, Berkshire Hathaway

Book I

Getting
Started
with High-
Powered
Investing

ETF	Indexed To	Expense Ratio	Avg. Cap Size	P/E Ratio	Top Holdings
Schwab U.S. Large-Cap Value ETF (SCHV)	Dow Jones U.S. Large-Cap Value Total Stock Market Index	0.07%	$56 billion	13	Exxon Mobil, GE, Chevron, IBM, Procter & Gamble

Small-cap blend funds

Some pretty good ETF options for people with limited portfolios include those listed in Table 3-5.

Table 3-5		Small-Cap Blend Funds			
ETF	Indexed To	Expense Ratio	Avg. Cap Size	P/E Ratio	Top Holdings
Vanguard Small-Cap ETF (VB)	CRSP U.S. Small-Cap Index	0.10%	$2.3 billion	15	Rock-Tenn Company, Onyx Pharmaceuticals, B/E Aerospace, Fortune Brands Home & Security, Cheniere Energy
iShares Morningstar Small Core Index ETF (JKJ)	Morningstar Small Core Index	0.25%	$2 billion	18	Abercrombie & Fitch Company, Alaska Air Group, Omega Healthcare Investors, JDS Uniphase, Acuity Brands
iShares S&P SmallCap ETF (IJR)	S&P SmallCap 600 Index	0.16%	$1.3 billion	18	Salix Pharmaceuticals, Cubist Pharmaceuticals, Gulfport Energy, Tanger Factory Outlet Centers, Proassurance

(continued)

Table 3-5 *(continued)*

ETF	Indexed To	Expense Ratio	Avg. Cap Size	P/E Ratio	Top Holdings
Schwab U.S. Small-Cap ETF (SCHA)	Dow Jones U.S. Small-Cap Total Stock Market Index	0.08%	$1.7 billion	16	Assured Guaranty Ltd, GameStop, Starwood Property Trust, Smithfield Foods, Alkermes

Strictly small-cap growth funds

If you have enough assets to warrant splitting up small value and small growth, go for those listed in Table 3-6.

Table 3-6		Small-Cap Growth Funds			
ETF	Indexed To	Expense Ratio	Avg. Cap Size	P/E Ratio	Top Holdings
Vanguard Small-Cap Growth ETF (VBK)	CRSP U.S. Small-Cap Growth Index	0.10%	$1.9 billion	17	Cheniere Energy, Tenet Healthcare, Fleetcor Technologies, Alaska Air Group, Mednax
iShares Morningstar Small Growth Index ETF (JKK)	Morningstar Small Growth Index	0.30%	$2.1 billion	24	3D Systems, CBOE Holdings, Hexcel Corp, Atmel Corp, SBV Financial Group
iShares S&P SmallCap 600 Growth ETF (IJT)	S&P SmallCap 600 Growth Index	0.25%	$1.4 billion	20	Salix Pharmaceuticals, Gulfport Energy, Hain Celestial Group, Old Dominion Freight Lines, Brunswick Corp

Book I

Getting
Started
with High-
Powered
Investing

ETF	Indexed To	Expense Ratio	Avg. Cap Size	P/E Ratio	Top Holdings
Guggenheim S&P SmallCap 600 Pure Growth ETF (RZG)	S&P SmallCap 600 Pure Growth Index Total Return	0.35%	$1.1 billion	20	Blucora, Tuesday Morning, Francescas Holdings, Winnebago Industries, On Assignment

Diminutive dazzlers: Small value ETFs

Look at the list of some of the companies represented in the Vanguard Small-Cap Value ETF listed in Table 3-7, and you probably won't recognize them. If you wanted to pick one of these companies to sink a wad of cash into, you'd probably be considered crazy. But if you wanted to sink that cash into the entire small value index, well, that's another matter. Assuming you can handle some risk, your odds of making money are pretty darned good — at least if history is your guide.

Whatever your total allocation to domestic small-cap stocks, 60 to 75 percent of that amount should be allocated to small value ETFs.

Table 3-7		Small Value ETFs			
ETF	Indexed To	Expense Ratio	Avg. Cap Size	P/E Ratio	Top Holdings
Vanguard Small-Cap Value ETF (VBR)	CRSP U.S. Small-Cap Value Index	0.10%	$1.7 billion	14	American Capital Ltd, Packaging Corporation of America, Two Harbors Investment Corp, Community Health Systems, Carlisle Companies

(continued)

Table 3-7 *(continued)*

ETF	Indexed To	Expense Ratio	Avg. Cap Size	P/E Ratio	Top Holdings
iShares Morningstar Small Value Index ETF (JKL)	Morningstar Small Value Index	0.30%	$2.1 billion	12	Tenet Healthcare, Community Health Systems, Assured Guaranty Ltd, Starwood Property Trust, Health Management Associates
iShares S&P SmallCap 600 Value Index ETF (IJS)	S&P SmallCap 600 Value Index	0.29%	$1.2 billion	16	ProAssurance Corp, EMCOR Group, Centene Corp, Piedmont Natural Gas Co, EPR Properties
Guggenheim S&P SmallCap 600 Pure Value ETF (RZV)	S&P SmallCap 600 Pure Value Index Total Return	0.38%	$607 million	20	Arkansas Best Corp, VOXX International Corp, Boyd Gaming, AAR Corp, Olympic Steel

Micro caps

Micro caps are companies larger than the corner delicatessen, but not by much. They're volatile little suckers, but as a group they offer impressive long-term performance figures. In terms of diversification, micro caps — in a conservative quantity — are a nice addition to most portfolios. Table 3-8 has some micro-cap ETFs to consider.

Book I

Getting
Started
with High-
Powered
Investing

Table 3-8	Micro-Cap Funds				
ETF	Indexed To	Expense Ratio	Avg. Cap Size	P/E Ratio	Top Holdings
iShares Russell Microcap Index ETF (IWC)	Russell Microcap Index	0.69%	$367 million	15	Radian Group, Aegerion Pharmaceuticals, ACADIA Pharmaceuticals, American Realty Capital Properties, Virtus Investment Partners
PowerShares Zacks Micro Cap ETF (PZI)	Zacks Micro Cap Index	0.91%	$427 million	13	Canadian Solar, ACADIA Pharmaceuticals, Hutchinson Technology, Zale Corp, Overstock. com
First Trust Dow Jones Select MicroCap ETF (FDM)	Dow Jones Select MicroCap Index	0.60%	$425 million	14	OfficeMax, Krispy Kreme Doughnuts, Headwaters, ACCO Brands, OFG Bancorp

Bond ETFs

For the most part, bonds are less volatile than stocks, and their returns over time tend to be less. But they're a key stabilizing force in a portfolio (refer to Chapter 2 of Book 1 to find out why). Bond ETFs include the following (refer to Table 3-9):

- ✔ **Treasuries:** If the creator/issuer of a bond is a national government, the issue is called a *sovereign* bond. The vast majority of sovereign bonds sold in the United States are Uncle Sam's own Treasuries.

- ✔ **Inflation-protected securities:** Technically, U.S. Treasury Inflation-Protected Securities (TIPS) are Treasuries, but they play a distinctly different role in your portfolio than the other Treasuries do. The gig with TIPS is this: They pay you only a nominal amount of interest (currently about 0.5 percent), but they also kick in an adjustment for inflation. If, for example, inflation is running at 4 percent, all things being equal, your TIPs will yield 4.5 percent.

✔ **Corporate bond ETFs:** You can buy a dizzying array of corporate bonds with varying maturities, yields, and ratings. Or you can buy a representative sampling through an ETF.

✔ **Investing in the entire U.S. bond market:** The broadest fixed-income ETFs are all-around good bets, especially for more modest portfolios.

Table 3-9	Bond ETFs			
ETF	*Indexed To*	*Expense Ratio*	*Current Yield*	*Average Weighted Maturity*
iShares Barclays 1–3 Year Treasury Bond ETF (SHY)	Barclays 1–3 Year U.S. Treasury Bond Index	0.15%	0.30%	1.9 years
iShares Barclays 7–10 Year Treasury ETF (IEF)	Barclays U.S. 7–10 Year Treasury Bond Index	0.15%	1.68%	7.6 years
iShares Barclays 20+ Year Treasury Bond ETF (TLT)	Barclays U.S. 20+ Year Treasury Bond Index	0.15%	2.75%	17.0 years
iShares Barclays TIPS Bond ETF (TIP)	Barclays U.S. Treasury Inflation-Protected Securities Index	0.20%	2.01% + adjustment for inflation	8.0 years
iShares iBoxx $ Investment Grade Corporate Bond ETF (LQD) (Average credit quality: BBB)	Markit iBoxx USD Liquid Investment Grade Index	0.15%	3.84%	7.8 years

ETF	Indexed To	Expense Ratio	Current Yield	Average Weighted Maturity
Vanguard Short-Term Corporate Bond Index ETF (VCSH) (Average credit quality: A)	Barclays U.S. 1–5 Year Corporate Bond Index	0.12%	2.01%	2.9 years
Vanguard Total Bond Market ETF (BND) (Average credit quality: AA)	Barclays U.S. Aggregate Float Adjusted Index	0.10%	2.51%	5.3 years
iShares Core Total US Bond Market ETF (AGG) (Average credit quality: A)	Barclays U.S. Aggregate Bond Index	0.08%	2.45%	4.9 years
Vanguard Short-Term Bond ETF (BSV) (Average credit quality: AA)	Barclays U.S. 1–5 Government/ Credit Float Adjusted Index	0.10%	1.41%	2.7 years

Real estate investing (REITs)

In a nutshell, *real estate investment trusts,* popularly known as *REITs* (rhymes with "Pete's"), are companies that hold portfolios of properties, such as shopping malls, office buildings, hotels, amusement parks, or timberland. Or they may hold certain real estate–related assets, such as commercial mortgages. Via a handful of ETFs listed in Table 3-10, you can buy a bevy of REITs.

The tax efficiency of ETFs will help cap any capital gains you enjoy on your REIT fund, but it won't do anything to diminish the taxes you'll be paying on the dividends. For that reason, all REIT funds — ETFs or otherwise — are best kept in tax-advantaged retirement accounts.

Table 3-10	REIT ETFs			
ETF	**Indexed To**	**Expense Ratio**	**Number of Holdings**	**Top Five Holdings**
Vanguard REIT Index ETF (VNQ)	MSCI U.S. REIT Index	0.12%	108	Simon Property Group, Equity Residential, Public Storage, Vornado Realty Trust, Boston Property
Focus Morningstar Real Estate ETF (FRL)	Morningstar Real Estate Index	0.12%	85	Simon Property Group, Equity Residential, Public Storage, Vornado Realty Trust, Boston Property
Vanguard REIT Index ETF (VNQ)	MSCI U.S. REIT Index	0.10%	124	Simon Property Group, HCP Inc, Public Storage, Ventas Inc, Prologis Inc
iShares Cohen & Steers REIT ETF (ICF)	Cohen & Steers Realty Majors Index	0.35%	31	Simon Property Group, Public Storage, HCP Inc, Ventas Inc, Prologis Inc

Chapter 4

All about Annuities

*I*n the years since the first edition of this book came out, Baby Boomers have begun to retire. They've saved trillions of dollars in 401(k) and 403(b) plans, but few have a strategy for stretching that money over what could be 20, 25, or even 30 years of retirement.

Annuities may be the answer. Annuities can help Baby Boomers (especially those without traditional pensions) protect their savings and/or convert savings into guaranteed lifelong income. Annuities aren't just for the Baby Boom generation. They can be a viable investment option for anyone who wants to protect his income in later years. This chapter gives you an overview of what annuities are, what they offer (both good and bad), and the general types of annuities you can choose from.

Introducing Annuities

Annuities are neither pure investments nor pure insurance. Instead, they have one foot in both worlds.

✔ An annuity is an *investment* in the sense that you give a sum of money to a financial institution with the hope that you'll get back more than what you put in. Your investment — or, in this case, a *premium* — can range in size from $2,000 to over $2 million. The financial institution — usually an insurance company — puts your money in its own general account (if you bought a fixed annuity) or in a separate account (if you bought a variable annuity).

✔ An annuity is *insurance* in the sense that your investment comes with a guarantee backed by the insurance company. The exact nature of the guarantee varies with the type of annuity. In fixed annuity contracts, for instance, your rate of return is guaranteed for a certain number of years. In the latest variable annuity contracts, you can lock in a guaranteed rate of return and get a guaranteed payout in retirement. With an income annuity, you get guaranteed income. All types of annuities include a death benefit, which pays a guaranteed amount of money to the beneficiary when the annuity owner dies. (Different types of annuities are explained in detail later in this chapter.)

Every annuity contains an option that allows you to convert your premium (and any additional gains that your contract earned over time) to a guaranteed income stream. In fact, annuities are the only financial product that can guarantee you a pension-like income for life. No more-efficient tool exists for converting a specific sum of money into a monthly income that lasts as long you live — even if you live to 105.

Like any other financial product, annuities involve tradeoffs between risk and return. The guarantees reduce your risk of losing money. But the cost of the guarantee may reduce the potential growth of your investment.

Looking at how annuities work

Annuities are intended to help you save for retirement and supplement your retirement income. Various types of annuities can make your retirement more secure by helping you do the following:

- ✔ **Save for retirement:** Before you retire, fixed deferred annuities — which include CD-type annuities, market value–adjusted fixed annuities, and indexed annuities — allow you to earn a specific (or adjustable) rate of interest on your money for a specific number of years, tax-deferred. They're also a safe place to park money during retirement.

- ✔ **Invest for retirement:** Before you retire, variable deferred annuities — baskets of mutual funds usually combined with one or more optional guarantees — allow you to invest your savings in stocks and/or bonds while deferring taxes on the capital gains, dividends, and interest that mutual funds typically generate every year.

- ✔ **Distribute your savings:** Many who retire with six-figure balances in their employer-sponsored retirement plans won't know how fast or slow to spend their savings. An income annuity or a variable deferred annuity with a lifetime income rider (sometimes referred to by the acronyms GLWB or GMIB) can provide structure to the process.

- ✔ **Insure you against longevity risk:** An income annuity can insure you against the risk of living so long that you run out of money. The income

Book I

Getting
Started
with High-
Powered
Investing

may begin within 13 months after you buy the annuity (an immediate annuity) or it may begin years later (a deferred income annuity).

✔ **Manage your taxes:** Everybody with a big 401(k) or 403(b) account will retire with a large income tax debt to the government, to be paid as the savings are spent. A life income annuity makes it easy to spread that tax liability evenly across your entire retirement.

To encourage saving, Uncle Sam lets you defer taxes on the growth of your investment in an annuity. To discourage you from spending your savings before retirement, the IRS exacts a penalty for withdrawals taken from annuities (as well as from other tax-deferred investments) before you reach age 59½.

Getting to know the participants

Every annuity has an owner, an annuitant, beneficiaries, and an issuer:

✔ **The owner:** The owner of an annuity is the person who pays the premiums, signs the application, and agrees to abide by the terms of the contract. The owner decides who the other parties of the annuity contract will be. Depending on the type of contract or the stage it's in, the owner can withdraw money or even sell the annuity. The owner is liable for any taxes that are due on the withdrawals.

✔ **The annuitant:** The annuitant is the person whose life expectancy is used to calculate the amount of each annuity payment. If and when the owner decides to start taking a guaranteed lifetime income from the annuity, the size of the annuity payments will be based on the annuitant's age and life expectancy — not the owner's (although, in most cases, the owner and annuitant are the same person).

✔ **The beneficiaries:** On the contract application, the owner needs to name an owner's beneficiary and an annuitant's beneficiary. The owner and annuitant can be each other's beneficiary, which can help keep things simple, but no one can be his or her own beneficiary.

✔ **The issuer:** The insurance company that issues the contract and puts itself on the hook for any guarantees in the contract is the issuer (also sometimes called the *carrier*).

You should always look for an issuer that's rated "excellent," "superior," or "very good" by the ratings agencies, such as A.M. Best (www.ambest.com) and Fitch (www.fitchratings.com), both of which make ratings available to members; you can sign up at either website for free. A high rating suggests — but doesn't guarantee — that the issuer will fulfill its promises to you and that you'll get your money back.

Noting common elements of all (or most) annuities

All annuities have a free look period, a death benefit, guarantees, and annuitization options. Most have surrender periods. Deferred variable annuities have accumulated unit values (AUVs). The following list provides basic information about these elements:

- ✔ **Free look period:** Whoever buys an annuity has between 10 and 30 days after receiving the contract in the mail to cancel the contract. Some immediate annuity contracts offer a rider that lets you cancel your contract within the first six months. Some fixed annuity contracts let you opt out during a brief "window" at the beginning of each contract year.

- ✔ **Death benefit:** Depending on whether the owner bought a "standard" death benefit or an "enhanced" death benefit, the death benefit may be equal to the original premium, to the maximum value of the contract on any contract anniversary, or to another amount. This amount is paid out to the beneficiaries upon the annuitant's death.

- ✔ **Guarantees:** Annuities offer one or more of the following guarantees:

  - A guarantee of a particular return

  - A guarantee against loss of principal

  - A guarantee that, if the owner dies during a bear market, her heirs won't suffer financially

  - A guarantee of lifetime income

- ✔ **Annuitization option:** All deferred annuities allow you to annuitize. To *annuitize* is to relinquish control over your money to the issuer in return for a guarantee that the issuer will pay you a fixed or variable income for a specific period, for the rest of your life, or as long as either you or your spouse is living.

- ✔ **Surrender period:** Most, but not all, annuities have surrender periods during which the issuer may levy a penalty, known technically as a contingent deferred sales charge (CDSC), if you withdraw more than 10 percent of your money per year from the contract. All deferred fixed annuities have CDSCs, and so do most deferred variable annuities that are purchased from agents or brokers.

- ✔ **Accumulation unit value (AUV):** The most important unit of measure for mutual fund shares is the *net asset value,* or NAV. After the financial markets close every business day and the final prices are fixed for the evening (except for after-hours trading), a mutual fund manager tallies up the value of all his investments and divides those millions or billions

Book I

Getting
Started
with High-
Powered
Investing

of dollars by the number of mutual fund shares outstanding. The result is the NAV. (Chapter 3 in Book I has more about NAVs and mutual funds.)

In the parallel universe of deferred variable annuities, mutual funds are called *subaccounts* and NAVs are called *accumulation unit values* (AUVs). A subaccount and a mutual fund may be managed by the same manager and invest in the same securities, but they will have different daily values. Certain fees are deducted every day from the subaccounts that are not deducted from the mutual fund accounts. Also, the mutual fund makes taxable distributions and the subaccount does not. Thus the NAV of a mutual fund and the AUV of a variable annuity are typically different, even when they own the same basket of securities.

Deciding Whether an Annuity Is Right for You

Annuities aren't for everyone. The very poor or the ultra-rich, for example, may not find much use for them. People who expect both Social Security and a handsome company pension in retirement may not need the extra guaranteed income that income annuities offer. Cockeyed optimists, who buy every dip in the Dow and purposely seek risk, may not want to bother with annuities because the cost of the guarantees can reduce their potential returns. Nor is every type of annuity right for everybody (you can check out different types of annuities later in this chapter).

Evaluating the pluses

Annuities offer a number of benefits, such as tax deferral, unlimited contributions, and the opportunity for guaranteed income. Some of these benefits are a result of federal tax law. Others come from the fact that annuities are insurance products as well as investments. Different types of annuities offer different types of advantages, as the following list explains:

- ✔ **Guaranteeing income after age 59½:** Annuities are the only financial product that can guarantee you an income for life (or two lives) or for a specific number of years. All annuities offer you the option to convert savings to income, and new types of annuities are making it easier to buy future income.

- ✔ **Deferring taxes:** When you buy a deferred annuity with money you have already paid taxes on, you can let the money grow and not pay taxes on the growth until years later — ordinarily after you reach age 59½.

Assuming that your tax rate during retirement will be lower than your tax rate while you're still working, you'll ultimately pay less in taxes. (***Note:*** You can't deduct your contributions to a deferred annuity from your taxable income the way you can deduct contributions to a traditional IRA or employer-sponsored retirement account.)

✔ **Allowing unlimited contributions:** You can contribute as much as you want to a deferred annuity. Most insurance companies reserve the right to review contributions over $1 million in advance — to prevent large-scale money laundering, in part — but they don't specifically discourage large deposits.

✔ **Reducing investment risk:** Unlike with investments, when you put your savings in a fixed deferred annuity, there's virtually no risk. Your contract guarantees you a specific return for at least one year and maybe more, and it promises that, no matter what, you won't lose money and you'll make a certain minimum amount. The guarantee is backed by the reserves of the insurance company that issues the annuity and sometimes by a guaranty fund maintained by the state you live in.

✔ **Paying death benefits:** When you buy a deferred annuity, you pay a small annual fee for a death benefit that ensures that, if you die while the annuity contract is in force, your beneficiaries will receive a certain minimum. The more you pay for the death benefit (you may have as many as three or four options), the richer the benefit.

✔ **Providing survivorship credits:** Income annuities that are guaranteed for life provide mortality credits (also called survivorship credits), which represent a transfer of money from annuity owners who have died to those who are still living.

✔ **Providing a retirement distribution method:** You may be one of the millions of Americans who, after compiling a six-figure nest egg in your employer's retirement plan, don't know how to begin converting it into an income. Buying an income annuity with a portion of your savings is a good way to enhance your retirement income and ensure that you will always have income (in addition to Social Security). For people who don't expect a defined benefit pension from a former employer, income annuities represent a way to purchase one.

Recognizing the minuses

Although annuities offer several benefits, they have a downside as well. When you buy an annuity, you're usually buying a guarantee, and guarantees always cost money and usually come with restrictions. Here are the minuses:

✔ **Higher expenses than mutual funds:** Although inexpensive products do exist, high fees are very common in the world of deferred variable annuities — especially if you buy your contract from a broker or other commission-earning intermediary. The insurance fees, distribution costs, investment fees, and rider fees can easily amount to more than 3 percent per year. The average annual expense ratio for variable annuities is about 2.4 percent.

High fees also contribute to the cost of immediate (income-generating) annuities, though the fees are not as apparent because they're built into the price you pay for your lifelong income stream. Depending on the insurance company's costs and perhaps its desire to make a sale, it may charge you from $140,000 to $150,000 for a $1,000-a-month lifelong income that starts at age 65. You won't receive an explanation why.

✔ **Reduced liquidity and control:** Annuities offer guaranteed benefits. Insurance companies can't provide those guarantees unless they can count on possessing your money long enough to collect fees and earn interest on it. For that reason, annuities offer less flexibility and access to your money *(liquidity)* than conventional risky investments such as mutual funds.

✔ **Annuity earnings are taxed as ordinary income:** Eventually you'll have to pay income taxes on the gains in your deferred annuity contract. If your taxable income is higher than about $160,000, the annuity profits will be taxed at the rate of 33 or 35 percent. By contrast, your profit on that single stock or mutual fund that you bought 20 years ago and sold last year will be taxed at the capital gains rate of only 15 percent.

✔ **Lack of transparency:** When you buy a fixed deferred annuity that guarantees a rate for only the first year, you don't know exactly what the rate will be during subsequent years. An issuer of indexed annuities (also known as *fixed indexed* or *equity indexed* annuities) also reserves the right to change the formula for crediting gains to you. In addition, no one but the managers and actuaries are privy to the many different formulas and factors that go into the pricing of products, and the benefits of today's popular deferred variable annuity contracts — which offer guaranteed lifetime income and access to your principal if you need it — require some very complex financial engineering and entail many different restrictions. The rules are described in the prospectus, but they can be extremely difficult or even impossible for the average person to understand.

✔ **Often not adjusted for inflation:** If your lifetime payment is not adjusted for inflation (and in most cases, it's not), you receive the same payment amount in year 20 as you do in year 1. Based on 3 percent long-term inflation, $1 will have the purchasing power of 0.74 cents in 10 years and 0.55 cents in 20 years.

Checking Out the Main Types of Annuities

If you prefer and are willing to pay for a safety net, you may consider an annuity. Like other forms of insurance, annuities may or may not seem worth the price. Ultimately, the decision to buy an annuity or not depends on the amount of financial risk you're willing to tolerate. This section explains the basic annuity options that are available.

Fixed deferred annuities

A fixed annuity is the insurance industry's version of a savings account. Technically, fixed annuities are *deferred* annuities. Owners defer their rights to convert the annuity's value to a retirement income stream for at least several years. In truth, few people ever convert them. Most people use them to save or to increase the stability of their investment portfolios. This section describes the pros, cons, and types of fixed deferred annuities.

Advantages and disadvantages

Like all investments, fixed annuities represent a mixture of trade-offs. On the plus side, they offer the following:

- **Safety:** Buying a fixed annuity with a multi-year guarantee (MYG) and holding it for the entire term is a safe, conservative way to grow your money.

- **Tax deferral:** Annuities, like investments that are held in IRAs and 401(k) plans, grow tax deferred, meaning that you don't have to report and pay taxes on them.

- **Stable rates:** When you buy an MYG fixed annuity, you know what interest rate return you'll receive and you know exactly what your investment will be worth at the end of the term.

- **Higher returns when the bond yield curve is steep:** A steep bond *yield curve* occurs when bonds of longer maturities (ten-year Treasury bonds, say) pay significantly higher rates of interest than bonds of shorter maturities (a three-month Treasury bill, for instance). At such times, fixed annuities often pay higher interest rates than certificates of deposit.

- **No probate:** If you die while owning a fixed annuity, your money goes straight to the beneficiaries you named on your contract; it doesn't go through the legal process known as *probate,* where creditors and relatives can lay claim to it.

✔ **The option to annuitize:** Like all annuity contracts, a fixed annuity can be converted to a retirement income stream.

Book I

Getting
Started
with High-
Powered
Investing

Fixed annuities also have their fair share of negatives:

✔ **Low liquidity:** If you take more than 10 percent of your money out of your fixed annuity during the surrender period, you'll pay a charge.

✔ **Uncertain returns:** With single-year-guarantee fixed annuities, you don't know exactly what the interest rate will be after the first year. Historically, the rates on single-year guarantee contracts tend to either stay the same or decline gradually after the first year.

✔ **Lower returns when the bond yield curve is flat:** When the yield curve is flat — when long-term interest rates are the same as or lower than short-term rates — you may be able to get a better rate from a certificate of deposit.

✔ **Federal penalty for early withdrawal:** If you withdraw money from a fixed annuity before you reach the age of 59½, you may have to pay a penalty, equal to 10 percent of the earnings withdrawn, to the IRS. However, under certain circumstances, such as illness, you can withdraw money from an annuity before age 59½ without a penalty.

Types of fixed deferred annuities

If you're interested in fixed deferred annuities, you have several options:

✔ **Single-year-guarantee fixed annuity:** In this type of annuity, the insurance company promises to pay you a certain rate of interest for one year. Each year, for the rest of the surrender period, the insurance company can raise or reduce the interest rate it pays you. In addition, single-year-guarantee fixed annuities often offer big first-year *bonus rates,* interest rates that last only for the first year. After that, the rate generally falls slightly from year to year, enabling the company to recover the cost of the bonus.

✔ **Multi-year-guarantee (MYG) fixed annuity:** In an MYG fixed annuity, you give a specific amount of money to an insurance company, and the insurer guarantees that your investment will earn a specific rate of compound interest for a specific number of years. MYG annuities are often called *CD-type* annuities or *tax-deferred CDs* because they serve the same purpose as a certificate of deposit. The beauty of MYGs is their transparency: What you see is what you get. You know the interest rate your money will earn and how long it will earn it.

✔ **Market value–adjusted (MVA) fixed annuities:** With a *market value–adjusted* (MVA) fixed annuity, you, not the insurer, assume the interest rate risk. In return, the insurance company pays you a slightly higher interest rate than it pays on non-MVA annuities, which are known as *book value* annuities. If you withdraw too much of your money (over

10 percent, in most cases) from your MVA annuity during the surrender period, you'll pay a surrender charge (a percentage equal to the number of years left in the surrender period, in many cases), and your account value will either be adjusted downward (if interest rates have risen since you bought your annuity) or upward (if rates have declined).

In addition to paying higher rates, MVA fixed annuities tend to have longer terms than other fixed annuities. So if you want to lock in current interest rates for a long time, an MVA fixed annuity may be right for you.

✔ **Floating rate and pass-through rate contracts:** A few fixed annuity contracts offer an interest rate that *floats* from month to month. If interest rates go up a bit, you earn a little more that month. If interest rates go down, you earn less. Certain floating-rate fixed annuities will give you a 30-day window once a year to take withdrawals without charging you a penalty or a market value adjustment.

You may also come across annuities that offer *pass-through* rates of interest. Instead of paying you a fixed rate and keeping the rest of what it earns on its bonds, the insurance company pays itself a fixed spread — perhaps 2 percent — and gives you the rest of what it earns. These annuities can be attractive because there's no upper limit on the amount of interest you can earn.

In these contracts, the insurance company will typically try for the highest possible returns by investing in *junk bonds,* which offer higher interest rates because there's a risk that the bond's issuer — the borrower — won't repay the lender, which in this case is the insurance company. These types of fixed annuities offer the potential for higher returns than conventional fixed annuities, as well as higher risk. But why *add* risk to a fixed annuity, whose principal virtue is safety? If you want more risk (and potentially more reward), consider investing a larger percentage of your money in stocks.

Indexed annuities

Indexed annuities — also called *equity indexed* annuities (EIAs) and *fixed indexed* annuities (FIAs) — are a type of fixed annuity. As such, they protect you from losing your investment and guarantee a minimum return. But they also offer you a chance to earn additional interest when the stock market goes up.

When you hand over a chunk of money — at least $2,000 or so — to the insurance company that issues your indexed annuity, the carrier uses your money for three purposes:

✔ It puts most of the money in bonds, which earn interest.

✔ It deducts fees to cover its own expenses.

✔ It uses a small percentage of the money to buy options on a stock index. The most widely used index is the S&P 500 Index, which reflects a rise or fall in the value of the shares of the 500 largest publicly-held companies in the U.S. (See Chapter 1 in Book I for an introduction to stock indexes.)

Book I

Getting Started with High-Powered Investing

When the value of an index goes up, owners of index options can earn large profits. If the index drops in value, the owners of index options can let the option expire unused. When the insurance company makes money on its index options, it passes a portion of the gains to the owner of the indexed annuity. If the index never goes up during the entire life of the indexed annuity contract, the contract owners won't lose anything and will still earn a small guaranteed minimum interest rate.

Here are some of the reasons you may consider buying an indexed annuity:

✔ **Protection from loss and guaranteed minimum return:** The great attraction of indexed annuities is that you gain when stocks go up but you don't lose when stocks go down. Even if the stock market declines in every year that you own your indexed annuity, you still earn a minimum annual return.

✔ **Higher potential returns than certain other investment vehicles:** Generally, indexed annuities are said to provide a rate of return somewhere between those of stocks and bonds.

✔ **Protection from sequence-of-returns risk:** A steep investment loss within five years before or after you retire can put you in a financial hole that you can't dig out of. This vulnerability is called *sequence-of-returns risk*. By keeping your money in an indexed annuity during that period, you can protect it from this risk while still being in a position to benefit from an increase in stock prices.

✔ **Tax deferral:** You pay no tax on your indexed annuity gains until you take withdrawals from the contract.

✔ **Lifetime income option:** Like almost all other annuities, indexed annuities give you the option to convert the value of your account to a guaranteed income that will last for a specific number of years or for as long as you live (or for as long as either you or your spouse is living).

Now, here are the cons:

✔ **Complexity:** Few people truly understand indexed annuities, and you'll have a heck of a time understanding or evaluating the many different formulas that indexed annuities use to calculate your return.

✔ **Unpredictability:** Because their performance is linked to the performance of stocks, indexed annuities don't give you the steady, reliable returns that you can expect from a fixed annuity. In addition, insurance companies can change the terms of the contract from year to year.

✔ **High commissions:** Insurance companies pay insurance agents commissions as high as 9 percent on the sale of indexed annuities.

✔ **Sold mainly by insurance agents:** Although these agents are, by and large, fine people, they don't have any responsibility to put your financial welfare ahead of theirs, as certain accredited financial advisors do.

✔ **Lack of liquidity:** Indexed annuities, especially contracts that include bonuses, tend to have long surrender periods during which you can't withdraw more than 10 percent of your premium without incurring penalties and/or losing a bonus.

✔ **No dividends to reinvest:** Because indexed annuities involve the purchase of index options rather than the actual purchase of stocks, owners of indexed annuities do not earn the dividends that usually come from owning stocks.

✔ **Short track record:** Indexed annuities were invented in 1996. They haven't been around long enough for anyone to be sure of their long-term value.

✔ **Federal penalty for withdrawals before age 59½:** Unless you qualify for one of the hardship-related exceptions, the Internal Revenue Service will charge a 10 percent penalty for any earnings you take out of any annuity before age 59½.

Variable annuities

Variable annuities (VAs) are mutual fund investments that have certain insurance-related guarantees, such as living benefits and death benefits. The following sections discuss these benefits as well as the pros and cons of VAs.

Guaranteed living benefits

Guaranteed living benefits (GLBs) can be used as a form of protection against investment losses or as a retirement income strategy. Because they can protect you from so-called sequence-of-returns risk — the chance that a bear market early in your retirement will permanently wreck your portfolio — they're worth your attention.

GLBs are designed to let investors have it all: protection from catastrophic loss, the potential for growth, and the assurance that if they die, their beneficiaries won't be left empty-handed. Table 4-1 lists the various kinds of GLBs.

VA pros and cons

There are several pros and cons of VA ownership that you need to carefully weigh before deciding on your investment strategy. The pros include:

Book I

Getting
Started
with High-
Powered
Investing

Table 4-1	Types of GLBs
Type	*Description*
Guaranteed minimum income benefit (GMIB)	Lets you annuitize (convert to a regular income) whichever is greater: the market value of your investments or a guaranteed minimum amount based on your principal plus a minimum guaranteed annual growth rate.
Guaranteed minimum withdrawal benefit (GMWB)	Protects your principal and guarantees that you'll receive it in equal installments until it's exhausted.
Guaranteed minimum withdrawal benefit — for life (GMWB for life)	Lets you withdraw a certain percentage of a guaranteed amount every year for life.
Guaranteed minimum accumulation benefit (GMAB)	Guarantees that, after a specified investment period, your investments won't lose money; some guarantee a certain amount of growth.
Guaranteed account value (GAV)	Guarantees your principal over the course of a specific investment period; may automatically lock in any gains at the end of each quarter or year.
Guaranteed payout annuity floor (GPAF)	Guarantees that your monthly income payment will never be less than a certain percentage — from 85 to 100 percent — of the first payment.

✔ Deferred taxes on dividends and capital gains

✔ Lifetime income options, including annuitization and GLBs

✔ A death benefit that protects heirs from market losses

✔ Investment options that provide control over retirement savings

✔ No limit on the contribution of pretax money

The cons of VA ownership include:

✔ High fees, especially if sold by commissioned brokers or agents.

✔ Earnings are taxed as income rather than as capital gains.

- ✔ Withdrawals of earnings before age 59½ may be subject to a 10 percent federal penalty, in addition to income tax.
- ✔ Investment risks are usually greater than with fixed-rate annuities.

Income annuities

Income annuities enable you to convert savings into a monthly, quarterly, or annual paycheck. You pay a lump sum — usually $100,000 or more — to an insurance company, and the insurer issues a contract that promises to pay you (or someone you choose) an income for an agreed-upon length of time. Income annuities are the only financial product that can offer you an income stream that's guaranteed by an insurance company to last as long as you live. Two main types of income annuities are available:

- ✔ **Immediate:** An immediate income annuity offers an income stream that begins soon after purchase.
- ✔ **Deferred:** A deferred income annuity (DIA) offers a retirement income stream that may begin from 13 months to several decades after purchase. Some DIAs can be funded with a series of payments over many years prior to retirement.

A *life* annuity *guarantees* that you will receive an income as long as you live (or as long as either you or your spouse is living). But this guarantee assumes that the insurance company will remain financially strong enough to meet its obligations for the next 30 years or more. If the insurer fails, your payments will be in jeopardy. That's why you must buy your annuity from a gilt-edged, A-rated company.

The simplest type of income annuity is a single premium income annuity, known as a SPIA (pronounced "*spee*-ah"). Income from a SPIA begins no later than one year after you purchase it. When brokers and advisers talk about SPIAs — and they rarely do — they usually mean annuities that offer a fixed payment every month. But you can also buy a SPIVA (a single premium immediate *variable* annuity) whose payout rate fluctuates with the stock market.

People tend to be wary of income annuities because they feel that if they die the insurance company will get their money. That's a healthy fear. But buying an income annuity doesn't necessarily mean losing control over all your money, or even all the money in your annuity. Most issuers of income annuities offer options that allow you to tailor your annuity to your own needs and comfort level. Keep in mind, however, that you'll get the highest monthly payment if you relinquish all control over your money. The more control you retain, the lower your income will be.

Book II
Futures and Options

Five Things to Review after a Trade

- **Exit and entry points:** Review your exit and entry points and then ask yourself whether you adapted the right strategy to the right market and whether you used the best possible method to protect yourself. Did you give yourself enough room to maneuver? For example, was your sell stop too tight? Should you have given the market more room?

- **Your charts:** Go back and look at the charts you used to make your trade to find out whether the market you were trading is acting similar to the way history shows it has acted in the past. If it isn't, try to figure out what's different about the market. Did you let your own personal judgment ruin your trade because you thought you knew better than the charts? Always trade what you see and not what you think you know.

- **Fundamentals:** Did you really understand what the fundamentals of the market were telling you? Did you understand the nuts and bolts of the industry? For example, did you pay attention to the part of the livestock cycle that the market was in when you traded hogs? Or did you check the weather reports before you shorted soybeans?

- **Market suitability:** Are you really suited for trading in a given market? Perhaps it moves too fast or too slow for you. If you're trading currencies, for example, can you handle moves that last for several days and keep your positions open overnight? Or does that frighten you and make you lose sleep?

- **Market volume and sentiment:** Did you consider the market's volume and the overall sentiment before you bought that top and got stopped out in a hurry? Low volume and high levels of pessimism often mean that a market has bottomed, whereas huge volume and a feeling of invincibility are the hallmark of a pending top.

If you're not careful, your foray into futures and options trading can be short and costly. To uncover the trading rules that help futures and options traders maximize their chances of success, head to www.dummies.com/extras/highpowered investingaio.

Chapter 1

Futures and Options Fundamentals

In This Chapter

▶ Grasping the basics of futures trading

▶ Getting a handle on options trading

▶ Figuring out whether futures or options trading is right for you

*B*efore you trade in futures and options, there's quite a bit you need to know. For starters, you need to understand what, exactly, futures trading and options trading are. Then you need to know how the futures and options markets work and who the major players are. And because trading involves speculating (more akin to gambling than investing), you absolutely need to know about volatility and risk. This chapter gives you just that kind of information. And because trading futures and options isn't for everyone, this chapter also helps you decide whether being a trader is the right move for you.

Getting the Lowdown on Futures Trading

Trading is not investing; it's speculating. When you *speculate*, you assume a business risk with the hope of profiting from market fluctuations. Successful speculating requires analyzing situations, predicting outcomes, and putting your money on the side of the trade that represents the way you think the market is going to go, up or down. Speculating also involves an appreciation of the fact that you can be wrong 70 percent of the time and still be a successful futures trader if you apply the correct techniques for analyzing trades, managing your money, and protecting your account.

Basically that means you have to chuck all your preconceptions about buy-and-hold investing, asset allocation, and essentially all the strategies that stock brokers put out for public consumption. Buy-and-hold doesn't work in the futures markets because futures are designed for trading.

Trading futures contracts is a risky business and requires active participation. You can trade successfully only if you're serious, well prepared, and committed to getting it right. That means that you have to develop new routines and master new concepts. You must be able to cultivate your trading craft by constantly reviewing and modifying your plan and strategies.

Futures are contracts for specific commodities that you buy or sell for delivery at a specified price and at a specified date some time in the future. To be a successful futures trader, you have to become connected with the world through the Internet, television, and other news sources so you can be up-to-date and intimately knowledgeable with regard to world events. Setting up for this endeavor also requires a significant amount of money. You need a computer, a trading program, and a brokerage account of some sort, not to mention how well capitalized you have to be to survive.

Getting used to going short

Going or selling short is the opposite of going long. *Going short* means that you're trying to make money when prices fall, whereas going long means that you're trying to make money when prices rise. In the stock market, going short involves borrowing shares of stock from someone, usually your brokerage firm, so you can sell them at a high price, wait for prices to fall, buy them back at the lower price, return the asset to the lender, and pocket the difference between what you sold it for and what you paid for it.

In the futures market, going short means that you're trying to make money as a result of falling contract prices. No borrowing is involved. Say you enter into a futures contract to sell 100 shares of Company A's stock for $50 a share with a delivery date of August 1, hoping the price will fall before you have to deliver the stock. On July 15, the price falls to, say, $45 dollars a share, so you buy the $5,000 contract back for only $4,500, making yourself $500 in the process. Although this may sound confusing, trading software simplifies the concept for futures traders by giving you a button choice for short selling (find out more about software in the later section "Choosing a futures broker"). You can also bet on the market falling by using options strategies. See the later section "Getting Up to Speed on Options" for more.

In futures trading, every transaction involves a trader who's trading short and one who's trading long. Before you consider trading futures contracts or, for that matter, aggressively trading stocks, make sure that you understand selling short.

Decoding a futures contract

Futures contracts are, by design, meant to limit the amount of time and risk exposure experienced by speculators and hedgers (these folks are discussed later in this chapter). As a result, futures contracts have several key characteristics that enable traders to trade them effectively:

✔ **Expiration:** All futures contracts are time-based; they *expire,* which means that at some point in the future they'll no longer exist. From a trading standpoint, the expiration of a contract forces you to make one of the following decisions:

- Sell the contract and roll it over (that is, buy another contract for the same asset but with a later maturity date)

- Sell the contract (taking your profits or losses) and just stay out of the market

- Take delivery of the commodity, equity, or product represented by the contract

✔ **Daily price limits:** Because of their volatility and the potential for catastrophic losses, futures contracts include limits that freeze prices but don't freeze trading. Limits are meant to let markets cool down during periods of extremely active trading. (Keep in mind that the market can trade at the limit price but not beyond it.) Some contracts have *variable limits,* meaning the limits change if the market closes at the limit. (For example, if the cattle markets close at the limit for two straight days, the limit is raised on the third day.)

✔ **Size of account:** Most brokerage firms require individuals to deposit a certain amount of money in a brokerage account before they can start trading. A fairly constant figure in the industry is $5,000.

Depositing only $5,000 with the brokerage firm probably isn't enough to provide you with a good trading experience. Some experienced traders say that $100,000 is a better figure to have on hand, and $20,000 is probably the least amount you can actually work with. These are not hard-and-fast rules, though.

E-mini contracts are smaller-value versions of larger contracts. They trade for a fraction of the price of the full-value instrument and thus are more suitable for small accounts. The attractive feature of e-mini contracts is that you can participate in the market's movements for lesser investment amounts. Be sure to check commissions and other prerequisites before you trade. E-minis are the commonly quoted overnight futures contracts on CNBC and online quote services.

Book II

Futures and Options

Futures exchanges: Where the magic happens

True futures contracts must be traded at an organized exchange, where trading takes place either via an open-cry system or an electronic system (see the next section for details). Several active futures and options exchanges exist in the United States. Each has its own niche, but some overlaps occur in the types of contracts that are traded. Here are the names to know:

- **Chicago Board of Trade** (CBOT, `www.cmegroup.com/company/cbot.html`): The CBOT brings to the table trades made in futures contracts for agriculturals, interest rates, Dow indexes, and metals.

- **Chicago Board Options Exchange** (CBOE, `www.cboe.com`): The premier options exchange market in the world, the CBOE specializes in trading options on individual stocks, stock index futures, interest rate futures, and a broad array of specialized products such as exchange-traded funds. *Note:* The CBOE is not a futures exchange but is included here to be complete, because futures and options can be traded simultaneously, as part of a single strategy.

- **Chicago Mercantile Exchange** (CME, `www.cmegroup.com`): The CME is the largest futures exchange in North America. CME merged with the CBOT, forming a formidable contender in the exchange industry. The merged entity operates both exchanges and trades on the New York Stock Exchange under the stock symbol NYSE: CME. Although they are one company, the two exchanges have separate trading floors and between them offer a wide variety of trading instruments including commodities, stock index futures, foreign currencies, interest rates, and environmental futures.

  Futures contracts for the S&P GSCI (formerly known as the Goldman Sachs Commodity Index) and options on the futures contracts that the CME listed also are traded here, along with real estate futures.

- **Kansas City Board of Trade** (KCBT, now a part of CME; `www.cmegroup.com/trading/agricultural/kcbt.html`): The KCBT is a regional exchange that specializes in wheat futures and offers trading on stock index futures for the Value Line Index, a broad listing of 1,700 stocks.

- **Minneapolis Grain Exchange** (MGEX, `www.mgex.com`): MGEX is a regional exchange that trades three kinds of seasonally different wheat futures, and offers futures and options on the National Corn Index and the National Soybeans Index.

- **New York Mercantile Exchange** (NYMEX, `www.cmegroup.com`): The NYMEX, also part of the CME, is the hub for trading in energy futures and metals.

Open-cry or electronic: Futures trading systems

Around the world, most futures exchanges now use electronic trading. The United States still uses the *open-cry system,* where traders on a trading floor or in a trading pit shout and use hand signals to make transactions or trades with each other. However, most U.S. futures markets also offer electronic trading, which is slowly taking over as the major method of order filling in both the futures and stock markets.

In the open-cry system, when you call your broker, he relays a message to the trading floor, where a runner relays the message to the floor broker, who then executes the trade. The runner then relays the trade confirmation back to your broker, who tells you how it went. Trade reporters on the floor of the exchange watch for executed trades, record them, and transmit these transactions to the exchange, which, in turn, transmits the price to the entire world almost simultaneously. The order of business is similar when you trade futures online, except that you receive a trade confirmation via an e-mail or other online communiqué.

One key difference between open-cry and electronic trading is the length of the trading day. Regular market hours usually run from 8:30 a.m. to 4:15 p.m. eastern time. CME Globex, the major electronic data and trading system, extends futures trading beyond the pits and into an electronic overnight session. Globex is active 23 hours per day, and contracts are traded on it for Eurodollars, S&P 500, NASDAQ-100, foreign exchange rates, and CME e-mini futures. You can also trade options and spreads on Globex.

When you turn to the financial news on CNBC before the stock market opens, you see quotes for the S&P 500 futures and others taken from Globex as traders from around the world make electronic trades. Globex quotes are real, meaning that if you keep a position open overnight, and you place a *sell stop* under it (which triggers selling the security when it reaches a particular price) or you place a buy order with instructions to execute in Globex, you may wake up the next morning with a new position or out of a position altogether.

CME Globex trading overnight tends to be thinner and, in some ways, more volatile than trading during regular market hours. A great free website to get real-time futures data overnight is www.investing.com.

The individual players: Hedgers and speculators

The two major categories of traders are hedgers and speculators. The two groups enter the futures market trying to accomplish different objectives.

- ✔ *Hedgers* trade not only in futures contracts but also in the commodity, equity, or product represented by the contract. They trade futures to secure the future price of the commodity of which they'll take delivery and then sell later in the cash market. By buying or selling futures contracts, they protect themselves against future price risks.

- ✔ *Speculators* bet on the price change potential for one reason only — profit. They don't care whether the prices are going up or down; they just want to ride the price trend of products for as long as possible, while always intending to cash in before the delivery date.

The interaction between speculators and hedgers is what makes the futures markets efficient. This efficiency and the accuracy of the supply-and-demand equation increase as the underlying contract gets closer to expiration and more information about what the marketplace requires at the time of delivery becomes available.

Futures contracts are attractive to *longs* (people looking to buy at the lowest possible price and sell at the highest possible price) and *shorts* (people selling commodities in the hope that prices fall) because they provide price and time certainty and reduce the risk associated with *volatility,* or the speed at which prices change up or down. Hedging can help lock in an acceptable *price margin* (the difference between the future price and the cash price for the commodity) and improve the risk between the cost of the raw material and the retail cost of the final product by covering for any market-related losses.

Note: Hedge positions don't always work, and in some cases, they can make losses worse.

Choosing a futures broker

If you decide to trade futures, you need to choose between a full-service broker and a discount broker. A full-service broker charges you a larger commission but is expected to provide you with good advice about your trades. Look for the following when choosing a full-service broker:

- ✔ **Access to all markets:** Even if you're interested in only a handful of markets right now, you may want to consider expanding your horizons in the future.

✔ **Access to the firm's research:** Some brokers offer discounts to newsletters and websites, while others offer direct access to their own research departments. Some offer live broadcasts from the trading pits.

✔ **Intelligent software and the full gamut of technical tools:** You want the ability to run multiple real-time charts with oscillators and indicators and receive intermarket analysis, as well as access to software and charting packages that let you *back test,* or review, the results of your trading strategies and indicators, as well as forward test your strategy. (*Forward testing* is based on the probability of certain conditions occurring in the future and indicates how much money — hypothetically — you'd make if certain things happened.)

Most brokers offer you a trial of their software and trading platforms if you register on their website. Take advantage of this capability.

Book II

Futures and Options

✔ **A 24-hour customer-service line:** This line of communication is crucial if you decide to exit a position overnight in the face of events that are costing you money.

✔ **The option to enter trades via the Internet or phone:** Access to both lets you make trades when the phones are busy or your Internet connection is down.

✔ **Acceptable fees:** Check all potential trading fees before you sign up and make a trade.

Be careful whenever you deal with brokers or other advisors because they sometimes earn large incentives for steering you in certain directions, regardless of whether taking those directions with your money is in your best interest.

Look on the U.S. Commodity Futures Trading Commission's (CFTC's) website (www.cftc.gov) under the "Consumer Protection" heading for current trading scams and for disciplinary actions taken against firms and brokers. On the National Futures Association's (NFA's) website (www.nfa.futures.org/basicnet), you can search for brokers, trading pools, and commodity trading advisors (CTAs). Also, if you're just getting started, going with a large, established broker can be a good idea. Large firms are not exempt from fraud but, because of their size, information about their practices is more readily available.

Going the route of the discount broker may be a better alternative if you're adventurous and do your homework, which includes practice trading in simulated accounts. A large number of discount brokers operate in the futures markets, and you can find most of them by using your favorite search engine or looking at advertisements in *Futures, Active Trader,* the *Wall Street Journal,* and other publications. Aside from the important aspects, such as service in general, availability of 24-hour service, commissions, and ease of access to the trading desk, discount brokers offer online trading services. You want to make sure that the trading platform the discount broker provides is easy to use and that the orders you place online are executed in a reasonable amount of time.

Getting Up to Speed on Options

Just like stocks and futures contracts, *options* are securities that are subject to binding agreements. The key difference between options and futures contracts is that options give you the *right* to buy or sell an underlying security or asset without being obligated to do so, as long as you follow the rules of the options contract. In addition, options are derivatives. A *derivative* is a financial instrument that gets its value not from its own intrinsic worth but rather from the value of the underlying security. Options on the stock of IBM, for example, are directly influenced by the price of IBM stock.

Because options come in two forms, calls and puts, adding them to your current investing and trading tools allows you to benefit from both bullish and bearish moves in any underlying asset you select. You can do this to limit your total assets at risk or to protect an existing position. The following sections explain option basics.

Options differ from stocks in terms of what they represent and how they're created. This differentiation results in additional rules for trading and decision-making beyond the basic buy or sell considerations. This book focuses on stock and index options, referred to as *listed options,* that use standard agreements and trade on exchanges.

Comparing call and put options

A listed stock option is a contractual agreement between two parties with standard terms. Buying an option gives you rights, and selling an option leaves you with obligations:

- ✔ **Call options:** When you own a call, you have the right to buy a certain stock at a specific price (called the *strike price*) by a certain date. A call option gains value when its underlying stock goes up (explaining why the call price goes up when the stock price goes up), but if the move in the stock is too late, the call can expire worthless. A call option allows you to invest a smaller amount and still benefit from an upward move in stock value because the price you have rights to is fixed while the value of the stock itself is increasing.

- ✔ **Put options:** As a put owner, you have the right to sell certain stock at a specific price by a specific date. A put option gains value when its stock moves down, but, as with call options, the move has to occur before the option contract expires. A put option on a stock you hold for the long-term gains value during downturns.

You have to exercise these rights within a certain period of time because contracts have a limited life. As a result, a primary risk you encounter with options is time risk. On the plus side, options have expiration periods as late as 9 months to 2½ years. Gaining skill as an options trader means selecting options with expiration dates that allow time for the anticipated moves to occur.

So you don't confuse your call and put rights, think about *calling* the stock away from someone (buying) and *putting* the stock to someone (selling).

Uncovering an option's value

Option prices are determined by the type of option (call or put), its strike price, the price of the underlying stock, and the time remaining to expiration. Prices are also determined by the volatility of that underlying stock. It turns out this last pricing component plays a pretty big role in options analysis and strategy selection.

Option valuation measures are available that help you determine whether an option price quoted in the market represents a reasonable value or not. The measures provide you with a feel for how decreasing time or changes in the stock's price or volatility impact the option's price. These measures are available for each individual option and are referred to as the option's Greeks because most of their names are derived from Greek letters. The next sections explain the Greeks and other factors that affect option values.

Introducing the Greeks

An option's Greeks provide you with the value of expected changes in the option, given changes in the underlying stock. They're derived from one of several option valuation models and are available to you from various sources, such as an option calculator. Most option exchange websites provide this tool (find out more about these exchanges later in this chapter).

Using an option calculator, you enter the price of the underlying stock, the option strike price, time to expiration, and the option quote. The calculator then provides each of the Greek values listed. The insight you gain from the Greeks includes the following:

✔ **Delta:** Represents the expected change in the option value for each $1 change in the price of the underlying stock. Delta is probably the most important Greek value for you to initially understand because it connects changes in the underlying stock's value directly to changes in the option value. Following are the delta value ranges for both calls and puts:

- **Calls:** 0 and 1.00 or 0 and 100
- **Puts:** 0 and −1.00 or 0 and −100

✔ **Gamma:** Represents the expected change in delta for each $1 change in the price of the underlying stock. By understanding and checking gamma, you reduce the chance of delta values getting away from you.

The delta for an *at the money* (ATM, when an option's strike price is identical to the price of the underlying security) option is approximately +/–0.50 regardless of the stock's past volatility. Option valuations assume that there's a 50 percent chance the stock will move up and a 50 percent chance it will move down.

✔ **Theta:** Represents the option's expected daily decline due to time.

✔ **Vega:** Represents the expected change in the option value due to changes in volatility expectations for the underlying stock.

✔ **Rho:** Estimates changes in the option value due to changes in the risk-free interest rate (usually T-bills). Option price changes attributable to interest rates are much smaller, so this last measure receives less coverage.

You can use option valuation models to determine whether a particular option is relatively expensive or cheap. Keep in mind, though, that the Greeks provide expected values; they by no means guarantee the future.

Connecting past movement to the future: Historical and implied volatility

Past movement in the underlying stock is used to determine the probability that a certain minimum or maximum price will be reached. As you know, past movement doesn't provide you with a map of what's going to happen during the next month, the next week, or even the next day, but that doesn't mean you can't look at past movement to evaluate the potential for certain price targets to be reached. Two key measures that relate past movement in a stock to movement that is expected in the future are historical volatility and implied volatility:

✔ **Historical volatility (HV),** also referred to as statistical volatility (SV), is a measure of past movement in a stock and is a rough gauge of future volatility. When compared to implied volatility, it is used to determine whether option prices are under- or overvalued. To calculate HV:

1. **Calculate the daily price change over a set number of days.**

2. **Calculate the average value for price change over that period.**

3. **Determine how each daily price change compares to that average value by taking the standard deviation for the price changes in the set.**

4. **Divide the value in Step 3 by 0.0630 to approximate an annualized standard deviation.**

Standard deviation measures how dispersed data is from its average value. When applying this measure to stocks, those with a higher HV are expected to make bigger daily moves that are less predictable than those with a smaller HV. Lower HV stocks have daily changes that stay close to the average daily change.

Note: Don't get hung up on the math — HV is calculated in this manner so you can make an apples-to-apples comparison of a stock's most recent movement versus its past movement. It also allows you to compare two different stocks.

✔ **Implied volatility (IV)** is the volatility implied by the current market price for the option and is related to the time remaining until expiration. IV is based on historical volatility, but it also incorporates supply and demand pricing pressures for the individual option. On a given day, you can identify a given stock's current price, the nature of its past movement, what kind of option it is and its strike price, and the number of days until that option expires. What you don't know, of course, is what the stock is going to do between now and expiration.

The biggest distinction between HV and IV is that HV relies on a specific formula — it uses past data for the stock. IV is based on this calculation, but is more abstract, reflects new information about the market, and has a psychological component. A large one-day move in a stock has some impact on its 100-day HV calculation, but the impact on the option's IV will likely be much more pronounced because of the uncertainty this one-day event brings.

Modeling option values

An option pricing model uses stock and option data to provide you with a theoretical value for the option. A few similar models exist, such as the one available on the Options Industry Council (OIC) website (`www.options education.org`), and you can access them via an options calculator. By comparing an option's theoretical value to its market price, you get a feel for whether the option is relatively expensive or cheap.

Different historical volatility (HV) values are available using a variety of time frames and typically include 10-day, 20-day, and 100-day. IV is an option-specific value based on the option's current price. Both HV and IV values are available to you from a variety of sources, including option analysis software.

Options mispricing

In a perfect world, HV and IV should be fairly close together, given the fact that they're supposed to be measures of two financial assets that are intrinsically related to one another: the underlying asset and its option. In fact, sometimes IV and HV actually are very close together. Yet the differences in these numbers at different stages of the market cycle can provide excellent trading opportunities. This concept is called *options mispricing*, and if you understand how to use it, options mispricing can help you make better trading decisions.

When HV and IV are far apart, the price of the option isn't reflecting the actual volatility of the underlying asset. For example, if IV rises dramatically and HV is very low, the underlying stock may be a possible candidate for a takeover. Under those circumstances, the stock probably has been stuck in a trading range as the market awaits news. At the same time, option premiums may remain high because of the potential for sudden changes with regard to the deal.

The bottom line is that HV and IV are useful tools in trading options. Most software programs can graph out these two variables. When they're charted, big spreads become easy to spot, enabling you to look for trading opportunities.

Calculating option risks

Both call and put options have risk that is limited to the initial investment. This initial investment can vary in size but is less than the investment required to control the same number of shares of the underlying stock. Although the risk is relatively smaller in terms of dollars, it's important to recognize that the likelihood of an option going to zero is much higher than the underlying stock going to zero.

The chance that an option will go to zero is 100 percent because an option eventually expires. At expiration, the option value goes to zero.

Here are the risks for call and put options:

- ✓ **Call option:** When the strike price for the call option is below the price for the underlying stock, it loses time value as expiration nears. (An option's *time value* is its cost minus its *intrinsic value,* the difference between the option's strike price and the price of the underlying asset.) Assuming the stock remains at the same price level, this time decay can result in losses for the trader, but the losses are limited because the option retains its intrinsic value. However, when the stock is trading below the strike price, the option's value is all time value. Assuming the stock remains at the same price level, time value diminishes as you get closer to expiration. Continuing in this manner results in a total loss of the initial investment.

  Most of the time a stock doesn't stand still; it vacillates. The underlying stock may increase in value and rise above a call strike price, or it may decline in value and fall below the strike price, which puts you in a situation where you can lose your entire investment as expiration nears.

Because an option eventually expires, you really need to understand option valuations so you don't pay too much for the time remaining. You can manage this time risk by exiting a long option at least 30 days before it expires. Within 30 days, the option's time value erodes at an accelerated pace.

✔ **Put option:** A put option loses time value as expiration nears, which can result in losses for the trader when the stock is trading above the option strike price. When trading below the strike price, the losses are limited because the option retains intrinsic value. However, when the stock is trading above the strike price, the option's value is all time value. Assuming the stock remains at the same price level, time value diminishes as you get closer to expiration. Continuing in this manner results in a total loss of the initial investment.

Because the stock has the same chance of rising as falling, there's a chance the underlying stock will increase in value, rising above a put strike price. As a result, you can lose your entire investment as expiration nears.

Book II

Futures and Options

Taking stock of the U.S. options exchanges

The U.S. has numerous options exchanges. Because of a large merger boom between security exchanges, the list changes periodically, as do the websites. The following list represents the players that are most likely to be around for a while. You can find an updated list at the Securities and Exchange Commission website: www.sec.gov/divisions/marketreg/mrexchanges.shtml.

✔ **Boston Options Exchange (BOX):** www.boxexchange.com

✔ **Chicago Board Options Exchange (CBOE):** www.cboe.com

✔ **International Securities Exchange (ISE):** www.ise.com

✔ **Nasdaq OMX PHLX Inc. (PHLX):** www.nasdaqomx.com

✔ **New York Stock Exchange (NYSE/Arca):** usequities.nyx.com

The different option exchange Internet sites provide common information, along with information specific to the exchange's listings. Each also seems to have a unique strength. Periodically check the sites for new tools and insights.

Creating option contracts

Stocks have a set number of shares available for trading. To increase this number, shareholders vote to authorize the issuance of additional stock.

Options are more flexible because new contracts are created to meet the demand for that particular contract. This flexibility impacts how you place an option order and makes it easier to sell an option you don't own. The following sections discuss several aspects of creating option contracts: opening and closing positions as well as covered and naked calls and puts.

The total stock issued for a company is referred to as the *authorized shares,* and shares available for trading are referred to as the stock's *float.* The possible number of option contracts available to trade is limitless because they're created by demand. The actual contracts in existence for a specific option is referred to as its *open interest.*

Opening and closing positions

Because option contracts are created as needed, you enter option orders in a unique way. You identify whether you're creating a new position or closing an existing position by including one of the following with your order:

- Buy to Open
- Sell to Close
- Sell to Open
- Buy to Close

For example, to purchase a call option, you enter the following order:

Buy to Open, 1 ABC Apr 08 30.00 strike call option

What you're directing the broker to do with this order is to "Buy 1 contract of an ABC 2008 April call option with a strike price of 30."

To exit, or close, the position at any point down the road you place this order:

Sell to Close, 1 ABC Apr 08 30.00 strike call option

When you sell an option you don't own (see the next section for details), you designate what type of transaction you're completing by using the same terminology to enter and exit the position:

Sell to Open, 1 FGH Jun 08 17.50 strike call option

Buy to Close, 1 FGH Jun 08 17.50 strike call option

Identifying whether an order opens or closes a position is important for contract recordkeeping. If you make a mistake during order entry and the trade is executed, the error should be readily fixable. Contact your broker as soon as possible to get the transaction corrected in your account and at the exchanges. (Get the scoop on options brokers later in this chapter.)

Covered and naked calls and puts

Selling a stock call option as an opening transaction obligates you to sell a certain amount of stock at the strike price at any point through the option's expiration date. From the time you sell it until expiration weekend, you're required to satisfy that obligation if a call option holder chooses to exercise his rights. This event is referred to as being *assigned* the option. Typically your broker contacts you informing you of the assignment.

Assuming you're assigned on a call option contract, one of two possibilities exist:

- ✔ You owned shares of the underlying stock in the account. These shares are then sold at the strike price, resulting in closing the stock position in your account.
- ✔ You did not own shares of the underlying stock, but the shares are sold at the strike price, creating a short stock position in your account.

Selling a call option when you own the underlying shares is referred to as a *covered* transaction because the stock is said to *cover* the short call position. If you don't own the stock, the option position is referred to as a *naked call*.

When selling a call option as an opening transaction without owning the stock, your risk is the same as holding a short stock position. Because a stock can technically keep rising, your risk is unlimited.

Selling a stock put option as an opening transaction obligates you to buy a certain amount of stock at the strike price at any point up through the option's expiration date. From the time you sell the put until expiration weekend, you're required to satisfy the obligation if a put option holder chooses to exercise her rights.

Typically you're assigned on a short put when the stock has suffered a decline. So you're purchasing stock at a higher level than its current market value. As with short call transactions, short put transactions can be covered or naked.

When selling a short put, you're obligating yourself to buy shares, so you cover the option with a short stock position in the underlying asset. Buying the shares closes this short stock position. If the short put is naked, assignment of the put creates a new long stock position in your account.

When you're short a stock option contract, you're at risk of assignment from the time you create the position through expiration of the contract. The only way you can alleviate yourself of the obligation is to exit the position by entering a Buy to Close order for the option. Contact your broker to find out the method that's used to assign short options. Almost all brokers use a random selection process.

Knowing a few important options trading rules

Whenever you begin trading a new market, you'll likely get some butterflies until the first few trades go off without a hitch. Watching everything unfold as you expected is always nice, but it actually requires some advance work on your end. This short list of options trading rules hopefully will increase your comfort level with initial executions, as well as considerations down the road:

- ✔ **Contract pricing:** Options in general trade in $0.05 and $0.10 increments rather than $0.01 increments the way stocks do.

- ✔ **Transaction premium:** The premium value you pay for an option is obtained by multiplying the option price quoted in the market by the option's *multiplier* (a number used to determine how much money you pay or receive when calling or putting a stock). This value is usually 100 for stock options. So when you purchase an option quoted at $2.80, you're actually paying $280 for the option, plus commissions.

- ✔ **Market conditions:** Different market conditions impact both the stock and options markets. These include

  - **Trading halts for a security or entire market:** If you hold options for a halted stock, the options are also halted. If the halt occurs before expiration, you still have the ability to exercise your contract rights. Generally, a trading halt doesn't restrict your right to exercise.

  - **Fast trading conditions for a security or securities:** When this happens, you'll likely experience significant delays in order execution and reporting. Unless you must exit a position for risk reasons, using market orders for options in fast markets is inadvisable.

  - **Booked order:** A *booked order* is one that improves the current market quote and updates it. The market maker isn't necessarily willing to take the trade at the quoted level, but another trader is. You can encounter problems with such orders because the size can be as small as one contract. If you enter a ten-contract order that matches the booked order price, only one of the ten contracts may be filled. The rest of your order may or may not be filled.

- ✔ **Best-execution:** *Execution quality* is a general term used to describe a broker's ability to provide trade completions at, or better than, the current market for the security. When you place an order to buy an option with an asking quote of $2.00, for example, your order is filled in a timely manner at $2.00 or better.

Choosing an options broker

If you're interested in trading options but aren't sure about your own ability to trade them, you need to find a good options broker/advisor to help you out. A broker can assist with strategy development, research, monitoring open positions, and working orders. (***Note:*** A futures broker usually can handle your options activity as it relates to futures and may be able to handle stock option transactions; selecting a futures broker is discussed earlier in this chapter.) If you want to do all that stuff yourself, then you just want to get access to the markets through the lowest-cost medium, usually an online discount broker.

Con artists and unscrupulous advisors lurk around every corner and prey on the unsuspecting and uninformed options trader, so do your homework. When selecting a broker/advisor, be sure to ask these important questions, which are applicable to broker and advisor candidates for online and managed accounts:

Book II

Futures and Options

 ✔ **What kinds of services does the brokerage firm offer?** If you decide to establish a managed account, make sure early on that you're getting your money's worth. Aside from getting good results, you're paying for customer service. Most advisors will meet with you at least on a yearly basis. Many meet with you on a quarterly basis. If you're an active trader and your advisor calls you with trades frequently, make sure that he's giving you winning trades. Otherwise, he's probably churning your account.

 ✔ **What commissions and other costs are charged and under what circumstances?** As part of your search, compare fees and services between the different advisor/broker candidates and match their results with their costs.

 ✔ **Is my broker registered with the U.S. Commodity Futures Trading Commission (CFTC) or National Futures Association (NFA)?** This is applicable to options on futures only. For stock options, Financial Industry Regulatory Authority (FINRA) and CBOE memberships are critical.

 If the broker is registered with one of these organizations, contact it to find out whether the firm or the broker is in good standing or whether public records of previous disciplinary actions exist. If disciplinary actions have been taken, ask for audited results (and check out the auditor because she may have had her own problems!).

 ✔ **What kind of results can I expect from the broker assigned to me?** Be careful of financial advisors who advertise instant riches based on small amounts of money and promise to return all of your money. No one can make such a promise. Also get to know who's doing the trading and what methods he's using before you give him any of your money.

In addition to asking questions, make sure that you tell your advisor how much risk you're willing to take and how involved you want to be. If your advisor takes actions that make you uncomfortable despite your requests regarding the amount of risk you're willing to take, it's time to say goodbye to that advisor. A good advisor tells you whether (or not) you're a good customer-match for the methods he's accustomed to using.

After you choose a broker, you must sign an options agreement before you can trade options. Option trading agreements are pretty stout, spelling out the risks of options trading and holding you liable for knowing the stuff on the agreement as well as stipulating that you'll make good on the promises you make in the agreement. You also must sign a margin agreement (because options trade mainly from margin accounts). A margin agreement is similar to a promissory note when you get a loan from the bank. Basically, you're promising to repay the loan, and the borrowed stock is collateral for the loan.

Deciding Whether to Trade Futures or Options

Futures traders, at least the ones who survive the initial stages of torment and can ride out the inevitable and discouraging down periods, are by nature risk-takers. And options are an integral part of the trading game that futures traders play, although it's worth noting that options and futures are viable stand-alone vehicles for trading. But is trading in futures or options right for *you?* The following questions help you answer that question:

- ✔ **How much money do you have?** Many experienced traders say that you need $100,000 to get started, but many talented traders have made fortunes after starting out with significantly less than $100,000. However, it would be irresponsible to lead you astray by giving you the impression that the odds are in your favor if you start trading with a very low level of capital. If you don't have that much money and aren't sure how to proceed, you need to either reconsider trading altogether, develop a stout trading plan and the discipline required to heed its tenets, or consider managed futures contracts.

- ✔ **How involved are you?** Trading futures or options is risky business and requires active participation. To be successful, you must be connected with the world through the Internet, television, and other news sources so you can be up-to-date and intimately knowledgeable with regard to world events. And this doesn't mean just picking up on what you get from occasionally watching the evening or headline news shows. You also must be able to develop your trading craft by constantly reviewing and modifying your plan and strategies.

- ✔ **Do you have the necessary technology?** You need an efficient computer system with enough memory to enable you to look at large amounts of data and run either multiple, fully loaded browsers or several monitors at the same time. You also need a high-speed Internet connection. And if you're serious about trading, you need two modes of high-speed Internet access so that you have a backup in the event that one goes down.

Chapter 2

Being a Savvy Futures and Options Trader

Successful futures and options traders can make money by anticipating market movement combined with following established trends and cutting losses. To understand what the markets are doing or anticipate where they're heading, you should be familiar with the current state of the global economy and the conflicting pressures that can impact it (financial crises, interest rates, and fiscal policy, for example), as well as the role of central banks in stabilizing those forces — all topics covered in this chapter.

Being a savvy futures and options trader also means being able to recognize economic trends early. To that end, this chapter also explains how to read and make sense of key economic reports.

Holding the Key: Interest Rates and the Money Supply

If you can figure out which way interest rates are headed and where money is flowing, most of what happens in the markets in general will fall into place, and you can make better decisions about which way to trade. Keep these relationships in mind:

✔ Futures markets often move based on the relationship between the bond market and the Federal Reserve. When either the Fed or the bond market moves interest rates in one direction, the other eventually follows.

✔ Higher interest rates tend to slow economic growth, whereas lower interest rates tend to spur economies.

Normally, you begin to see markets come to life at some point before or after the Fed makes a move. So get in the habit of watching all the markets together. When the Fed starts to ease rates, look at what happens to commodities like copper, gold, oil, and so on. The commodities markets provide you with confirmation of what the markets in general are expecting as the Fed makes its move.

Since the 2008 financial crises, central banks have kept interest rates at artificially low levels in order to keep economies from sinking lower. This is not a normal historical period. At some point, interest rates will rise again and then the normal relationships between markets will likely be restored. Figuring out early in that transition period which markets will reverse course and to what degree will be extremely important. For example, if central banks begin to raise interest rates, under normal circumstances, you can expect to see bond prices fall and stocks to follow.

In the following sections, you find out the role of central banks in setting interest rates and supplying money, and you track the money supply through various stages.

Respecting the role of central banks

Central banks around the globe, including the Federal Reserve in the U.S., are designed to make sure that their respective domestic economies run as smoothly as possible. Their overarching goal is to keep in check the boom-and-bust cycles in the global economy. So far this goal is only an intention because boom-and-bust cycles remain in place and are now referred to as the *business cycle.* In most countries, central banks are expected at the very least to combat inflationary pressures. *Inflation* is usually defined as a monetary phenomenon in which prices rise because too much money is in circulation, and that money's chasing too few goods.

To understand the role of central banks, consider the actions of the Federal Reserve during the 2007–2008 financial crisis. When global markets began to crash, the Federal Reserve lowered interest rates aggressively and immediately. This action served to keep the damage from becoming worse as money (liquidity) disappeared from the financial markets and the global economies. The central banks injected money into the system to keep it from collapsing.

Under more normal times, the objectives of the Fed are to fight inflation and maintain full employment in order to keep the consumption-based U.S. and global economies moving. As the events of 2007–2008 and beyond have revealed, the Fed is also the lender of last resort and source of money in times of crises as a way of maintaining the stability of the financial system and containing systemic risk.

After a central bank starts down a certain policy route, it usually stays with it for months or years, creating an intermediate-term trend on which to base the direction of trading. The Federal Reserve has essentially kept interest rates at zero since the 2007–2008 crisis. Nothing has changed at the time of this writing in April 2013.

Book II

Futures and Options

Following the money supply

The *money supply* is how much money is available in an economy to buy goods, services, and securities. The money supply is as important as the supply of goods in determining the direction of the futures and options markets. The three money supply figures to watch are

- ✔ **M0:** The total of all physical currency plus the currency in accounts held at the Federal Reserve that can be exchanged for physical currency

- ✔ **M1:** The M0 minus those portions of M0 held as reserves or cash held in vaults plus the amounts in all checking and current accounts

- ✔ **M2:** The M1 plus money housed in other types of savings accounts, such as money-market funds and certificates of deposit (CDs) of less than $100,000

The following sections explain how the money supply relates to inflation, commodity tendencies, and financial markets.

The key to making money by using money supply information is to have a good grip on whether the Fed actually is putting money into the system or taking it out. What's even more important is how fast the Fed is doing whatever it's doing at the time. The market, by its actions, factors in what it thinks the money supply is doing, what effects it will have on the economy, and the way the world works. All you have to do is pay attention and follow the overall trend of the market.

The multiplier effect

The wildest thing about money is how one dollar counts as two dollars whenever it goes around the loop enough times in an interesting little concept known as the *multiplier effect.* For example, say the Fed buys $1 worth of bonds from Bank X, and Bank X lends it to Person 1. Person 1 buys something from Person 2, who deposits the dollar in Bank 1. Bank 1 lends the money to Person 3, who deposits it in Bank 2, where the $1, in terms of money supply, is now $2 because it has been counted twice. By multiplying this little exercise by billions of transactions, you can arrive at the massive money supply numbers in the United States.

Equating the money supply and inflation

The *monetary exchange equation* explains the relationship between money supply and inflation:

$$\text{Velocity} \times \text{Money Supply} = \text{Gross Domestic Product (GDP)} \times \text{GDP Deflator}$$

Velocity, a measure of how fast money is changing hands, records how many times per year the money actually is exchanged. *GDP* is the sum of all the goods and services produced by the economy. The *GDP deflator* is a measure of inflation.

Here's what's important about the money supply as it relates to futures and options trading: A rising money supply, usually spawned by lower interest rates, tends to spur the economy and eventually fuels demand for commodities. Whenever the money supply rises to a key level, which differs in every business cycle, inflationary pressures eventually begin to appear, and the Fed starts reducing the money supply. The more money that's available, the more likely that some of it will make its way into the futures and options markets.

During *deflation*, the money supply shrinks because nobody wants to buy anything. Deflation usually results from *oversupply,* or a glut of goods in the marketplace. In deflation, consumers put off buying things in the hope that prices will fall farther. In *reflation,* central banks start pumping money into the economic system, hoping that lower borrowing costs will spur demand for goods and services, create jobs, and create a stronger economy.

Linking the money supply and commodity tendencies

As a general rule, futures prices respond to inflation. Some tend to rise, such as gold, and others tend to fall, such as the U.S. dollar. Each individual area of the futures market, though, is more responsive to its own fundamentals and its own supply-and-demand equation at any given time. With that noted, here is a quick-and-dirty guide to general money supply/commodity tendencies:

- ✔ Metals, agricultural products, oil, and livestock contracts generally tend to rise along with money supply.

- ✔ Bond prices fall and interest rates or bond yields rise in response to inflation.

- ✔ Stock index futures tend to rise when interest rates — either from the Fed or market rates in the bond and money markets — fall, and they tend to fall when interest rates rise to a high-enough level.

- ✔ Currencies tend to fall in value during times of inflation.

In a global economy, many of these dynamics occur simultaneously or in close proximity to each other, which is why an understanding of the global economy is more important when trading futures than when trading individual stocks.

Book II

Futures and Options

Connecting the money supply to financial markets

When central banks buy bonds from banks and dealers, they're putting money into circulation, enabling people and businesses to borrow money more easily. As a result, commodity markets tend to rise because they thrive on money. The commodity markets' actions are directly related to interest rates, underlying supply, and the perceptions and actions of the public, governments, and traders as they react to *supply* (how much is available and how fast it's going to be used up) and, to a lesser degree, *demand* (how long this period of rising willingness to buy is likely to last). In some cases, such as after the 2007–2008 financial crisis, these relationships aren't as reliable and markets tend to trade based on the perception of large trading firms that use computer algorithms to move prices. This trend toward higher levels of volatility caused by computer trading has accelerated over the years after the 2007–2008 financial crisis.

Traditionally, the higher the money supply, the easier it is to borrow, and the higher the likelihood that commodity markets will rise. As more money chases fewer goods, the chances of inflation rise, and the central banks begin to make borrowing money more difficult.

In the post 2007–2008 financial crisis world, bank and brokerage lending standards have changed, making the borrowing of money difficult in some cases. This has been more pronounced in the real economy away from the trading floors. As a result, the best way to trade is to understand that knowing traditional relationships is important, but watching price action is still the best way to trade.

Digesting Economic Reports

Each month a steady flow of economic data is generated and released by the U.S. government and the private sector. These reports are a major influence on how the futures and the financial markets move in general and a source of the *cyclicality,* or repetitive nature, of market movements.

You can access the calendar of report release dates in many places: your broker's website, the *Wall Street Journal,* Marketwatch.com, and other major news outlets, either posted for the month or for a particular day of the week.

The employment report

Released on the first Friday every month, the U.S. Department of Labor's employment report, formally known as the Employment Situation Report, sets the trend for overall trading in the entire arena of the financial markets for several weeks after its release. The employment report is most important when the economy is shifting gears. When consecutive reports show that a dominant trend is in place, the trend of the overall market tends to remain in the same direction for extended periods of time. The reversal of such a dominant trend can often be interpreted as a signal that bonds, stock indexes, and currencies are going to change course.

Traders use the employment report as one of several important clues to predict the future of interest rates and the overall economy. For trading purposes, pay attention to these two major components of the employment report:

- ✔ **The number of new jobs created:** This number tends to predict which way the strength of the economy is headed.

- ✔ **The unemployment rate:** The trend in the unemployment rate is more important than the actual monthly number. Full employment (an employment rate of around 95 percent) usually is a sign that interest rates are going to rise.

The unemployment rate is less reliable and important as a trading variable than the number of new jobs created. The politicians in Washington often spin this number for their own agenda's purposes. This number is easily manipulated by the way the statistics are plugged into the formula that's used to calculate it.

The Consumer Price Index

The Consumer Price Index (CPI) is the main inflation report for the futures and financial markets. Unexpected rises in this indicator usually lead to falling bond prices, rising interest rates, and increased market volatility.

As a trader, you want to know what the core CPI number is — that is, prices at the consumer level without food and energy factored in — because this core number gives you a clearer perspective of the other information, which, seen alone, may give an inaccurate picture of what's really going on. Here are some other key factors to consider regarding the CPI:

- ✓ Prices at the consumer level aren't as sensitive to supply and demand as they are to retailers' ability to pass their own costs on to consumers.

- ✓ Supply tends to be more important than demand.

- ✓ Inflationary expectations and consumer prices are related.

- ✓ By the time prices begin to rise at the consumer level, the supply-and-demand equation, price discovery, and pressure on the system have been ongoing at other levels of the price chain for some time.

Book II

Futures and Options

The release of the CPI usually moves the markets for interest-rate, currency, and stock index futures, and it's one of the best reports with which to trade option strategies. (For more about option strategies, see Chapters 3 and 4 in Book II.)

The Producer Price Index

The Producer Price Index (PPI) measures prices at the producer level (the cost of raw materials to companies that produce goods). The market is interested in two things contained in this report:

- ✓ **How fast these prices are rising:** If a rise in PPI is significantly large in comparison to previous months, the market checks to see where it's coming from: Does some other piece of information or a deeper understanding of the report's data change the initial interpretation of what's happening?

- ✓ **Whether producers are passing along any price hikes to their consumers:** If prices at the core level are tame, traders will conduct business based on the information they have in hand, at least until the CPI is released — usually one or two days after the PPI is released.

The purchasing managers' reports

The Institute for Supply Management's (ISM's) Report on Business, which measures the health of the manufacturing sector in the United States, is based on the input of purchasing managers surveyed across the country. The report addresses 11 categories, including the widely watched headline, the purchasing managers' index (PMI). The data for the entire report are included with a summary of the economy's current state and pace near the headline.

To understand the ISM report, which is available at the ISM website (www.ism.ws), first find out whether the main index and the subsectors are above or below 50. A number above 50 on the PMI means that the economy is growing.

International PMI numbers, such as China's reports, can also move U.S. and other global markets.

Consumer confidence reports

Consumer confidence reports come from two sources:

- ✔ **The Conference Board, Inc.,** a private research group, publishes a monthly report based on survey interviews of 5,000 consumers. The key components of the Conference Board survey are the monthly index, current conditions, and consumers' outlook for the next six months.

- ✔ **The University of Michigan** conducts its own survey of consumer confidence and publishes several preliminary reports and one final report per month. The key components of the University of Michigan survey are the Index of Consumer Sentiment, the Index of Consumer Expectations, and the Current Economic Conditions.

The Beige Book

The Summary of Commentary on Current Economic Conditions, otherwise known as the *Beige Book,* is released eight times per year and is a summary of current economic activity in each of the Federal Reserves' 12 federal districts. This summary is based on anecdotal information from Fed bank presidents, key businesses, economists, and market experts, among other sources. Traders look for any mention of labor shortages and wage pressures in the Beige Book. If any such trends are mentioned, bonds may sell off because rising wage pressures are taken as a sign of building inflation in the pipeline.

Housing starts

Big moves often occur in the bond market after the monthly release of numbers for housing starts. Housing starts are compiled by the U.S. Commerce Department and reported in three parts: building permits, housing starts, and housing completions. The markets focus on the percentage of rise or fall in the numbers from the preceding month for each component.

The Index of Leading Economic Indicators

The Index of Leading Economic Indicators, a lukewarm indicator, is more likely to move the markets whenever it clearly diverges from data provided by other indicators. In calculating its Index of Leading Economic Indicators, the Conference Board (see the earlier section "Consumer confidence reports") looks at ten key indicators such as the index of consumer expectations, the real money supply, the interest-rate spread, stock prices, vendor performance, average weekly initial claims for unemployment insurance, and more.

Gross Domestic Product

The report on Gross Domestic Product (GDP) measures the sum of all the goods and services produced in the United States. Although GDP can yield confusing and mixed results on the trading floor, it sometimes is a big market mover when it's far above or below market expectations.

Oil supply data

The Energy Information Administration (EIA), a part of the U.S. Department of Energy, and the American Petroleum Institute (API) release oil supply data for the preceding week at 10:30 a.m. eastern time every Wednesday. Traders want to know the following:

- **Crude oil supply:** The crude oil supply is the basis for the oil markets. Every week, oil experts and commentators guess what the number will be. A *build* occurs when the stockpiles of crude oil in storage are increasing. Such increases are considered *bearish* or negative for the market because large stockpiles generally mean lower prices at the pump. A *drawdown,* on the other hand, is when the supply shrinks. Traders like drawdown situations because prices tend to rise after the news is released.

- **Gasoline supply:** Gasoline supplies are more important as the summer driving season approaches.

- **Distillate supply:** Distillate supply figures are more important in winter because they essentially represent a measure of the heating oil supply.

The market has changed because of problems with refinery capacity in the United States, the aftereffects of two major hurricanes (Katrina and Rita) in 2005 in the Gulf of Mexico region, and the growing economies in places like India, China, and Brazil. Expect volatility in the markets and supply numbers to evolve over the next few years.

A bevy of other reports

A hodgepodge of data trickles in throughout the month about retail sales, personal income, industrial production, and the balance of trade. Of these four reports, the one most likely to get the most press is the balance of trade report. Because the Chinese economy is getting so much attention these days, the currency and bond markets may move dramatically whenever the balance of trade report shows a much greater than expected trade deficit or trade surplus. If several consecutive reports show that the United States is reversing its trend toward more imports than exports, you may see a major set of moves in the futures markets.

(Psycho)-Analyzing the Market

The stock market has a mind of its own and it pays to remember that, especially when you think you have the next move figured out. You may expect a decline when weak economic numbers are released, only to be surprised by the rally that follows. Or you may expect to see a boring day after a profitable earnings report is released, and then your jaw may drop with the ensuing decline that's attributed to this news.

Embracing the idea that the market has a mind of its own is easier when you consider that human behavior drives it. Although some argue that the market is efficient, all you have to do is watch the way an index moves after big reports are released to get the feeling that something very irrational is going on.

Many rules-based approaches allow you to make money in the markets, but that doesn't mean the market moves in a predictable way. In fact, market participants bring a good amount of irrationality to the game. Multiply one irrational person many times over and you have a crowd moving prices up or down, quickly or slowly, depending on the day.

The following sections describe a few methods for analyzing irrational market behavior: sentiment analysis, call and put monitoring, and volatility analysis.

Defining sentiment

There are ways to monitor market conditions and crowd behavior to better understand why the market reacts the way it does. One helpful step in this process is identifying which human emotion is in command at the time: greed or fear.

Sentiment broadly describes the overriding bias for the market, be it bullish or bearish. Greed (with a touch of fear) generally drives the former, whereas it's all about fear when markets decline. Month after month, year after year, and decade after decade, these greed-fear patterns repeat regardless of economic changes that occur along the way.

Sentiment tools use stock and options statistics to provide you with information about crowd activity during advances and declines. Most of this data is available from exchange websites (like those in Chapter 1 of Book II) or technical charting packages.

When employing sentiment analysis, you try to identify periods when greed has become unsustainable or fear is just about exhausted. It's sort of like musical chairs . . . at some point the music stops and everyone is scrambling for a spot so he can participate in the next round or move. You just want to be prepared so that you can respond quickly when a change in direction does take place. Focusing on market sentiment may allow you to do just that.

Sentiment analysis attempts to measure bullish and bearish actions versus what's being said about the market or even its current direction. Watch for things such as the following:

- Bullish commentary contradicted by unusually high put volume (flip to Chapter 1 in Book II for an introduction to puts and calls)
- A mild economic report that produces a wild swing in the market

The options market gives you quick indications about trader sentiment:

- Are traders bullish (buying calls/selling puts)?
- Are they bearish (buying puts/selling calls)?

Option data primarily provide insight to fear. Historical volatility and volume measures give you a feel for how much emotion was involved with moves in the past. Implied volatility levels let you know what's anticipated for the road ahead. (Chapter 1 in Book II discusses historical and implied volatility in more detail.)

Watching call and put activity

Investors are generally bullish. Because the markets spend more time going up rather than down, this is a pretty rational result. The reason it pays to note market bullishness is because typically call volume exceeds put volume, reflecting the tendency for the market to advance. It provides you with an

Book II

Futures and Options

option activity baseline. When people start getting nervous, as they will, put volume increases. Monitoring the put-to-call relationship, you can identify extreme levels corresponding with market reversals. Indicators may use call and put volume, or put volume alone, to measure fear or complacency in the market. For more details, go to the Chicago Board Options Exchange (CBOE) website at `www.cboe.com/data/PutCallRatio.aspx`.

Using volatility to measure fear

Market participants generally head for the exit much faster than they commit new money to stock positions. As a result, markets generally fall much faster than they rise. This scenario can be seen with increased volatility as daily and weekly swings move in a larger range. Using volatility sentiment measures helps you recognize declines that are nearing exhaustion.

Volatility really just gives you information about the price range for a particular security. You can use a variety of trading periods to calculate an annualized value, allowing you to compare movement for different securities. Historical volatility (HV) can be plotted on a chart enabling you to view trends and gain a sense of how current volatility stacks up to previous periods.

Implied volatility (IV) is an option pricing component that's referred to as a plug figure. It's the volatility level that accounts for the current option price after all other, more tangible pricing factors (for example, price, time, and interest rates) are valued. IV incorporates HV because it's reasonable to expect the stock to move in a manner that's similar to, although not necessarily the same as, past movement.

IV can also be plotted on a chart allowing you to view trends and relative levels. Such charts highlight strong seasonal tendencies for certain stocks.

You want to understand IV so you can make the best decisions when buying and selling options. Your chances of being wrong about the direction of an index or stock are two out of three, but the following generally hold true:

- ✔ When IV is relatively low and increases quickly, it adds value to both calls and puts.
- ✔ When IV is relatively high and decreases quickly, it decreases value for both calls and puts.

Pending news and reports, along with unexpected events, can spike IV. After the news or event is in the past and an initial reaction occurs in the stock, IV declines as quickly as it spiked. Changes in IV that are more gradual may also occur, in either direction.

Spelling fear the Wall Street way: V-I-X

VIX stands for *volatility index:* a blended, implied volatility value calculated using specific S&P 500 Index option contracts. VIX is used as a sentiment indicator. You may have heard references to the VIX by market analysts commenting on conditions.

Because statistical volatility usually climbs when securities decline, you should expect IV to increase too. The following holds for VIX readings:

✔ A climbing VIX reflects bearish conditions in SPX (the S&P 500 Index) and typically the market as a whole.

✔ A declining VIX reflects neutral to bullish conditions in SPX and typically the market as a whole.

Overly bearish sentiment is reflected by high VIX levels. Eventually the bearish fear is exhausted, a reversal in stocks occurs, and the VIX declines.

Book II

Futures and Options

Adding Technical Analysis to Your Toolbox

After you become better acquainted with the basic drivers and influences of a particular market and how that information — key market-moving reports, the major players involved, and the general fundamentals of supply and demand — fits into the big picture of the marketplace in general, the next logical step is to become acquainted with how the fundamentals are combined with the data that is compiled in price charts. And that leads you to the field of *technical analysis:* the use of price charts, moving averages, trendlines, volume relationships, and indicators for identifying trends and trading opportunities in underlying financial instruments.

Technical analysis is the key to success in the futures and options markets. The more you know about reading charts, the better your trading results are likely to be. Aside from its key role in decision-making, technical analysis is also a tool that leads you toward exploring more information about why the pattern suggests that you need to buy, sell, or sell short the underlying instrument.

 By becoming proficient at reading the charts of various security prices, you gain quick access to significant amounts of information, such as prices, general trends, and info about whether a market is sold out and ready to rally or *overbought,* meaning few buyers are left and prices can fall. By combining your knowledge of the markets and trading experiences with excellent charting skills, you vastly improve your market reaction time and your ability to make informed trades.

Book X is devoted to technical analysis. Head there for the nuts and bolts of how to use technical analysis to chart and recognize patterns.

Chapter 3

Basic Trading Strategies

A main reason investors choose options as a trading vehicle is that they give you leverage while limiting risk. The simplest option strategy is buying call options, because the upside potential is theoretically limitless, while the downside risk is your option premium. This is usually the first strategy that beginners use when they enter this sector and is best used when you're expecting the underlying asset to rally.

A second use of call options is option writing. In this case, you're looking to protect a long position by selling a call option to someone and collecting the premium. Option writing works better in markets that are falling or moving sideways. You're hoping that the underlying market goes mostly nowhere and that the option expires worthless, while you pocket the premium.

Put option strategies are another alternative. Generally useful in falling markets, they tend to be riskier than call-related strategies. When you buy a put option, you accomplish essentially the same thing as short selling without some of the more complicated details. Put options also give you leverage because you don't have to spend as much money as you would trying to short sell a stock.

This chapter covers these basic option strategies. And because trading on margin is a key concept to futures and options trading, it starts there.

 Paper trading — simulating or practicing trades on paper before you make real trades — is *never* a bad idea. If you're a beginner who insists on trading real money, trade only in small lots or small amounts of money, one contract at a time. Finding a good options advisor/broker, one with a conscience who can run your option strategies for you — at least until you get your feet wet — is another worthy consideration; Chapter 1 in Book II provides pointers on finding an options broker.

Trading on Margin

To be a successful futures and options trader, you need to understand the ins and outs of trading on margin. Trading on margin enables you to *leverage* your trading position — that is, control a larger amount of assets with a smaller amount of money. Margins in the futures market generally are low; they tend to be near the 10 percent range, so you can control, or trade, $100,000 worth of commodities or financial indexes with only $10,000 or so in your account. The downside is that if you don't understand how trading on margin works, you can take on some big losses in a hurry.

You can reduce the risk of buying futures on margin by

- ✔ Trading contracts that are lower in volatility
- ✔ Using advanced trading techniques such as *spreads,* or positions in which you simultaneously buy and sell contracts in two different commodities or the same commodity for two different months, to reduce the risk

Margin requirements for different options and strategies sometimes are difficult to calculate and may vary among different brokers. Before setting up an account, read the options and margin agreements from your broker carefully so that you fully understand margin requirements for each individual class of options you're trading.

Trading on margin in the stock market is a different concept than trading on margin in the futures market. The following sections explore the differences.

Looking at margin limits

In the stock market, the Federal Reserve sets the allowable margin at 50 percent; to trade stocks on margin, you must put up 50 percent of the value of the trade. Futures margins are set by the futures exchanges and are different for each different futures contract. Margins in the futures market can be raised or lowered by the exchanges, depending on current market conditions and the volatility of the underlying contract.

Futures markets margins by design are lower than other margins, because futures contracts are meant to be highly leveraged trading instruments, and their main attraction is the potential they have for yielding large profits with small cash requirements. The flip side, of course, is the risk involved.

If the life of the option is nine months or less, you can't purchase options on margin as you can stocks. However, if the option has a life of greater than nine months, the broker can lend you 25 percent.

Options already have a great deal of leverage and risk built into them. To keep traders from taking risks that can lead to their losing the entire value of their account, the Securities and Exchange Commission (SEC) allows brokers to lend only up to 25 percent of the required margin to options traders, which means you must keep 75 percent of the value of your positions in your account to be able to continue trading options on margin.

Mulling over the multiple meanings of "margin"

Book II

Futures and Options

Generally, when you deposit a margin on a stock purchase, you buy partial equity of the stock position and owe the balance as debt. In the futures market, a margin acts as a security deposit that protects the exchange from default by the customer or the brokerage house.

When you trade futures on margin, in most cases you buy the right to participate in the price changes of the contract. Your margin is a sign of good faith, or a sign that you're willing to meet your contractual obligations with regard to the trade.

Buying Calls

Call buying is different from call writing, because it isn't usually used by traders as a hedge against risk. Instead, call buying is used to make money on stocks that are likely to go up in price. Call buying is the most common technique used by individual investors, but beware that success in this form of trading requires good stock-picking skills and a sense of timing.

The following sections describe reasons and tips for buying calls, note how to calculate break-even prices, explain the use of delta to time your purchases, and show you how to follow up after you buy.

Understanding reasons and getting some pointers for buying calls

The main attraction of buying call options is the potential for making large sums of money in short amounts of time, while limiting downside risk to only the original amount of money that you put up when you bought the option. Here are two reasons for buying call options:

✔ **You expect the stock to rise.** ABC stock is selling at $50, and you buy a six-month call, the December 55, at $3. You pay $300 for the position. For the next six months you have a chance to make money if the stock rises in price. If the stock goes up 10 points, or 20 percent, your option also will rise, and because of leverage, the option will be worth much more. If the price drops below $55 by the expiration date, all you lose is your original $300 if you didn't sell back the option prior to that.

✔ **You expect to have money later and don't want to miss a move up in a stock.** Say, for example, that you expect a nice sum of money in a couple of weeks, and a stock you like is starting to move. You can buy an option for a fraction of the price of the stock. When you get your money, if you're still interested, you can exercise your option and buy the stock. If you're wrong, you lose only a fraction of what you would have by owning the stock.

When you buy a call option, you pay for it in full. You don't have to post margin.

Here's some advice to keep in mind when buying call options:

✔ Choose the right stock. Buy call options on stocks that look ready to break out. To figure out which stocks meet that criterion, you need to become familiar with charting techniques and technical analysis (see Book X).

✔ Use charts over fundamentals when you trade call options.

✔ Out-of-the-money calls have greater profit potential and greater risk.

✔ In-the-money calls may perform better when the stock doesn't move as you expected.

✔ Don't buy cheap call options just because they're cheap.

✔ Near-term calls (those with shorter time periods in which to exercise the option) are riskier than far-term calls.

✔ Intermediate-term calls may offer the best risk/reward ratio.

Calculating the break-even price for calls and puts

Before you buy any call option, you must calculate the break-even price by using the following formula:

Strike price + Option premium cost + Commission and transaction costs = Break-even price

So if you're buying a December 50 call on ABC stock that sells for a $2.50 premium and the commission is $25 for 100 shares, your break-even price per share would be

$50 + $2.50 + 0.25 = $52.75 per share

That means that to make a profit on this call option, the price per share of ABC has to rise above $52.75.

To calculate the break-even price for a put option, you subtract the premium and the commission costs. For a December 50 put on ABC stock that sells at a premium of $2.50, with a commission of $25 for 100 shares, your break-even point per share would be

$50 − $2.50 − 0.25 = $47.25 per share

That means the price per share of ABC stock must fall below $47.25 for you to make a profit.

Make sure that you understand the fee structure used by your broker before making any option trades. Fees differ significantly from one broker to the next. Brokers frequently charge *round-trip fees,* which refer to the fees that you're charged on the way in and on the way out of an options trading position. To figure out round-trip commission fees in the break-even formula, simply double the commission cost.

Using delta to time call-buying decisions

Delta (explained in Chapter 1 of Book II) measures the amount by which the price of the call option will change, up and down, every time the underlying stock moves 1 point.

In a day-trading situation, Lawrence McMillan, author of *Options as a Strategic Investment* (published by Prentice-Hall Press), recommends trading the underlying stock. This strategy follows the key concept of using delta: The shorter the term of the strategy, the greater your delta should be. The delta of the underlying stock is 1.0. Thus, the stock is the most volatile instrument and is best suited for day-trading.

How long you expect to hold an option determines in part which option to buy. Here are some general rules to follow when using delta to time your call buying:

✔ For trades that you expect to hold for a week or less, use the highest delta option you can find, because its moves will correlate the closest with the underlying asset. In this case, short-term, in-the-money options are the best bet.

Book II

Futures and Options

- For intermediate-term trading, usually weeks in duration, use options with smaller deltas. McMillan recommends using at-the-money options (that is, those for which the strike and market price are identical) for this time frame.

- For longer-term trading, choose low-delta options, either slightly out-of-the-money or longer-term at-the-money options.

Following up after buying a call option

Keep these rules in mind after you buy a call option:

- If the underlying stock tanks, the best course is to sell the call option and cut your losses.

- If the option rises in price, especially if it doubles in a short period of time, take some profits.

- It's better to sell a call than to exercise it because the commission costs to buy the stock when you exercise the call are usually more than what it costs to sell the option. Also, if you then turn around and sell the stock, you'll pay more of a commission at that time as well.

- If you buy several options and the stock rises significantly, you can take partial profits by selling a portion of your overall position. For example, if you bought five calls and the position is profitable, you can sell three calls and ride the profit train with the remaining ones.

- If you decide to do nothing, you can lose everything at expiration. But if you sell your profitable initial position and stay out of the options in that particular stock, you can keep your profit. (For my money, a good profit in my pocket is better than a great one that may never come.) So note that at the beginning of an options trading strategy, keeping it simple is the best way to go. As you become more experienced, you can start making more sophisticated bets.

Writing Calls

When you *write a call,* you sell someone the right to buy an underlying stock from you at a specific price (called the *strike price*) that's specified by the option series, or contract traded on that particular exchange. As the writer, you are now *short* the option. The buyer of your call is *long* the option. You also are obligated to deliver the stock if the buyer decides to exercise the call option.

As a call writer, you're hoping that

- ✔ The stock goes nowhere.
- ✔ You collect the premium.
- ✔ The option expires worthless so you don't have to come up with shares of the stock to settle when the holder exercises the call, which is what can happen with naked call writing.

The following sections distinguish naked and covered call options, provide pointers for writing calls, show you how to diversify, and explain how to follow up after you write a call.

Choosing to be naked or covered

When you write a *naked call option,* you're selling someone else a chance to bet that the underlying stock is going to go higher in price. The catch is that you don't own the stock, so if the buyer exercises the option, you need to buy the stock at the market price to meet your obligation. When you write a *covered call option,* you already own the shares. If you're exercised against, you just sell your shares at the strike price.

Covered call writing is a perfect strategy if you're looking to smooth out your portfolio's performance and collect the extra income from the call premiums. When the call expires worthless, you get to keep the stock (which you already own) and collect all the dividends that accrued during the time the call was in play. When you write naked calls (in which you don't own the stock), if the call expires worthless, you still keep the premium.

Writing covered calls is a safer strategy than writing naked calls. If the holder exercises a naked call option, you have to buy the stock before you can deliver it to him. If the stock price has risen in the interim, you can sustain a serious loss in meeting the exercise. You can get around losing a lot of money when writing naked calls by figuring out your break-even point and unwinding the position if the price reaches that point. Getting out of the trade at your break-even point enables you to decide what you're willing to lose before ever making a trade.

Doing your homework

When you write calls, think of your stock and your option as two different parts of one single position. Each part has its own role to play and is dependent on the other to perform a complete job for your portfolio.

Each part also has its own cost, so you need to know the price of the stock when you bought it and add in the price of the premium that you gain when you sell the call.

Before you write a call, figure out how much you get from the strike price and the premium if the call option is exercised against you. Always know your worst-case scenario before you hit the trade button. Here are some additional tips to keep in mind about writing calls:

- A low volatility stock is perfect for call option writing.

- Writing in-the-money options generally lets you collect a better premium than writing out-of-the-money options; however, the profit potential is greater when you write out-of-the-money call options. (***Note:*** For *in-the-money* call options, the strike price is below the market price; for put options, being *in-the-money* means the strike price is above the market price. In either case, the general significance is that your option is worth money. Being out-of-the-money means the opposite.)

- For the covered-call strategy to work best, try to execute the trades — buy the stock and write the call option — at the same time by establishing a *net position* in which your goal is to achieve your *net price,* or the price you set as your investment goal for the order. You can establish a net position by placing a *contingent order* with your broker, which stipulates how you want the order executed.

   Note: Contingent orders — also referred to as *net orders* — are not guaranteed by the broker. They're also referred to as *not-held orders,* because if the broker thinks the order is too difficult to fill, you'll receive a "nothing done" report, and the order won't be filled.

   If you're unwilling to sell the stock against which you're writing the covered call, you shouldn't even consider writing the option. You'll probably get hurt if someone exercises a call against you.

- If you change your mind after selling an option, you can buy it back in the marketplace. The buyer can also sell his options to the marketplace. This rule applies to both puts and calls.

Protecting your trade by diversification

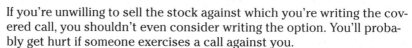

A diversification strategy is pretty simple, and it works best when you own more than a couple hundred shares of a stock. In this strategy, you sell more than one covered call at different strike prices and for different time frames. Again, the goal is to spread out your risk against volatility and your risk against the call you sold being exercised. You accomplish this strategy by writing in-the-money calls on some stocks and out-of-the-money calls on other stocks in your portfolio.

Setting up this strategy is difficult because writing out-of-the-money calls theoretically works better when you write them against stocks that do well. In other words, you're forced to decide which stocks you think are likely to do better than others, which is difficult to do in a simple stock-picking strategy without the option strategy. Conversely, writing in-the-money calls works better for stocks with low volatility. One way to get around this problem is to write half of the position against in-the-money and half against out-of-the-money on the same stock.

Following up after writing a call

Your job as an options trader starts when you make the transaction. The heavy lifting is what lies ahead — managing the position, which is more difficult in some ways than opening the position. Here are two important things to know about managing the position:

- ✔ What to do if a stock rises after you've written a covered call
- ✔ What to do as the covered call approaches expiration

Knowing what to do when the stock rises

If your stock goes up, you can just let the buyer have it at the higher price. You made your premium, and you sold your stock at a price that you were comfortable with. If you want to be aggressive, you can buy back your option and *roll up,* or write another call at a higher strike price. When you do, though, you incur a debit in your trade, because you have to put more money into the account.

Rolling up can be risky, because you can end up with a loss. Lawrence McMillan, author of *Options as a Strategic Investment*, suggests that you shouldn't roll up whenever you can't withstand a 10-percent correction in the stock's price.

Rolling forward when the expiration time nears

Rolling forward is what you may want to do as your option's expiration time nears. When you roll forward, you buy back your option and sell a new one with a longer term but the same strike price. Although you could let the stock be called away, if your stock has low volatility and your option strategy has been working for you, rolling forward usually is best. How you make your decision is based on your projected costs of commissions and fees, and what your break-even point will be for the position.

If you're writing calls, make sure you're willing to let the underlying stock get called away. Otherwise, you're likely to become sorry at some point. If the position is going against you and you keep rolling up and forward, you're probably only making matters worse. At some point, you will hit the panic button and buy back your calls at a loss. You'll probably start selling put options to generate some credits, but you'll also end up placing yourself in a position that can wipe out your whole account.

Considering Basic Put Option Strategies

When you buy a put option, you're hoping that the price of the underlying stock falls. You make money with puts when the price of the option rises, or when you exercise the option to buy the stock at a price that's below the strike price and then sell the stock in the open market, pocketing the difference. By buying a put option, you limit your risk of a loss to the premium that you paid for the put. (Puts are sometimes thought of as portfolio insurance because they give you the option of selling a falling stock at a predetermined strike price.)

If, for example, you bought an ABC December 50 put, and ABC falls to $40 per share, you can make money either by selling a put option that rises in price or by buying the stock at $40 on the open market and then exercising the option, thus selling your $40 stock to the writer for $50 per share, which is what owning the put gave you the right to do.

The following sections discuss buying and selling puts, exercising put options, and handling profits from puts.

Making the most of your put option buys

Out-of-the-money puts are riskier but offer greater reward potential than in-the-money puts. The flip side is that if a stock falls a relatively small amount, you're likely to make more money from your put if you own an in-the-money option.

Call options (discussed earlier in this chapter) tend to move more dramatically than puts. You can buy the right put option, and the underlying stock may fall significantly, yet the market may decide that the put option should rise only 1 or 2 points. In an ideal world, you'd expect to be greatly rewarded for buying a put option on a stock that collapses. But, in the world of options pricing, things aren't always what you'd expect them to be because of the vagaries of trading, the time to expiration, and other major influences on option pricing. To avoid disappointment, you're better off buying in-the-money puts unless the probability that the underlying stock is going to fall by a significant amount is extremely high.

In contrast to call options, you may be able to buy a longer-term put option for a fairly good price. Doing so is a good idea, because it gives you more time for the stock to fall. Buying the longer-term put also protects you if the stock rises, because its premium will likely drop less in price.

Dividends make put options more valuable, and the larger the dividend, the more valuable the put becomes. When stocks go ex-dividend, the day the dividend gets paid out, the amount of the dividend reduces the price of the stock. As the stock falls, the put increases in value. The prices of puts and calls are not reduced by dividends. Instead, the price reflects the effect of the dividend on the stock. Call prices fall as the stocks pay out their dividends. Put prices rise as of the ex-dividend date.

Book II

Futures and Options

Buying put options

Buying a put option without owning the stock is called *buying a naked put*. Naked puts give you the potential for profit if the underlying stock falls. But if you own a stock and buy a put option on the same stock, you're protecting your position and limiting your downside risk for the life of the put option.

A good time to buy a put on a stock that you own is when you've made a significant gain, but you're not sure you want to cash out; your put option acts as an insurance policy to protect your gains. You can also use puts to protect against short-term volatility in long-term holdings; if your put goes up in value, you can sell it and decrease the paper losses on your stock. You decide which put option to buy by calculating how much profit potential you're willing to lose if the stock goes up.

Out-of-the-money puts are cheap, but they won't give you as much protection as in-the-money puts until the stock falls to the strike price. In-the-money puts are more expensive but can provide better insurance.

Selling naked and covered puts

Selling naked put options is similar to buying a call option, because you make money when the underlying stock goes up in price. Selling a naked put means you're selling a put option without being short the stock, and in the process, you're hoping that the stock goes nowhere or rises, which enables you to keep the premium without being *assigned* (in other words, being required to satisfy the obligation if an option holder chooses to exercise his rights). If the stock falls in a big way, and you get assigned, you can face big losses from having to buy the stock in the open market to sell to the party exercising the put you sold.

You need to put up collateral to write naked puts, usually in an amount that equals 20 percent of the current stock price plus the put premium minus any out-of-the-money amount. Here's how it works: ABC is selling at $40 per share, and a four-month put with a strike price of $40 is selling for 4 points. You have the potential to make $400 here (every options contract for stocks gives you the opportunity to speculate on 100 shares of the stock) or the potential for a huge loss if the stock falls. Your loss is limited only because the stock can't go below zero. The amount of collateral you'd need to put up would be $400, plus 20 percent of the price of the stock, or $80. The minimum you'd have to put up, though, would be 10 percent of the strike price plus the put premium, even if the amount is smaller than what you just calculated.

Selling covered puts is not particularly recommended for beginners. A put sale is *covered*, not by owning the stock, but rather by having an open short position on the underlying stock. Your margin is covered if you're also short the stock. This strategy has unlimited upside risk and limited profit potential if the underlying stock rises because the short sale will accrue losses. The position is equivalent to a naked call write, except the covered put writer has to pay out the dividend of the underlying stock if the stock pays a dividend.

Exercising your put option

Put and call options rarely are exercised in the stock market. Most option traders take the gains on the options if they have them or cut their losses short as early as possible if the market goes against them. But if you're the holder of a put option and you decide to exercise it, you're selling the underlying stock at the strike price, and you can sell the stock at the strike price any time during the life of the option. If you write, or sell, the put, you're assigned the obligation of buying the stock at the strike price.

You can sell stock that you own at the strike price or buy stock in the open market if you don't own it, as in the case of a naked strategy, and then sell it at the strike price. You notify your broker how you'll deliver or receive the stock. You must make sure that you can satisfy any margin or other requirement involved, and the exercise procedure and share transfer will be handled by the broker.

Dealing with a huge profit in a put option

If you're lucky enough to get a nice drop in a stock on which you own a put option, you can do several things:

- ✔ **Do nothing.**
- ✔ **Take profits.** Doing so guarantees that you lock in a gain if you execute the trade in a timely manner.

✔ **Sell your in-the-money put and buy an out-of-the money put.** By opting for this strategy, you're taking partial profits and then extending your risk and your profit potential if the stock continues to fall.

✔ **Create a spread strategy by selling an out-of-the-money put against the one you already own.** This strategy adds an important new wrinkle to the possible strategies you can use. Your options are to

- **Sell a different put option than the one you already own.** You can, for instance, sell a December 45 put to offset the already profitable December 50 put that you own, all so that you make some money off the sale and lock in some of the costs of having bought the original December 50 put. If the stock goes above 50, you lose everything. But if the stock falls below 45 and stabilizes, you make the 5-point maximum profit from the spread, which is the best of all worlds in this strategy.

- **Buy a call option.** You can buy a December 45 call to limit your risk if the stock rises. (See the earlier section about writing calls.) Your cost is 5 points. This spread guarantees you 5 points no matter where the stock closes at expiration.

Spreads get the best results when the stock stabilizes in price after the spread is put on. But it's more important that the stock price stays in the profit range of the spread.

The IRS taxes short-term and long-term profits on every sale of every trade you make, except in a retirement account for which the IRS taxes you when you withdraw the money. Some tax-specific details you need to know if you're trading put options include the following:

✔ Buying put options has no tax consequences if you're a long-term holder, usually greater than six months.

✔ If you forfeit any accrued time during the holding period, or if you're a short-term holder of the stock and you buy a put option, holding time won't begin to accrue again until you sell the put or it expires.

Be sure to consult with your accountant before you trade any options.

Chapter 4

Advanced Speculation Strategies

In This Chapter
▶ Engaging in contrarian trading
▶ Investigating interest rate futures
▶ Fixating on stock index futures

*I*n this chapter, you get into the big money with advanced speculation strategies, getting the lowdown on interest-rate futures and taking stock of stock index futures. These markets, in addition to the currency market (which you can read about in Book IV), often set the tone for the trading day in all markets because they form a focal point or hub for the global financial system. What's good about these markets is that they're great places for you to get started in futures trading, so you get tips for doing just that. But first, you discover the benefits of thinking (and trading) like a contrarian.

Thinking Like a Contrarian

Contrarians trade against the grain at key turning points when shifts in market sentiment become noticeable. A contrarian, for example, may start looking for reasons to sell when everyone else is bullish or may consider it a good time to buy when pessimism about the markets is so thick that you can cut it with a knife. The most important aspect of contrarian thinking is to be able to spot important turning points that can lead to profitable trades.

Sentiment trading is inexact and can lead to losses whenever you pull the trigger too early during the cycle; therefore, you need to combine sentiment analysis and technical analysis to become a better trader. This section takes you through the major aspects of contrarian thinking and explains how to make it part of your trading arsenal.

Picking apart popular sentiment surveys

You use sentiment surveys to gauge when a particular market is at an extreme point: either too bullish or too bearish. The major weakness of these surveys is that their popularity hinders their ability to truly mark major turning points. Still, when used within the context of good technical and fundamental analysis, they can be useful. Two popular sentiment surveys affect the futures markets: Market Vane (www.marketvane.net) and Consensus, Inc. (www.consensus-inc.com). Both offer sentiment data on items such as the following:

- **Precious metals:** Silver, gold, copper, and platinum

- **Financial instruments:** Eurodollars, the U.S. dollar, Treasury bills (T-bills), and Treasury bonds (T-bonds)

- **Currencies:** The U.S. dollar, Euro FX, British pound, Deutschemark, Swiss franc, Canadian dollar, and Japanese yen

- **Agricultural products:** Soybean products, meats, grains, other foods (such as sugar, cocoa, and coffee), and more

- **Stock indexes:** The S&P 500 and NASDAQ-100 stock indexes

- **Energy complex:** Crude oil, natural gas, gasoline, and heating oil

Snapshots of both surveys for stocks, bonds, Eurodollars, and Euro currency are available weekly in *Barron's* magazine under the Market Lab section or at Barron's Online, www.barrons.com. What you'll find when reading *Barron's* or another such publication are percentages of market sentiment, such as oil being 75 percent bulls, or bullish, which simply means that 75 percent of the opinions surveyed by the editors of Market Vane or Consensus are bullish on oil.

When using sentiment surveys to help guide your decision-making, keep these points in mind:

- **Sentiment survey readings must be at extreme levels to be useful.** Sentiments below 35 to 40 percent for any given category usually are considered bullish, for example, because few advisors are left to recommend selling.

- **Avoid trading on sentiment data alone, because doing so can be too risky.** After you find out the market sentiment, you need to perform a bit of technical analysis and fundamental analysis (covered in Books X and VII, respectively). A high bullish reading in terms of sentiment, for example, should alert you to start looking for technical signs that a top is in place, checking to see whether key support levels or trendlines have been breached or whether the market is struggling to make new highs.

Looking at trading volume as a sentiment indicator

Trading volume is a direct, real-time sentiment indicator. As a general rule, high trading volume signals that the current trend is likely to continue. Still, good volume analysis takes other market indicators into account. When analyzing volume, be sure that you

- ✔ Don't think about hard-and-fast rules. Instead, put the current volume trends in the proper context with relationship to the market in which you're trading. It's important to note, for example, that trends tend to either start or end with a volume spike climax (typically twice the 20- or 50-day moving average of daily volume).

- ✔ Remember the differences in the way that volume is reported and interpreted in the futures market compared with the stock market.

- ✔ Check other indicators to confirm what volume is telling you.

- ✔ Ask yourself whether the market is vulnerable to a trend change.

- ✔ Consider key support and resistance levels.

- ✔ Protect your portfolio by being prepared to make necessary changes.

Figure 4-1, which shows the S&P 500 e-mini futures contract for September 2005, portrays an interesting relationship between volume, sentiment, and other indicators. In April, the market made a textbook bottom. Notice how the volume bars at the bottom of the chart rose as the market was reaching a selling climax, as signified by the three large candlesticks, or trading bars. This combination of signals — large price moves and large volumes when the market is falling — is often the prelude to a classic market bottom because traders panic and sell at any price just to get out of their positions.

Notice how the volume trailed off as the market consolidated, or started moving sideways, making a complex bottom that took almost two weeks to form. When markets consolidate (that is, when buyers and sellers are in balance), they're catching their breath and getting set up for their next move. Consolidation phases are unpredictable and can last for short periods of time, such as hours or days, or longer periods, even months to years.

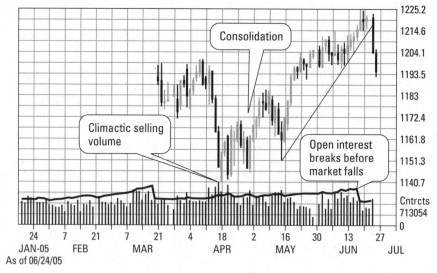

Figure 4-1:
Volume and
the e-mini
S&P 500
September
2005 futures.

A third important volume signal occurred in late May and early June as the market rallied. Notice how volume faded as the market continued to rise. Eventually, the market fell and moved significantly lower as it broke below key trendline support. Finally, note that open interest fell during the last stage of the rally in late June, which usually is a sign that more weakness is likely, because fewer contracts remain open, suggesting that traders are getting exhausted and are less willing to hold on to open positions.

Using volume indicators in the futures markets has limitations. The example in Figure 4-1 needs to be viewed within the context of these limitations:

✔ The release of volume figures in the futures market is delayed by one day.

✔ Higher volume levels steadily migrate toward the closest *delivery month*, or the month in which the contract is settled and delivery of the underlying asset takes place. That migration is important for traders because the chance of getting a better price for your trade is higher when volume is better.

✔ *Limit days* (especially limit up days), or days in which a particular contract makes a big move in a short period of time, can have very high volume, thus skewing your analysis. Limit up or limit down days tend to happen in response to a single or related series of events, external or internal, such as a very surprising report. A *limit up* day, when the market rises to the limit in a short period of time, usually is a signal of strength in the market. When markets crash, you can see *limit down* moves that then trigger *trading collars* (periods when the market trades but prices don't change) or complete stoppages of trading.

Signaling a potential trend reversal: Open interest

One of the most useful tools you can have when trading futures, *open interest* is the total number of options and/or futures contracts that are not closed or delivered on a particular day. It's the most beneficial tool for analyzing poten-tial trend reversals in futures markets. Open interest applies to futures and options but not to stocks and does the following:

Book II

Futures and Options

- ✔ Measures the total number of short and long positions (*shorts* and *longs*). In the futures markets, the number of longs always equals the number of shorts. So when a new buyer buys from an old buyer who is cashing in, no change occurs in open interest.

- ✔ Varies based on the number of new traders entering the market and the number of traders leaving the market.

- ✔ Rises by one whenever one new buyer and one new seller enter the market, thus marking the creation of one new contract.

- ✔ Falls by one when a long trader closes out a position with a trader who already has an open short position.

Charting open interest on a daily basis in conjunction with a price chart helps you keep track of the trends in open interest and how they relate to market prices. Barchart.com (www.barchart.com) offers excellent free futures charts that give you a good look at open interest.

The following sections describe open interest signals in three market scenarios: rising markets, sideways markets, and falling markets.

Rising markets

In a rising market, open interest is fairly straightforward:

- ✔ **Bullish open interest:** When open interest rises along with prices, it sig-nals that an uptrend is in place and can be sustained. This bullish sign also means that new money is moving into the market. Extremely high open interest in a bull market, however, usually is a danger signal.

- ✔ **Bearish open interest:** Rising prices combined with falling open interest signal a short-covering rally in which short sellers are reversing their positions so that their buying actually is pushing prices higher. In this case, higher prices aren't likely to last because no new buyers are entering the market.

✔ **Bearish leveling or decline:** A leveling off or decrease in open interest in a rising market often is an early warning sign that a *top* (the peak, or high point, of the trading price) may be nearing.

Sideways markets

In a sideways market, open interest gets trickier, so you need to watch for the following:

✔ **Rising open interest during periods when the market is moving sideways (or in a narrow trading range):** This scenario usually leads to an intense move after prices break out of the trading range — up or down.

When dealing with sideways markets, be sure to confirm open-interest signals by checking them against other market indicators, such as pricing trends.

✔ **Down-trending price breakouts (breakdowns):** Some futures traders use breakouts on the downside to set up short positions, thus leaving the public wide open for a major sell-off.

✔ **Falling open interest in a trader's market:** When it happens, traders with weak positions are throwing in the towel, and the pros are covering their short positions and setting up for a market rally.

Falling markets

In falling markets, open-interest signals are a bit more complicated to decipher:

✔ **Bearish open interest:** Falling prices combined with a rise in open interest indicate that a downtrend is in place and being fueled by new money coming in from short sellers.

✔ **Bullish open interest:** Falling prices combined with falling open interest signal that traders who didn't sell their positions as the market broke — hoping the market would bounce back — are giving up. In this case, you need to start anticipating, or even expecting, a trend reversal toward higher prices after this give-up phase ends.

✔ **Neutral:** If prices rise or fall but open interest remains flat, a trend reversal is possible. You can think of these periods as preludes to an eventual change in the existing trend. Neutral open-interest situations are good times to be especially alert.

✔ **Trending down:** A market trend that shifts downward at the same time open interest reaches high levels can be a sign that more selling is coming. Traders who bought into the market right before it topped out are now liquidating losing positions to cut their losses.

Combining volume and open interest

You can combine open interest and volume to predict a trend change. Generally, volume and open interest need to be heading in the same direction as the market. Rising markets should have rising volume and open interest accompanying the rise of prices — a sign of strength. A rising market with shrinking volume and falling open interest usually is one that's heading for a correction. Table 4-1 summarizes the relationship between volume and open interest.

Table 4-1	The Relationship between Volume and Open Interest		
Price	*Volume*	*Open Interest*	*Market Trend*
Rising	Up	Up	Strong
Rising	Down	Down	Weak
Declining	Up	Up	Weak
Declining	Down	Down	Strong

Checking out put/call ratios as sentiment indicators

The *put/call ratio,* the most commonly used sentiment indicator for trading stocks, can also be useful in trading stock index futures because it lets you pinpoint major inflection points in trader sentiment. At extremes, put/call ratios can be signs of excessive fear (a high level of put buying relative to call buying) and excessive greed (a high level of call buying relative to put buying). *Note:* These indicators aren't as useful as they once were, due to the more sophisticated hedging strategies now used in the markets.

As a futures trader, put/call ratios can help you make several important decisions about

- ✔ Tightening your stops on open positions
- ✔ Setting new entry points if you've been out of the market
- ✔ Setting up hedges with options and futures
- ✔ Taking profits

The Chicago Board Options Exchange (CBOE) updates the put/call ratio throughout the day at its website (www.cboe.com/data/IntraDayVol. aspx) and provides final figures for the day after the market closes (5 p.m. central time). Check the put/call ratios after the market closes.

Put/call ratios are best used as alert mechanisms for potential trend changes and in conjunction with technical analysis. So be sure to look at your charts and take inventory of your own positions during the time frame in which you're trading futures contracts. The sections that follow describe important ratios you need to become familiar with when trading stock index futures.

Total put/call ratio

The total put/call ratio is calculated using the following equation:

Total put options purchased ÷ Total call options purchased

The total ratio includes options on stocks, indexes, and long-term options bought by traders on the CBOE. Although you can make sense of this ratio in many ways, it's often useful when the ratio rises above 1.0 and when it falls below 0.5. Above 1.0, the ratio usually means too much fear is in the air and the market is trying to make a bottom. Readings below 0.5 usually mean that too much bullishness is in the air and the market may fall.

Index put/call ratio

The index put/call ratio is a good measure of what futures and options players, institutions, and hedge-fund managers are up to. Above 2.0, this indicator traditionally is a bullish sign; below 0.90, it becomes bearish and traditionally signals that some kind of correction is coming.

Because these numbers aren't as reliable as they used to be, consider them only as reference points and never base any trades on them alone. Don't forget that put/call ratios need to be correlated with chart patterns.

A word about abnormal ratios

Ignoring abnormal put/call ratio readings can cost you significant amounts of money in a hurry. When you see abnormally high or low put/call ratios, make sure you're ready to handle dramatic changes and immediately look for weak spots in your portfolio. Abnormal activity should trigger ideas about hedging. When you see abnormal put/call ratio numbers, consider

- ✔ Tightening stops on your open stock index futures positions.

- ✔ Looking for ways to hedge your portfolio (employing option strategies, for example, or buying or selling short positions in other markets).

- ✔ Reversing positions. If you have a short position in the market, be ready to go long; if you have a long position, be ready to go short.

Using soft sentiment signs

Soft sentiment signs — the subtle, nonquantitative factors that most people tend to ignore — can be anything from the shoeshine boy giving stock tips or a wild magazine cover (classic signs of a top) to people jumping out of windows during a market crash (a classic sign of the other extreme). Although you shouldn't make them a mainstay of your trading strategy, they can be helpful; consider them an alert that something dramatic is going to happen.

You can find soft sentiment signs in the following places:

- **Magazine covers and website headlines:** Every time crude oil rallies, I start looking for crazy headlines. When crude oil reached what was then an all-time high on June 17, 2005, *Time's* cover featured the late Mao Tse-tung, *BusinessWeek* had senior citizens, and *Newsweek* had dinosaurs. None of them even mentioned oil — a good soft sentiment sign that the oil market still had some room to rise.

- **Congressional investigations and activist protests:** Political activity and outrage are usually a sign that things are at a fever pitch, and the trend can change, possibly in a hurry. As a contrarian, understand that the public going wild over an issue can be a sign that a major turning point is on the way in the market.

Book II

Futures and Options

Exploring Interest Rate Futures

The bond market rules the world. Everything that anyone does in the financial markets anymore is built upon interest rate analysis. When interest rates are on the rise, at some point, doing business becomes difficult. When interest rates fall, economic growth is eventually energized. The relationship between rising and falling interest rates makes the markets in interest rate futures, Eurodollars, and Treasuries (bills, notes, and bonds) important for all consumers, speculators, economists, bureaucrats, and politicians.

Bonding with the universe

The center of the bond market is its relationship with the United States Federal Reserve (the Fed) and the way the Fed conducts interest rate policies. (See Chapter 2 in Book II for more information on the Fed.) Grasping the connection between the bond market, the Fed, and the rest of the financial markets is fundamental to understanding how to trade futures and options and how to invest in general. The following sections discuss the most important aspects of how they all work together.

When you buy a bond, you get a fixed return as long as you hold that bond until it matures or, in the case of some corporate or municipal bonds, until it's called in. If you're getting a 5 percent return on your bond investment and inflation is growing at a 6 percent clip, you're already 1 percent in the hole, which is why bondholders hate inflation.

The Fed and bond market roles

The Fed cannot directly control the long-term bond rates that determine how easy (or difficult) it is to borrow money to buy a new home or to finance long-term business projects. What the Fed *can* do is adjust short-term interest rates, such as the interest rate on *Fed funds,* the overnight lending rate used by banks to square their books, and the *discount rate,* the rate at which the Fed loans money to banks to which no one else will lend money. As the Fed senses that inflationary pressures are rising, it starts to raise interest rates. When the Fed raises the Fed funds and/or the discount rates, banks usually raise the *prime rate,* the rate that targets their best customers. At the same time, credit card companies raise their rates.

As the bond market senses an increase in inflationary pressures, bond traders sell bonds, and market interest rates rise, triggering rate increases for mortgages and car loans, which usually are tied to a bond market benchmark rate.

When it recognizes that inflation is lurking, sometimes the bond market takes action ahead of the Fed, and bond prices fall and market rates rise (such as the yield on the U.S. 10-year T-note). If the Fed's indicators agree with the bond market's analysis, the Fed raises rates. Whenever the Fed disagrees with the markets, it usually signals those disagreements through speeches from Fed governors or even the chairman of the Fed. These disagreements usually occur at the beginning or at the end of a trend in interest rates.

Interest rate futures and you

Interest rate futures serve one major function: They enable large institutions to neutralize or manage their price risks. As an investor or speculator who trades interest rate futures, your motivations are different. For you, the market is a way to make money based on the system's inefficiencies, which often are created by the current relationship between large hedgers, the Fed, and other major players, such as foreign governments. Generally, you want to watch for opportunities to trade the long-term issues when interest rates are falling and to stay on the shorter-term side of the curve when interest rates are rising.

Going global with interest rate futures

Globalization has increased the number of short-term interest rate contracts that trade at the Chicago Mercantile Exchange (CME) and around the world. Just about every country with a convertible currency has some kind of bond or bond futures contract that trades on an exchange somewhere around the world. The following sections offer snapshots of some of the more liquid contracts.

Fed funds futures

Fed funds futures trade on the CME and are an almost pure bet on what the Federal Reserve is expected to do with future interest rates. Fed funds measure interest rates that private banks charge each other for overnight loans of excess reserves.

Each Fed funds contract lets you control $5 million and is cash settled. The tick size as described by the Chicago Board of Trade (CBOT) is "$20.835 per ½ of one basis point (½ of ¹⁄₁₀₀ of 1 percent of $5 million on a 30-day basis rounded up to the nearest cent)." Margins are variable, depending on the tier in which you trade, and they range from $104 to $675. A *tier* is just a time frame. The longer the time frame before expiration, the higher the margin. (For full information, you can visit the CBOT's margin page; to access it, go to the website of the CBOT's new owner, the CME Group, at www.cmegroup. com.) Fed funds contracts are quoted in terms of the rate that the market is speculating on by the time the contract expires, and they're based on the formula found at the CBOT: "100 minus the average daily Fed funds overnight rate for the delivery month (for example, a 7.25 percent rate equals 92.75)."

Book II

Futures and Options

LIBOR futures

LIBOR futures are one-month interest rate contracts based on the London Interbank Offered Rate (LIBOR), the interest rate charged between commercial banks. LIBOR futures have 12 monthly listings. Each contract is worth $3 million. The role of LIBOR futures is to offer professionals a way to hedge their interest portfolio in a similar fashion to that offered by Eurodollars.

The minimum increment of price movement is 0.0025 (¼ tick = $6.25) for the front month expiring contract and 0.005 (½ tick = $12.50) for all other expirations. The major difference: Margin requirements are less for LIBOR, at $473 for initial and $350 for margin maintenance, compared with margins of $945 and $700 for respective Eurodollar contracts.

If you're new to trading, a good way to choose between the highly liquid and popular Eurodollar and LIBOR contracts — which offer essentially the same type of trading opportunities — is to paper trade both contracts after doing some homework on how each contract trades.

Eurodollar contracts

A *Eurodollar* is a dollar-denominated deposit held in a non-U.S. bank. Eurodollars are the most popular futures trading contract in the world because they offer reasonably low margins and the potential for fairly good return in a short period of time. A Eurodollar contract gives you control of $1 million Eurodollars and is a reflection of the LIBOR rate for a three-month, $1 million offshore deposit. Following are some facts about Eurodollars:

- With Eurodollars, a point = one tick = 0.1 = $25. Eurodollars can trade in ¼ or ½ points, which are worth $6.25 and $12.50, respectively.

- Eurodollar prices are a central rate in global business and are quoted in terms of an index. If the price on the futures contract is $9,200, for example, the yield is 8 percent.

- Eurodollars trade on the CME with contract listings in March, June, September, and December. Different Eurodollar futures contracts suit different time frames. For full details, check with your broker about which contracts are available, or go to the CME website at www.cmegroup.com.

- Trading hours for Eurodollars are from 7:20 a.m. to 2 p.m. central time on the trading floor, but they can be traded almost 24/7 on the CME Globex electronic trading platform (www.cmegroup.com/globex). For Eurodollars, Globex is shut down only between 4 and 5 p.m. daily.

Small traders usually trade Eurodollars, while pros with large sums and more experience tend to trade LIBOR. No matter what contract you trade, though, think in terms of short holding periods. Consider how much you may actually have to pay up (if you're long) if you don't sell before the contract rolls over (the amount specified by the contract — $3 million).

Treasury bill futures

A 13-week T-bill contract is considered a risk-free obligation of the U.S. government. In the cash market, T-bills are sold in $10,000 increments; if you pay $9,600 for a T-bill in the cash market, an annualized interest rate of 4 percent is implied. At the end of the 13 weeks, you get $10,000 in return.

Risk-free means that if you buy the T-bills, you're assured of getting paid by the U.S. government. Trading T-bill futures, on the other hand, isn't risk-free. Instead, T-bill futures trades essentially are governed by the same sort of risk rules that govern Eurodollar trades. T-bill futures are 13-week contracts based on $10,000 U.S. Treasury bills; have a face value at maturity of $1,000,000; and move in ½-point increments (½ point = 0.005 = $12.50) with trading months of March, June, September, and December.

Bonds and Treasury notes

The 10-year U.S. Treasury note has been the accepted benchmark for long-term interest rates since the United States stopped issuing the long bond (30-year U.S. Treasury bond) in October 2001. Thirty-year bond futures and 30-year T-bonds (issued before 2001) still are actively traded, and new 30-year T-bonds hit the market in early 2006.

Bond and note futures are big-time trading vehicles that move fast. Each tick or price quote, especially when you hold more than one contract and the market is moving fast, can be worth several hundred dollars. Here are some other facts about 10- and 30-year interest rate futures that you need to know:

- ✔ The 10-year contract is traded under the symbols *TY* (pit trading) and *ZN* (electronic trading). The 30-year bond contract is traded under the symbols *US* (pit trading) and *ZB* (electronic trading).

- ✔ They have no price limits and are valued at $100,000 per contract.

- ✔ They're quoted in terms of 32nds. One point is $1,000, and one tick must be at least

    - ½ of ¹⁄₃₂, or $15.625, for a 10-year issue

    - ¹⁄₃₂, or $31.25, for a 30-year issue

    For example, a price quote of "84-16" represents 84 and ¹⁶⁄₃₂ together, and the value is $84,500: (84 × $1,000) + (16 × 31.25).

- ✔ They're traded on the CME from 7:20 a.m. to 2 p.m. central time Monday through Friday. Electronic trades can be made from 7 a.m. to 4 p.m. central time Sunday through Friday. Trading in expiring contracts closes at noon central time on the *last trading day,* which is the seventh business day before the last business day of the delivery month.

Book II

Futures and Options

Euroyen contracts

Euroyen contracts represent Japanese yen deposits held outside of Japan. Open positions in these contracts can be held at CME or at the SIMEX exchange in Singapore. Euroyen contracts are listed quarterly, trade monthly, and offer expiration dates as far out as three years. That long-term time frame can be useful to professional hedgers with specific expectations about the future.

CETES futures

CETES futures are 28-day and 91-day futures contracts that are based on Mexican Treasury bills. These instruments are denominated and paid in Mexican pesos, and they reflect the corresponding benchmark rates of interest rates in Mexico.

Eurobond futures

Longer-term global plays include Eurobond futures. The Eurobond market is composed of bonds issued by the Federal Republic of Germany and the Swiss Confederation. Eurobonds come in four different categories with different durations: Euro Shatz (1.75 years), Euro Bobl (4.5–5.5 years), Euro Bund (8.5–10 years), and Euro Buxl (24–35 years). The contract size is for 100,000 euros or 100,000 Swiss francs, depending on the issuer. Eurobonds can be traded in the United States. The basic strategies are similar to U.S. bonds because they trade on economic fundamentals and inflationary expectations, and they respond to European economic reports similar to the way U.S. bonds respond to U.S. reports.

Yielding to the curve

The *yield curve* is a graphical representation comparing the entire spectrum of interest rates available to investors. Several informative shapes can be seen on the yield curve. Three important ones are

- ✔ **Normal curves:** The *normal curve* rises to the right, and short-term interest rates are lower than long-term interest rates. This kind of movement is usually a sign of normal economic activity, where growth is ongoing and investors are being rewarded for taking more risks by being given extra yield in longer-term maturities.

- ✔ **Flat curves:** In a *flat curve,* short-term yields are equal or close to long-term yields, a sign that the economy is slowing or that the Fed has been raising short-term rates.

- ✔ **Inverted curves:** An *inverted curve* shows long-term rates falling below short-term rates, which can happen when the market is betting on a slowing of the economy or during a financial crisis when traders are flocking to the safety of long-term U.S. Treasury bonds.

Figures 4-2 and 4-3 are illustrations of the U.S. Treasury yield curve and rate structure at a time when inflationary expectations are under control and the economy is growing steadily. The curve and the table are from July 1, 2005, just two days after the Fed raised interest rates for the ninth consecutive time in a 12-month period. Figure 4-3 depicts a standard, table-style snapshot of all market maturities for the U.S. Treasury. You can view an up-to-date version at `bonds.yahoo.com/rates.html`.

As you review Figures 4-2 and 4-3, notice that the longer the maturity, the higher the yield — a relationship that's normal for interest-paying securities. Also notice that, starting with the 3-month Treasury bill (T-bill) and ending with the 30-year bond, all yields rose (compared with the previous week and month) after the Fed raised interest rates.

According to Mark Powers in *Starting Out in Futures Trading* (McGraw-Hill), keeping track of the yield curve lets you

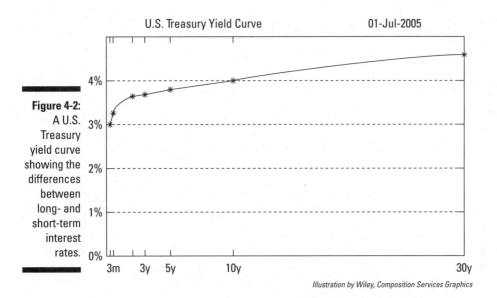

Figure 4-2: A U.S. Treasury yield curve showing the differences between long- and short-term interest rates.

Illustration by Wiley, Composition Services Graphics

Book II

Futures and Options

Figure 4-3: A U.S. Treasury summary showing common maturity listings and price changes.

U.S. Treasury Bonds				
Maturity	Yield	Yesterday	Last week	Last month
3 Month	3.00	2.96	2.93	2.81
6 Month	3.21	3.18	3.12	2.98
2 Year	3.73	3.62	3.56	3.46
3 Year	3.76	3.64	3.60	3.50
5 Year	3.82	3.69	3.68	3.61
10 Year	4.04	3.91	3.91	3.88
30 Year	4.29	4.18	4.21	4.23

Illustration by Wiley, Composition Services Graphics

✔ Focus on the cash markets. Doing so enables you to put activity in the futures markets in perspective and provides clues to the relationship between prices in the futures markets.

✔ Watch for prices rising above or falling below the yield curve, info that can indicate good opportunities to buy or sell a security.

✔ Know that prices above the yield curve point to a relatively underpriced market and that prices below the curve point to a relatively overpriced market.

Deciding your time frame

From a trader's standpoint, you want to consider trading the short term, the intermediate term, or the long term. Each position has its own time, place, and reasoning, stemming from how much money you have to trade, your individual risk tolerance, and whether your analysis leads you to think that the particular area of the curve can move during any particular period of time. The general rule is that the longer the maturity, the greater the potential reaction to good or bad news on inflation. In other words, the farther out you go on the curve, the greater the chance for volatility.

Eurodollars are the best instrument for trading the short term because they're *liquid* investments (that is, easy to buy and sell). Eurodollars are well suited for small traders because margin requirements tend to be smaller and the movements can be less volatile.

For long- and intermediate-term trading, you can use the 10-year T-note and 30-year T-bond futures. Both can be quite volatile because large traders and institutions usually use them for direct trading and for complicated hedging strategies.

Sticking to sound interest rate trading rules

When trading international interest rate contracts, you must consider the effects of currency conversion. If you just made a 10 percent profit trading Eurobonds but the Euro fell 10 percent, your purchasing power hasn't grown. When getting ready to trade, make sure that you do the following:

- ✔ Calculate your margin requirements so that you know how much of a cushion for potential losses you have available before you get a margin call and are required to put up more money to keep a position open.

- ✔ Factor in how much of your account's equity you plan to risk before you make your trade.

- ✔ Canvass your charts so that you know support and resistance levels on each of the markets that you plan to trade, and then set your entry points above or below those levels, depending on which way the market breaks.

- ✔ Be ready for trend reversals, especially when the market appears to be comfortable with its current trend.

- ✔ Understand what the economic calendar has in store on any given day so that you can be prepared for the major volatility that can occur on the days economic news is released.

✔ Pick your entry and exit points, including your worst-loss scenario — the possibility of taking a margin call.

✔ Decide what your options are if your trade goes well and you have a significant profit to deal with.

Focusing on Stock Index Futures

Stock index futures are futures contracts based on indexes that are composed of stocks. The S&P 500 futures contract, for example, is based on the popular S&P 500 stock index, a group of 500 commonly traded stocks. When you trade stock index futures, you're betting on the direction of the contract's value, *not* on the individual stocks that make up the index.

As a percentage of the total number of futures contracts traded, stock index futures are by far the largest category of futures contracts traded. Here are some of the more common reasons to trade stock index futures:

✔ **Speculation:** When you speculate, you're making an educated guess about the direction of a market. You can deliver trading profits to your accounts by going long or short on index futures or by betting on prices rising or falling, respectively.

✔ **Hedging:** In a *hedge,* you use stock index futures and options to protect an individual security in your portfolio or, in some cases, your entire portfolio from losing value.

✔ **Tax consequences:** Short-term gains in the futures markets may be taxed at lower rates than stock market capital gains.

The IRS has a complex set of rules for taxing gains in the futures markets and specific forms (such as IRS Form 4797 Part II for securities or Form 6781 for commodities) that you must become familiar with. To be safe and stay on the right side of tax law, check with your accountant *before* you start trading.

✔ **Lower commission rates:** Although not as widespread a practice as it was before online discount brokers became a mainstay, many futures brokerages offer lower commission rates, a factor that becomes more important as you trade large blocks or quantities of stocks.

✔ **Time factors:** If something happens overnight, when the stock market is closed, and you want to hedge your risk, you can trade futures on Globex, a 24-hour electronic trading system, while Wall Street sleeps.

You don't need to trade every major index contract in the world to be successful; just find one or two with which you're comfortable and that enable you to implement your strategies. This section focuses on the S&P 500 stock index futures. Any of the lessons that are described with respect to the S&P 500 can be applied to just about any contract.

Looking into fair value

Fair value is the theoretically correct value for a futures contract at a particular point in time. You calculate fair value using a formula that includes the current index level, index dividends, number of days to contract expiration, and interest rates. Fair value is a benchmark that can be helpful in analyzing the markets. When a stock index futures contract trades below its fair value, for example, it's trading at a *discount.* When it trades above its fair value, it's trading at a *premium.*

Knowing the fair value is most helpful in gauging where the market is headed. Because stock index futures prices are related to spot-index prices, changes in fair value can trigger price changes. Here's how it works:

- ✔ If the futures contract is too far below fair value, the index (cash) is sold and the futures contract is bought.

- ✔ If the futures contract is too high versus its fair value, the futures contract is sold and the index (cash) is bought.

- ✔ If enough sell programs hit the market hard enough over an extended period of time, you can see a *crash,* a situation where market prices fall dramatically.

- ✔ If enough buy programs kick in, the market tends to rally.

Fair value is the number that the television stock analysts refer to when discussing the action in futures before the market opens.

Considering major stock index futures contracts

You can trade many different stock index contracts, but they all share the same basic characteristics. The sections that follow describe many of these general issues and address particular differences with descriptions of other individual contracts.

S&P 500 futures

The biggest stock index futures contract, the S&P 500 (SP) trades on the Chicago Mercantile Exchange (CME). This index is made up of the 500 largest stocks in the United States. It's a *weighted* index, which means that component companies that have bigger *market capitalizations,* or market values, can have a much larger impact on the movements of the index than components with smaller market capitalizations. Table 4-2 lists some of the particulars about the S&P 500 Index.

Table 4-2	S&P 500 Futures Details
Characteristic	*Description*
Composition	400 industrial companies, 40 financial companies, 40 utilities, and 20 transportation companies
Valuation	1 tick = 0.1 index points = $25; a move of a full point is worth $250
Contracts	Worth 250 times the value of the index (when the index value is 1,250, for example, a contract is worth 250 × $1,250, or $312,500)
Trading times	8:30 a.m. to 3:15 p.m. central time; 3:30 p.m. to 8:15 a.m. central time on Globex
Contract limits	No more than 20,000 net long or short contracts at any one time for an individual contract
Price limits	Set on a quarterly basis; find the price limits on the CME's website (www.cmegroup.com)
Final settlement	Based on a Special Opening Quotations (SOQ) price, a value calculated on the opening prices for each of the stocks in an index on the day that the contract expires
Margin requirements	Variable
Cash settlement	Applies to all stock index futures

Book II

Futures and Options

NASDAQ-100 futures

The NASDAQ-100 index futures contract (ND) works similarly to the S&P 500 futures contract. Here's what you need to know:

- **Composition:** The NASDAQ-100 stock index is made up of the 100 largest stocks traded on the NASDAQ system, including large technology and biotech stocks.

- **Valuation:** The ND is valued in minimum ticks of 0.25 that are worth $25.

- **Contract limits:** No individual can hold more than 10,000 net long or short contracts at any one time.

✔ **Margin requirements:** Margins required for NASDAQ-100 index futures are similar to the S&P 500 index futures. In June 2013, the initial margin for the ND contract was $12,100, and the maintenance margin was $11,000.

E-mini S&P 500 and e-mini NASDAQ-100

The e-mini S&P 500 (ES) contract and the e-mini NASDAQ-100 (NQ) are among the most popular stock index futures contracts because they enable you to trade the market's trend with only a fifth of the requirement. The mini contracts are marketed to small investors, and they offer some advantages. However, they also carry significant risks because they're volatile and still have fairly high margin requirements. In addition, during extremely volatile market environments, e-minis can move even more aggressively than the respective index contracts on which they're based.

Other particulars about the e-mini contracts:

✔ **Valuation:** One tick on ES is 0.25 of an index point and is worth $12.50. One tick on NQ is 0.50 of an index point and is worth $10.

✔ **Contracts:** The value of an ES contract is $50 multiplied by the value of the S&P 500 index. The value of an NQ contract is $20 multiplied by the value of the NASDAQ-100 index.

✔ **Trading times:** The e-mini contracts trade nearly 24 hours per day, with a 30-minute maintenance break in trading from 4:30 to 5:00 p.m. central time daily.

✔ **Monthly identifiers:** Monthly identifiers for both mini contracts are *H* for March, *M* for June, *U* for September, and *Z* for December.

✔ **Margin requirements:** Margins for the ES and NQ contracts are less than for the normal-sized contracts. As of June 2013, the ES required $3,850 for initial margin and $3,500 for maintenance, and the NQ required $2,420 and $2,200, respectively.

The day-trading margin is less than the margin to hold an overnight position in S&P 500 e-mini futures. Traders, though, are obligated to pay for the difference between the margins for entry and exit points, which means that if you lose, you're likely to pay up in a big way at the end of the day.

When you own normal-sized contracts and e-mini contracts in one or the other of the underlying indexes, position limits apply to both positions, meaning that each of the contracts is counted as an individual part of the overall position. The combined number of contracts can't exceed the 20,000 contract limit for the S&P 500–based index and the 10,000 contract limit for the NASDAQ-100–based index.

Book III
Commodities

Five Reasons to Invest in Commodities

- **The global population explosion:** The United Nations (UN) estimates that the global population will grow to about 9 billion people by 2050. Significant population growth translates into greater global demand for commodities. This large population growth is a key driver for the increasing demand for commodities, which will continue to put upward pressure on commodity prices.

- **Urbanization:** Sixty percent of the world's population is expected to live in urban areas by the year 2030. Urbanization is highly significant for commodities because people who live in urban centers consume a lot more natural resources than those who live in rural areas. Industrial metals such as copper, steel, and aluminum are going to be in high demand to construct apartment buildings, schools, hospitals, cars, and so on.

- **Industrialization:** A new wave of industrialization is taking place in the 21st century; it's transforming a large number of developing countries into more industrialized countries, and raw materials are fueling this transformation.

- **Safe haven for investments:** Investors view certain commodities, such as gold and silver, as reliable stores of value, so they flock to these assets when times aren't good. When currencies slide, nations go to war, or global pandemics break out, you can rely on gold, silver, and other commodities to provide you with financial safety.

- **A hedge against inflation:** One of the only asset classes that benefits from inflation is commodities. In fact, increases in the prices of basic goods (commodities such as oil and gas) actually contribute to the increase of inflation. One way to not only protect yourself from inflation but also profit from it is to invest in gold.

In the commodities market, you have several investment vehicles to choose from. Find ten important ones in a free article at www.dummies.com/extras/highpoweredinvestingaio.

Chapter 1

Getting an Overview of Commodities

*I*n the years since the first edition of this book, commodities have grown into their own legitimate and respected asset class. Trade magazines and financial newsletters frequently include feature-length articles on the topic. Financial TV stations regularly report oil, gold, and copper prices on the crawling ticker. And no global macro money manager can claim continued success without constantly keeping a pulse on commodities.

Why are commodities, long regarded as an inferior asset class, quickly moving to the investing mainstream? Good performance. Investors like to reward good performance, and commodities have performed well in recent years. In addition, investors can more easily access these markets: Plenty of new investment vehicles, from exchange-traded funds (ETFs) to master limited partnerships (MLPs), have been introduced to satisfy investor demand.

Commodities as an asset class have been plagued by a lot of misinformation, and it's sometimes difficult to separate fact from fiction or outright fantasy. This chapter sheds some light on commodities so you can invest with confidence.

Defining Commodities and Their Investment Characteristics

Put simply, commodities are the raw materials we humans use to create a livable world. We've been exploiting earth's natural resources since the beginning of time; we use energy to sustain ourselves, metals to build weapons and tools, and agricultural products to feed ourselves. These three classes of commodities — energy, metals, and agricultural products — are the essential building blocks of the global economy (see the later section "Checking Out What's on the Menu" for more details).

Chapter 2 of Book III offers general information on how to invest in these kinds of products, and Chapters 3 through 5 give you the details about investing in specific types of commodities. All the commodities covered meet the following criteria:

- ✔ **Tradability:** I include a commodity if it has a futures contract assigned to it on one of the major exchanges (see Book II), if a company processes it, or if an ETF tracks it.

- ✔ **Deliverability:** All the commodities have to be physically deliverable. I include crude oil because it can be delivered in barrels, and I include wheat because it can be delivered by the bushel. However, I don't include currencies, interest rates, and other financial futures contracts because they're not physical commodities.

- ✔ **Liquidity:** Liquidity is critical because it gives you the option of getting in and out of an investment without having to face the difficulty of trying to find a buyer or seller for your securities. Thus, every commodity in this book has an active market, with buyers and sellers constantly transacting with each other.

As an asset class, commodities have unique characteristics that separate them from other asset classes and make them attractive, whether as independent investments or as part of a broader-based investment strategy.

Gaining from inelasticity

In economics, *elasticity* seeks to determine the effects of price on supply and demand. Goods that are elastic tend to have a high correlation between price and demand, which is usually inversely proportional: When the price of a good increases, demand tends to decrease. This makes sense because you're not going to pay for a good that you don't need if it becomes too expensive. Capturing and determining that spread is what elasticity is all about.

Inelastic goods, however, are goods that are so essential to consumers that changes in price tend to have a limited effect on supply and demand. Most commodities fall in the inelastic goods category because they are essential to human existence.

For instance, if the price of ice cream were to increase by 25 percent, chances are you'd buy less ice cream because it's not a necessity. However, when the price of unleaded gasoline increases by 25 percent, you may not be happy, but you still fill your tank because gas is a necessity. Of course, the demand for gasoline isn't *absolutely* inelastic; a point will come when you decide that it's simply not worth paying the amount you're paying at the pump, and you'll begin looking for alternatives. But the truth remains that you're willing to pay more for gasoline than for other products you don't need (such as ice cream); that's the key to understanding price inelasticity.

Most commodities are fairly inelastic because they're the raw materials that allow you to live the life you strive for. Without these precious raw materials, you wouldn't be able to heat your home in the winter. In fact, without cement, copper, and other basic materials, you wouldn't even have a house to begin with! And then, of course, there's the most essential commodity of all: food. Without food you'd cease to exist.

Offering a safe haven for investors

During times of turmoil, commodities tend to act as safe havens for investors. When currencies slide, when nations go to war, or when global pandemics break out, you can rely on gold, silver, and other commodities to provide you with financial safety. For example, after September 11, 2001, the price of gold jumped as investors sought safety in the metal.

Have part of your portfolio in gold and other precious metals so that you can protect your assets during times of turmoil. Turn to Chapter 4 in Book III for more on investing in precious metals.

Hedging against inflation

One of the biggest things you need to watch out for as an investor is the ravaging effects of inflation. Inflation can devastate your investments, particularly paper assets such as stocks. The central bankers of the world — smart people all — spend their entire careers trying to tame inflation, but despite their efforts, inflation can easily get out of hand. You need to protect yourself against this economic enemy.

Ironically, one of the only asset classes that actually *benefits* from inflation is — you guessed it — commodities. Perhaps the biggest irony of all is that increases in the prices of basic goods (commodities such as oil and gas) actually contribute to the increase of inflation. For example, there's a positive correlation between gold and the inflation rate. During times of high inflation, investors load up on gold because it's considered a good store of value.

Taking time to bring new sources online

The business of commodities is a time- and capital-intensive business. Unlike high tech or other "new economy" start-ups (such as e-commerce), bringing commodity projects online takes a lot of time. It can take up to a decade, for example, to bring new sources of oil online.

What does this mean to you as an investor? When you're investing in commodities, you have to think long-term. If you're used to investing in tech stocks or if you're an entrepreneur involved in e-commerce, you need to radically change the way you think about investing when you approach commodities.

Moving in different cycles

"Sell in May and go away" is an old Wall Street adage referring to stocks; because historically the stock market hasn't performed well during the summer months, the thinking goes, you should sell your stocks and get back into the game in the fall. This adage doesn't apply to commodities because commodities move in different cycles than stocks. Some commodities perform really well during the summer months. Unleaded gasoline tends to increase in price during the summer due to increased driving.

Checking Out What's on the Menu

Book III covers several commodities. Here's a listing of all the kinds of commodities you can expect to encounter while going through these pages.

Energy

Energy, which has always been indispensable for human survival, makes for a great investment (see Chapter 3 of Book III for details). From fossil fuels to renewable energy sources, it has attracted a lot of attention from investors who seek to profit from the world's seemingly unquenchable thirst for energy.

✔ **Crude oil:** Crude oil is the undisputed heavyweight champion in the commodities world. More barrels of crude oil are traded every single day (87 million and growing) than any other commodity. Accounting for 40 percent of total global energy consumption, crude oil provides some terrific investment opportunities.

✔ **Natural gas:** This fossil fuel, in both its gaseous and liquid form (liquefied natural gas [LNG]), is a major commodity in its own right and used for everything from cooking food to heating houses during the winter.

✔ **Coal:** Coal accounts for more than 20 percent of total world energy consumption. In the United States, the largest energy market, 50 percent of electricity is generated through coal. Because of abundant supply, coal is making a resurgence.

✔ **Uranium/nuclear power:** Due to improved environmental standards within the industry, nuclear power use is on the rise.

✔ **Electricity:** Electricity is a necessity of modern life, and the companies responsible for generating this special commodity have some unique characteristics.

✔ **Solar and wind power:** For a number of reasons that range from environmental to geopolitical, demand for renewable and alternative energy sources such as solar and wind power are increasing.

✔ **Ethanol:** Ethanol, which is produced primarily from corn or sugar, is an increasingly popular fuel additive that offers investment potential.

Book III

Commodities

Metals

Metallurgy has been essential to human development since the beginning of time. Societies that have mastered the production of metals have been able to thrive and survive. Similarly, investors who have incorporated metals into their portfolios have been able to generate significant returns (see Chapter 4 in Book III for the scoop).

✔ **Gold:** For centuries, people have been attracted to its quasi-indestructibility and have used it as a store of value. Gold is a good asset for hedging against inflation and also for asset preservation during times of global turmoil.

✔ **Silver:** Silver, like gold, is another precious metal that has monetary applications. Silver also has applications in industry (such as electrical wiring), placing it in a unique position of being coveted for both its precious metal status and its industrial uses.

✔ **Platinum:** Platinum, the rich man's gold, is one of the most valuable metals in the world, used for everything from jewelry to the manufacture of catalytic converters.

- ✔ **Steel:** Steel, which is created by alloying iron and other materials, is the most widely used metal in the world and is used to build everything from cars to buildings.

- ✔ **Aluminum:** Perhaps no other metal has the versatility of aluminum; it's lightweight yet surprisingly robust and is the second most widely used metal (right behind steel).

- ✔ **Copper:** Copper, the third most widely used metal, is a great conductor of heat and electricity, making it the metal of choice for industrial uses.

- ✔ **Palladium:** Palladium is part of the platinum group of metals, and almost half of the palladium that's mined goes toward building automobile catalytic converters. As the number of cars with these emission-reducing devices increases, the demand for palladium will increase as well, making this an attractive investment.

- ✔ **Nickel:** Nickel is in high demand because of its resistance to corrosion and oxidation. Steel is usually alloyed with nickel to create stainless steel, which ensures that nickel will play an important role for years to come.

- ✔ **Zinc:** The fourth most widely used metal in the world, zinc's resistance to corrosion makes it ideal for use in the process of galvanization, in which zinc coating is applied to other metals, such as steel, to prevent rust.

Agricultural products

Food is the most essential element of human life, and the production of food presents solid money-making opportunities (flip to Chapter 5 in Book III for details).

- ✔ **Coffee:** Coffee is the second most widely produced commodity in the world, in terms of physical volume, behind only crude oil. Folks just seem to love a good cup of coffee, and this provides good investment opportunities.

- ✔ **Cocoa:** Cocoa production, which is dominated by a handful of countries, is a major agricultural commodity, primarily because it's used to create chocolate.

- ✔ **Sugar #11 and #14:** Sugar is a popular food sweetener. Sugar #11 represents a futures contract for global sugar (refer to Book II for more on futures). Sugar #14 is specific to the United States and is a widely traded commodity.

- ✔ **Frozen concentrated orange juice (FCOJ) — types A and B:** FCOJ-A is the benchmark for North American orange juice prices because it's grown in the hemisphere's two largest regions: Florida and Brazil. FCOJ-B, like

FCOJ-A, is a widely traded contract that represents global orange juice prices. This contract gives you exposure to orange juice activity on a world scale.

- **Corn:** Corn's use for culinary purposes is perhaps unrivaled by any other grain, which makes corn a potentially lucrative investment.

- **Wheat:** According to archaeological evidence, wheat was one of the first agricultural products grown by man. It's an essential staple of human life and makes for a great investment.

- **Soybeans and their derivatives, like soybean oil and soybean meal:** Soybeans have many applications. Soybean oil, also known as vegetable oil, is derived from actual soybeans, is used for cooking purposes, and has become popular in recent years with the health-conscious dietary movement. Soybean meal is used as feedstock for poultry and cattle.

- **Live and feeder cattle:** For investors involved in agriculture, using the live cattle futures contract to hedge against price volatility is a good idea. Whereas the live cattle contract tracks adult cows, the feeder cattle contract hedges against the risk associated with growing calves.

- **Lean hogs:** Lean hogs are an essential commodity, making them a good trading target.

- **Frozen pork bellies:** Frozen pork bellies are essentially nothing more than good old bacon. This industry is cyclical and subject to wild price swings, which provides unique arbitrage trading opportunities.

Putting Risk in Perspective

Many investors are scared of investing in commodities because of their reputation for being risky. Of course, investing in commodities does present risks — all investments do. This section explains what the risks are and how you can minimize and manage them.

Futures markets are one way to get involved in commodities, but trading futures is not for everyone. By their very nature, futures markets, contracts, and products are extremely complex and require a great deal of mastery even by the most seasoned investors. If you don't feel you have a good handle on all the concepts involved in trading futures, don't jump into futures or you may lose a lot more than your principal (because of the use of leverage and other characteristics unique to the futures markets). If you're not comfortable trading futures, don't sweat it. You can invest in commodities in multiple other ways. If you're ready to start investing in the futures markets, however, you need to understand those markets (head to Book II) and have a solid grasp of technical analysis (see Book X).

Looking at the pitfalls of using leverage

In finance, *leverage* refers to the act of magnifying returns through the use of borrowed capital. Leverage is a powerful tool that gives you the opportunity to control large market positions with relatively little upfront capital. However, leverage is the ultimate double-edged sword because both your profits and losses are magnified to outrageous proportions.

Just as you're able to trade on margin when you invest in stocks (see Chapter 3 in Book II for details), you can trade commodities on margin as well. However, the biggest difference between using margin with stocks and with commodities is that the margin requirement for commodities is much lower than margins for stocks, which means the potential for losses (and profits) is much greater in commodities.

The minimum margin requirements for commodity futures vary but are, on average, lower than those for stocks. You have to have at least 50 percent of the capital in your account before you can enter into a stock position on margin, but the margin requirement for soybeans in the Chicago Board of Trade, for example, is 4 percent. With only $400 in your account, you can buy $10,000 worth of soybeans futures contracts! If the trade goes your way, you're a happy camper. But if you're on the losing side of a trade on margin, you can lose much more than your principal.

When you're trading on margin, you may get a *margin call* from your broker requiring you to deposit additional capital in your account to cover the borrowed amount. The balance on futures accounts is calculated at the end of the trading session. If you get a margin call, you need to take care of it immediately. So if you're trading commodities on margin, you may have to come up with a nice chunk of change — even more than if you're trading stocks on margin.

Because of the use of margin and the extraordinary amounts of leverage you have at your disposal in the futures markets, you should be extremely careful when trading commodity futures contracts. In order to be a responsible investor, I recommend using margin only if you have the necessary capital reserves to cover any subsequent margin calls you may receive if the market moves adversely.

Assessing the real risks behind commodities

Investing is all about managing the risk involved in generating returns. This section lays out some common risks you face when investing in commodities and some small steps you can take to minimize these risks.

Sovereign government risk

Sovereign government risk is more important than other types of risks because it involves the balance sheet of sovereign governments. During the 2008 financial crisis, banks were in a position to bail out consumers; when banks started to fail, governments began to bail out the banks. However, when governments start to fail, few institutions can bail them out. This type of risk became more evident in European countries, which for geographic, demographic, and economic reasons, no longer enjoy the place in the sun they once occupied. As a result, these countries may start defaulting. In addition to liquidity risks, they pose a solvency risk; that is, they simply cannot pay back their borrowers.

Many countries in Europe, such as Greece, Portugal, Spain, Ireland, and, to some extent, Italy and France (Germany being the main exception) — are facing severe budget cuts and unprecedented decreases in government expenditure programs. As their unfavorable demographic trends further accelerate and their manufacturing base is eroded by more competitive spheres in Asia and other emerging markets, expect to see more belt-tightening in Europe over the next five years. In a post-2008 world, carefully examining the countries you're investing in is necessary.

Geopolitical risk

One of the inherent risks of commodities is that the world's natural resources are located on various continents, and the jurisdiction over these commodities lies with sovereign governments, international companies, and many other entities. For example, to access the large deposits of oil located in the Persian Gulf region, oil companies have to deal with the sovereign countries of the Middle East that have jurisdiction over this oil.

Book III

Commodities

International disagreements over the control of natural resources are common. Sometimes a host country simply kicks out foreign companies involved in the production and distribution of the country's natural resources. In 2006, Bolivia, which contains South America's second-largest deposits of natural gas, nationalized its natural gas industry and kicked out the foreign companies involved. In a day, a number of companies, such as Brazil's Petrobras and Spain's Repsol, were left without a mandate in a country where they had spent billions of dollars developing the natural gas industry. Investors in Petrobras and Repsol paid the price.

To minimize the risk posed by geopolitical uncertainty, invest in companies with experience and economies of scale. For example, if you're interested in investing in an international oil company, go with one that has an established international track record. A company like ExxonMobil, for instance, has the scale, breadth, and experience in international markets to manage the geopolitical risk it faces. A smaller company without this sort of experience faces more risk than a bigger one. In commodities, size does matter.

Speculative risk

The commodities markets, just like the bond and stock markets, are populated by traders whose primary interest is in making short-term profits by speculating whether the price of a security will go up or down. Although speculators provide much-needed liquidity to the markets (particularly in commodity futures markets), they also tend to increase market volatility, especially when they begin exhibiting what former Federal Reserve Chairman Alan Greenspan termed "irrational exuberance." The amount of speculative money involved in commodity markets is in constant fluctuation, but as a general rule, most commodity futures markets contain about 75 percent commercial users and 25 percent speculators.

Too much speculative money coming into the commodities markets can have detrimental effects when speculators drive the prices of commodities in excess of the fundamentals. If you see too much speculative activity, it's probably a good idea to simply get out of the markets.

If you trade commodities, find out as much as possible about who the market participants are so that you can distinguish between the commercial users and the speculators. Check out the Commitment of Traders report, put out by the U.S. Commodity Futures Trading Commission (CFTC) and available online at www.cftc.gov/cftc/cftccotreports.htm.

The risk of fraud

Although the CFTC and other regulatory bodies do a decent job of protecting investors from market fraud, the possibility of becoming a victim always exists. Your broker may hide debts or losses in offshore accounts, for example.

One way to prevent being taken advantage of is to be extremely vigilant about who you do business with. Make sure that you thoroughly research a firm before handing over your money. I go through the due diligence process you should follow when selecting managers in the next section. Unfortunately, occasionally, no amount of research or due diligence is able to protect you from fraud — it's just a fact of the investment game.

Managing risk

You can't completely eliminate risk, but you can sure take steps to help you reduce it. This section goes through time-proven and market-tested ways to minimize risk.

Due diligence: Just do it

Many investors buy on hype; they hear a certain commodity mentioned in the press, and they buy just because everyone else is buying. Buying on impulse is one of the most detrimental habits you can develop as an investor. Before you put your money into anything, you need to find out as much as possible about this potential investment.

Because you have a number of ways to invest in commodities (which I discuss in Chapter 2 of Book III), the type of research you perform depends on the approach you take. The following sections go over the due diligence to perform for each investment methodology.

Futures markets

The futures markets provide liquidity and allow hedgers and speculators to establish benchmark prices for the world's commodities. If you're interested in investing through commodity futures, you need to ask a lot of questions before you get started. Consider some of these questions:

- On what exchange is the futures contract traded?
- Is there an accompanying option contract for the commodity?
- Is the market for the contract liquid or illiquid? (You want it to be liquid, just in case you're wondering.)
- Who are the main market participants?
- What's the expiration date for the contract you're interested in?
- What's the open interest for the commodity?
- Do any margin requirements exist? If so, what are they?

To find out more about trading futures contracts, as well as options, be sure to read Book II.

Managed funds

If you're not a hands-on investor or you simply don't have the time to actively manage your portfolio, you may want to choose to invest in a managed fund.

Before you invest in a managed fund, find out as much as you can about the fund's manager. Ask a few questions:

- What is the manager's track record?
- What's his investing style —conservative or aggressive — and are you comfortable with it?

✔ Does he have any disciplinary actions against him?

✔ What do clients have to say about him? (Ask to speak to one of the manager's existing clients.)

✔ Is he registered with the appropriate regulatory bodies?

✔ What fees does he charge? (Watch out for hidden fees by asking whether any fees aren't disclosed.)

✔ How much in assets does he have under management?

✔ What are his after-tax returns? (Make sure that you specify *after*-tax returns, because many managers post returns only before taxes are considered.)

✔ Are minimum time commitments involved?

✔ Are penalties assessed if you withdraw your money early?

✔ Are minimum investment requirements applied?

Commodity companies

One way to get exposure to commodities is to invest in companies that process commodities. This indirect way to access raw materials is a good approach for investors who are comfortable in the equity environment. Ask a few questions before you buy the company's stock:

✔ What are the company's assets and liabilities?

✔ How effective is the management with the firm's capital?

✔ Where will the firm generate future growth?

✔ Where does the company generate its revenue?

✔ Has the company run into any regulatory problems in the past?

✔ What is the company's structure? (Some commodity companies are corporations, whereas others act as limited partnerships.)

✔ How does the company compare with competitors?

✔ Does the company operate in regions of the world that are politically unstable?

✔ What is the company's performance across business cycles?

You can get the answers to these questions by looking through the company's annual report (Form 10K) and quarterly reports (Form 8K).

Understanding the commodity itself

Whether you decide to invest through futures contracts, managed funds, or commodity companies, you need to gather as much information as possible about the underlying commodity itself. This caveat is perhaps the most important piece of the commodities puzzle because the performance of any investment vehicle you choose depends on the actual fundamental supply-and-demand story of the commodity.

Ask yourself a few questions before you start investing in a commodity, whether it's coffee or copper:

- ✔ Which country or countries hold the largest reserves of the commodity?
- ✔ Is the country politically stable, or is it vulnerable to turmoil?
- ✔ How much of the commodity is actually produced on a regular basis? (Ideally, you want to get data for the daily, monthly, quarterly, and annual basis.)
- ✔ Which industries or countries are the largest consumers of the commodity?
- ✔ What are the primary uses of the commodity?
- ✔ Do any alternatives to the commodity exist? If so, what are they, and do they pose a significant risk to the production value of the target commodity?
- ✔ Do seasonal factors affect the commodity?
- ✔ What's the correlation between the commodity and comparable commodities in the same category?
- ✔ What are the historical production and consumption cycles for the commodity?

These questions are only a few to ask before you invest in any commodity. Ideally, you want to gather this information before you start trading.

Diversifying your portfolio

One of the best ways to manage risk is to diversify. This strategy applies on a number of levels: diversify *among* asset classes, such as bonds, stocks, and commodities; and diversify *within* an asset class, such as diversifying commodity holdings among energy and metals.

Book III

Commodities

For diversification to minimize risk, you want to have asset classes that perform differently. One of the benefits of using commodities to minimize your overall portfolio risk is that commodities tend to behave differently than stocks and bonds. For example, as you can see in Figure 1-1, the performance of commodities and equities is remarkably different. This fact means that when stocks aren't doing well, you'll at least have your portfolio exposed to an asset class that is performing.

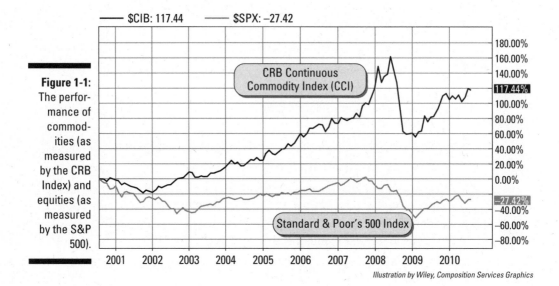

Figure 1-1: The performance of commodities (as measured by the CRB Index) and equities (as measured by the S&P 500).

Illustration by Wiley, Composition Services Graphics

Chapter 2

Adding Commodities to Your Portfolio

In This Chapter

▶ Gaining exposure to commodities in a variety of ways

▶ Investigating exchanges around the world

▶ Placing orders at the exchange

The goal of this chapter is to help you figure out how much of your portfolio you should devote to commodities and introduce you to the vehicles that let you invest in them — from mutual funds to master limited partnerships. If you've ever wondered how to get commodities into your portfolio, you can't afford to skip this chapter!

Many investors who like the way commodities anchor their portfolios have about 15 percent exposure to commodities. But if you're new to commodities, start out with a relatively modest amount, anywhere between 3 and 5 percent, to see how comfortable you feel with this new member of your financial family. Test out how commodities contribute to your overall portfolio's performance. If you're satisfied with what you see, gradually increase the percentage.

Checking Out Methods for Investing in Commodities

You have several methods at your disposal, both direct and indirect, for getting exposure to commodities. This section goes through the different ways you can invest in commodities.

Having a diversified portfolio is important because it helps reduce the overall volatility of your market exposures. Holding unrelated assets in your portfolio increases your chances of maintaining good returns when a certain asset underperforms.

Buying commodity futures

The futures markets are the most direct way to get exposure to commodities. Futures contracts allow you to purchase an underlying commodity for an agreed-upon price in the future.

In the futures markets, individuals, institutions, and sometimes governments transact with each other for price-hedging and speculating purposes. An airline company, for instance, may want to use futures to enter into an agreement with a fuel company to buy a fixed amount of jet fuel for a fixed price for a fixed period of time. This transaction in the futures markets allows the airline to hedge against the volatility associated with the price of jet fuel. Although commercial users are the main players in the futures arena, traders and investors also use the futures market to profit from price volatility through various trading techniques.

Following are some things to know about trading commodities in the futures market (head to Book II for in-depth information about futures contracts):

- ✓ **The futures markets are administered by the various commodity exchanges, such as the Chicago Mercantile Exchange (CME) and the Intercontinental Exchange (ICE).** Head to the later section "Examining the Major Commodity Exchanges" for details on these and other exchanges, the role they play in the markets, and the products they offer.

- ✓ **A number of organizations regulate the futures markets, including the Securities and Exchange Commission (SEC) and the Commodity Futures Trading Commission (CFTC).** These organizations monitor the markets to prevent market fraud and manipulation and to protect investors.

- ✓ **Trading futures isn't for everyone.** Futures markets, contracts, and products are extremely complex and even experienced investors need a high level of skill to master them. If you don't have a good handle on all the ins and outs of trading futures, you stand to lose a lot more than your principal. If you're not comfortable trading futures, don't worry about it. You can invest in commodities in several other ways.

Accessing commodity markets via funds

If you think delving into commodity futures isn't for you (see the preceding section), you can access the commodity markets through commodity mutual funds and commodity exchange-traded funds (ETFs). If you've invested before, you may be familiar with these two investment vehicles (see Chapter 3 in Book I for an introduction).

Commodity mutual funds

Commodity mutual funds are exactly like average, run-of-the-mill mutual funds, except that they focus specifically on investing in commodities. You can choose from several funds, although the two biggest ones are the PIMCO Commodity Real Return Strategy Fund and the Oppenheimer Commodity Strategy Total Return Fund:

✔ **PIMCO:** The largest commodity-oriented fund in the market, the PIMCO Commodity Real Return Strategy Fund seeks to broadly mirror the performance of the Dow Jones-UBS Commodity Index Total Return. As such, the fund invests directly in commodity-linked instruments such as futures contracts, forward contracts, and options on futures. Because these contracts are naturally leveraged, the fund also invests in bonds and other fixed-income securities to act as collateral to the commodity instruments.

✔ **Oppenheimer Commodity Strategy Total Return Fund:** Considerably smaller than the PIMCO fund, this fund tracks the performance of the Dow Jones-UBS Commodity Index, which tracks a broad basket of 24 commodities. Oppenheimer requires a little less capital up front than PIMCO but is slightly more expensive because of the front-load charges and its expense ratio.

To find out more about commodity mutual funds, go to the Morningstar website (www.morningstar.com), an excellent resource for investors that includes lots of information related to commodity mutual funds, such as the latest news, updates, load charges, expense ratios, and other key data. It also uses a helpful five-star ratings system to rate mutual funds and includes an Analyst Rating system.

Book III

Commodities

Exchange-traded funds

Exchange-traded funds (ETFs) have become popular with investors because they provide the benefits of investing in a fund with the ease of trading a stock. This hybrid instrument is one of the best ways for investors to access the commodities markets. You currently have at your disposal ETFs that track baskets of commodities through commodity indexes, as well as ETFs that track single commodities such as oil, gold, and silver. Table 2-1 lists some popular commodity ETFs.

Table 2-1	Commodity ETFs
ETF	**Description**
PowerShares DB Commodity Index Tracking (DBC)	Tracks the performance of the DBIQ Optimum Yield Diversified Commodity Index Excess Return
United States Oil Fund (USO)	Mirrors the movements of the WTI crude oil on the NYSE Arca

(continued)

Table 2-1 *(continued)*

ETF	Description
SPDR Gold Shares (GLD)	Tracks the performance of gold bullion
iShares Gold Trust (IAU)	Tracks the performance of gold futures contracts on the COMEX
iShares Silver Trust (SLV)	Tracks the performance of silver

Investing in commodity companies

Another route you can take to get exposure to commodities is to buy stocks of commodity companies. These companies are generally involved in the production, transformation, or distribution of various commodities.

This route is perhaps the most indirect way of accessing the commodity markets because, in buying a company's stock, you're getting exposure not only to the performance of the underlying commodity that the company is involved in, but also other factors, such as the company's management skills, creditworthiness, and ability to generate cash flow and minimize expenses. (Check out Chapter 2 in Book I for an introduction to stocks.)

Here are a couple of options:

- **Publicly traded companies:** Publicly traded companies can give you exposure to specific sectors of commodities, such as metals, energy, or agricultural products. Within these three categories, you can choose companies that deal with specific methods or commodities, such as refiners of crude oil into finished products or gold-mining companies.

- **Master limited partnerships:** A *master limited partnership* (MLP) is a hybrid instrument that offers you the convenience of trading a partnership like a stock. You get the best of both worlds: the liquidity that comes from being a publicly traded entity and the tax protection of being a partnership. Some of the popular assets that MLPs invest in include oil and gas storage facilities and transportation infrastructure such as pipelines.

One of the biggest advantages of MLPs is that, as a unit holder, you are taxed at only the individual level. This structure is different than if you invest in a corporation, because cash back to shareholders (in the form of dividends) is taxed at both the corporate level and the individual level. MLPs don't pay any corporate tax, which is a huge benefit for your bottom line.

Making physical commodity purchases

The most direct way of investing in certain commodities is to actually buy them outright. Precious metals such as gold, silver, and platinum are a great example of this. As the price of gold and silver has skyrocketed recently, you may have seen ads on TV or in newspapers from companies offering to buy your gold or silver jewelry. As gold and silver prices increase in the futures markets, they also cause prices in the *spot markets* (markets in which commodities or securities are sold for cash and delivered immediately or in the very near future) to rise (and vice versa). You can cash in on this trend by buying coins, bullion, or even jewelry.

This investment strategy is suitable for only a limited number of commodities, mostly precious metals like gold, silver, and platinum. Unless you own a farm, keeping live cattle or feeder cattle to profit from price increases doesn't make much sense. And I won't even mention commodities like crude oil or uranium!

Owning a piece of an exchange

Commodity exchanges, outlined in the next section, are becoming popular vehicles through which investors access the commodity markets.

Sometimes, with all the commotion associated with the trading floors on commodity exchanges, it's easy to forget that an exchange is a business like any other business. Exchanges have employees, board members, revenues, earnings, expenses, and so on. Whereas a car manufacturer sells cars to customers, commodity exchanges sell commodity contracts to customers. Of course, they charge fees for this service.

For most of their existence, exchanges have been privately held companies whose business side remained under close wraps. However, because of the increasing popularity of commodities and the rise of the electronic trading platform, many commodity exchanges are now becoming public companies with shareholders and outside investors. You can cash in on this trend by becoming a shareholder in one of these exchanges.

In 2003, the Chicago Mercantile Exchange (the nation's largest commodity exchange in terms of volume) went public under the name CME Group. Its shares are traded on the New York Stock Exchange under the ticker symbol CME. CME went public at a price of $43 a share. By March 2006, the stock price of CME reached an astonishing $435 a share! That's more than a 1,000 percent increase in a period of three years. Encouraged by these results, a number of other commodity exchanges went public soon after, and more are following suit. Other exchanges that have gone public include the Chicago Board of Trade (CBOT) and the Intercontinental Exchange (ICE).

Before you purchase stock in one of the commodity exchanges, make sure you perform a thorough analysis of the stock and the company fundamentals. A stock never goes up in a straight arrow — it always retreats before reaching new highs. Sometimes, it doesn't reach new highs at all. I recommend you follow a stock on paper — that is, follow its movements without actually owning the stock — for a period of at least two weeks. That way you can get a feel for how the stock moves with the rest of the market. Doing so allows you to pinpoint the right entry and exit points.

Examining the Major Commodity Exchanges

A number of commodity exchanges operate worldwide and specialize in all sorts of commodities. The following sections discuss key exchanges as well as two important regulatory organizations.

Exchanges in the United States

Before 2007, the industry was characterized by several players, each dominant in a particular segment of the market. In 2007, the industry experienced a significant and game-changing consolidation period during which the number of players decreased and the number of product offerings from each remaining body increased significantly. This consolidation permanently altered the exchange landscape and, in a certain way, made it easier for investors and traders to get access to these markets: The remaining exchanges became one-stop shops offering a variety of different products.

Although the industry had been ripe for consolidation for some time, the main catalyst for change was the advent of electronic and Internet-based trading platforms. One of the main factors of the digital revolution has been the migration of trade flow from floor exchanges to electronic platforms, a shift that has resulted in decreased volumes on traditional floor exchanges such as the New York Mercantile Exchange (NYMEX) and increased flow in electronic-based exchanges such as the Intercontinental Exchange (ICE).

During the consolidation, two main players emerged: the Chicago Mercantile Exchange (CME) and the ICE (note that both the CME and the ICE offer interactive, online-based trading platforms).

- ✔ **The CME** acquired the Chicago Board of Trade (CBOT) and the NYMEX, including the COMEX division (the metals complex of the NYMEX), making it the largest commodities exchange globally.

- ✔ **The ICE** acquired the New York Board of Trade (NYBOT) and the Winnipeg Commodity Exchange (WCE). The ICE is now a dominant player in energy (crude oil, coal, natural gas) and agricultural commodities (cocoa, coffee, cotton).

The main commodity exchanges in the United States are located in New York and Chicago, with a few other exchanges in other parts of the country. Table 2-2 lists the major commodity exchanges in the United States, along with the commodities traded in each one. *Note:* This list contains only a small sampling of the commodities these exchanges offer. The CME, for example, offers more than 100 futures products that track everything from milk and feeder cattle to nonfarm payrolls and currencies. Visit the exchanges' websites for a comprehensive listing of their product offerings.

Table 2-2	**The Major U.S. Commodity Exchanges**
Exchange Name	*Sampling of Commodities Traded*
Chicago Board of Trade (CBOT); www.cmegroup.com/company/cbot.html	Corn, ethanol, oats, rice, soybeans, wheat, gold, silver
Chicago Mercantile Exchange (CME); www.cmegroup.com/trading/agricultural	Feeder cattle, frozen pork bellies, lean hogs, live cattle, butter, milk, lumber
Intercontinental Exchange (ICE); www.theice.com	Crude oil, cocoa, coffee, cotton, electricity, frozen concentrated orange juice, grains, natural gas, sugar, ethanol
Kansas City Board of Trade (KCBT); www.cmegroup.com/trading/agricultural/kcbt.html	Natural gas, wheat
Minneapolis Grain Exchange (MGE); www.mgex.com	Corn, soybeans, wheat
New York Mercantile Exchange (NYMEX); www.cmegroup.com/company/nymex.html	Aluminum, copper, gold, palladium, platinum, silver, crude oil, electricity, gasoline, heating oil, natural gas, propane

In the U.S., the technical name for a commodity exchange is a *Designated Contract Market* (DCM). DCM is a designation that the Commodity Futures Trading Commission (CFTC) assigns to exchanges that offer commodity products to the public. If an exchange doesn't have the designation DCM, stay away from it!

Although most commodities in the United States are traded on only one exchange — the feeder cattle contract is traded only on the CME, for example — certain commodities are traded on more than one exchange. In that case, you want to trade the most liquid market. To find the most liquid market for a commodity, consult the CFTC (www.cftc.gov), which keeps information on all the exchanges and their products.

A sampling of international exchanges

Although the bulk of commodity trading is done in the United States — the largest consumer market of commodities — other countries also have commodity exchanges. If you're in the United States, you may want to consider investing in overseas exchanges for diversification purposes. Table 2-3 lists some of these international commodity exchanges.

Table 2-3	Sampling of International Commodity Exchanges	
Exchange Name	*Country*	*Commodities Traded*
European Energy Exchange; www.eex.com	Germany	Electricity
London Metal Exchange; www.lme.com	United Kingdom	Aluminum, copper, lead, nickel, tin, zinc
Natural Gas Exchange; www.ngx.com	Canada	Natural gas
Tokyo Commodity Exchange; www.tocom.or.jp	Japan	Aluminum, gold, palladium, platinum, silver, crude oil, gasoline, kerosene, rubber

Regulatory organizations for commodity exchanges

Commodity exchanges are under strict oversight, to protect all market participants and ensure transparency in the exchanges. These main regulatory organizations have oversight of commodity exchanges in the United States:

✔ **Commodity Futures Trading Commission (CFTC):** The CFTC (`www.cftc.gov`) is a federal regulatory agency whose main purpose is to regulate the commodity markets and protect all market participants from fraud, manipulation, and abusive practices. Any exchange that conducts business with the public must be registered with the CFTC.

✔ **National Futures Association (NFA):** The NFA (`www.nfa.futures.org`) is the industry's self-regulatory body. It conducts audits, launches investigations to root out corrupt practices in the industry, and enforces the rules related to trading commodities on the various exchanges. It also regulates every firm or individual who conducts business with you as an investor — including floor traders and brokers, futures commission merchants, commodity trading advisors, commodity pool operators, and brokers.

Opening an Account and Placing Orders

When you decide you're ready to start trading exchange-traded products, you have to open a trading account with a commodity broker who's licensed to conduct business on behalf of clients at the exchange.

The technical term for a commodity broker is a *futures commission merchant* (FCM). The FCM is licensed to solicit and execute commodity orders and accept payments for this service. Before choosing a commodity broker to handle your account, perform a thorough and comprehensive analysis of its trading platform. You want to get as much information as possible about the firm and its activities. A few things you should consider are the firm's history, clients, licensing information, trading platform, regulatory data, and employee information.

The following sections help you select the right type of trading account and place orders.

Choosing the right account

When you're ready to open an account and start trading, you can choose from a number of different brokerage accounts. Most firms offer you at least two types of accounts, depending on the level of control you want to exercise over the account:

✔ **Self-directed accounts:** If you feel confident about your trading abilities, have a good understanding of market fundamentals, and want to get direct access to commodity exchange products, then a self-directed account is for you. In this type of account, also known as a *non-discretionary individual account,* you call the shots and make all the trading decisions.

Before you open a self-directed account, talk to a few commodity brokers because each firm offers different account features. Specifically, ask about any minimum capital requirements the firm has, account maintenance fees, and the commission scale the firm uses.

✔ **Managed accounts:** In a managed account, you essentially transfer the responsibility of making all buying and selling decisions over to a trained professional. This type of account is ideal if you don't follow the markets on a daily basis, are unsure about which trading strategy will maximize your returns, or simply don't have the time to manage a personal account.

Before you open a managed account, determine your investment goals, time horizon, and risk tolerance, and find a commodity trading advisor (CTA) who will manage your account based on your personal risk profile. A CTA is a securities professional who's licensed by the Financial Industry Regulatory Authority (FINRA) and the National Futures Association (NFA) to offer advice on commodities and accept compensation for investment and management services.

Before contracting with anyone, however, find out about any minimum capital requirements, commissions, or management fees you may face.

Placing orders

Your trading account is your link to a commodity exchange. The broker's trading platform gives you access to the exchange's main products, such as futures contracts, options on futures, and other derivative products. Because the products traded on commodity exchanges are fairly sophisticated financial instruments, you need to specify a number of parameters in order to purchase the product you want.

As an investor, you can choose from a number of different contracts — from plain vanilla futures contracts to exotic swaps and spreads. Whichever contract(s) you choose, you need to follow specific entry order procedures. Here is a list of the parameters you need to indicate to place an order at the exchange:

✔ **Action:** Indicate whether you're buying or selling.

✔ **Quantity:** Specify the number of contracts you're interested in buying or selling.

✔ **Time:** Futures contracts have delivery months, and you must specify the delivery month. You should also specify the year because many contracts represent delivery points for periods of up to five years (or more).

✔ **Commodity:** You must specify the underlying commodity that the contract represents. It could be crude oil, gold, or soybeans, for example. You may also want to indicate on which exchange you want to place your order, especially since more and more of the same commodities are being offered on different exchanges.

✔ **Price:** Unless you're placing a *market order* (which is executed at current market prices), indicate the price at which you want your order to be filled.

✔ **Type of order:** Indicate how you want to buy or sell the contract. Several types of orders are available, from plain vanilla market orders to more exotic ones such as *Fill or Kill* (FOK). Table 2-4 lists the different types of orders.

✔ **Day or open order:** Indicate how long you want your order to remain open. In a *day order,* your order expires if it isn't filled by the end of the trading day. An *open order* remains open unless you cancel the order, the order is filled, or the contract expires.

Table 2-4	Types of Orders
Order	**Description**
Fill or Kill (FOK)	Your order is to be filled right away at a specific price. If a matching offer is not found within three attempts, your order will be cancelled, or "killed."
Limit (LMT)	Your order is to be filled only at a specified price or better. If you're on the buy side of a transaction, you want your limit buy order placed at or below the market price. If you're on the sell side, you want your limit sell order at or above the market price.
Market (MKT)	Your order will be filled at the current market price.
Market if Touched (MIT)	You specify the price at which you want to buy or sell a commodity. When that price is reached (or "touched"), your order is automatically filled at the current market price. A buy MIT order is placed below the market; a sell MIT order is placed above the market.
Market on Close (MOC)	You select a specific time to execute your order, and your order will be executed at whatever price that particular commodity is commanding at the end of the trading session.
Stop (STP)	Your order is placed when trading occurs at or through a specified price. A buy stop order is placed above the market, and a sell stop order is placed below market levels.

(continued)

Book III

Commodities

Table 2-4 *(continued)*

Order	Description
Stop Close Only (SCO)	Your stop order will be executed only at the close of trading and only if the closing trading range is at or through your designated stop price.
Stop Limit (STL)	After the stop price is reached, the order will become a limit order and the transaction will be executed only if the specified price at which you want the order to go through has been reached.

Here's a sample order:

Buy ten June 2013 COMEX Gold at $550 Limit Day Order

Translation: You're buying ten contracts for gold on the COMEX with the delivery date of June 2013. You're willing to pay $550 or less per troy ounce per contract. (A *troy ounce* is the measurement unit for gold at the COMEX.) Because this is a day order, your order will expire at the end of the day if it isn't filled.

Chapter 3

The Power House: Making Money in Energy

*E*nergy is the largest commodities asset class and presents some solid investment opportunities. This chapter helps you discover the ins and outs of the energy markets and shows you ways to profit in this sector, from trading crude oil futures contracts to investing in diversified electric utilities.

Investing in Crude Oil

Crude oil is undoubtedly the king of commodities, in terms of both its production value and its importance to the global economy. It's the most-traded nonfinancial commodity in the world, and it supplies 40 percent of the world's total energy needs — more than any other single commodity. About 87 million barrels of crude oil are traded on a daily basis, and crude oil is also the base product for a number of indispensable goods like gasoline, jet fuel, and plastics.

In the following sections, you get some background information on global crude oil consumption and production, and you find out how to invest in big oil.

Facing the crude realities

Having a good understanding of global consumption and production patterns is important if you're considering investing in the oil industry.

Global oil reserves and production

As demand for crude oil increases, countries that have large deposits of this natural resource stand to benefit tremendously. One way you can benefit from this trend is to invest in countries and companies with large reserves of crude oil. To determine which countries are exploiting their reserves adequately, you also need to look at actual production. Having large reserves is meaningless if a country isn't tapping those reserves to produce oil.

Table 3-1 lists the countries with the largest proven crude oil reserves, as well as the top ten producers of crude oil. Consider the fact that Venezuela, Libya, and Nigeria are on the top-ten reserves list but are not among the top ten producers, whereas three of the top ten producers — the United States, China, and Mexico — don't rank among the top ten in terms of reserves. Note that the reserve figures may change as new oilfields are discovered and as new technologies allow for the extraction of additional oil from existing fields.

Table 3-1		Oil Reserves and Production by Country		
Oil Reserves*			**Production****	
Rank	**Country**	**Proven Reserves (Billion Barrels)**	**Country**	**Daily Production (Thousand Barrels)**
1	Venezuela	297.6	Saudi Arabia	11,545.7
2	Saudi Arabia	267.9	United States	11,124.1
3	Canada	173.1	Russia	10,397.0
4	Iran	154.6	China	4,416.2
5	Iraq	141.4	Canada	3,869.0
6	Kuwait	104.0	Iran	3,538.4
7	United Arab Emirates	97.8	United Arab Emirates	3,213.2
8	Russia	80.0	Iraq	2,986.2
9	Libya	48.1	Mexico	2,936.0
10	Nigeria	37.2	Kuwait	2,796.8

Source: U.S. Energy Information Administration

*2013 numbers

**2012 numbers

If you're an active oil trader with a futures account, it's crucial that you follow the daily production numbers, available through the U.S. Energy Information Administration (EIA) website at www.eia.gov. The futures markets are particularly sensitive to these numbers, and any event that takes crude off the market can have a sudden impact on crude futures contracts. (For an introduction to futures, check out Book II.)

Demand figures

The United States tops the list of oil consumers and has been the single largest consumer of crude oil for the last 25 years. Although a lot of folks pay attention to the demand increase from China and India, most of the demand for crude oil (and the resulting price pressure) still comes from the United States.

Demand figures are important because they indicate a steady and sustained increase in crude demand for the mid to long term, which is likely to maintain increased pressure on crude prices. Table 3-2 lists the top ten consumers of crude oil in the world.

Table 3-2	Largest Consumers of Crude Oil, 2012	
Rank	*Country*	*Daily Consumption (Million Barrels)*
1	United States	18.5
2	China	10.2
3	Japan	4.7
4	India	3.6
5	Russia	3.2
6	Brazil	2.8
7	Saudi Arabia	2.8
8	Germany	2.4
9	Canada	2.3
10	South Korea	2.2

Source: U.S. Energy Information Administration

Book III

Commodities

Always design an investment strategy that will profit from long-term trends. The steady increase in global demand for crude oil is a good reason to be bullish on oil prices.

Imports and exports

Knowing the top exporting countries allows you to zero in on the countries that are actually generating revenues from the sale of crude oil to other countries. You can get in on the action by investing domestically in these countries.

Imports are as important as exports in your calculations. Countries that are main importers of crude oil are primarily advanced, industrialized societies like Germany and the United States, which are rich enough that they can absorb crude oil price increases. As a general rule, however, importers face a lot of pressure during any price increases, which sometimes translates into lower stock market performances in the importing countries. Table 3-3 shows the top oil exporting and importing countries.

Table 3-3		Top Ten Oil Exporters and Importers		
	*Exports**		*Imports***	
Rank	*Country*	*Daily Oil Exports (Thousand Barrels)*	*Country*	*Daily Oil Imports (Thousand Barrels)*
1	Saudi Arabia	8,684	United States	2,579.9
2	Russia	7,201	Netherlands	2,079.2
3	UAE	2,590	Singapore	1,348.2
4	Kuwait	2,410	Japan	1,310.8
5	Nigeria	2,254	China	971.5
6	Iraq	2,235	France	834.8
7	Iran	1,829	South Korea	794.0
8	Angola	1,778	Germany	758.1
9	Venezuela	1,712	United Kingdom	680.4
10	Norway	1,646	Mexico	607.4

Source: U.S. Energy Information Administration
*2012
**2010

Crude quality

Crude oil is classified into two broad categories: light and sweet, and heavy and sour. The two criteria most widely used to determine the quality of crude oil are density and sulfur content:

✔ **Density:** This usually refers to how much a crude oil will yield in terms of products, such as heating oil and jet fuel. A lower-density crude oil, known as *light crude,* tends to yield higher levels of products. A high-density crude oil *(heavy crude)* has lower product yields.

✔ **Sulfur content:** Sulfur is a corrosive material that decreases the purity of a crude oil. Crude oil with high sulfur content, which is known as *sour,* is much less desirable than crude oil with low sulfur content, known as *sweet* crude.

A company involved in the production of light, sweet crude will generate more revenue than one involved in the processing of heavy, sour crude. This doesn't mean you shouldn't invest in companies with exposure to heavy, sour crude; you just have to factor the type into your investment strategy.

Making big bucks with big oil

The price of crude oil has skyrocketed during the first years of the 21st century (see Figure 3-1); if this trend is any indication of what's in store for oil, you definitely want to develop a winning game plan to take advantage of it.

Book III

Commodities

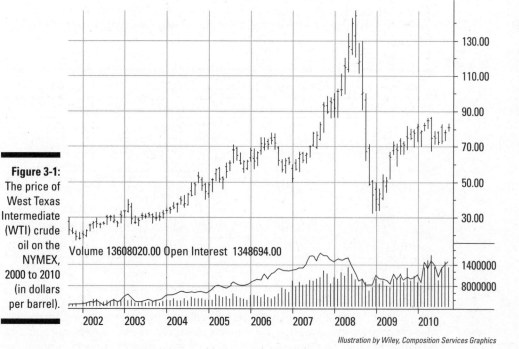

Figure 3-1: The price of West Texas Intermediate (WTI) crude oil on the NYMEX, 2000 to 2010 (in dollars per barrel).

Illustration by Wiley, Composition Services Graphics

The integrated oil companies, sometimes known as *big oil* or *the majors,* are involved in all phases of the oil production process — from exploring for oil, to refining it, to transporting it to consumers. ExxonMobil, Chevron, and BP are all "big oil" companies. The following sections discuss buying into individual companies, oil company exchange-traded funds (ETFs), and companies in emerging markets.

In addition to big oil companies, a number of other companies are involved in specific aspects of the process of crude oil. Companies like Valero, for example, are primarily involved in refining, and others such as General Maritime own fleets of tankers that transport crude oil and products. I discuss how to invest in these companies — the refiners, transporters, and explorers — in the later section "Putting Your Money in Energy Companies."

Buying into individual oil companies

The major oil companies have been posting record profits. In 2005, ExxonMobil, for example, earned more than $30 billion on revenues of $301 billion! The company posted net income of $40.1 billion in 2007 and $45 billion in 2008. Another big oil company, ConocoPhillips posted net income of $4.8 billion in 2009.

As global demand continues and supplies remain limited, big oil companies are likely to keep generating record revenues and profits. Table 3-4 lists some of the companies that you may want to include in your portfolio. For a more comprehensive list, check out Yahoo! Finance's section on integrated oil companies at biz.yahoo.com/ic/120.html.

Table 3-4	Major Integrated Oil Companies, 2005 Figures		
Oil Company	*Ticker*	*Revenues*	*Earnings*
BP	BP	$239 billion	$16 billion
ExxonMobil	XOM	$301 billion	$30.5 billion
Chevron	CVX	$167 billion	$10 billion
ConocoPhillips	COP	$152 billion	$5 billion
Eni	E	$95 billion	$5 billion
Petrobras	PBR	$91 billion	$15 billion
PetroChina	PTR	$70 billion	$18 billion

Most of these traditional oil companies have now moved into other areas in the energy sphere. These companies not only process crude oil into different products, but they also have vast petrochemicals businesses as well as growing projects involving natural gas and, increasingly, alternative energy sources. Investing in these oil companies gives you exposure to other sorts of products in the energy industry as well.

Choosing oil company ETFs

If you can't decide which oil company you want to invest in, you have several other options at your disposal. One option is to buy exchange-traded funds (ETFs) that track the performance of a group of integrated oil companies. (ETFs are discussed in detail in Book I, Chapter 3.) Here are a few oil company ETFs to consider:

- ✔ **Energy Select Sector SPDR (NYSEARCA:XLE):** The largest energy ETF in the market, XLE ETF is part of the S&P's family of *Standard & Poor's Depository Receipts* (SPDR), commonly referred to as *spiders,* and tracks the performance of a basket of oil company stocks, including the majors ExxonMobil and Chevron, as well as oil services companies such as Halliburton and Schlumberger.

- ✔ **iShares S&P North American Natural Resources SectorIndex (IGE):** The IGE ETF mirrors the performance of the S&P North American Natural Resources Sector Index, which tracks the performance of companies like ConocoPhillips and Chevron, as well as refiners such as Valero and Suncor.

- ✔ **iShares S&P Global Energy Sector Index (IXC):** This ETF mirrors the performance of the S&P Global 1200 Energy Sector Index. Buying this ETF gives you exposure to companies such as ExxonMobil, Chevron, ConocoPhillips, and Royal Dutch Shell.

Investing overseas

Another great way to capitalize on oil profits is to invest in an emerging-market fund that invests in countries that sit on large deposits of crude oil and that have the infrastructure in place to export crude oil. Here are a couple of emerging-markets funds that give you indirect exposure to booming oil-exporting countries (flip to Book VI for the full scoop on emerging markets):

- ✔ **Wells Fargo Advantage Emerging Markets Equity Fund (EMGYX)**
- ✔ **Fidelity Emerging Markets Fund (FEMKX)**

Book III

Commodities

Trading Natural Gas

Natural gas accounts for approximately 25 percent of energy consumption. Because of its importance as a source of energy, natural gas makes for a good investment.

Liquefied natural gas, or LNG, is nothing but natural gas in a liquid state. LNG is easy to transport — an important characteristic as meeting increasing demand requires transporting natural gas across vast distances, like continents and oceans.

The majority of natural gas in the United States is transported through pipe-lines in a gaseous state. LNG is usually transported in specially designed tankers to consumer markets. Some of the major operators of natural gas pipelines that transport both natural gas and LNG are entities known as *master limited partnerships* (MLPs). You can profit from moving natural gas across the United States by investing in MLPs.

The following sections describe natural gas applications and explain how to invest in natural gas.

Recognizing natural gas applications

Because it's one of the cleanest-burning fossil fuels, natural gas has become increasingly popular as an energy source. In the United States alone, natural gas accounts for nearly a quarter of total energy consumption, second only to petroleum. The primary consumers of this commodity are the industrial sector, residences, commercial interests, electricity generators, and the transportation sector.

Industrial uses

The industrial sector is the largest consumer of natural gas, accounting for almost 40 percent of total consumption, using it for processing food, melting glass and metal, incinerating waste, fueling industrial boilers, and more.

Although industrial uses of natural gas have always played a major role in the sector, their significance has increased over the last several years, and the industrial sector's demand for natural gas use is projected to continue. (Actually, demand for natural gas products as a whole will increase through-out the first quarter of the 21st century.) This increased demand should put upward price pressure on natural gas.

Residential uses

Residential usage accounts for almost a quarter of total natural gas consumption, with a large portion of homes in the United States and other countries using natural gas for both cooking (about 70 percent of U.S. households) and heating (over 50 percent).

One way to benefit from the use of natural gas as a heating fuel is to identify peak periods of natural gas consumption. Specifically, demand for natural gas for heating increases in the northern hemisphere during the winter seasons. One way to profit in the natural gas markets is to calibrate your strategy to this cyclical, weather-related trend.

Commercial uses

Commercial users, such as hospitals and schools, account for almost 15 percent of total natural gas consumption. Because commercial users also include restaurants, movie theaters, malls, and office buildings, demand for natural gas from these key drivers of the economy rises during times of increasing economic activity. This means that, all things being equal, you should be bullish on natural gas during times of economic growth.

One place to look for important economic clues that affect demand for natural gas is the Energy Information Administration (EIA), a division of the U.S. Department of Energy (DOE). The EIA provides a wealth of information regarding consumption trends of key energy products, such as natural gas, from various economic sectors. For information on the commercial usage of natural gas, visit www.naturalgas.org.

Electricity generation

Natural gas is quickly becoming a popular alternative to coal burning to generate electricity; just under 25 percent of natural gas usage goes toward generating electricity. In the United States, natural gas is used to support approximately 10 percent of electricity generation, a figure that is expected to increase dramatically in the coming years (see Figure 3-2).

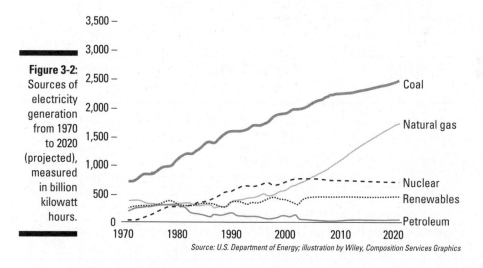

Figure 3-2: Sources of electricity generation from 1970 to 2020 (projected), measured in billion kilowatt hours.

Source: U.S. Department of Energy; illustration by Wiley, Composition Services Graphics

Book III

Commodities

Transportation uses

Natural gas is used in approximately 3 million vehicles worldwide as a source of fuel. These *natural gas vehicles* (NGVs) run on a grade of natural gas called *compressed natural gas* (CNG). Although this usage accounts for only about

5 percent of total natural gas consumption, demand for NGVs could increase as they become a viable (cheaper) alternative to vehicles that use gasoline (a crude oil derivative). As of 2010, for example, more than 11 million NGVs were in circulation worldwide.

Keep a close eye on technological developments that affect natural gas usage in the transportation sector. If natural gas were to grab a slice of the transportation market, which now accounts for almost two-thirds of crude oil consumption, prices for natural gas could increase dramatically. One place to check out the latest info on NGVs is NGV Global, formerly known as the International Association for Natural Gas Vehicles; the website is www.iangv.org.

Investing in natural gas

The future for natural gas looks bright. The total natural gas consumption on a global scale in 2006 was approximately 110 trillion cubic feet (110 Tcf). By 2010, that figure increased to 120 Tcf. By 2020 that figure is estimated to increase more than 50 percent — at a rate of 2.3 percent annually — to a total of 156 Tcf. More important than knowing that demand for natural gas will remain steady until 2025 is figuring out which countries and companies will be meeting this demand. Table 3-5 lists the countries with the largest reserves of natural gas in the world.

Table 3-5		Top Ten Natural Gas Reserves and Production by Country, 2011		
	Reserves		*Production*	
Rank	*Country*	*Proven Reserves (Trillion Cubit Feet)*	*Country*	*Total Production (Billion Cubit Feet)*
1	Russia	1,680.0	United States	28,479
2	Iran	1,045.7	Russia	23,686
3	Qatar	895.8	Iran	7,915
4	United States	304.6	Algeria	6,714
5	Saudi Arabia	275.7	Canada	6,669
6	United Arab Emirates	227.9	Qatar	5,184

Rank	Reserves		Production	
	Country	Proven Reserves (Trillion Cubit Feet)	Country	Total Production (Billion Cubit Feet)
7	Nigeria	186.9	Norway	5,062
8	Venezuela	178.9	China	3,629
9	Algeria	159.0	Saudi Arabia	3,617
10	Iraq	111.9	Indonesia	3,255

Source: U.S. Energy Information Administration

You can get exposure to the huge natural gas market in a couple of ways: by trading futures contracts or by investing in companies that are involved in the production and development of natural gas fields in the countries listed in Table 3-5.

Trading natural gas futures

The most direct method of investing in natural gas is to trade futures contracts on one of the designated commodities exchanges (see Chapter 2 in Book III for more about these exchanges). The CME Group (formerly the Chicago Mercantile Exchange), the exchange for energy products, gives you the option to buy and sell natural gas futures and options.

The natural gas futures contract is the third-most-popular energy contract on the CME, right behind crude oil and heating oil. It's traded under the ticker symbol NG, and it trades in increments of 10,000 MMBtu (1 mmBtu = 1 million British thermal units). You can trade it during all the calendar months, to periods up to 72 months after the current month.

The CME offers a mini version of this contract for individual hedgers and speculators. Check out the natural gas section of the CME website for more on this contract: www.cmegroup.com/trading/energy/natural-gas/natural-gas.html.

Trading natural gas futures contracts and options isn't for the fainthearted. Even by commodities standards, natural gas is a notoriously volatile commodity, subject to wild price fluctuations. If you're not an aggressive investor willing to withstand the financial equivalent of a wild roller-coaster ride, natural gas futures may not be for you.

Book III

Commodities

Investing in natural gas companies

Investing in companies that process natural gas offers you exposure to this market through the expertise and experience of industry professionals, without the volatility of the futures market. Some natural gas companies are involved in the production of natural gas fields, while others are responsible for delivering natural gas directly to consumers. Following are *fully integrated* natural gas companies, which means they're involved in all the production, development, transportation, and distribution phases of natural gas. Investing in these companies provides you with a solid foothold in this industry:

- ✔ **Alliant Energy (NYSE: LNT):** Provides consumers in the Midwest United States with natural gas and electricity derived from natural gas. A good choice if you want exposure to the North American natural gas market. www.alliantenergy.com

- ✔ **Nicor Gas (NYSE: GAS):** Provides natural gas to more than 2 million consumers, primarily centered in the Illinois area. Another good regional investment. nicorgas.aglr.com

For a complete listing of companies involved in natural gas production and distribution, look at the American Gas Association website: www.aga.org.

Bowing to Ol' King Coal

Coal, which accounted for 23 percent of total fossil fuel consumption in the United States in 2009, is used primarily for electricity generation and steel manufacturing. It's an increasingly popular fossil fuel because of its large reserves. Companies in the United States have long touted the benefits of moving toward a more coal-based economy because the United States has the largest coal reserves in the world.

Demand for coal is expected to increase dramatically during the first quarter of the 21st century. Most of this growth will come from the emerging-market economies, particularly the economies of China and India, which will account for approximately 75 percent of the increased demand for coal. (China is currently the largest consumer of coal in the world, ahead of the United States, India, and Japan.)

Coal is measured in short tons. One *short ton* is the equivalent of 2,000 pounds. In terms of energy, one short ton of *anthracite,* the coal of highest quality, contains approximately 25 million British thermal units (Btu) of energy.

This demand for coal has resulted in strong price movements in the commodity itself. Before the 2008 Global Financial Crisis, prices for coal experienced a major uptrend, going from $50 per short ton in 2006 to almost $200 per short ton in 2008. The financial crisis resulted in a severe quasicrash scenario for coal prices, as was the case for several other important commodities. Expect much more activity surrounding this commodity in the future.

In the following sections, you find out about coal reserves and production, and you discover how to invest in coal.

Considering coal reserves and production

If you're going to invest in coal, you need to know which countries have the largest coal reserves. Just because a country has large deposits of a natural resource, however, doesn't mean that it exploits them to full capacity. Therefore, there is a significant gap between countries with large coal reserves and those that produce the most coal on an annual basis. Russia, for example, ranks second in terms of reserves but comes in sixth on the production side. Table 3-6 lists the top ten countries with the largest coal reserves, as well as the top coal-producing countries.

Book III

Commodities

Table 3-6		Coal Reserves and Production by Country		
	Reserves*		**Production****	
Rank	**Country**	**Reserves (Million Short Tons)**	**Country**	**Production (Thousand Short Tons)**
1	United States	260,551	China	3,991,050
2	Russia	173,074	United States	1,016,399
3	China	126,215	India	693,592
4	Australia	84,217	Australia	475,872
5	India	66,800	Indonesia	452,132
6	Germany	44,863	Russia	387,121
7	Ukraine	37,339	South Africa	287,650
8	Kazakhstan	37,038	Germany	216,375

(continued)

Table 3-6 *(continued)*

| | Reserves* | | Production** | |
Rank	Country	Reserves (Million Short Tons)	Country	Production (Thousand Short Tons)
9	South Africa	33,241	Poland	158,428
10	Serbia	14,179	Kazakhstan	134,008

Source: Source: U.S. Energy Information Administration
* 2008 figures
** 2012 figures

If you're going to invest in a company that processes coal, select a company with a heavy exposure in one of the countries listed in Table 3-6. Before you invest in companies involved in the coal business, however, find out which type of coal they produce, which can help you better understand the company's business and profit margins. You can find this type of information in a company's annual and quarterly reports.

Investing in coal

You can get access to the coal markets by either trading coal futures or investing in coal companies:

✔ **Coal futures:** Coal has an underlying futures contract that trades on the CME Group (formerly the Chicago Mercantile Exchange). The coal futures contract on the CME tracks the price of the high-quality Central Appalachian coal (CAPP), sometimes affectionately called *the big sandy*. The CAPP futures contract is the premium benchmark for coal prices in the United States. It trades under the ticker symbol QL and is tradable during all the calendar months of the current year, in addition to all calendar months in the subsequent three years. Additional information on this futures contract is available on the CME website: www.cmegroup.com.

Most of the traders in this market represent large commercial interests that transact with each other, which means that you may not be able to get involved directly in this market without large capital reserves to compete with the commercial interests.

✔ **Coal companies:** One of the best ways to invest in coal is by investing in a company that mines it. The following three companies are among the best:

- **Arch Coal (NYSE: ACI):** Smaller in size than Peabody or Consol, Arch Coal (www.archcoal.com) operates more than 30 mines on the continental United States and controls more than 3 billion short tons of reserves.

- **Consol Energy (NYSE: CNX):** Headquartered in Canonsburg, PA, Consol Energy (www.consolenergy.com) has significant operations in the coal mines of Pennsylvania and the neighboring coal-rich states of West Virginia and Kentucky. As of 2009, it controlled 8 billion short tons of coal reserves, with operations in over 17 mines across the United States. CNX is well positioned to take advantage of the booming domestic coal market.

- **Peabody Energy (NYSE: BTU):** This is the largest coal company in the United States with approximately 15 billion short tons of coal reserves, generating approximately 10 percent of the electricity in the United States. The company has mining operations in the United States and Australia. www.peabodyenergy.com

If you want to invest in coal companies with a more international exposure to markets in Russia, China, and other coal-rich countries, consult the World Coal Association (www.worldcoal.org).

Looking at Other Energy Sources

Although crude oil, natural gas, and coal are always in the spotlight, they aren't the only energy commodities you can consider. The following sections touch on nuclear power, renewable energy, and other sectors of the energy market that may be worth your investment dollars.

Embracing nuclear power

Nuclear power generates more than 20 percent of the electricity in the United States; in countries like France, nuclear power generates more than 75 percent of electricity! Accounting for about 5 percent of total global energy consumption, nuclear power is expected to remain at stable levels until 2030. But if the price of fossil fuels (oil, natural gas, and coal) rises dramatically enough to start affecting demand, nuclear power may play an important role in picking up the slack.

One way you can profit from increased interest in nuclear power is to invest in uranium, the most widely used fuel in nuclear power plants. Because uranium isn't a widely tradable commodity, the best way to profit from this trend is to invest in companies that specialize in mining, processing, and distributing uranium for civilian nuclear purposes. A few companies in this sector include:

- ✔ **Cameco Corp. (NYSE: CCJ)**
- ✔ **Strathmore Minerals Corp. (Toronto: STM)**
- ✔ **UEX Corp. (Toronto: UEX)**

For more information on nuclear power, check out the EIA's web page with all sorts of practical information on this industry at `www.eia.gov/nuclear`. Another great source for everything regarding uranium and nuclear power is The Ux Consulting Company (`www.uxc.com`).

Trading electricity

Investing in coal and in nuclear power are ways to invest in electricity. But you can invest directly in the power industry by trading in the electricity futures market and investing in utilities:

- ✔ **Trading electricity futures:** The most direct way of investing in electricity is . . . to buy it! The CME Group (formerly the Chicago Mercantile Exchange) offers a futures contract that tracks the price of electricity as administered by PJM Interconnection. PJM is a *Regional Transmission Organization* (RTO) that oversees the largest electric grid system in the world and services more than 50 million customers in the United States. It's responsible for generating more than 700 million megawatt-hours of electricity across 55,000 miles of transmission lines. Because of its dominance in the U.S. electricity market, the PJM electricity futures contract on the CME/NYMEX provides you with a widely recognizable and tradable electricity benchmark.

  The PJM contract is traded in units of 40 mWh (megawatt-hours) under the ticker symbol JM. For more information on this specific contract, check out the CME Group website, `www.cmegroup.com`.

- ✔ **Investing in utilities:** I like utilities for a number of reasons, particularly for their very high dividend payout. Averaging 3.5 percent, the industry's dividend yield is one of the highest of any industry. Table 3-7 lists some utilities to consider, along with their dividend yield. In addition to juicy dividend yields, utilities offer you solid capital appreciation opportunities.

Table 3-7	Publicly Traded Utilities, 2010 Dividend Yields	
Utility	*Ticker*	*Dividend Yield*
Consolidated Edison	NYSE: ED	4.29%
Dominion Resources	NYSE: D	4.04%

Utility	Ticker	Dividend Yield
Duke Energy Corp.	NYSE: DUK	4.59%
Entergy Corp.	NYSE: ETR	4.86%
Great Plains Energy	NYSE: GXP	3.85%
PG&E Corp.	NYSE: PCG	4.08%

Tapping into renewable energy sources

Currently, renewable sources of energy make up about 13 percent of total energy use in the world, but they have the potential to grow as nonrenewable energy sources are depleted. The following sections highlight solar and wind energy.

If you're interested in keeping up-to-date on the latest developments in the renewable energy space, check out the U.S. Department of Energy's Energy Efficiency and Renewable Energy (EERE) initiative (www.eere.energy.gov).

Spotlighting solar energy

Solar power currently accounts for only 1 percent of total energy consumed in the United States, but it's one of the fastest growing energy areas.

Currently, the equity markets give you a direct way to get exposure to the solar industry. Following are some of the top names in the industry to choose from:

- **First Solar, Inc. (NASDAQ: FSLR):** FSLR is involved in the manufacture and sales of photovoltaic solar panels to governments, corporate entities, and private individuals. With net profit margins in excess of 22 percent (2010 figures), this company offers solid exposure to the photovoltaic market segment.

- **Suntech Power Holdings (NYSE: STP):** Suntech, a world leader in the development, design, and implementation of solar photovoltaic systems and products, provides both construction services and engineering and maintenance services to its clients around the world. It has operations in Germany, the United States, Australia, South Africa, Japan, and South Korea.

Eyeing the potential of wind energy

Wind energy — generated by huge wind machines (similar to traditional windmills) that are placed side by side in *wind farms* — is getting increasing attention from investors. Currently, very few publicly traded companies deal specifically in wind power. However, many industrial companies are beginning to implement large-scale investments in wind energy production.

With rising energy prices, wind energy may get more focus. If you're interested in investing in wind power and want to keep on top of any emerging trend, check out the American Wind Energy Association (www.awea.org), which keeps a database of private companies involved in wind energy that may go public one day.

Putting Your Money in Energy Companies

One way to play the energy markets is to invest in the companies involved in the production, transformation, and distribution of the world's most important energy commodities. Each of the companies operating in these segments of the market offers unique money-making investment opportunities. Finding out about specialized energy and oil companies that are critical links in the global crude oil supply chain can help you develop a targeted investment strategy.

Profiting from oil exploration and production

The exploration and discovery of oil is a very lucrative segment in the oil business, and you can invest in companies that specialize in the exploration and production of oilfields, known in the business as *E&P*. Oil wells are found in one of two places: on land or on sea.

- ✔ **Onshore drilling:** Although most industry insiders agree that a majority of onshore oil wells have been discovered, you can still benefit by investing in companies that are involved in the exploitation and production of onshore oilfields.

- ✔ **Offshore drilling:** In recent years, offshore drilling has generated a lot of interest among investors, and a flurry of activity has been taking place in this sector as oil on land becomes more and more scarce.

Table 3-8 lists some of the leading companies in off- and onshore drilling.

Table 3-8	E&P Companies Worth a Look	
Company	*Expertise*	*Notes*
Offshore Operations		
Diamond Offshore Drilling (NYSE: DO)	Drilling in ultra-deep water	With 50 offshore rigs, DO has a wide global footprint, with deepwater drilling operations in Brazil, Scotland, Australia, and the Gulf of Mexico.
Noble Corporation (NYSE: NE)	Implementing technologically oriented solutions	Noble has a fleet of more than 60 vessels and operations stretching from Brazil to the North Sea.
Transocean Inc. (NYSE: RIG)	Operating under harsh and extreme weather conditions	The largest company in terms of market capitalization and the size and scope of its operations, it has operations in the U.S. Gulf of Mexico, Brazil, South Africa, the Mediterranean Sea, the North Sea, Australia, and Southeast Asia, and, since a 2007 merger with GlobalSanteFe, the Middle East and Canada.
Onshore Operations		
Nabors Industries (NYSE: NBR)	Engaging in heavy-duty and horizontal drilling activities	Nabors is one of the largest land-drilling contractors in the world.
Patterson-UTI Energy Inc. (NASDAQ: PTEN)	Drilling new wells and servicing and maintaining existing oil wells	Patterson-UTI has extensive operations in North America and is part of the S&P 400 MidCap Index.

Book III

Commodities

If you want to dig deeper into the offshore E&P sector, you can check out the website www.rigzone.com, which includes up-to-date information on the offshore industry and the oil industry as a whole.

You can also invest in companies that focus on oilfield maintenance and services. As fewer and fewer oilfields are discovered, the world's major oil companies are looking for ways to maximize existing oilfields. Therefore, the role of the oilfield services companies will become increasingly important in the future. Consider these top companies if you're looking to invest in oilfield services:

- **Baker Hughes, Inc. (NYSE: BHI)**
- **Halliburton Co. (NYSE: HAL)**
- **Schlumberger Ltd. (NYSE: SLB)**

Investing in refineries

To be useful, crude oil must be refined into consumable products such as gasoline, diesel and jet fuel, automotive lubricating oil, propane and kerosene, and a myriad of other products. For this reason, refineries are a critical link in the crude oil supply chain. Given the importance of the crude oil derivative products, you can make a lot of money investing in refineries. Most major integrated oil companies, like ExxonMobil and BP, have a large refining capacity. A more direct way to profit from refining activity is by investing in independent refineries, such as these:

- **Valero Energy Corp. (NYSE: VLO)**
- **Sunoco Inc. (NYSE: SUN)**
- **Tesoro Corp. (NYSE: TSO)**

When considering investing in companies that operate refineries, pay attention to three criteria (included in a company's annual or quarterly reports):

- **Refinery throughput:** The capacity for refining crude oil over a given period of time, usually expressed in barrels
- **Refinery production:** Actual production of crude oil products, such as gasoline and heating oil
- **Refinery utilization:** The difference between production capacity (the throughput) and what's actually produced

The EIA compiles data on all U.S. refineries at www.eia.doe.gov/neic/rankings/refineries.htm.

Chapter 4

Pedal to the Metal: Investing in Metals

*I*nvestors able to master the fundamentals of the metals markets have been handsomely rewarded. Gold, silver, and platinum have industrial applications, but their primary value comes from their ability to act as stores of value, in addition to their use in jewelry. Steel, aluminum, and copper, although not as glamorous as their precious metal counterparts, are perhaps even more precious to the global economy. Other important metals, like palladium, zinc, and nickel, are also essential building blocks of the global economy. In this chapter, I cover all these metals that can play an important role in your portfolio.

Metals are classified into two broad categories: *precious metals* and *base metals*. This classification is based on a metal's resistance to corrosion and oxidation: Precious metals have a high resistance to corrosion, whereas base metals have a lower tolerance.

Going for the Gold

Perhaps no other metal — or commodity — in the world has the cachet and prestige of gold. Coveted and valued for its unique metallurgical characteristics, gold also has a number of applications in industry and jewelry that have increased its demand.

Gold is such a hot commodity because it's nearly indestructible and can retain its luster over thousands of years. It's one of the rarest natural resources on earth (all the gold in the world wouldn't even fill up four Olympic-size swimming pools!). Pure gold (24 karat) is very malleable and prized by craftsmen around the world (one ounce of gold can be transformed into more than 96 square feet of gold sheet!). And it's highly ductile. (*Ductility* measures how much a metal can be drawn out into a wire.) One ounce of gold can be converted into more than 50 miles of gold wire, which can then be applied in electronics.

Because of these characteristics, gold is used for jewelry (accounting for more than 70 percent of gold's total consumption), electronics, and dentistry. Gold also has many monetary uses: Many central banks hold reserves of gold; it's one of the only commodities that the investing public holds in its physical form; and it's used in coinage.

In the following sections, you find out how gold is measured and valued, and you discover a few methods for buying into the gold market.

Measuring and valuing gold

Gold, like most metals, is measured and weighed in *troy ounces* (oz). One troy ounce is the equivalent of 31.10 grams. When you buy gold for investment purposes, such as through exchange-traded funds (ETFs) or gold certificates, troy ounces are the measurement of choice. When you want to refer to large quantities of gold, such as the amount of gold a bank holds in reserve or the amount of gold produced in a mine, the unit of measurement you use is *metric tons.* One metric ton is equal to 32,150 troy ounces.

If you've ever bought gold jewelry, you've certainly heard of the measurement call *karats* (sometimes spelled *carats*). This measurement indicates the purity of gold. The purest form of gold is 24-karat gold (24K). Everything below that number denotes that the gold is *alloyed,* or mixed, with another metal. The purer the gold, the higher its value.

Buying into the gold market

You can invest in gold in a number of ways: physical gold, gold ETFs, gold mining companies, and gold futures contracts.

Purchasing physical gold

One way to invest in gold is to actually buy it. You can purchase gold coins or bars and store them in a safe location as an investment:

✔ **Gold coins:** One of the easiest ways to invest in physical gold is by buying gold coins. Here are the most popular types of gold coins:

- **Gold Eagle:** Issued by the U.S. government, the 22-karat Gold Eagle comes in various sizes including 1 ounce, ½ ounce, ¼ ounce, and $^1/_{10}$ ounce.

- **Gold Maple Leaf:** Issued by the Royal Canadian Mint, this 24-karat coin is the purest gold coin on the market.

- **Gold Krugerrand:** Issued by the South African government, it's one of the oldest gold coins issued in the world and has a fineness of 0.916. (*Fineness* is the ratio of the primary metal to any additives or impurities.)

✔ **Gold bars:** Gold bars are ideal if you're interested in purchasing larger quantities of gold. Gold bars come in all shapes and sizes. They can be as small as 1 gram or as large as 400 troy ounces. Most gold bars are high quality with a fineness of 0.999 and above (24 karats).

For a comprehensive listing of gold bars, peruse *The Industry Catalogue of Gold Bars Worldwide* at `www.grendon.com.au/goldbarscat.htm`. (FYI, the term *gold bullion* simply refers to large gold bars.)

✔ **Gold certificates:** Gold certificates enable you to own physical gold without actually taking possession of it. The gold itself is usually stored in a safe location by the authority that issues the gold certificates. The gold standard of gold certificates is the Perth Mint Certificate Program (PMCP), administered by The Perth Mint, Australia's oldest and most important mint. You may retrieve or sell your gold at any point. For more on this program, check out The Perth Mint's website at `www.perthmint.com.au`.

To purchase physical gold, or even gold certificates, you need to go through a gold dealer such as Kitco (`www.kitco.com`). Before doing business with any gold dealer, find out as much information about the business and its history as possible. You can check out different gold dealers by going through the Better Business Bureau at `www.bbb.org`.

Investing in gold ETFs

Currently you have two gold ETFs to choose from:

✔ **SPDR Gold Shares (NYSE: GLD):** The SPDR gold ETF is the largest gold ETF on the market today. Launched in late 2004, it holds about 29 million ounces of physical gold in secured locations. The price per ETF unit is calculated based on the average of the bid/ask spread in the gold spot market. This fund is a good way of getting exposure to physical gold without actually owning it.

✔ **iShares Gold Trust (AMEX: IAU):** The iShares gold ETF holds a little more than 5.7 million ounces of gold in its vaults. The per-unit price of the ETF seeks to reflect the current market price in the spot market of the ETF gold.

Because both ETFs track the price of gold on the spot market, their performance is remarkably similar — at times, it's actually identical. If you're struggling to decide between the two, consider that SPDR holds more physical gold and, more importantly, offers you more liquidity than the iShares ETF. (Keep in mind, though, that its expense ratio is also higher: 40 percent versus 25 percent.)

Holding stock in gold companies

A number of companies specialize in mining, processing, and distributing gold. A few recommendations:

✔ **Newmont Mining Corporation (NYSE: NEM):** Newmont (www.newmont.com), one of the largest gold mining companies in the world, has operations in Australia, Indonesia, Uzbekistan, the United States, Canada, Peru, and Bolivia. It is the largest gold producer in South America and has exploration programs in Ghana that could turn out to be very promising for the company.

✔ **Barrick Gold Corporation (NYSE: ABX):** Barrick (www.barrick.com), a Canadian company, has operations in Canada, the U.S., Argentina, Peru, Chile, Tanzania, South Africa, Australia, and Papua New Guinea, as well as a foothold in the potentially lucrative Central Asian market, where it has joint operations in Turkey, Russia, and Mongolia. Barrick also has one of the lowest production costs per ounce of gold in the industry.

✔ **AngloGold Ashanti Ltd. (NYSE: AU):** AngloGold (www.anglogold.com) operates more than 20 mines and has significant operations in Africa and South America in areas that have major gold deposits, as well as additional operations in Australia and North America. It is a wholly owned subsidiary of Anglo American PLC, a global mining giant covered in the later section "Putting Stock in Diversified Mining Companies."

✔ **New Gold, Inc. (AMEX: NGD):** Founded in 2005, New Gold (www.newgold.com) is a junior gold-mining company headquartered in Vancouver, British Columbia. It currently operates three highly profitable mines in California, Mexico, and Australia; the cash costs per ounce for each of these mines are among the industry's lowest, translating into high margins. In addition, NGD is in the process of exploiting two additional mines, one in Canada and the other in Chile.

These companies don't give you direct exposure to gold, as gold certificates or bars do, for example. Also, by investing in these stocks, you expose yourself to regulatory, managerial, and operational factors. Research the company before you invest. For guidance on how to do so, head to Book VII. Although that book deals with value investing, it offers lots of information about how to evaluate a company's performance and stability.

Getting in the game through gold futures contracts

With gold futures contracts, you invest in gold directly through the futures markets (see Book II for details). Three gold futures contracts are widely traded in the United States:

- **COMEX Gold (COMEX: GC):** The most liquid gold contract in the world, this contract is traded on the COMEX division of the New York Mercantile Exchange (NYMEX). Although large commercial consumers and producers, such as jewelry manufacturers and mining companies, use these contracts primarily for price hedging purposes, you can also purchase the contract for investment purposes. Each contract represents 100 troy ounces of gold.

- **NYSE Liffe Mini-Gold (NYSE: YG):** This gold contract is very attractive because you can trade it online through the New York Stock Exchange. In addition, at a contract size of 33.2 troy ounces, the mini is popular with investors and traders who prefer to trade smaller-size contracts.

- **CME/CBOT E-Micro Gold (CBOT: MGC):** Launched in 2010, this gold contract trades on the COMEX section of the CME Group (formerly the Chicago Mercantile Exchange). The contract's popularity has been growing with its electronic execution traded on the CME Globex platform. At a contract size of 10 troy ounces, the E-Micro is popular with investors and traders who prefer to trade an even smaller-size contract than the Mini-Gold's 33.2 troy ounces.

Book III

Commodities

Taking a Shine to Silver

Silverware and jewelry aren't the only uses for silver. As a matter of fact, silverware is only a small portion of the silver market. A large portion of this precious metal goes toward industrial uses, such as conducting electricity; creating bearings; and welding, soldering, and brazing (the process by which metals are permanently joined together). Because of its numerous practical applications and its status as a precious metal, investing in silver can bolster your portfolio.

Assessing silver applications

Silver has a number of uses that make it an attractive investment. Here are the most important ones, which account for more than 95 percent of the total demand for silver:

- **Industrial:** Silver has a number of applications in the industrial sector, including creating control switches for electrical appliances and connecting electronic circuit boards.

- ✔ **Jewelry and silverware:** Silver plays a large role in creating jewelry and silverware.

- ✔ **Photography:** In photography, silver is compounded with halogens to form *silver halide,* which is used in photographic film. The demand for silver by the photo industry is slowly decreasing, however, because of the popularity of digital cameras, which don't use silver halide. (Photography's demand for silver halved between 2006 and 2010, going from 20 to less than 10 percent.)

Getting a sliver of silver in your portfolio

Because of its precious metal status, you can use silver as a hedge against inflation and to preserve part of your portfolio's value. And because it has important industrial applications, you can use it for capital appreciation opportunities. The following sections provide a few methods for buying into the silver market.

To find out more about silver and its investment possibilities, go to the Silver Institute's website (www.silverinstitute.org), where you can find a comprehensive database on the silver market.

Buying physical silver

Like gold (discussed earlier in this chapter), you can invest in silver by actually buying the stuff. Most dealers that sell gold generally offer silver coins and bars as well. Here are two products to consider as investments:

- ✔ **Silver maple coins:** These coins, a product of the Royal Canadian Mint, are the standard for silver coins around the world. Each coin represents 1 ounce of silver and has a purity of 99.99 percent, making it the purest silver coin on the market.

- ✔ **100-oz. silver bars:** These bars are what their name indicates: 100-ounce bars of silver. Before buying, check the bar to make sure it's pure silver. (You want 99 percent purity or above.)

Pure silver is sometimes alloyed with another metal, such as copper, in order to make it stronger and more durable. The term *sterling silver* refers to a specific silver alloy that contains 92.5 percent silver and 7.5 percent copper or other base metals. If you're considering silver jewelry as an investment, sterling silver won't provide you with as much value in the long term as buying pure silver.

Considering a silver ETF

One of the most convenient ways to invest in silver is to go through an exchange-traded fund (ETF). The iShares Silver Trust (AMEX: SLV) holds silver bullion in a vault and seeks to mirror the spot price of that silver based on current market prices.

Looking at silver mining companies

Another alternative investment route is to go through companies that mine silver. The following companies specialize in mining this precious metal. Even though they may not be household names, they're potentially good investments nevertheless:

- ✔ **Pan American Silver Corporation (NASDAQ: PAAS):** This well-managed company, based in Vancouver, operates six mines in some of the most prominent locations in the world, including Peru, Mexico, and Bolivia. See www.panamericansilver.com.

- ✔ **Silver Wheaton Corp. (NYSE: SLW):** Silver Wheaton (www.silver wheaton.com), one of the few companies focusing exclusively on developing and mining silver, has operations in geographically diverse areas that stretch from Mexico to Sweden.

Tapping into silver futures contracts

The silver futures contracts, like gold futures, provide you with the most direct access to the silver market. Following are the most liquid silver futures contracts:

- ✔ **COMEX Silver (COMEX: SI):** The standard futures contract for silver, this contract is traded on the COMEX division of the New York Mercantile Exchange (NYMEX) and represents 5,000 troy ounces of silver per contract.

- ✔ **NYSE Liffe Mini-Silver (NYSE: YI):** The Mini-Silver contract that trades on the New York Stock Exchange represents a stake in 1,000 troy ounces of silver with a purity of 99.9 percent. This contract is available for electronic trading.

Putting Your Money in Platinum

Platinum, sometimes referred to as "the rich man's gold," is one of the rarest and most precious metals in the world. If you were to put all the platinum that has ever been mined in an Olympic-size swimming pool, it wouldn't even cover your ankles! Platinum also has superior characteristics to most metals: It's more resistant to corrosion, doesn't oxidize in the air, and has stable chemical properties.

Platinum is also the name of the group of metals that includes platinum, palladium, rhodium, ruthenium, osmium, and iridium. In this section, you find out about the metal only — not the group of metals. (I do cover palladium in the later section "Appreciating Palladium.")

Poring over some platinum facts

Deposits of platinum ore are extremely scarce and, more important, are geographically concentrated in a few regions around the globe, primarily in South Africa, Russia, and North America. Platinum's rarity is reflected in its price per troy ounce. For example, the price of platinum in August 2013 was around $1,500 per troy ounce! By comparison, silver during the same period cost around $25 per troy ounce.

Platinum has several uses. Here are the most important ones:

- **Catalytic converters:** As environmental fuel standards become more stringent, expect the demand from this sector to increase.
- **Jewelry:** Jewelry once accounted for more than 50 percent of the total demand for platinum. Although that number has decreased, the jewelry industry is still a major purchaser of platinum metals.
- **Industrial:** Platinum has wide applications in industry, being used in everything from personal computer hard drives to fiber optic cables.

A change in demand from any one of these industries affects the price of platinum. The International Platinum Group Metals Association (www.ipa-news.com) maintains an updated database of the uses of platinum. Check out the site for more information on platinum supply and demand.

Going platinum

Platinum's characteristics as a highly sought-after precious metal with industrial applications make it an ideal investment. Fortunately, you can invest in platinum in a number of ways. Here are two:

- **Buying into platinum mining companies:** Here are a couple of companies you can check out that can give you direct exposure to platinum mining activities:

- **Stillwater Mining Company (NYSE: SWC):** Stillwater Mining (`www.stillwatermining.com`), headquartered in Billings, Montana, owns the rights to the Stillwater mining complex in Montana, which contains one of the largest commercially viable platinum mines in North America.

- **Anglo American PLC (NASDAQ: AAUK):** Anglo American (`www.angloamerican.com`) is a diversified mining company that has activities in gold, silver, platinum, and other precious metals. It's worth a look because it has significant interests in South African platinum mines, the largest mines in the world.

✔ **Purchasing a platinum futures contract:** The New York Mercantile Exchange (NYMEX) offers a platinum futures contract. Because of increased demand from the industrial sector and other fundamental supply and demand reasons, the price of the NYMEX platinum futures contract has experienced a significant upward shift in recent years. The NYMEX platinum futures contract represents 50 troy ounces of platinum and is available for trading electronically. It trades under the ticker symbol PL.

Adding Some Steel to Your Portfolio

Steel, iron alloyed with other compounds (usually carbon), is still the most widely produced metal in the world today. In a high-tech world dominated by software and technological gadgets, this age-old metal is making a resurgence as advanced developing countries — China, India, and Brazil — barrel down a path toward rapid industrialization.

Getting the steely facts

Steel production today is dominated by China, which produces three times more steel than Japan, the second largest producer. The United States is still an important player in the steel industry, and other countries worth mentioning include Russia, Germany, and South Korea.

If you're interested in exploring additional statistical information relating to steel production and manufacturing, check out these resources: the World Steel Association (`www.worldsteel.org`), the International Steel Statistics Bureau (`www.issb.co.uk`), and the Association for Iron & Steel Technology (`www.aist.org`).

Book III

Commodities

Holding stock in steel companies

Currently, no underlying futures contract for steel exists. However, a number of exchanges have expressed interest in developing a steel futures contract, so keep an eye out for such a development. For now, the best way to get exposure to steel is by investing in companies that produce steel, specifically, globally integrated steel companies. The following are good investments that are not only the best-run companies but also show the greatest potential for future market dominance:

- ✔ **U.S. Steel (NYSE: X):** U.S. Steel (`www.ussteel.com`) is the seventh largest steel-producing company worldwide, involved in all aspects of the steel-making process from iron ore mining and processing to the marketing of finished products.

- ✔ **Nucor Corp. (NYSE: NUE):** Nucor (`www.nucor.com`) operates almost exclusively in the United States, offering exposure to the U.S. steel market. It's also one of the only companies to operate mini-mills domestically, which many people argue are more cost-efficient than the traditional blast furnaces.

- ✔ **Gerdau (NYSE: GGB):** Gerdau (`www.gerdau.com`) is a Brazilian, vertically integrated steel producer with operations across several countries. It has mills in Brazil, Argentina, Mexico, Colombia, and the United States.

- ✔ **ArcelorMittal (NYSE: MT):** In 2006, the two largest steel companies in the world merged. The resulting company, ArcelorMittal (`corporate.arcelormittal.com`), controls more than 10 percent of the world's steel market (in terms of output) and produces approximately 120 million metric tons of steel annually.

Including Aluminum in Your Investments

Aluminum, generally measured in *metric tons* (MT), is lightweight, resistant to corrosion, durable, and sturdy. It's the second most widely used metal in the world, right after steel (see the preceding section), and is used in a number of sectors. It's used in transportation (car bodies, axles, and, in some cases, engines, as well as large commercial aircraft), packaging (aluminum wrap and foil, beverage cans, and rivets), and construction (buildings, oil pipelines, and bridges). Aluminum is also used in electrical powerlines, machinery, and consumer goods. The underlying demand from rapidly industrializing nations such as China and India has resulted in upward price pressures on the metal.

To find out more about the aluminum industry, check out these organizations: the International Aluminum Institute (`www.world-aluminium.org`), the Aluminum Association (`www.aluminum.org`), and B2b alunet.com (`www.alunet.com`).

Considering aluminum companies

One way to invest in aluminum is to invest in companies that produce and manufacture aluminum products. Here are two that make the cut:

- ✔ **Alcoa (NYSE: AA):** The world leader in aluminum production, Alcoa (www.alcoa.com) is involved in all aspects of the aluminum industry and produces primary aluminum, fabricated aluminum, and alumina. The company has operations in more than 40 countries and services a large number of industries, from aerospace to construction. Alcoa is a good choice if you're looking to get the broadest exposure to the aluminum market.

- ✔ **Aluminum Corporation of China (NYSE: ACH):** ACH (www.chalco.com.cn/zl/web/chinalco_en.jsp) is primarily engaged in the production of aluminum in the Chinese market. This company, which trades on the New York Stock Exchange, provides a foothold in the aluminum Chinese market, which has the potential to be the biggest such market in the future. Besides this competitive advantage, ACH boasts profit margins that, during the writing of this book, were in excess of 20 percent.

Trading aluminum futures

You can invest in aluminum through the futures markets. Previously, two major contracts for aluminum were the London Metal Exchange (LME) and the COMEX division of the New York Mercantile Exchange (NYMEX). However, the COMEX contract was eliminated in 2009. As a result, the go-to contract is now the LME.

The LME aluminum contract is the most liquid in the world. It represents a size of 25,000 tons, and its price is quoted in U.S. dollars.

Seeing the Strengths of Copper

Copper, the third most widely used metal in the world, has applications in many sectors and is sought after because of its high electrical conductivity, resistance to corrosion, and malleability. Copper is used for a wide variety of purposes, from building and construction to electrical wiring, engineering, and transportation. Because of the current trends of industrialization and urbanization across the globe, demand for copper has been — and will remain — very strong. Demand for copper from China, India, and other advanced developing countries is increasing, which has put upward pressure on the price of copper.

To find out more about copper usage, consult the Copper Development Association (www.copper.org).

Investing in copper companies

You can invest in copper by getting involved in companies that specialize in mining and processing copper ore. An industry leader involved in all aspects of the copper supply chain is Freeport-McMoRan Copper & Gold Inc. (NYSE: FCX). Freeport-McMoRan (www.fcx.com) is one of the lowest-cost producers of copper in the world. It has copper mining and smelting operations across the globe, and it has a significant presence in Indonesia and Papua New Guinea. The company specializes in the production of highly concentrated copper ore, which it then sells on the open market. FCX also has some operations in gold and silver. The company acquired Phelps Dodge, one of the oldest mining companies in the United States, in 2007.

Buying copper futures contracts

A futures market is available for copper trading. Most of this market is used by large industrial producers and consumers of the metal, although you can also use it for investment purposes. You have two copper contracts to choose from:

- ✔ **LME Copper (LME: CAD):** The copper contract on the London Metal Exchange (LME) accounts for more than 90 percent of total copper futures activity. It represents a lot size of 25 tons.

- ✔ **CME/COMEX Copper (COMEX: HG):** This copper contract trades in the COMEX division of the CME Group (formerly the Chicago Mercantile Exchange). The contract, which trades during the current month and subsequent 23 calendar months, is traded both electronically and through the open outcry system. It represents 25,000 pounds of copper traded under the symbol HG.

Appreciating Palladium

Palladium, which belongs to the group of platinum metals, is a popular alternative to platinum in the automotive and jewelry industries. Its largest use is in the creation of pollution-reducing catalytic converters. Because of palladium's malleability, corrosion resistance, and price (it's less expensive than platinum: $741 per ounce versus $1,521 per ounce, according to 2013 figures), it's increasingly becoming the metal of choice for the manufacture of these devices. Palladium is also used in dentistry and electronics.

When pollution-reducing regulation was established in the United States in the 1970s, demand for palladium skyrocketed. All things equal, if emissions standards are further improved and require a new generation of catalytic converters, demand for palladium will increase again. Another reason to be bullish on palladium is that the number of automobiles, trucks, and other vehicles equipped with platinum- and palladium-made catalytic converters is increasing, particularly in China. So if you invest in palladium, make sure you keep an eye on automobile manufacturing patterns.

The palladium market is essentially dominated by two countries: Russia and South Africa. These two countries account for more than 85 percent of total palladium production. Any supply disruption from either country has a significant impact on palladium prices.

One of the best — albeit indirect — methods of getting exposure to the palladium markets is by investing in companies that mine the metal. A number of companies specialize in this activity; following are the two largest companies that trade publicly on U.S. exchanges:

- **Stillwater Mining Company (NYSE: SWC):** Stillwater Mining is the largest producer of palladium outside of South Africa and Russia. It produces approximately 500,000 ounces of palladium a year, primarily through North American mines.

- **North American Palladium (AMEX: PAL):** North American Palladium (www.napalladium.com), headquartered in Toronto, has a significant presence in the Canadian palladium ore mining business. It's the largest producer of palladium in Canada, with production in 2012 totaling almost 164,000 ounces.

Several international companies have significantly larger palladium mining activities than these two. Here are a couple of international palladium companies to consider. (Before investing, make sure you're aware of the many regulatory differences between U.S. and overseas markets.)

- **Anglo American Platinum Ltd. (South Africa):** Anglo American Platinum Ltd. (www.angloplatinum.com) is one of the largest producers of palladium in the world. With its operations located primarily in South Africa, Anglo American Platinum Ltd. is your gateway to South African palladium. Its shares are traded on the Johannesburg Stock Exchange (JSE), as well as the London Stock Exchange (LSE).

Book III

Commodities

✔ **Norilsk Nickel (Russia):** Norilsk Nickel (www.nornik.ru/en), the largest producer of palladium in the world, dominates the Russian palladium industry. While the company has large palladium mining activities, it's also a major player in copper and nickel ore mining. The company's shares are available through the Moscow Inter-bank Currency Exchange (MICEX).

For folks who are comfortable in the futures markets, the CME Group offers a futures contract that tracks palladium. This contract represents 100 troy ounces of palladium and trades both electronically and during the open outcry session. It trades under the symbol PA.

Keeping an Eye on Zinc

Zinc is the fourth most widely used metal, right behind iron/steel, aluminum, and copper. Zinc, which has unique abilities to resist corrosion and oxidation, is used for metal *galvanization,* the process of applying a metal coating to another metal to prevent rust and corrosion. Galvanization is by far the largest application of zinc (accounting for 47 percent of zinc usage), but zinc has other applications as well: brass and bronze coatings and zinc alloying, for example.

The best way to invest in zinc is by going through the futures markets. The London Metal Exchange (LME) offers a futures contract for zinc, which has been trading since the early 1900s and is the industry benchmark for zinc pricing. The contract trades in lots of 25 tons and is available for trading during the current month and the subsequent 27 months.

Noting the Merits of Nickel

Nickel is sought-after for its ductility, malleability, and resistance to corrosion. Although nickel has a number of important uses, the creation of stainless steel remains its primary application (accounting for 65 percent of its market consumption). Nickel is also used in non-ferrous alloys, ferrous alloys, and electroplating, among other things.

Australia has the largest reserves of nickel, and its proximity to the rapidly industrializing Asian center — China and India — is a strategic advantage. Another major player in the nickel markets is Russia; the Russian company Norilsk Nickel (covered in the earlier section on palladium) is the largest producer of nickel in the world. Nickel mining is a labor-intensive industry, but countries that have large reserves of this special metal are poised to do very well.

The London Metal Exchange (LME) offers a futures contract for nickel. The nickel futures contract on the LME provides you with the most direct access to the nickel market. It trades in lots of 6 tons, and its tick size is $5.00 per ton. It trades during the first month and in 27 subsequent months.

Putting Stock in Diversified Mining Companies

Trading metals outright — through the futures markets — can be tricky for the uninitiated trader. An alternative way of opening up your portfolio to metals is by investing in companies that mine metals and minerals. Following are the top diversified companies (that is, they're involved in *all* aspects of the metals production process: processing, transportation, distribution, and so on):

✔ **BHP Billiton:** One of the largest mining companies in the world, BHP Billiton (www.bhpbilliton.com), headquartered in Melbourne, Australia, has mining operations in more than 25 countries including Australia, Canada, the United States, South Africa, and Papua New Guinea. The company processes a large number of metals, including aluminum, copper, silver, and iron; it also has small oil and natural gas operations in Algeria and Pakistan. The company is listed on the New York Stock Exchange (NYSE) under the symbol BHP. In recent years, it has benefited handsomely from the increasing prices of commodities such as copper and aluminum.

✔ **Rio Tinto:** Rio Tinto (www.riotinto.com) boasts operations in Africa, Australia, Europe, the Pacific Rim, North America, and South America. The company is involved in the production of a number of commodities, including iron ore, copper, aluminum, and titanium. In addition, Rio Tinto has interests in diamonds, manufacturing almost 30 percent of global natural diamonds, processed primarily through its mining activities in Australia. Rio Tinto trades on the New York Stock Exchange (NYSE) under the ticker symbol RIO.

✔ **Anglo American:** Anglo American (www.angloamerican.com) has operations in all four corners of the globe and operates in more than 20 countries. It is involved in the production and distribution of a wide array of metals, minerals, and natural resources including gold, silver, and platinum as well as diamonds and paper packaging. (It owns 45 percent of De Beers, the diamond company.) The company is listed in the London Stock Exchange under the ticker symbol AAL. In addition, it has American Depository Receipts listed in the OTC Pink Sheets that trade under the symbol AAUKY.

Book III

Commodities

Chapter 5

Down on the Farm: Trading Agricultural Products

In This Chapter

▶ Investing in soft commodities: Coffee, cocoa, sugar, and orange juice

▶ Exploring ags: Corn, wheat, and soybeans

▶ Trading livestock: Cattle and lean hogs

Food is the most essential resource in human life. Investing in this sector can also help improve your bottom line. This chapter introduces the major sectors in this sub-asset class and shows you how to profit from tropical commodities like coffee and orange juice, grains such as corn and wheat, and livestock.

Profiting from the Softs: Coffee, Cocoa, Sugar, and Orange Juice

The commodities in this section — coffee, cocoa, sugar, and frozen concentrated orange juice — are known as *soft commodities.* Soft commodities are those commodities that are usually grown, as opposed to those that are mined, such as metals, or raised, such as livestock. The *softs,* as they are sometimes known, represent a significant portion of the commodities markets. They're indispensable and cyclical, just like energy and metals, but they're also unique because they're edible and seasonal. *Seasonality* is actually a major distinguishing characteristic of soft commodities because they can be grown only during specific times of the year and in specific geographical locations — usually in tropical areas (which is why these commodities are also known as *tropical commodities*). In this section, you find out that there's nothing soft about these soft commodities.

Feeling the buzz from coffee

Coffee is the second most widely traded commodity in terms of physical volume, behind only crude oil (see Chapter 3 of Book III). Like a number of other commodities, coffee production is dominated by a handful of countries. Brazil, Vietnam, and Indonesia are the largest producing countries, but other coffee producers include Colombia, India, Ethiopia, Mexico, Honduras, Guatemala, and Uganda.

Just like choosing the right flavor when buying your cup of coffee, knowing the different types of coffees available for investment is important. The world's coffee production is pretty much made up of two types of beans:

✔ The *Arabica bean* accounts for more than 60 percent of global coffee production, is the premium (and therefore most expensive) coffee bean, and serves as the benchmark for coffee prices all over the world.

✔ The *Robusta bean* is easier to grow than Arabica coffee and is less expensive.

You can invest in coffee production by buying coffee in the futures markets or by investing in companies that specialize in running gourmet coffee shops. To find out more about coffee markets, consult the International Coffee Organization (www.ico.org) and the National Coffee Association USA (www.ncausa.org).

The coffee futures contract: It could be your cup of tea

The coffee futures markets are used to determine the future price of coffee, to protect producers and purchasers of coffee from wild price swings, and to allow individual investors to profit from coffee price variations. The most liquid coffee futures contract is available on the Intercontinental Exchange (ICE; www.theice.com).

One of the oldest futures contracts in the market today is the CME Group's coffee futures contract (www.cmegroup.com). Here are its contract specs:

✔ **Contract ticker symbol:** KC

✔ **Contract size:** 37,500 pounds

✔ **Underlying commodity:** Pure Arabica coffee

✔ **Price fluctuation:** $0.0005/pound ($18.75 per contract)

✔ **Trading months:** March, May, July, September, December

Because of seasonality, cyclicality, and geopolitical factors, coffee can be a volatile commodity subject to extreme price swings. Make sure to research the coffee markets inside and out before investing. (See Book II for an introduction to futures.)

Investing in gourmet coffee shops

Coffee is serious business: The coffee craze has gripped the United States (the largest consumer of coffee in the world) and is spreading throughout Europe and newly developing countries like India and China. You can profit by investing in the companies that are capitalizing on the gourmet coffee-shop trend:

- ✔ **Starbucks Corp. (NASDAQ: SBUX):** With more than $10 billion in revenue, Starbucks (www.starbucks.com) dominates the entire coffee supply chain, from purchasing and roasting to selling and marketing.

- ✔ **Green Mountain Coffee Roasters, Inc. (NASDAQ: GMCR):** Green Mountain Coffee (www.greenmountaincoffee.com), headquartered in Vermont, operates in the distribution of specialized coffee products to a number of entities, such as convenience stores, specialty retailers, and restaurants.

Heating up your portfolio with cocoa

Book III

Commodities

Cocoa is a fermented seed from the cacao tree, which is usually grown in hot and rainy regions around the equator. The first cacao tree is said to have originated in South America, but today the cocoa trade is dominated by African countries. Lead cocoa-producing countries include Ivory Coast, Ghana, Indonesia, Nigeria, Cameroon, Brazil, and Ecuador.

For a more nuanced understanding of the cocoa market and the companies that control it, check out these resources: the World Cocoa Foundation (www.worldcocoafoundation.org), the International Cocoa Organization (www.icco.org), and the Alliance of Cocoa Producing Countries (www.copal-cpa.org).

The ICE offers a futures contract for cocoa — the most liquid one in the market:

- ✔ **Contract ticker symbol:** CC
- ✔ **Contract size:** 10 metric tons
- ✔ **Underlying commodity:** Generic cocoa beans
- ✔ **Price fluctuation:** $1 per ton ($10 per contract)
- ✔ **Trading months:** March, May, July, September, December

Like coffee, the cocoa market is subject to seasonal and cyclical factors that have a large impact on price movements, which can be pretty volatile.

Being sweet on sugar

Although sugar production began more than 9,000 years ago in southeastern Asia, today, Latin American countries dominate the sugar trade. Brazil is the largest sugar producer in the world; the other nine in the top ten include the E.U., India, China, Thailand, the U.S., South Africa, Mexico, Australia, and Russia.

If you're interested in investing in sugar, the ICE offers two futures contracts: Sugar #11 (world production) and Sugar #16 (U.S. production). Here are the contract specs for these two sugar contracts.

Contract Spec	Sugar #11	Sugar #16
Ticker symbol	SB	SF
Contract size	112,000 pounds	112,000 pounds
Underlying commodity	Global sugar	Domestic (U.S.) sugar
Price fluctuation	$0.01/pound ($11.20 per contract)	$0.01/pound ($11.20 per contract)
Trading months	March, May, July, October	January, March, May, July, September, November

Historically, Sugar #16 tends to be more expensive than Sugar #11. However, Sugar #11 accounts for most of the volume in the ICE sugar market.

Squeezing healthy profits from orange juice

Orange juice is one of the only actively traded contracts in the futures markets that's based on a tropical fruit. Oranges are widely grown in the western hemisphere; Brazil is by far the largest producer of oranges, although the United States — primarily Florida — is also a major player. Other major producers of oranges include India, Mexico, and China.

Because oranges are perishable, the futures contract tracks *frozen concentrated orange juice* (FCOJ), which is suitable for storage and fits one of the criteria for inclusion in the futures arena: that the underlying commodity be deliverable. This contract is available for trade on the ICE and tracks Florida/Brazil/Costa Rica/Mexico oranges (FCOJ-A). Here are the contract specs:

- ✓ **Contract ticker symbol:** OJ
- ✓ **Contract size:** 15,000 pounds
- ✓ **Underlying commodity:** FCOJ from Brazil, Florida, Costa Rica, Mexico
- ✓ **Price fluctuation:** $0.0005/pound ($7.50 per contract)
- ✓ **Trading months:** January, March, May, July, September, November

The production of oranges is very sensitive to weather. Make sure to take into consideration weather and seasonality when investing in FCOJ futures.

Trading Ags: Corn, Wheat, and Soybeans

The major agricultural commodities that trade in the futures markets, sometimes simply known as *ags,* are very labor intensive and are subject to volatility because of underlying market fundamentals. However, they also present solid investment opportunities.

For additional information on agricultural commodities in general, check out the following resources: the National Grain and Feed Association (www.ngfa.org), the U.S. Department of Agriculture (USDA) (www.usda.gov), the USDA National Agricultural Library (www.nal.usda.gov), and the USDA National Agricultural Statistics Service (www.nass.usda.gov).

Fields of dreams: Corn

Corn is definitely big business, valued at over $20 billion a year by the U.S. Department of Agriculture. In 2012, world corn production stood at almost 860 million metric tons. Historically, the United States has dominated the corn markets, and it still does due to abundant land and helpful governmental subsidies. China is also a major player and exhibits a lot of potential for being a market leader in the coming years. Other notable producers include Brazil, Mexico, Argentina, and France.

The most direct way of investing in corn is by going through the futures markets. Both high-grade number 2 and number 3 yellow corn are traded in the futures markets. In addition, corn futures contracts are usually measured in

Book III

Commodities

bushels; large-scale corn production and consumption is generally measured in metric tons. A corn contract exists, courtesy of the Chicago Mercantile Exchange (CME), to help farmers, consumers, and investors manage and profit from the underlying market opportunities:

- ✔ **Contract ticker symbol:** C
- ✔ **Electronic ticker:** ZC
- ✔ **Contract size:** 5,000 bushels
- ✔ **Underlying commodity:** High-grade No. 2, No. 1 yellow corn at a premium, or No. 3 yellow corn at a discount
- ✔ **Price fluctuation:** $0.0025/bushel ($12.50 per contract)
- ✔ **Trading months:** March, May, July, September, December

Like other agricultural commodities, corn is subject to seasonal and cyclical factors that have a direct, and often powerful, effect on prices. Prices for corn can go through roller-coaster rides, with wild swings in short periods of time. For more information on the corn markets, check out the following sources: the National Corn Growers Association (www.ncga.com), the Corn Refiners Association (www.corn.org), and the USDA Economic Research Service (www.ers.usda.gov/briefing/corn).

The bread basket: Wheat

Wheat is the second most widely produced agricultural commodity in the world (on a per volume basis), right behind corn and ahead of rice. World wheat production was more than 697 million metric tons in 2011–2012, according to the USDA.

The major wheat producers are a surprisingly eclectic group. The advanced developing countries of China and India are the two largest producers, while industrial countries like Russia, the U.S., France, Canada, and Germany also boast significant wheat production capabilities. Pakistan, Australia, and Ukraine round out the top ten producers.

Wheat is measured in bushels for investment and accounting purposes. Each bushel contains approximately 60 pounds of wheat. As with most other agricultural commodities, metric tons are used to quantify total production and consumption figures on a national and international basis.

The most direct way of accessing the wheat markets, short of owning a wheat farm, is by trading the wheat futures contract. The CME offers a futures contract for those interested in capturing profits from wheat price movements — whether for hedging or speculative purposes. Here are the specs for the CME futures contract:

- ✔ **Contract ticker symbol:** W
- ✔ **Electronic ticker:** ZW
- ✔ **Contract size:** 5,000 bushels
- ✔ **Underlying commodity:** Premium wheat
- ✔ **Price fluctuation:** $0.0025/bushel ($12.50 per contract)
- ✔ **Trading months:** March, May, July, September, December

Wheat production, like that of corn and soybeans, is a seasonal enterprise subject to various output disruptions that can have a magnified effect on futures prices. To find out more about the wheat market, check out these sources: the Wheat Foods Council (www.wheatfoods.org), the National Association of Wheat Growers (www.wheatworld.org), and U.S. Wheat Associates (www.uswheat.org).

Masters of versatility: Soybeans

Book III

Commodities

Soybeans are used for everything from poultry feedstock to the creation of vegetable oil. You can trade soybeans themselves, soybean oil, and soybean meal.

To get more background information on the soybean industry, check out these resources: the American Soybean Association (www.soygrowers.org), the Iowa Soybean Association (www.iasoybeans.com), the annual *Soy Stats* reference guide (www.soystats.com), and the Soy Protein Council (www.spcouncil.org).

Soybeans

Although most soybeans are used for the extraction of soybean oil (used as vegetable oil for culinary purposes) and soybean meal (used primarily as an agricultural feedstock), whole soybeans are also a tradable commodity.

The United States dominates the soybean market, accounting for more than 50 percent of total global production. Brazil is a distant second, with about 20 percent of the market. The crop in the United States begins in September, and the production of soybeans is cyclical.

The most direct way for you to trade soybeans is through the Chicago Board of Trade (CBOT) soybean futures contract:

- ✔ **Contract ticker symbol:** S
- ✔ **Electronic ticker:** ZS
- ✔ **Contract size:** 5,000 bushels
- ✔ **Underlying commodity:** No. 2 yellow at contract price, No. 1 yellow at a premium, and No. 3 yellow at a discount
- ✔ **Price fluctuation:** $0.0025/bushel ($12.50 per contract)
- ✔ **Trading months:** January, March, May, July, August, September, November

Soybean oil

Soybean oil, more commonly known as vegetable oil, is an extract of soybeans. Soybean oil is the most widely used culinary oil in the United States and around the world. Soybean oil is also becoming an increasingly popular additive in alternative energy sources technology, such as biodiesel. An increasing number of cars in the United States and abroad, for example, are being outfitted with engines that allow them to convert from regular diesel to soybean oil during operation.

Demand for soybean oil has increased in recent years as demand for these cleaner-burning fuels increases and as automotive technology is more able to accommodate the usage of such biodiesels.

If you want to trade soybean oil, you need to go through the CME, which offers the standard soybean oil contract. Here is the contract information:

- ✔ **Contract ticker symbol:** BO
- ✔ **Electronic ticker:** ZL
- ✔ **Contract size:** 60,000 pounds
- ✔ **Underlying commodity:** Premium crude soybean oil
- ✔ **Price fluctuation:** $0.0001/pound ($6.00 per contract)
- ✔ **Trading months:** January, March, May, July, August, September, October, December

For more info, take a look at the National Oilseed Processors Association, an industry group (www.nopa.org).

Soybean meal

Soybean meal is another extract of soybeans. Soybean meal is a high-protein, high-energy-content food used primarily as a feedstock for cattle, hogs, and poultry.

To invest in soybean meal, you can trade the soybean meal futures contract on the CME. Here is the information to help you get started trading this contract:

- ✔ **Contract ticker symbol:** SM
- ✔ **Electronic ticker:** ZM
- ✔ **Contract size:** 100 tons
- ✔ **Underlying commodity:** 48 percent protein soybean meal
- ✔ **Price fluctuation:** $0.10/ton ($10.00 per contract)
- ✔ **Trading months:** January, March, May, July, August, September, October, December

You can get more information regarding soybean meal from the Soybean Meal INFOcenter (www.soymeal.org).

Making Money Trading Livestock

Like the tropical and grain commodities, livestock is a unique category in the agricultural commodities sub-asset class. It's not a widely followed area of the commodities markets — unlike crude oil, for example, you're not likely to see feeder cattle prices quoted on the nightly news — but this doesn't mean you should ignore this area of the markets. That said, raising livestock is a time-consuming and labor-intensive undertaking, and the markets are susceptible and sensitive to minor disruption. This section covers the markets for cattle (both live cattle and feeder cattle) and lean hogs.

Even by agricultural futures standards, livestock futures are notoriously volatile and should be traded only by traders with a high level of risk tolerance. Trading agricultural futures requires an understanding of the cyclicality and seasonality of the underlying commodity as well as large capital reserves to help offset any margin calls that may arise from a trade gone bad. If your risk tolerance isn't elevated or you aren't comfortable in the futures arena, don't trade these contracts because you could be setting yourself up for disastrous losses. Venture into this area of the market only if you have an iron-clad grasp on the concepts behind futures trading — and a high tolerance for risk.

One resource that provides fundamental data relating to the consumption and production patterns of livestock and other commodities is the *CRB Commodity Yearbook,* compiled by the Commodity Research Bureau (www.crbtrader. com). This book includes a large number of data on some of the most important commodities, including the identification of seasonal and cyclical patterns affecting the markets.

Staking a claim on cattle

Throughout the ages, cows have been valued not only for their dietary value, but also their monetary worth. They're low-maintenance animals with a high products output: They eat almost nothing but grass, yet they're used to produce milk, provide meat, and, in some cases, create leather goods. This input-to-output ratio means that cows occupy a special place in the agricultural complex.

Two futures contracts exist for the cattle trader and investor: the live cattle and the feeder cattle contracts, which both trade on the Chicago Mercantile Exchange (CME).

Live cattle

The live cattle futures contract is widely traded by various market players, including cattle producers, packers, consumers, and independent traders. One reason for the popularity of the live cattle contract is that it allows all interested parties to hedge their market positions in order to reduce the volatility and uncertainty associated with livestock production in general and live cattle growing in particular. Here are the specs of this futures contract:

- ✔ **Contract ticker symbol:** LC

- ✔ **Electronic ticker:** LE

- ✔ **Contract size:** 40,000 pounds

- ✔ **Underlying commodity:** Live cattle

- ✔ **Price fluctuation:** $0.00025/pound ($10.00 per contract)

- ✔ **Trading months:** February, April, June, August, October, December

If you trade this contract, keep the following market risks in mind: seasonality, fluctuating prices of feedstock, transportation costs, changing consumer demand, and the threat of diseases (such as mad cow disease).

Feeder cattle

The feeder cattle contract is for calves that weigh in at the 650- to 849-pound range, which are sent to the feedlots to get fed, fattened, and then slaughtered.

Because the CME feeder cattle futures contract is settled on a cash basis, the CME calculates an index for feeder cattle cash prices based on a seven-day average. This index, known in the industry as the *CME Feeder Cattle Index,* is an average of feeder cattle prices from the largest feeder cattle producing states in the United States, as compiled by the U.S. Department of Agriculture (USDA). You can get information on the CME Feeder Cattle Index through the CME website at `www.cmegroup.com/trading/agricultural/livestock/feeder-cattle.html`.

To get livestock statistical information, you should check out the U.S. Department of Agriculture's statistical division. Its website is `www.marketnews.usda.gov/portal/lg`.

Here are the specs of this futures contract:

- ✔ **Contract ticker symbol:** FC
- ✔ **Electronic ticker:** GF
- ✔ **Contract size:** 50,000 pounds
- ✔ **Underlying commodity:** Feeder cattle
- ✔ **Price fluctuation:** $0.00025/pound ($12.50 per contract)
- ✔ **Trading months:** January, March, April, May, August, September, October, November

Two important traits characterize the feeder cattle contract. Like many meat commodities, it's fairly volatile. It's also a thinly traded contract — in other words, it doesn't have as much liquidity as some of the other CME products.

Seeking fat profits on lean hogs

The lean hog futures contract (which is a contract for the hog's carcass) trades on the CME and is used primarily by producers of lean hogs — both domestic and international — and pork importers/exporters. Here are the contract specs for lean hogs:

- ✔ **Contract ticker symbol:** LH
- ✔ **Electronic ticker:** HE
- ✔ **Contract size:** 40,000 pounds
- ✔ **Underlying commodity:** Lean hogs
- ✔ **Price fluctuation:** $0.00025 per hundred pounds ($10.00 per contract)
- ✔ **Trading months:** February, April, May, June, July, August, October, December

Book III

Commodities

Perhaps no other commodity, agricultural or otherwise, exhibits the same level of volatility as the lean hogs futures contract. One reason for the low liquidity is that, compared to other products, this contract is primarily used by commercial entities seeking to hedge against price risk. Commodities that are actively traded by both individual speculators and commercial entities are far more liquid and thus less volatile. If you trade this contract, keep in mind that you're up against some very experienced and large players in this market.

Book IV
Foreign Currency Trading

Five Habits of Successful Currency Traders

✔ **Trade with a plan:** No currency trader lasts very long without a well-conceived game plan for each trade. Successful currency traders have a specific plan of attack for each position, including position size, entry point, stop-loss exit, and take-profit exit.

✔ **Anticipate event outcomes:** Successful forex traders look ahead to future events and consider how much the market has (or hasn't) priced in an expected outcome. They also consider the likely reactions if the event matches, or fails to match, those expectations. Then they construct trading strategies based on those alternative outcomes.

✔ **Stay flexible:** Rather than wait for price action to take them out of their trade, successful currency traders adapt to incoming news and information and quickly abandon an open position if events run counter to it. They remain alert to fresh opportunities that may develop in the market, and they keep sufficient margin available so that they're prepared to react when things change.

✔ **Focus on a few pairs:** Many successful forex traders focus on only one or two currency pairs for most of their trading. Doing so enables them to get a better feel for those markets in terms of price levels and price behavior. It also narrows the amount of information and data they need to monitor.

✔ **Protect profits:** Successful traders take profit regularly, whether it's a partial take-profit (reducing the size of a winning position) or squaring up completely and stepping back after a profitable market movement. Above all, when a trade is in the money, successful traders focus on keeping what they've made; they don't give it up for the chance to make a little more.

web extras

In the foreign currency market, trading mistakes can be costly or, in worst-case scenarios, devastating. To discover how to avoid such mistakes, go to www.dummies.com/extras/highpoweredinvestingaio.

Chapter 1

Your Forex Need-to-Know Guide

*T*he foreign exchange *(forex or FX)* market has exploded onto the scene and is the hot new financial market. It has been around for years, but advances in electronic trading have made it available to individual traders on a scale unimaginable just a few years ago. Because it's relatively new, a lot of people are still in the dark when it comes to exactly what the currency market is: how it's organized, who's trading it, and what a trading day looks like when the market never closes. This chapter sheds a bit of light on these topics.

Getting a Quick Overview of Currency Trading

Currency trading is speculation, pure and simple. The securities you're speculating with are the currencies of various countries. For that reason, currency trading is about both the dynamics of market speculation, or trading, and the factors that affect the value of currencies.

Speculating, or active trading, is about taking calculated financial risks in an attempt to realize a profitable return, usually over a very short time horizon. It's not gambling (playing with money even when you know the odds are stacked against you) or investing (minimizing risk and maximizing return, usually over a long time period).

Often called the *forex market* (or FX market), the foreign exchange market is the largest and most liquid of all international financial markets. It's the crossroads for international capital, the intersection through which global commercial and investment flows have to move. The following sections describe the market, its liquidity, and its key players.

Entering the interbank market

When people talk about the "currency market," they're referring to the *interbank market,* whether they realize it or not. The interbank market is where the really big money changes hands. Minimum trade sizes are one million of the base currency, such as €1 million of EUR/USD (euro/U.S. dollar) or $1 million of USD/JPY (U.S. dollar/Japanese yen). (EUR/USD and USD/JPY are examples of currency pairs, the topic of discussion in the later section "Checking Out Currency Pairs and Prices.") Much larger trades — between $10 million and $100 million, for example — are routine and can go through the market in a matter of seconds. For the individual trading FX online, the prices you see on your trading platform are based on the prices being traded in the interbank market.

As the prefix suggests, the *interbank* market is "between banks," with each trade representing an agreement between the banks to exchange the agreed amounts of currency at the specified rate on a fixed date. The interbank market is alternately referred to as the *cash market* or the *spot market* to differentiate it from the currency futures market, which is the only other organized market for currency trading. (Flip to Book II for an introduction to futures.)

The sheer size of the interbank market is what helps make it such a great trading market, because investors of every size are able to act in the market, usually without significantly affecting prices. Daily trading volumes are enormous by any measure, dwarfing global stock trading volumes many times over. In 2010, for example, daily FX trading volumes reached nearly $4 trillion. To give you some perspective on that size, it's about 10 to 15 times the size of daily trading volume on all the world's stock markets combined.

The interbank market developed without any significant governmental oversight and remains largely unregulated. In most cases, no regulatory authority apart from local or national banking regulations exists for spot currency trading. Interbank trading essentially evolved based on credit lines between international banks and trading conventions that developed over time.

Firms such as FOREX.com, Saxo Bank, and Oanda have made the forex market accessible to individual traders and investors. You can now trade the same forex market as the big banks and hedge funds.

Trading in the interbank market

The interbank market is an over-the-counter (OTC) market, which means that each trade is an agreement between the two counterparties to the trade. The trades involve no exchanges or guarantors, just each bank's balance sheet and the promise to make payment.

The bulk of spot trading in the interbank market is transacted through electronic matching services, such as EBS and Reuters Dealing. Electronic matching services allow traders to enter their bids and offers into the market, *hit bids* (sell at the market), and *pay offers* (buy at the market). Price spreads vary by currency pair and change throughout the day depending on market interest and volatility. (You get the scoop on currency pairs later in this chapter.)

In recent years, the major international FX trading banks have also developed electronic trading platforms that function via the Internet, enabling their customers to bypass banks' trading desks and deal directly in the market, potentially accessing more advantageous prices.

Looking at liquidity

Liquidity, liquidity considerations, and market interest are among the most important factors affecting how prices move, or *price action.* From a trading perspective, liquidity is a critical consideration because it determines how quickly prices move between trades and over time. A highly liquid market like forex can see large trading volumes transacted with relatively minor price changes. An illiquid, or *thin,* market will tend to see prices move more rapidly on relatively lower trading volumes. A market that trades only during certain hours (futures contracts, for example) also represents a less liquid, thinner market.

Although the forex market offers exceptionally high liquidity on an overall basis, liquidity levels vary throughout the trading day and across various currency pairs. As an individual trader, factor when and how prices are likely to move in the timing of your trades.

Meeting the key players: Hedgers, hedge funds, big-time investors, and you

Participants in the forex market generally fall into one of two categories:

- ✔ **Financial transactors:** Like hedgers and financial investors, financial transactors are active in the forex market as part of their overall business but not necessarily for currency reasons. An electric utility operator in the United States may need EUR to buy a German-made turbine for a new generator, for example. Financial transactors are important to the forex market for several reasons:

- Their transactions can be extremely sizeable, typically hundreds of million or billions.

- Their deals are frequently one-time events.

- They're generally not price sensitive or profit maximizing.

✔ **Speculators:** These folks are in forex trading purely for the money. The lion's share of forex market turnover — nearly 90 percent, according to BIS data — comes from speculators.

The following list looks at all these players:

✔ **Hedgers:** Hedgers in the forex market look to insure themselves against adverse price movements in specific currency rates.

✔ **Financial investors:** More often than not, financial investors look at currencies as an afterthought because they're more focused on the ultimate investment target, be it Japanese equities, German government bonds, or French real estate.

When a company seeks to buy a foreign business that uses a different currency, the trade may have a substantial foreign exchange implication.

✔ **Hedge funds:** Hedge funds (covered in detail in Book V) are a type of *leveraged fund* that borrow money for speculation based on real assets under management. For instance, hedge funds with $100 million under management can *leverage* those assets (through margin agreements with their trading counterparties) to give them trading limits of anywhere from $500 million to $2 billion. Hedge funds are subject to the same type of margin requirements as you are, just with a whole lot more zeroes involved.

The other main type of leveraged fund is known as a *commodity trading advisor* (CTA). A CTA is principally active in the futures markets. But because the forex market operates around the clock, CTAs frequently trade spot FX as well.

In the forex market, leveraged funds can hold positions anywhere from a few hours to days or weeks. When you hear that leveraged names are buying or selling, it's an indication of short-term speculative interest that can provide clues as to where prices are going in the near future.

✔ **Day-traders:** This is where you fit into the big picture of the forex market. Most of that speculation in the forex market is short-term in nature: minute-to-minute or hour-to-hour, but rarely longer than a day or two. From the interbank traders who are scalping EUR/USD (high-frequency, in-and-out trading for few pips — the smallest price increments in the currency) to the online trader looking for the next move in USD/JPY, short-term day-traders are the backbone of the market.

Checking Out Currency Pairs and Prices

Forex markets refer to trading currencies by *pairs,* with names that combine the two different currencies being exchanged for one another. Additionally, forex markets have given most currency pairs nicknames or abbreviations, which reference the pair and not necessarily the individual currencies involved. This section gives you a brief overview of the currency pairs; go to Chapter 2 of Book IV for in-depth information. You also find out how to read currency prices here.

 Activity in the forex market frequently functions on a regional "currency bloc" basis. The bulk of trading takes place between the USD bloc (U.S. dollars), the JPY bloc (Japanese yen), and the EUR bloc (euros), which represent the three largest global economic regions. Trading in the currencies of smaller, less-developed economies, such as Thailand or Chile, is often referred to as *emerging-market* or *exotic* currency trading and may involve currencies with local restrictions on convertibility or limited liquidity, both of which limit access and inhibit the development of an active market. (Check out Book VI for details on emerging markets.)

Introducing currency pairs

There are anywhere from 30 to more than 100 different currency pairs — pitting the U.S. dollar (USD) against other countries' currencies or pitting two non-USD currencies against each other — depending on which forex brokerage you deal with.

Major and minor currency pairs

The bulk of spot currency trading, about 75 percent by volume, takes place in the so-called major and minor currencies. The major and minor currency pairs all involve the U.S. dollar on one side of the deal. Table 1-1 lists the most frequently traded currency pairs, what they're called in conventional terms, and what nicknames the market has given them. *Note:* The designations of the major currencies are expressed using International Standardization Organization (ISO) codes for each currency.

Book IV

Foreign Currency Trading

Table 1-1	The Major and Minor U.S. Dollar Currency Pairs		
ISO Currency Pair	*Countries*	*Long Name*	*Nickname*
EUR/USD	Eurozone*/United States	Euro-dollar	N/A
USD/JPY	United States/Japan	Dollar-yen	N/A
GBP/USD	United Kingdom/United States	Sterling-dollar	Sterling or Cable
USD/CHF	United States/Switzerland	Dollar-Swiss	Swissy
USD/CAD	United States/Canada	Dollar-Canada	Loonie
AUD/USD	Australia/United States	Australian-dollar	Aussie or Oz
NZD/USD	New Zealand/United States	New Zealand-dollar	Kiwi

The Eurozone is made up of all the countries in the European Union that have adopted the euro as their currency. As of this printing, the Eurozone countries are Austria, Belgium, Cyprus, Estonia, Finland, France, Germany, Greece, Ireland, Italy, Luxembourg, Malta, the Netherlands, Portugal, Slovakia, Slovenia, and Spain.

Cross-currency pairs

A cross-currency pair (*cross* or *crosses* for short) is any currency pair that does not include the U.S. dollar. The most actively traded crosses focus on the three major non-USD currencies (EUR, JPY, and GBP) and are referred to as *euro crosses, yen crosses,* and *sterling crosses.* The remaining currencies (CHF, AUD, CAD, and NZD) are also traded in cross pairs. Tables 1-2, 1-3, and 1-4 highlight the key cross pairs in the euro, yen, and sterling groupings, respectively, along with their market names. (Nicknames never quite caught on for the crosses.) Table 1-5 lists other cross-currency pairs.

Table 1-2	Euro Crosses	
ISO Currency Pair	*Countries*	*Market Name*
EUR/CHF	Eurozone/Switzerland	Euro-Swiss
EUR/GBP	Eurozone/United Kingdom	Euro-sterling
EUR/CAD	Eurozone/Canada	Euro-Canada
EUR/AUD	Eurozone/Australia	Euro-Aussie
EUR/NZD	Eurozone/New Zealand	Euro-Kiwi

Table 1-3	Yen Crosses	
ISO Currency Pair	*Countries*	*Market Name*
EUR/JPY	Eurozone/Japan	Euro-yen
GBP/JPY	United Kingdom/Japan	Sterling-yen
CHF/JPY	Switzerland/Japan	Swiss-yen
AUD/JPY	Australia/Japan	Aussie-yen
NZD/JPY	New Zealand/Japan	Kiwi-yen
CAD/JPY	Canada/Japan	Canada-yen

Table 1-4	Sterling Crosses	
ISO Currency Pair	*Countries*	*Market Name*
GBP/CHF	United Kingdom/Switzerland	Sterling-Swiss
GBP/CAD	United Kingdom/Canada	Sterling-Canadian
GBP/AUD	United Kingdom/Australia	Sterling-Aussie
GBP/NZD	United Kingdom/New Zealand	Sterling-Kiwi

Table 1-5	Other Crosses	
ISO Currency Pair	*Countries*	*Market Name*
AUD/CHF	Australia/Switzerland	Aussie-Swiss
AUD/CAD	Australia/Canada	Aussie-Canada
AUD/NZD	Australia/New Zealand	Aussie-Kiwi
CAD/CHF	Canada/Switzerland	Canada-Swiss

Cross trades can be especially effective when major cross-border mergers and acquisitions (M&A) are announced. If a UK conglomerate is buying a Canadian utility company, the UK company is going to need to sell GBP and buy CAD to fund the purchase. The key to trading on M&A activity is to note the cash portion of the deal. If the deal is all stock, the companies involved won't need to exchange currencies, so you shouldn't expect an impact in the forex market.

Base and counter currencies

According to market quoting convention, the first currency in the pair is known as the *base currency*. The base currency is what you're buying or selling when you buy or sell the pair. It's also the *notional,* or *face,* amount of the trade. So if you buy 100,000 EUR/JPY, you've just bought 100,000 euros and sold the equivalent amount in Japanese yen. If you sell 100,000 GBP/CHF, you've just sold 100,000 British pounds and bought the equivalent amount of Swiss francs.

The second currency in the pair is called the *counter currency,* or the *secondary currency.* The counter currency is the denomination of the price fluctuations and, ultimately, what your profit and losses will be denominated in. If you buy GBP/JPY, it goes up, and you take a profit, your gains are not in pounds but in yen.

Reading currency prices

Online brokerages display currency prices. Although different online forex brokers use different formats to display prices on their trading platforms, the info is the same.

Two prices appear for each currency pair. The price on the left-hand side is called the *bid,* and the price on the right-hand side is called the *offer* (some call this the *ask*). Some brokers display the prices above and below each other, with the bid on the bottom and the offer on top. The easy way to tell the difference is that the bid price will always be lower than the offer price.

The price quotation of each bid and offer you see has two components:

- ✔ **The big figure:** The first three digits of the overall currency rate. It's usually shown in a smaller font size or even in shadow.

- ✔ **The dealing price:** The last two digits of the overall currency price. It's brightly displayed in a larger font size (see Figure 1-1).

Figure 1-1: A dealing box from the FOREX. com trading platform for EUR/USD.

FOREX.com

A spread is the difference between the bid price and the offer price. Think of it as the commission that the online brokers charge for executing your trades. Spreads vary from broker to broker and by currency pairs at each broker as well. Generally, the more liquid the currency pair, the narrower the spread; the less liquid the currency pair, the wider the spread. This is especially the case for some of the less-traded crosses.

Around the World in a Trading Day

The forex market is open and active 24 hours a day from the start of business hours on Monday morning in the Asia-Pacific time zone straight through to the Friday close of business hours in New York. At any given moment, depending on the time zone, dozens of global financial centers — such as Sydney, Tokyo, and London — are open, and currency trading desks in those financial centers are active in the market. In addition to the major global financial centers, many financial institutions operate 24-hour-a-day currency trading desks, providing an ever-present source of market interest. The following sections explain how the markets open and what this process means to you as a currency trader.

Opening the trading week

No designated time officially starts the trading day or week, but for all intents and purposes, the market action kicks off when Wellington, New Zealand, the first financial center west of the international dateline, opens on Monday morning local time. Depending on whether daylight saving time is in effect in your own time zone, it roughly corresponds to early Sunday afternoon in North America, Sunday evening in Europe, and very early Monday morning in Asia. The Sunday open represents the starting point where currency markets resume trading after the Friday close of trading in North America (5 p.m. eastern time [ET]). Here's what you need to know:

✔ This is the first chance for the forex market to react to news and events that may have happened over the weekend. Prices may have closed New York trading at one level, but depending on the circumstances, they may start trading at different levels at the Sunday open. The risk that currency prices open at different levels on Sunday versus their close on Friday is referred to as the *weekend gap risk* or the *Sunday open gap risk*. A *gap* is a change in price levels where no prices are tradable in between.

As a strategic trading consideration, you need to be aware of the weekend gap risk and know what events are scheduled over the weekend. Of typical scheduled weekend events, the most common are quarterly Group of Seven (G7) or G20 meetings and national elections or referenda. Just be sure you're aware of any major events that are scheduled. Unscheduled, surprising events may also occur over a weekend: rumors of a major bank in trouble, protest riots, and natural disasters, to name just a few.

REMEMBER

Book IV

Foreign Currency Trading

✔ The opening price spreads in the interbank market are much wider than normal, because only Wellington and 24-hour trading desks are active at the time. Opening price spreads of 10 to 30 points in the major currency pairs (described earlier in this chapter) are not uncommon in the initial hours of trading. When banks in Sydney and other early Asian centers enter the market over the next few hours, liquidity begins to improve and price spreads begin to narrow to more normal levels.

Because of the wider price spreads in the initial hours of the Sunday open, most online trading platforms do not begin trading until 5 p.m. ET on Sundays, when sufficient liquidity enables the platforms to offer their normal price quotes. Make sure you're aware of your broker's trading policies with regard to the Sunday open, especially in terms of order executions.

Trading in the Asia-Pacific session

The principal financial trading centers in the Asia-Pacific session are Wellington, New Zealand; Sydney, Australia; Tokyo, Japan; Hong Kong; and Singapore. In terms of the most actively traded currency pairs, that means news and data reports from New Zealand, Australia, and Japan are going to be hitting the market during this session.

✔ New Zealand and Australian data reports are typically released in the early morning local time, which corresponds to early evening hours the day before in North America.

✔ Japanese data is typically released just before 9 a.m. Tokyo time, which equates to roughly 7 or 8 p.m. ET the day before. Some Japanese data reports and events also take place in the Tokyo afternoon, which equates to roughly midnight to 4 a.m. ET.

The overall trading direction for the NZD, AUD, and JPY can be set for the entire session depending on what news and data reports are released and what they indicate. In addition, news from China, such as interest rate changes and official comments or currency policy adjustments, may also be released.

With the rapid growth of China over the last decade, Chinese news and data have become critical drivers of global markets. China also holds more than $2.6 trillion in currency reserves, with more than half allocated to U.S. Treasury debt, so any news of shifts in China's currency reserve management policies can trigger strong shifts in major currencies, especially the USD.

Trading in the European/London session

About midway through the Asian trading day, European financial centers begin to open up, and the market gets into full swing. The European session overlaps with half of the Asian trading day and half of the North American trading session, which means that market interest and liquidity is at its absolute peak during this session.

News and data events from the Eurozone, Switzerland, and the United Kingdom are typically released in the early-morning hours of the European session. As a result, some of the biggest moves and most active trading take place in the European currencies (EUR, GBP, and CHF) and the euro cross-currency pairs (EUR/CHF and EUR/GBP).

Because of the larger size of the European/London session volume, market moves that started earlier in Asia can become much more pronounced after Europe/London gets started.

Asian trading centers begin to wind down in the late-morning hours of the European session, and North American financial centers come in a few hours later, around 7 a.m. ET.

Trading in the North American session

Because of the overlap between North American and European trading sessions, the trading volumes are much more significant. Some of the biggest and most meaningful directional price movements take place during this crossover period.

The North American morning is when key U.S. economic data is released and the forex market makes many of its most significant decisions on the value of the U.S. dollar. Most U.S. data reports are released at 8:30 a.m. ET, with others coming out between 9 and 10 a.m. ET. Canadian data reports are also released in the morning, usually between 7 and 9 a.m. ET. There are also a few U.S. economic reports that variously come out at noon or 2 p.m. ET, livening up the New York afternoon market.

London and the European financial centers begin to wind down their daily trading operations around noon eastern time each day. The London close (or *European close,* as it's known) can frequently generate volatile flurries of activity.

Book IV

Foreign Currency Trading

On most days, market liquidity and interest fall off significantly in the New York afternoon, which can make for challenging trading conditions. On quiet days, the generally lower market interest typically leads to stagnating price action. On more active days, when prices may have moved more significantly, the lower liquidity can spark additional outsized price movements, as fewer traders scramble to get similarly fewer prices and liquidity.

Lower liquidity and the potential for increased volatility are most evident in the least-liquid major-currency pairs, especially USD/CHF and GBP/USD and their crosses, like EUR/GBP or EUR/CHF.

North American trading interest and volume generally continue to wind down as the trading day moves toward the 5 p.m. New York close, which also sees the change in value dates take place. (See the later section "Understanding rollovers" for more on rollovers and value dates.) But during the late New York afternoon, Wellington and Sydney have reopened and a new trading day has begun.

The Mechanics of Currency Trading

The biggest mental hurdle facing newcomers to currencies, especially traders familiar with other markets, is the idea that each currency trade consists of a simultaneous purchase and sale. The purchase of one currency involves the simultaneous sale of another currency. This is the *exchange* in *foreign exchange.* To put it another way, if you're looking for the dollar to go higher, the question is "Higher against what?" The answer has to be another currency. In relative terms, if the dollar goes up against another currency, it also means that the other currency has gone down against the dollar. The following sections outline the other conventions fundamental to currency trading.

Grasping the long, short, and square of it

Forex markets use the same terms to express market positioning as most other financial markets. But because currency trading involves simultaneous buying and selling, being clear on the terms helps — especially if you're totally new to financial market trading.

- ✔ **Going long:** A *long position,* or simply a *long,* in the currency market refers to having bought a currency pair. When you're long, you're looking for prices to move higher, so you can sell at a higher price than where you bought. When you want to close a long position, you have to sell what you bought. If you're buying at multiple price levels, you're *adding to longs* and *getting longer.*

- ✔ **Getting short:** In currency trading, a *short position,* or simply a *short,* means you've sold a currency pair: You've sold the base currency and bought the counter currency (these terms are explained earlier in this chapter). When you've sold a currency pair, it's called *going short* or *getting short,* and it means you're looking for the pair's price to move lower so you can buy it back at a profit. If you sell at various price levels, you're *adding to shorts* and *getting shorter.*

In currency trading, going short is as common as going long. "Selling high and buying low" is a standard currency trading strategy.

✔ **Squaring up:** Having no position in the market is called being *square* or *flat.* Having an open position that you want to close is called *squaring up.* If you're short, you need to buy to square up. If you're long, you need to sell to go flat. The only time you have no market exposure or financial risk is when you're square.

Understanding rollovers

One market convention unique to currencies is rollovers. A *rollover* is a transaction where an open position from one *value date* (settlement date) is rolled over into the next value date. Rollovers represent the intersection of interest-rate markets and forex markets, because what you're actually trading is good old-fashioned cash. Being long a currency (cash) is like having a deposit in the bank. Being short a currency is like having borrowed a loan. Just as you'd expect to earn interest on a bank deposit or pay interest on a loan, you should expect an interest gain/expense for holding a currency position over the change in value date.

Rollovers only occur if you hold an open position at the 5 p.m. ET NY close. Being long in the higher-interest-rate currency and short in the lower-yielding currency typically results in a positive rollover, meaning you should see a small improvement in the average rate of your position or your account balance, depending on how your brokerage handles rollovers. Being short the higher-yielding currency and long the lower-interest-rate currency typically costs money.

If you're a day trader and you're square at the end of each day (5 p.m. ET), you'll never have to deal with rollovers. If you're holding positions medium to long term (for days or weeks), then rollovers are a potential cost/benefit to your account. Rollovers are expressed in pips or points (explained later in this chapter), and as of this writing, differences between major currency interest rates are negligible, meaning rollover rates should typically be less than a pip (plus or minus) for a one-day rollover.

Getting up close and personal with profit and loss

If you're going to trade currencies actively, you need to familiarize yourself with profit and loss (P&L). The following sections describe leverage, margin balances, liquidations, unrealized versus realized P&L, and pips.

Amplifying risk and reward with leverage

Online margin trading is usually based on *leverage,* where the brokerage effectively lets you borrow more money than you have deposited as collateral. Leverage refers to the ratio of that loan to your collateral. A leverage ratio of 50:1, for example, means that your collateral can be leveraged 50 times. More concretely, if you open an account with $1,000, you could trade a position size as large as $50,000. At 100:1, that same $1,000 margin deposit could control a position size of $100,000. But those calculations miss the point.

The important thing to know about leverage is that it amplifies any gains or losses equally. If your trade is profitable, great. You just made more than you otherwise could have. But if your trade misses, the result is a larger loss than you may be willing or able to tolerate. Above all, don't be deluded into trying to maximize position size.

Many newcomers to the currency market seek out the highest leverage ratios available, sometimes opening accounts offshore in questionable jurisdictions. Use leverage sparingly; that 50:1 is more than ample to trade actively, yet prudently.

Risk management is the key to any successful trading plan. Without a risk-aware strategy, margin trading can be an extremely short-lived endeavor. With a proper risk plan in place, you stand a much better chance of surviving losing trades and making winning ones. You can find information on risk management in Chapter 4 of Book IV.

Understanding margin balances and liquidations

When you open an online currency trading account, you need to pony up cash as collateral to support the margin requirements established by your broker. That initial margin deposit becomes your opening *margin balance* and is the basis on which all your subsequent trades are collateralized. Unlike futures markets or margin-based equity trading, online forex brokerages do not issue *margin calls* (requests for more collateral to support open positions). Instead, they establish ratios of margin balances to open positions that must be maintained at all times.

Understanding how P&L works is especially critical to online margin trading, where your P&L directly affects the amount of margin you have to work with. Changes in your margin balance determine how much you can trade and for how long you can trade if prices move against you. Stay focused on your P&L targets when devising a trade strategy and what those results mean for your margin balance.

Be sure you completely understand your broker's margin requirements and liquidation policies. Some brokers' liquidation policies allow for all positions to be liquidated if you fall below margin requirements. Others close out the biggest losing positions until the required ratio is satisfied again. You can find the details in the fine print of the account opening contract that you sign.

Comparing unrealized and realized profit and loss

Most online forex brokers provide real-time mark-to-market calculations showing your *margin balance,* which is the sum of your initial margin deposit, your unrealized P&L, and your realized P&L. *Mark-to-market* is the calculation that shows your unrealized P&L based on where you could close your open positions in the market at that instant. *Realized P&L* is what you get when you close out a trade position or a portion of a trade position.

Your unrealized P&L will continue to fluctuate based on the remaining open positions, and so will your total margin balance. If you have a winning position open, your unrealized P&L will be positive, and your margin balance will increase. If the market is moving against your positions, your unrealized P&L will be negative, and your margin balance will be reduced. Currency prices are constantly changing, so your mark-to-market unrealized P&L and total margin balance are also constantly changing.

Calculating profit and loss with pips

Profit-and-loss calculations are pretty straightforward in terms of math — they're all based on position size and the number of pips you make or lose. A *pip* (or point) is the smallest increment of price fluctuation in currency prices. Different currency pairs have a different number of digits behind the decimal point. In all cases, that last, itty-bitty digit is the pip. (Most online brokerages have recently decimalized forex pips, but I focus on the main pip for clarity's sake.) Here are some major currency pairs and crosses, with the pip underlined:

- ✓ **EUR/USD:** 1.305<u>3</u>
- ✓ **USD/CHF:** 1.056<u>7</u>
- ✓ **USD/JPY:** 84.2<u>3</u>
- ✓ **GBP/USD:** 1.508<u>5</u>
- ✓ **EUR/JPY:** 110.6<u>5</u>

Looking at EUR/USD, if the price moves from 1.3053 to 1.3073, it has just gone up by 20 pips. If it goes from 1.3053 down to 1.3003, it has just gone down by 50 pips. To turn that pip movement into a P&L calculation, all you need to know is the size of the position. For a 100,000 EUR/USD position, the 20-pip move equates to $200 (EUR 100,000 × 0.0020 = $200). For a 50,000 EUR/USD position, the 50-point move translates into $250 (EUR 50,000 × 0.0050 = $250).

Book IV

Foreign Currency Trading

Online currency trading platforms calculate the P&L for you automatically, but they do so only *after* you enter a trade. To structure your trade and manage your risk effectively, you need to calculate your potential P&L outcomes *before* you enter the trade.

Forces behind Forex Rates

On a daily basis, currency traders have to sort through myriad economic reports, interpret the comments of political and financial officials from around the world, take stock of geopolitical developments, and assess movements in other financial markets. They do all this to help them determine what direction major currencies are likely to move.

Currencies and interest rates

Interest rates are important to currencies because they influence the direction of global capital flows and serve as benchmarks for what investors expect to earn investing in a particular country. Currencies with higher yields (higher interest rates) tend to strengthen versus lower-yielding (lower-interest-rate) currencies, and vice versa. The following sections explain what you need to know.

The future is now: Interest rate expectations

When it comes to currencies and interest rates, forex markets are focused more on the direction of future interest rate moves (higher or lower) than they are on the current levels. Even though a currency may have a low interest rate, market expectations of higher interest rates in the future frequently will cause the currency to appreciate. The opposite is also true: A currency with a relatively high interest rate frequently weakens if the market expects interest rates in that country to move lower in the future.

The *outlook period,* or the time frame in which markets are expecting interest rates to change, can span several months or quarters into the future. The farther out the expected changes are on the horizon, however, the more limited the impact on the currencies in the here and now.

Make the connection: Relative interest rates

Currency traders usually pay very little attention to absolute interest rates and prefer to home in on one currency's interest rate in relation to other currencies' interest rates:

✔ **Interest-rate differentials:** The difference between the interest rates of two currencies, known as the *interest-rate differential,* is the key spread to watch. An increasing interest-rate differential generally favors the higher-yielding currency, while a narrowing interest-rate differential tends to favor the lower-yielding currency.

✔ **Nominal and real interest rates:** The interest rate to focus on is not always just the *nominal interest rate* (the base interest rates you see, such as the yield on a bond). Markets focus on *real interest rates* (inflation-adjusted rates, which are the nominal interest rate minus the rate of inflation [usually the consumer price index]).

Monetary policy

The most significant overall determinant of a currency's value relative to other currencies is the nature and direction of monetary policy set by a country's central bank. *Monetary policy* is the set of policy actions that central banks use to achieve their legal mandates. Most central banks function under legislative mandates that focus on two basic objectives: to promote price stability (also known as restraining inflation) and to promote sustainable economic growth, sometimes with an explicit goal of promoting maximum employment.

Central bankers like to focus primarily on inflation, and the primary lever of monetary policy is changes to benchmark interest rates, such as the federal funds rate in the United States or the refinance rate in the Eurozone. Changes in interest rates effectively amount to changes in the cost of money, where higher interest rates increase the cost of borrowing and lower interest rates reduce the cost of borrowing.

Identifying monetary policy cycles

Changes in monetary policy usually involve many small shifts in interest rates (because central bankers are increasingly reluctant to shock an economy by adjusting interest rates too drastically) that play out over extended periods of time, ranging from quarters to years. Still, given the significance of monetary policy to currencies, currency traders devote a great deal of attention to trying to divine the intentions of central bankers. Fortunately, central bankers communicate with the markets in a number of ways: rate decisions, policy statements or guidance, and public speeches (see the next section for details).

Currency traders need to be aware of and constantly follow the current market thinking on the direction of interest rates because of the strong relationship between interest rates and currency values. The best way to do this is to follow market commentaries in print and online news media, always keeping in mind that such outlets (especially print) are usually one step behind the current market. Some of the best sites for timely insights and market reporting are Bloomberg.com, Reuters.com, and MarketWatch.com. Best of all, these sites are free.

Interpreting monetary policy communications

Central bankers are keenly aware that their comments have the ability to move, and potentially disrupt, financial markets all over the world. So they choose their words very carefully, leaving traders to act as interpreters. Before you start interpreting monetary policy statements and commentary, it helps to know the following:

- ✔ **When the head of the central bank gives an update on the economy or the outlook for interest rates, listen up.** A scheduled speech by the chair of the Fed, for instance, is likely to be preceded by market speculation similar to that of a major economic data report. And the reaction to those comments can be equally sharp.

- ✔ **Markets typically refer to central bankers in terms of being hawks or doves.** A *hawk* is someone who generally fixates on fighting inflation. A *dove* tends to stress growth and employment. If a hawk is slated to speak on the outlook for monetary policy, and he downplays the threats from inflation or suggests that inflationary pressures may be starting to recede, pay attention. Markets will jump all over dovish comments coming from a hawk, and vice versa.

Assessing official currency policies and rhetoric

After considering interest rates and monetary policy communications, the next biggest influences on currency values are government policies or official stances regarding the value of individual currencies. National governments have a great deal at stake when it comes to the value of their currencies. After all, in a sense, a nation's currency is the front door to its economy and financial markets. If the currency is viewed as unstable or too volatile, it's tantamount to slamming the front door shut. And no major economy can afford to do that today.

Investigating types of currency market intervention

Intervention refers to central banks buying or selling currencies in the open market to drive currency rates in a desired direction. Direct intervention in the market is usually taken only as a last resort. It also may be a stopgap measure to stabilize markets upset by extreme events, such as a terrorist attack or rumors of a financial institution's failure. When it's not necessitated by emergency circumstances, markets are generally aware of the increasing risks of intervention.

Open market intervention can take several different forms, all depending on which and how many central banks are participating:

- ✔ **Unilateral intervention:** Intervention by a single central bank to buy or sell its own currency. Unilateral intervention is generally the least effective form of intervention, because the government is perceived (usually correctly) to be acting alone and without the support of other major governments.

- ✔ **Joint intervention:** When two central banks intervene together to shift the direction of their shared currency pair. This is a clear sign to markets that the two governments are prepared to work together to alter the direction of that pair's exchange rate.

- ✔ **Concerted intervention:** When multiple central banks join together to intervene in the market simultaneously. The most powerful and effective type of intervention, concerted intervention suggests unity of purpose by multiple governments. It's the equivalent of a sledgehammer to the head. Concerted intervention frequently results in major, long-term trend changes.

In terms of the impact of intervention, different governments are given different degrees of respect by the market. Due to the frequency of past interventions and constant threats of it, the Japanese tend to get the least respect. The Bank of England, the Swiss National Bank, and the European Central Bank (ECB) are treated with considerably more respect by markets, with the ECB being the linchpin of credibility for the Eurozone. Finally, when the U.S. Treasury (via the Fed) intervenes, it's considered a major event, and the market usually respects the intervention.

Financial stability

The Great Financial Crisis of 2008–2009 triggered a massive global recession, the likes of which had not been seen since the Great Depression of the 1930s. As a result, major governments' finances were thrown into disarray, as tax revenues plunged and spending was maintained or increased through fiscal stimulus. Suddenly the creditworthiness and financial stability of major national governments was being questioned by global markets.

A currency's perceived value is intrinsically linked to the faith investors have in the financial stability of the nation(s) standing behind it. If investors fear a *sovereign debt default,* meaning government bonds won't be paid back, they're likely to sell both those bonds and the country's currency. The result can be a market frenzy in which government bond prices crash, sending yields soaring

Book IV

Foreign Currency Trading

and increasing the government's borrowing costs, effectively forcing the government out of global capital markets and leading to a default.

The Eurozone debt crisis of 2009–2012 is the most obvious recent example, where bond investors fled Greek and Irish government debt, among others, raising borrowing costs to unaffordable levels and forcing those governments to seek a bailout from wealthier Eurozone members. From the start of the Greek debt crisis in November 2009 until a temporary bailout mechanism was established in May 2010, the euro weakened against the USD by more than 20 percent, and fell even more against other currencies.

Debts, deficits, and growth

In the aftermath of the Great Financial Crisis, highly indebted European countries are certainly not alone in having investors question their financial stability. Debt levels in the United States and Japan are routinely cited as potential negatives, weighing on sentiment for those currencies from time to time.

As part of your analysis of individual currencies, you need to be aware of the financial stability of the key currency countries. The metrics to keep in mind are as follows:

- **Debt to GDP ratio:** A measure of the total amount of government debt relative to the size of the economy. Debt/GDP ratios over 85 to 90 percent of GDP tend to put countries under the credit-risk microscope (see the next section).

- **Deficits as a percent of GDP:** Current and projected deficits add to the total amount of government debt, which can increase the debt/GDP ratio, potentially destabilizing a country's credit outlook.

- **Growth rates (GDP):** Low or negative growth can undermine a nation's GDP relative to its debt service obligations, increasing the burdens of debt service and raising the risk of default.

Credit risk

Just as with monetary policy and interest rate developments, financial stability evolves over a long time period. But day-to-day developments impact the markets' view of individual countries' financial stability. How can you monitor the current state of the markets' views of a nation's creditworthiness? Keep an eye on the following credit risk measures through market news reports and economic commentaries:

- ✔ **Credit ratings:** The sovereign debt ratings issued by Moody's, Standard & Poor's (S&P), and Fitch carry a lot of weight. Prior to a ratings change (an upgrade or a downgrade), the credit rating agencies typically issue an announcement that a country's debt ratings are under review and offer a bias to that review, such as "Portugal sovereign debt placed on review; outlook negative." Such announcements can have a significant impact on the currency involved.

- ✔ **Yield spreads:** These are the difference between the yields (interest rates) of one government's bonds relative to an ostensibly safer country's bonds. A widening spread indicates increasing credit concerns, as the bonds of the weak country are sold, sending yields higher, and bonds of the safe country are bought, sending those yields lower. Yield spreads fluctuate on a daily and intra-day basis, with widening spreads indicating deteriorating credit risk and narrowing spreads indicating greater relief.

- ✔ **Credit default swaps (CDS):** These derivatives are basically an insurance policy in the event of a default, where the buyer pays a premium and the seller is obligated to make good on the bond in the event of a default. CDS are an active speculative counterpart to the underlying bonds themselves, and may often lead bond market moves. Rising CDS indicate increasing credit risk, and falling CDS rates, expressed in basis points (bps), signal lesser concern.

- ✔ **Debt auction results:** Governments borrow money through regularly scheduled auctions or *issuances,* where the government offers its debt for sale to global investors. The extent of demand and the price investors are willing to pay (the yield) are the key measures here. Demand is gauged according to the *bid/cover ratio,* meaning how much is bid, or sought, relative to the amount being offered. The higher the bid/cover ratio, the greater the demand and supposed security.

Geopolitical risks and events

In the context of currency markets, geopolitics tends to focus on political, military/security, or natural disruptions to the global economy or individual regions or nations. Elections in individual countries, including by-elections and legislative referenda, also fall under the geopolitical risk umbrella, especially when the outcome may lead to a change in government or economic policies. Because currency markets are the conduits for international capital flows, they're usually the first to react to international events, as global investors shift assets in response to geopolitical developments.

Book IV

Foreign Currency Trading

Chapter 2

Major and Minor Currency Pairs

*T*he vast majority of trading volume takes place in the *major* currency pairs: EUR/USD, USD/JPY, GBP/USD, and USD/CHF. These currency pairs account for about two-thirds of daily trading volume in the market and are the most watched barometers of the overall forex market. When you hear about the dollar rising or falling, it's usually referring to the dollar against these other currencies.

Of course, speculative trading opportunities extend well beyond just the four major *dollar pairs* (currency pairs that include the USD). For starters, three other currency pairs — commonly known as the *minor* or *small* dollar pairs — round out the primary trading pairs that include the USD. This chapter takes a look at the various major and minor currency pairs to show how they fit into the overall market.

Banking on the Big Dollar: EUR/USD

EUR/USD is by far the most actively traded currency pair in the global forex market. *EUR/USD* is the currency pair that pits the U.S. dollar against the single currency of the Eurozone, the euro. The *Eurozone* refers to a grouping of countries in the European Union (EU); currently the euro is the official currency of 17 of the 28 E.U. member states. All together, the Eurozone constitutes a regional economic bloc roughly equal to the United States in both population and total GDP.

Trading fundamentals of EUR/USD

Standard market convention is to quote EUR/USD in terms of the number of USD per EUR. For example, a EUR/USD rate of 1.3000 means that it takes $1.30 to buy €1.

EUR/USD trades inversely to the overall value of the USD, which means when EUR/USD goes up, the euro is getting stronger and the dollar weaker. When EUR/USD goes down, the euro is getting weaker and the dollar stronger. If you believe the U.S. dollar is going to move higher, you look to sell EUR/USD. If you think the dollar is going to weaken, you look to buy EUR/USD.

EUR/USD has the euro as the base currency and the U.S. dollar as the secondary or counter currency (see Chapter 1 of Book IV for the basics on these terms). That means

- ✔ **EUR/USD is traded in amounts denominated in euros.** In online currency trading platforms, standard lot sizes are €100,000, and mini lot sizes are €10,000.

- ✔ **The pip value, or minimum price fluctuation, is denominated in USD.**

- ✔ **Profit and loss accrue in USD.** For one standard lot position size, each pip is worth $10; for one mini lot position size, each pip is worth $1.

- ✔ **Margin calculations in online trading platforms are typically based in USD.** At a EUR/USD rate of 1.3000, to trade a single mini lot position worth €10,000, it'll take $260 in available margin (based on 50:1 leverage). That calculation changes over time, of course, based on the level of the EUR/USD exchange rate. A higher EUR/USD rate requires more USD in available margin collateral, and a lower EUR/USD rate needs less USD in margin. (Flip to Chapter 1 in Book IV for more about margin.)

Having a sense of which currency is driving EUR/USD at any given moment is important so you can better adapt to incoming data and news. If it's a EUR-based move higher, for instance, and surprisingly positive USD news or data is released later in the day, guess what? You have counter-trend information hitting the market, which could spark a reversal lower in EUR/USD (in favor of the dollar). By the same token, if that U.S. data comes out weaker than expected, it's likely to spur further EUR/USD gains, because EUR buying interest is now combined with USD selling interest.

Liquidity in EUR/USD is unmatched by other major currency pairs. This trait is most evident in the narrower trading spreads regularly available in EUR/USD. Normal market spreads are typically around 1.5 to 2.5 pips versus 3 to 4 pips in other major currency pairs. Tight spreads make EUR/USD a great choice for high-frequency trading.

The euro serves as the primary foil to the U.S. dollar when it comes to speculating on the overall direction of the U.S. dollar in response to U.S. news or economic data. If weak U.S. economic data is reported, traders are typically going to sell the dollar, which begs the question, "Against what?" The euro is the first choice for many, simply because it's there. It also helps that it's the most liquid alternative, allowing for easy entry and exit.

The EUR/USD reacts to more than just U.S. economic data or news. Eurozone news and data can move EUR/USD as much as U.S. data moves the pair. But the overall tendency still favors U.S. data and news as the driving force of short-term price movements. Here's a list of the major European data reports and events to keep an eye on:

- European Central Bank (ECB) interest rate decisions and press conferences after ECB Central Council meetings
- Speeches by ECB officials and individual European finance ministers
- EU-harmonized consumer price index (CPI), as well as national CPI and producer price index (PPI) reports
- EU Commission economic sector confidence indicators
- Consumer and investor sentiment surveys separately issued by three private economic research firms known by their acronyms: Ifo, ZEW, and GfK
- Industrial production

Trading behavior of EUR/USD

The deep liquidity and tight trading spreads in EUR/USD make the pair ideal for both shorter-term and longer-term traders. The price action behavior in EUR/USD regularly exhibits a number of traits you should be aware of.

Trading tick by tick

In normal market conditions, EUR/USD tends to trade tick by tick, as opposed to other currency pairs, which routinely display sharper short-term price movements of several pips. In trading terms, if EUR/USD is trading at 1.2910/13, traders will be looking to sell at 13, 14, 15, and higher, while buyers are waiting to buy at 9, 8, 7, and lower.

Fewer price jumps and smaller price gaps

The depth of liquidity in EUR/USD reduces the number of price jumps (quick movements in prices over a relatively small distance — roughly 10 to 20 pips — in the course of normal trading) or price gaps (when prices instantaneously adjust over a larger price distance, typically in response to a news event or data release) in short-term trading.

Price jumps/gaps do occur in EUR/USD, but they tend to be generated primarily by news/data releases and breaks of significant technical levels, events which can usually be identified in advance.

Backing and filling

TIP

When it comes to EUR/USD price action, *backing and filling* (when prices moving rapidly in one direction reach a short-term stopping point when opposite interest enters the market) is quite common. It tends to be more substantial than in most currency pairs, meaning a greater amount of the directional move is retraced (see Figure 2-1). EUR/USD not backing and filling the way you expect means the directional move is stronger and has greater interest behind it.

Figure 2-1:
A one-minute EUR/USD chart showing periods of backing and filling price action after short-term directional moves. Backing and filling occurs in price declines, too.

Source: www.eSignal.com

Because EUR/USD tends to retrace more of its short-term movements, you can usually enter a position in your desired direction by leaving an order to buy or sell at slightly better rates than current market prices may allow. If the post–08:30 ET U.S. data price action sees EUR/USD move lower, and you think getting short is the way to go, you can leave an offer slightly above the current market level (roughly 5 to 10 pips) and use it to get short instead of reaching out and hitting the bid on a down-tick. If your order is executed, you've got your desired position at a better rate than if you went to market, and you're probably in a better position rhythm-wise with the market (having sold on an up-tick). Alternatively, you can take advantage of routine backing and filling by dealing at the market, selling on up-ticks and buying on down-ticks.

Prolonged tests of technical levels

When it comes to trading around technical support and resistance levels, EUR/USD can try the patience of even the most disciplined traders because EUR/USD can spend tens of minutes (an eternity in forex markets) or even several hours undergoing tests of technical levels. (See Book X for a primer on technical analysis.) This characteristic goes back to the tremendous amount of interest and liquidity that defines the EUR/USD market. All those viewpoints come together in the form of market interest (bids and offers) when technical levels come into play. The result is a tremendous amount of market interest that has to be absorbed at technical levels, which can take time.

Be patient. The EUR/USD can spend hours trading in relatively narrow ranges or testing technical levels. The key in such markets is to remain patient based on your directional view and your technical analysis. You should be able to identify short-term support that keeps an upside test alive or resistance that keeps a down-move going. If those levels fail, the move is stalling at the minimum and may even be reversing.

GBP/USD and USD/CHF as leading indicators

Given the tremendous two-way interest in EUR/USD, gauging whether a test of a technical level is going to lead to a breakout or a rejection can be very difficult. To get an idea of whether a test of a technical level in EUR/USD is going to lead to a break, professional EUR/USD traders always keep an eye on GBP/USD and USD/CHF (discussed later in this chapter), because they tend to be leading indicators for the bigger EUR/USD and dollar moves in general.

If GBP/USD and USD/CHF are aggressively testing (trading at or through the technical level with very little pullback) similar technical levels to EUR/USD (for example, daily highs or equivalent trendline resistance), then EUR/USD is likely to test that same level. If GBP/USD and USD/CHF break through their technical levels, the chances of EUR/USD following suit increase. By the same token, if GBP/USD and USD/CHF are not aggressively testing the key technical level, EUR/USD is likely to see its similar technical level hold.

GBP/USD and USD/CHF lead times can be anywhere from a few seconds or minutes to several hours or even days. Just make sure you're looking at the equivalent technical levels in each pair.

When it comes to determining whether EUR/USD has broken a technical level, use a 10- to 15-pip margin of error. (Shorter-term traders may want to use a smaller margin of error.) Some very short-term traders and technical purists like to pinpoint an exact price level as support or resistance. If the market trades above or below their level, they'll call it a break and that's that. But the spot forex market rarely trades with such respect for technical levels to make such a clear and pinpointed distinction. And given the amount of interest in EUR/USD, it's especially prone to hazy technical lines in the sand.

Book IV

Foreign Currency Trading

Exploring Where East Meets West: USD/JPY

USD/JPY (pitting the U.S. dollar against the Japanese yen) is one of the more challenging currency pairs among the majors. Where other currency pairs typically display routine market fluctuations and relatively steady, active trading interest, USD/JPY seems to have an on/off switch. It can spend hours and even days in relatively narrow ranges and then march off on a mission to a new price level. The key to developing a successful trading game plan in USD/JPY is to understand what drives the pair and the how price action behaves.

Trading fundamentals of USD/JPY

The Japanese yen is the third major international currency after the U.S. dollar and the European single currency, the euro. USD/JPY accounts for 14 percent of daily global trading volume, according to the 2010 Bank for International Settlements (BIS) survey of foreign exchange markets. Japan stands as the third largest national economy after the United States and EUR groupings.

Standard market convention is to quote USD/JPY in terms of the number of JPY per USD. For example, a USD/JPY rate of 85.30 means that it takes ¥85.30 to buy $1.

USD/JPY trades in the same direction as the overall value of the USD, and inversely to the value of the JPY. If the USD is strengthening and the JPY is weakening, the USD/JPY rate will move higher. If the USD is weakening and the JPY is strengthening, the USD/JPY rate will move lower.

USD/JPY has the U.S. dollar as the base currency and the JPY as the secondary or counter currency. This means

- **USD/JPY is traded in amounts denominated in USD.** In online currency trading platforms, standard lot sizes are $100,000, and mini lot sizes are $10,000.

- **The pip value, or minimum price fluctuation, is denominated in JPY.**

- **Profit and loss accrue in JPY.** For one standard lot position size, each pip is worth ¥1,000; for one mini lot position size, each pip is worth ¥100. To convert those amounts to USD, divide the JPY amount by the USD/JPY rate.

- **Margin calculations are typically calculated in USD.** So the calculation is a straightforward one, using the leverage rate to see how much margin is required to hold a position in USD/JPY. At 50:1 leverage, $200 of available margin is needed to open a mini-size position of 10,000 USD/JPY.

The following sections discuss a few more detailed fundamentals of USD/JPY trading.

The heavy influence of U.S. interest rates

If the main driver of USD/JPY had to be identified, it would easily be the movements in U.S. interest rates. The main reason for this is the massive amount of U.S. government debt held by the Japanese government and Japanese investors. The Bank of Japan (BOJ) alone holds nearly $900 billion worth of U.S. Treasury debt. If U.S. interest rates begin to fall, the prices of U.S. government bonds rise, increasing the USD-value of Japan's U.S. debt holdings. To offset, or hedge, their larger USD-long currency exposure, Japanese reserve managers need to sell more USD. This causes USD/JPY to closely track U.S. Treasury yields.

Political sensitivity to trade

USD/JPY is the most politically sensitive currency pair among the majors. Japan remains a heavily export-oriented economy, accounting for more than 40 percent of overall economic activity. This reliance on exporting means the JPY is a critical policy lever for Japanese officials to stimulate and manage the Japanese economy — and they aren't afraid to get involved in the market to keep the JPY from strengthening beyond desired levels.

A weak currency makes a nation's exports cheaper to foreigners and, all other things being equal, creates a competitive advantage to gain market share. On the flip side, a JPY that's too strong makes Japanese exports more expensive and may hurt the export sector and squeeze corporate profitability. That's one reason Japanese stock markets typically decline when the JPY strengthens sharply (USD/JPY lower).

The routine involvement of the Japanese Ministry of Finance in the forex market

Currency intervention is usually a last resort for most major national governments. Instead, the Japanese Ministry of Finance (MOF) engages in routine verbal intervention to influence the level of the JPY.

The Japanese financial press devotes a tremendous amount of attention to the value of the JPY, similar to how the U.S. financial media cover the Dow or S&P 500. Press briefings by MOF officials are routine. These statements move USD/JPY on a regular basis. In addition, the MOF has also been known to utilize covert intervention through the use of sizeable market orders by the pension fund of the Japanese Postal Savings Bank, known as Kampo. This is sometimes referred to as *semiofficial intervention* in various market commentaries.

MOF comments are quite frequent and can shift market sentiment and direction as much as, or more than, fundamental data. The key data reports to focus on coming out of Japan are

- ✔ Bank of Japan policy decisions, monthly economic assessments, and Monetary Policy Committee (MPC) member speeches

- ✔ The Tankan Report (a quarterly sentiment survey of Japanese firms by the BOJ — the key is often planned capital expenditures)

Book IV

Foreign Currency Trading

✔ Industrial production

✔ Machine orders

✔ Trade balance and current account

✔ The All-Industry Index and Tertiary Industry (service sector) Index

Japanese asset management trends

Due to historically high saving rates, Japanese asset managers and investors control trillions of dollars' worth of assets, mostly invested in bonds. With exceptionally low rates available in Japan, Japanese assets are frequently looking abroad for better-yielding returns. When the risk environment is calm, they tend to be regular sellers of JPY against most other currencies. But if the risk environment deteriorates suddenly, those JPY are quickly bought back and JPY-crosses can collapse.

Japanese financial institutions also tend to pursue a highly collegial approach to investment strategies. The result for forex markets is that Japanese asset managers frequently pursue similar investment strategies at the same time, resulting in tremendous asset flows hitting the market over a relatively short period of time. This situation has important implications for USD/JPY price action (see the next section).

Price action behavior of USD/JPY

As noted earlier, USD/JPY seems to have an on/off switch when compared to the other major currency pairs. Add to that the fact that USD/JPY liquidity can be similarly fickle. Sometimes, hundreds of millions of USD/JPY can be bought or sold without moving the market noticeably; other times, liquidity can be extremely scarce. This phenomenon is particularly acute in USD/JPY owing to the large presence of Japanese asset managers and the Japanese investment community's tendency to move en masse into and out of positions.

Short-term trends, followed by sideways consolidations

The result of this concentration of Japanese corporate interest is a strong tendency for USD/JPY to display short-term trends (several hours to several days) in price movements, as investors pile in on the prevailing directional move. This tendency is amplified by the use of standing market orders from Japanese asset managers.

For example, if a Japanese pension fund manager is looking to establish a long position in USD/JPY, he's likely to leave orders at several fixed levels below the current market to try to buy dollars on dips. If the current market is at 83.00, he may buy a piece of the total position there, but then leave orders to buy the remaining amounts at staggered levels below, such as 82.75, 82.50, 82.25, and 82.00. If other investors are of the same view, they'll be bidding below the market as well.

If the market begins to move higher, the asset managers may become nervous that they won't be able to buy on weakness. Thus, they raise their orders to higher levels or buy at the market price. Either way, buying interest is moving up with the price action, creating a potentially accelerating price movement. Any counter-trend move is met by solid buying interest and quickly reversed.

Such price shifts tend to reach their conclusion when everyone is onboard — most of the buyers who wanted to buy are now long. At this point, no more fresh buying is coming into the market, and the directional move begins to stall and move sideways. The early buyers may be capping the market with profit-taking orders to sell above, while laggard buyers are still buying on dips. This leads to the development of a consolidation range, which can be as narrow as 40 to 50 pips.

Short-term traders can usually find trading opportunities in such consolidation ranges, but medium- and longer-term traders may want to step back and wait for a fresh directional movement.

The importance of technical levels

If you're a regular trader or investor and you don't work at a Japanese bank, you can tell where the orders are by focusing on the technical levels. Perhaps no other currency pair is as beholden to technical support and resistance as USD/JPY. In large part, this correlation has to do with the prevalence of substantial orders, where the order level is based on technical analysis. USD/JPY displays a number of other important trading characteristics when it comes to technical trading levels:

- ✔ USD/JPY tends to respect technical levels with far fewer false breaks.

- ✔ USD/JPY's price action is usually highly directional (one-way in terms of traffic) on breaks of technical support and resistance.

- ✔ Orders frequently define intraday highs and lows and reversal points. When you look at charts involving JPY, note tops/bottoms that are close to round-number price levels because significant orders may be there.

Book IV

Foreign Currency Trading

USD/JPY trading considerations

USD/JPY's tendency is to either be active directionally or consolidating — the on/off switch. A good way to approach USD/JPY is on a more strategic, hit-and-run basis — getting in when you think a directional move is happening and standing aside when you don't. Look for breaks of trendlines, spike reversals, and candlestick patterns as your primary clues for spotting a pending directional move. Here are some suggestions:

- ✓ **Actively trade trendline and price-level breakouts.** One trigger point for jumping into USD/JPY is breaks of trendlines and key price levels, such as daily or weekly highs/lows. Because a significant amount of market interest is required to break key technical levels, look at the actual breaks as concrete evidence of sizeable interest rather than normal back-and-forth price action.

- ✓ **Jump on spike reversals:** After USD/JPY has seen a relatively quick (usually within two to three hours) move of more than 70 to 80 pips in one direction, be on the lookout for any sharp reversals in price. Spike reversals of 30 to 40 pips that occur in very short time frames (5 to 20 minutes) are relatively common in USD/JPY. But you pretty much have to be in front of your trading screen to take advantage of these, because they're a short-term phenomenon by their very nature.

- ✓ **Monitor EUR/JPY and other JPY crosses:** USD/JPY is heavily influenced by cross flows and can frequently take a back seat to them on any given day. In evaluating USD/JPY, always keep an eye on the JPY crosses and their technical levels. EUR/JPY is the most actively traded JPY cross, and its movements routinely drive USD/JPY on an intraday basis. Be alert for when significant technical levels in the two pairs coincide, such as when both USD/JPY and EUR/JPY are testing a series of recent daily highs or lows. A break by either can easily spill into the other and provoke follow-through buying/selling in both.

Mixing It Up with the Other Majors: GBP/USD and USD/CHF

GBP/USD (affectionately known as *sterling* or *cable*) and USD/CHF (called *Swissy* by market traders) are counted as major currency pairs, but their trading volume and liquidity are significantly less than EUR/USD and USD/JPY. As a result, their trading characteristics are very similar to each other.

The British pound: GBP/USD

Trading in cable (pitting the British pound versus the U.S. dollar) presents its own set of challenges, because the pair is prone to sharp price movements and seemingly chaotic price action. But it's exactly this type of price behavior that keeps the speculators coming back — when you're right, you know very quickly, and the short-term results can be significant.

Trading fundamentals of GBP/USD

The UK economy is the second largest national economy in Europe, after Germany, and the pound is heavily influenced by cross-border trade and mergers and acquisitions (M&A) activity between the United Kingdom and continental Europe. Upwards of two-thirds of UK foreign trade is conducted with EU member states, making the EUR/GBP cross one of the most important trade-driven cross rates.

The 2010 BIS survey of foreign exchange turnover showed that GBP/USD accounted for 9 percent of global daily trading volume, making cable the third most active pairing in the majors. But you may not believe that when you start trading cable, where liquidity seems always to be at a premium. Relatively lower liquidity is most evident in the larger bid-offer spread, which is usually 3 to 5 pips compared to 2 to 3 pips in EUR/USD and USD/JPY.

GBP/USD is quoted in terms of the number of dollars it takes to buy a pound, so a rate of 1.5515 means it costs $1.5515 to buy £1. The GBP is the primary currency in the pair and the USD is the secondary currency. That means

- ✔ **GBP/USD is traded in amounts denominated in GBP.** In online currency trading platforms, standard lot sizes are £100,000, and mini lot sizes are £10,000.

- ✔ **The pip value, or minimum price fluctuation, is denominated in USD.**

- ✔ **Profit and loss accrue in USD.** For one standard lot position size, each pip is worth $10; for one mini lot position size, each pip is worth $1.

- ✔ **Margin calculations are typically calculated in USD in online trading platforms.** Because of its high relative value to the USD, trading in GBP pairs requires the greatest amount of margin on a per-lot basis. At a GBP/USD rate of 1.5500, to trade a one-mini-lot position worth £10,000, it takes $310 in available margin (based on 50:1 leverage). That calculation changes over time, of course, based on the level of the GBP/USD exchange rate. A higher GBP/USD rate requires more USD in available margin collateral, and a lower GBP/USD rate needs less USD in margin.

Trading alongside EUR/USD, but with a lot more zip!

Cable is similar to the EUR/USD in that it trades inversely to the overall USD, except that it exhibits much more abrupt volatility and more extreme overall price movements. If U.S. economic news disappoints, for instance, both cable and EUR/USD will move higher. But if EUR/USD sees a 60-point rally on the day, cable may see a 100+ point rally.

Regarding liquidity, in terms of daily global trading sessions (see Chapter 1 in Book IV for details), cable volume is at its peak during the UK/European trading day, but that level of liquidity shrinks considerably in the New York

Book IV

Foreign Currency Trading

afternoon and Asian trading sessions. During those off-peak times, cable can see significant short-term price moves simply on the basis of position adjustments (for example, shorts getting squeezed out).

Important UK data reports

Another important difference between cable and EUR/USD comes in their different reactions to domestic economic/news developments. Cable tends to display more explosive reactions to unexpected UK news/data than EUR/USD does to similar Eurozone news/data. Key UK data reports to watch for are

✔ Bank of England (BOE) Monetary Policy Committee (MPC) rate decisions, as well as speeches by MPC members and the BOE governor

✔ BOE MPC minutes (released two weeks after each MPC meeting)

✔ Inflation gauges, such as the consumer price index (CPI), the producer price index (PPI), and the British Retailers Consortium (BRC) shop price index

✔ Retail sales and the BRC retail sales monitor

✔ Industrial and manufacturing production

✔ The BOE quarterly inflation report

Safe haven or panic button: USD/CHF

The Swiss franc (CHF) has a reputation for being a *safe-haven currency,* meaning investors flock to it in times of geopolitical tensions or uncertainty. That reputation is largely a relic of the Cold War. More recently, however, in the aftermath of the Great Financial Crisis (GFC) and the Eurozone debt crisis of 2009–2012, the Swiss franc has emerged as a perceived safer alternative to the other major currencies, all of which are burdened by troubled economic outlooks and high debt levels. But there's nothing magically safe about CHF, as other currencies like AUD (the Australian dollar) and CAD (the Canadian dollar) have similarly outperformed the beleaguered majors.

Trading fundamentals of USD/CHF

In terms of overall market volume, USD/CHF accounts for only 4 percent of global daily trading volume according to the 2010 BIS survey (and was eclipsed by AUD/USD [6 percent] and USD/CAD [5 percent]). With such a small share of market turnover, you may be wondering why it's considered a major pair in the first place. And that's probably the key takeaway from this section: In terms of liquidity, Swissy is not a major.

USD/CHF is quoted in terms of the number of CHF per USD. At a USD/CHF rate of 0.9800, it costs CHF0.9800 to buy $1. USD/CHF trades in the overall direction of the U.S. dollar and inversely to the CHF. If the USD/CHF rate moves higher, the USD is strengthening and the CHF is weakening.

The USD is the primary currency in the pairing, and the CHF is the secondary currency. That means

- **USD/CHF is traded in amounts denominated in USD.** In online currency trading platforms, standard lot sizes are $100,000, and mini lot sizes are $10,000.

- **The pip value, or minimum price fluctuation, is denominated in CHF.**

- **Profit and loss accrue in CHF.** For one standard lot position size, each pip is worth CHF10; for one mini lot position size, each pip is worth CHF1. To convert those amounts to USD, divide the CHF amount by the USD/CHF rate.

- **Margin calculations are typically calculated in USD.** So the calculation is a straightforward one, using the leverage rate to see how much margin is required to hold a position in USD/JPY. At 50:1 leverage, $200 of available margin is needed to open a mini lot–size position of 10,000 USD/CHF.

Keeping the focus on Europe

Switzerland conducts the vast share (about 80 percent) of its foreign trade with the Eurozone and remaining EU countries. When it comes to the value of the CHF, the Swiss are most concerned with its level against the EUR as opposed to the USD. The Swiss National Bank (SNB), the Swiss central bank, tends to get involved in the forex market only when the Swiss franc is either too strong or too weak against the euro.

The European debt crisis came to the fore in late 2009, and the EUR began to weaken sharply against CHF, falling below the key 1.5000 EUR/CHF level. The SNB began ratcheting up its rhetoric opposing CHF strength relative to the EUR, but the market forces were simply too great — the EUR was being dumped and CHF embraced. The SNB felt compelled to undertake unilateral intervention to stem CHF strength, but was ultimately overwhelmed and EUR/CHF fell to below 1.2500 despite nearly $200 billion being spent on intervention. This is another example of unilateral intervention proving ineffective, at least in the medium term.

In the summer of 2011, despite months of SNB threats to take decisive action to stem CHF strength, EUR/CHF fell below the 1.2000/2500 level, a perceived line in the sand for the SNB. EUR/CHF fell to within a hair's breadth of parity (1.0000) in August 2011, finally prompting the SNB to take off the gloves. In

Book IV

Foreign Currency Trading

September 2011, the SNB took the unprecedented step of imposing a floor of 1.2000 in EUR/CHF (a ceiling for CHF), and vowed to sell unlimited amounts of CHF against other major currencies to enforce the policy. The market reaction was immediate, and EUR/CHF adjusted to above 1.2000 in very short order.

Important Swiss economic reports

Swiss data tends to get lost in the mix of data reports out of the United States and the Eurozone, with many in the market looking at Switzerland as a de facto Eurozone member. In that sense, market reactions to Swiss data and events primarily show up in EUR/CHF cross rates. The important Swiss data to keep an eye on are

- ✔ SNB rate decisions and speeches by directorate members
- ✔ The KOF Leading Economic Indicator
- ✔ Retail sales
- ✔ Trade balance
- ✔ PPI and CPI
- ✔ The unemployment rate

Price action behavior in GBP/USD and USD/CHF

The GBP/USD and USD/CHF share similar market liquidity and trading interest, which are the main drivers of price action. In both pairs, liquidity and market interest tend to be the thinnest among the majors, especially outside of European trading hours. As a result, both pairs typically trade with wider 3- to 5-pip prices relative to narrower spreads in EUR/USD and USD/JPY. The most important trading characteristics of cable and Swissy are as follows:

- ✔ **Price action tends to be jumpy, even in normal markets.** Cable and Swissy are like long-tailed cats in a room full of rocking chairs — extremely nervous. In a relatively calm market, you can see prices in these two pairs jump around by routine 2- to 3-pip increments, which can be even more pronounced when prices are moving in response to news or data.

- ✔ **Price action tends to see one-way traffic in highly directional markets.** When news or data move the market, the price changes in Swissy and cable are apt to be the most abrupt. On top of that, cable and Swissy remain highly directional and tend to see minimal pullbacks or backing and filling.

✔ **Cable and Swissy are leading indicators for EUR/USD.** For example, if bids in USD/CHF keep appearing in a relatively orderly fashion, say every 1 to 2 pips on a downswing, it's a sign that the move is not especially extreme. On the other hand, prices dropping by larger increments and displaying very few bounces is a strong indication that a larger move is unfolding.

✔ **False breaks of technical levels occur frequently.** Cable and Swissy have a nasty habit of breaking beyond technical support and resistance levels, only to reverse course and then trade in the opposite direction. And we're not talking about just a few points beyond the level here, but more like 25 to 30 pips in many cases.

✔ **Spike reversals are very common.** The tendency of cable and Swissy to overshoot in extreme directional moves and to generate false breaks of technical levels means that spike reversals appear frequently on short-term charts. Though the size of the spikes varies depending on the market circumstances and current events, spike reversals of more than 30 to 40 points on an hourly closing basis should alert you to a potentially larger reversal taking place. The bigger the spike reversal, the more significance it holds for the future direction.

GBP/USD and USD/CHF trading considerations

The routine short-term volatility of cable and Swissy suggests several important tactical trading refinements. The overarching idea in the following suggestions is to adjust your trading strategies to weather the erratic price action and higher overall volatility in these pairs in comparison to the larger EUR/USD:

✔ **Reduce position size relative to margin.** This first consideration is especially important in cable, due to its high relative value to the USD. With GBP/USD trading around 1.60 to the dollar (£1 = $1.60) a single, mini lot position (£10,000) eats up $320 in required margin at 50:1 leverage. A similar-size position in EUR/USD (at 1.30) requires only $260 in margin. If you're going to trade in cable, you need more margin than if you stay with EUR/USD, USD/JPY, or Swissy. Cable and Swissy's higher volatility also argue for overall smaller position sizes. A smaller position allows you to better withstand their short-term volatility and gives you greater staying power relative to margin.

✔ **Allow a greater margin of error on technical breaks.** In cable and Swissy, tests of technical levels frequently result in false breaks as stops are triggered. If your stop loss is too close to the technical level, it's ripe

Book IV

Foreign Currency Trading

for the picking by the market. Factoring in a margin of error when placing stop-loss orders can help — it allows you to withstand any short-term false break. Using a margin of error may also require you to reduce your position size to give you greater flexibility and margin staying-power.

✔ **Anticipate overshoots and false breaks for position entry.** When you're looking to enter a position by selling on rallies or buying on dips, you're probably focused on selling at resistance and buying on support. You can take advantage of cable and Swissy's tendency to overshoot or make false breaks of technical levels by placing your limit order behind the technical level (above resistance, below support). If cable and Swissy break through the level, you're able to enter at a better price than if you'd adhered to the technical level alone.

Alternatively, you can enter a portion of your desired position at the technical level and enter the rest at better prices if the level is breached, improving the average rate of your position. Worst-case scenario, the market fills you for only half of your desired position and then reverses. Best-case scenario, you establish your full desired position at a better rate than you expected and the market reverses. If the market keeps going against you, at least your average position rate is better than it otherwise would have been.

✔ **Be quick on the trigger.** Cable and Swissy tend to move very quickly and may not spend a lot of time around key price levels. This characteristic favors traders who are decisive and quick to enter and exit positions. Another way you can take advantage of the short-term volatility of cable and Swissy is by using resting orders (preset orders that cover longer-term open positions) to get in and out. A standing limit order (to buy or sell at a specified price or better) accomplishes trades automatically and instantly if the price deals. Trailing stops (stop-loss orders set as a percentage below the market price) are especially useful when you have a position that's moving the right way.

✔ **Resist the contrarian urge following large directional moves.** After an extended directional price move, many traders may feel inclined to trade in the opposite direction, if only for a short-term correction. Resist that urge in cable and Swissy. On days with large directional price moves of more than 100 pips, cable and Swissy often finish out the trading day at the extremes of the price move (meaning at the highs on an up-move and at the lows on a decline). So even if you sell the high of a move up, you're unlikely to get any joy on the day.

✔ **Pick your spots wisely.** Instead of simply jumping into cable or Swissy, do a fair amount of watching and studying to get a handle on where appropriate entry points are. Short-term volatility in cable and Swissy make for treacherous short-term trading conditions. You'll greatly improve your chances of catching a favorable move if you step back and look at the medium- and longer-term pictures (four-hour and daily) instead of getting caught up in the short-term volatility.

Trading the Minor Pairs: USD/CAD, AUD/USD, and NZD/USD

The minor dollar pairs are USD/CAD (the U.S. dollar versus the Canadian dollar), AUD/USD (the Australian dollar versus the U.S. dollar), and NZD/USD (the New Zealand dollar versus the U.S. dollar). The minor currency pairs are also commonly referred to as the *commonwealth currencies* or the *commodity currencies*.

USD/CAD and AUD/USD account for 5 and 6 percent of global daily trading volume, respectively, according to the 2010 Bank for International Settlements (BIS) survey of forex market volumes. NZD/USD accounts for less than 2 percent each of spot trading volume. But these three pairs offer more than ample liquidity to be actively traded and can offer significant trading opportunities, both for short-term traders and medium- to longer-term speculators.

Trading fundamentals of USD/CAD

The Canadian dollar (nicknamed the *Loonie*) trades according to the same macroeconomic fundamentals as most major currencies. So closely follow Bank of Canada (BOC) monetary policy developments, current economic data, inflation readings, and political goings-on, just as you would with any of the majors.

The trajectory of the Canadian economy is closely linked to the overall direction of the U.S. economy. The United States and Canada are still each other's largest commercial trading partners, and the vast majority of Canadians live within 100 miles of the U.S./Canadian border. Even the BOC regularly refers to the U.S. economic outlook in its forecasts of Canadian economic prospects. It's a long-term dynamic, making for plenty of short-term trading opportunities.

Trading USD/CAD by the numbers

The standard market convention is to quote USD/CAD in terms of the number of Canadian dollars per USD. A USD/CAD rate of 1.0200, for instance, means it takes CAD1.02 to buy USD1. The market convention means that USD/CAD trades in the same overall direction of the USD, with a higher USD/CAD rate reflecting a stronger USD/weaker CAD and a lower rate showing a weaker USD/stronger CAD.

USD/CAD has the USD as the primary currency and the CAD as the counter currency. This means

✔ **USD/CAD is traded in amounts denominated in USD.** For online currency trading platforms, standard lot sizes are USD100,000, and mini lot sizes are USD10,000.

- ✔ **The pip value, or minimum price fluctuation, is denominated in CAD.**

- ✔ **Profit and loss register in CAD.** For a standard lot position size, each pip is worth CAD10, and each pip in a mini lot position is worth CAD1. A USD/CAD rate of 1.0200 (which will change over time, of course) equates to a pip value of USD9.80 for each standard lot and USD0.98 for each mini lot.

- ✔ **Margin calculations are typically based in USD, so seeing how much margin is required to hold a position in USD/CAD is a simple calculation using the leverage ratio.** At 50:1 leverage, for instance, $2,000 of available margin is needed to trade 100,000 USD/CAD, and $200 is needed to trade 10,000 USD/CAD.

USD/CAD is unique among currency pairs in that it trades for spot settlement only one day beyond the trade date, as opposed to the normal two days for all other currency pairs. The difference is due to the fact that New York and Toronto, the two nations' financial centers, are in the same time zone, allowing for faster trade confirmations and settlement transfers. For spot traders, the difference means that USD/CAD undergoes the extended weekend (three-day) rollover after the close of trading on Thursdays, instead of on Wednesdays like all other pairs, assuming no holidays are involved.

Canadian events and data reports to watch

On top of following U.S. economic data to maintain an outlook for the larger economy to the south, pay close attention to individual Canadian economic data and official commentaries, particularly the following:

- ✔ Bank of Canada (BOC) speakers, rate decisions, and economic forecasts
- ✔ The employment report
- ✔ The gross domestic product (GDP) reported monthly
- ✔ International securities transactions
- ✔ International merchandise trade
- ✔ Wholesale and retail sales
- ✔ CPI and BOC CPI
- ✔ Manufacturing shipments
- ✔ The Ivey Purchasing Managers Index

Trading fundamentals of AUD/USD

The Australian dollar is commonly referred to as the *Aussie,* or even just *Oz* for short. These terms refer to both the AUD/USD pair and Australian dollar cross pairs. Aussie trading volume accounts for a little over 5 percent of daily global spot turnover, but it's still a regular mover, both against the U.S. dollar and on the crosses, so it makes an active currency pair for speculators.

The boom in Asian regional growth over the past decade and high levels of global economic growth have benefited the Australian economy in recent years. Those high levels of growth have brought with them relatively high levels of inflation, prompting the Reserve Bank of Australia (RBA) to repeatedly hike interest rates. In addition to commodity prices and the outlook for global demand, the interest-rate outlook is especially critical to the value of the Aussie.

Aussie trading is heavily influenced by cross trading, especially against the yen, because the AUD/JPY cross captures one of the highest interest differentials between major currencies. AUD/JPY has been a favorite among traders pursuing the carry trade, so you want to monitor important AUD/JPY technical levels.

Aussie trading is also regularly influenced by New Zealand economic data, but the flow is usually more significant in the opposite direction, where Aussie data will exert a larger pull on NZD prices, given the larger size of the Australian economy. Still, when trading Aussie, it helps to be aware of upcoming NZD data, because the two tend to move together in regional sympathy. (NZD is discussed later in this chapter.)

Trading AUD/USD by the numbers

Market quoting conventions for trading in AUD/USD are to quote the pair in terms of the number of USD per AUD. An AUD/USD rate of 0.7000 means it takes USD0.70 (or 78¢) to buy AUD1. This is the same convention as GBP/USD.

AUD/USD trades in the opposite direction of the overall value of the USD and in the same direction as the value of the AUD. A higher AUD/USD rate means AUD is stronger/USD weaker, and a lower AUD/USD rate means AUD is weaker/USD stronger.

AUD is the primary currency in the pair, and USD is the counter currency, which means

- ✔ **AUD/USD is traded in amounts denominated in AUD.**

- ✔ **The pip value is denominated in USD.**

- ✔ **Profit and loss accrue in USD.** For a 100,000 AUD/USD position size, each pip is worth USD10, and each pip on a 10,000 AUD/USD position is worth USD1.

- ✔ **Margin calculations are typically in USD on online trading platforms.**

Book IV

Foreign Currency Trading

As of September 2013, AUD/USD is trading around 0.9200, meaning a standard lot position size (AUD 100,000) requires USD1,840 in available margin (AUD 100,000 × 0.9200 = USD92,000 ÷ 50 = USD1,840), and a mini lot (AUD 10,000) needs USD184 in available margin.

Australian events and data reports to watch

Australian data and events regularly transpire during the New York late afternoon or early evening, which is early morning the next day in the land down under. Keep an eye on the following:

- Reserve Bank of Australia (RBA) and treasury speakers, RBA rate decisions, and monetary policy outlooks

- Trade balance (monthly) and current account balance (quarterly)

- Employment reports (full-time/part-time)

- Westpac consumer and National Australia Bank (NAB) business confidence indices

- CPI and producer price index (PPI) reports

- Retail sales and housing market data

Trading fundamentals of NZD/USD

The New Zealand dollar is nicknamed the *Kiwi*, which refers to both the NZD and the NZD/USD pair. Given the relatively small size of the New Zealand economy, the Kiwi is probably the most interest-rate sensitive of all the currencies.

The New Zealand economy has undergone a virtual transformation over the past two decades, moving from a mostly agricultural export orientation to a domestically driven service and manufacturing base. The rapid growth has seen disposable incomes soar; with higher disposable incomes have come persistently high levels of inflation. The Reserve Bank of New Zealand (RBNZ), the central bank, has frequently been among the more hawkish central banks.

In addition to all the standard New Zealand economic data and official pronouncements you need to monitor, Kiwi trading is closely tied to Australian data and prospects, due to a strong trade and regional relationship. No set formula exists to describe the currencies' relationship, but a general rule is that when it's a USD-based move, Aussie and Kiwi tend to trade in the same direction as each other relative to the USD. But when Kiwi or Aussie news comes in, the AUD/NZD (Aussie/Kiwi) cross exerts a larger influence.

Trading NZD/USD by the numbers

AUD/USD and NZD/USD are both quoted in the same way; refer to the earlier section for details on the AUD/USD pairing. NZD/USD rates reflect the number of USD per NZD. The Kiwi trades in the opposite direction of the overall value of the USD, so a weaker USD means a higher Kiwi rate, and a lower Kiwi rate represents a stronger USD.

The NZD is the primary currency in the pair, and the USD is the counter currency, which means

- ✔ **NZD/USD is traded in position sizes denominated in NZD.**

- ✔ **The pip values are denominated in USD.**

- ✔ **Profit and loss accrues in USD.** On a 100,000 NZD/USD position, each pip is worth USD10; on a 10,000 position size, each pip is worth USD1.

- ✔ **Margin calculations are typically based in USD on margin trading platforms.**

Using an NZD/USD rate of 0.7000 and a leverage ratio of 50:1, a 100,000 Kiwi position requires USD1,400 in margin, while a 10,000 NZD/USD position would need only USD140 in margin.

New Zealand events and data reports to watch

RBNZ commentary and rate decisions are pivotal to the value of the Kiwi, given the significance of interest-rates to the currency. Finance ministry comments are secondary to the rhetoric of the independent RBNZ but can still upset the Kiwi cart from time to time. Additionally, keep an eye on the following:

- ✔ Consumer prices, housing prices, and food prices

- ✔ Retail sales and credit-card spending

- ✔ Westpac and ANZ (Australia and New Zealand Banking Group) consumer confidence indices

- ✔ The quarterly GDP and the monthly trade balance

- ✔ The National Bank of New Zealand (NBNZ) business confidence survey

Trading considerations in USD/CAD, AUD/USD, and NZD/USD

These three currency pairs share many of the same trading traits and even travel as a pack sometimes — especially Aussie and Kiwi, given their regional proximity and close economic ties. Whether they're being grouped as the commodity currencies, the commonwealth currencies, or just smaller regional currencies versus the U.S. dollar, they can frequently serve as a leading indicator of overall USD market direction.

Liquidity and market interest are lower

One of the reasons these pairs tend to exhibit leading characteristics is due to the lower relative liquidity of the pairs, which amplifies the speculative effect on them. If sentiment is shifting in favor of the U.S. dollar, for example, the effect of speculative interest — the fast money — is going to be most evident in lower-volume currency pairs.

In general, you need to be aware that overall liquidity and market interest in these pairs is significantly lower than in the majors. On a daily basis, liquidity in these pairs is at its peak when the local centers (Toronto, Sydney, and Wellington) are open. London market makers provide a solid liquidity base to bridge the gap outside the local markets, but you can largely forget about USD/CAD during the Asia-Pacific session, and the Aussie and Kiwi markets are problematic after the London/European session close until their financial centers reopen a few hours later. The net result is a concentration of market interest in these currency pairs among the major banks of the currency countries, which has implications of its own (see the later section "Technical levels can be blurry").

Price action is highly event driven

As a result of the overall lower level of liquidity in these currency pairs, in concert with relatively high levels of speculative positioning (at times), you have the ultimate mix for explosive reactions after currency-specific news or data comes out. Significant data or news surprises, especially when contrary to expectations and likely market positioning, tend to have an outsized impact on the market. Traders positioning in these currencies need to be especially aware of this impact and to recognize the greater degree of volatility and risk they face if events don't transpire as expected.

A data or event surprise typically leads to a price gap when the news is first announced. If the news is sufficiently at odds with market expectations and positioning, subsequent price action tends to be mostly one-way traffic, as the market reacts to the surprise news and exits earlier positions. If you're caught on the wrong side after unexpected news in these pairs, you're likely better off getting out as soon as possible rather than waiting for a correction to exit at a better level. The lower liquidity and interest in these currency pairs mean you're probably not alone in being caught wrong-sided, which tends to see steady, one-way interest, punctuated by accelerations when additional stop-loss order levels are hit.

All politics (and economic data) is local

Domestic political developments in these smaller-currency countries can provoke significant movements in the local currencies. National elections, political scandals, and abrupt policy changes can all lead to upheavals in the value of the local currency. The effect tends to be most pronounced on the downside of the currency's value (meaning that bad news tends to hurt a currency more than good news — if there ever is any in politics — helps it). Of course, every situation is different, but the spillover effect between politics and currencies is greatest in these pairs, which means you need to be aware of domestic political events if you're trading in them.

In terms of economic data, these currency pairs tend to participate in overall directional moves relative to the U.S. dollar until a local news or data event triggers more concentrated interest on the local currency. If the USD is under pressure across the board, for instance, USD/CAD is likely to move lower in concert with other dollar pairs. But if negative Canadian news or data emerges, USD/CAD is likely to pare its losses and may even start to move higher if the news is bad enough. If the Canadian news is CAD-positive (say, a higher CPI reading pointing to a potential rate hike), USD/CAD is likely to accelerate to the downside, because USD selling interest is now amplified by CAD buying interest.

Other trading options: Cross-currency pairs and the Scandies

More trading options are available than the major and minor currency pairs. You have options in the currency of Scandinavian nations that haven't adopted the EUR, referred to as the *Scandies,* as well as the *cross-currency* pairs, or *crosses* for short, which pit two non-USD currencies against each other:

✔ **Scandies:** A few of the Scandinavian, or Nordic, countries — namely Sweden ("Stocky," for the Swedish krona), Norway ("Nokkie," for the Norwegian krone), and Denmark ("Copey," for the Danish krone) — chose not to join the monetary union that led to the euro. Trading volumes in the Scandies are generally light but sufficient enough to offer additional speculative trading opportunities depending on the circumstances. Most of the trading in the Scandies is done versus EUR, driven by intra-European divergences in either growth or interest rate outlooks. Generally speaking, trading the USD versus the Scandies tends to mimic EUR/USD, but in mirror image due to quoting conventions.

✔ **Cross-currency pairs:** A cross-currency pair is any currency pair that doesn't have the U.S. dollar as one of the currencies in the pairing (see Chapter 1 in Book IV for more info). The catch is that cross rates are derived from the prices of the underlying USD pairs. For example, one of the most active crosses is EUR/JPY, pitting the two largest currencies outside the U.S. dollar directly against each other. But the EUR/JPY rate at any given instant is a function (the product) of the current EUR/USD and USD/JPY rates. The most popular cross pairs involve the most actively traded major currencies, like EUR/JPY, EUR/GBP, and EUR/CHF.

Technical levels can be blurry

The relatively lower level of liquidity and market interest in these currency pairs makes for sometimes-difficult technical trading conditions. Trendlines and retracement levels in particular are subject to regular overshoots. Prices may move beyond the technical level — sometimes only 5 to 10 pips, other times for extensive distances or for prolonged periods — only to reverse course and reestablish the technical level later.

If the price break of a technical level is quickly reversed, it's a good sign that it was just a position-related movement. If fresh news is out, however, you may be seeing the initial wave of a larger directional move.

Chapter 3

Gathering and Interpreting Economic Data

*F*undamental economic data reports are among the most significant information inputs because policymakers and market participants alike use them to gauge the state of the economy, set monetary policy, and make investment decisions. From a trader's perspective, data reports are the routine catalysts that stir up markets and get things moving.

In this chapter, you discover how to factor the various reports into a broader view of the economic outlook for each particular country. This chapter also covers the major data reports from the United States and around the world to give you an idea of what they cover and how the forex market interprets them. *Remember:* Even more important than the data itself is the market's reaction to the data.

Making Sense of Economic Data

If you're like most people, you probably have a decent idea of what certain economic reports mean, like the unemployment rate or the consumer price index (CPI). But like lots of people, you probably don't have a strong idea of how to put the data together to make sense of it all. Having a fundamental model to put the data in perspective is critical to understanding what the data means and how the forex market is likely to react to the data.

Interpreting data with a basic model

In this section, I suggest a basic model to interpret the deluge of economic indicators you encounter in the forex market. Although it's not the be-all and end-all of economic theory, this model is a solid framework on which to hang the economic indicators and see how they fit together. (***Note:*** This model leaves out government to simplify matters.) Following are the areas to focus on:

✔ **The labor market:** Jobs and job creation are the keys to the medium- and long-term economic outlook for any country or economic bloc. Signs of broader economic growth are seen as tentative or suspect unless job growth is also present. Both scenarios have major implications for interest-rate moves and investment themes, which are key currency drivers.

From the currency-market point of view, labor-market strength is typically seen as a currency positive, because it indicates positive growth prospects going forward, along with the potential for higher interest rates based on stronger growth or wage-driven inflation. Labor-market weakness is typically viewed as a currency negative.

✔ **The consumer:** The economies of the major currencies are driven overwhelmingly by *personal consumption* (also known as *private consumption, personal spending,* and similar impersonal terms), which refers to how people spend their money. Are they spending more or less? Also, what's the outlook for their spending — to increase, decrease, or stay the same? If you want to gauge the short-run outlook of an economy, look no further than how the individual consumer is faring.

✔ **The business sector:** Firms contribute directly to economic activity through *capital expenditures* (for example, building factories, stores, and offices; buying software and telecommunications equipment) and indirectly through growth (by hiring), expanding production, and producing investment opportunities.

Manufacturing and export sectors are more significant in many non-U.S. economies than they are in the United States.

✔ **The structural indicators:** *Structural indicators* are data reports that cover the overall economic environment. Structural indicators frequently form the basis for currency trends and tend to be most important to medium- and long-term traders. The main structural reports focus on

- **Inflation:** Whether prices are rising or falling, and how fast.

- **Growth:** Indicators of growth and overall economic activity, typically in the form of gross domestic product (GDP) reports, pointing out whether the economy is expanding or contracting, and how fast.

- **Trade balance:** Whether a country is importing more or less than it exports. The currency of a country with a *trade deficit* (the country imports more than it exports) tends to weaken while the currency of a country with a *trade surplus* (the country exports more than it imports) tends to appreciate.

- **Fiscal balance:** The overall level of government borrowing and the market's perception of financial stability. Countries with high debt levels run the risks of a weakening currency.

Assessing economic data reports from a trading perspective

When you assess economic data reports, you have to consider not only the imperfections of economic data gathering but also how markets interpret individual data reports. The following sections look at important data-reporting conventions and how they can also affect market reactions.

Understanding and revising data history

Economic data reports have a history, and the market reacts strongly when data comes in surprisingly better or worse than expected. The sustainability of the reaction, however, varies greatly depending on the circumstances. If retail sales are generally increasing, for instance, does a one-month drop in retail sales indicate that the trend is over, or was it a one-off decline due to bad weather keeping shoppers at home?

When you're looking at upcoming economic data events, be aware not only of what's expected, but also what, if any, trends are evident in the data series. The more pronounced or lengthy the trend is, the more likely the reactions to out-of-line economic reports will prove short-lived. The more uneven the recent data has been, the more likely the reaction to the new data will be sustained.

When interpreting incoming economic data, see whether the data from the prior period has been revised. Unfortunately, no rule prevents earlier economic data from being changed. When prior-period data is revised, the market will tend to net out the older, revised report with the newly released data, essentially looking at the two reports together for what they suggest about the data trend. A general rule is that the larger the revision to the prior report, the more significance it will carry into the interpretation of the current release. In general, current data reports tend to receive a higher weighting by the market, if only because the data is the freshest available, and markets are always looking ahead.

Book IV

Foreign Currency Trading

Getting to the core

A number of important economic indicators are issued on a headline basis and a core basis. The *headline* reading is the complete result of the indicator; the *core* reading is the headline reading minus certain categories or excluding certain items. Most inflation reports and measures of consumer spending use this convention.

In the case of inflation reports, many reporting agencies strip out or exclude highly volatile components, such as food and energy. By excluding items that are prone to market, seasonal, or weather-related disruptions, the core reading is believed to paint a more accurate picture of structural, long-term price pressures, which is what concerns monetary policymakers the most. In the United States, for instance, the consumer price index (CPI) is reported on a core basis excluding food and energy, commonly cited as *CPI ex-F&E*. Looking at consumer spending reports, the retail sales report in the United States is reported on a core basis excluding autos (retail sales ex-autos), which are large-ticket items heavily influenced by seasonal discounting and sales promotions.

Markets tend to focus on the core reading over the headline reading in most cases. The result can be large discrepancies between headline data and the core readings, and market reactions are similarly disjointed, with an initial reaction based on the headline reading and subsequent reaction based on the core.

Market-Moving Economic Data Reports from the United States

This section surveys the major economic data reports that come out of the United States. The purpose for doing this is twofold: to introduce you to the major economic reports issued by every major currency country, using U.S. data as the example, and to let you in on the finer points of how the market views the important data reports. Head to later sections in this chapter for a country-by-country look at major non-U.S. data reports.

Labor-market reports

Job creation/destruction is the single-most important driver of overall economic growth. Every major economy issues updates on its labor market by reporting the number of jobs added/lost, the unemployment rate, or some variation of those. The following are the key U.S. employment reports.

U.S. monthly employment report

The U.S. jobs report, considered among the timeliest of economic indicators (it's released on the first Friday of each month), is subject to large revisions to prior periods and significant statistical volatility. The main components of the report include

- ✔ **Change in non-farm payrolls (NFP):** Shows the number of jobs gained or lost in the prior month. The market's initial reaction is based on the difference between the actual and the forecast change in NFP.

- ✔ **The unemployment rate:** Measures unemployed individuals seeking work as a percentage of the civilian labor force, with increasing rates typically interpreted as a sign of weakness in the labor market and the economy overall, and declining rates considered a positive sign.

- ✔ **Average hourly earnings:** Measures the change in employee wages and is looked at as an indicator of whether incomes are rising or falling and the implications for consumer spending.

- ✔ **Average weekly hours:** Measures the average number of hours worked each week and is looked at as a rough gauge of the demand for labor, with increasing weekly hours seen as a positive for the labor market.

ADP national employment report

This report (put together by the payroll processing company of the same name) measures only private jobs and excludes government hiring. It has a spotty track record of predicting the NFP for any given month, but it shows a stronger correlation over longer time frames. Because of that uncertainty, market reaction to the ADP is typically minor and short-lived, but many economists' NFP forecasts are still adjusted to reflect large ADP *misses* (when the data is significantly above/below consensus estimates).

Weekly initial unemployment claims

Initial jobless claims represent first-time filings for unemployment insurance. Although the changes in initial claims can be volatile on a week-to-week basis, sharp increases or declines get the market's attention, producing a market reaction on their own, as well as causing estimates of upcoming monthly NFP reports to be downgraded or upgraded.

A second part of the weekly claims report is *continuing claims,* which is a measure of the total number of people receiving unemployment benefits, excluding first-time filers. Increases in continuing claims typically suggest deterioration in the job market; declines in continuing claims are viewed as an improvement.

Consumer-level data reports

Personal consumption accounts for two-thirds or more of most developed nations' economies, so how consumers are doing has a big impact on the economic outlook and the direction of interest rates, which are both key drivers of forex rates. Here are the main U.S. data reports focusing on personal consumption.

Consumer sentiment

The market pays attention to consumer confidence indicators even though little correlation exists between how consumers say they feel and how they actually go on to spend. In fact, consumer sentiment is frequently the result of changes in gasoline prices, how the stock market is faring, or what recent employment indicators suggested. More reliable indicators of consumer spending are money-in-the-pocket gauges like average weekly earnings, personal income and spending, and retail sales reports. The following are key confidence gauges:

- **Consumer confidence index:** A monthly report issued by the Conference Board. The surveys ask households about their outlooks for overall economic conditions, employment, and incomes.

- **University of Michigan consumer sentiment index:** Comes out twice a month: a preliminary reading in the middle of the month and a final reading at the start of the next month.

- **ABC Consumer Confidence:** A weekly confidence report you can use to update your expectations of upcoming monthly consumer confidence and University of Michigan reports.

Personal income and personal spending

These two monthly reports provide an indication of how much money is going into and out of consumers' pockets. *Personal income* includes all wages and salaries, along with transfer payments (such as Social Security or unemployment insurance) and dividends. *Personal spending* is based on personal consumption expenditures for all types of individual outlays.

The greater the increases in personal income, the more optimistic the consumption outlook will be, and vice versa. But it's important to note that inflation-adjusted incomes are the key. If incomes are just keeping pace with inflation, the outlook for spending is less positive.

Retail sales

The monthly advance retail sales report is the primary indicator of personal spending in the United States, covering almost every purchase Americans make, from gas-station fill-ups to dinner and a movie. Retail sales are reported on a headline basis as well as on a core basis (which excludes automobile purchases), but the market focuses mainly on the core number to get a handle on how the consumer is behaving.

Retail sales reports are subject to a variety of distorting effects, most commonly from weather. Stretches of bad weather, such as major storms or bouts of unseasonable cold or heat, can impair consumer mobility or alter shopping patterns, reducing retail sales in the affected period. Sharp swings in gasoline prices can also create illusory effects, such as price spikes leading to an apparent increase in retail sales due to the higher per-gallon price, while overall non-gas retail sales are reduced or displaced by the higher outlays at the pump.

Durable goods orders

Durable goods measure the amount of orders received by manufacturers that produce items made to last at least three years (washing machines, furniture, and so on). Durable goods are reported on a headline basis and on a core basis, excluding transportation (ex-transportation — mostly aircraft).

Because durables are generally bigger-ticket purchases, they're also looked at as a leading indicator of overall consumer spending.

Housing-market indicators

The real estate or housing market is a major factor behind consumer spending because the home typically represents the largest asset on a household's balance sheet. Rising home prices are seen to support consumption through the *wealth effect* (the richer you feel, the more likely you are to spend), whereas falling house prices can be a major drag on personal spending. A raft of monthly housing market reports monitor the sector, based on whether the homes are new or existing:

- ✔ **Existing-home sales** (condos included) account for the lion's share of residential real-estate activity — about 85 percent of total home sales. Median home prices and the inventory of unsold homes are important clues to how the housing market is evolving. Existing-home sales are counted after a closing; pending home sales are counted when a contract is signed to buy an existing home.

- ✔ **New-home sales** account for about 15 percent of residential home sales. New-home sales are counted when a contract is signed to purchase the new home, which means that contract cancellations (not reported) may result in lower actual sales than originally reported.

- ✔ **Housing starts** measure the number of new-home construction starts that took place in each month, reported on an annualized rate. Housing starts are considered a leading indicator of new-home sales but more recently have been looked at as an indication of home builder sentiment.

- ✔ **Building permits** are the starting point of the whole new-housing cycle. Because they are required before construction can begin on new homes, they're viewed as another leading indicator of housing starts and new-home sales.

Business-level data reports

Getting a handle on how businesses are faring is an important clue to the strength of the economy, which in turn drives the outlook for interest rates and the overall investment environment. The following series of data reports offer insights into how companies are responding at the enterprise level.

Book IV

Foreign Currency Trading

Institute for Supply Management reports

The Institute for Supply Management (ISM) calculates several regional and national indices of current business conditions and future outlooks based on surveys of purchasing managers. ISM readings are based on a boom/bust scale, with 50 as the tipping point — a reading above 50 indicates expansion, whereas a reading below 50 signals contraction. The main ISM reports to keep an eye on are the

- **Chicago Purchasing Managers Index (PMI):** The Chicago PMI remains the key regional manufacturing activity index because the Chicago area and the Midwest region are still significant hubs of manufacturing activity in the United States. The Chicago PMI is frequently viewed as a leading indicator of the larger national ISM manufacturing report.

- **ISM manufacturing report:** This report is the monthly national survey of manufacturing activity and is one of the key indicators of the overall manufacturing sector. The report includes a prices-paid index, which is viewed as an interim inflation reading, along with other key subsector measurements.

  The market tends to react pretty strongly to sharp changes in the report or if the ISM is moving above or below 50, but because the manufacturing sector accounts for a relatively small portion of overall U.S. economic activity, the importance of the ISM manufacturing gauge tends to be exaggerated.

- **ISM nonmanufacturing report:** This monthly report covers the other 80 percent of the U.S. economy, namely the service sector. Although the ISM manufacturing report gets more attention, the ISM nonmanufacturing report is the one to focus on.

Regional Federal Reserve indices

A number of the Federal Reserve district banks issue monthly surveys of business sentiment in their regions, usually concentrated on the manufacturing sector. Responses above zero indicate that conditions are improving, and readings below zero indicate deterioration. The main regional Fed indices to watch are the

- **Philadelphia Fed index:** Covers the manufacturing sector in Pennsylvania, New Jersey, and Delaware, and includes sub-indices focusing on new orders, employment, inventories, and prices, among others.

- **New York Empire State index:** Assesses New York state manufacturers' current and six-month outlooks.

- **Richmond Fed manufacturing index:** A composite index based on new orders, production, and employment, covering the Middle Atlantic states.

Industrial production and capacity utilization

Industrial production measures the amount of output generated by the nation's factories, mines, and utilities on a monthly basis and is viewed as an indication of changes in the broader economy. Changes here could signal a larger swing in the economic outlook.

The capacity utilization report is looked at for what it suggests about inflationary pressures. High levels of capacity utilization (above 80 percent) may indicate price pressures are building and send a warning sign to policymakers. Lower levels of capacity utilization may signal the absence of inflationary pressures and allow monetary policymakers to keep interest rates lower.

The Fed's Beige Book

The Beige Book is a compilation of regional economic assessments from the Fed's 12 district banks, which develop their summaries based on surveys and anecdotal reporting of local business leaders and economists. The Beige Book, released prior to the Federal Open Market Committee (FOMC) meetings, serves as the basis of economic discussions at the meeting. Markets look at the Beige Book's main findings to get a handle on how the economy is developing as well as what issues the FOMC might focus on.

The key for the market is to assess the main themes of the report, such as

- ✔ **Economic growth (or lack thereof):** Is the economy expanding or contracting? How fast, and how widespread?

- ✔ **Strength by sector:** Which sectors are strongest, and which sectors are weakest?

- ✔ **Inflation:** Are there any signs of inflation?

- ✔ **Employment:** How does the labor market look?

Structural data reports

Structural data reports, which are the big-picture, macroeconomic data that depict the longer-term economic outlook (refer to the earlier section "Interpreting data with a basic model"), can be some of the most significant drivers of central bank monetary policy.

Inflation gauges

Inflation reports are used to monitor overall changes in price levels of goods and services and as key inputs into setting interest rate expectations. Increases in inflation are likely to be met with higher interest rates by central-bank policymakers seeking to stamp out inflation, whereas moderating or declining inflation readings suggest generally lower interest-rate expectations.

A number of different inflation reports exist, each focusing on a different source of inflation or stage of the economy where the price changes are appearing. The main inflation reports to keep an eye on are the

- ✔ **Consumer price index (CPI):** Measures the cost of a basket of goods and services at the consumer or retail level — the prices that we're paying. The CPI is looked at as the final stage of inflation.

- ✔ **Producer price index (PPI):** Measures the change in prices at the producer or wholesale level, or what firms are charging one another for goods and services. The PPI may serve as a leading indicator of overall inflation.

- ✔ **Personal consumption expenditure (PCE):** Although roughly equivalent to the CPI, measuring changes in the price of a basket of goods and services at the consumer level, PCE is preferred by the Federal Reserve as its main inflation gauge because the composition of items in the PCE basket changes more frequently than that of the CPI, reflecting evolving consumer tastes and behavior.

Gross domestic product

Gross domestic product (GDP) measures the total amount of economic activity over a specified period, usually quarterly and adjusted for inflation. The percentage change in GDP from one period to the next is looked at as the primary growth rate of an economy. (**Note:** GDP is frequently calculated on a quarterly basis but reported in *annualized* terms. That means a 0.5 percent quarterly GDP increase would be reported as a 2 percent annualized rate of growth for the quarter: 0.5 percent × 4 quarters = 2 percent. The use of annualized rates is helpful for comparing relative growth among economies.)

In most countries, GDP is reported on a quarterly basis, so it's taken as a big-picture reality check on overall economic growth. The market's economic outlook is heavily influenced by what the GDP reports indicate. Better-than-expected growth may spur talk of the need for higher interest rates, whereas steady or slower GDP growth may suggest easier monetary policy ahead.

Trade and current account balances

Two of the most important reports for the forex markets, because of their direct and potentially long-term currency implications, are trade and current account balances:

- ✔ **Trade balance** measures the difference between a nation's exports and its imports. A nation that imports more than it exports has a *trade deficit;* a nation that exports more than it imports has a *trade surplus*.

- ✔ **Current account balance** is a broader measure of international trade and includes financial transfers as well as trade in goods and services. Current accounts are also either in deficit or surplus, reflecting whether a country is a net borrower from or lender to the rest of the world.

Countries with persistently large trade or current account deficits tend to see their currencies weaken relative to other currencies, whereas currencies of countries running trade surpluses tend to appreciate.

Government debt and budget deficits

The aftermath of the Great Financial Crisis of 2008–2009 (GFC) has exposed high debt and deficit levels in many major economies, especially in the United States, Europe, the United Kingdom, and Japan. Fears of a debt *restructuring* (where terms of a bond are altered) or default can seriously undermine confidence in a national currency, leading to an extended bout of weakness, as was seen with the euro in the 2010 European debt crisis.

No single data release adequately covers the debt situations in major economies. Instead, monitoring the debt/deficit picture of key countries depends on a series of news and data flows:

- ✔ **Budget and deficit forecasts:** Issued by individual governments and the International Monetary Fund, these reports are the best way to stay on top of evolving fiscal changes.

- ✔ **Government bond yields, spreads, and CDS (credit default swaps):** As investors' fears increase over the creditworthiness of governments, they sell those countries' bonds, driving yields higher. *Yield spreads* are another measure of risk, noting the difference between the yields of an embattled nation and a safer alternative. Credit default swaps are a form of insurance that pays investors in the event of a default — the higher they are, the greater the perceived risk.

- ✔ **Government debt auctions:** When governments seek to borrow in capital markets, lack of demand or too high a price can shut them out and possibly trigger a default. Watch for indicators of demand, like the *bid/cover ratio,* which measures the amount of bids submitted relative to the issuance amount (the higher the better) and pricing (the higher the yield demanded, the greater the risk).

- ✔ **Sovereign credit ratings:** Major credit rating agencies, like Moody's S&P and Fitch, may announce periodic credit reviews of sovereign debt, possibly suggesting a downgrade.

Book IV

Foreign Currency Trading

Major International Data Reports

The main data reports of other major national economies essentially mirror the U.S. data reports, but with some minor differences in calculation methods or reporting. In other words, the CPI report out of the United Kingdom is looked at the same way as the CPI report is viewed in the United States — as a measure of consumer-level inflation. The next few sections highlight the main data reports of other national economies beyond what is covered earlier.

Eurozone

The main data reports out of the Eurozone are remarkably similar to those of the United States. The key difference is that individual European countries report national economic data, which comes out alongside Eurozone-wide reports from Eurostat or the European Central Bank (ECB).

Because the Eurozone has a common currency and central bank, the forex market focuses primarily on indicators that cover the entire region, such as Eurozone industrial production and CPI. Among individual national reports, the market concentrates on data from the largest Eurozone economies, mainly Germany and France. Keep an eye on all the major reports coming out of those countries because they can generate sizeable reactions based on the idea that they're leading indicators of Eurozone-wide data.

The only European reports that may escape your attention due to unusual names are the principal European confidence indicators. These reports can generate sizeable reactions depending on how they compare to forecasts:

- ✔ **ZEW survey:** Measures growth expectations over the next six months by institutional investors and analysts. The survey is done for Germany and the whole Eurozone.

- ✔ **IFO and GfK surveys:** Monthly corporate sentiment surveys that query businesses across Germany on current sentiment and how business is expected to develop over the next six months.

- ✔ **Purchasing Managers Indexes (PMIs):** Monthly PMIs for the manufacturing and service sectors for Germany, France, and the whole Eurozone, similar to the ISM in the United States (see the earlier section "Institute for Supply Management reports").

- ✔ **Eurozone Confidence:** Monthly confidence surveys for a variety of sectors: consumer, services, industrial, and overall economic sentiment.

Japan

The Japanese economy is still heavily export-oriented. In addition to following all the usual reports, pay special attention to industrial production and manufacturing data because of their large role in the economy. Outside the standard reports to watch, keep an eye on the following:

- ✔ **Tankan index:** This quarterly survey of business outlooks covers current conditions and future prospects from both large manufacturers and large nonmanufacturers.

✔ **Trade balance:** The size of Japan's monthly trade balance surplus carries indications for the health of the export sector.

✔ **All-industry and tertiary industry (services) indices:** These serve as monthly sentiment gauges of industrial and service-sector firms.

United Kingdom

In addition to the usual major government-issued data reports, be alert for the following reports that can frequently trigger sharp reactions in British pounds (GBP):

✔ **Bank of England (BOE) Minutes:** Shows the voting results for the most recent decisions of Monetary Policy Committee (MPC) meetings. Market expectations and GBP are frequently upended when the policy discussion or vote shows a split leaning in the direction of an interest rate change.

✔ **BOE Quarterly Inflation Report:** Shows forecasts for growth and inflation over the next two years. This report can have a significant impact on the interest rate outlook and GBP.

✔ **Purchasing Managers Indexes (PMIs):** Monthly PMIs for the manufacturing, construction, and service sectors.

✔ **GfK consumer confidence and Nationwide consumer confidence:** Two separate, monthly, consumer-sentiment gauges.

✔ **CBI distributive trades survey and industrial trends survey:** The distributive trades survey is a measure of retail and wholesale sales, and the industrial trends survey is a survey of manufacturers' current and future outlook. They're put out by the Confederation of British Industry (CBI).

Canada

Canadian data mirrors U.S. data in many respects, but here are a few other important Canadian indicators to watch:

✔ **International securities transactions:** Shows net investment flows into and out of Canada on a monthly basis. High inflows typically support the Canadian dollar (the CAD), and outflows tend to hurt it.

✔ **The Ivey Purchasing Manager index:** A monthly gauge of Canadian business outlooks, covering purchases, employment, inventories, deliveries, and prices.

Australia and New Zealand

Australian data reports exert a strong influence on the Aussie (the Australian dollar), similar in many respects to how UK data affects the pound. In particular, keep an eye on

- ✔ **The Reserve Bank of Australia (RBA) rate decisions and RBA Minutes:** The RBA's statement following a rate decision, and the subsequent release of the minutes two weeks later, can drive interest rate expectations and AUD big-time.

- ✔ **Westpac consumer confidence and National Australia Bank (NAB) business confidence:** Two separate monthly sentiment gauges.

New Zealand data is similarly provocative for the Kiwi (the New Zealand dollar). In addition to the main data reports and Reserve Bank of New Zealand (RBNZ) statements, keep an eye on the following Kiwi-specific data:

- ✔ **NZ Card Spending:** A monthly report covering purchases using credit, debit, and store cards

- ✔ **ANZ Consumer Confidence:** A monthly survey of New Zealand consumer sentiment

China

China is the world's second largest national economy after the United States, and data out of China has taken on increased prominence, with global markets frequently reeling on weaker China data or surging on stronger reports. The Chinese growth outlook affects global markets through a number of different channels. Stronger Chinese growth is good for global trade and tends to positively influence stock markets around the world. Chinese demand for commodities also has implications for individual commodity markets and commodity-producing countries such as Australia and South Africa. As a result, financial markets around the world are increasingly driven by Chinese growth prospects.

In terms of economic reports, Chinese data that reflects growth are the most significant, with the trade surplus, industrial production, manufacturing PMIs, and quarterly GDP as the keys.

The Chinese still manage their currency and it's not accessible to individual traders. But Chinese data can have an impact far beyond its borders due to its newfound prominence in the global economy.

Chapter 4

Advice for Successful Forex Trading

Sun Tzu, author of the ancient *The Art of War,* a book of military strategy, observed that every battle is won or lost before it even begins. That same rationale applies to trading. And just as an army must know its strengths and weaknesses to succeed, you have to get to know yours, too. This chapter looks at various forex trading styles, provides tips to develop trading discipline, and offers a practical plan for analyzing markets with an eye to spotting trade opportunities. It also takes a hard look at risks beyond just losing money, so you can be prepared for bumps in the road.

Finding a Trading Style That Suits You

The forex market's trading characteristics have something to offer every trading style (long-term, medium-term, or short-term) and approach (technical, fundamental, or a blend). In deciding what style or approach is right for you, the starting point is not the forex market itself, but your own individual circumstances and way of thinking.

Step 1: Know thyself

Before you can identify a trading style and approach that works best for you, you need to give some serious thought to what resources you have available to support your trading. In other words, what can you afford?

- **Money:** When it comes to money, trading capital has to be *risk capital:* money that, if lost, will not materially affect your standard of living. (Obviously, borrowed money is *not* risk capital — never use borrowed money for speculative trading.) When you determine how much risk capital you have available for trading, you'll have a better idea of what size account you can trade and what position size you can handle.

- **Time:** If you're a full-time trader, you have lots of time to devote to market analysis and actually trading the market. But if your full-time job is something other than trading, you have to do your market research in your free time. Be realistic when you think about how much time you'll be able to devote on a regular basis, keeping in mind family obligations and other personal circumstances.

Step 2: Technical or fundamental analysis?

Ask yourself on what basis you'll make your trading decisions: fundamental analysis, which relies on evaluating the underlying value and future potential of the security, or technical analysis, which uses the tracking of price fluctuations to predict or identify market trends? (For details on the different styles, go to Books VII and X, respectively.)

Sometimes forex markets seem to be more driven by fundamental factors; other times, technical developments seem to be leading the charge. So rather than take sides, why not follow an approach that *blends* the two disciplines? Approaching the market with a blend of fundamental and technical analysis can improve your chances of both spotting trade opportunities and managing your trades more effectively.

Step 3: Pick a style, any style

After you've given some thought to the approach you favor (technical, fundamental, or a blend), the next step is to settle on a trading style that best fits those choices. The next sections explain three main trading styles, with degrees of exposure to market risk. Keep in mind that styles frequently overlap, and you can adopt different styles for different trade opportunities or different market conditions.

Short-term, high-frequency trading

Short-term trading in forex typically involves holding a position for only a few seconds or minutes and rarely longer than an hour. The goal is to profit by repeatedly opening and closing positions after gaining just a few pips, frequently as little as one or two pips. (A *pip* is the smallest increment of price fluctuation in currency prices.) In the interbank market, extremely short-term, in-and-out trading is referred to as *jobbing the market;* online currency traders call it *scalping.* Traders who follow this style have these characteristics:

- **They're among the fastest and most disciplined of traders.** Their goal is to capture only a few pips on each trade. Rapid reaction and instantaneous decision-making are essential to successfully jobbing the market. Their motto is "Take the money and run" — repeated a few dozen times a day.

- **They have an intuitive feel for the market.** Some practitioners refer to it as *rhythm trading.* If you were to ask a scalper for her opinion of a particular currency pair, she would be likely to respond along the lines of "It feels *bid*" or "It feels *offered*" (meaning, she senses an underlying buying or selling bias in the market — but only at that moment). If you ask her again a few minutes later, she may respond in the opposite direction.

- **They have no allegiance to any single position.** They couldn't care less if the currency pair goes up or down. They're strictly focused on the next few pips.

Trading a short-term strategy online requires individual traders to invest more time and effort in analyzing the overall market, especially from the technical perspective. Other tips for the short-term trader:

- Trade only the most liquid currency pairs, such as EUR/USD, USD/JPY, EUR/GBP, EUR/JPY, and EUR/CHF, and focus your trading on only one pair at a time. (See Chapter 2 in Book 1V for details on major currency pairs.)

- Trade only during times of peak liquidity and market interest, and avoid trading around data releases.

- Look for a brokerage firm that offers click-and-deal trading so you're not subject to execution delays or requites.

- Preset your default trade size so you don't have to keep specifying it on each deal, and adjust your risk and reward expectations to reflect the dealing spread of the currency pair you're trading.

Medium-term momentum trading

Medium-term positions are typically held for periods ranging anywhere from a few minutes to a few hours, but usually not much longer than a day. As with short-term trading, the key distinction for medium-term trading is not the length of time the position is open but the amount of pips you're seeking/risking.

Book IV

Foreign Currency Trading

Going long in the forex market

Long-term trading seeks to capitalize on major price trends, which are in turn the result of long-term macroeconomic factors:

✔ **Interest rate cycles:** Where are the two currencies' relative interest rates, and where are they likely to go in the coming months?

✔ **Economic growth cycles:** What's the outlook for relative growth over the next several months?

✔ **Currency policies:** Are the currencies considered to be excessively overvalued or undervalued by the major global trading powers?

✔ **Structural deficits or surpluses:** Do the currencies have any major structural issues that tend to see currencies weaken or strengthen, such as fiscal deficits/surpluses or trade deficits/surpluses?

Although the typical players in long-term currency trading are hedge funds and big institutional types, with proper risk management, individual margin traders can seek to capture longer-term trends. The key is to hold a small enough position relative to your margin that you can withstand volatility of as much as 5 percent or more. Mini accounts, which trade in lot sizes of 10,000 currency units, are a good vehicle to take advantage of longer-term price trends.

Also consider taking advantage of significant price changes when they're in your favor in the medium term. *Trading around a core position* refers to taking profit on a portion of your overall position after favorable price changes. You continue to hold a portion of your original position — the core position — and look to reestablish the full position on subsequent market corrections. The risk with trading around a core position is that the trend may not correct after you've taken partial profit, never giving you the chance to reestablish your desired full position. But you're still holding the core of your position, and the fact that the market hasn't corrected means your core position is doing just fine.

The essence of medium-term trading (sometimes referred to as *momentum trading* and *swing trading*) is determining where a currency pair is likely to go over the next several hours or days and constructing a trading strategy to exploit that view.

Medium-term trading requires many of the same skills as short-term trading, but it also demands a broader perspective, greater analytical effort, and a lot more patience. Medium-term traders typically pursue one of the following overall approaches, but there's also plenty of room to combine strategies:

✔ **Trading a view:** Having a fundamental-based opinion on which way a currency pair is likely to move (although view traders still need to be aware of technical levels).

✔ **Trading the technicals:** Spotting trade opportunities on charts (but these traders still need to be aware of fundamental events).

✔ **Trading events and data:** Basing positions on expected outcomes of events, like a central bank rate decision or a G7 meeting. Event/data traders typically open positions well in advance of events and close them when the outcome is known.

✔ **Trading with the flow:** Trading based on overall market direction (trend) or information of major buying and selling (flows). Flow traders tend to stay out of short-term range-bound markets and jump in only when a market move is underway.

Long-term trading

Long-term trading in currencies is generally reserved for hedge funds and other institutional types with deep pockets. Long-term trading in currencies can involve holding positions for weeks, months, and potentially years at a time. Holding positions for that long necessarily involves being exposed to significant short-term volatility that can quickly overwhelm margin trading accounts and isn't for the inexperienced trader. To find out more about this trading style, head to the nearby sidebar "Going long in the forex market."

Developing Trading Discipline

No matter which trading style you decide to pursue, you need an organized *trading plan,* a well-thought-out approach to executing a trade strategy, or you won't get very far. Any trading plan has three simple components:

✔ **Determining position size:** How large a position will you take for each trade strategy? Position size is half the equation for determining how much money is at stake in each trade.

✔ **Deciding where to enter the position:** Exactly where will you try to open the desired position? What happens if your entry level isn't reached?

✔ **Setting stop-loss and take-profit levels:** Exactly where will you exit the position, both if it's a winning *(take-profit)* position and if it's a losing *(stop-loss)* position? Stop-loss and take-profit levels are the second half of the equation that determines how much money is at stake in each trade.

Developing a trading plan and sticking to it are the two main ingredients of trading discipline, *the* defining characteristic of successful traders. Traders who follow a disciplined approach are the ones who survive year after year and market cycle after market cycle. They can even be wrong more often than right and still make money because they follow a disciplined approach. Yet establishing and maintaining trading discipline is an elusive goal for many traders. The following sections explain a few principles of developing trading discipline.

Book IV

Foreign Currency Trading

Taking the emotion out of trading

When it comes to trading in any market, don't underestimate the power of emotions to distract and disrupt. Because you can't take all the emotion out of trading, the best you can hope to achieve is limiting their impact on your trading. Do the following:

- ✔ **Focus on the pips and not the dollars and cents.** Don't be distracted by the exact amount of money won or lost in a trade. Instead, focus on where prices are and how they're behaving.

- ✔ **Remind yourself it's not about being right or wrong; it's about making money.** At the end of the day, the market doesn't care if you were right or wrong, and neither should you. The only true way of measuring trading success is in dollars and cents.

- ✔ **Accept that you're going to lose in a fair number of trades.** Taking losses is as much a part of the routine as taking profits, and you can still be successful over time.

- ✔ **Don't personalize what happens in the market.** The market isn't out to get you; it's going to do what it does whether you're involved in it or not. Interpret events professionally, just as you would the results of any other business venture.

Managing your expectations

Before you get involved with trading currencies, you need to have a healthy sense of what to expect when it comes to trading outcomes. The trading style that you pursue dictates the relative size of profits and losses that you can expect to experience. If you're trading on a short- to medium-term basis, look at average daily trading ranges to get a good idea of what to expect.

The *average daily trading range* is a mathematical average of each day's trading range (high to low) over a specified period. Keep in mind that this figure is just a statistical average — there will be days with larger ranges and days with narrower ranges. Also, average daily ranges will vary significantly by currency pair.

Balancing risk versus reward

Trading is all about taking on risk to generate profits. Some trading books advise people to use a risk/reward ratio, like 2:1, meaning that if you risk $100 on a trade, you should aim to make $200 to justify the risk. Others counsel never to risk more than a fixed percentage of your trading account on any single trade. But a better way to think about risk and reward is to look at each trade opportunity on its own and assess the outcomes based on technical analysis. This approach has the virtue of being as dynamic as the market, allowing you to exploit trade opportunities according to prevailing market conditions.

Another factor to consider in balancing risk and reward is the use of leverage. In online currency trading, generous leverage ratios of 100:1 or 200:1 are typically available. The higher the leverage ratio, the larger the position you can trade based on your margin. But leverage is a double-edged sword because it also amplifies profits and losses. The key is to limit your overall leverage utilization so you're not putting all your eggs in one basket. If you open the largest position available based on your margin, you'll have very little cushion left in case of adverse price movements.

Keeping your ammunition dry

One of the biggest mistakes traders make is known as overtrading. *Overtrading* typically refers to trading too often in the market or trading too many positions at once. Both forms suggest a lack of discipline — throwing handfuls of darts at a board and hoping something sticks. *Keeping your ammunition dry* refers to staying out of the market, watching and waiting, and picking your trades more selectively.

Using your margin collateral sparingly

The margin you're required to post with your forex broker is the basis for all your trading. The amount of margin you put up determines how large a position you can hold and for how long (in pips) if the market moves against you. Unless you just won the lottery, your margin collateral is a precious, finite resource, so you have to use it sparingly.

Holding open positions not only exposes you to market risk but can also cost you market opportunities. After you enter a position, your available margin is reduced, which in turn lowers the amount of available positions you can establish. If you're routinely involved in the market because you don't want to miss out on the next big move, you actually run the risk of missing out on the next big move because you may not have enough available margin to support a position for the big move.

Missing a few opportunities — deliberately

Don't be afraid to miss out on some trade opportunities. No one ever catches all the moves. Instead, focus on your market analysis and pinpoint the next well-defined trading opportunity. (Find out about spotting trade setups in the upcoming section "Analyzing trade setup to determine position size.")

Book IV

Foreign
Currency
Trading

One virtue of trading less frequently is that your market outlook isn't skewed by any of the emotional entanglements that come with open positions. If you ask a trader who's long EUR/USD what he thinks of EUR/USD, surprise, surprise — he's going to tell you he thinks it's going up. That's called *talking your book*. But being out of the market, or being *square,* allows you to step back and analyze market developments with a fresh perspective. That's when you can spot opportunities more clearly and develop an effective trade strategy to exploit them.

Making Time for Market Analysis

The more regular your analysis, the greater the feel you'll develop for where the market has been and where it's likely to go. Also, the more regularly you update yourself on the market, the less time it takes to stay up to speed. At the minimum, be prepared to devote at least an hour every day to looking at the market and keeping tabs on upcoming data and events. A routine for reliable market analysis includes

- ✔ Multiple-time-frame technical analysis, which enables you to recognize price channels. (Both are explained in the following sections.)

- ✔ Candlestick analysis after each daily and weekly close. (Head to Chapter 3 in Book X for information on candlestick analysis.)

- ✔ Reading economic data reports that have come out overnight (flip to Chapter 3 in Book IV for details on these reports).

- ✔ Assessing the likely market impact of upcoming data reports and events.

- ✔ Reviewing market commentaries to stay on top of major themes and overall market sentiment.

 If the time you have to devote to market analysis is limited, focus your energies on only one or two currency pairs. As you become more adept at analysis — or if your available time increases — you can follow and analyze additional currency pairs.

Performing multiple-time-frame technical analysis

You need to perform multiple-time-frame technical analysis to identify support and resistance levels and to track overall price developments. (For key technical analysis principles and charting techniques, go to Book X.)

Multiple-time-frame technical analysis is nothing more complicated than looking at charts using different time frames of data. The basic idea is to look at the big picture first to identify the key longer-term features and then drill down into shorter data time frames to pinpoint short-term price levels and trends. My own preference is to focus on daily, 4-hour, and 30-minute time frames, but you can use whichever time frames you think best match your trading style (these styles are described earlier in this chapter).

Whichever time frames you end up working with, be sure to include longer time frames, like daily and weekly, so you can get a sense of where the most significant price levels are. The strength and significance of support and resistance levels are a function of the time frame in which they're evident, with longer-term technical levels holding greater meaning than shorter ones. You don't want your focus to become so narrow that you lose sight of the big picture and go with a break of short-term resistance, for instance, when major daily or weekly resistance is just beyond.

Make sure the charting system you're using has the ability to save trendlines across time frames, meaning that a trendline you draw on a daily chart should also appear on the four-hour and hourly charts, and vice versa. Also, make sure the charting system has the ability to save the entire chart so you don't have to redraw the trendlines every time you pull up the same chart. On subsequent updates, keep the trendlines that still appear to be valid (meaning that price action has not broken through them), and erase trendlines that are no longer active or have been broken. Over time, you'll get an idea of how good you are at spotting meaningful trendlines by the frequency with which you have to discard old trendlines.

Looking for price channels

A *price channel* is a series of parallel trendlines that encapsulate price action over a discernible period. Channels form in all time frames, with long-term channels on a daily chart highlighting multiday or multiweek trading ranges, and short-term channels on an hourly chart revealing steady buying or selling during a trading session. Price channels can also form in any direction, from horizontal to steeply sloping up or down and anything in between. The whole point of looking for and drawing channel lines, of course, is to highlight additional sources of support or resistance.

The way to identify price channels is through visual inspection, using your eyes and imagination, as well as a fair amount of trial and error. Drawing channels is made much easier by the Copy a Line and Parallel Line functions, which are standard in most charting systems.

Book IV

Foreign Currency Trading

You can use channels as part of your trading strategy to guide both position entry and exit. Short-term traders in particular like to use channels to trade around a core position, for example, selling short on trendline resistance and buying a portion of the position back if prices drop to channel support. If the channel continues to hold, they'll resell on gains back toward trendline resistance, reestablishing their core short position. When channels break, it's also a sign that prices are accelerating in the direction of the trend, as shown by the channel, or that the trend is reversing as prices break out of the channel in the opposite direction.

Managing Your Trading Risk

Experienced traders calculate the risk they're facing in every trade before they ever enter it. By approaching the forex market with risk management as your first thought, you can get some trades wrong and still survive to get other trades right.

Because you're dealing with finite resources — namely, the amount of risk capital you've devoted to your trading — you have a definite limiting factor to your trading. If you eat through your trading capital, you're done. So the starting point of a risk-aware trading plan has to focus on the downside risks. It may not be as much fun as thinking about making millions, but it makes you a better trader.

Analyzing trade setup to determine position size

A *trade setup* is a trade opportunity that you've identified through your analysis. In every trade setup, you need to identify the price point where the setup is invalidated — where the trade is wrong. If you're looking to sell a currency pair based on trendline resistance above, for example, price gains beyond the trendline invalidate your rationale for wanting to be short. So the price level of the trendline is the line in the sand for the overall strategy.

Now comes the entry point for the trade. Say that current market prices are 50 pips below the trendline resistance you've identified. That means the market could move higher by 50 pips and your trade setup would still be valid, but you'd be out of the money by 50 pips. You now have a clear delineation of how much risk your trade setup requires you to assume. If you get in now, you're risking at least 50 pips. Alternatively, you could reduce that risk by waiting and using an order to try selling at better levels — say, 25 pips higher. If the market cooperates and your limit-entry order is filled, you're now risking only 25 pips before your trade setup is negated.

So how large a position should you commit to the trade? From a risk stand-point, it all depends on where you're able to enter the trade relative to your *stop-out level,* the point at which the broker closes your active position because the equity in your account falls below the minimum required for margin. To protect against a stop out, you can set a stop-loss order.

Putting the risk in cash terms

After you've identified where your stop-loss point is — where the trade setup is negated — and where you're able to enter, you're able to calculate the amount of risk posed by the trade. Say you're inclined to enter the position at current market levels, and your stop is 50 pips away. If you're trading a standard-size account (100,000 lot size), and the trade is in NZD/USD (where profit and loss accrue in USD), each lot translates into risking $500 (100,000 × 0.0050 NZD/USD pips = $500). If your margin balance is $10,000, you're risking 5 percent of your trading capital in a one-lot trade (frequently cited in trading literature as the maximum risk in any one trade).

Considering other opportunity risks

Risk in the trading plan is not confined simply to losing money on the trade. There are also opportunity risks from trade setups that you're not able to enter.

Identifying the trade entry points

Identifying where to get into the trade is one of the most important steps in any trading plan. Technical analysis (see Book X) is the primary means of identifying entry levels. When looking to identify entry points, focus on the following technical levels:

✔ Trendlines in various time frames (daily, four-hour, and hourly)

✔ Hourly highs and lows for short-term intraday position entries

✔ Daily highs and lows for medium- to longer-term positions

✔ Congestion zones

✔ Fibonacci retracements of prior price movements (38.2 percent, 50 per-cent, 61.8 percent, and 76.4 percent)

✔ Spike highs and lows

If you're not familiar with Fibonacci retracements (which refer to a theory that prices are likely to retrace a large portion of an original move based upon certain ratios), check out www.fibonacci.com.

Establishing stop losses with foresight

The stop-loss level is the starting point in any trade plan from an overall risk perspective. It's the point where the trade setup is negated and the strategy fails. When considering where to place the stop level, be aware that the currency market, like most financial markets, has a tendency to try to take out levels where stop losses are likely to be located. Nothing is worse than having the right strategy but being taken out by a short-term, stop-loss-driven price move that eventually reverses and goes in the direction of your outlook.

To guard against the risk of being unnecessarily whipsawed out of a position, approach selecting your stop-loss level from a defensive point of view. Anticipate that the market *will* test the level where the trade setup is invalidated, such as trendline support or hourly lows. Then consider this question: If the market tests that level, how far must the market go before it's really considered a break?

No set formula exists for this calculation, but allowing for a margin of error can sometimes prevent a stop loss from being triggered unnecessarily. The margin of error you apply depends on the general volatility of the currency pair you're trading, as well as on the overall market volatility at the time of the trade.

Setting take-profit objectives dynamically

When you establish the take-profit objective, use a market-based approach, one that considers where the market is likely to go based on where it's been (technical analysis) and overall market conditions. The idea is to be *realistic* about how much you can take out of the market, not *idealistic* about how much the market will reward you. Focus on technical support and resistance levels as the primary guideposts in the progress of market movements.

Another important consideration in dynamically managing your profit objectives is time. Be aware of and anticipate upcoming events and market conditions. If you've been long for a rally during the North American morning, what's likely to happen when European markets begin to close up for the day? If you're positioned in USD/JPY in the New York afternoon, and Japanese industrial production is slated to be released in a few hours, what can you expect in the interim? Stay flexible and dynamic, just like the market.

Chapter 5

Putting Your Trading Plan in Action

In This Chapter

▶ Opening a position at the right time and with the right strategy

▶ Making sure you enter everything correctly

▶ Actively administering your trades

▶ Taking profits — or not

▶ Doing some post-trading analysis

*T*his is what it all comes down to. You've done the research, you've looked at the charts, you've developed your strategic trade plan, and now it's time to put it to work. If you thought economic data mining and chart analysis were the hard part, wait until your adrenaline starts pumping after you've entered the trade. This chapter takes you through the concrete steps of opening a position in the forex market, monitoring the trade while it's active, closing it out, and doing a post-trade analysis to refine your trading going forward.

Getting into the Position

You can make trades in the forex market one of two ways: You can trade *at the market,* or at the current price, using the click-and-deal feature of your broker's platform; or you can employ orders, such as stop-loss entry orders, limit orders, and one-cancels-the-other orders (OCOs). But there's a lot more to it than that. Certain trade setups suggest a combination of both methods for entering a position, while others rely strictly on orders to capture rapid or unexpected price movements. Then there's the fine art of timing the market to get in at the best price at the moment.

Buying and selling at the current market

Many traders like the idea of opening a position by trading at the market as opposed to leaving an order that may or may not be executed. They prefer the certainty of knowing that they're in the market. If this describes you, before actually executing your first trade, fine-tune your entry by getting a good handle on the short-term price action. To do this, look at shorter-term charts, such as 5 or 15 minutes, to get an idea of where prices have been trading recently. (Flip to Book X for details on technical analysis charts.) Chances are you'll observe a relatively narrow range of price action, typically between 10 and 20 pips. (A *pip* is the smallest increment of price fluctuation in currency prices.) Unless the situation is urgent, a little patience can go a long way toward improving your entry level. Why buy at 1.1550 when you have a viable chance to buy at 1.1535?

Let the routine price fluctuations work to your advantage by trying to buy on down-ticks and sell on up-ticks in line with your overall strategy. Selecting your trade size in advance helps — so when the price gets to your desired level, you need to click only once to execute the trade. As you watch the price action, keep a disciplined price target in mind, both in your favor and in case prices start to move away from your entry level.

Averaging into a position

Averaging into a position refers to the practice of buying/selling at successively lower/higher prices to improve the average rate of the desired long/short position. Say you buy one lot of USD/JPY (pitting the U.S. dollar against the Japanese yen) at 120.50 and another lot at 120.30; you're long two lots at an average price of 120.40 ([120.50 + 120.30] ÷ 2 = 120.40).

Here's how it works. You were long one lot from 120.50. To add to the position at 120.30, the market had to be trading lower, which also means you were looking at an unrealized profit/loss (P/L) of –20 pips on your initial position from 120.50. After you buy the second lot, your unrealized P/L has not changed substantially, but your position size has just doubled, which means your risk has also just doubled. If the market rebounds from 120.30, your unrealized loss will be reduced. But if the market continues to decline, your losses are going to be twice what they were had you not added on to your position.

Many trading books recommend avoiding averaging into, or adding on to, a losing position — and with good reason. The tactic can lead to dramatically higher losses on smaller incremental price movements.

Trading breakouts

A *breakout* or *break* refers to a price movement that moves beyond, or breaks out of, recent established trading ranges or price patterns captured with trendlines. Breakouts can occur in all time frames. The longer the time frame, the more significant the breakout in terms of the overall expected price movement that follows. In terms of entering a position, breakouts frequently represent important signals to get in or out of positions. The following sections provide pointers on trading breakouts.

Trading breakouts is a relatively aggressive trading strategy. Until you've gained some experience in the forex market, you're probably better off focusing only on breaks of levels identified by trendline analysis in longer time frames, such as daily charts, or breaks of longer-term price levels, like daily or weekly highs/lows. They may not occur as frequently, but they tend to be more reliable.

Identifying potential breakout levels

The first step in trading on a breakout is to identify where breakouts are likely to occur. The easiest way to do this is to draw trendlines that capture recent high/low price ranges, which, in many cases, form a sideways or horizontal range of prices. Horizontal ranges are mostly neutral in predicting which direction the break will occur.

Other ranges form price patterns with sloping trendlines on the top and bottom, such as flags, pennants, wedges, and triangles. These patterns have more predictive capacity for the direction of the eventual breakout and even the distance of the breakout. (Go to Book X to find out about common patterns.)

The time frame determines the overall significance of the breakout and goes a long way toward determining whether you should make a trade based on it. Very short time frames (less than an hour) have much less significance than a break of a four-hour range or a daily price pattern. The length of time that a price range or pattern has endured also gives you an idea of its significance. A break of a range that has formed over the past 48 hours has less significance for price movements than the break of a range that's persisted for the past 3 weeks.

Trading breaks with stop-loss entry orders

After you identify a likely breakout point, you can use a resting stop-loss entry order placed just beyond the breakout level to get into a position when a breakout occurs.

Book IV

Foreign Currency Trading

- To get long for a break to the upside, you leave a stop-loss entry order to buy at a price just above the upper level of the range or pattern.

- To get short for a break lower, you leave a stop-loss entry order to sell at a price just below the lower level of the range or pattern.

When placing a stop-loss entry order to trade a breakout level, be aware of any major data or news events that are coming up. If your stop-loss entry order is triggered as a result of a news event, the execution rate on the order could be subject to slippage, which may wipe out any gains from getting in on the breakout.

Trading the retest of a breakout level

The other way to trade a breakout is after the breakout has occurred. A *retest* refers to a frequent price reaction after breakouts, where prices eventually reverse course, return to the break level, and retest it to see whether it will hold. In the case of a break to the upside, for example, after the initial wave of buying has run its course, prices may stall and trigger very short-term profit-taking selling. The tendency is for prices to return to the breakout level, which should now act as support and attract buying interest.

Not every breakout sees prices return to retest the break level. Some retests may retrace only a portion of the breakout move, stopping short of retesting the exact break level, which is typically a good sign that the break is for real and will continue. Other breakouts never look back and just keep going.

Guarding against false breaks

Breakouts are relatively common events in currency trading, especially from a very short-term perspective. But not every breakout is sustained. When prices break through key support or resistance levels, but then stop and reverse course and ultimately move back through the break level, it's called a *false break*. To protect against false breaks, you need to follow up your stop-loss entry with a contingent stop-loss exit order to close out the position if the market reverses course.

Although there's no surefire way to tell whether a breakout is a false break or a valid one that you should trade, here are a few points to keep in mind:

- The shorter the time frame you're looking at, the greater the potential for a false break.

- The more important the price level that's broken, the more likely it is to provoke a market response and to be sustained.

- The longer the breakout level is held, the more likely the breakout is to be valid.

✔ Relatively volatile currency pairs, such as GBP/USD (pitting the British pound versus the U.S. dollar) and USD/CHF (pitting the U.S. dollar versus the Swiss franc), are more prone to false breaks than others, especially in short-term time frames.

✔ Sustained breakouts tend to have a fundamental catalyst behind them — a significant piece of news that has altered the market's outlook, resulting in the breakout.

Making the Trade Correctly

When using an online trading platform, entering a position is as easy as making a few simple mouse clicks. At the same time, the simplicity and speed of online trading platforms make those simple mouse clicks a done deal that puts your trading capital at risk. That's why it's important to understand from the get-go that any action you take on a trading platform is your responsibility. You may have meant to click Buy instead of Sell, but no one knows for sure except you.

Most every online trading brokerage now provides for click-and-deal trade execution. *Click and deal* refers to trading on the current market price by clicking either the Buy button or the Sell button in the trading platform. Before you can click and deal, you have to do the following:

✔ **Select the right currency pair.** When the market gets hectic, and you're switching between your charts and the trading platform, you can easily mistake EUR/USD (pitting the euro versus the U.S. dollar) for EUR/CHF (pitting the euro versus the Swiss franc) if you're not careful.

✔ **Select the correct trade amount.** Make sure you've specified the correct amount you want to trade. Different platforms have different ways of inputting the trade amount.

✔ **Double-check your selections.** This is your money; be certain now or be sorry later. In case you think input errors can't happen to you, think about the equity trader at a New York investment bank who meant to sell 10 million shares of a stock but ended up entering 10 *billion*. By the time the trade was stopped, the system had sold several hundred million shares. Ouch!

✔ **Be sure you know which side of the price you want to deal on.** If you want to buy, you need to click the higher price — the trading platform's offer. If you want to sell, you have to click the lower price — the platform's bid. Most platforms have labeled the sides of the prices from the user's perspective, with the bid side labeled Sell, and the offer side labeled Buy.

Book IV

Foreign Currency Trading

Attempts to trade at the market can sometimes fail in very fast-moving markets when prices are adjusting quickly, like after a data release or break of a key technical level or price point. Part of this stems from the *latency effect* of trading over the Internet, which refers to time lags between the platform price reaching your computer and your trade request reaching the platform's server. If you continually get failed trade responses, check the speed of your Internet connection.

Whatever the outcome of your trade request, you need to be sure you receive a response from the trading platform. If you don't get a response back within a few seconds, call your broker immediately and confirm the status of the trade request.

Here are some additional important tips to keep in mind when placing and managing your orders:

- **If you make a mistake, fix it as soon as you discover and confirm it.** Don't try to trade your way out of it. Don't try to manage it. Don't start rationalizing that it may work out anyway. No trader is error-proof, and you're bound to make a mistake someday. Just cover the error and get your position back to what you want it to be. Covering errors immediately is one of the few hard-and-fast rules I subscribe to in trading any market.

- **Note the expiration of your orders.** Order expirations are typically one of the following:

  Good-'til-cancelled (GTC): The order remains active until *you* cancel it.

  Good 'til the end of the day (EOD): The order automatically expires at the end of the trading day.

  If you have an intraday position with a stop loss good until EOD, and you later decide to hold the position overnight, you need to revise the expiration. On some trading platforms, GTC orders automatically expire after an extended period of time, such as 90 days, so be clear on your broker's policy.

- **Cancel unwanted orders.** Some trading platforms allow orders to be *associated with a position,* meaning that the order remains valid as long as the position is open. Such *position orders* also usually adjust the order amount if you increase or reduce the associated position. Other orders are *independent of positions,* so even if you close out your position, the independent orders remain active. Make sure you understand the difference between the two types, and be sure to cancel any independent orders if you close the positions they were based on, such as take profits, stop losses, or OCOs.

Managing the Trade

The forex market isn't a roulette wheel where you place your bets, watch the wheel spin, and simply take the results. It's a dynamic, fluid environment where new information and price developments create new opportunities and alter previous expectations. Actively managing a trade when you're in it is just as important as the decision-making that went into establishing the position in the first place.

Monitoring the market

No matter which trading style you follow, you want to keep up with market news and price developments while your trade is active. Unexpected news that impacts your position may come into the market at any time.

✔ **Rate alerts:** One way to follow the market from a distance is to set rate alerts from either your charting system or your trading platform. A *rate alert* is an electronic message that alerts you when a price you've specified is touched by the market in a particular currency pair. Rate alerts are a great way to keep tabs on the market's progress, but keep in mind that they don't take the place of live orders and should never be substituted for stop-loss orders.

✔ **News and data developments:** Ideally, you should be aware of all data reports and news events scheduled to occur during the anticipated time horizon of your trade strategy (see Chapter 3 in Book IV for more about data reports). You should also have a good understanding of what the market is expecting in terms of event outcomes to anticipate how the market is likely to react. Additionally, if your trade rationale is reliant on certain data or event expectations, you need to be especially alert for upcoming reports on those themes.

Updating your trade plan over time

Several market reactions are as much the result of time as they are of the event itself. For example, routine daily events, such as option expirations and the daily closing of the currency futures market, can spur a flurry of activity, and as the time for scheduled news or data events approaches, price movements can become more erratic. Time can also increase or decrease the significance of price movements that have already occurred, frequently providing trading signals as a result. So pay attention to time as you update your trade plan with the help of the following sections.

Book IV

Foreign Currency Trading

Recognizing that trendlines move over time

If you're basing your trading strategies on trendline analysis, you need to be aware that price levels derived from trendlines change depending on the slope of the trendline. The steeper the slope of the trendline, the more the relevant price level will change over time; the less slope, the more gradually the price levels will change with time. No matter what time frame you're trading, be sure to factor in the shifting levels of trendlines if they're part of your trade strategy. In particular, consider the following:

- ✔ **Short-term and overnight positions:** Consider where trendline support or resistance will be over the next 6 to 12 hours, while your position is still active even though you may not be able to actively follow the market. Consider using a *trailing stop* (a stop-loss order set as a percentage below the market price) as a proxy for changes in trendline-based support/resistance levels.

- ✔ **Limit-entry orders:** If your limit buying/selling order is based on a sloping trendline, periodically adjust your order so that it's still in play according to changes in the trendline.

- ✔ **Breakouts:** A significant trendline that looks to be a mile away one week may suddenly be within striking distance in the following week or two weeks, substantially altering the market's outlook. Alternatively, the market may be focused on a price high/low as a breakout trigger, when a sloping trendline touching that high/low may actually be the catalyst for a breakout. (Breakouts are discussed earlier in this chapter.)

Adjusting your trade plan over impending events

As you develop your trading plan, look ahead to see what data and events are scheduled during the expected life of the trade. Doing so reduces the chances that your trade strategy will be upset by largely predictable events. More important, you'll be able to anticipate likely catalysts for price shifts, which will give you greater insight into subsequent price movements.

Before major data and events, the market frequently goes into a sideways holding pattern. The event speculators have all put on their positions, and the rest of the market is waiting for the data to decide how to react. These holding patterns can develop hours or days in advance, depending on what event is coming. Especially if you're trading from a short-term perspective, be prepared for these doldrums and consider whether riding through them is worthwhile.

Updating order levels as prices progress

When you're in a position and the market is moving in your favor, be flexible in adjusting take-profit targets and amending stop-loss orders to protect your profits. You also need to be prudent: Don't adjust your take-profit targets without also adjusting your stop-loss order in the same direction. If you're long and you raise your take profit, raise your stop loss too. If you're short and you lower your take profit, lower your stop-loss order as well.

Increasing take-profit targets

You've put together a well-developed trade strategy ahead of your trade, so now that you're in the trade, why would you change your take-profit objective? Only for some very good reasons, like the following:

- ✔ **Major new information:** *Major* means it has to come from the very top echelons of decision-making, like the Fed chairman, the European Central Bank (ECB) president, or other central bank chiefs; the U.S. Treasury secretary; or the G7. Surprise interest rate changes or policy shifts are always candidates.

- ✔ **Thinner-than-usual liquidity:** Reduced liquidity conditions can provoke more extensive price movements than would otherwise occur, because fewer market participants are involved to absorb the price shocks. Reduced liquidity is most evident during national holidays, seasonal periods (late summer, Christmas/New Year's), the end of the month, the end of the quarter, and certain Fridays.

- ✔ **Breaks of major technical levels:** Trendlines dating back several months or years, retracement levels of major recent directional moves, and recent extreme highs and lows are likely to trigger larger-than-normal price movements.

- ✔ **The currency pair:** The more illiquid and volatile the currency pair you're trading, the greater the chances for an extreme move. GBP, CHF, and JPY are the most common culprits among the majors.

Tightening stop-loss orders to protect profits

To protect profits, adjust your stop losses to lock in gains. When formulating your overall trade plan, consider what price levels need to be surpassed to justify moving your stop loss. If it happens in the market, you'll be ready and know exactly what to do.

Focus on hourly and daily trendline levels, daily highs/lows, and breaks of Fibonacci retracement levels (see www.fibonacci.com if you're unfamiliar with these retracements). When these technical support/resistance points are exceeded, it's an indication that the market has seen fit to move prices into a new level in the overall direction of the trade. When that happens, consider moving your stop-loss order to levels just inside the broken technical level. If the market has second thoughts about sustaining the break, your adjusted stop will then take you out of the trade.

Book IV

Foreign Currency Trading

Another way to lock in profits in a more dynamic fashion is by using a trailing stop-loss order. After a technical level in the direction of your trade is overcome, you may consider instituting a trailing stop to replace your fixed stop-loss order. Set the trailing distance to account for the distance between the current market and the other side of the technical break level.

Closing Out the Trade

On the most basic level, every trade ends with either a profit or a loss. Sure, some trades finish *flat,* which is when you exit the trade at the same price you entered, producing no gain or loss. Most of the time, though, you're going to be dealing with the agony or ecstasy of either being stopped out or taking profit.

Taking profits

Taking profit is usually a positive experience for traders. But if the market continues to move in the direction of your trade after you've squared up and taken profit, you may begin to feel as though you're missing out or even losing money. At these times, you want to avoid making rash trading decisions. Even if the market continues to move in the direction of your earlier position, don't reenter the same position until you've taken the time to reevaluate the market objectively. Also, avoid the urge to suddenly take a position in the opposite direction. The key is to treat each trade independently, recognizing that the outcome of one trade has no bearing on the next trade. Here are some suggestions:

- ✔ **Take partial profits:** One way to stay in the market with a profitable position and hang on for a potentially larger move is to take partial profits on the overall position. Taking partial profits requires the ability to trade in multiple lots — at least two. The idea is that as prices move in favor of your trading position, you take profit on just a portion of your total position.

   Whenever you take partial profits, modify the size of your stop-loss and other take-profit orders to account for the reduction in your total position size. Some online brokers offer a position-based order-entry system, whereby your order size automatically adjusts based on any changes to the remaining open position.

- ✔ **Stop out before things get worse:** Stop losses are a necessary evil for every trader, big or small. You can never know beforehand where a price movement will stop, but you can control where you exit the market if prices don't move as you expect. Stop losses are an important tool for preventing manageable trading losses from turning into disastrous ones.

Trailing stop-loss orders are often used to protect profits and enable traders to capture larger price movements. They're no surefire guarantee that you'll be able to stay on board for a larger directional price move, but they do provide an element of flexibility that you should consider in adjusting your trade plan.

✔ **Let the market trigger your stop-loss/take-profit order:** When you've identified a trade opportunity and developed a risk-aware trading plan, you're going to have active orders out in the market to cover your position one way or the other (stop loss or take profit). Depending on your trading style and the trade setup, you can reasonably follow a set-it-and-forget-it trade strategy whereby your orders watch the market and your position for you.

Medium- to longer-term traders are more likely to rely on set, or *resting,* market orders to cover open positions due to the longer time frame of such trade strategies and the burdens of monitoring the market overnight or for longer stretches of time. If you use resting orders, also use rate alerts to update you on specific price movements (see the earlier section "Monitoring the market") so that you can act when necessary. Shorter-term traders are more apt to be in front of their trading monitors while their trade is still open, but they should always still have an ultimate set of orders (stop-loss and take-profit) to cover the trade.

Although you may want to be flexible with where you leave your take-profit order, always have a stop-loss order in place to protect you in case of unexpected news or price movements. If you're trading the market from the long side (meaning you think prices in a currency pair are likely to move higher), you need to pinpoint the ultimate price level on the downside, which negates this short-term view.

Getting out when the price is right

The most reliable market information is the prices themselves. Sharp price reactions are usually strong indicators of significant market interest that's either pushing prices faster in the same direction or repelling them in the opposite direction. As you monitor your position in the market, stay closely attuned to significant price reactions, such as spike reversals or price gaps, with a good benchmark being typically more than 20 points over a few minutes. The sharp move in prices may be due to news or rumors, or it may just be a pocket of illiquidity. Either way, the sharp price move carries its own significance that is information to you. There's no set way such moves always play out, but if you're alert for them, you'll have one more piece of information to help you decide when and how to exit your position.

If the rapid price movement is in your favor, you can look at it as a new high-water mark, or as a new support or resistance level. If the move is reversed, the tide is reversing, and you should consider exiting sooner rather than later. If the tide doesn't reverse, you'll have a solid, short-term price level on which to base your decisions going forward. If the price move is against you, you may want to consider that the market isn't cooperating and adopt a more defensive strategy, such as tightening stop losses, reducing your position, or exiting altogether.

Getting out when the time is right

The time of day and the day of the week can frequently determine how prices behave and how your ultimate trade strategy plays out. If you're trading ahead of major data releases, for example, you need to be aware that price action is going to be affected in the run-up to the scheduled release, not to mention in its aftermath. Similarly, if you've been positioned correctly for a directional price move in the New York morning, for example, you need to be aware that a price reaction may occur as European traders begin to wind up their trading on any given day. When it comes to adjusting your trading plan or closing out your position, it frequently pays to be a clock watcher.

Analyzing after the Trade

Good traders learn from their mistakes and try to avoid repeating them in the future. Bad traders keep making the same mistakes over and over again until they give up in frustration or are forced to for financial reasons. The best way to learn from each trading experience — both the good and the bad ones — is to make post-trade analysis part of your regular trading routine.

Identifying what you did right and wrong

Regardless of the outcome of any trade, look back over the whole process to understand what you did right and wrong. In particular, ask yourself the following questions:

> ✔ **How did you identify the trade opportunity?** If more of your winning trades are being generated by technical analysis, you'll probably want to devote more energy to that approach, for example.

✔ **How well did your trade plan work out?** Was the position size sufficient to match the risk and reward scenarios, or was it too large or too small? Could you have entered at a better level? What tools might you have used to improve your entry timing? Was your take profit realistic or pie in the sky? Use the answers to these questions to refine your position size, entry level, and order placement going forward.

✔ **How well did you manage the trade after it was open?** Were you able to effectively monitor the market while your trade was active? Did you modify your trade plan appropriately along the way? Did you close out the trade based on your trading plan, or did the market surprise you somehow? Based on your answers, you'll discover what role your emotions may have played and how disciplined a trader you are.

Updating your trading record

Recollections of individual trades can be hazy sometimes. Some traders may tend to favor remembering winning trades, while others may remember only the losing trades. The only way to get to the heart of the matter is to look at the numbers — the results of your trades over a specific time period, such as a month. A trading record doesn't lie, but you still have to interpret it properly to glean any useful lessons from it. Depending on your trading style, the best approach is to analyze your trading record from two different angles, which have a common denominator — average wins and average losses.

✔ **Long-term and medium-term traders** tend to have fewer overall trades because they're more likely to be looking at the market from a more strategic perspective, picking trade opportunities more selectively. If that's you, tally your results on a per-trade basis, totaling up separately the number of winning trades and the number of losing trades, along with the amount of pips gained or lost (to examine strategy accuracy independent of position size), and cash profits and losses (to account for position size and risk management). Divide the amount of profits by the number of winning trades to find your average winning trade amount. Do the same with your losing trades.

✔ **Short-term traders** tend to have a larger number of trades due to their short-term trading style. If that's you and you're making only one or two trades a day, you may want to follow the method described in the preceding bullet item. If you're a more active day-trader, measure your results on a per-day basis to get an idea of how successful you are at trading in multiple positions on any given day. Tally up the results of each trading day over the course of a month to come up with the same numbers outlined in the preceding bullet item: total numbers of winning and losing trades, average pips gained or lost, and average win and loss amounts.

Book IV

Foreign Currency Trading

Focus on what you're doing right, but also figure out what you're doing wrong. Refine your analysis of your trading results by breaking them down to smaller categories, such as day of the week and currency pair or even trade size. Are your losing days or trades concentrated on certain days of the week or certain currency pairs? Does the position size of each trade have any relationship to wins and losses? Your post-trade analysis will only help you if you're diligent and honest about keeping it accurate and up-to-date. By faithfully monitoring your trading activity, you improve your skills, learn from your mistakes, and gain confidence in your market abilities.

Book V
Hedge Funds

Five Reasons Why Hedge Funds Require Savvy Investors

✔ **They have few investor protections.** Depending on the amount of assets in the fund, hedge funds may not have to register with the U.S. Securities and Exchange Commission (SEC), which protects individual and institutional investors in the United States, although many do anyway. Nor do hedge fund investors receive the same federal and state protections that typically apply to mutual fund investors.

✔ **They require large up-front investments.** Minimum investments are rarely less than $25,000; many funds want investors to commit at least $1 million.

✔ **They lock up investments for long periods of time.** Most hedge funds place limits on how often investors can get their money out because they want to take advantage of as many investment opportunities as possible, including illiquid securities that may be hard to value.

✔ **They may take on incredible risk.** Although traditional hedge funds use short selling, futures, and portfolio diversification to reduce risk, some hedge funds use high levels of leverage, exotic futures strategies, and aggressive investment techniques to generate high rates of return. *Remember:* The term "hedge fund" applies to any lightly regulated investment partnership, regardless of the amount of risk in the partnership.

✔ **They invest without tax considerations.** Investors who have to pay taxes pay taxes each year on their hedge funds' gains, whether or not they received any of the gains in cash. And some investment strategies may generate high returns with few offsetting expenses, leading to large tax liabilities.

 web extras

A lot of misinformation surrounds hedge funds: what they are, how they work, and so on. To get the real scoop and debunk common myths, go to www.dummies.com/extras/highpoweredinvestingaio.

Chapter 1

Getting the 411 on Hedge Funds

In This Chapter
▶ Discovering basic characteristics and types of hedge funds
▶ Distinguishing between absolute-return funds and directional funds
▶ Perusing the fee structure of hedge funds
▶ Getting a handle on how a hedge fund works
▶ Ensuring that a hedge fund is right for your needs

You see hedge funds in the news all the time, but it's hard to know exactly what they are. That's because, at its essence, a hedge fund is a bit of a mystery. A *hedge fund,* generally speaking, is a lightly regulated investment partnership that invests in a range of securities in an attempt to increase expected return while reducing risk. And that can mean just about anything.

This chapter covers basic things you need to know if you're considering buying into a hedge fund. It tells you what a hedge fund is and explains who the people involved in hedge funds are, what you have to do to qualify as a hedge fund investor, and more.

Defining Hedge Funds

The term *hedge fund* means different things to different people. In the investment world, "I run a hedge fund" has the same meaning as "I'm a consultant" in the rest of the business world. Still, one definition that most folks can agree on is a fairly general one: A *hedge fund* is a lightly regulated, private investment partnership that uses a range of investment techniques and invests in a wide array of assets to generate a higher return for a given level of risk than what's expected of normal investments. In many cases, but hardly all, hedge funds are managed to generate a consistent level of return, regardless of what the market does.

The following sections describe hedge funds in more detail and list the people who work with them.

Hedging: The heart of the hedge fund matter

To understand what a hedge fund is, obviously, it helps to know what hedging is. *Hedging* means reducing risk, which is what many hedge funds are designed to do. Although risk is usually a function of return (the higher the risk, the higher the return), a hedge fund manager has ways to reduce risk without cutting into investment income. She can look for ways to get rid of some risks while taking on others with an expected good return.

Return is a function of risk, and risk remains, no matter the hedge fund strategy. The challenge for the hedge fund manager is to eliminate some risk while gaining return on investments — not a simple task, which is why hedge fund managers get paid handsomely if they succeed.

Characteristics of hedge funds

A hedge fund differs from traditional investment accounts like mutual funds, pensions, and endowments because it has more freedom to pursue different investment strategies. In some cases, these unique strategies can lead to huge gains while the traditional market measures languish. The amount of potential return makes hedge funds more than worthwhile in the minds of many accredited and qualified investors. Basically, hedge funds are

✔ **Illiquid:** Hedge funds are *illiquid*. Most hedge fund managers limit how often investors can take their money out; a fund may lock in investors for two years or more. In other words, investing in a hedge fund is a long-term proposition because the money you invest may be locked up for years.

✔ **Exempt from most regulatory oversight:** Hedge funds don't have to register with the U.S. Securities and Exchange Commission (SEC), nor are the funds and their managers required to register with the Financial Industry Regulatory Authority (FINRA) or the Commodity Futures Trading Commission, the major self-regulatory bodies in the investment business. However, many funds register with these bodies anyway, to give investors peace of mind and many protections otherwise not afforded to them (not including protection from losing money, of course). Whether registered or not, hedge funds can't commit fraud, engage in insider trading, or otherwise violate the laws of the land.

✔ **Accessible only to qualified investors:** In order to stay free of the yoke of strict regulation, hedge funds agree to accept money only from accredited or qualified investors — people and institutions with high net worths. The later section "Making Sure a Hedge Fund Is Right for You" defines the requirements for each.

✔ **Aggressive investment strategies:** To post a higher return for a given level of risk than otherwise expected, a hedge fund manager has a broad array of investment techniques, such as short selling and leveraging, at his disposal that aren't feasible for a tightly regulated investor. This fact is where a hedge fund's relative lack of regulatory oversight becomes important.

✔ **Secretive about performance and strategies:** Some hedge funds are very secretive, and for good reason: If other players in the market know how a fund is making its money, they'll try to use the same techniques, and the unique opportunity for the front-running hedge fund may disappear. Hedge funds aren't required to report their performance, disclose their holdings, or take questions from shareholders. However, that doesn't mean hedge fund managers refuse to tell you anything. A fund must prepare a partnership agreement or offering memorandum for prospective investors that explains the following:

   • The fund's investment style

   • The fund's structure

   • The fund manager's background

✔ A hedge fund should also undergo an annual audit of holdings and performance and give this report to all fund investors. But the hedge fund manager doesn't have to give you regular and detailed information, nor should you expect to receive it. (See the nearby sidebar "Getting info from hedge fund managers" for details on communicating with fund managers.)

What gets investors excited about hedge funds is that the funds seem to have fabulous performances at every turn, no matter what the market does. But the great numbers you see in the papers can be misleading because hedge fund managers don't have to report performance numbers to anyone other than their fund investors. Those who do report their numbers to different analytical, consulting, and index firms do so voluntarily, and they're often the ones most likely to have good performance numbers to report. Add to that the fact that hedge fund managers can easily close shop when things aren't going well; after a fund is shut down, its data isn't reported anymore (if it ever was), and poorly performing funds are most likely to close. What all this means is that measures of hedge fund performance have a bias toward good numbers.

Getting info from hedge fund managers

Many hedge fund managers prefer to sit in front of trading screens and make investment decisions all day. They prefer not to sit in meetings, hold the hands of their nervous clients, or make presentations to marketing departments. Many hedge fund investors, on the other hand, want regular contact with the people managing their money, and they want the niceties of notes, golf outings, and occasional dinners.

The partnership agreement you sign will probably discuss what kind of communication the hedge fund manager wants to arrange and how often he'll make contact. If you feel like you have to have regular, face-to-face communication with the hedge fund manager you associate with, make sure a manager is amenable to this request before you commit your money.

Even if she isn't big on face-to-face meetings, your hedge fund manager should offer you written reports:

✔ **Quarterly report:** This report should explain the fund's investment performance to date, giving you a sense of where the returns are relative to the appropriate investment benchmarks and letting you know how the market outlook suits the fund's strategy.

✔ **Annual report:** Once a year, your fund manager should give you a comprehensive report on the fund's performance, including the total value of the assets under management and the total fees charged. Although you probably won't get a comprehensive list of holdings, you should get enough information on industry and asset classes to get a sense of the fund's overall risk-and-return profile, which helps you evaluate how the fund's performance fits your portfolio needs. An outside auditor should prepare this report.

Alpha: What hedge funds are all about

Hedge fund managers all talk about alpha. Their goal is to generate alpha, because alpha is what makes them special. But what the heck is it? Unfortunately, alpha is one of those things that everyone in the business talks about but no one really explains.

Alpha is a term that originated in the Modern (or Markowitz) Portfolio Theory (MPT), which explains how an investment generates its return. The equation used to describe the theory contains four terms:

✔ The risk-free rate of return

✔ The premium over the risk-free rate that you get for investing in the market

✔ Beta, the sensitivity of an investment to the market

✔ Alpha, the return over and above the market rate that results from the manager's skill or other factors

Today, people aren't always thinking of MPT when they use *alpha*. Instead, many people use it as shorthand for whatever a fund does that's special. In basic terms, alpha is the value that the hedge fund manager adds. If a hedge fund hedges out all its market risk, its return comes entirely from alpha.

The people in your hedge fund neighborhood

Many different people work for, with, and around hedge funds. The following list gives you a little who's who so you understand the roles of the people you may come into contact with and of people who play a large role in your hedge fund.

- ✓ **Fund partners:** Most hedge funds are structured as lightly regulated (if at all) investment partnerships, but that doesn't mean that the partners within a fund are equal:

  - • **General partners:** A hedge fund's *general partners* are the founders and money managers of the fund. They form the fund, control the fund's investment strategy, collect the fees charged, pay the bills, and distribute the bonuses. In exchange for control, general partners take on unlimited liability in the fund, which means that their personal assets are at stake if the fund's liabilities exceed its assets. Many general partners own their stakes through S corporations or other structures that shield their personal assets.

  - • **Limited partners:** The *limited partners* (often shortened to *limiteds*) of a hedge fund are the people who invest in the fund. Limited partners have little or no say in the fund's operations. And the fund may restrict ongoing communication with the general partners to only a few times per year. But in exchange for these limitations of control, limited partners have limited liability. You can lose only the amount you invest in the fund and no more.

- ✓ **Managers:** The person who organizes the hedge fund and oversees its investment process is the *fund manager* — often called the *portfolio manager* or even PM for short. The fund manager may make all the investment decisions, handling all the trades and research himself, or he may opt to oversee a staff of people who give him advice.

- ✓ **Lawyers:** Although hedge funds face little to no regulation, they have to follow a lot of rules in order to maintain that status. Hedge funds need lawyers to help them navigate the regulation exemptions and other compliance responsibilities they face, and hedge fund investors need lawyers to ensure that the partnership agreements are in order and to assist with due diligence.

> ✔ **Consultants:** Due to the amount of money involved, many hedge fund investors work closely with outside consultants who advise them on their investment decisions, market for accredited investors, and make sure that they're meeting their investors' needs. Consultants can also help investors make sound investment decisions, ensure that they follow the law, give advice on the proper structure of their portfolios in order to help them meet their investment objectives, and so on.

Introducing Basic Types of Hedge Funds

You can sort hedge funds into two basic categories: absolute-return funds and directional funds. The following sections look at the differences between the two.

Absolute-return funds

Sometimes called a *non-directional fund,* an *absolute-return fund* is designed to generate a steady return no matter what the market is doing. An absolute-return fund has another moniker: a *pure-alpha fund.* In theory, the fund manager tries to remove all market risk (in other words, beta risk) in order to create a fund that doesn't vary with market performance. If the manager removes all the market risk, the fund's performance comes entirely from the manager's skill, which in academic terms is called *alpha* (discussed earlier in this chapter).

An absolute-return strategy is most appropriate for a conservative investor who wants low risk and is willing to give up some return in exchange.

Some people say that absolute-return funds generate a bond-like return because, like bonds, absolute-return funds have relatively steady but relatively low returns. The return target on an absolute-return fund is usually higher than the long-term rate of return on bonds, though. A typical absolute-return fund target is 6 to 8 percent, which is above the long-term rate of return on bonds and below the long-term rate of return on stocks. (Flip to Chapter 2 in Book I for details about bonds and stocks.)

Directional funds

Directional funds are hedge funds that don't hedge — at least not fully. Managers of directional funds maintain some exposure to the market, but they try to get higher-than-expected returns for the amount of risk that they take. Because directional funds maintain some exposure to the stock market, they're sometimes called *beta funds* and are said to have a *stock-like return*. A fund's returns may not be steady from year to year, but they're likely to be higher over the long run than the returns on an absolute-return fund.

A directional fund's return may be disproportionately larger than its risk, but the risk is still there. These funds can also swing wildly, giving a big return some years and plummeting big in others. Longer-term investors may not mind as long as the upward trend is positive.

Fee, Fi, Fo, Cha Ching! Hedge Fund Fees

Hedge funds are expensive, for a variety of reasons. If a fund manager figures out a way to get an increased return for a given level of risk, he deserves to be paid for the value he creates. In addition to the management and performance fees the fund manager receives, there are a variety of other fees as well. All are discussed in the following sections.

Management fees

A hedge fund can be an expensive business to run. The general partners of the fund have to worry about paying for many areas of the business, including the rent and utility costs of the office space; the price of research services, specialized software, and brokerage commissions; salaries for the fund managers and staff; and fees for the lawyers and accountants who provide professional services for the fund.

Most funds charge management fees of about 1 percent to 2 percent of the fund's assets, usually at the end of the fiscal year. Some charge higher fees — especially if they follow strategies that involve expensive research and related expenses, such as shareholder activism. Other funds keep the fee relatively low by paying only some expenses out of the fee; the funds pay for other bills, especially legal and accounting expenses, directly out of the funds' own assets.

A hedge fund manager receives a management fee no matter how the fund performs. However, if the fund's assets increase, the fee does, too. Two percent of $60 million is more than 2 percent of $50 million, so a 20-percent investment return translates into a 20-percent increase in management fees.

Sales charges

Hedge funds incur expenses throughout the year. Some funds may need money up front in order to operate, so they charge upfront *sales charges* — often at the same scale as the management fees (1 percent to 2 percent, which comes out of the amount invested). The sales charge allows the fund to cover its expenses and pay its staff until the management fees and performance fees come in.

Performance fees

Hedge fund managers charge *performance fees* as a reward for getting excellent returns for their investors. One of the many appeals of hedge funds is that hedge fund managers' incentives are aligned with their investors' goals. If the fund doesn't make money, the fund manager doesn't get paid.

Many hedge funds are structured under the so-called *2 and 20* arrangement, meaning that the fund manager receives an annual fee equal to 2 percent of the assets in the fund and an additional bonus equal to 20 percent of the year's profits.

Performance fees come with a downside for fund managers: The fund gets paid only if it turns a profit, and most funds set what's called a *high water mark.* The fund can charge a performance fee only if the fund's assets return to where they were before the fund started losing money. If it had $10 million in year one and lost 10 percent, making the asset value $9 million, the manager can't charge a performance fee until the assets appreciate back to $10 million.

Redemption fees

Many hedge funds charge *redemption fees* when their investors withdraw their money. These fees may be another 1 percent to 2 percent of assets. Hedge funds want to impress upon their limited partners that investment is a long-term proposition, so they can't get out easily. Also, the general partners have to deal with sales and administrative costs involved with raising the money to meet the redemption. Another reason funds charge redemption fees is that they can; doing so also increases the money that the fund manager earns.

A hedge fund that charges a redemption fee may waive it if it has held the investment for a certain amount of time or if you provide a certain amount of notice about when you plan to withdraw the funds.

Commissions

If you employ a broker or consultant to find a suitable hedge fund for you and she introduces you to the general partners, she will expect to be paid for said services. The consultant may charge you a flat fee, or she may take a percentage of the assets invested.

Understanding How Hedge Funds Work

A hedge fund manager's job is to survey the world's markets to find investments that meet the fund's risk and return parameters. To perform this feat, the fund manager has to have a system in place for determining what to invest in and for how long. He looks for opportunities to make money in an asset that's going to change in price, and he looks to reduce the risk of the portfolio. Anyone who invests money has several available techniques for increasing returns and reducing risk. Some hedge fund managers simply do better research, and others rely on technical analysis, short selling, and leverage to generate the returns that their clients expect.

The following sections give you a basic overview of the different financial assets available and tell you how fund managers may value them. Armed with this information, you can make better investment decisions for yourself and ask better questions of a hedge fund manager.

Examining asset options

Most investors should hold a diversified mix of securities in order to get their optimal risk and return payoff. The exact proportion depends on your needs. Likewise, hedge fund managers have different targets for risk and return, and they turn to different assets in order to meet their targets.

A hedge fund or a group of hedge funds may use the assets you see here in many different ways. Hedge fund managers often use traditional assets in nontraditional ways, for example, so there are no hard and fast rules to rely on. Chapter 3 in Book V covers some of the investment strategies and styles that hedge funds use.

> ✔ **Traditional asset classes:** Most funds have some investment positions in ordinary investment classes, such as stocks, bonds, and cash equivalents like short-term loans (expected to mature within 30 days or even overnight), long-term bonds that are about to mature, uninsured bank CDs, and government securities that will mature within 90 days.

Just because a hedge fund invests in securities doesn't mean it's playing it safe. Some hedge funds buy very ordinary and safe securities, such as U.S. government bonds, but they goose up the returns — and the risk — by using borrowed money to finance almost the entire position.

✔ **Alternative assets:** An *alternative investment* is anything other than stocks, bonds, or cash. Hedge fund managers, sniffing out opportunities to meet their investment objectives, often turn to the alternative assets such as real estate, commodities (discussed in detail in Book III), venture capital, derivatives (financial contracts that draw their value from the value of an underlying asset, security, or index), futures and options (discussed in Book II), warrants and convertible bonds, forward contracts, and swaps.

✔ **Custom products and private deals:** Hedge funds often participate in private transactions and offbeat investments so they can meet their desired risk and return characteristics better than they can with readily traded securities. Following are a few such private transactions, but you may come across many others:

- *Mezzanine financing,* a combination of debt and equity used to support a company until it can go to the public markets

- *Payment-in-kind bonds,* in which instead of paying interest on its debt, the company in financial trouble gives its bondholders other bonds or securities

- *Tranches* (classes of bonds, each of which may have a different interest rate and payment terms)

- *Viaticals,* life insurance policies purchased from the insured as investments

Researching a security's value

Each hedge fund manager needs a system for figuring out the price at which to buy or sell a security. The following sections outline common analytical approaches.

Top-down analysis

This type of analysis examines the overall state of the economy and uses the findings to identify specific assets that are expected to benefit or suffer from changes in the overall state of the economy, like price increases, employment levels, and interest rates. Top-down investing is sometimes called *theme investing* because a fund manager looks for a handful of broad trends and invests based on those trends. The fund may look to benefit from an aging population, higher energy prices, or increased defense spending, for example.

Following are the different levels of economic analysis within top-down research:

- **A microeconomic approach:** This strategy looks at the structure of small units in the economy, such as individual companies or households.

- **A macroeconomic approach:** This tactic looks at the overall national or even global economy.

- **Cyclical versus secular trends:** A *cyclical trend* is related to economic cycles. For example, when employment improves, more people are working, and these new employees need clothes to wear to work, so they buy more threads, increasing revenue for apparel companies. A *secular trend* represents a fundamental shift in the market, regardless of the cyclical trends. A secular trend in the clothing industry, for example, is the move toward casual dress in the office, a trend that, in the 1990s, led to strong sales at retailers that sold casual apparel, but falling sales at traditional suit makers.

  The challenge for an investor is separating the cyclical economic trend, which is temporary, from the secular economic one, which is not.

- **Demographics:** Understanding the nature of the demographics within a population can help hedge fund managers make better decisions and separate cyclical from secular trends. For example, young populations tend to have cheap, unskilled workers, and older demographics usually have highly skilled, experienced, and expensive work forces. Young people tend to borrow money to spend; older people spend their savings; and people in the middle tend to set aside more than they spend.

Bottom-up analysis

A *bottom-up* analyst looks for individual companies that he expects to do especially well or especially poorly in the future. The analyst first examines the company itself — its financial statements, its history, its product line, the quality of its management, and so on — and then makes a judgment about the company's value on its own merits. He incorporates broad market trends only as they directly affect the business, which sets bottom-up analysis apart from top-down analysis.

Some bottom-up analysts look only at a company's reported financial statements, ignoring other aspects of its business. These people look for evidence of fraud, unsustainable growth, or hidden assets. This examination is known as *accounting research.* Often accountants themselves, the accounting analysts who examine the companies understand the many nuances and judgment calls that go into preparing financial statements. In most cases, the goal of accounting research is to identify potential short ideas.

Quantitative research

Quantitative research looks strictly at numbers. These numbers may represent accounting figures (for example, accounts receivable relative to sales), or they may be sensitivity factors (for example, how much a company's profit changes when oil prices increase by 1 percent). Quantitative analysts, often called *quants,* tend to put the information they find into complex mathematical models, and the solutions that result correspond to the securities that investors should put into their portfolio.

Technical analysis

Technical analysis involves looking at charts of the price and volume of trading in a security. The charts show the historic supply and demand for the security, which may indicate where future prices are heading. The information shows a measure of sentiment. Analysts look to any number of questions: Is the number of buy orders increasing? Are the orders increasing while the price goes up or while the price goes down? Is the stock's price rising steadily, or does it go up in bursts around news announcements? Technical analysts use the answers to these types of questions to make investment decisions. Few funds rely on technical analysis exclusively, but many use it regularly as a check on their fundamental research. For information on how to perform this type of analysis, go to Book X.

Algorithmic and high-frequency trading

Many hedge funds have developed automated trading programs, known as algorithms (often shortened to "algos"), which buy and sell securities when predetermined signals are hit. Algos scan news headlines, social media feeds, and price data, then get to work when the time is right. They often execute a high volume of trades in a very short period of time — high-frequency trading. This is a growing hedge fund strategy and a growing source of volatility in the financial markets.

Putting the findings to work

So, what happens when a hedge fund's research identifies some great opportunities in different assets? Well, the fund takes a position. It can go long (buy in hopes that the asset goes up) or go short (sell in hopes that the asset goes down). The fund can also trade securities, monitor positions that may pay off in the future, or look for other ways to turn the information into a return for the hedge fund investor.

The long story: Buying appreciating assets

When a hedge fund manager or other investor buys a security, she's said to be *long.* An investor has only one reason to go long: She thinks that the asset will go up in price. Some hedge fund managers look for longs that will work over an extended period of time — possibly years — and others prefer to make their profits over very short stretches of time — possibly seconds.

The short story: Selling depreciating assets

Hedge funds can make money by selling securities, and not necessarily securities that they own. A *short seller* borrows a security from someone else (usually from a brokerage firm's inventory) and then sells it. After a while — ideally, after the security goes down in price — the short seller buys back the security in the market and repays the loan with the asset that he originally borrowed. The lender doesn't have to repay the original dollar value, just the security in question. The profit (or loss) is the difference between where the short seller sold the security and where he bought it back, less commissions and interest charged by the lender. (See Chapter 3 in Book V for more on short selling.)

A fund exacts a *naked short* when it sells a security that it hasn't borrowed in hopes that it will go down fast enough that the fund can buy back the security and settle with the buyer. Naked shorting is against exchange regulations in most markets, but it still happens. The advantage for the fund is that it can sell short without paying interest to the lender, and it can sell short even if no lender will loan the security to the fund. The downside is that if the fund can't repurchase the security in time to settle its sale, the exchanges will find out and probably shut down the fund. Because of the illicit nature of the technique, you shouldn't invest in any fund that admits to naked shorting.

Making Sure a Hedge Fund Is Right for You

Hedge funds aren't for everyone. If you don't meet the SEC's definition of an accredited investor, you can't invest in a hedge fund. And some hedge funds go beyond the SEC requirements, making sure that all investors are qualified purchasers.

In addition, hedge funds are both illiquid and lightly regulated. Because your money is likely to be tied up for an extended period and the fund itself won't necessarily fall under the scrutiny of any regulatory body, the onus is on you to be a savvy investor. Before signing an agreement with any hedge fund manager — even the one your investment banker friend swears by — you need to take a close look at your own specific financial goals, figure out how much you can afford to invest in a hedge fund scheme, and consider what type of asset allocation is most likely to mesh with the other investments in your portfolio.

The following sections explain the requirements and other things you should think about before diving in.

Being accredited or qualified

An *accredited investor* is one who

- ✔ Has a net worth of more than $1 million, owned alone or jointly with a spouse
- ✔ Has earned $200,000 in each of the past two years
- ✔ Has earned $300,000 in each of the past two years when combined with a spouse
- ✔ Has a reasonable expectation of making the same amount in the future

For investment institutions, such as pensions, endowments, and trusts, the primary qualification is having $5 million in assets.

Many hedge funds set a more stringent standard than the SEC, asking that investors be *qualified purchasers* under their own internal guidelines. Typically, qualified purchasers are individuals with at least $5 million in investable assets. Trusts, endowments, and pensions must have at least $25 million in investable assets. Investors who meet a firm's qualified-purchaser standards are sometimes called *super accredited*.

Because of their illiquidity, hedge funds are seldom appropriate for an entire investment portfolio. In almost all cases, hedge funds offer their maximum portfolio benefit in relatively small doses. In fact, hedge funds are mostly designed as investment vehicles for *excess capital:* money that the investor doesn't need now and doesn't need to support near-term spending.

If you don't qualify for a hedge fund as an accredited or qualified investor, you can use hedge fund strategies within a small portfolio. Chapter 3 in Book V outlines many of the strategies that hedge funds use to gain a high return. You can also invest in mutual funds that use hedge fund strategies. Some mutual fund companies offer funds designed to capture the benefits of hedge funds within the highly regulated mutual fund structure.

Determining your financial goals

The answers to two questions go a long way toward determining how to invest your money and what to invest it in: "When do you need your money?" and "What do you need your money for?" Your answers influence the risk you can take, the return you need to shoot for, the asset classes that are open to you, and how much time you can allocate toward the investment.

Generally speaking, investable money falls into three categories:

- **Temporary (or short-term) funds** that you'll need in a year. Hedge funds want money that investors can set aside for long periods.

- **Matched assets** that you invest to meet a specific liability, like a college education. Whether a hedge fund is an appropriate match for an upcoming financial need depends in large part on the risk profile of the hedge fund. An absolute-return fund, which is designed to have low risk and a steady, low return, is usually a good match with an intermediate-term obligation. Directional funds, which pursue high-risk strategies in exchange for higher expected returns, are a better match for financial needs that reach far into the future. (Both types of funds are described earlier in this chapter.)

- **Permanent funds** that you invest for such a long term that, for all practical purposes, you'll never spend them. Instead, investors plan to spend only the income generated from the investments' interest and dividends. Permanent funds are often great investment candidates for hedge funds. Most hedge funds are designed to generate steady capital gains, and they limit withdrawals, so your fund's money should build up over time.

Few managers structure hedge funds to generate income, so if producing income is one of your key investment objectives, you should allocate your funds to other types of investments, such as bonds or dividend-paying stocks (introduced in Chapter 2 of Book I).

Finding the right asset allocation mix

Different assets — real (tangible) and financial (securities) — have different sources of return and present different tradeoffs, and you want a balance of them in your portfolio. Table 1-1 summarizes many types of financial assets.

Table 1-1	Characteristics of Different Financial Assets		
Financial Asset	*Primary Source of Return*	*Relative Level of Return*	*Relative Level of Risk*
Stocks (equities)	Capital gains	High	High
Bonds (fixed income)	Income	Medium	Medium
Cash	None	Low	Low
Real estate	Income, store of value	Medium	Medium
Commodities	Store of value, possible appreciation	Medium	Medium

When choosing a hedge fund to fit into your portfolio, you need to think about how it will act with the other investments in your portfolio because different asset classes interact with your other investments differently. For example, if you mostly invest in domestic stocks and bonds, you may want to put your hedge fund allocation into macro funds because those will have more international exposure — a strategy that will reduce the risk of your overall portfolio better than a U.S. long-short equity fund.

You also want to find a fund whose strategy jibes with your investment needs — a task that's fairly difficult when hedge fund managers often don't want to tell investors what strategies they're following or where they invest their money. Chapter 2 in Book V gives a list of questions you can ask as you interview prospective hedge fund managers to gather the information you need.

Think about the following:

- **Matching goals to money:** *Asset allocation* is the process of matching your investment goals to your money in order to meet your goals with the lowest possible amount of risk. If you need to generate $100,000 in pretax annual income from your investments and current interest rates are at 4 percent, for example, you should put $4 million in fixed-income securities with an average coupon (annual interest rate) of 4 percent. If you need $10 million in 20 years to meet a contractual obligation and think that an 8 percent return is acceptable as long as you experience little variation between your expected return and the return that you get, then you should put $2.2 million in a hedge fund with an absolute-return strategy.

The exact amounts and investments you choose will vary with your means and your goals. Any professional advisors you work with should take the time to find out what you need. Beware of advisors who try to sell you products without finding out what your needs are. It's not only against regulations (a violation of the know-your-customer and suitability rules), but also bad for you.

- **Chasing return versus allocating assets:** "I don't care what fund you put me in, as long as it performs well. How about this fund that was up 40 percent last year?" Whoa, cowboy! Unfortunately, that's a common strategy among investors, and it's a dangerous one. Known as *chasing return,* this strategy ignores long-term goals, near-term constraints, and good investing principles in hopes of landing the big bucks right now.

Return chasers are doomed to fail in the long run, and often in the short run, too. Markets move in cycles, so last year's hot performer will probably cool off this year. Moving your money around too much leads to plenty of taxes and commission charges that eat into your investment base. And without a sense of how much money you really need, when you need it, and with what degree of certainty you're operating, you risk choosing investments that miss your goals by a mile.

Chapter 2

Taking the Plunge with Hedge Funds

An open-end mutual fund (described in Book I, Chapter 3) continuously offers stock to the public. You simply find a fund that interests you, fill out a form, write your check, and voilà! You're a mutual fund shareholder. A hedge fund, which is a private-investment partnership, is nothing like that.

To help you navigate your way into and around hedge funds, this chapter explains how to choose the fund that's right for you, how to purchase a stake in the fund, what to do after you're a partner, and how to read the hedge fund reports. Finally, as an investor who's (hopefully!) making money, you need to know what your tax obligations are. This chapter covers that topic, too.

Investor, Come on Down! Pricing Funds

When you buy into a hedge fund or cash out your shares, you need to know what the shares are worth. When a fund forms, setting the price is simple: The total value of the fund is the total value of the cash put into it. If the fund disbands, setting the prices is also simple: The hedge fund manager sells all the securities, pays all the bills, and distributes the remainder proportionately. Of course, you also need to know what the shares are worth to calculate performance. (See Chapter 4 in Book V for more information on performance calculation.)

This section covers net asset value calculation, including dealing with illiquid securities and side pockets. With the use of these tools, you'll have a sense of how the fund comes up with the value of your investment.

Calculating net asset value

Hedge funds are priced on their *net asset value.* Also called *book value,* net asset value is the total of all the fund's assets minus all the fund's liabilities. The catch is finding the value for all the fund's securities, calculated at the end of each trading day, when the end of the trading day varies depending on when markets close around the world.

- ✔ If a fund invests entirely in one market and one type of investment, the pricing is straightforward. The New York Stock Exchange closes at 4 p.m. Eastern Time, so if all your investments trade there, you simply price at the close.

- ✔ When your investments trade on different exchanges, pricing is more difficult. One way to calculate net asset value is to add the values at the closing time for each relevant market. The price then would be the sum of the prices at each market's close (ignoring after-market trading).

No calculation method is inherently better; the key is that the method is disclosed and applied consistently. Be sure to ask the fund manager when and how the fund calculates the value. It should be spelled out in the contracts that you sign when you enter the fund.

Valuing illiquid securities

Because hedge funds can limit how often clients withdraw money, and because they tend to take a broad view of possible investments, they often put money in *illiquid securities* — investments that don't trade very often and are difficult to sell on short notice.

Short-term buying and selling can have an enormous impact on the prices of securities. If an asset trades all the time, the value is widely known. If an asset doesn't trade often, however, you have little observable, unbiased market indicator of what the true price should be. To get around this situation, hedge funds have many techniques to assign values to illiquid securities (see Chapter 4 in Book V for more details):

- ✔ **Net present value:** The discounted value of all the expected cash flows
- ✔ **Black-Scholes:** A complicated mathematical model used to find the value of an option

✔ **Relative valuation:** Basing the security's price on a similar security that trades frequently

If a hedge fund you're interested in invests in illiquid securities, find out what its policy for valuation is. And know that you take on some risk if the fund buys a lot of these assets; the price assigned by the fund may not hold when the illiquid securities have to be sold.

Surveying side pockets

A *side pocket* in a hedge fund is a group of securities held by only some of the fund's investors. Hedge funds set up side pockets — also called *designated investments* or *special investments* — for two main reasons:

✔ **To hold illiquid securities away from money that investors can redeem:** For example, the fund may allow investors to pull money out of the main part of the fund once per quarter, but it may decide that investors can redeem funds in the side pocket only once every two years. Likewise, new fund investors can't enter into the side pocket so that the valuation of those investments doesn't become an issue for them. If you invest in a fund that's just starting out, part of your investment may be held in a side pocket.

✔ **To allow certain fund investors access to securities that other investors may not have:** The fund may provide performance enticements or other special benefits that attract specific investors. A fund may also set up a side pocket to meet the needs of a large institutional investor that can put a great deal of money into the fund.

Side pockets are priced separately from the rest of the fund. Because they're often set up just to hold illiquid investments, their price may be more uncertain.

Due Diligence: Picking a Hedge Fund

Because hedge funds are structured as partnerships (see Chapter 1 in Book V), you enter into a relatively intimate business relationship with the fund manager when you buy into the fund. The better prepared you are, the better the relationship will be. Although a consultant may help you evaluate a fund manager, you still need to do your own research. The following sections explain how.

Knowing what to ask

One of the first steps in determining whether a particular hedge fund makes sense for you is to ask a lot of questions. After you prove to the hedge fund manager that you're both an accredited investor and able to invest in the fund now (see Chapter 1 in Book V), you'll probably receive an offering document that tells you about the fund. No matter how thorough the offering document is, you'll have to sit down for an interview with the fund manager or submit a list of questions to the fund's staff.

The following sections provide you with some questions to get you started. Your offering document will cover some; some you'll ask in an interview; and some you may have to find answers to on your own. You probably want to get an answer for each one, and you may well come up with other questions to ask.

Getting to know the hedge fund manager on the other side of the table is a good idea. When you talk to a fund manager, you get a sense of what doing business with this person will be like. You want to make sure that the fund fits your needs and that you're comfortable with the fund's strategy and the fund manager's personality.

Investment strategy

You want to get a feel for the fund manager's objective, his analytical style, and how he views himself and the fund. You also need an understanding of how the portfolio is constructed and the positions it holds, the tax suitability of the fund, and how liquidity is managed. The following questions help you get to the heart of investment strategy:

- ✔ What's your investment objective? How do you achieve alpha (see Chapter 1 in Book V)?

- ✔ How did you construct your portfolio? How and why is it rebalanced?

- ✔ What's your analysis and investment style? What would cause you to deviate from your style?

- ✔ If you use computer models, do you ever override or change them?

- ✔ What's the average number of positions your fund holds? How long do you hold a typical position? What's the level of portfolio turnover?

- ✔ Do you use *sub-advisors* (money managers who handle a portion of the portfolio)? When and why? How do you compensate them?

- ✔ Do you see yourself as a trader, an investor, or an analyst?

- ✔ Why is your fund different from others with the same investment style? What edge do you have over other managers?

- ✔ Is your fund more suitable for taxable investors or for tax-exempt ones?

- ✔ How does your fund keep enough liquidity to meet allowed withdrawals?

Performance

You want to know how well the fund performs in both the best and the worst of times, and why some times — and holdings — are better than others. You also want to know how the fund is valued, and by whom. Find out by asking these questions:

- What have been your worst and best months? Why?

- Did you earn your performance evenly in the past year, or did you have one or two really good months? If so, what made those months so good for your strategy?

- What was the time (the *peak-to-trough range*) between your best month and your worst month?

- What holdings have worked out the best for you? Which one was your worst ever? Why?

- Who calculates your fund's returns? How often? Where does this person get her data: from the prime broker or from the fund manager?

- How do you value the portfolio? When do you price it? How do you handle illiquid securities?

- Is your performance GIPS (Global Investment Performance Standards) compliant? If not, why not? Do you report your performance to Morningstar or other tracking services?

Risk management

You want to know how the fund regards risk and the fund manager's strategies for managing it. The following questions address those issues:

- How does your fund use leverage (see Chapter 3 in Book V)? What's the average leverage? What's the maximum leverage allowed? How often are you near those limits?

- Does your fund always have some leverage?

- Does your fund borrow from one bank or broker, or from several?

- What's your maximum exposure to any one security? Any one market? How often are you near those limits?

- How much of your borrowing is overnight? Short-term? Long-term? How has that changed over time?

- How do you define risk? What's your firm's attitude toward risk?

- What risks have you identified? What are your strategies for managing them?

- What happens if a trader exceeds his limits?

- What are your long-tail risk scenarios?

- Do you use derivatives to hedge? To speculate?

- Do you try to profit from, or hedge against, interest-rate risk? Currency risk? Market risk?

Fund operations

Fund operations revolve around such areas as accounting, legal, administrative, auditing, and data-protection services. You want to find out as much as possible about who's who. Consider the following questions:

- Who are your fund's founders? Are they still with you? If they've left, why did they leave and where did they go?

- How do you compensate your traders? What's the turnover of your investment staff? Of your total staff?

- How much do the fund principals have invested in the fund? Is this a good portion of their net worth?

- How do you keep the front and back office separated?

- Who is the asset custodian?

- What are your data-backup and disaster-recovery plans? How quickly could you get back into business if your building shut down?

- Who takes over if the fund manager is incapacitated or dies? What is the key person risk?

- What are your data-security practices?

- Is the fund audited annually? If not, why not? If yours is a new fund, have you lined up an auditor to do an audit at the end of the year?

- What's your accounting firm? Your law firm? Your prime broker? Your administrative-services firm?

Compliance and transparency

It's a good idea to find out how compliance is viewed and to know up-front how much you can expect to be informed going forward. Investigate with these questions:

- What are your compliance policies and procedures? May I see them?

- Are you registered with the Securities and Exchange Commission? With the Commodity Futures Trading Commission? Why or why not?

- How much disclosure and reporting can I expect? How much transparency should any hedge fund investor expect?

Poring over fund literature

After you arm yourself with the right questions and get some answers (see the preceding sections), your next step is to check up on the information you receive. One way to do this is by reviewing the firm's literature. These legal documents lay out the investment policies that govern the fund and its operations. You may also receive PowerPoint slides or other sales materials that explain the fund's investment policies and operations with less legalese. The information in these legal documents and marketing materials includes the fund's investment strategy and fees, as well as biographical information on the people who run the fund.

Picking up the phone

Another important step in the due-diligence process is to call former employees of the fund and others to verify the information that you've received through interviews and literature and that appears on the hedge fund manager's résumé. The fund manager should give you reference names and contact information for the resources you want to investigate. Here's a list of people you should call:

- **Former employees:** They may restrict their details to only dates of hire and positions held, but that information is useful — especially if it doesn't match with what the hedge fund manager tells you. If you can talk to a former fund colleague in depth, consider asking about things like how the fund manager researched and made trades, how the fund manager worked with both staff members and clients, and how the fund manager affected this person's performance in his old position.

- **Universities and colleges listed on the hedge fund manager's résumé:** Verify the degrees that the hedge fund manager claims from the schools that he says he attended.

- **Current investors:** You may also be able to talk to current investors in the hedge fund. If so, you should ask them why they chose this fund, whether the fund's performance has met their expectations, and what type of communication they've received from the hedge fund manager.

Sometimes, criminals hire an accomplice and give the person a cellphone and a script to use when the phone rings. Even if the list has a former employee's or current investor's direct line or personal cellphone, go through the organization's main switchboard and ask to be connected. In the unlikely event that a fraud is being perpetrated, you can catch it faster this way.

Searching Internet databases

Are the folks in charge of the hedge fund who they say they are? One way to find out is to do some simple Internet searches and look beyond the first pages of results you see. Most likely, your search will turn up nothing interesting, but that's what you want. And sometimes, page 4 or page 6 of the search shows something that the fund manager would like to hide.

Internet databases sometimes have incorrect information, and they can be thrown off if the person that you're looking for has a common name. Consider any information that you find to be a point for further questioning and research, not an automatic reason to accept or reject the fund.

Some of the sites that show up may be products of the hedge fund manager herself; what you want are sites that objective outsiders have prepared. Here are some recommended database sites:

- **LexisNexis** (`www.lexisnexis.com`): A huge database of court records, public records, and news stories that you can search for free. You can then buy the documents you need at about $3 each.

- **FINRA BrokerCheck** (`brokercheck.finra.org`): An online service that lets you check employment and disciplinary history of managers who are registered at this site.

- **U.S. Securities and Exchange Commission** (`www.sec.gov`): Offers information on funds registered with the SEC as well as searchable enforcement records (`www.sec.gov/divisions/enforce.shtml`) that tell you if a registered fund has had problems or if the fund manager ran into trouble while at another job.

- **National Futures Association** (`www.nfa.futures.org/basicnet`): A database that enables you to look up information about the people and funds registered with the Commodity Futures Trading Commission.

Seeking help from associated service firms

Most hedge funds rely heavily on outside service organizations. As a prospective hedge fund investor, you should know who the people in these firms are and what they do. The hedge fund manager should give you a list of the fund's service providers, and you should call at least a few to verify the services provided:

- **The prime broker:** The brokerage firm that handles most of the securities trades that the fund makes. The prime broker may also handle administrative services, such as taking in new investments, dispersing any funds withdrawn, and sending out periodic statements. (A dedicated administrative-services provider can also handle these functions.)

REMEMBER

The folks who actually handle the fund's cash, taking in investments and disbursing withdrawals, should be part of an outside organization. Consider it a red flag if the hedge fund you're investigating does its own administrative work. At a minimum, separate legal subsidiaries that have guidelines to ensure that transactions happen at arm's length should provide the fund's administrative services.

✔ **A law firm:** Assists with the fund's regulatory compliance activities. Even an unregistered fund has laws that govern its activities.

✔ **An accounting firm:** Assists with the fund's valuation of assets, calculation of returns, and preparation of tax forms.

✔ **Sub-advisors:** Manage certain types of assets.

✔ **An actuary or other risk-management consultant:** Helps the fund calculate the risk it takes.

Purchasing Your Stake in a Hedge Fund

After a hedge fund investor and a hedge fund manager decide to work together, the next stage in the process is the purchase. The investor (lucky you!) and the manager have forms to fill out, and, of course, you have to transfer some money. The following steps outline the process.

1. **Provide the necessary documents.**

   To comply with government regulations, the hedge fund's staff must verify that they know who the investors in the fund are and where their money came from. Therefore, you have to provide the following when you open a hedge fund account:

   • Name

   • Date of birth

   • Street address

   • Place of business

   • Social Security number or taxpayer identification number

   • Copies of financial statements from banks, brokerages, and other accounts showing that you're accredited and that you have enough money to meet the initial investment

• Driver's license and passport, if you're opening an individual account; if you're opening an institutional account, certified articles of incorporation, a government-issued business license, or a trust instrument

2. **Fill out tax forms.**

   As a partner, you report your share of the fund's earnings to the IRS, even if you haven't received any cash. This reporting structure is different from most other forms of investment income.

   The fund itself doesn't pay the taxes — you do. For more on your tax obligations, see the later section "Understanding Your Tax Responsibilities."

3. **Sign the partnership agreement, thus agreeing to the terms and certifying that you're an accredited investor (see Chapter 1 in Book V).**

   The partnership agreement is a contract (also called a *subscription agreement* or a *private-placement memorandum*) that specifies contractual obligations that both you and the hedge fund's general partners have to meet. The hedge fund contract sets forth many pieces of information you need to know, like the fund's general partners, its status with regulators, the fees that the fund charges and how it calculates them, the fund's limits on withdrawals, and the fund's procedure for handling any conflict.

   The contract is more or less standard, but it's written to favor the general partners' interests. Have a lawyer with you when going over the contract. A lawyer may be able to negotiate changes on different provisions, such as withdrawal procedures or disclosure levels, to get them working in your favor.

4. **Deposit your cash.**

   The money you put up goes to the fund's prime broker, which holds it in escrow until the fund is ready to add new money. To minimize the cash-flow effects on investment returns, the fund may add money only once a month, once a quarter, or once a year.

   If you already have an account for your other investments at the same firm as the fund's prime brokerage, you'll have an easy transfer. If your money comes from a bank or another brokerage firm, you may be required to obtain signature guarantees before you can transfer the funds.

Handling Liquidity after Your Initial Investment

Choosing and entering a hedge fund is a big, tough process, but your work doesn't stop after you hand over your investment and ride out the minimum lockup period (during which you don't have access to your funds). Your hedge fund will (hopefully) generate money for your investment, giving you additional investment opportunities. The fund may allow you to withdraw funds so you can meet other objectives (but it comes with a price). The fund may also start sending you checks to reduce its burden, or it may decide to disband altogether. The following sections discuss factors that can affect your investment objectives after you enter into a hedge fund.

Considering other investment opportunities

After you meet the strict requirements to get into a hedge fund and find the right fund for your investment objectives, you can begin to enjoy the perks of the fund: additional investment opportunities, like these:

- ✔ Your hedge fund manager may look to raise more money from his current investors in order to pursue interesting investment strategies that he sees in the market.

- ✔ You may come into money that you want to add to the fund and let your fund manager know. He may not need the money now, but he may want it in the near future.

- ✔ Even if the fund doesn't want to take on more money, the manager may allow you to buy shares from another investor — another good way to make additional investments after you enter a fund.

From the fund manager's perspective, cash in the fund is a problem unless he can invest it to meet the risk-and-return profile that investors expect. Your fund manager plans to reinvest the returns from the hedge fund. Every time the fund manager receives an interest payment or sells an investment at a profit, you make money that goes into the fund. Your underlying investment increases as long as the fund has a positive return.

Withdrawing funds

At some point, you may need to pull out money from your hedge fund. To do so, you'll probably have to send written notice to a hedge fund manager in advance of your withdrawal. The manager may lay out very specific terms for how you should send the request (for example, certified postal mail). The turnaround time between when the manager receives the request and when he approves the withdrawal may be a month. (A hedge fund's offering documents should set out how often you can make withdrawals, how you should request a withdrawal, and the length of time between your request and disbursement.)

The fund manager has some options when it comes to raising your withdrawal funds: He may meet your request with cash on hand, sell off some assets to raise the cash, or sell your shares to another investor. Then you'll receive the proceeds from the bank or prime broker that handles the fund's investments.

A hedge fund manager may not want to sell investments just to meet your withdrawal request because it may screw up a carefully crafted investment position or require him to sell an asset at a near-term loss. Also, some fund investments are illiquid, meaning that they're difficult to sell on demand. As a result, a fund manager may view your withdrawal as something that will hurt the fund's remaining investors. To offset the hurt, some hedge funds impose withdrawal fees, especially if investors want to pull out more than a small amount.

Your fund manager may also hold back some of your money until the fund's accountants have a chance to calculate the performance of the fund up to the date of your withdrawal. It isn't easy to calculate the value of some investments like venture capital, so the fund manager wants to wait until he knows the value before settling up with you.

Receiving distributions

Although few hedge funds are designed as income investments, they sometimes send checks to their investors. The checks may be distributions of income, or they may be returns of capital. The difference may appear academic on the surface, but it affects your portfolio — especially when it comes time to pay your taxes. Which distribution is which, and why do the funds start sending you checks like Grandma on your birthday? Read on to find out!

- ✔ **Income:** *Income* is money generated from interest, dividends, rental payments, and similar sources. Hedge funds usually reinvest income into their funds, but sometimes they pay it out to their investors. You may receive a check to help you meet your tax obligations, or your fund may send it to manage the size of its investable assets.

- ✔ **Returns of capital:** *Capital gains* are profits made when an investment goes up in price. These gains are *paper gains* when the fund still holds the asset that goes up in price, and *realized gains* when the fund sells the asset, locking in the profit in the process. Realized gains are taxable, but paper gains are not. In most cases, hedge funds want to reinvest their capital gains into new investments. However, your hedge fund may send you a check for your capital gains, reducing the amount of principal in the fund.

You may think that income and capital gains are the same thing, but they aren't. The government taxes them at different rates, and people handle them differently for accounting purposes. In most cases, capital gains are taxed at lower rates than income, which is enough of a reason to keep them separated. See the later section "Understanding Your Tax Responsibilities" for more information.

Managers of top-performing funds have been known to kick investors out. (The offering documents that you sign when you enter the fund explain if and when the fund manager can do this.) The policy may screw up your portfolio, and all the paper gains will suddenly fall into the realized (taxable) category.

Moving on after disbandment

For many reasons — mostly related to poor performance — a fund manager may decide to disband the fund and return the money to investors. When your fund disbands because of poor performance, you're happy to get your money back. But a fund may disband for other reasons, such as having difficulty raising and earning enough money to make the venture worthwhile. Two main problems exist with fund abandonment:

- ✔ **Poor performance may be a temporary blip.** A given investment strategy may be having an off year, which actually presents a good opportunity to buy assets cheap in order to take advantage of better performance in the near future. If the fund closes, its investors lose the opportunity to buy low in order to sell high. This is one reason that funds like having as long a lockup period as possible.

- ✔ **It may not be easy for you to find a new investment that meets your risk-and-return needs.** The likelihood of you finding another suitable investment is called *reinvestment risk.*

If disbandment looks like a possibility for your fund, you really can't do anything except start looking for new places to put your money. Disbandment is one of the risks you take when you invest in hedge funds.

Reading the Hedge Fund Reports

Hedge funds don't like to talk about what they do. You can attribute their preference for mystery to a few reasons: They're organized as private partnerships; they may not be registered with the Securities and Exchange Commission; and they may have figured out proprietary strategies to take advantage of market inefficiencies. If they tell the world what they're doing, they risk losing their money-making secrets.

However, you have legitimate reasons to know what's happening in the fund. Not only are you putting your money at risk, but you also may need to report to others or certify that you've met your fiduciary responsibilities if you work with an endowment or charitable organization, for example. If you have fiduciary responsibilities, transparency — or the lack of it — may affect your ability to do your job.

This section discusses position transparency, risk transparency, and window dressing and how they affect fiduciary responsibility — a consideration when choosing whether to invest in hedge funds or which hedge funds to invest in.

Appraising positions

When a hedge fund releases a list of the investments it owns, it has *position transparency.* You can look at the list to see what stocks sit in the account, what bonds the fund holds, what currencies it's exposed to, and other information. You can combine this information with any other holdings you have to ensure that the fund is meeting your overall investment risk-and-return objectives. Position transparency can also show whether the fund is complying with any unique requirements that you may have.

Interpreting risk

By using tactics such as *leverage* (or borrowing) and agreements such as *derivatives* (contracts based on the value of an underlying asset), a hedge fund may present a different risk level than its holdings list indicates. The risk may be more or less than the investor realizes. The bad news is that you don't have an easy way to measure the amount of risk in a hedge fund.

Although some hedge fund managers simply refuse to give investors information on risk, saying that the information is proprietary, most try to give their investors some information they can use:

- ✔ **Value at risk (VaR),** a single number that gives the likelihood of the portfolio losing a set amount of money over a set period (say, ten days). One problem with VaR is that the likelihood will never be zero. Another is that the hedge fund manager may give you information on VaR at a given point in time, but that number can change rapidly as market conditions change.

- ✔ **Stress testing,** where the fund manager runs computer models to find out how a hedge fund's portfolio may perform in different economic conditions. The results of stress testing give you some parameters to use in determining how much risk an investment has. Keep in mind, however, that stress testing can't test for every possible event.

If you need to know the risk of the hedge fund that you're investing in, you should deal only with funds that give you risk information.

Avoiding window dressing

Hedge funds rarely give transparency in real time. A hedge fund won't tell anyone what's happening on any particular day. Some hedge fund managers take advantage of this position to make their portfolios look good on the days that they must report. This tactic is known in the investing world as *window dressing*.

Highly nefarious forms of window dressing occur — for example, fund managers ignoring restrictions established in a partnership agreement that ban investments in some industries or geographical regions in order to take advantage of opportunities and then selling them the day before having to report the fund's holdings. However, a common form of window dressing takes place when a hedge fund manager sells all the positions that turned out to be bad ideas right before the reporting date.

No matter how you look at it, window dressing is a manipulation of the truth. Avoid hedge funds that practice it.

Understanding Your Tax Responsibilities

Hedge fund investment returns come in two forms: capital gains and income (see the earlier section "Receiving distributions" for details). The U.S. tax code treats these returns differently. The following sections go into detail on both capital gains and income taxes.

Keep these things in mind as you sort out your tax responsibilities:

✔ Different investment techniques have different tax effects. Some hedge fund strategies make great money, but not after the fund pays taxes. If you have to pay taxes, you need to make sure your hedge fund is managed with that responsibility in mind.

✔ You may have to pay taxes on your share of your hedge fund's income and capital gains each year, whether you take any money out of the fund or not. And you aren't done after the Feds get their cut; your state probably wants a share of your profit, too, and the city or county where you live may also take a piece of your investment profits. There are too many state considerations to cover in this book; just make sure you look into it, for your own sake.

✔ It's a good idea to work with a hedge fund manager who has enough experience to understand the tax implications of different trading strategies. Because taxes can eat into an investment return, hedge fund investors who pay taxes should ask potential hedge fund managers about the tax implications of the strategies their funds use.

Making sense of capital gains taxes

Most hedge funds generate at least some returns from capital gains. A *capital gain* is the increase in value of an asset over time. If you buy a share of stock at $10, hold it while the company introduces great new products and generates tons of profits, and then sell it after the stock reaches $52, you have a capital gain of $42. You don't pay taxes until you sell the asset. Your basis is the price you paid to acquire the asset, and your gain is the price you sell it at minus the basis. The advantage of capital gains is that the government taxes them at a lower rate than income.

Capital gains are classified as short-term or long-term, based on how long you hold your investment. *Long-term capital gains* come from assets that you hold for more than one year, and *short-term capital gains* come from assets that you hold for one year or less. You can net capital gains against capital losses. If you lose money when you sell one investment, you can deduct that loss against a gain incurred when you sell another. You can use up to $3,000 of excess losses to offset ordinary income and carry any additional loss amount into future years to offset gains or deduct against ordinary income. You can also net any short-term capital losses against long-term capital gains, which may reduce your liability. Long-term capital gains are taxed at lower rates than short-term capital gains.

Investors in a hedge fund are expected to pay taxes on those gains each year out of other sources of funds (the fund manager probably won't distribute money to investors so they can pay the taxes).

Tax laws change every year. Be sure to check the IRS's latest guidance on investment tax issues at www.irs.gov.

Taxing ordinary income

Many investment gains are classified as ordinary income. *Income* is money that an asset generates on a regular basis — interest on a bond, dividends on common stock, or rent from a commercial real estate stake. You report this income on your taxes, and you pay the same rate on it that you pay on earned income from your job. The good news? You can deduct any investment interest you pay, such as interest paid in leveraging or short selling strategies.

The government taxes qualified *dividends,* payouts of company profits, at a lower rate than other investment income because the company that issues the dividend has already paid taxes on its profits before it issues the dividend out of what's left over. The maximum tax rate on qualified dividend income as of this writing is 23.8 percent. (With a *qualified dividend,* you've held the stock for a specified minimum amount of time, currently at least 61 days, and the sales have no puts, calls, or short sales associated with them.)

A hedge fund that generates much of its return from interest income carries a higher tax burden than one that generates return from qualified dividend income or from long-term capital gains.

Chapter 3

A Potpourri of Hedge Fund Strategies

. . . .

In This Chapter

▶ Understanding how hedge funds can be an asset class on their own

▶ Using arbitrage in hedge funds

▶ Checking out short selling, leveraging, and other equity strategies

▶ Observing how hedge funds profit from the corporate life cycle

. . . .

*H*edge funds are wildly different from each other. Because hedge funds are lightly regulated investment partnerships and can take advantage of more investment strategies than other highly regulated investment vehicles, different funds are bound to invest in different ways.

This chapter looks at how you can include hedge funds in your investment portfolio to increase your return for a given level of risk. It also explains arbitrage, the primary investment strategy of many hedge funds, as well as equity-based hedge funds and hedge funds that make money through venture capital and loans. If you want to invest in a hedge fund, you need to know about these various strategies so that you have a better understanding of what a particular hedge fund may be doing. The more you know, the better your questions — and decisions — will be.

Viewing Hedge Funds as an Asset Class

Asset classes are distinctly different from each other, with unique risk-and-return profiles. For example: Bonds are loans, and their prices are affected by changes in interest rates and the borrower's ability to make payments. Stocks, on the other hand, are partial shares of ownership in a company; the company's profits and prospects affect the price of stocks.

One of the biggest debates in the hedge fund world is whether hedge funds represent a separate, new asset class, or whether they simply represent another vehicle to manage the traditional asset classes of stocks, bonds, and cash. This debate is more than an academic argument, because which side you come down on can affect the way you make decisions about your money.

An investor should structure her investment portfolio to reflect the risk and return that she needs. If a hedge fund appears in its own asset class, other assets that the investor selects to offset the portfolio's risk-and-return characteristics need to appear in the portfolio. In fact, adding different kinds of assets to a portfolio can reduce risk without affecting expected return.

Here's a breakdown of what happens when a hedge fund is in its own class and what happens when it isn't:

- ✔ If a hedge fund is its own asset class, with its own risk-and-return profile, it can diversify the risks of other assets in the portfolio. For this reason, many large pension and endowment funds have been putting money into hedge funds that feature an absolute-return style and listing them as separate asset classes.

- ✔ If a hedge fund isn't its own asset class, it increases the risk in the portfolio. Investors would have to add other assets to offset that risk. For this reason, many hedge fund investors don't break out their investments in hedge funds; they opt to include them with their domestic equity or international markets assets when they report their holdings.

Hedge fund managers have a ton of discretion, and they sometimes change strategies or attempt trades in new areas. You may think you're buying one type of fund but end up in something different. Your hedge fund's investment agreement may specify limitations, but it may not. You can exit the fund if you don't like the new strategy, but only when the lock-up period expires (see Chapter 1 in Book V for more about the illiquidity of hedge funds).

Moving together: Correlation

If return is a function of risk, how can adding different assets to your portfolio reduce risk without affecting return? The answer: *correlation*. Correlation shows how much two assets move together. If they move in tandem, the assets are perfectly correlated. If two assets aren't perfectly correlated, some of the movement in one offsets the movement in another.

An investment manager can run a computer program that analyzes the correlations of all her assets under consideration and determines how much of an investor's portfolio should be in each in order to generate the *minimum-variance portfolio*. This portfolio has less risk — but not less return — than the average risk and return of all of its assets.

Buying Low, Selling High: Arbitrage

Arbitrage is the process of buying an asset cheap in one market and selling it for a higher price in another. In theory, arbitrage opportunities don't exist because markets are perfectly efficient, right? In reality, arbitrage takes place every single day, which forces markets into efficiency. However, the price differences needed for arbitrage are often small and don't last long. For this reason, successful arbitrageurs have to be paying constant attention to the market, and they have to be willing to act very quickly. They have no room for indecision.

People often misuse the word "arbitrage" to describe any kind of aggressive trading. If you hear a hedge fund manager say that his fund uses arbitrage, ask what kind of arbitrage is involved.

Whether you buy into the idea of arbitrage depends on your feelings about market risk: the idea that market prices reflect all known information about a stock.

✔ Someone who believes in market efficiency would say that arbitrage is imaginary because someone would've noticed a price difference between markets already and immediately acted to close it off.

✔ People with a less rigid view would say that arbitrage exists, but the opportunities for taking advantage of it are very few and far between.

✔ People who don't believe in market efficiency would say that arbitrage opportunities happen all the time. These people believe that someone in one of the markets knows something, and if you can figure out what that person knows, you may have a solid advantage in the marketplace.

The following sections distinguish true arbitrage from risk arbitrage, list arbitrage tools, describe types of arbitrage, and explain arbitrage transaction costs.

Separating true arbitrage from risk arbitrage

True arbitrage is riskless trading. The purchase of an asset in one market and the sale of the asset in another happen simultaneously. The fund manager can count on profit as long as the trades go through immediately. True, riskless arbitrage is possible, but rare. No hedge fund that pursues only riskless arbitrage will stay in business for long.

Here's a classic example of true arbitrage: A hedge fund trader notices that a stock is trading at $11.98 in New York and $11.99 in London. He buys as many shares as possible in New York, borrowing money if necessary, and immediately sells those shares in London, making a penny on each one. This type of arbitrage transaction has no risk, so people often describe it as "finding money on the sidewalk." In most cases, these trades are driven by computer algorithms that search the markets for price discrepancies and take action in the blink of an eye — literally, not figuratively.

Most arbitrageurs practice *risk arbitrage,* which, like true arbitrage, seeks to generate profits from price discrepancies; however, risk arbitrage involves taking some risk (go figure!). Risk arbitrage still involves buying one security and selling another, but an investor doesn't always buy the same security, and he doesn't necessarily buy and sell at the same time. For example, a fund manager may buy the stock of an acquisition target and sell the stock of an acquirer, waiting until the acquisition finalizes before closing the transaction, making (he hopes) a tidy profit in the process.

In many cases, the risk taken is that of time. The trade may work out but not as soon as the hedge fund manager hopes. In the meantime, his portfolio's performance may suffer or loans taken to acquire the position may be called in. It's one thing to be right; however, it's another thing entirely to be right in time for the decision to matter.

Cracking open the arbitrageur's toolbox

Opportunities for riskless trading are very few and far between. Therefore, to find risky arbitrage opportunities, hedge funds look at similar securities, and they look for ways to profit from price discrepancies while offsetting much of the risk. The arbitrageur's favorite tools for offsetting risk include the following:

- ✔ **Derivatives:** A *derivative* is a financial instrument (like an option, a future, or a swap) that derives its value from the value of another security. A stock option, for example, is a type of derivative that gives you the right, but not the obligation, to buy shares of the stock at a predetermined price. Because derivatives are related to securities, they can be useful in risk arbitrage. A fund manager may see a price discrepancy between a derivative and an underlying asset, creating a profitable trading opportunity.

  With their value so closely linked to the value of other securities, derivatives offer many opportunities for constructing risk arbitrage trades. And with a wider range of low-risk arbitrage opportunities, a fund stands a better chance of making money.

✔ **Leverage:** *Leverage,* discussed in the upcoming section "Investigating Equity Strategies," is the process of borrowing money to trade. Because a hedge fund puts only a little of its own capital to work and borrows the rest, the return on its capital is much greater than it would be if it didn't borrow any money. Because leverage allows a hedge fund to magnify its returns, it's a popular tool for arbitrage.

The downside of leverage is that, along with magnifying returns, it also magnifies risk. The fund has to repay the borrowed money, no matter how the trade works out.

✔ **Short selling:** *Short selling* gives fund managers a way to profit from a decline in a security's price (see the later section "Investigating Equity Strategies" for details). The short seller borrows the declining security (usually from a broker), sells it, and then repurchases the security in the market later in order to repay the loan. If the price falls, the profit is the difference between the price when the fund manager sold the security and the price when she repurchased it. If the price goes up, though, that difference is the amount of the loss. By shorting an asset, the seller gives up the risk of the price going down, which can offer both a way to exploit a price discrepancy and a way to manage the risk of the transaction.

✔ **Synthetic securities:** A *synthetic security* is one created by matching one asset with a combination of a few others that have the same profit-and-loss profile. For example, you can think of a stock as a combination of a *put option,* which has value if the stock goes down in price, and a *call option,* which has value if the stock goes up in price. (Flip to Book II for more about these options.) By designing transactions that create synthetic securities, a hedge fund manager can create more ways for an asset to be cheaper in one market than in another, thus increasing the number of potential arbitrage opportunities. Many of the arbitrage styles that you can read about in the following sections involve synthetic securities.

Recognizing arbitrage types

Arbitrageurs use the tools of arbitrage in many different ways. Most arbitrage funds pick a few strategies to follow, although some may stick to only one and others may skip from strategy to strategy as market conditions warrant. Most hedge funds use some forms of arbitrage, and some may use arbitrage as their primary source of investment returns.

The following sections outline all the varieties of arbitrage transactions that a hedge fund may use as part of its investment strategy, arranged in alphabetical order. The strategies vary in complexity and in how often a fund can use them, but all are designed to take advantage of profits from security price discrepancies.

Capital-structure arbitrage

The *capital structure* of a firm represents how the company is financed. Does it have debt? How much? Does it have stock, and if so, how many classes? When a company has many different securities trading, arbitrageurs look for price differences among them. The thinking is that if all the securities are tied to the same asset — the company's business — they should trade in a similar fashion.

For example, say that the MightyMug Company has common stock outstanding, as well as 20-year corporate bonds at 7.5 percent interest. The stock price stays in line with market expectations, but the company bonds fall in value more than expected given changes in interest rates. An arbitrageur may buy the bonds and short the stock, waiting for the price discrepancy between the two securities to return to its normal level. That means that the bonds will have increased in price, so he can sell them at a profit, and the stock will have fallen in price, so he buys it back to cover the short and locks in a profit.

Convertible arbitrage

Some companies issue *convertible bonds* (sometimes called a *convertible debenture*) or *convertible preferred stock.* The two types of securities are very similar: They pay income to the shareholders (interest for convertible bonds and dividends for convertible preferred stock), and they can be converted into shares of common stock in the future. Convertible securities generally trade in line with the underlying stock, but if the convertible gets out of line, an arbitrage opportunity presents itself.

Suppose that an arbitrageur notices that a convertible bond is selling at a lower price than it should be, given the interest rates and the price of the company's common stock. So she buys the bonds and sells the stock short. The trade cancels out the stock exposure, reducing the transaction risk and leaving only the potential for profit as the bond's price moves back into line.

Fixed-income arbitrage

Fixed-income securities give holders a regular interest payment. Because interest rates affect so many different securities — bonds, currencies, and derivatives, for example — they're a common focus for arbitrageurs. With *fixed-income arbitrage,* the trader breaks out the following:

- The time value of money
- The level of risk in the economy
- The likelihood of repayment
- The inflation-rate effects on different securities

If one of the numbers is out of whack, the trader constructs and executes trades to profit from it. For example, if a hedge fund trader tracking interest rates on U.S. government securities notices that one-year treasury bills are trading at a higher yield than expected, he may decide to short the two-year treasury notes and buy the one-year treasury bills until the price difference falls back where it should be.

Index arbitrage

A *market index* is designed to represent the activity of the market. Futures contracts are available on most indexes, for example. These derivatives (covered in Book II) are based on the expected future value of the index. Sometimes, the value of the futures contract deviates from the value of the index itself. When that happens, the arbitrageur steps in to make a profit.

Most indexes have many securities (the S&P 500 Index has 500 stocks in it!), so buying a load of them can be expensive. That's why only the largest hedge funds are active in index arbitrage. Some funds do a version of index arbitrage using exchange-traded funds; although these should match the index that they're based on, sometimes they don't.

Liquidation arbitrage

Liquidation arbitrage is a bet against the breakup value of a business. Imagine that an arbitrageur researches a company to see what it would be worth if it were sold. If she sees value in the company's various components that is greater than the current market value of the stock, she may buy shares of the company in anticipation that someone will come along and take over the company at a price that reflects its value.

Merger arbitrage

Merger arbitrage is about profiting from a company's acquisition *after* a merger has been announced. A merger announcement includes the name of the acquiring company, the name of the company being acquired, the price of the transaction, the currency (cash, stock, debt), and the date the merger is expected to close. Any of these variables can change — the acquiring company may decide that the deal is a bad one and walk away, for example — and all these variables create trading opportunities, although not all are riskless.

When companies announce a big merger, traders sometimes get caught up in the mood of the moment and engage in *garbatrage*. That is, everyone gets so excited that even businesses with no real connection to the merger become part of the speculation. For example, if a drug company buys a shampoo manufacturer, the shares of any and all beauty-products manufacturers may go up, causing folks to pay too much money because not all the shares will be worth their newly inflated price.

Option arbitrage

Options (discussed in Book II) come in many varieties, even if they exist on the same underlying security. They come in different types: *puts* (bets on the underlying security price going down) and *calls* (bets on the underlying security price going up). They have different prices, at which a holder can cash in the option for the underlying security, and different expiration dates. You can exercise some options, known as *European options,* at any time between the date of issue and the expiration date, and you can exercise others, known as *American options,* only at the expiration date. Needless to say, having so many securities that are almost the same creates plenty of opportunities for a knowledgeable arbitrageur to find profitable price discrepancies.

If, for example, a hedge fund's options trader notices that the options exchanges are assuming a slightly higher price for a security than in the security's own market, he may decide to buy the underlying security and then buy a put and sell a call with the same strike price and expiration date. The put–call transaction has the same payoff as shorting the security, so the trader has effectively bought the security cheap in one market and sold it at a higher price in another.

Pairs trading

Pairs trading is a form of long-short hedging (described in the upcoming section "Looking at long-short funds") that looks for discrepancies among securities in a given industry sector. If one security appears to be overvalued relative to others, a savvy arbitrageur will short that security and then buy another security in the group that seems to be undervalued.

Factoring in transaction costs

What goes into the cost of arbitrage trading? Quite a lot, actually:

- **Staff:** The overhead of having traders on staff, including salaries, bonuses, and benefits.
- **Information systems:** The cost of having the information systems in place to monitor several markets in real time, enabling the hedge fund and a broker to execute an arbitrage trade almost instantaneously. (The free quotes that investors can find online through such sources as Yahoo! Finance [finance.yahoo.com] are delayed for 15 to 20 minutes, depending on where the security trades. Real-time quotes are expensive.)
- **Commissions:** The commissions for brokers who execute the transaction.

Because of transaction costs associated with arbitrage, hedge funds tend to either commit heavily to arbitrage or avoid it entirely. If you plan on investing in a hedge fund that expects to generate most of its profits from arbitrage, be sure to ask about these factors when you shop for a hedge fund. (Chapter 2 in Book V has full details on picking a hedge fund.)

Investigating Equity Strategies

Equity-based hedge funds (hedge funds that invest in equities) start with the same investment strategies as mutual funds, brokerage accounts, or other types of investment portfolios that invest in equities. But they use two unique strategies — short selling and leveraging — to change the risk profiles of their investments in stocks. Depending on your hedge fund's strategy and market expectations, it may have greater or less risk than the market, in part because of the use of these strategies. And you can assume that most hedge funds are using some leverage and some short selling to reach their risk and return objectives.

Almost all hedge funds use some short selling and leverage in order to increase return for a given level of risk. Therefore, if you're interested in hedge funds, you should find out as much as you can about short selling and leverage so that you have a better understanding of what hedge funds do:

- ✓ **Short selling:** Borrowing an asset (like a stock or bond), selling it, and then buying it back to repay the loaned asset. If the asset goes down in price, the hedge fund makes the difference between the price where it sold the asset and the price where it repurchased the asset. Of course, if the asset appreciates in price, the hedge fund loses money. The opposite of short is long, so an investor who is *long* is an investor who owns the asset.

  If much of your portfolio sits in an S&P 500 Index fund — a fund that invests in all the securities in the S&P 500 in the same proportion as the index in order to generate the same return — you have significant exposure to the stock market, which means you have market risk. One way to reduce that risk without giving up your expected return is to seek out equities with a different risk profile. Short selling gives you more places to look.

- ✓ **Leverage:** Borrowing money to invest, often from brokerage firms. Leverage increases your potential return — and your risk. Hedge funds use leverage, but so do other types of accounts, and many individual investors use it, too.

The following sections detail equity strategies that involve short selling and leverage; they discuss long equity investment styles, market-neutral portfolios, long-short funds, market calls, and buying on margin.

Surveying the investment styles of long equity managers

Long equity managers, those equity investors who don't short stocks (and thus are rarely hedge fund managers, although a small number of hedge fund managers are long-only), fall into several broad categories and employ several styles, often called *style boxes*. Fund managers use these categories to guide their choices for the long portions of their portfolios (the securities that they own, not those that they short) or to determine the risk that they can reduce with hedging strategies. At a minimum, you want to recognize the terms covered in this section when they come up in conversation.

Few hedge funds use the strategies in this section exclusively. Hedge fund managers are in the business of using exotic investment techniques in order to beat the market — and to justify their high fees.

Trying on a large cap

A *large-cap fund,* which may be a hedge fund, a mutual fund, or another type of investment portfolio, invests in companies with a market capitalization (shares outstanding multiplied by current price) of $5 billion or more. These companies tend to be multinational behemoths with steady performance and fortunes tied to the global economy. You can find these companies in the S&P 500, the Fortune 500, and on every other 500 list, save the Indy 500.

Many large-cap managers engage in a strategy called *closet indexing:* They buy shares in the largest companies in the S&P 500 in more or less the same proportion as the S&P index. The result is that the portion of the portfolio containing the large-cap shares has almost identical risk and return as the index but for the higher fee that an active manager receives. A hedge fund manager who does closet indexing isn't hedging, so she isn't doing what you pay her to.

Fitting for a small, micro, or mid cap

A *small-cap stock* is a share of a company with a market capitalization of under $1 billion. These companies tend to be growing faster than the market as a whole, and they aren't as closely covered by investment analysts as larger companies, so their shares may not be as expensive as those in similar but better-known companies.

Some fund managers concentrate on investing in company stocks with a market cap of under $100 million, believing that's where the real money-making opportunities lie because these stocks are even less covered than small-cap stocks, so the managers may be getting in on the ground floor. This style of investing, known as *micro cap,* is similar to venture capital and requires that the fund manager do careful research, because other investors may be showing little interest in the company.

What's in between $5 billion and $1 billion? Mid-cap investments, which have characteristics of both large-cap and small-cap stocks. Easy, huh? Some small- and mid-cap companies will grow and graduate to the next level. However, some mid-cap companies used to be large-cap companies before they ran into trouble, and some small caps are former mid caps whose growing days are over.

If a hedge fund manager mentions capitalization as a style, ask how the fund defines the cutoffs. Because the industry has no standard cutoff for small-, mid-, and large-cap stocks, different analysts and money-management firms set their own parameters.

Investing according to growth and GARP

A *growth fund* looks to buy stock in companies that are growing their revenue and earnings faster than the market as a whole. Hedge funds expect these equities to appreciate more than the market and to have some life to them, making them longer-term holdings.

Growth stocks tend to be more expensive than stocks in companies that are growing at a normal rate. For this reason, many fund managers try to find cheap growth stocks, following a strategy called *growth at the right price* (or *growth at a reasonable price [GARP]*). The fund manager attempts to combine growth with low price-to-earnings ratios in order to earn a greater-than-market return for a market rate of risk.

Swooping in on lowly equities with value investing

Value investors are the most traditional of equity investors. Hedge fund managers who consider themselves value investors look for stocks that are cheap based on accounting earnings or asset values. They shoot for companies that have solid assets, plenty of cash, and inferiority complexes because the market doesn't recognize them. Value investors care more about what a business would look like dead, with the assets sold and the proceeds distributed to shareholders, than what it would look like if it grew in the future. (For more on value investing, go to Book VII.)

Keeping options open for special style situations

A special-situations investor doesn't like to declare allegiance to any one style of equity investing; he prefers to look at stocks that seem likely to appreciate. A sharp manager may want to keep his options open, especially at a larger firm that can afford investment analysts and traders who have their own investment niches. Other managers may want flexibility to move between styles whenever the current en vogue style isn't working out.

Although keeping all investment options open may seem like a good idea, special-situations investors can end up chasing ideas all over the place. With no discipline to help them determine valuation, these investors may end up buying high and selling low, which is a sure path to ruin. If you interview a special-situations fund manager because you're interested in his fund's ability to handle your money, ask how he makes his investing decisions.

Creating a market-neutral portfolio

With a typical, diversified equity portfolio, you can earn only the market rate of return. Although you take on the same amount of risk as the market, that may be more risk than you want. For these reasons, many hedge funds have a market-neutral strategy. You expect a *market-neutral portfolio* to generate a positive return, regardless of what the market does. This doesn't mean that a market-neutral portfolio will generate a higher return than the market, although it should when the market loses money.

A fund manager has to tweak a market-neutral portfolio to maintain its neutrality, so the manager needs a system for the tweaking process. The three common styles of market-neutral investing are creating beta-neutral, dollar-neutral, and sector-neutral portfolios.

Being beta-neutral

Many hedge fund managers use beta as the neutral point when figuring out ways to make their portfolios market-neutral. Beta is the relationship of a security to the market as a whole. Under the Modern (Markowitz) Portfolio Theory (MPT), the market has a beta of 1, and a stock that's correlated with the market also has a beta of 1. A security that's negatively correlated with the market has a beta of –1. A *beta-neutral portfolio,* therefore, is made up of securities that have a weighted average beta of 0. In other words, the portfolio has no market exposure.

Few 0-beta securities exist in the market, because if a security is part of the market, it almost definitely has some bit of exposure to it. That's why almost every investment went down in the September 2008 market crash. The closest asset to a 0-beta security is a short-term U.S. treasury security, which has a very low return. Of course, a beta-neutral hedge fund has to generate a return greater than treasuries in order to attract assets!

To maintain 0 beta while maximizing return, a fund manager can run a program that comes up with optimal portfolio weighting. In some ways, a beta-neutral portfolio is as much about programming as it is about picking stocks, because the weightings are very difficult to calculate by hand. Finding negative-beta stocks, on the other hand, is easy. Shorting a stock is the same as reversing its beta, so a fund manager can generate negative-beta securities by taking short positions in stocks with positive betas.

Establishing dollar neutrality

In a *dollar-neutral portfolio,* the hedge fund manager holds the same amount of money in short positions — that is, in securities that he borrowed and then sold in hopes that they would go down in price so the fund could repurchase them at a lower price to repay the loan — as in long positions, securities that the fund owns outright. With this strategy, the portfolio's expected return isn't highly exposed to the market, because the portfolio should benefit no matter what direction the market moves. An investor follows this strategy to eliminate market risk from a portfolio. Of course, if you want to have market risk, this feature would be a disadvantage.

Staying sector-neutral

Certain industries represented in the investment indexes perform differently than others, which can make index performance more volatile than a true market investment should be. The people who select the stocks for the indexes have been known to make additions and subtractions that make the indexes perform better, even if the indexes become less representative of the market and the economy.

To structure his portfolio free of political influences, generating less risk than may be found in an index fund in the process, a hedge fund manager can weight each industry sector equally so that Internet stocks don't crowd out automaker stocks, for example. This is called *sector neutrality.* Although it doesn't eliminate market risk, it does reduce it. Many hedge fund managers combine sector neutrality with other portfolio strategies, such as arbitrage (described earlier in this chapter) or leverage.

Looking at long-short funds

A *long-short fund* is actually a traditional hedge fund: It buys and sells stocks according to its risk profile and market conditions. A long-short fund manager looks for overvalued assets to sell and undervalued assets to buy. The valuation may be relative to the current assets and earnings of the securities or relative to the future prospects for the companies. Matching the two allows for reduced risk and increased returns — the very stuff of the hedge fund game.

Some hedge fund managers allocate parts of their portfolios to pure short selling. (The other part of the portfolio is long but not matched to the short assets, so this is a type of long-short fund.) These managers want to increase their risk (and thus their expected returns) by finding overvalued securities in the market and then selling them short. This strategy isn't for the faint of heart, because the most a stock can go down is 100 percent, to 0, but the most it can go up is infinity. That's why most hedge fund managers view short selling as part of a hedged portfolio, not the centerpiece of it.

The flip side of this is a long strategy called a *short squeeze,* in which a hedge fund or other portfolio manager looks for stocks that have been shorted. At some point, all the short sellers have to buy back the stocks to repay the lenders. This means that someone can buy up enough of the stock to push the prices higher, causing investors on the short side to start losing money. As the shorts lose money, the managers can buy shares to cover the loans and get out of the positions; their buying drives the prices even higher.

Most short sellers do excellent research. An unscrupulous few have been known to drive asset prices down by starting ugly rumors and spreading outright lies. As a result, short selling isn't a game for the faint of heart.

Making market calls

A traditional hedge fund — namely, a long-short hedge fund (see the preceding section) — hedges risk. A modern, lightly regulated partnership may enlist all sorts of risky strategies to increase return. As long as the fund doesn't closely correlate the risk with the other holdings in the portfolio, it can meet its goal of reducing risk. What's more, a strategy keyed off of market performance doesn't require the portfolio manager to determine how the market is moving. But some investors want more. They want return tied to the market in one form only: a return that beats the market handily.

But here's the thing: How do you call the market (read: foresee the future)? Anyone who can call the market consistently is retired to a beachfront estate in Maui, not running a hedge fund. Some hedge fund managers are close to affording a beach hideout, but others are still trying to beat the market in order to get there. Trying to call the market is a perilous enterprise.

Predicting the market is nearly impossible to do in the long run. Don't expect a hedge fund you're interested in to beat the market, and be leery of a fund manager who claims to be a seer. Instead, think about how the hedge fund will help you manage risk.

Some of the things that hedge fund managers look for when they make decisions about buying and selling securities include the following:

✔ **Investing with event-driven calls:** An *event-driven* manager looks at situations he expects to happen in the market, guesses how the market will react, and invests accordingly. A manager always has two moving pieces when making event-driven calls: predicting the event and determining what the market expects the event to be. Such an event may be an upcoming election, the death of an ailing world leader, or a hurricane that knocks out some offshore oil drills.

✔ **Taking advantage of market timing:** A hedge fund manager who *times* the market allocates different portions of his portfolio to different asset classes. The exact proportion for each class varies with different market indicators. The idea is to have plenty of money in assets that the fund manager expects to do well and to put less money in assets that aren't supposed to do as well.

The difference between a market-timing strategy and an event-driven strategy is that an event-driven manager looks for individual securities that he expects to do well based on specific events; the market timer looks for changes in general economic trends, such as inflation and unemployment — often signaled by technical indicators — which show up on stock trading charts analyzed by using technical analysis. (See Book X for more information on technical analysis.)

Buying on margin to put the power of leverage to use

Even a simple investing strategy — such as buying stocks in the S&P 500 Index in the same proportion in order to replicate the index's performance — can take on new risk and return levels through the use of leverage. Maybe you've heard the phrase "using other people's money"; that's what leveraging is. An investor borrows money to make an investment, getting maximum return for a minimal amount of cash up-front. Of course, this strategy can also lead to a maximum loss. You can use leverage in an equity portfolio to maximize return. But be forewarned: It's a strategy that also increases your risk.

The simplest way to use leverage is to borrow money from the brokerage firm that holds the investment account — called buying securities *on margin*. The Federal Reserve Board sets the amount that a hedge fund can borrow. The Board requires individual investors to have 50 percent of the purchase prices on account at the time they place their margin orders; they may borrow the rest of the money from their brokerage firms. Hedge funds and other large investors are often allowed to borrow more.

After the leverage takes place, the margin borrower must meet ongoing margin requirements. As the security bought on margin fluctuates in price, the 50 percent purchase-price level kept on account may fall to only

---

Gaining return with other forms of borrowing

Larger hedge funds can find banks, financial institutions, and even other hedge funds willing to lend them money that they can use to buy securities. If you're investing in a hedge fund, you should expect that the fund has more sources of funds than just margin accounts.

Private banks often loan hedge fund investors money to get into a fund or a fund of funds. In this case, the investor's personal wealth is leveraged over and above whatever leverage the fund has. The same risks apply: If the investment goes up, the loan leads to a greater rate of return, but if the investment heads south, the investor still has to repay the loan.

---

30 percent of the money owed. In this case, the borrower gets a *margin call* and has to add money to the account to get it back to the minimum maintenance level. Otherwise, the brokerage firm will cash out the borrowed position. The New York Stock Exchange (NYSE) and Financial Industry Regulatory Authority (FINRA) set minimum margin requirements, although many brokerage firms have the ability to set higher levels based on their risk-management requirements and their comfort levels with the clients.

As long as a borrowed security appreciates by more than the cost of the borrowing, the margin position makes money. But because the borrowing fund has to pay interest, margin buying is a money-losing proposition if the security doesn't go up.

Participating in Corporate Life Cycles

The hedge fund you're interested in may be taking roles in corporate transactions. The following sections describe these transactions so you'll understand what a hedge fund that follows this type of strategy is doing with your money. The many stages of the corporate life cycle give hedge funds plenty of opportunities to make money. Some funds concentrate on corporate finance transactions, and others view that strategy as one of many ways to make money.

Venture capital: Helping businesses break to the next level

Hedge funds often invest in venture capital. *Venture capital,* sometimes known as *private equity,* is money given to entrepreneurs to fund new companies — money that comes with strings attached. An investor who gives the money wants to ensure that the business succeeds. It isn't uncommon, for example, for venture capitalists to make their investments on the condition that the founders leave their companies so seasoned managers can replace them.

Venture investments can help a company grow faster than it could otherwise, and investors can bring expertise — and potential clients — to the start-ups. Some of the biggest technology companies in the United States, like Intel, Oracle, Apple, and Google, were started with venture capital. The payoff to those investors (and investors in those investors) was huge, which is the attraction of the investment.

Here are some things to know about venture capital investing:

- ✔ Venture investors count on acquiring some companies that will fail in their portfolios, offset by the few companies that hit it big.

- ✔ Venture capital comes in different forms. Investors from a hedge fund may give the money to a young company as equity, making the hedge fund one of the owners of the company. The capital can also be debt that converts into equity if the company goes public or sells out to a larger company. The structure depends on the start-up company's business and state of profitability.

- ✔ Venture-capital investors need a liquidity event to make money. This event occurs when a company is sold to a larger one or when it issues stock through an initial public offering, or IPO. Until that event happens, the venture investor won't make much money.

Following are the most common forms of venture capital that you're likely to encounter when scoping out hedge funds (including private equity, which deals with established companies, making it not quite venture capital, but close):

- ✔ **Late-stage venture:** For new companies that have gotten over the initial hurdles of setting up the business and attracting customers but still need more money to grow before going public or being acquired. Venture investors see a little less risk with some huge upside.

- ✔ **Mezzanine capital:** For young companies that need just enough financing to move to the stage where they can go public or be attractive acquisitions. This is the least risky stage of venture capital. Hedge funds are interested in these companies because returns are likely to be higher than with public companies.

- ✔ **Private equity:** For publicly traded companies that can't raise money efficiently through a public offering. These transactions carry lower potential returns than venture capital because they carry less risk (the company is established), but they often carry higher returns than shares of common stock in similar companies because selling private equity is harder.

✔ **Seed capital:** Money used to take an idea and turn it into a business. Few hedge funds provide seed capital because they prefer to wait to see whether a company has a chance of surviving.

Short-term transactions: Replacing banks?

Hedge funds may have money to lend, or they may need money to invest. When it comes to short-term transactions — sometimes as short as overnight — hedge funds often replace banks in the role of taking deposits and lending money.

✔ **Borrowing money:** In the effort to make the largest possible amount of money at the lowest possible rate, hedge funds borrow from other hedge funds, from banks, from brokerage firms, and sometimes from large corporations. Many corporations lend out money, often for only overnight, that would otherwise just be sitting around. This amount of time may be exactly enough for a hedge fund to take advantage of a profitable price discrepancy between two securities. In such transactions, most hedge funds use *leverage* to increase their potential return, which means that they borrow money to buy securities, increasing the amount of money that they can make relative to the amount of money actually in the funds. (See the earlier section "Investigating Equity Strategies" for an introduction to leverage.)

✔ **Lending money:** If a hedge fund manager sees money in one account that isn't being used for one of the fund's investments, he may decide to loan it out, even for a short period, to get some amount of return. Hedge funds receive interest when they loan out money; of course, the funds take on the risk that the borrowers won't repay the money.

Gaining return from mergers and acquisitions

Hedge funds are often players in *mergers* (combinations of equal companies) and *acquisitions* (when larger companies purchase smaller companies) by providing funding and speculating on the outcomes. Funds look for certain situations and use certain strategies to increase return and put money in your pocket:

✔ **Leveraged (management) buyouts:** Sometimes, members of a company's management group, having grown fed up with shareholders and the hassles of having publicly traded shares, believe they could make more money if they ran the company themselves, so they decide to raise the money to take over. Because it involves heavy borrowing, this type of transaction is called a *leveraged buyout* (LBO) in the United States (in Europe, it's called a *management buyout* [MBO]). Many hedge funds invest in LBO debt because it tends to be riskier than most corporate debt. The risk comes from the management group's decision to borrow most or all of the money needed for the acquisition.

✔ **Buyout funds:** *Buyout funds* are investment pools formed by hedge fund managers and other private investors for the express purpose of funding leveraged buyouts and business expansions.

✔ **Bridge lending:** Hedge funds that want to loan money may work with companies that are looking to acquire other companies and, at least in the short run, need some financing to acquire shares in the market or otherwise support a bid for another company. A loan from a hedge fund in this situation is called a *bridge loan* or *bridge financing*.

✔ **Merger arbitrage:** *Merger arbitrage* is a low-risk trading strategy designed to profit after a corporate merger or acquisition is announced. In general, the shares of the company about to be acquired trade at a discount to the offer price because you take on some risk that the deal won't go through. A hedge fund trader buys the stock of the target company and sells the stock of the acquirer, waiting until the deal is announced for the gap to close at a nice profit.

Investing in troubled and dying companies

Insiders often use a slang term for investment pools that seek out troubled businesses and troubled countries: *vulture funds.* In some ways, vulture funds are the opposite of venture capital funds (described earlier in this chapter): The venture funds profit as companies get going, and vulture funds profit at the end of the corporate life cycle. If a fund's traders see that a nation's currency has weakened or that some bonds are in risk of default, they swoop in, buy as much as they can, and use their positions as negotiating leverage to get a profit for the fund. Fund traders may also take large positions in the equity and debt of a troubled company and then force management to sell off divisions and other assets. Several investment strategies prey on troubled businesses, including hostile takeovers and liquidation arbitrage:

✔ **Hostile takeovers:** A *hostile takeover* occurs when a company or an investment group acquires enough common stock in a company to get control of its board of directors. In some cases, the company or investment group believes that it can operate the business more profitably. In other cases, the acquirer simply wants to sell off the company's assets at a profit. A hedge fund may offer financing to another takeover group, or it can buy enough stock to be a part of one. Both strategies can be profitable.

✔ **Liquidation arbitrage:** *Liquidation arbitrage* is an investment technique that looks to profit from the breakup of a firm. An investor does careful research to determine exactly how a company's market value differs from the value of the sum of its parts. If the investment fund, often a hedge fund, finds an opportunity where the actual value of the company looks very different from the market value, the fund can acquire enough shares to force management to break up the company or at least sell off some of the assets at a gain for shareholders.

Chapter 4

Evaluating Hedge Fund Performance

Calculating investment performance seems easy: You take your balance at the end of the year, divide it by your balance at the start of the year, subtract 1, and voilà! But what if you add to your investment in the middle of the year in order to net a bigger return? What if your hedge fund manager had to cash out other shareholders? Quickly, you're left with algebra unlike any you've seen since high school. Because of all the possible complications, many researchers in the investment industry are trying to standardize calculations, and others are asking pointed questions to make solid comparisons.

This chapter looks at how a hedge fund measures and evaluates its performance, as well as what questions you need to ask your prospective fund partners about performance calculation. Evaluating a hedge fund's performance helps you determine whether the fund is the right fit for your investment objectives. It also tells you whether the hedge fund manager is doing well relative to the risk taken, which is why you invest in the fund in the first place.

Measuring a Hedge Fund's Return and Risk

In general, less risk is preferable to more, and more return is preferable to less. Some people invest in hedge funds to reduce risk, preferring *nondirectional* or *absolute-return funds* (see Chapter 1 in Book V); other investors aim to increase return regardless of risk by investing in *directional funds.* These funds maintain exposure to the market rate of return, and you have no guarantee that the direction of the return will be up.

The following sections give you the methods used to measure return and risk within a hedge fund, presenting the different forms of return, factoring in fees, and explaining how risk factors into performance.

Reviewing the return

Return is a measure of past performance, not a predictor of future results. What a hedge fund did last year doesn't matter; this year is an entirely different ballgame. Whether you're a current or a prospective investor, past return numbers are only rough indicators of what you can expect.

That doesn't mean, however, that return figures are worthless. Return measures tell you how a fund did over a time period, and you can compare that number to your expectations and your needs. What muddies the picture is that a hedge fund manager may have been lucky or unlucky, or he may have an investment style that does very well in some market conditions and not so well in others. That's why return is only one piece in the evaluation of a portfolio's performance. The following sections explain how to calculate return and some associated fees.

Calculating the return

When calculating investment return, fund managers typically do the following:

- ✔ **Value the assets to determine what the fund holds and what its holdings are worth:** The best method is to use *market value* — what the security would sell for on the market today — but some funds use their initial costs instead for assets that don't trade easily, like real estate. Sometimes, a hedge fund estimates the value of an illiquid asset; that estimation may be close to reality or may be used simply to make the fund look good.

- ✔ **Choose the dates to set the fund's time period:** A year in an accounting calendar may be 360 days long, and a month could end not on the last day of the month but on the last business day or the last Friday. As long as the hedge fund manager discloses the beginning and ending dates and applies the method consistently, it doesn't matter how she sets the fund's time periods.

When you're doing comparisons, make sure that you compare numbers for the same time periods. A shady fund manager may change the ending date for a quarter to avoid a big market decline on the last calendar day, for example.

✔ **Pick a calculation methodology:** Give someone with a numerical bent a list of numbers and a calculator and she can come up with several different relationships between the numbers. Although various calculation methods are possible, most people who analyze investment returns — also called the *compound average growth rate* (CAGR) — prefer to use a time-weighted, compound average approach.

The time-weighted return calculation produces a simple percentage, using the following formula, where *EOY* stands for "end of year asset value," and *BOY* is "beginning of year asset value." The result is the percentage return for one year:

$$\frac{EOY-BOY}{BOY}$$

If you want to look at your return over a period of several years, you need the following formula, which looks at the compound return rather than the simple return for each year; here *EOP* stands for "end of the total time period," *BOP* stands for "beginning of the total time period," and *N* is the number of years that you're looking at:

$$\sqrt[N]{\frac{EOP}{BOP}} - 1$$

This approach isn't as flashy as some others — you can do it with the same cheap scientific calculator you used in high school chemistry — but it gives you a more precise way to figure out how a fund performs over a range of market cycles.

Calculating fees

One big nuance with return calculations is whether or not you include fees, which can be hefty: A typical hedge fund charges a 1 or 2 percent management fee and takes a 20 percent cut of profits (see Chapter 1 of Book V). Other funds take much more. Here are two terms to know:

✔ **Gross of fees:** If a fund manager reports returns *gross of fees,* he hasn't taken out most of the fees. Trading costs should be removed because those commissions and fees are necessary to building the portfolio. Although they're usually relatively small, they can be high if the fund makes many small, frequent trades or if it uses unusual strategies that carry high commissions. However, the manager shouldn't remove the investment management fees and cuts of profits.

One reason to report numbers gross of fees is that different investors may be paying different fees. A hedge fund may agree to reduce the profit fee charged to a *fund of funds* (which invests in several different hedge funds) or a single large investor in exchange for its investment. So, although most investors may have an arrangement for a 2-percent management fee and a 20-percent share of profits, some may be paying only "1 and 18."

✔ **Net of fees:** In a *net-of-fees* performance calculation, the fund manager removes all the fees charged by the fund. This method may not reflect the return that any one investor receives, because different investors may have different fee schedules. Anyone evaluating a net-of-fee rate of return has to ask whether different investors pay different fees, because any one investor's realized returns may be higher or lower.

Sizing up the risk

An investor must consider return relative to what a manager had to do to get it, which is why you have to compare return to the amount of risk taken. The problem is that measurements of risk are inherently subjective. What's risky to one investor may not be risky to you. In finance, the dispute over how to define risk has led to a range of measures, which I describe in the following sections.

Standard deviation

In finance, risk is usually considered to be a function of *standard deviation* — a statistic that shows how much your return may vary from the return that you expect to get. Say, for example, that you expect a security to have an average return of 10 percent over two years. If it returns 10 percent the first year and 10 percent the second year, no deviation exists between any one return and the average return. But if the security returns 20 percent one period and 0 percent the next, it still returns an average of 10 percent but with big deviations from the 10-percent mean. The more a security swings around the expected return, the riskier it is.

Beta

A refinement of the standard deviation measurement is *beta,* which compares the standard deviation of an investable asset or fund to the standard deviation of the market itself. In most cases, the performance of an index measures the "market" (in the sense that the index is a sample of investable assets, not an agglomeration of all the possible assets that you can invest in), like the Standard & Poor's 500 (S&P 500) in the United States or the Nikkei in Japan.

A fund with a beta of 1 moves right in step with the market. A fund with a beta greater than 1 moves more sharply up or down — whichever way the market goes. A beta of less than 1 means the fund moves in the same direction as the market, but less sharply. And if beta is negative, it should move in the opposite direction of the market.

Peak-to-trough ranges

A simple way to look at the volatility of a long-standing hedge fund is to compare the distance between the *peak* — the year with the highest return — and the *trough* — the year with the lowest return. The greater the distance between the peak and the trough, and the closer together the two are, the riskier the fund is.

For a hedge fund with a short operating history, you can look at the peak and trough months rather than years.

Stress tests

A *stress test* helps answer the question, "How much money will I lose if things go terribly wrong?" The test is a computer simulation that models what could happen to a hedge fund's portfolio under a variety of different scenarios, such as a dramatic increase in interest rates, the euro falling apart, or the government of Mexico defaulting on its bonds. Based on the sensitivity that the different fund investments have to the tested factors, the stress test shows how much the factors may affect the portfolio's return. The less effect the events have, the less risky the fund — assuming that the right stresses have been tested.

Stress tests are expensive to run, and even the best are based on guesses about the future. Still, the information from a test can be useful, especially for a fund that intends to retain exposure to a certain set of market factors.

Value at risk

Value at risk (VAR) is a single number that represents how much you can expect a portfolio to lose over a given time period. For example, a hedge fund may say that it has a 95 percent confidence level that its portfolio has a 10-day VAR of losing $10 million. This translates to the following: Based on the securities held in the portfolio and on market conditions, the fund manager is 95 percent certain that the most the fund could lose over the next 10 days is $10 million.

The value is a statistical calculation involving several equations, so calculating it by hand is very difficult; in most cases, you have to rely on the hedge fund for VAR information. You see it quoted with similar margins of error that you see with political polls.

Using Benchmarks to Evaluate a Fund's Risk and Return

Investment performance is relative — relative to your needs and expectations and relative to what your return would've been had you invested your money elsewhere. That's why you have to compare your return and risk numbers to something. But what? In many cases, hedge fund investors compare performance to a market index. Some compare performance to that of similar hedge funds or to an expected return based on the fund's style. All these types of comparisons have their advantages and disadvantages.

A fund can beat its benchmarks and all its peers and still lose money. The fund manager may be happy; the consultants and brokers who recommended the hedge fund may be happy; but the investors who put money into the fund may be fuming.

Looking into indexes

The most common way to compare investment performance is with a market index. *Market indexes* are the measures of the overall market that you hear quoted all the time in the news, like the Standard & Poor's 500 (S&P 500) and the Dow Jones Industrial Average.

Indexes aren't perfect for comparison purposes, however. One big problem is that investors often look at the wrong indexes for the type of investments that they have. For example, an investor may compare the performance of a macro fund that invests all over the world to the S&P 500 when he should use a global index that includes a range of securities.

In many cases, you should compare a fund to a mixture of indexes. For example, you should compare a macro fund that invests

> 30 percent in international equities
>
> 30 percent in international bonds
>
> 40 percent in currencies

to

> 30 percent of the return on an international equity index
>
> 30 percent of the return on an international bond index
>
> 40 percent of the return on a currency index

Preparing indexes is a big business, and the different companies that calculate and maintain indexes put different conditions on their use. Anyone offering an S&P 500 Index fund has to pay a fee to Standard & Poor's, for example. Therefore, when a hedge fund presents its results relative to a given index, it may do so for different reasons:

- ✔ Because that index is the best choice
- ✔ Because the index's performance makes the fund look good
- ✔ Because another index service was too expensive to use

Verify that your hedge fund uses the same benchmarks every time it reports. A fund that changes its benchmarks may be trying to make its performance look good, or it may be changing its investment style, which means it may no longer match the profile of the fund you need in your portfolio.

Indexes can be calculated in several different ways, and understanding them can give you a sense of why a fund manager may choose one over the other.

✔ **Market capitalization–weighted index:** *Market capitalization* is the total value of a security. The market capitalization of a common stock, for example, is the total number of shares outstanding multiplied by the price per share. In a *market capitalization–weighted index,* different securities are entered in proportion to their total market value. One example of a market capitalization–weighted index is the S&P 500.

A market capitalization–weighted index is a good representation of how the market as a whole trades, but it may place too much emphasis on the price fluctuations of the largest companies. The NASDAQ Composite Index, which represents the value of all the companies traded on NASDAQ, is disproportionately exposed to the trading of Microsoft and other huge high-tech and biotech companies. Those huge technology companies are mainstays on NASDAQ, but most of the companies on that exchange are quite small.

✔ **Price-weighted index:** A *price-weighted index* includes one of each security from the group being measured. For example, a price-weighted stock index includes one share of each of the companies it tracks, and a price-weighted bond index includes one share of each of the bonds it tracks. The Dow Jones Industrial Average is an example of a price-weighted index.

The price-weighted index is independent of the total capitalization of the included securities, so securities with a high price may be overweighted.

Even if they include the same securities, price-weighted and market capitalization indexes can post different results.

Picking over peer rankings

If you just want the risk and return that comes with an index, you won't consider paying a hedge fund's high fees. And if you make the decision that a hedge fund is the way to go with your money, you'll want to know how your fund does against other hedge funds that you could've invested in instead. That's why you look at peer group rankings.

Many hedge funds report their results to services, like Morningstar (www.morningstar.com), where the analysts rank funds based on their risk-and-return parameters. For example, the service ranks arbitrage funds against other arbitrage funds, and long-short funds against other long-short funds. (Flip to Chapter 3 in Book V for details on arbitrage and long-short funds.) With the information from the services, you can see whether your fund is one of the better or worse ones within a specific style. Unlike Morningstar's mutual fund information, you have to pay to see these rankings.

One problem with peer rankings of hedge funds is that reporting is optional, which makes the picture you see less rounded. A fund that doesn't do so well is less likely to report its numbers for a ranking, so the average performance may have an upward bias. A fund in the bottom half of a published ranking isn't in the bottom half of all hedge funds within that style; it's just in the bottom half of funds that reported. You can bet that plenty of funds in that style are worse; they're just in hiding.

Standardizing performance calculation

Hedge fund managers have many options to use when calculating and comparing risk and return, and they have an incentive to choose the methods that make them look better than the alternatives. To help U.S. investment advisors present their numbers fairly and to make it easy for investors to compare the performance of different firms, the CFA Institute created Global Investment Performance Standards (or GIPS), which include the following:

- ✔ Accurate data collection, with records to support the information
- ✔ Market-value accounting
- ✔ Accrual accounting for the value of any assets that generate income
- ✔ Monthly portfolio valuation, ending on the last business day or last calendar day of the month
- ✔ Time-weighted returns
- ✔ Results that are net of investment expenses
- ✔ Results shown for the last five years (or from the fund's inception if it's less than five years old), with annual results given for each year

Compliance with the standards is voluntary, but it allows fund managers to market their results to current and prospective investors as being "GIPS Compliant" or "GIPS Verified." Still, some hedge funds ignore GIPS, sometimes for good reasons; among them are expense (it can be costly to calculate results in a way that qualifies for the GIPS label) and unsuitability (the methodology was designed for investment-management firms that handle several different portfolios in-house; many hedge funds are one-portfolio operations).

Putting risk and return into context with academic measures

Given that hedge funds have huge minimum-investment requirements (see Chapter 1 in Book V), investors have a lot of money at stake. Many hedge fund investors, like employees of pension funds or charitable endowments, have responsibilities to the people who rely on their funds. For these reasons, investors need to know what the risk-and-return numbers mean and how they reflect on hedge fund managers' performances. Several equations developed in ivory towers can help you figure out why a hedge fund did as well as it did, and this section shows you what they are.

Academic approaches to finance have their problems because they're based on the assumption that rational investors are trading in efficient markets. Look at the following approaches with this limitation in mind:

- **Sharpe measure:** This measure is the amount of performance that a fund earns over and above the risk-free rate of return (which, for investors based in the United States, is the interest rate on Treasury bills) divided by the standard deviation of returns. (*Standard deviation* is a mathematical measure of how much one number in a set varies from the average of all the numbers in the set.)

  This measure shows whether the portfolio's return for taking risk came by increasing the amount of risk in the portfolio or from the fund manager's skill (known as *alpha;* see Chapter 1 in Book V), which allowed her to get a better return than expected from the amount of standard deviation in the securities held by the portfolio. A higher number is better than a lower one, because a higher number indicates that the hedge fund manager is getting more return for the risk that she's taking.

- **Treynor measure:** This measure, a variation of the Sharpe measure, looks at how a hedge fund performed for the risk it took over and above the risk of the market as a whole — not just at how it performed relative to the risk-free rate of return. For example, if the fund returned 15 percent, the market rate of return was 10 percent, and the fund's standard deviation was 20 percent, the Treynor measure would be (15 – 10) ÷ 20, or 25 percent. This is better than a fund with a Treynor measure of 15 percent, and worse than a fund with a Treynor measure of 35 percent.

- **Jensen's alpha:** This method uses the capital assets pricing model (CAPM) rather than Sharpe's or Treynor's measures of performance. The CAPM involves *alpha,* which measures how much an investment returns over and above its *beta* (its exposure to the market). If a portfolio has a positive alpha, the portfolio manager did a good job. If the portfolio's alpha is zero or negative, maybe the manager's fees weren't deserved.

✔ **The appraisal ratio:** This measure divides the fund's alpha by the nonsystematic risk of the portfolio. The *nonsystematic risk* is risk that the manager could've diversified by adding more securities to the portfolio but didn't. The return from the risk isn't so much due to the portfolio manager's skill as to the portfolio manager's decision not to diversify the portfolio. Suppose, for example, that a hedge fund manager decides to invest only in oil company stock. Beta isn't the best comparison, because the fund's portfolio is far narrower than the entire investment market. Some of that risk is unnecessary, and the manager could remove it through diversification. The appraisal ratio is an attempt to separate the diversifiable risk from the true alpha — the true extra performance due to a portfolio manager's skill.

Taking a Reality Check on Hedge Fund Returns

One reason so many investors are interested in hedge funds is because they think hedge funds are raking in enormous investment returns that other investors can't get. Certainly, some hedge funds bring in enormous investment returns, and the nature of a hedge fund's structure supports the idea that other investors are shut out (see Chapter 1 in Book V for info on the structure of hedge funds). But the reality is that many hedge funds don't perform in the stratosphere, which is why you need to know what you want from your investments before you commit. The following sections aim to put you in touch with your investment needs by bringing to light many facts about hedge fund returns.

Risk and return tradeoff

Some hedge funds post poor results relative to a stock-market index because they're designed to perform very differently. Investment return is a function of risk; the more risk a fund takes, the greater its expected return. A hedge fund's goal is to post a return that's greater than expected for a given level of risk. Some funds choose high risk levels in the hopes of even higher returns, and others maintain very low risk levels and generate relatively low returns.

Many investors are content with an 8 percent return year in and year out, but others would find this incredibly disappointing. Before you commit to a hedge fund, you need to know your investment objectives inside and out; refer to Chapter 1 in Book V.

Survivor bias

Many hedge fund managers limit how often investors can make withdrawals, but they can't lock up an investor's money forever. A fund may require that an investor keep his money in for two years, but if performance is bad in both years, you can bet that the investor will yank the money as soon as the time period expires. In addition, hedge fund managers charge high fees, but they can collect a profit payout only if the funds show a profit. If a fund isn't doing so well, its investors will go, and the fund manager will want out, too, so he can make some money elsewhere. Hedge Fund Research, a firm that tracks hedge funds, estimated that 873 hedge funds folded in 2012.

When looking at long-term results for hedge funds, note that the worst performing funds all probably dropped out of the game after two years. The funds that are still in business have less competition and, because they're still in business, they already have better-than-average status. However, unless they're looking for new investors, they'll force you to invest in a newly formed fund, which may end up a survivor — or one that eventually shuts down.

Performance persistence

One huge problem for any hedge fund and its investors is following one good year with another. Is a great number the result of luck, or is it due to the portfolio manager's skill? Will the manager's luck hold out next year? Will a skilled portfolio manager face bad luck next year? It's really hard to demonstrate *performance persistence*, that is, the ability to post good performance year after year.

A 2000 study published by Vikas Agarwal of Georgia State University and Narayan Naik of the London Business School found no evidence of persistence in the funds they studied. One year's performance wasn't an indicator of the next year's, and the relationship between performance one year and the next weakened as more time periods were included in the study. What does this mean? If a hedge fund has the kind of extraordinary return that grabs headlines this year, it probably won't bring in those spectacular returns the next year.

Style persistence

The problem of a fund manager changing style to get performance is called *style persistence*. Some funds show persistence because the fund changes its investment style with the market, which lets the fund post good numbers. The problem with this strategy is that consultants, academics, and others who evaluate returns may not know what to do with the fund. Academic performance studies, in particular, control for different risk measures, which affects the performance persistence that they report. Still, some investors may want a hedge fund that's flexible and can post a consistent return no matter what. Other investors may need a fund to limit its investments or maintain a consistent risk profile so that it complements other parts of their portfolios.

Hiring a Reporting Service to Track Hedge Fund Performance

Given all the information-collecting options covered in this chapter, how in the world are you supposed to keep track of everything to find out how a hedge fund actually performs? Along with the numbers that the fund manager presents, you can find several consulting firms and reporting services that monitor how hedge funds perform, analyze their results, and evaluate their risk and return based on the styles that the fund managers follow.

The following list is by no means exhaustive and doesn't represent an endorsement. But it can give you some ideas of where to start if you want to enlist some help to evaluate hedge fund performance. Be forewarned: Most of these companies charge for their services — and charge a lot; and some require that you be an accredited investor to access information.

- ✔ **Greenwich Alternative Investments** (www.greenwichai.com): One of many hedge fund services that operates in two businesses: a consulting firm that advises investors on hedge fund investments, and a hedge fund performance-analysis service

- ✔ **eVestment** (eVestment.com): Maintains a database of quantitative and qualitative information about hedge funds, submitted by the funds themselves, and carries news and information about the industry (even offering a free daily report)

- ✔ **Hedge Fund Research** (www.hedgefundresearch.com): Compiles detailed databases of hedge fund performance and administration

- ✔ **HedgeWorld** (www.hedgeworld.com): Offers a variety of free and paid reports on performance

- ✔ **Morningstar** (www.morningstar.com): Offers access to a database of information on 7,000 hedge funds, funds of hedge funds, and commodity trading advisors

Book VI
Emerging Markets

Five Ways to Invest in Emerging Markets (In Addition to Stocks)

- ✔ **Exchange-traded funds (ETFs):** ETFs are designed to perform the same as a market index: They should go up when the index goes up and down when the index goes down. The key advantage is that you can buy or sell ETFs at any point in the trading day, long or short, with cash or on margin, through a regular brokerage account. Many of the ETF sponsors have funds that invest in different emerging market indexes, some diversified and some specific to one country.

- ✔ **Banks:** Because banks are major beneficiaries of a country's economic growth, buying shares of stock in them can be a great way to invest in emerging markets. In addition, banks offer certificates of deposit (CDs) and other types of accounts that you may be able to use to invest in an emerging market's currency, possibly at higher interest rates than you can earn at home.

- ✔ **Currency mutual funds:** One way to invest in emerging market bank accounts and in currency is through a *currency mutual fund,* which is a pool of money collected from thousands of investors that allows investors to build a more diversified portfolio than they may otherwise be able to build.

- ✔ **Real estate:** Land is the one thing they aren't making any more of, as the joke goes, which makes it an appealing investment overseas. Among your investment alternatives are owning the land outright, investing in real estate investment trusts (REITs), and buying shares in construction companies and banks.

- ✔ **Microfinance:** *Microfinance* is the practice of making very small loans to very small entrepreneurs. Microfinance combines investment and philanthropy in one transaction, with the potential for the best or the worst of each. Microfinance not only offers investment opportunities but also presents a way to think of the scale of commerce in an emerging- or frontier-market economy.

web extras

For a free article on currency categories, head to www.dummies.com/extras/highpoweredinvestingaio.

Chapter 1

Introducing Emerging Market Investing

In This Chapter

▶ Explaining different market categories

▶ Understanding and handling the risks of emerging market investing

▶ Identifying emerging markets with investment potential

*I*nvestors are always looking for the Next Big Thing, and the Next Big Thing is happening right now in places of the world that you may have overlooked. People are developing new ideas and reaching new markets far from where you live. Emerging markets have great growth potential, and many of them are developing amazing new technologies, partly because they're not tied to existing infrastructure. If you have no phone lines, going wireless makes more sense than building land lines first. If you have no electric power plants, why not go straight to solar?

This chapter starts your tour of emerging markets and the key issues facing them. You don't need a passport, only a desire to discover more about the economic opportunities in the world today.

Defining Emerging Markets

Developing markets fall into three categories:

- ✔ **Emerging markets:** Countries that have growing economies and a growing middle class

- ✔ **Frontier markets:** Nations that are very small, are at an early stage of economic development, or have tiny stock markets

- ✔ **Pre-emerging markets:** Nations that are the poorest of the poor and whose markets have few opportunities for investors but are worth watching

Due to space constraints, this book focuses primarily on emerging markets. The following sections explain the growth opportunities in emerging markets, distinguish investment categories in these markets, and list countries in both emerging and frontier markets.

Displaying great growth opportunities

Developing markets are where the growth opportunities are now. A full 43 percent of the world's wealth is in those nations, and most of the world's people — 5.5 billion, in fact — are in such countries as well. The world's developing nations are growing faster than the developed ones. That faster growth can lead to higher profits than you may get from similar investments in the established markets found in North America, Western Europe, Australia, and Japan. Bottom line: The needs in emerging markets are creating exciting opportunities for investors. Meeting the needs of the world's emerging middle class is enough work to keep many companies profitable for decades to come.

Here's why these markets should interest you:

- ✔ **Uncorrelated returns:** One of the many attractions of emerging markets is that the risks are very different from those in developed countries. The United States and Western Europe have similar economic cycles, for example, but the United States and South Africa are in different cycles. One country is fully developed and last had a revolution more than 230 years ago. The other is rapidly developing after a peaceful revolution just 20 years ago. (You can find out more about risk and return in emerging markets in the upcoming section "Considering and Managing Risk in Emerging Markets.")

- ✔ **New technologies:** One reason companies in emerging markets have pursued new technologies is because many of these countries have poor infrastructure. That poor infrastructure has turned into a strange advantage because innovators aren't tied to an existing way of doing things. The result is that some of the best technologies for mobile telephones and solar power have come out of emerging markets, which have few land lines or electrical generation facilities.

- ✔ **New markets:** The world no longer follows the old mercantile model, in which rich countries bought materials in poor countries, took them back home to their factories, and then brought the manufactured goods back to the poor countries to trade. Instead, everyone trades with one another. A company in China working on low-cost solar power has a ready market in Nigeria. An Indian company that develops a $2,000 car for the new middle class there can sell it in Indonesia and Malaysia, too. A Mexican cement manufacturer can find customers in the United States and in El Salvador.

For a detailed look at the investment opportunities unique to emerging markets, head to the later section "Finding Key Opportunities for Investment in Emerging Markets."

Knowing the big categories of investment

Basically, you can invest in emerging markets in two ways — buy securities as an investment or invest directly as a business.

✔ **Purchasing securities:** The most common way for individual investors to participate in emerging markets is through purchases of *securities* such as stocks, bonds, or mutual funds, which give people exposure to the potential in emerging markets without the headaches of actually running a business. You have a huge range of ways to invest in securities in emerging markets.

Book VI

Emerging Markets

  • You can invest from your home country through mutual funds or international securities listed on domestic exchanges. You can buy securities traded in other markets if your broker can handle the trade (and most can these days).

  • You can find hedge funds that accept minimum investments of millions of dollars that seek out opportunities in emerging markets (see Book V for information on hedge funds), or you can commit just a few dollars to a microfinance fund to help very small businesses get underway.

  • You can make related investments such as cash or real estate.

And in most cases, you can buy or sell with little fuss when your circumstances — or those in the target country — change. Chapters 3 and 4 in Book VI explain specific investment options.

One way to invest in the more than 2 billion people who want the same consumer goods that Americans and Europeans enjoy is to invest in multinational corporations. Most of the largest food-, beverage-, and consumer-product companies have a presence in emerging markets, and in many cases, they get much of their growth from sales in those places.

✔ **Owning a business:** *Foreign direct investment* involves starting a business, opening a subsidiary, making an acquisition, or otherwise expanding an operating company into an emerging market. It involves making a major commitment of time, money, and energy to a country that may not have a lot of experience hosting international businesses. Foreign direct investment isn't easy to get started in or to pull out of if the project fails. For the most part, only large companies pursue direct investment, although some entrepreneurs have been known to run off and start new ventures in lands far from home.

Due to the challenges inherent in foreign investment, this book focuses on investing in securities rather than foreign direct investment. Keep in mind, however, that much of the information here — specifically regarding the risks involved — applies to direct investment as well as securities.

Identifying emerging and frontier markets

Emerging markets run the gamut. Some are Middle Eastern. Others are European nations that weren't aligned with the Soviet Union but that were never exactly poor, either. Others may be found among long-established nations in South America. Some are countries that were Communist but that are now embracing capitalism. And some are nations in that vast Third World category that are now meeting or surpassing more established nations in terms of economic growth.

Emerging markets don't have to be hours away by plane. Every country has lesser-developed regions, and every city has lesser-developed neighborhoods. And you can invest in these areas without taking on the currency risk or political risk of investing in other countries by opening an account at a community deposit financial institution, which is a bank that lends money for mortgages and businesses in a specific neighborhood. Or you can buy stock in real estate and banking companies that specialize in community redevelopment.

To know what an emerging market is, you need to understand developed markets. In general, a *developed market* is one of the 34 nations that belong to the Organisation for Economic Cooperation and Development (OECD). These nations are usually thought of as fully developed countries, considering that OECD membership is for countries that have demonstrated a commitment to democracy and a market economy, at least as defined by the countries in North America and Western Europe that set up the group.

Emerging markets aren't quite fully developed but are making efforts toward developing further. These are countries that have some infrastructure, some stable government systems, strong human capital, and success with economic growth.

One of the simplest ways to determine whether a market is emerging is to see whether it appears in a financial index that tracks emerging markets, such as the MSCI Emerging Markets Index or the MSCI Frontier Markets Index. You can let MSCI Barra, one of the larger financial index and data firms, do the classification work for you by checking out its list of countries at www.mscibarra.com/products/indices/tools/index_country_membership/emerging_markets.html.

The following sections further define and list emerging markets and frontier markets (which are a type of emerging market).

Emerging markets

To be truly emerging, a country's economic growth should be expanding beyond its borders. It should be producing enough goods that it can export products to other countries, becoming an active participant in global trade.

It should have people who can take the jobs that local companies are creating. And it should be open to capital and investments from outside the country, whether by individuals, financial institutions, or multinational corporations.

There's one other catch: An emerging market has to have a stock market so that investors can buy and sell securities. Chapter 2 in Book VI covers the following 21 emerging markets in more detail:

- Brazil
- Chile
- China
- Colombia
- Czech Republic
- Egypt
- Hungary
- India
- Indonesia
- Malaysia
- Mexico
- Morocco
- Peru
- Philippines
- Poland
- Russia
- South Africa
- South Korea
- Taiwan
- Thailand
- Turkey

Frontier markets

Frontier markets are a subset of emerging markets. These countries are in the earliest stage of development, but they do have a stock market and investable securities. Growth can be explosive, and the profit potential is enormous. That means the risk is high, too. These countries may have small economies, impoverished human capital, and weak infrastructure to support investors, any of which can lead to curtailed growth. Here are the frontier markets:

- ✔ Argentina
- ✔ Bahrain
- ✔ Bangladesh
- ✔ Bulgaria
- ✔ Croatia
- ✔ Estonia
- ✔ Jordan
- ✔ Kazakhstan
- ✔ Kenya
- ✔ Kuwait
- ✔ Lebanon
- ✔ Lithuania
- ✔ Mauritius
- ✔ Nigeria
- ✔ Oman
- ✔ Pakistan
- ✔ Qatar
- ✔ Romania
- ✔ Serbia
- ✔ Slovenia
- ✔ Sri Lanka
- ✔ Trinidad and Tobago
- ✔ Tunisia
- ✔ Ukraine
- ✔ United Arab Emirates
- ✔ Vietnam

Finding Key Opportunities for Investment in Emerging Markets

Emerging and frontier markets have opportunities for growth that often aren't available in more-developed economies. These come from three main sources: new, pervasive technologies; the improved spending power of a growing middle class; and gains from greater trading activity with other countries. When you look at investments, you want to look at how these changes create growth opportunities.

Leapfrogging technologies

Are you waiting for the app that lets you use your cellphone line as a debit card, allowing you to take money from your checking account to pay for your groceries without any additional card or fuss? It's already the standard form of payment in Kenya, but barely found in the U.S.

One of the greatest opportunities in emerging markets is to be on the ground floor of companies that are working on technologies that aren't yet economically feasible for big multinational corporations to try. Some of these technologies are low, and some are high. Investments in the securities of the companies that make these technologies may be a profitable path for playing in emerging markets.

Book VI

Emerging Markets

Here are some of the characteristics related to technological advancements in emerging markets:

✔ **The technology that succeeds often emphasizes products that are smaller and more basic than the products in developed economies.** In fact, some products may seem like a step backward to people in developed countries, but they can be vital to making life better for those living in less-developed countries. Here are two examples:

- **Farming equipment:** The world's premier agricultural equipment companies are based in the United States and have been exporting equipment to developed nations for years. The equipment is so good that Chinese companies haven't tried to match it. Instead, the equipment that Chinese agricultural equipment companies make is designed for small farmers with simple, low-cost operations. This Chinese equipment is much in demand in Africa.

- **Water pumps:** In Africa, KickStart (www.kickstart.org) offers a water pump for just a few hundred dollars that looks like a StairMaster workout machine. Made in China, it allows small farmers with more labor than capital to harness their energy in order to water more soil than they could do by hand.

✔ **Many new technologies can't offer 100 percent reliability.** If you have no electricity, a solar system that works 85 percent of the time is a huge improvement in your life. That product won't work for people with reliable electric power, but how long will it be before companies in developing countries making solar cells that work 85 percent of the time come up with solar cells that work 99.99 percent of the time? That's where the technology opportunity is in emerging markets.

Companies that master low technology often go on to design and build better products that can be sold to customers in developed countries at lower prices than they see now. At one time, Japan was a developing country, and Toyota made inexpensive cars that the Detroit firms weren't interested in building. Toyota is now the largest automaker in the world, and Japan has one of the world's most developed economies.

✔ **The high rate of education and the low cost of living in some emerging market countries have helped them attract companies that want to take advantage of these factors to become high-tech leaders.** This is especially true of places where English or a European language is commonly spoken. Successful high-technology ventures generate big profits and create excellent, high-paying jobs. Hence, economic development officers are always looking for ways to attract high-tech ventures.

Be aware that their hopes are sometimes inflated. India became a technology hotbed because the country has an educated workforce that speaks English and a network of citizens who worked for technology companies in other countries and who became advocates for their compatriots back home. Another country, one with an agricultural economy and a low literacy rate in any language, may dream of the jobs that helped build India's middle class, but it isn't going to be a hotbed of semiconductor design any time soon. So protect yourself and don't invest on wishes and dreams, as delightful as they may be.

Growing the middle class

To a certain extent, an emerging market is really a market where a middle class is emerging. As jobs and opportunities are created, more people move out of poverty and into a comfortable middle zone where they can afford some luxuries that were previously unimaginable. They go out and spend their money, creating more economic activity. They need refrigerators, washing machines, and cars. They have money to pay their children's school fees and to give their children shoes and toys. Eventually, they want designer purses, big-screen televisions, and annual vacations, too.

As a country's economy improves, the poorest people tend to become less poor, and even they have more money to spend. Even a small improvement in income represents a huge increase in purchasing power. Yes, the money goes to subsistence needs, especially food, but even that spending power represents an improvement in an economy and in the health of the people.

Improving trade opportunities

Before they enter frontier or emerging market status, many markets are closed to outsiders. If people in a country are unable to produce whatever goods they need, they just do without. Open trade, however benefits both the importer and the exporter. It lets people capitalize on their skills. If they're good at making something, they can keep doing that even if they make more of a good than people at home can use. And if they need something, they can buy it from those who produce it, wherever they are.

Here are some facts to understand about trade and emerging markets:

- ✔ If a nation's businesses can produce something at a lower cost than it can be produced elsewhere, even after adjusting for extra time and higher error rates, the country is going to benefit from trade. And that's where emerging markets find their niches. Companies in the United States, Europe, and Japan make the best-quality cars in the world, but not everyone in the world wants the best-quality car. Some people are willing to accept a lower-quality car, made by less-skilled labor, in order to have basic transportation.

- ✔ *Free trade* is trade between nations free of quotas (limits on the number of an item that can be brought into a country each year) and tariffs (tax, usually known as a *duty,* charged to importers of an item). Tariffs may be low enough to simply offset some of the payrolls lost when the item was produced overseas, or they may be so high that it makes no sense at all to buy the imported item. In addition to tariffs, governments sometimes protect local industries through regulation. Regulation is one subtle way to create a barrier to trade without a tariff or a quota.

  Because trade moves better when it's free of restrictions, 159 nations have joined the World Trade Organization (www.wto.org), which negotiates the rules of trade among nations and settles disputes as they arise.

- ✔ *Fair trade* is a movement to give producers of agricultural products and handicrafts in developing nations some of the advantages of their competitors in developed countries in order to make the terms of trade equal. Many of the organizations involved in fair trade operate programs on an ad hoc basis, but some international federations are trying to improve markets and to create branding that would attract buyers in developed countries. One such group is Fairtrade Labelling Organizations International: www.fairtrade.net.

Book VI

Emerging Markets

Considering and Managing Risk in Emerging Markets

Investing in emerging markets is exciting. You get to find out about new places and participate in the movement of billions of people out of poverty and into a more prosperous life. And you may be able to reduce your portfolio risk and increase its return at the same time. However, investing in emerging markets has its own issues, and the more you know about them, the fewer surprises you'll have. The following sections identify the risks and offer suggestions on managing them.

Knowing the risks

Emerging markets offer amazing opportunities for investors who want to make money and maybe even change the world. But they also have some risks that investors new to the category may not have considered.

Political and social risks

In any country, investors have to be concerned about changes in the political climate or in the way that society is organized. Even changes that make most people better off may leave a few behind, and sometimes those left behind are investors.

Many emerging markets began their economic improvement because of a major political change. For example, the emerging markets in Eastern Europe were once Communist nations but are now parliamentary democracies with market economies. The economic climate is really exciting for the people who live in these countries, not to mention for the people who invest in them. However, such profound changes create risk, and many nations in Eastern Europe have had economic and social upheaval on the way to economic stability.

Politics being politics, things may turn against investors. A country could experience an event, such as a war, ethnic unrest, or a natural disaster, that destabilizes the economy and pushes commerce down the list of priorities. Investors, especially those outside the country, won't necessarily be a consideration for a government tackling what it sees as bigger issues.

Corruption

In many emerging markets, corruption is a fact of business. In some cases, it's rooted in cultural differences, where people receive tips for services that wouldn't be rewarded anywhere else. In other cases, corruption is rampant because ineffective institutions have forced people to figure out ways to work around them. And in still other cases, the problem is nothing more than basic human nature combined with lax law enforcement.

Corruption affects a business's ability to present fair financial statements. It adds costs that may not be predictable or manageable. It can throw in surprises and make contracts void in court. Although a bribe may seem to be the quickest way to get business done, corruption is costly in the long run. As a rule, the less corruption a country has, the better its economy. Academic research shows that the less corruption a country has, the less volatile its investment returns are.

Currency risk

In most emerging markets, you use a currency other than your own. That means that your investment returns are affected by changes in the value of both your currency and the emerging market currency.

When you invest in another country, you almost always have to buy that country's currency to buy the investment. Then when you sell the investment to use the proceeds elsewhere, you also sell the currency. The change in the currency's value while you own the investment may enhance — or diminish — the investment's value.

In general, if an economy grows and has a lot of economic activity, its currency should be in great demand and should become more valuable. But currencies sometimes become less valuable over time. This drop in value may be because of economic changes or because the currency becomes overvalued and corrected, or it may just be that the emerging market currency is fine but your home currency has become more valuable for other reasons.

You can reduce the risk with hedging techniques. Keep in mind, however, that doing so may eliminate some of the return and diversification benefits.

Liquidity risk

Buying and selling securities in emerging markets isn't always easy. Some markets are just very small! Jamaica, for example, has a total market capitalization of $6.4 billion. Compare that to one company, Apple Computers, at $391.9 billion! Getting a position in some of these markets may be difficult, and you may have a hard time selling your position when you're ready to get out. This is known as *liquidity risk*.

Here are some factors contributing to the liquidity risk:

- **Thin markets:** Many emerging markets are *thin,* as the traders like to say, which means that few people are buying and selling securities on a regular basis.

- **Limits on how much you can take with you:** Some countries have laws that limit the amount of currency people can take out of the country, which means you may be able to sell your investment, but you may be prohibited from taking the cash home. Countries have these laws to help manage their exchange rates and to ensure good account balances in local banks.

- **Restrictions on buying and selling:** Some nations may restrict who can invest and who can sell. In these nations, when it's time to sell, you may not be allowed to, or you may not be allowed to sell your entire position at one time. You need to know the laws of the country in which you invest and react accordingly.

If you limit your emerging market commitment to the part of your portfolio that's intended for long-term goals, low liquidity will be less of an issue because you're less likely to have to sell your positions on short notice.

Information problems

With reliable information, you can assess the risks and the potential return of your investments. In emerging markets, getting good information can be difficult. A country may have loose accounting standards, little media oversight, and few objective investment analysts paying attention to how companies are doing.

Even when the information is available, you have to work harder to get it. And information is expensive. You must expend time and energy to find media that report on a nation in a language you understand, to become familiar with the differences in legal and accounting practices, and to make sure that the investment you make is for real.

In most cases, information problems result in merely unpleasant surprises, but in a few cases, emerging market investments have turned out to be outright scams. Investors fall into the trap because they don't have enough information, don't ask the right questions, or ignore the obvious. One easy first question to consider is why you're being offered this fabulous investment opportunity. Is it because you have special expertise? Are you associated with an investment company that has been active in the region? If the answers don't add up or if the opportunity seems too good to be true, steer clear.

Managing risks in emerging markets

The preceding list of risks shouldn't dissuade you from investing in emerging markets. After all, these growing economies are great places to look for wonderful investment opportunities. But it should motivate you to take necessary precautions: Do your homework, use advisors who are knowledgeable about the markets that you're considering, diversify, and examine nations' memberships in economic organizations. By managing the risks associated with emerging markets, you can make the most of the opportunities that are presented to you.

Doing your homework

Doing careful research can help you better identify your sources of risk and return, which in turn can help you better understand when — and how much — to buy and sell. Doing your homework starts with a good understanding of the country and the industry that you're investing in.

For starters, peruse Chapter 2 in Book VI, which offers an overview of different emerging markets. You can also head online for a list of resources that you can use to get more information at www.dummies.com/extras/highpoweredinvestingaio.

When you start your research into the country and industry, ask some basic questions: Who runs the government? Is the government committed to development? Who competes for customers and funds with the investment that you're considering?

Because markets change quickly, especially new markets, be sure to rely on news sources for up-to-date information. Two great places to start are the website for *The Economist* magazine, www.economist.com, and the Wall Street Journal Online, www.wsj.com. *The Economist* is published in London and offers great weekly coverage of business and political issues all over the world. The *Wall Street Journal* covers business and investing issues worldwide and has some of the best coverage of Asia around.

The next step is looking at the financials of the investment that you're considering. How will it make money? How much funding will it need to grow?

Finally, keep in mind that research is an ongoing process. You need to keep it up to see whether situations have changed. Maybe you want to commit more money to a market or investment, or maybe you want to cut back. The more you know, the better decisions you can make.

Considering a nation's membership in economic organizations

The OECD, introduced in the earlier section "Identifying emerging and frontier markets," represents the nations that are commonly thought of as developed. Some organizations related to the OECD are the G-7, which stands for the *Group of 7* and includes the countries with the world's largest economies; the G-8, which is the G-7 plus Russia; and the G-20, which includes 19 nations and the European Union. These organizations work to promote international financial stability more than international development, and OECD members collect and share information about their economies in order to develop new policies for themselves and to assist in the development of the rest of the world.

Table 1-1 is a list of nations and the organizations each belongs to. The categories can help you organize your thoughts about where to invest.

Much of your success in investing in emerging markets comes from identifying the countries that are growing now and that are likely to continue to grow in the future. Even a mediocre company can grow as it goes along for the ride in a growing country, but a great company can be held back in a mediocre country. As you look at this list, think about what it would take for a country to move up or down a category. How likely is such a change? What would happen to your investments if such a change took place?

Table 1-1   Ladder of International Organizations: Member Nations

Nation	OECD	MSCI Emerging Markets Index	G-7	G-8	G-20
Argentina					x
Australia	x				x
Austria	x				
Belgium	x				
Brazil		x			x
Bulgaria					
Canada	x		x	x	x
Chile	x	x			
China		x			x
Colombia		x			
Cyprus					
Czech Republic	x	x			
Denmark	x				
Egypt		x			
Estonia	x				
Finland	x				
France	x		x	x	x
Germany	x		x	x	x
Greece	x				
Hungary	x	x			
Iceland	x				
India		x			x
Indonesia		x			x
Ireland	x				
Israel	x				
Italy	x		x	x	x
Japan	x		x	x	x
Latvia					
Lithuania					
Luxembourg	x				
Malta					
Malaysia		x			

Nation	OECD	MSCI Emerging Markets Index	G-7	G-8	G-20
Mexico	x	x			x
Morocco		x			
Netherlands	x				
New Zealand	x				
Norway	x				
Peru		x			
Philippines		x			
Poland	x	x			
Portugal	x				
Romania					
Russia		x		x	x
Saudi Arabia					x
Slovak Republic	x				
Slovenia	x				
South Africa		x			x
South Korea	x	x			x
Spain	x				
Sweden	x				
Switzerland	x				
Taiwan		x			
Thailand		x			
Turkey	x	x			x
United Kingdom	x		x	x	x
United States	x		x	x	x

The borders between developed and emerging markets blur, and nations often move between them. Iceland, for example, is an OECD nation that had a strong, developed economy at the end of the 20th century and into the 21st. Several of its major banks collapsed in 2008, taking down its currency and its economic prospects and, for practical purposes, moving it back to emerging markets or even frontier status, at least as of this writing. If you can identify a market that's likely to be promoted, you may find a great market to invest in.

The OECD is great for researchers because it collects so much data on economic affairs; to find out more about the economic state of the developed world, check out the website at www.oecd.org.

Using intermediaries or advisors

The emerging markets you're interested in may be far from where you live and show up in the news less often or not at all. This lack of exposure can make research difficult and put you at a disadvantage. To get around this situation, consider using an intermediary. The most popular intermediaries are emerging market mutual funds and exchange-traded funds (ETFs) that pool money from many different investors. The fund managers concentrate on emerging markets and have access to research and travel budgets that you may not have. Their job is to find investment opportunities and assess risks so that their clients can make money, so they can devote more time and effort than you may be able to on your own.

If you have a great deal of money to invest, you can work with a private investment fund or a wealth manager with a specialty in emerging markets. A *private investment fund* is similar to a mutual fund in that it pools money from many different investors, but it may have more flexibility. In exchange, you need to commit a great deal of money.

Some brokers, wealth mangers, and other financial advisors specialize in emerging markets. These people usually charge a percentage of assets under management for their services. Before paying, make sure they're doing the work that they claim to do. Ask to see verified performance records and talk to their references. Otherwise, you may be better off in an emerging market mutual fund, even though it seems less glamorous than having your own personal money guy.

Flip to Chapter 3 in Book I for an introduction to mutual funds and ETFs.

Diversifying your investments

In any market, the easiest way to improve your long-term return and manage your risk is to diversify. If you limit your emerging market investments to the long-term, risk-bearing part of your portfolio, and if you invest in a range of countries and industries, your overall risk is greatly reduced because you have the rest of your portfolio in less-risky, more-liquid assets.

When you diversify, don't just go after a grab bag. Instead, look at a mix of emerging markets. They range from almost developed to barely modern, from natural-resources economies to technology-driven economies, from hard currencies to those that are difficult to exchange. If you have exposure to a little bit of each, then the unique risks in any given market will be offset by unique advantages in others.

A mutual fund or an ETF invests in a variety of securities, but it's not necessarily a diversified investment. Some emerging market funds invest only in one country, and that country's major businesses may all be in the same industry. With such a fund, you have more diversification than if you purchase shares of stock in one country, but you aren't well diversified across emerging markets.

Chapter 2

A Guided Tour through the World's Emerging Markets

In This Chapter

▶ Blazing economic trails in Brazil, Russia, India, and China

▶ Tapping emerging markets in Europe

▶ Checking out markets in the Middle East and Africa

▶ Investing in the Americas

▶ Exploring opportunities in Asia

*T*he world's emerging markets are typically divided into two groups: the four largest (Brazil, Russia, India, and China, known collectively as BRIC) and everywhere else. The term *BRIC* was coined by Goldman Sachs, but the nifty word that results isn't the only reason these countries are grouped together. All have huge populations, are rich in natural resources, and have enormous growth potential. The other emerging markets have reasonable political stability, a good business climate, and people who are raring to make a go of it in the world's economy. This chapter offers the key information you need to know if you're interested in investing in these markets.

Building with the BRICs: Brazil, Russia, India, and China

BRIC stands for Brazil, Russia, India, and China. These countries stand apart from other emerging markets because they are much larger in terms of population, size, and economic potential. Combined, they have 42 percent of the world's population and 23 percent of the world's total output of goods and services. All four markets are moving out of years of various levels of collective ownership to create robust private sectors with great opportunities for investors. Table 2-1 shows where these nations stand on some key measures. (*Note:* MSCI is an investment research firm that calculates indexes on financial markets around the world; see www.msci.com.)

Table 2-1	A Snapshot of the BRICs			
Measure	**Brazil**	**Russia**	**India**	**China**
Type of government	Federal Republic	Federation	Federal Republic	Communist
Gross domestic product (GDP)	$2.36 trillion	$2.50 trillion	$4.78 trillion	$12.38 trillion
Population/ median age	201 million/ 30.3 years	143 million/ 38.8 years	1.2 billion/ 26.7 years	1.3 billion/ 36.3 years
GDP per capita (purchasing power parity basis)	$12,000	$17,700	$3,900	$9,100
Area (square kilometers)	8.5 million	17.1 million	3.3 million	9.6 million
MSCI one-year return, 2012, local currency	5.93%	5.14%	27.86%	18.73%
MSCI one-year return, 2012, U.S. dollars	–3.50%	9.60%	23.93%	18.97%
MSCI annualized five-year return, 2007–2012, local currency	4.09%	12.59%	2.22%	5.95%
MSCI annualized five-year return, 2007–2012, U.S. dollars	–6.74%	–12.07%	–8.46%	–5.84%

Because of their scale, these countries have a good shot at becoming fully developed and may also become true economic superpowers. China's GDP is second only to the United States right now; the country may end up with the world's largest economy without its people having anywhere near the wealth that Americans enjoy. If you're an investor looking for high long-term growth rates, you have to look at these countries.

But the BRICs do pose some risk. Managing a nation with 400 million poor people, as is the case in India, is difficult for any politician. How do you keep people satisfied when they see enormous wealth around them? How do you build and maintain infrastructure in a country like Russia, which is spread out over 17.1 million square kilometers?

The BRICs aren't the only emerging markets; you can read about others in the later section "Examining Non-BRIC Emerging Markets." But because Brazil, Russia, India, and China dominate discussions about the developing world, their success or failure reflects on the other markets. Even if you choose not to invest in these countries, you should know something about them.

Burgeoning Brazil

Brazil is on its way to being one of the richest and most developed countries on earth. The largest country and economy in South America, Brazil is the fifth largest nation in the world in terms of both area and population. The country is blessed with a diverse array of natural resources that allow it to meet many of its own needs while building a broad industrial base. Brazil will show its strengths to the rest of the world as the host nation for both the 2014 World Cup and the 2016 summer Olympic games.

Although Brazilians are a mix of ethnicities and religions, those characteristics don't divide the people. Instead, the country's tensions are between the rich and the poor. The situation has improved, though, because economic development has led to a rising middle class and a more equal distribution of income. Brazil has friendly neighbors and few border disputes, which makes it easier for the government to concentrate on internal issues. If the government continues to rebuild institutions and maintain its credibility, Brazil may become the envy of the world.

Industries and opportunities

Brazil has a really diverse mix of industries, but the largest companies are found in aircraft manufacturing, oil, and mining. All three were once government companies that have been privatized. They are

- ✓ **Embraer** (www.embraer.com), maker of commercial aircraft, especially jets for mid-range distances
- ✓ **Petrobras** (www.petrobras.com.br/en), one of the world's largest investor-owned oil companies

✔ **Vale** (www.vale.com), the second-largest mining company in the world, with operations in Brazil and around the world that produce iron ore, nickel, coal, aluminum, and other materials

Brazil has both mineral wealth and some of the world's finest conditions for agriculture, with rich soil and a tropical climate that allows for year-round growing. Brazil is the world's largest exporter of coffee, sugar, chickens, beets, and orange juice. Brazil's reserves of oil and natural gas are enough to make the country self-sufficient, with some left over for export at current usage rates. Because some of the recent oil finds are offshore and in deep water, Brazil probably can't feasibly develop them right now, but it is also a leading ethanol producer, and its sunny climate and 7,491 kilometers of coastline could be beneficial should solar and wind power become more widespread.

Assessment of risks

As amazing as the potential is for Brazil, plenty of issues could hold the country back.

✔ Crime related to illegal drug trade is the most notorious, but Brazil's deep divisions between the rich and the poor have also resulted in various forms of crime. Both have scared off tourists and business travelers alike.

✔ Brazil has poor infrastructure, and land ownership, especially in the jungle lands in the interior, is often ambiguous and plagued by squatting, poaching, and violent retaliations.

✔ Many countries have found only too late that big events like the Olympics are money losers.

Running with Russia

Russia is the world's largest country in terms of land, with a complicated and fascinating history. Under Soviet rule from 1922 to 1991, the country had a Communist regime in which bureaucrats in Moscow, rather than the market, planned the economy. Despite problems inherent with this system, Russia developed a decent infrastructure, including an outstanding educational system.

At the fall of the Soviet Union, restrictions on speech, travel, and association were loosened, and the country's economy became privatized and driven by markets. This transition from Communism was disruptive, to say the least, shaking up the Russian economy, culture, and society. Today, however, the country's economy is strong, and investors are finding new opportunities.

Industries and opportunities

Russia's primary industry is the production of oil and gas. The country has rich reserves and pipelines in place to serve Europe, India, and China. The other major industries in Russia are mining and steel production, which are also resource businesses.

The Russian companies that prove most exciting to international investors these days are the energy companies. The big ones are

- **Gazprom** (www.gazprom.com), which produces and transports natural gas

- **Lukoil** (www.lukoil.com), the world's second-largest publicly traded oil company, which has an integrated exploration, production, and distribution system

- **Rosneft** (www.rosneft.com), the Russian national oil company, with the government holding about 75 percent of its shares and the rest trading in the public market.

Russia has ports to the northwest on the Baltic Sea, to the southwest on the Caspian Sea, and to the east along the Pacific Ocean. In addition, the nation has tremendous resources: It has rich agricultural soil, can sustain its own people, can provide food and materials to developed and developing nations worldwide, and is a net exporter of grain and timber. Russia has also been a special beneficiary of growth in India and China because those nations need Russia's resources.

Assessment of risks

Russia has plenty of risk:

- **An aging population and a brain drain:** The average age of the population in Russia is 38.8 years, and the population is only stabilizing now after years of decline due to a low birthrate and out migration. One risk associated with this scenario is whether Russia will have enough workers and consumers to support a more diversified economic base.

- **Corruption and crime:** Like many formerly Communist countries, Russia has a long-standing culture of corruption; the country ranks 133 out of 176 nations on Transparency International's 2012 Corruption Perceptions Index (a low ranking is better than a high one).

- **Reliance on one key industry:** The Russian economy is based on oil and gas. That's mostly good, because global demand for carbon-based fuel is huge and growing. However, by being so narrowly focused, the Russian economy is directly exposed to price fluctuations.

Investing in India

India is a diverse country that has always been open to the rest of the world, and its progress shows the power of a diverse, open economy. India's 1.2 billion people are crammed into just 3.3 million square kilometers of space. The country is the largest democracy in the world in terms of population. Although only 60 percent of the people are literate, most who have an education understand English — it's one of two official languages of the government — making India the largest English-speaking nation in the world after the United States.

Following its independence from the United Kingdom in 1947, the country experimented with Soviet-style socialism and central planning in the hope of solving its immense poverty problem, but in 1991, it kicked off a program of economic liberalization that has led to rapid growth. Its large population and its low starting point mean that India can sustain much faster average long-term growth than most other countries on earth.

India has its own numbering system that can confuse the heck out of anyone who isn't used to it. The system uses a number that's between a thousand and a million: the *lakh,* which is equal to one hundred thousand. If a company reports earnings of 20 lakhs rupees, that means it earned 2 million of them. Another number, the *crore,* is equal to 10 million. A company with assets of 100 crores rupees has 1 billion rupees in assets.

Industries and opportunities

India's basic industrial companies are huge because India is huge, but they aren't all growing rapidly or able to compete on a global stage. Instead, the companies that have made a mark on commerce in India and elsewhere have mostly been in newer industries, especially high technology. India has become a world center for software development, business process automation, and high-tech customer service. India is the only BRIC where English is widely spoken, giving Indian businesses a key advantage when dealing with customers in the United States and the UK.

India's largest companies make products and services that are well known outside of India. These include:

- **Infosys** (www.infosys.com) has more than 100,000 employees and brings in about $5 billion in annual revenue from its information technology, engineering, and consulting services.

- **Reliance** (www.ril.com) was formed as a holding company with several different businesses, including the oil, gas, chemicals, textile, and retail business (called Reliance Industries) and the cellphone and information technology business (Reliance Communications).

- **Tata** (www.tata.com) is a conglomerate that owns brands all over the world, ranging from Eight O'Clock Coffee and Tetley Tea to Jaguar and Land Rover cars. Its global operations include information technology, engineering, and energy, and much of the company's growth has been through acquisitions of businesses outside of India.

India has huge scale, and it's growing off of a small economic base. Even small improvements in income, when multiplied across more than a billion people, add up to big money. That opportunity is huge and its improving infrastructure, as well as businesses that address the needs of people at the bottom of the economic pyramid, open up opportunities for investors.

Assessment of risks

Despite India's growth and prospects, the country has some real challenges that could derail its progress:

- ✔ **Ethnic tensions:** Myriad religious and ethnic groups mostly get along, but not always, and the tensions can get ugly, leading to several assassinations of prime ministers, wars with Pakistan, and terrorist attacks instigated by various nationalist and separatist groups. This problem is made worse by a large number of unmarried young men, a consequence of India's cultural preference for sons.

- ✔ **Petty corruption:** India is notorious for its petty corruption, inefficient operations, and incompetent bureaucracy. It takes a long time to get things done there. The World Bank ranks India 132 out of 185 nations for the ease of running a business, worse than any of its BRIC counterparts. Almost any commercial activity involves a chain of inefficiencies. Unless these issues are addressed, India's growth rate will be held back.

- ✔ **Extreme poverty:** More than a quarter of the population lives below the official poverty line of $1 per day in purchasing power. India's GDP per capita ($3,900) is one of the lowest rates in the world.

- ✔ **Poor educational system:** About 40 percent of the people in India can't read or write. A handful of universities are outstanding, but most are not — and most Indians don't have enough education to qualify for admission to any university anywhere. The shortage of skilled workers is driving up wages for Indians who do have an education and leaving everyone else behind.

Book VI

Emerging Markets

Checking out China

When people think about emerging markets, they tend to think about the People's Republic of China, if only because it's so big. With more than a billion people, its GDP per capita is just $9,100 — but its GDP in total is the third highest in the world, behind the European Union and the United States. Break the EU into its constituent countries, and China's GDP ranks second.

China is an officially Communist nation, and the government maintains a tight control over the people's lives. Some families are penalized for having more than one child, internal migration is controlled (at least officially), and the media — including the Internet — is censored. At the same time, the government has promoted private ownership, international investment, and entrepreneurial ventures.

Industries and opportunities

China is the world's workshop, with the people manufacturing or assembling almost everything we use, including your clothes, your shoes, and, if you're reading on an electronic device, the device in your hand. Chinese companies have two markets: the more than a billion people in China who have a lot of pent-up demand for consumer goods, and everyone else in the world. Chinese manufacturers are adept at making super-cheap, quasi-disposable goods, as well as high-technology devices with nearly zero defects.

Although China is known for manufacturing, the economy is well diversified. China has banks, retailers, agriculture, and mining businesses. Many Chinese companies operate quietly, performing contract design and manufacturing for big commercial brands in the United States and Europe, although others, like Lenovo and Haier, operate under their own names. The largest Chinese companies, though, are major businesses started by the government that are now at least partially privatized. They include

- **Sinopec** (english.sinopec.com), the China Petroleum and Chemical Corporation, is an integrated oil producer that owns oil fields but that specializes in all the downstream products: oil-field equipment, chemicals, fertilizers, and 30,000 service stations throughout China.

- **China National Petroleum** (www.cnpc.com.cn/en) competes with Sinopec. Its shares trade as PetroChina (www.petrochina.com.cn/ptr), a subsidiary that holds the assets and liabilities of the exploration, development, refining, marketing, and chemical businesses. In 2010, it was the world's largest company by market capitalization.

- **Industrial and Commercial Bank of China** (www.icbc.com.cn/icbc/sy/default.htm), the largest bank in the world and one of four major banks in China, was mostly untouched by the 2008 financial crisis. It ranked at the top of Forbes Magazine's Global 2000 list of the world's top companies for 2013.

Although China is an emerging market success, the country has plenty of room to grow before it's considered a developed economy. Two factors that will create more investment opportunities are China's population and its foray into privatization.

- Most of China's 1 billion consumers have a decent income by emerging market standards. In addition, these people have been productive, making money and saving it, waiting for the day when consumer products are easy to get. And that's happening quickly. China is a nation that needs a billion cars, a billion televisions, a billion refrigerators. And it can afford all these products — or it will be able to soon.

- Although many of China's largest industries have been privatized, many Chinese people are still assigned to work units in government enterprises. However, the government is working hard to convert companies to private ownership structures. As that happens, China likely will see more growth and innovation, and international investors will have more access to securities in order to get exposure to China.

Assessment of risks

China's transition to an open economy has been huge and mostly trouble-free, but that may not continue, due to demographics, the environment, and politics:

✔ **Demographic imbalances:** China's one-child policy has contributed to an aging of the population and a situation in which the country soon may not have enough workers to cover pensions and other state-provided benefits. In addition, because of a traditional preference for sons over daughters, China has 1.06 males for every female, an imbalance that is even starker among the young; for people under age 15, China has 1.17 males for every female. As the population starts to skew older and male, it will shrink, and that may cause the economy to shrink, too.

✔ **Environmental damage:** China's economic miracle has come at a high cost to the land, the air, and the water. The country is losing agricultural soil to erosion and industrialization. The water table is dropping, and access to clean water is limited. The air quality is terrible. Increased production and consumption is likely to tax China's resources further. The country isn't as rich in resources as Russia or Brazil, nor does it have the luxury of space that Russia does. If the government and the people don't commit to improving the environment, China's progress could dry up — literally.

✔ **Potential for unrest:** One issue is that many Chinese workers feel under-paid. They work long hours, and their products sell for higher prices overseas. They want to make more money. Combined with retailers and manufacturers attempting to offset the rising wage rate (caused by the shortage of workers) by looking elsewhere for low-cost labor, worker dissatisfaction is growing, and some companies have experienced strikes.

Another issue is how long the Chinese people accept restrictions on speech and tight government control over their lives. As China engages in more trade with the world and has access to more ideas, the people may want more freedom. Already, the Chinese government has had a series of fights with such Internet companies as Google over what people in China can access.

Examining Non-BRIC Emerging Markets

Whether you're looking for a mutual fund or have been told by your boss to check out some interesting emerging markets, this section gives you some basic background information to get you started. For each country, you'll find vital facts and statistics, including the 2012 MSCI equity market return, which is the return on the MSCI Equity Index for that country in 2012.

Exploring Eastern and Southern Europe

In the 20th century, the nations of Eastern and Southern Europe were damaged by two world wars and the control of the Soviet Union. Now free to pursue their economic destinies, the people of these nations have been catching up, big time, by rebuilding their economies and making friends (and trading partners) with their wealthier neighbors in the rest of Europe. Table 2-2 provides a rundown of key stats for the markets in this area.

Europe is facing serious economic problems, and the unified currency that many countries on the continent use — the euro — looks unstable. The problems of the countries that use the euro are spilling to other nations on the continent, making everyone weaker in absolute terms. Relatively speaking, though, these non-euro European emerging markets look pretty good. That doesn't necessarily mean that these are bad investments, just that things are changing. Change, of course, is a constant in emerging markets.

Table 2-2	Emerging Markets in Eastern and Southern Europe			
Country	**Government**	**Major Industries**	**GDP per Capita/ Median Age**	**MSCI 2012 Equity Market Return (in U.S. dollars)**
Czech Republic	Parliamentary democracy	Armaments, glass, machinery and equipment, metallurgy, motor vehicles	$27,200/41.4 years	−3.10%
Hungary	Parliamentary democracy	Chemicals (especially pharmaceutical), construction materials, metallurgy, mining, motor vehicles, processed foods, textiles	$19,800/40.8 years	18.66%

Country	Government	Major Industries	GDP per Capita/ Median Age	MSCI 2012 Equity Market Return (in U.S. dollars)
Poland	Republic	Beverages, chemicals, coal mining, food processing, glass, iron and steel, machine building, shipbuilding, textiles	$21,000/39.1 years	32.07%
Turkey	Parliamentary democracy	Construction, electronics, food processing, lumber, mining (boron, chromate, coal, and copper), motor vehicles, paper, petroleum, steel, textiles	$15,000/29.2 years	60.53%

Moving into markets in the Middle East, North Africa, and South Africa

Sometimes referred to by the acronym MENA (Middle East-North Africa), this region is one of great risk offering potentially huge returns. Many, although not all, of the countries in the region draw their economic power from petroleum.

The Middle East and North Africa have suffered from enormous upheaval. Many of these nations allow polygamy, which has led to a surplus of unmarried men. Many of these men are educated but they can't find suitable work. Many nations have experienced ongoing upheaval and protests (starting with the "Arab Spring" of 2011), which have hindered economic growth.

Africa has enormous potential, and South Africa shows how economic growth happens; it's the dominant economy south of the Sahara. After Nelson Mandela was elected president in 1994, he did a masterful job of bringing the people together and creating a culture of reconciliation. But that doesn't mean that it's all sunshine and ponies in modern South Africa. The people have a high rate of HIV infection, community crime is a serious problem, and educated people of all ethnicities are tempted to leave for opportunities elsewhere. Still, the country's peaceful transition is amazing; South African leaders raised their standards, reassured their citizens, and convinced businesses and consumers all over the world to trade with the nation again. The 2010 World Cup took place in South Africa, bringing in tourist dollars, infrastructure improvements, and positive public relations. The ports, soil, climate, and minerals that attracted colonists are still in place and the envy of most of the world.

Table 2-3 shows the key stats of a few emerging markets in the Middle East, North Africa, and South Africa.

Table 2-3	Emerging Markets in the Middle East, North Africa, and South Africa			
Country	*Government*	*Major Industries*	*GDP per Capita/ Median Age*	*MSCI 2009 Equity Market Return (in U.S. dollars)*
Egypt	Republic	Cement, chemicals, construction, energy, food processing, hydrocarbons, light manufacturing, metals, pharmaceuticals, telecommunications, textiles, tourism, transportation	$6,600/24.8 years	44.49%

Country	Government	Major Industries	GDP per Capita/ Median Age	MSCI 2009 Equity Market Return (in U.S. dollars)
Morocco	Constitutional monarchy	Construction, energy, food processing, leather goods, phosphate rock mining and processing, textiles, tourism	$5,300/27.7 years	−16.47%
South Africa	Republic	Electronics, fertilizer, motor vehicles and parts, textiles	$11,300/25.5 years	14.79%

Navigating North and South America

In general, countries in the Americas are rich in natural resources and human capital. They're also plagued with government deficits and historic credit problems. Interest rates tend to be higher here than elsewhere in the world, which is attractive to bond investors but also a sign of risk and potential currency problems. Table 2-4 shows the numbers.

Table 2-4   Emerging Markets in North and South America

Country	Government	Major Industries	GDP per Capita/ Median Age	MSCI 2012 Equity Market Return (in U.S. dollars)
Chile	Republic	Fishing, mining (especially for copper), wine	$18,400/33.0 years	5.59%
Colombia	Republic	Agriculture, metals, petroleum, textiles	$10,700/28.6 years	31.55%

(continued)

Table 2-4 *(continued)*

Country	Government	Major Industries	GDP per Capita/ Median Age	MSCI 2012 Equity Market Return (in U.S. dollars)
Mexico	Federal republic	Food and beverages, iron and steel production, motor vehicle manufacturing	$15,300/27.7 years	27.07%
Peru	Constitutional republic	Fishing, mining, textiles	$10,700/26.7 years	15.51%

Finding action in Asia

When you think of emerging markets, think of Asia, home to China, India, and more than half of Russia — as well as several more emerging markets covered in this section. China and Japan dominate the region's economy and geopolitics, and most Asian countries have complicated relationships with those two nations. Other factors that Asian markets have in common? Low interest rates, export-driven economies, and an emphasis on high technology. Table 2-5 lists the stats.

Table 2-5 **Emerging Markets in Asia**

Country	Government	Major Industries	GDP per Capita/ Median Age	MSCI 2013 Equity Market Return (in U.S. dollars)
Indonesia	Republic	Apparel, cement, chemical fertilizers, food, mining, petroleum and natural gas, plywood, rubber, textiles, tourism	$5,000/28.9 years	2.41%

Country	Government	Major Industries	GDP per Capita/ Median Age	MSCI 2013 Equity Market Return (in U.S. dollars)
Malaysia	Constitutional monarchy	Automation, electronics, machinery, rubber products, telecommunications	$16,900/27.4 years	10.76%
The Philippines	Republic	Business outsourcing, electronics, food processing, textiles	$4,300/23.3 years	43.86%
South Korea	Republic	Electronics, industrial machinery, motor vehicles, telecommunications	$32,400/39.7 years	20.16%
Taiwan	Multiparty democracy	Information technology, petrochemicals, textiles	$38,500/38.7 years	13.45%
Thailand	Constitutional monarchy	Agriculture, banking, chemical products, electronics, machinery and industrial tools, tourism	$10,000/35.1 years	30.85%

Chapter 3

Picking Bonds, Stocks, and Mutual Funds in Emerging Markets

In This Chapter

▶ Buying and selling emerging market bonds and stocks

▶ Surveying the wide world of open-end and closed-end mutual funds

▶ Getting a handle on international exchanges

*B*onds and stocks are the most traditional investments. They're basic ways for companies to finance their growth, and they're popular with investors in developed markets. Emerging market investors can buy bonds and stocks, too, although they need to know about some differences. As an investor outside of a country, for example, you may not be able to buy bonds and stocks directly, and the risk levels are probably higher than you're used to. Plus, fewer bonds and stocks are available for purchase in emerging markets than in developed ones. But those differences are what help make the markets interesting.

So yes, buying bonds and stocks in emerging markets can be more complicated than buying them in developed markets — but it can also be rewarding.

Still, many investors find that selecting individual stocks and bonds is difficult and may require more money than they have to create a diversified portfolio. After all, you have to have a lot of assets to buy a lot of investments to get good diversification, and you have to spend a lot of time doing the research. That's more of a commitment than many emerging market investors want to make. Mutual funds, both open-end and closed-end, offer a relatively simple way to create a diversified portfolio of emerging markets and emerging companies.

The information in this chapter can help you make solid decisions when it comes to buying securities — whether they're bonds, stocks, or mutual funds — in emerging markets.

Pursuing Emerging Market Bonds

A *bond* is a loan; the buyer gives money to the issuer, and then the issuer repays the loan over time. Each interest payment is known as a *coupon,* and the bond's price at issue is known as the *principal.* The interest rate at the time the bond is issued is called the *coupon rate;* after the bond is issued, the price goes up and down so that the realized interest is in line with the market rate of interest. When interest rates go up, bond prices go down. When interest rates go down, bond prices go up. That relationship holds in every market in every time period. (Refer to Book I, Chapter 2 for more general information on bonds.)

No matter the market, bonds are less risky than stocks because the bondholders are first in line for cash. If the issuer goes bankrupt, those who own bonds are paid before any money goes to shareholders. But keep in mind that investing in emerging markets is riskier than investing in a developed market, so emerging market bonds may have risk that's closer to Fortune 500 equity. If that risk is just right for you, the following sections help you understand how bonds work in emerging markets.

Sorting out key bond categories

Bonds come in two flavors: government and corporate. They differ not only based on who issues the bond but also based on how they trade and what happens when and if the issuer can't pay. Here are the basics:

- ✔ **Government bonds:** In many emerging market countries, the government is the primary economic agent. It may own utilities, banks, and construction firms because the private sector is too small to provide these services. One way to invest in the growth of the country's economy is through bonds issued by the government itself, also known as *sovereign debt.* Government bonds tend to trade in large volumes and generally have less risk than corporate bonds in the same market. They have some of their own risks, though, which I cover in the later section "Noting the effects of inflation on bonds."

Debt issued by foreign governments is often used to pay U.S. and European contracting companies for their infrastructure development services. If you're interested in investing in emerging market infrastructure, you may be able to do it with engineering and construction firms that are based in major markets but that draw much of their revenue from emerging markets. You can do some basic screening on a financial website such as Yahoo! Finance (`finance.yahoo.com`) if you're looking for the names of such companies.

> ✔ **Corporate bonds:** Corporations issue corporate bonds to finance their growth and expansion. Many companies prefer to use debt rather than equity to expand because in many countries, interest expenses are tax-deductible, and as long as a company doesn't go bankrupt, debt allows the current owners to stay in control.

Matching bonds and currencies

Bonds have a lot of exposure to changes in exchange rates. When you hold a bond, every time the borrower makes an interest payment or repays the principal, you receive cash. If you need to exchange that cash, then the value of every payment will change based on what the exchange rate is at the time that you receive your money.

If you don't like that risk, you can own a diversified portfolio of bonds in different currencies, or you can buy an emerging market bond that's priced in your own currency. Many governments and large corporations want investors in other countries to buy their bonds, so they often sell bonds in U.S. dollars, euros, and yen. So if, for example, you want to invest in Brazil but don't want exposure to the real (the Brazilian currency), you can buy Brazilian government dollar bonds.

Book VI

Emerging Markets

Noting the effects of inflation on bonds

One way for a government to pay off its debts is to pay back the debt with cheaper money; a government has the ability to create inflation (for example, by printing more money) in order to accomplish this goal. Your return is reduced, but the government's leaders have the satisfaction of keeping their reputation for repaying their bills. Hence, one risk you must factor in as a buyer of sovereign debt is that the money may get repaid with funds that are less valuable when converted to your home currency.

Inflation is a bigger risk for government debt buyers than default is. (See the next section for more on bond default.)

Inflation is okay in small doses, but in massive quantities, it drowns an economy and sinks the value of a market's bonds. Any amount of inflation causes a currency to depreciate relative to other currencies, all else being equal. The higher the inflation, the lower your return. Even bonds issued in your currency are affected by inflation because it reduces the purchasing power of the principal and interest payments.

One way to evaluate the risk of bonds in an emerging market is to look at the percentage of debt that a country has relative to its gross domestic product (GDP). The higher that number, the more likely a nation is to try to inflate its way out of debt.

Dealing with default

When a company or government can't pay the principal or interest on its loans, the bond goes into *default*. With a corporate bond, the bondholders will press the company to come up with a plan to pay off the debt or to liquidate the company. The exact process and legal remedies vary from country to country, but you stand a chance at getting some money back. Keep these points in mind:

- ✔ **Seniority:** Whether the troubled bonds are issued by a corporation or a government, your first question is whether you, as an international investor, will be treated the same as investors who live in the country. The order of repayment in bankruptcy is known as *seniority,* and it's possible that citizens are senior to outsiders.

- ✔ **Difference between defaults of corporate versus government bonds:** Foreign governments may default on bonds, but the governments won't go away. They have to come back to borrow money or otherwise deal with the financial markets, so they have to somehow make good to their creditors. Exactly how and when, though, is a tricky question. With corporate debt, on the other hand, bondholders may be left with nothing after the bankruptcy process is finished.

With government debt, the International Monetary Fund (IMF) often directs the restructuring of government bonds that are in default. The IMF works with major creditors, which are often other governments, to try to find a way to make sure that the debt is repaid without excessive inflation or hardship. The folks at the IMF don't always succeed, though, and they're not always loved for their efforts.

Buying Emerging Market Stocks

As a market becomes more commercialized, more stock is issued for international investors to purchase, sometimes by the government itself. Most emerging markets have outperformed the developed markets in recent years. By many measures, such as price-to-earnings and price-to-book-value ratios, stocks in emerging markets are less expensive, too. And emerging markets have new companies and new ideas that are great profit opportunities for stock investors.

With a stock, your potential profits are unlimited. That's the excitement! If the company goes bankrupt, however, shareholders are repaid only after all the creditors and bondholders are, so they'll most likely receive nothing. Following are some other things to know about investing in stocks in emerging markets:

- ✔ **Role rights as a shareholder may be limited.** As owners in the business, shareholders are usually allowed to vote on such major corporate governance matters as who should serve on the board of directors and whether a major merger should take place. In many markets, however, overseas investors aren't allowed to vote on corporate matters. Even when they're able to vote, their position may be dwarfed by the shares of a controlling family or corporation. The less say you have in how a company is run, the less valuable your shares are. Keep this in mind when you invest in emerging market stocks.

- ✔ **Short selling is difficult in most emerging markets.** When you short a stock, you borrow shares, sell them, and then repurchase shares at a later time to pay back the loan. If the price falls between the time that you sell the shares and the time that you repurchase them, you make money.

- ✔ **Splits may increase the value of your holdings.** On occasion, a company may split the number of shares outstanding. If you own 100 shares of a company worth 150 South African rand each, for example, you'd have a total investment of 15,000 rand. If the company does a two-for-one stock split, your new stake would be 200 shares worth 75 rand each, for a total investment of 15,000 rand. In other words, a stock split is neutral for your pocketbook. However, local investors often like splits and misunderstand their effect, so the total value of the shares you hold may be worth more after a split.

The following sections delve more deeply into other things you need to know if you buy stocks in emerging markets.

Calculating the float

A stock's *market capitalization* is the price of a share times the number of shares outstanding. It may look plenty big, on par with those of companies you trade every day in developed markets, but keep looking. In any market — but especially in emerging markets — a good chunk of the stock may be held by a controlling family or company. These investors aren't likely to sell shares, and if they do, then something really big is going on with the business. The number of shares left over for you to trade, known as the *float,* may be very small.

Calculating the float is pretty easy. First you find the total number of shares outstanding, and then you reduce that number by the number of shares that won't likely be traded because of family ownership or another controlling investor. Those are the shares that are available to you to buy.

Trading depository receipts

A depository receipt is a way for a company overseas to attract international investors on its own terms. Here's how it works: Shares of the company are placed in trust at a bank that organizes depository receipts. The bank then turns around and issues certificates representing shares in the company (sometimes one, sometimes more) that then trade in local currency on the local stock exchange or over-the-counter. Certificates that are arranged in the United States are known as ADRs (American depository receipts); in Europe, they're EDRs (European depository receipts); and elsewhere, GDRs (global depository receipts).

Depository receipts tend to trade at a premium to home-country shares because they involve no special transaction costs. They're bought and sold through American (or European or global) brokers with the same commissions and trading requirements as a U.S. (or European or Japanese) company has. If the depository receipts are listed on a stock exchange, the company has to meet the exchange listing requirements, which also means that investors have more information than they may otherwise have. The company doesn't have to offer the same financial information as a company with a regular exchange listing, however.

Jumping on initial public offerings

As a country grows, the government may decide to get out of the business of running corporations and arrange initial public offerings (IPOs). This is especially true for a nation discarding a legacy of socialism or moving from underdeveloped to developing.

 These offerings don't come along often, but when they do, they're a great opportunity for investors to get in on the ground floor. In many cases, certain politicians or influential families end up having voting control, so little is shared but the potential for profit. The IPOs are usually covered with much fanfare in the financial press, so if you stay on top of news about the markets, you'll know about them.

Corporations sometimes go public in the United States because U.S. investors have a greater appetite for start-up companies than do investors in many other markets. When a company goes public in the United States, it has to publish the same financial information no matter where it's headquartered, so investors have a good sense of how to value the company. That reduces the risk.

Diversifying with Mutual Funds

If individual stocks and bonds aren't your thing, consider investing in mutual funds. They're the most popular kids at the party for investors who are new to emerging markets or who can't — or choose not to — commit tons of money and energy to them. Mutual funds allow thousands of investors to get together to create a diversified portfolio with a professional manager who does nothing but research emerging markets. The following sections offer the details (refer to Book I, Chapter 3 for general information on investing in mutual funds.)

Book VI

Emerging Markets

Choosing open-end funds

The number of mutual funds on the market is staggering. At the end of 2012, the Investment Company Institute reported that 8,752 funds were on the market. Where do you begin?

Each fund has a different investment style, fee structure, and management team, and those factors influence how appropriate the fund is for you. For example, if your interest is emerging markets in Asia, do you want a fund that also invests in Japan? Probably not, because Japan is a developed market, not an emerging one. Likewise, if you want to generate income from your investment, you'll probably be more interested in an emerging market bond fund than in a stock fund, because bonds are more likely to earn income than stocks are.

This section discusses *open-end mutual funds,* which are investments that collect money from many different people and invest it in different securities that fit the fund's stated investment objectives. The people who own shares in the fund can buy or sell them any day that the market is open. (You can find out about *closed-end funds* later in this chapter.)

The main offering document for a mutual fund is called the *prospectus,* and it tells you all you need to know. It explains the fund's investment objective, management style, performance history, and fee structure. You want to review this information before you invest in a mutual fund.

Investment style

When you start looking at mutual funds, you'll see that they're categorized into narrow categories, and even then, you'll have a lot of funds to compare. But your interest in emerging markets makes your task simpler. Go to the lists of international funds. At some fund companies and with some research services, emerging market funds are separated from other funds that invest overseas. Other times, all international options are kept together, so you have to look at the fund name or the prospectus to find out how it invests.

Because the mutual fund industry has to find ways to categorize the thousands of funds, you find emerging market funds grouped in different ways. Here a few of the pros and cons of the different investment categories for emerging markets:

- **Diversified emerging market funds:** These funds invest in any emerging market that strikes the fund manager's fancy, often allocating to countries in a similar proportion to the MSCI Emerging Markets Index. These funds have great diversification and give you wide exposure to the changing global economy, but you can't concentrate on any markets that you find to be especially attractive. These funds may be too broad to be managed well.

- **Regional emerging market funds:** Is your interest in Africa? Latin America? Asia? Then you may want to consider a fund that invests only in one region. These funds have some diversification, and they let you concentrate on the regions where you see the most opportunities, but you may pick up some developed countries in the mix. In addition, problems in one country can bring down the performance of unrelated companies in unrelated countries that happen to be nearby.

- **Country-specific funds:** These funds invest in only one country. These funds specialize in the markets you may care about, giving you exposure to the market without limiting your investment to just one company. However, they offer fewer diversification benefits, and fund managers may face difficulty finding enough good investments in some of the smaller countries to satisfy investor demand.

Research expertise

Mutual fund companies employ armies of analysts, traders, and portfolio managers who learn about the markets, tear through financial statements, and meet company management. They have the time and the expertise to navigate through the issues involved in emerging market investing.

Before you invest in a fund, find out about the manager's expertise in emerging markets and in other funds. Is the fund manager a specialist, or does she have responsibilities for completely different types of funds?

Emerging market expertise can be so specialized that many fund companies don't claim to have it. Instead, they hire *sub-advisors* — investment management companies based in or near the emerging markets, with great experience in those countries. The employees of the sub-advisory firm have the great knowledge and contacts that, hopefully, lead to better investment decisions with your money.

Fund family issues

Although each mutual fund is legally a separate company, with its own board of directors and officers, the reality is that mutual funds have next-to-no independence. Large corporations that are in the business of managing money organize almost all mutual funds. This structure may influence the funds that are available to you, especially if you're investing as part of an employer-sponsored retirement plan.

- ✔ **Dedicated international investors:** Some mutual fund companies have a robust approach to global investing, with a team of analysts and portfolio managers who concentrate on markets outside of the United States. These firms often have offices in other countries and more than a dozen stock and bond funds in different developed and emerging market categories. These funds are more likely to have good options for emerging market investors than fund companies with less emphasis on international investing, although not always.

- ✔ **General fund companies offering emerging market funds:** Because customers want international investments, some fund companies offer them even if these funds aren't really part of their core expertise. They may hire a fund manager with experience, or they may use a sub-advisor. Although you're less likely to find a great emerging market fund at one of these companies, you may, especially if the sub-advisor is a good one.

Fees

Mutual funds offer investors great convenience and professional management. Naturally, you have to pay for these services! In addition to the regular fees mutual funds charge (refer to Book I, Chapter 3), also be aware that emerging market funds tend to have higher fees than other types of funds because the research is more difficult. There just isn't as much information out there on the companies and countries. The fund managers probably travel to see what's happening for themselves, and that gets really expensive. Hence, emerging market funds are likely to have much higher expense ratios than funds that invest in developed countries. (Expense ratios include all of a fund's fees, not just its management fees.)

The higher expenses are worth it if you get the returns that you expect. That's why looking at a fund's performance is important. Head to the later section "Evaluating funds of all types" for information on how to do that.

Some emerging market open-end funds

If you're considering mutual funds as a way to play in emerging markets, the following list is for you! This list has several emerging market funds, grouped by the companies that issue them. These firms have a lot of international investing expertise. This list is hardly exhaustive, nor is it an endorsement; it's just a place for you to start your research:

- ✔ **Aberdeen:** Aberdeen (www.aberdeen-asset.us) is the U.S. subsidiary of an asset management firm based in the United Kingdom. It has several load funds that invest in emerging markets. Funds include the Aberdeen China Opportunities Fund, Aberdeen Emerging Markets Fund, and Aberdeen Asia-Pacific (ex-Japan) Equity Institutional Fund.

- ✔ **Fidelity:** As the world's largest mutual fund company, Fidelity (www.fidelity.com) has 31 no-load international funds, including several committed to emerging markets. Funds include the Fidelity China Region Fund; Fidelity Emerging Europe, Middle East, Africa Fund; Fidelity Emerging Markets Fund; Fidelity New Markets Income Fund; and Fidelity Southeast Asia Fund.

- ✔ **Franklin Templeton:** Franklin Templeton (www.franklintempleton.com) was one of the first mutual fund companies to make a big commitment to emerging markets. The company offers several load-carrying international funds, most of which invest in the world's new economies. Funds include the Templeton BRIC Fund, Templeton China World Fund, Templeton Emerging Markets Small-Cap Fund, and Templeton Frontier Markets Fund.

- ✔ **T. Rowe Price:** This company (individual.troweprice.com/public/Retail) offers a full range of no-load funds that invest in almost any market you can think of. T. Rowe Price has 20 mutual funds, several of which invest in emerging markets with blessedly self-explanatory names. Funds include the T. Rowe Price Africa and Middle East Fund, T. Rowe Price Emerging Europe Fund, T. Rowe Price Emerging Markets Bond Fund, T. Rowe Price Emerging Markets Stock Fund, T. Rowe Price Latin America Fund, and T. Rowe Price New Asia Fund.

- ✔ **Vanguard:** Vanguard (www.vanguard.com) doesn't have deep international expertise. What the company is good at is low-cost index mutual funds, designed to mimic the performance of one of the world's many market benchmarks. The Vanguard Emerging Markets Stock Index Fund, based on the MSCI Emerging Markets Index, is an easy way to get the return of the index in mutual fund form.

Exploring closed-end funds

Open-end mutual funds are far more common than *closed-end funds*. With a closed-end fund, the fund holds an initial public offering. The amount of money raised becomes the initial net asset value of the fund. The fund managers then go to work finding great places to invest the money. If the fund's shareholders want to sell their funds, they do so through their brokers. If new investors want to buy into the funds, they place an order — just as they would for any other publicly traded stock.

The pricing of closed-end funds

In open-end mutual funds, the shares are issued and redeemed by the fund company. The mutual fund's price per share is its *net asset value* (NAV). That's the total value of the fund's investments divided by the total number of shares outstanding. Every night, the fund company buys and sells shares so that anyone who wants to get into — or get out of — the fund can do so at the net asset value.

The closed-end fund company posts its net asset value every night, but the share price may be very different. In most cases, the share price is lower.

In academic finance theory, market prices are accurate because they reflect all known information about an asset. This is known as the *efficient markets hypothesis*. It's plenty controversial; one of the known deviations from market efficiency is that closed-end funds almost always trade at a discount from their net asset value. If markets were really efficient, then a closed-end fund's price would be the NAV.

Many people are scared of closed-end funds because of the price discount, which may be one reason that there's a discount in the first place. However, closed-end funds may be a great choice for you as an emerging market investor because the manager of a closed-end fund doesn't have to worry about money going into or out of the fund — the number of shares is already fixed. That means she can invest in securities that don't trade very often, giving her more ways to make money in a market with thin trading. She can think about the long-term value of the assets, rather than her short-term cash management concerns.

Some emerging market closed-end funds

The Closed-End Fund Center (www.cefa.com), a membership organization for managers of closed-end funds, lists 18 different closed-end emerging funds. Table 3-1 offers a sample of the membership. (See the earlier section "Investment style" for definitions of the types of funds.) Check these funds out before you invest in them!

Closed-End Fund	Type	Ticker Symbol
Aberdeen Chile	Country	CH
Aberdeen Emerging Markets Smaller Company Opportunities	Diversified	ETF
Central Europe, Russia, and Turkey (managed by DWS Investments)	Regional	CEE
Herzfeld Caribbean Basin	Regional	CUBA
India Fund (managed by Aberdeen)	Country	IN
Mexico Fund (managed by its own staff)	Country	MXF
Morgan Stanley East Europe	Regional	RNE
Templeton Dragon Fund	Country	TDF
Templeton Emerging Markets	Regional	EMF
Turkish Investment Fund (managed by Morgan Stanley Investment Management)	Country	TKF

Table 3-1   Sample of Emerging Market Closed-End Funds

Evaluating funds of all types

The preceding sections include some lists of funds to get you started, but here's the reality: No matter when you read this book, the names of some of the funds will have changed, new funds will be available that you should consider, and some funds on the list will have such dismal performance or such high fees that you won't want to own them.

And after you buy a fund, you need to decide when to sell. That decision may be driven by your own needs (for example, you may want to change the overall risk in your portfolio as you get closer to retirement age), or it may be that your needs are the same, but the fund no longer fits.

When you evaluate a fund, you're looking at two things: how the fund suits your risk and return needs, and how the fund performs relative to other funds investing in the same markets.

You can turn to several great resources, including information from the fund company itself. Two sources of information about funds from all sponsors are Morningstar and Yahoo! Finance:

- ✔ **Morningstar** (www.morningstar.com) specializes in research on funds of every stripe. Its analysts conduct extensive research on each fund and then pull all their findings together into ratings, style categories, and easy-to-use screens and reports. Some information is free to all comers, more is free to those who register on the site, and even more is available to people who subscribe to its premium services.

- ✔ **Yahoo! Finance** (http://finance.yahoo.com) has detailed price and financial information on just about every company registered with the U.S. Securities and Exchange Commission, which includes every type of fund mentioned in this chapter. Much of the information comes from the public filings, and you can sort through it to find funds that may fit your interests. Best of all, it's all free.

Be sure that you look at performance after fees. Mutual funds tend to have high fees, which isn't a problem if the investment returns are high enough to cover them and if you receive something in exchange for your money.

Navigating International Securities Exchanges

Traditionally, a security is traded on an *exchange,* which is an organization set up to allow people to buy and sell. Exchanges grant trading privileges to different brokerage firms so that they can execute orders for their customers. The alternative to exchange trading is *over-the-counter trading,* in which networks of buyers and sellers find one another in order to get trades done. Over-the-counter trading has exploded as information technology has improved. Many over-the-counter networks have requirements for participating members in order to ensure that no one is ripped off, so the lines between the exchanges and the networks have blurred.

You don't necessarily need to have a brokerage account in the country where you trade, by the way. Many major brokers in developed markets have exchange membership or trading privileges all over the world. If they don't have their own seat on an exchange, they may be able to do it through a partnership with another firm, an arrangement known in the trade as a *correspondent broker.*

The following sections describe the regulation of exchanges in emerging markets, dual-listed securities, and the accuracy of price quotes.

Figuring out who's regulating whom

Securities exchanges are often for-profit businesses that need to generate a return for shareholders while fending off competition. That's fine, but they also perform an important function in keeping capital flowing in a country so that businesses can expand. In order to ensure that they function, they are regulated. Stock exchanges have two types of regulation:

- ✔ **From the national government:** The government almost definitely has basic rules for how the exchange should operate. The regulatory body may be the central bank or a dedicated regulatory agency. It sets and enforces rules on how much information companies need to give to investors, how quickly trades are settled, whether margin and short selling are permitted, and what qualifications brokers have to meet. Some exchanges are more closely regulated than others, but all have at least some government oversight.

- ✔ **From the exchange's internal regulation process:** Each exchange has rules for the standards that companies have to meet in order to be listed, for trading hours and procedures, and for obtaining permission to work as a broker or trader on the exchange. If you're investing in a country where the laws are weak, the exchange's governance structure should be more important to you.

Trading on material nonpublic information, also known as *insider trading,* is legal in some countries. In other places, it's illegal or prohibited by the exchanges, but the rules against it aren't enforced. It's clearly illegal in the United States, but understand that in other markets, you may well be buying or selling against people who have more information than you do, and that makes it especially dangerous to trade against the price trend.

Dealing with dual listings

Often, securities are listed on more than one exchange. For example, a Chinese company may list its shares in Hong Kong, Shanghai, and New York. The only difference between the shares is the exchange rate, because the shares trade in local currency on the markets where they're listed.

Because dual-listed securities have to meet the exchange-listing requirements on every exchange, investors often prefer them to other emerging market securities. After all, the more listing requirements a company has to meet, the more information about it is in the market that investors can use. And all else being equal, dual-listed securities tend to trade at a premium to other securities because of this.

Getting accurate price quotes

The academics like to say that all the information about a security is included in its price. If it's cheap, it's cheap for a reason, they say, because as long as people are free to buy and sell in a market with perfect information, prices will change to reflect changes in news. In actively traded markets, especially those in developed economies, prices more or less work as the academics say, mostly going up when the news is good and down when the news is bad. In emerging and frontier markets, though, prices may not reflect all the information about a company's prospects. For that matter, the prices you see before you place orders may have nothing to do with the prices you receive when your orders are executed. The markets may not have the trading activity needed to force prices to respond to information, or there may be limits on the types of information that different people receive.

Here are two ways to evaluate the quality of the prices in a market:

- ✔ **Check the website of the country's stock exchange to see how often its prices are updated.** Do they change minute by minute, day by day, or week by week? The less often a trade takes place, the less accurate the prices are.

- ✔ **Look for the size of the spread between the bid and the ask.** The *spread* is the difference between the bid and the ask. The wider the difference between these two numbers, the less often the stock trades — and the less accurate the price quote is likely to be.

Book VI

Emerging Markets

Chapter 4

High Finance in Emerging Markets

In This Chapter

▶ Parsing partnership fund options

▶ Partnering with governments, local investors, and NGOs

▶ Sidestepping high-finance pitfalls

*E*merging markets are for investors of all sizes, but some of the greatest opportunities are for those who have the most money to commit. These *private investment partnerships* are designed for high-net-worth individuals, pensions, foundations, endowments, and other people and organizations that have a lot of money they can afford to lock up for a long time. The funds may have higher returns for a given level of risk, but they may be less flexible than other types of investments.

Think of these private partnerships as the VIP room of high finance. These investments can be a great way to get into a market big and early. In some cases, investors really do get access to better opportunities and superior risk-adjusted returns. In other cases, though, investors get behind the velvet rope only to find out that the drinks are more expensive but the service is no better.

In this chapter, you get an overview of the investment funds available to you if you have millions of dollars to invest. I give you the information to understand what makes sense for you — as well as what may not — in order to help you make better decisions.

Delving into the World of High Finance

In high finance, the catchall phrases are *alternative investments* and *private partnerships*. These funds are alternatives to stocks, bonds, and other traditional investments, and they're structured as partnerships that aren't traded on public exchanges. The following sections compare different types of private partnerships and describe their basic structure.

The buzzword on these investments is *alpha.* Alpha is a term in a financial equation called the *capital assets pricing model,* which proposes that most investment returns come from the market itself but that portfolio managers may be able to add something extra. Alpha is a way of measuring the added return on an investment that comes from the manager's skill. Consider it the secret ingredient. When you talk to money managers, you hear a lot of discussion about alpha. (Flip to Chapter 1 in Book V for more about alpha.)

Comparing some common emerging market partnership funds

The most popular type of private partnership these days is a hedge fund, but it's hardly the only one out there. Venture capital and private equity funds also play in some emerging markets. These funds all have a similar structure (as explained later in this chapter) but have different operating philosophies.

Note that you can't just call up these companies and invest in them. These aren't like mutual funds (introduced in Book I, Chapter 3). Investors have to be accredited or qualified (see the nearby sidebar "Investor accreditation" for details) before these types of funds will even approach them. If you're an accredited or qualified investor, you probably have a financial advisor who can help you make introductions by vouching for your status.

Investor accreditation

In the United States, investors can't participate in such private investment partnerships as hedge funds or venture capital funds unless they meet the Securities and Exchange Commission's standards for *accredited investors.* An individual qualifies with a net worth (assets minus liabilities) of $1 million or more, excluding the value of the person's primary residence, or with an income of at least $200,000 ($300,000 joint with a spouse) in each of the two most recent years. The idea isn't to shut out the little guy so much as to make sure that the people who invest in these funds know what they're doing, because they don't have the same protections as people who invest in stocks, bonds, or mutual funds. The assumption is that people with more money have more experience in investing and can afford good advisors, which may or may not be true. Some private partnerships ask for documentation; others simply set a minimum investment that's so high (for example, $10 million) that anyone who participates would have to be accredited.

Hedge funds

In their original incarnation, *hedge funds* (the subject of Book V) were designed to generate steady returns no matter what the market did. These days, many funds take significant amounts of risk and have returns that fluctuate all over the place. You may be okay with such fluctuations if you like the flexibility and the long-term risk and return trade-off.

Some hedge funds specialize in emerging markets and aren't interested in investments elsewhere. Others, known as *macro funds,* invest in pretty much any market that offers the possibility of a profit, which often means the emerging markets.

Book VI

Emerging Markets

In general, hedge fund managers look for markets where they can easily buy and sell securities. They may look for long-term commitments from the people who invest in their funds, but they aren't necessarily interested in the long term when they do their trading. Because of that, they tend to be more active in currency and debt than in stock. The currency markets, covered in Book IV, offer the greatest liquidity, and government bonds are a close second. More liquidity makes for more opportunities to make money.

Most hedge funds move money in and out of markets quickly, using borrowed money to increase their commitments to different investments. If a fund manager sees a good opportunity, he'll buy. If the situation changes, he'll sell. Because they turn their investments over on short notice, hedge funds aren't always beloved. In fact, many people in Asia blame hedge funds for the 1997–1998 currency crisis that damaged many economies there, even though the funds didn't make policy, only profits.

Hedge funds that buy stock tend to look only at the largest of the emerging markets because they need to put a lot of money to work. Because many fund managers see higher profit potential from stocks in emerging markets than from stocks in developed markets, they invest in emerging markets wherever they believe they can acquire a good-sized position. That's why, for example, you're more likely to see hedge funds invest in Brazil than in Botswana.

Venture capital funds

Venture capital funds, which many high-net-worth investors invest in, provide financing to companies at the early stages of their existence. Because most new businesses fail, venture investing is risky. However, those businesses that succeed often succeed spectacularly, and investing early in a company like Google can make up for an awful lot of trips to bankruptcy court. The goal is to get a company to the point where it can make an *initial public offering* (the first time that a company sells shares of stock to the public) or be sold to a larger company.

Emerging markets have great opportunities for new businesses, and that makes them really appealing to venture capitalists. They don't have to find the next Google; they can find something a lot simpler and still make money. However, emerging markets aren't perfect for venture capital. In many countries, entrepreneurs would be happy with loans of just a few hundred or a few thousand dollars. They often don't have a cohort of professional managers that venture capitalists typically hire, and the legal systems in emerging markets are rarely ready to accommodate the needs of a venture capital–funded start-up. If you're considering venture capital in emerging markets, you need to assess the opportunity's conditions and your own risk tolerance.

Expatriates are behind a lot of venture investments; successful immigrant executives in the United States, especially in the technology industry, often know of good start-ups in their home countries and work with the venture capitalists to arrange for the investments.

Private equity funds

Private equity funds provide capital to existing companies. They may help a company expand, they may help it avoid bankruptcy, or they may buy out the founder's share of the business. They tend to be active in emerging markets because private equity has many of the advantages of venture capital with few of the headaches that go with starting up a business. A private equity firm can make money from an investment as a business grows, but it doesn't have to find managers or provide a lot of operating advice.

The managers of these funds are usually comfortable with the logistics of running a business because many of them are retired corporate executives. That expertise is important, because in an emerging market, investors may be running a business for a long time.

Figuring out funds of funds

Often, folks who qualify as investors in private partnerships don't want to commit as much money as the fund managers want them to. Or, they may want greater diversification than they can receive by investing in only one fund. That's why *funds of funds* were invented. These funds pool money from a group of accredited investors and then allocate it to different private partnerships. They're especially common for hedge funds, but they also exist for venture capital and private partnerships that specialize in emerging markets.

Looking into the structure of limited partnerships

The highfalutin funds of high finance don't trade on organized exchanges. You can't just fill out an application and send in a check, or go to your brokerage account and click a few buttons. Instead, investing in these funds is akin to going into business with the organizers. You're making a commitment to them, and they to you. The following sections explain the different types of partners and the fees charged in a limited partnership.

Meeting the partners

The people who organize these funds are known as the *general partners*. They have investment expertise but need money to invest. They take on the risk of the business and receive the first cut of the profits in return. The *limited partners,* on the other hand, give up risk in exchange for turning over control to the general partners. They can lose the money they invest, but no more, which makes their investment much less risky than the general partners' investment. In most cases, investors in hedge funds or venture capital funds are limited partners.

The general partners don't have to take any investor who comes along. Some of these funds are like private clubs, where only friends or friends of friends are able to invest. Other funds are more widely accessible, with general partners who are comfortable having partners that they don't know personally. They just want to make sure that all potential investors they consider are accredited (see the earlier sidebar "Investor accreditation" for details).

When investing in these funds, you'll write a check eventually. Instead of an account application, you sign a partnership agreement that specifies the fees, the investment style, and the rules about making withdrawals or deposits. The terms for fees, withdrawals, and minimum investment may be negotiable, so it doesn't hurt to ask for changes that you'd like to see.

Finding out about fees

General partners, who are the people who set up and manage their funds, earn compensation in two forms:

- **Management fees:** The *management fee* is used to cover the costs of operating the business: paying rent on the office, subscribing to trading platforms (computer systems used to make high-speed trades), sending analysts on research trips, and the like. This fee is usually charged as a percentage of total assets in the fund, with 2 percent being a typical rate.

✔ **Performance fees:** The *performance fee* is a cut of each year's profits, sometimes 20 percent or so. This fee, which is also known as the *carry* or *carried interest,* is usually a good thing because it gives the fund manager an incentive to generate great performance for you, the investor. However, the performance fee also cuts into your return. If the fund manager has a mediocre year, your return could be downright miserable after that 20 percent is taken out.

Fund investors sometimes refer to the fee structure as the *2 and 20,* referring to a 2 percent management fee and a 20 percent cut of portfolio profits. Of course, the actual fee structure could be 1 and 10, 3 and 30, or 2 and 15. What's important is that you receive value for the fees you pay.

Working with Local Partners

Hedge funds, venture capital funds, and related investments are set up for long-term investments. These funds often can't sell their investments easily, so the fund managers need to make sure that they feel comfortable with the people they'll be working with. Just as general and limited partners go into business together (see the earlier section "Meeting the partners"), an entire partnership goes into business with the firms that it invests in and with those who have a key stake in the business. The key partners for emerging market funds are local governments, local investors, and nongovernmental organizations (NGOs). These people influence the fund's success or failure.

Governments

Whether explicitly or implicitly, a country's government plays a role in any emerging market investment. Because the government determines regulations, investors need to cooperate with the people in charge. In many cases, government leaders aren't thrilled to have high financiers from developed economies mucking around their country. Their key concern is *hot money:* funds that make huge investments when the market is going up and then pull out everything at the first sign of trouble — a strategy that can wreak incredible havoc in an emerging market.

Investors in publicly traded stocks and bonds already have government acceptance, as the very process of setting up a framework for securities trading is a bureaucratic dream! Markets work only if they have enough regulation to make sure that everyone coughs up the goods and the cash that they've agreed to, and that's a key function of government.

Private investors don't necessarily need government approval to get underway. However, regulators and politicians can come in after the fact and interfere, requiring licenses, refusing to protect contracts, or even preventing investors from removing money from the country.

Governments don't always thwart investors. In many cases, they become partners with them, which can add a whole layer of profit potential — and complication — to the deal. Emerging market governments often turn to outside investors like you to help fund infrastructure projects, for example, with the government itself as the ultimate payer.

On occasion, an emerging market government invests alongside private investors in a private company, especially if it deems the project to be in the national interest. A related transaction is known as *BOT,* for *Build-Operate-Transfer.* In these deals, a private company builds the project, such as a road or a power plant. It handles the initial operation and then transfers it to the government. These deals aren't common, but they do happen, and private partnerships are likely to know about them before anyone else.

Local investors

Managers of hedge funds, venture capital funds, or private equity funds in emerging markets often work with local investors to help find deals and to be a co-investor in different transactions. These people have tacit knowledge that an outsider may never be able to gain, and they can help smooth the way to better transactions, reducing risk and increasing the potential for return.

Expatriates often invest in private funds that invest in their home country, or they make the same investments that the private funds are making. These people often have the contacts and knowledge to increase the likelihood of success. They aren't exactly local, but they have local experience. If the expatriates are excited, you should be, too. And if the expatriates are staying away from a market, then it's probably not a great place to invest.

Some local investors see outside investors as competition. In many emerging markets, the richest and most successful companies are dynastic holding companies that would like to acquire some of the same businesses that venture capital and private equity funds are eyeing. This competition can make it more difficult to get a deal done, especially because these holding companies are likely to have really tight ties to the local government.

Nongovernmental organizations

In many cases, the private investment funds with the big bucks are partners with the major NGOs, like the World Bank or foreign government aid agencies. These organizations fund a range of infrastructure and economic development projects — water purification plants, industrial parks, highways, and just about anything else that makes it easier to live and work in a country.

The NGOs often look for private investors as a check on the economic viability of a project, which is why they often like to bring them in. A lot of aid organizations get so carried away with the opportunity to do good that they've been known to take on projects that make no economic sense and end up hurting the country in the long run. The better NGOs are well aware of this pitfall. Private investors are more concerned with risk and return than they are with romantic notions of doing good (although many would like to do good in the world). If they aren't interested in co-investing, then it's probably not a good project.

One organization that has long worked to bring private sector investors to the developing world is the World Bank's own investment bank, the International Finance Corporation (also known as the IFC). While the World Bank finances government projects, the IFC works only with private companies. In many cases, it invests in partnerships with other investor groups. It also issues bonds and other securities to help finance its investing activities, and it publishes a lot of great information about investing in emerging markets. You can find out more on its website, www.ifc.org.

Avoiding Potential Traps in High-Finance Investing

Private investment partnerships aren't for everyone. Even some of the people who have the money to invest in them prefer to put their money into investments with fewer restrictions. They want to know all about the investments in a fund and want to have the right to sell when they want to sell. Not all private partnerships tell these investors all they want to know.

In some cases, the fund managers just like the aura of mystery, but in most cases, these restrictions have practical reasons. These funds don't buy and hold registered securities the way that a mutual fund does (I discuss that type of investment in Chapter 3 of Book VI.) Instead, they often buy shares in operating businesses or pursue unusual trading strategies. They can't sell their investments easily, and they don't want to share details of trades that could be copied by others.

These issues aren't necessarily bad ones, unless they surprise you. Forewarned is forearmed, and this section explains some of the common drawbacks to private investment partnerships, especially those that invest in emerging markets.

Transparency issues

Investors in private partnerships should do plenty of due diligence before writing the check. Find out who the fund managers are, what experience they have, what banks and brokerage firms handle the money, and who will be providing legal and accounting advice. Also, get information on the investment strategy.

As a limited partner, you won't be able to call the shots in the fund, and you won't get a call every time the fund makes a trade. However, you should know what the fund is planning to invest in. Is the fund looking at providing venture capital to late-stage technology companies in all markets, emerging and developed? Does it invest in emerging market government bonds, including private placements on NGO-backed infrastructure projects? Does it trade currencies and interest-rate futures? You need this type of information before you invest in order to assess whether the fund is appropriate for you, and you need it afterward to evaluate the fund's performance.

For example, many investors in Long-Term Capital Management, a now-closed hedge fund, were surprised to discover that the firm had huge exposure to the Russian bond market. When Russia defaulted in 1998, Long-Term Capital Management's investments fell in value and the firm failed. No fraud was involved.

Private doesn't mean *top secret*. If you're going to invest in one of these funds, for yourself or on behalf of an organization that you're involved with, be sure that you understand what the fund invests in and how it makes decisions. Bernard Madoff said he ran a hedge fund, but he was actually operating the largest pyramid scheme in history. When clients asked him about his investment style, he said that it was none of their business. He had something to hide.

In addition to knowing about a fund's investment strategy, you need to know how often you'll receive performance reports, what those reports include, and how often audits are done. The fund manager may not want to disclose actual investment positions; are you okay with that? In any event, you want information on the fund's assets and liabilities, how its assets are allocated to different types of investments, and what its income and capital gains are.

Limits on liquidity

Liquidity refers to the ease of buying or selling an investment, and it's a concern for private partnerships in two ways — the way it affects the fund itself and the way it affects the fund's investors.

Liquidity and the fund

Many emerging markets don't have enough securities or enough trading volume to make complex strategies work. (That's one reason that many hedge funds use currency to invest in emerging markets; they can trade currency in big volume over a short time period.) If it's hard to buy and sell the types of investments that the fund hopes to invest in, the fund may have trouble making a return for investors. After the fund makes an investment, it may not be able to sell it any time soon.

Venture capital and private equity funds usually can't sell their investments until the company holds an initial public offering or is sold to someone else. It's not unusual for these investments to be in place for five or even ten years.

Liquidity and the fund investor

Because private partnerships often have their funds locked away in different investments, they don't always have the cash on hand to return to their investors. After you're invested in a fund, you may not be able to get out for years. These funds are designed for the long run, so be sure that you understand how the fund's general partners define that time frame before you invest. Some funds limit your withdrawals during the first year or so, a period known as a *lock-up;* after that, the fund may let you withdraw money once a quarter or once a year as long as you give advance notice. Some venture funds don't return investments and profits until they've been able to exit all the fund's investments.

Sometimes, a private partnership can't find suitable investments for the money that investors put in, so it returns funds. You get your cash, but you have to go out and find another place to invest it.

Governance in a limited partnership structure

For tax reasons, investment partnerships are often based in an offshore financial center, so they may be governed mostly by the laws of the country of incorporation. They may also be governed by the laws of the country where the partnership is sold. For example, a fund marketed in the United States to U.S. investors has to comply with certain laws about disclosure and marketing, the most important being that the fund can be marketed only to accredited investors. If the fund is sold to investors in other countries, those laws may or may not apply.

Many larger funds are set up with a master-feeder structure. The main fund is based in an offshore financial center, and it operates a handful of feeder funds for investors in other countries. U.S. investors invest in the U.S. feeder, European investors invest in the EU feeder, and so on. This prevents problems with contradicting laws and ensures that each group of investors gets what it needs to be compliant with the laws of the group's own country.

A fund may also be subject to the laws of the countries where it does its investing. For example, if a hedge fund operates a trading desk in Dublin, it has to comply with EU securities laws. If a venture capital firm finds solar-power start-ups in Kenya, it needs to comply with Kenyan laws to ensure that the investments are valid.

Book VII
Value Investing

Five Intangible Signs of Value

- ✔ **A franchise:** Market power is tantamount to lasting earnings power, and a franchise (a market position that's difficult or impossible to duplicate) is the cornerstone of market power. An obvious, defensible franchise puts a company in a much better position to preserve and grow value.

- ✔ **Price control:** A company in control of its product prices probably possesses franchise power and is using it effectively. A company that markets its products and competes on virtues other than price has good market position. That company is more likely to preserve and grow future profit margins.

- ✔ **Market leadership:** Market share is important in achieving price control and economies of scale in producing, marketing, and delivering products. A company with a large market share has an advantage, while companies with a small or declining market share must pay up just to catch up.

- ✔ **Candid management:** Strong management and good leadership are often obvious just from a company's behavior. Management that communicates with the press, with shareholders, and with its customers is probably doing a good job and has nothing to hide.

- ✔ **Customer care:** Companies that appreciate the value of their customer base and capitalize on that value are better positioned for long-term success. These companies know their customers and treat them as something more important than advertising targets. They also can claim strong and unusual brand loyalty.

The master of value investing is Warren Buffett. Read about his rise to superstardom in the finance world at www.dummies.com/extras/highpoweredinvestingaio.

Chapter 1

An Introduction to Value Investing

In This Chapter

▶ Defining value investing

▶ Brushing up on value investing math

▶ Deciding whether you're a value investor

*N*o doubt, somewhere during your investing career you've heard something about value investing. You may know it's "what Warren Buffett does," or maybe you've seen mutual funds described as "value-oriented." You have a pretty good idea what the word *value* means in ordinary English, but how does it apply to investing? What *is* value investing, anyway? This chapter answers that question and helps you decide whether you're a value investor at heart.

What Value Investing Is — And Isn't

Broadly defined, value investing is an investing approach and style blending many principles of business and financial analysis to arrive at good investing decisions. To be more specific, value investing is buying shares of a business as though you were buying the business itself. Value investors emphasize the intrinsic value of assets and current and future profits, and they pay a price equal to or less than that value.

Note the key phrases "buying . . . a business," "intrinsic value," and "pay a price equal to or less than that value." These are explicit tenets of the value investing approach, and underlying them all is the notion of conscious appraisal — that is, the idea of a rigorous and deliberate attempt to measure business value.

Obviously, price enters the value investor's appraisal, but notice that it appears at the end of the definition. Value investors go to the stock market only to buy their share of the business. They don't look at the market as a first indicator of whether or not to invest.

The following sections describe the principles and specific traits of value investing.

Important value investing principles

With the definition of value investing as an appetizer, here's a main course of value investing principles:

- ✔ **Buying a business:** Investing in stocks is really like buying a business. No matter how large or small the company you're investing in, you want to find out as much as possible about it before you commit your capital. You look at business fundamentals — the intrinsic value of assets and future profit prospects. You seek to understand the company's strategy and competitive advantages. You assess whether the stock price is at or below your appraisal. Engaging in these activities is the difference between value investing and most other investing forms that involve picking popular stocks to invest in.

- ✔ **Making a conscious appraisal:** If you were interested in buying a business and thought the corner hardware store looked attractive, how much would you be willing to pay for it? You'd likely be influenced by the sale price of other hardware stores and by opinions shared by neighbors and other customers. But you would still center your attention on the intrinsic economic value — the worth and profit-generation potential — of that business, and a determination of whether that value justified the price. Value investors refer to this process as an *appraisal* of the business. They rely on publicly available facts and figures to conduct a true numbers assessment — an appraisal of *intrinsic* value, not just the market price.

- ✔ **Going beyond the fundamentals:** Value investing begins with a basic analysis of business fundamentals (the metrics and measures that define business performance, like profitability, productivity, and capital structure), but it goes further: looking at a company's "story" to determine whether the fundamentals will hold up or, better yet, improve. The goal is not just to understand the *current* — but also the *future* — value of the business.

- ✔ **Ignoring the market:** As a general rule, value investors ignore the market and tune out brokers, advisors, and commentators. In other words, they focus on the company itself, *not* on the market, although they may listen to folks in the industry, customers, or people who know a lot about competitors. If value investors have done their homework right, what the market does to their stocks on a daily basis is irrelevant.

Note the use of the term *daily* in the preceding paragraph. External factors, like interest rates and economic crises, can affect stock prices. So paying some attention to the markets makes sense, especially in the long term. But daily fluctuations should be ignored. Value investors wait anywhere from a few years to forever for their investments to mature.

✓ **Questing consistency:** Most value investors like a high degree of consistency in returns, profitability, growth, asset value, management effectiveness, customer base, supply chain, and most other aspects of the business. Striving for consistency is an attempt to minimize risk and provide a margin of safety for the investment. Although value investors do invest in risky enterprises, the price paid for earnings potential must correctly reflect the risk. Consistency need not be absolute, but predictable performance is important.

The nitty-gritty of value investing's traits

Value investing isn't only about long-term investing, low price-to-earnings (P/E) ratios, cheap stocks, and diversification. And it isn't the opposite of investing in growth, as the popular "style boxes" applied to mutual funds would have you believe. The following list helps define value investing by providing a more nuanced explanation of its characteristics:

Book VII

Value Investing

✓ **Long-term investing:** Although most value investments *are* long-term, not all long-term investments are good values, and not all value investments are long-term. Indeed, as business cycles shorten, what is excellent today may soon look like a flash in the pan as technologies and marketplace acceptance change. Warren Buffett deals with this problem by avoiding technology stocks and other businesses he doesn't understand, but even businesses in other sectors see their products changing ever more quickly. Whereas once you could buy only one "flavor" of Tide detergent, dozens are now available, and they change all the time.

When buying a business, look long term, but realize that businesses and their markets change. Always be prepared to sell if assumptions change. Never forget the example of Eastman Kodak. Today's transition from a PC-based to a tablet- and cloud-based computing environment and the revival of domestic energy production also illustrate this point.

✓ **Low P/E ratios:** Oil companies, banks, food producers, steel companies — they all have had P/E ratios below market averages. But does that mean they're good values? Sometimes, but not always. Although a low P/E ratio can be part of the investing equation, especially when deciding when the stock price is right, it's far from the whole story. Banks traded with low P/Es and high dividend payouts, but that didn't protect them in the 2008–2009 Great Recession.

- **The opposite of growth:** You've no doubt heard some version of "Stock ABC is a growth stock, and stock XYZ is a value stock." So value stocks aren't supposed to grow? The truth is that for most companies, growth is an integral part of the business's value. In fact, the potential for growth defines some companies as good values, especially when current assets and perhaps even current business levels alone don't justify the price. Growth creates value.

- **Cheap stocks:** Above all, value investors seek to buy businesses at or below their appraised value in order to provide a *margin of safety.* Because even the best business appraisal is imprecise, value investors like to have a cushion for error in case things don't turn out as appraised.

- **Diversification:** You hear all the time about the importance of diversification when investing. But the masters of value investing have shown that diversification only serves to dilute returns. If you're doing the value investing thing right, *you are picking the right stocks at the right price,* so you don't need this extra insurance. That said, perhaps diversification isn't a bad idea until you prove yourself a *good* value investor. The point: Diversification *per se* is not a value investing technique.

A Short Math Primer for the Value Investor

Value investing is inherently analytical and numbers-based. To become fluent in the value investing thought process, you need to grasp a few key math principles. The following four lessons bubble up to the top as the most important; other principles and computational shortcuts can be found in the most recent edition of *Value Investing For Dummies* by Peter J. Sander and Janet Haley (Wiley).

Lesson 1: Time value of money

A dollar today isn't worth the same amount as a dollar yesterday, nor is it worth the same amount as a dollar tomorrow. Invested money appreciates with time.

An investment that has a present value of $10 will (hopefully) grow over time, so its future value will include the initial $10 plus all returns generated.

Invested money grows and compounds. You have the growth on the original investment, plus the return and growth on returns already earned. A snowball rolling downhill is a good analogy: As the ball gets bigger, it picks up ever-larger amounts of snow. How much? Compounding formulas, which are driven by rate of return and the amount of time, supply the answer. The following sections give you the scoop.

The magic compounding formula

Suppose that someone promises to pay you $10 five years from now. Are you $10 wealthier? No. To have $10 in the future, you need to put only some fraction of that $10 in the bank today. The exact fraction depends on the same factors that drive future value: rate of return and time. At 10 percent, you would need to deposit only $6.21 today to have $10 five years from now. Same concept, but this time, the approach is from the opposite direction. Instead of asking, "What is my $10 worth in five years?" you ask, "What would I need today to have $10 in five years?"

The fundamental time-value-of-money, or *compounding,* formula provides an indispensable foundation for value investors. In this formula, *FV* is future value, *PV* is present value, *i* is the interest rate (rate of return), and *n* is the number of years invested:

$$FV = PV \times (1 + i)^n$$

Book VII

Value Investing

When calculating the return for more than one year, you simply multiply *PV* by $(1 + i)$ factored by the number of years: 5 years, for example, is $PV \times (1 + i) \times (1 + i) \times (1 + i) \times (1 + i) \times (1 + i)$. Each $(1 + i)$ indicates another year of *compounding* interest. The *FV* of $10 invested at 10 percent interest over 5 years is

$$FV = \$10 \times (1 + 0.10)^5$$

or

$$\$10 \times (1.61), \text{ or } \$16.10$$

Understanding the formula, the dynamics, and the factors that drive or have the most influence on the result is just as important as memorizing the formula so that you can do lots of math problems. But you need a lot more than this formula to select stocks and be successful.

The power of i and n

The nature of the $(1 + i)^n$ expression in the formula produces a fascinating result. If *i* is small, no matter how large the *n*, the end result doesn't grow much. Likewise, if *n* is small, the value of *i* doesn't matter much. The power of compounding assumes its full glory (and your investments reach their full girth) as *i* and *n* get larger. The *and* is important! Value investors look for a few more *i* points of return *and* to hold the productive investment for as many *n* years as possible.

Because *n* is an exponent, it exerts the greatest power and influence on your investing portfolio. Time is an investor's best friend. As Warren Buffett says, "Time is the friend of the good business, and the enemy of the poor one." No wonder value investors tend to be long-term investors! Upshot: Find the best possible *i* and then let *n* happen.

Lesson 2: Rate of return done right

What the rate of return on an investment is depends on how it's calculated. Say that you have a friend who brags about buying a house for $150,000 and selling it ten years later for $600,000. She may call that a 300 percent return: an average of 30 percent per year. But when you evaluate the home purchase as an investment (compared to other investments), you must include the compounding effect to have an accurate, apples-to-apples comparison. If that $150,000 were invested ten years ago in such a way as to allow returns to compound, what rate of return would have produced $600,000?

To calculate true compounded, or geometric, rates of return, you use this formula, where *n* equals the number of years:

Compounded rate of return = [(Ending value/Beginning value)$^{(1/n)}$] − 1

In the example, $600,000/$150,000 is 4. Take 4 to the 1/10th power (use your calculator) and get 1.149. Subtract 1, and get 0.149, or 14.9 percent. Obviously, your friend's home purchase was still lucrative, but 14.9 percent return doesn't make headlines the way 30 percent would.

Lesson 3: How buying cheap really pays

The principle behind the maxim to "buy low and sell high" is obvious. But in the irrationally exuberant markets of 1999 and 2000, this old standard gradually gave way to "buy high, sell higher." Traders (and novice investors experiencing the markets for the first time) bought stocks because they were going up, defying value investing logic. The problem with this strategy is that the higher a price you pay for a stock, the *less likely* it is to achieve a high rate of return.

Suppose that a stock has an intrinsic value of $75. If you pay $100 for it, you're essentially betting that something good will happen to dramatically increase intrinsic value — or that some greater fool is out there to pay $110. But suppose that you were to buy the same stock at $50 as a *value play,* meaning that you think it's undervalued. The chance for a 50 percent return — reverting to intrinsic value — is much higher than with the at-value or overvalued $100 stock.

Follow these strategies:

- ✔ **Look for the opportunity to achieve superior *i*.** To get superior *i*, you buy a stock with good fundamentals, *including* growth. Doing so, you get the growth rate and, as a bonus, you also get the return to intrinsic value, which can increase returns substantially. The lower the price paid, the higher the likelihood of above-average returns.

- ✔ **Buy cheap.** Take a look at Table 1-1. Note how long-term profits jump as the rate of return grows beyond the market average and time has an opportunity to work its magic. An investor consistently beating the market by 2 percent achieves 20 percent greater return in 10 years ($3,106/$2,594), 43 percent in 20 years, and 72 percent in 30 years. An investor beating the market by even higher percentages would enjoy even greater returns.

Book VII

Value Investing

Table 1-1	Compounded Effects of Incremental Annual Returns, $1,000 Invested							
	1 Year	2 Years	5 Years	10 Years	15 Years	20 Years	30 Years	40 Years
Market return 10%	$1,100	$1,210	$1,611	$2,594	$4,177	$6,727	$17,449	$45,259
Beat the market by 2%	1,120	1,254	1,762	3,106	5,474	9,646	29,960	93,051
Beat by 6%	1,160	1,346	2,100	4,411	9,266	19,461	85,850	378,721
Beat by 10%	1,200	1,440	2,488	6,192	15,407	38,338	237,376	1,469,772

Lesson 4: Beware of large numbers

In investing, like life, some numbers are too good to be true and can't go on forever. Why not? In a word, *sustainability.* Suppose that your company has $100 million in sales today. To achieve a 30 percent growth rate, it has to achieve $130 million in sales next year, $169 million in sales in the second year, and so on.

To calculate future sales needed to sustain a particular percentage of growth, you use this formula:

$$FV = PV \times (1 + i)^{(n-1)}$$

You use $n - 1$ for the exponent because you're talking about growth *after* the first year. So for this example, future sales in 10 years = $100M \times (1 + 0.30)^9$, or $1.06 *billion.* In 20 years, that becomes $14.6 billion, with an average incremental growth of $764 million annually and about $4.4 billion in the 20th year.

If you're the sales manager assigned the glorious task of meeting shareholder expectations for growth, where can you find the incremental sales? Your company has conquered the world, but Earth is a small planet. Extraterrestrial markets are still pre-emergent. So what happens? Growth rates likely start to decline. Maintaining the growth rate requires greater and greater chunks of incremental dollars, which becomes increasingly difficult as markets become saturated.

Smart value investors recognize the increasing difficulty in maintaining high growth rates, so they project lower rates in years further out.

Over the years, there has been a noticeable trend toward diminished growth when a company hits the $20 billion, and then again the $40 billion, sales mark. Companies with $20 billion in sales and 20 percent growth rates suddenly see growth rates fall off the table and must buy growth through potentially harmful acquisitions. Why? Markets become saturated, and large incremental sales in core businesses become more difficult to find. Additionally, these companies, because of their sheer size, have more difficulty organizing themselves to execute dynamic and aggressive sales plans. The lesson: Conservative or even zero growth estimates are in order, especially beyond the five- to ten-year horizon.

Are You a Value Investor?

If you're asking yourself the same question, following are seven character traits found in most value investors. You don't have to display every one to be a good value investor, but you want to see yourself in at least some of them:

✔ **Bargain hunter:** You tend to check the price of the hotel across the street before you check into your chosen hotel.

✔ **Do-it-yourselfer:** You want to check the numbers yourself and build your own assessments as a way to better understand a company and its fundamentals.

✔ **Like margins of safety:** You actually slow down when it rains.

✔ **Long-term focus:** You'd rather make a lot of money slowly than a little flashy money in one day.

✔ **Business, not price, oriented:** You focus on the underlying business, not the price or superficial image.

✔ **Numbers oriented:** You're willing to investigate the numbers (or employ software packages that do this task for you) to find out about company business fundamentals and performance.

✔ **Contrarian:** You don't follow the crowd and purposefully stay away from what's exciting and hip (popular stocks aren't normally bargains).

Book VII

Value Investing

Chapter 2

A Value Investor's Guide to Financial Statements

In This Chapter

▶ Finding need-to-know info about a company's financial performance

▶ Reading annual reports, balance sheets, earnings statements, and cash flow statements

▶ Recognizing how accounting practices impact company valuation

*V*alue investors need to know about the companies they invest in. Fortunately, an enormous amount of financial information about companies is available and easy to find. Unfortunately, it's *too much* information for most of us. Worse, it's possible to present legally correct information in ways that make the true meaning hard to decipher.

The challenge is to acquire the right information about a company and then to convert it into actionable investing knowledge that

✔ Reveals the true character and dynamics of a business, its intrinsic value, and, more importantly, its *future* value

✔ Conclusively indicates whether the company is one you'd want to own and therefore would be a good place to invest

The goal of this chapter is to provide a guide for separating the wheat from the chaff, giving you a basic overview of financial statements and sharing some tricks of the trade and creative accounting practices that can and do deceive the inattentive investor from time to time.

What a Value Investor Looks For

Investing combines art and science. Quantifiable and unquantifiable facts are put into the pot, and the resulting stew is interpreted according to taste. The "science" is using numbers, facts, and formulas to measure business value.

The "art" is taking all the facts and measurements together and weighing them according to intuition and experience in order to judge a most likely outcome or set of outcomes.

Accessing facts and more facts

All value investors need facts about a company's financial and operating performance. These facts provide the foundation for value analysis and are available from the company itself as financial statements or from one of many information sources that repackage company-provided data for investor use:

- ✔ **Financial results:** Financial statements provide a picture of company assets, liabilities, earnings, and growth, and include the balance sheet, the earnings statement, and the statement of cash flows. Later sections of this chapter examine each of these documents in detail.

- ✔ **Financial trends:** Capturing and measuring change as it occurs over time is helpful. For the value investor, the key is to see where a company has been for the last five, ten, or more years. Unfortunately, good trend data, and especially good trend analysis and information that spans an adequate number of years, is hard to come by.

- ✔ **Ratios:** From raw financial data, a value investor can construct *ratios* — relationships between facts that offer clues to financial safety, quality, profitability, and efficiency, thus providing a clearer picture of company value. Find out more about ratios in Chapter 3 of Book VII.

- ✔ **Percentages:** Like ratios, percentages relate facts to other facts; they help paint a clearer picture of company performance and normalize data for comparison. Examples include return on equity (ROE), return on assets (ROA), and gross and net profit margin. ROE, ROA, and margins are explored in depth in Chapter 4 of Book VII.

- ✔ **Marketplace facts:** Because marketplace facts can often be a leading indicator of future financial results, you want to understand metrics like market share, customer base, and unit sales growth wherever possible. Unfortunately, companies aren't required to report such facts and often choose not to do so for competitive reasons. You have to rely on what a company does disclose and on market analysis done by third parties.

- ✔ **Operating facts:** Certain kinds of operational facts or metrics — like number of employees, stores, plants, or square feet as measures of size of operations — can be used as a measure of comparing companies or to support financial analysis. From there, you can determine *productivity* or *efficiency* — how much revenue, profit, and so on is produced per unit of operational activity. Hence, some people call these *unit* measures.

Seasoned investors find the right sources for the right information at the right time at the right cost, and use those sources consistently. You can gather the kind of information outlined in this section through the following sources:

- ✔ **Annual and quarterly reports:** Most U.S. companies are required by law to provide these reports. See the upcoming section "Poring over the annual report" for more information on the annual report.

- ✔ **Financial portals:** These gateways provide a great quick overview or update, usually with links to more detailed information. Yahoo!Finance (finance.yahoo.com) is one example.

- ✔ **Broker websites:** Many enable some investing analysis. The quality and ease of use of their tools varies, and in many cases you have to have an account to get the good stuff, such as professional analysis or stock screeners.

- ✔ **Research services:** Many are available to professional investors and offer huge packages of investment information, but at a high cost. Value Line (www.valueline.com) is the one moderately priced (under $1,000) research service designed especially for value investors.

Trial versions of the *Value Line Investment Survey,* including the more selective *Value Line 600* package, are available at a moderate price. Many libraries and brokerage firms with physical offices still carry the printed versions on their shelves. You may want to try this path before committing your dollars.

Book VII

Value Investing

The soft stuff

In addition to financial information, value investors want to get a sense of a company's management effectiveness and market position. To understand a company's products and markets, you can look at its website; its advertising and marketing campaigns; the company's own description of its products; and what you see, hear, and experience on the street.

You can gauge management effectiveness by looking at a company's financials and financial ratios, previous marketplace and financial decisions, business execution, acquisitions and mergers, public statements, and other "track record" items. Many value investors look at management ownership of company stock as a signal of management commitment. (You get a closer look at these intangibles in Chapter 4 of Book VII.)

The list of "soft stuff" sources is almost endless. Among the many sources are the following:

✔ **Financial and investing websites**, such as Yahoo!Finance, MarketWatch (www.marketwatch.com), TheStreet.com (www.thestreet.com), and The Motley Fool (www.fool.com), provide more thorough analysis generally from a value perspective.

✔ **Business journals**, including standbys like the *Wall Street Journal* and *Business Week,* as well as *Kiplinger's, Smart Money,* and *Money* magazines, offer high-quality appraisal of companies.

✔ **Trade journals and websites** that follow particular industries give you that industry's perspective.

✔ **Company conference calls with investors,** usually held at the time of quarterly earnings releases, relate the company's perspective.

Don't forget the power of "on the street" info. Particularly with consumer-focused companies, you can discover a lot about how a company markets its products, how well those products are selling, and even how employees feel about the company and its business by simply watching it do business. Also, when you read publications like the *Wall Street Journal,* don't go to the "Money & Investing" section first as most investors do — read the "Marketplace" section first.

Dissecting Financial Statements

A company's financial reports, described in the following sections, serve a critical function: to reflect the economic reality of a company and its business. Be aware, however, that although these reports are supposed to present a fair, unbiased view of company performance, a degree of latitude and flexibility exists in how reporting is actually done. This flexibility exists mostly in the valuation of assets and the determination of revenue and cost.

As a value investor, you need to be smart about what and how much to question in a financial report. The smart value investor knows what to look for in a statement and what levers a company's management can throw to convey a certain image. It's okay to be a skeptic, but it's probably not productive to dispute every figure in the report. As with so much else in life, focus on what's important.

Poring over the annual report

Annual reports, although they contain basic financial information, have become more of a marketing brochure. Value investors are better served by looking at what's known as a *Form 10-K* annual report, which is the version of the document required by the Securities and Exchange Commission (SEC). The 10-K is a longer, harder read, but it provides much more in-depth financial data, product and market data, and management discussion of the financials than does the standard annual report.

The best way to get 10-Ks reliably and quickly is to go to a company's "investor relations" website, but the SEC also has a website to make the required filings public: Electronic Data Gathering And Reporting (EDGAR) at `sec.gov/edgar.shtml`.

Most annual reports contain the elements that follow. From one company to the next, these elements won't look the same, be the same size, be in the same order, or contain the same information. But these pieces will likely be present in some form:

- **Highlights:** This section summarizes significant financial results: sales, earnings, and a few productivity measures key to a company's industry. Four or five years of history are often included.

- **Letter to shareholders:** This letter presents a chipper one- or two-page summary, usually from the CEO, describing the past year and the year ahead. Although some managers are frank in describing and confronting a company's difficulties, others are not. Look for clear language without panacean jargon or buzzwords; many investors also look for willingness to discuss bad stuff in these letters — a sign of management honesty and integrity.

- **Business summary:** This objectively worded section covers the business, its products, markets, competition, and factors like seasonality, patents, and international exposure that may affect the business. It's usually followed by a summary of the management team, which is in turn followed by a fairly detailed discussion of potential risks to the business. The business summary section is one of the best ways for an investor to gain business understanding.

- **Management's discussion and analysis:** This section usually begins with a management discussion and analysis of the company's financials. The discussion covers specific financial statement components, including sales, costs, expenses, assets, liabilities, liquidity, and perhaps market expansion risks.

- **The statements:** Several versions of consolidated financial data are presented. Financials invariably include the following:

  - The *balance sheet* shows all assets, liabilities, and owners' equity.

  - The *earnings statement* (also called the *income statement*) captures a company's performance over an interval of time. Pay attention to the sales or revenues, cost of those sales, other expenses, and the

Book VII

Value Investing

difference between sales and costs — gross profit, operating profit, and finally, net profit, or *earnings*.

- The *statement of cash flows* also captures company activity and performance over a time interval, but this time it's done in cash terms. (Head to the later section "Understanding the earnings statement" to see why cash and accounting flows can be different.)

Most reports also include a statement of shareholders' equity, a statement of working capital, or some other summary of changes in the financials.

✔ **Common size statements:** These are standard financial reports with all information presented as percentages. They're useful for comparing companies.

✔ **Notes:** This section contains more detail than the financial statements themselves and can give a lot of important detail or "color" to support the statements. This section also shows the accounting practice a company uses in preparing a statement, as well as one-time situations such as acquisitions, discontinued businesses, and asset write-downs — or changes in accounting methods.

✔ **Auditor's review:** This section provides concrete evidence of review and acceptance of a company's accounting and financial practices. Pay attention to the *exceptions.* The standard auditor's review is three paragraphs. If the words "qualified" or "adverse" creep into the third paragraph, or if there's a fourth paragraph, watch out.

Reading the balance sheet

A balance sheet is a listing of assets against the liabilities and equity that fund those assets, taken at a specific point in time. For investment and legal reporting purposes, these snapshots are generally taken at the end of each fiscal quarter and at fiscal year-end.

A core financial equation forms the heart of the balance sheet:

Assets = liabilities + owners' equity

A balance sheet must balance: For every asset dollar, a dollar must be contributed through either borrowing (increased liabilities) or additional funding by the owners (owners' equity).

The balance sheet can be a powerful indicator of business health. But keep in mind that it doesn't tell much about the future of the business or about future income. On a balance sheet, value investors and business analysts look for the following:

✔ The composition of assets, liabilities, and owners' equity (lots of inventory and little cash can be a bad sign)

✔ Trends (increasing debt and decreasing owners' equity — also bad)

✔ Quality (whether stated values reflect actual values)

Each of these examinations is done with an eye toward what the figure probably should be for a company in that line of business. A company like Starbucks, with frequent small cash sales, shouldn't have a large accounts receivable balance. A retailer should have sizeable inventories, but they shouldn't be out of line for the industry or category. A semiconductor manufacturer has a large capital equipment base but should depreciate it aggressively to account for technology change.

To determine whether balance sheet numbers are in line, most analysts apply specifically defined ratios to the numbers. Ratios serve to draw comparisons among companies and their industry. By doing so, they show whether performance is better or worse than industry peers. See Chapter 3 in Book VII for a discussion of ratio analysis.

The following sections go into more detail on assets and liabilities.

A swift kick in the assets

An *asset* is anything a company uses to conduct its business toward producing a profit. From an accounting standpoint, an asset must have value, produce a return for the business, be in the company's control, and be recordable. Following is a list of different assets:

✔ **Cash and cash equivalents:** Value investors like cash. Cash is security and forms the strongest part of the safety net that value investors seek. Value investors question a cash balance only if it appears excessive against the needs of the business. If a value investor sees an excess in cash, she's likely to ask "why?" Could the company not put that cash to better work elsewhere? Why isn't it being returned to shareholders? Most companies don't retain that much cash, but if they do, it becomes a red flag.

✔ **Accounts receivable:** *Accounts receivable* represent funds owed to the business, presumably for products delivered or services performed. As individuals, everyone likes to be owed money — until we're owed *too much* money. The same principle applies to businesses. You should be aware of situations in which companies aren't collecting on their bills or are using accounts receivable to create credit incentives for otherwise questionable customers to buy their product. Pay attention to the following:

- **The size of accounts receivable relative to sales and other assets:** Is a company extending itself too much to sustain or grow the business?

- **Trend:** Is the company continuously owed more and more, with potentially greater and greater exposure to nonpayment?

- **Quality of accounts receivable:** If accounts receivable balances grow, and particularly if large reserves show up on the earnings statement (as "allowance for doubtful accounts" or something similar), consider it a red flag.

✔ **Inventory:** *Inventory* is all valued material procured by a business and resold, with or without value added, to a customer. It's divided into *retail inventory* (goods bought, warehoused, and sold through stores) and *manufacturing inventory* (raw material, work in process, and finished goods inventory awaiting shipment). Companies live and die by their ability to effectively manage inventory. The key for most companies is to match inventory as closely as possible to sales. To measure inventory, look at *turnover* (annual sales divided by the dollar amount of the asset on the books). The greater the turnover, the more efficient the utilization of that asset.

✔ **Deferred taxes and other current assets:** Deferred taxes are essentially estimated taxes paid before a tax liability is actually determined. For the most part, you shouldn't worry about these items; seldom do they comprise more than 5 percent of stated assets.

✔ **Fixed assets:** Fixed assets include things that fall into the category of "property, plant, and equipment": land, buildings, machinery, fixtures, office technology, and similar items owned by the firm for productive use. To appropriately value fixed assets, you need to be familiar with the two basic types of depreciation: *straight-line depreciation,* in which an equal amount of asset value is expensed each year until the asset value reaches zero, and *accelerated depreciation,* in which the asset is expensed proportionately more in the early years of its life.

Depreciation is the leading difference between stated earnings and cash flows and can mean the difference between survival and failure for a company recording net income losses.

✔ **Investments:** Many companies commit surplus cash to more substantial long-term investments, which can serve many purposes: to achieve returns, to participate in the growth of a related or unrelated industry, or to eventually obtain control of the company. Favorable tax treatment of dividends and gains makes investing in companies still more attractive. Investment value is disclosed in the 10-K, but you need to read carefully to find the information. Watch out for declining fair values and particularly for large *gross unrealized losses* — future write-offs and asset value impairment loom large. Bottom line: Gauge the size of investments on the balance sheet, look for detail, and understand management's intent in making the investments.

✓ **Intangibles:** Also called "soft" assets, these assets don't have a physical presence but are critical in acquiring and maintaining sales and producing a competitive edge: patents, copyrights, franchises, brand names, and trademarks, for example.

Most companies classify assets as current or noncurrent. *Current assets* are short-term items generally held for a year or a business cycle. Think of current assets (especially cash) as the lifeblood of the business flowing to and from customers, to and from suppliers, and around to the different locations in the business operation to produce the greatest possible business and customer benefit. Conversely, *noncurrent assets* include longer-term fixed assets and a catch-all of other types of assets not normally vital to day-to-day operations.

To assign value to assets, look at three defining characteristics of any asset: size, trend, and quality. Table 2-1 is useful as a simple reference to convert reported asset values to liquidating value, a conservative base for intrinsic valuation (discussed in Chapter 4 of Book VII). Professionals may use evolved versions, but this table is still a handy tool.

Table 2-1	Valuing Balance Sheet Assets	
Type of Asset	*% Range of Liquidating Value to Book Value*	*Comments*
Cash, cash equivalents	100%	More is better. Watch out for the post-IPO "stash."
Accounts receivable	75 to 95%	Look at write-offs.
Inventory	50 to 75%	Less for businesses with high obsolescence exposure. Look at write-offs.
Fixed assets	1 to 50%	Depends on what kind of asset and where it is. Watch for obsolescence.
Intangibles	1 to 90%	Usually lower for acquisitions, higher for patents and trademarks. Fast depreciation (really, amortization) is better.

Liabilities: Does the company owe money?

Liabilities are fairly straightforward: If you owe, you owe. Although different things can be done to state asset values differently, the same doesn't happen with liabilities. The effect of liabilities on a company's intrinsic value is straightforward.

Excessive use of debt signals potential danger if things don't turn out the way a company expects them to. It reduces flexibility, and, unlike assets, the value of which may be estimated and thus may have a real value that's somewhat less than stated, liabilities are always "real" — that is, the company is truly liable for the total amount stated in a liability figure. Finally, value investors don't like surprises, and a company with uncertain prospects and a lot of debt may not make it onto their list. Industry standards and common sense apply to debt-to-equity ratios.

Like assets, liabilities come in two basic flavors: current and long term. Current liabilities are liabilities for which payment is due normally in less than a year. Long-term liabilities are long-term debts. Here are the details:

- ✔ **Payables (current liabilities):** Almost every corporation has *payables,* money owed to others for products purchased or services rendered. The liability is created when the service or product arrives; a cash payment follows to discharge the liability. Nearly all companies maintain a regular balance of current accounts payable, interest payable, and the like. If payment is received in advance, as with a deposit, the unearned portion is tracked as a liability.

  Value investors don't need to take much note of current liabilities other than perhaps to spot large changes or trends. Investors should also realize that current liabilities aren't necessarily a bad thing and can result in higher effective returns on ownership capital with relatively low cost and risk.

- ✔ **Long-term liabilities:** Long-term corporate liabilities represent contracted commitments to pay back a sum of money over time with interest. As with short-term liabilities, you don't need to look too closely at the quality of these long-term liabilities, or even the amount, if it's reasonable by previous company or industry standards. Trends can be important, however. Increased reliance on long-term debt may be a sign of trouble. In addition, a company constantly changing, restructuring, or otherwise tinkering with long-term debt may be sending tacit trouble signals.

Understanding the earnings statement

Earnings are *the* driving force and macro indicator of a company's success. Used by investors of all kinds, earnings statements are among the most widely examined of company publications. For value investors, earnings statements are indispensable. The following list highlights important attributes to look for in an earnings statement:

- ✔ **Growth:** The long-term growth of a stock price is driven by growth in the business. The value investor works to obtain a deep understanding of business growth, growth trends, and the quality of growth. The value investor assesses growth and growth patterns, judges the validity of growth reported, and attempts to project the future.

- ✔ **Consistency:** Long-term growth should be sustainable and consistent. A big pop in earnings one year followed by malaise for the next two does not paint a pretty picture. Consistency in sales and sales growth, profit margins and margin growth, and operating expense and expense trends is highly prized. The less consistency, the more difficult it is to predict the future five or ten years and beyond, and the less attractive a company looks to value investors.

- ✔ **Comparative components and trends:** Value investors look at individual lines in the earnings statement, not just the bottom line. Improving gross margins — especially sustained improvement — signals strong business improvement. Value investors also constantly compare companies in like industries. Gross margins of competing computer manufacturers, for instance, tell a lot about who has the best market position, production and delivery process, and business model.

As you examine earnings statements, keep in mind that they're not always broken down the same way. Although the bottom line is the bottom line, the intermediate steps may be different. One company's operating earnings may include marketing costs, while another's may not, for example. In addition, two companies that appear (and even are classified) in the same industry may have differences large enough to raise caution. The upshot: You must understand businesses before comparing them.

The bottom line and other lines

The *bottom line* refers to the net earnings or income after all expenses, taxes, and extraordinary items are factored in. The bottom line is the final net measure of all business activity. Other important lines in the earnings statement reveal key factors and trends in the business. You'll see these lines or items in various forms on financial statements depending on the statement and sometimes the industry.

There are many ways to measure income. Among them are

- ✔ **Gross profit:** Gross profit (simply the sales minus the direct cost of producing the company's product or service) is the purest indicator of business profitability. (Direct cost includes labor, material, and expenses directly attributable to producing the product.) Value investors closely watch gross margin trends as an indicator of market dominance, price control, and future profitability.

Book VII

Value Investing

✔ **Operating profit:** Operating profit is gross profit minus *period expenses* — overhead or marketing costs not directly attributable to product production. Operating profit gives a more complete picture of how the business is performing on a day-to-day basis. Period expenses typically include selling, general, and administrative expenses (SG&A), and amortization. Typically excluded are financing costs, such as interest and taxes, as well as items deemed extraordinary.

✔ **Net income:** This represents the net result of all revenues, expenses, interest, and taxes.

The top line

Sales and revenues make up the *top line* of any business and represent accounting dollars generated for business products sold or services performed. With business-to-business (b-to-b) businesses or those selling into a distribution channel (a wholesaler or retailer), revenue recognition can be more complex.

Accounting revenue is normally recorded at the time of sale or service completion. (With accrual accounting, it doesn't matter whether the company has been *paid* yet.) But in some situations, the delivery process isn't complete, and that may call revenue validity into question. If a distributor doesn't have to pay until a product is resold, or if the manufacturer is still required to perform significant services, such as configuration, installation, or even warranty work, a sale to a distributor or customer may be exaggerated if fully recorded as a sale. Similarly, sales to subsidiaries or affiliated companies shouldn't be considered sales. Sales for consideration other than money, such as advertising exposure, may also be suspect.

But for the most part, sales are sales. In many businesses, such as transportation or utilities, they may be called *revenues,* but they're the same thing. Occasionally you'll see an allowance for returns broken out; otherwise, you can usually safely assume that the allowance for returns is included in the sales figure as a negative amount.

When comparing sales figures or projecting trends, compare apples to apples. If significant acquisition, divestiture, or extraordinary change occurs in the business, make sure to take it into account.

Cost of goods sold

Cost of goods sold, or CGS, is the cost of acquiring goods and raw material plus labor and direct overhead expended to add value for sale, and it's an important driver of business success. For all but a few companies with high intellectual property or service content, CGS is the largest piece of the revenue pie. CGS varies widely by industry and industry cost structure, making apples-to-apples comparisons and trend analysis especially critical to effective business appraisal.

Different accounting treatments can affect CGS. LIFO (last in, first out) and FIFO (first in, first out) are different ways of valuing balance sheet inventory and can affect CGS. Be careful to understand which accounting method is used before comparing companies and watch for changes in accounting methods that may shift reporting bias.

Gross margin

Gross margin, or *gross profit,* is simply the sales minus the cost of goods sold. It is the basic economic output of the business before overhead, marketing, and financing costs enter the picture. Gross profit takes on added meaning when taken as a percentage. This percentage — and trends in the percentage — speaks volumes for the health and direction of the business.

Operating expenses

Every company incurs *operating expenses* (also called *indirect costs*): the costs of doing business that are not directly related to producing and selling individual units of product or service. Standard types of operating expenses include the following:

- ✓ **Selling, general, and administrative (SG&A) costs:** SG&A includes marketing and selling costs, including advertising; sales and sales forces; marketing and promotion campaigns; and a host of other administrative and corporate expenses such as travel, websites, office equipment, and so on. Many investors use SG&A as a barometer of management effectiveness — a solid management team keeps SG&A expenses in check.

- ✓ **Research and development:** Manufacturing and technology companies in particular need to invest in future products. Because these investments occur long before product production, and because many of them never pan out into saleable products, companies are allowed to expense research and development (R&D) as a period expense. Appropriate levels of R&D expense vary widely by industry.

  Because you won't know the details of R&D expenditures, watch the trend and changes in R&D as a percent of sales. Increasing R&D percentages reflect an increasing cost of doing business and possibly ineffective R&D; decreasing R&D as a percent may reflect sacrificing the future for the present. Also note that companies without a significant R&D effort may not report it as a separate line. In some financial statements, it's called *product development,* or it may be bundled into some other expense line.

- ✓ **Depreciation:** In addition to affecting inventory (refer to the earlier section "A swift kick in the assets"), depreciation can have a net effect on property, plant, and equipment as an earnings statement item. Depreciation (referring to physical fixed assets) and amortization (referring to intangible assets) represent the accountant's assignment of the cost of a long-lived asset to specific business periods and are usually broken out on the earnings statement, but they may be buried in a consolidated SG&A or other operating-expense line.

✔ **Impairments, investments, and other write-downs:** When the value of an asset changes significantly in the eyes of management, a company can elect to take a write-down recognizing the change. The *write-down* shows up as a decrease in asset value on the balance sheet for the asset category involved and as a (usually) one-time expense somewhere on the earnings statement. Write-downs are normally reported as a separate line and are well-documented in the notes. Write-down behavior provides insight into management behavior and effectiveness as well as overall business consistency. For value investors, knowing the detail or amount may not be as important as knowing the pattern.

Understanding write-offs and one-time charges when building intrinsic value models is critically important (more in Chapter 4 of Book VII). Many intrinsic value models base forward projections on the most recently reported net income numbers. Most financial portals and automated investment analysis tools simply take the latest year's earnings figure from a database. If that figure was significantly reduced (or enhanced) by extraordinary items, a large (and compounded!) error in the intrinsic value assessment can occur.

✔ **Goodwill:** Goodwill assets are obtained by acquiring other companies and arise when more is paid for an acquired company than it is worth in hard assets. Acquired goodwill assets often have real value — brand equity, customer base, and so forth — but more often than not, the amount booked exceeds this value, and goodwill is used as a plug-in figure to account properly for the purchase.

Like depreciation and impairments, goodwill amortizations are accounting phenomena and don't result in a cash transaction. Goodwill amortization affects earnings, not cash flow. You can decide how you want to appraise goodwill, but conservatism is usually best.

Operating income

Operating income is simply sales minus cost of goods sold, minus operating expenses. Because it includes noncash amortizations, it is a fully loaded view of operating performance in the business. If you closely observe the effects of amortizations, special write-downs, and accounting changes, you can better understand operating income and operating income trends.

Interest and taxes

Interest income comes primarily from cash and short-term investments held on the balance sheet, while interest expense comes from short- and long-term debt balances. Interest reporting is usually done as *net* interest — that is, by combining interest income and expense into a net figure.

Taxes are quite complicated, and the details go beyond the scope of this book. An income tax provision normally is recorded as a single line item on the earnings statement, consisting of federal, state, and local taxes put together.

You don't need to pay too much attention to these areas except where interest expenses are disproportionately high and growing. In most situations, value investors treat taxes as a given, unless the company has recently been through tough times and has a lot of write-offs to carry forward. When that happens, taxes can be artificially low for a while; investors must take into account what will happen when levels return to normal.

Income from continuing operations

What results from netting out interest and taxes from operating income is *income from continuing operations*. This figure gives a good picture of company performance, from not only an operating perspective but also a financial one. Income from continuing operations tells shareholders what their investments are returning after everyone, including Uncle Sam and his brethren, is paid.

Extraordinaries

Extraordinary items are tied to unusual and nonrecurring events. *Unusual* events aren't related to typical activities of the business, at least going forward. *Nonrecurring* events aren't expected to occur again. Extraordinary items commonly result from business closures ("discontinued operations"); major restatements due to changes in accounting rules, debt restructurings, or other complex financial transactions; layoffs and other employee transactions; and so on. Extraordinary items generally are *not* supposed to include asset write-downs (such as receivables, inventory, or intangibles), foreign currency gains or losses, or divestitures.

Book VII

Value Investing

Some companies interpret the accounting rules and guidelines more strictly than others, so watch for extraordinary expenses that aren't so extraordinary. If, for example, earnings are consistently a dollar a share each quarter with a consistent $4 year-end write-off year after year, the true value generated by the business is closer to zero than four.

There you have it: Net income

Sales minus CGS, minus operating expenses, minus interest and taxes, minus or plus extraordinaries gives you a company's net income, sometimes referred to as "income attributable to common shareholders" or some similar phrase. Net income represents the final net earnings result of the business on an accounting — not necessarily a cash — basis.

Net earnings are usually divided by the number of shares outstanding to arrive at *earnings per share* — the common barometer heard in nearly all financial reports. Most analysts and investors focus on *diluted* earnings per share, which figures in outstanding employee stock options and other equity grants beyond actual shares outstanding in the share markets.

Reading cash flow statements

A business needs cash to operate. A business generating positive cash flow is much healthier than one bleeding cash and borrowing or taking cash from investors to stay afloat. But because of noncash items, earnings statements don't give a complete cash picture. So value investors use the statement of cash flows as a standard part of the financial statement package. The statement of cash flows tracks cash obtained in, or used for, three separate kinds of business activity: operations, investing, and financing.

Cash flow from operations

Similar to operating income (described earlier in this chapter), cash flow from operations tells you what cash is generated from, or provided by, normal business operations, and what cash is consumed, or used in, the business. Cash flow information contains these figures:

- **Net income from continuing operations:** Calculating cash flow from operations starts with this number.

- **Adjustments for depreciation and amortization:** Depreciation and amortization are accounting, not cash, transactions. So here is where depreciation and amortization dollars are added back in — dollars that came out of accounting income but had no corresponding cash payment.

- **Changes in working capital items:** Working capital items include accounts receivable and inventory, and *changes* in these items either produce or consume cash. Getting used to the logic takes a while, but a positive number here means that the item *sourced* or *generated* cash; a negative number means that the item *used* cash. A negative figure for inventory, for example, means that the business used cash to buy more inventory. A positive figure means that inventory balances were reduced, freeing up cash for other uses.

- **Total cash flow from operating activities:** Essentially, this is cash generated by ongoing day-to-day business activities. Negative operating cash flow is a dismal sign — the company is consuming capital just to execute its day-to-day operations.

Cash flow from investing activities

The second section of the statement of cash flow shows, among other things, cash used for investments in the business, including capital expenditures for plants, equipment, and other longer-term product assets. While cash flow from operations should be positive, cash flow from investing activities is often negative because growing companies need more physical investments — property, plant, and equipment (PP&E) — to sustain growth.

By comparing net cash flows from operations and net cash flows from investing activities, you can get a first glance at whether a business is productive and healthy. If positive cash flows from operations exceed negative cash flows from investing activities, the business produces more cash than it consumes. But don't jump to a favorable conclusion too quickly; a surplus cash situation must be sustained to be meaningful.

Free cash flow

Earn income, pay for costs of doing business, and what's left over is yours to keep as an owner. What's left over is the free cash flow. Pretty simple. Free cash flow is a good indication of what a company really has left over after meeting obligations, and thus could theoretically return to shareholders. For that reason, free cash flow is sometimes called *owners' earnings* — earnings that can actually be withdrawn by the owners as beneficiaries of the business.

Cash flow from financing activities

Financing activities tell where a firm has obtained capital in the form of cash to fund the business. Proceeds from the sale of company shares or bonds (long-term debt) are a *source* of cash. If a company pays off a bond issue, pays a dividend, or buys back its own stock, that's a *use* of cash for financing.

Book VII

Value Investing

A consistent positive cash flow from financing activities indicates excessive dependence on credit or equity markets. Typically, this figure oscillates between negative and positive. A big positive spike reflects a big bond issue or stock sale. In such a case, check to see whether the resulting cash is used for investments in the business (probably okay) or to make up for a shortfall in operating cash flow (probably not okay). If the generated cash flows go straight to the cash balance, you should wonder why a company is selling shares or debt just to increase cash, although often the reasons are difficult to know. Perhaps an acquisition?

The Games Companies Play

Accounting rules, while improved in recent years, still allow enough flexibility to give companies latitude to manage their business and decide what to recognize, and when and how. Understanding company accounting and reporting policies — and conservative versus aggressive bias — has always been considered a good value investing practice.

This section explores some occasional accounting practices used to make business results look better. It's called *accounting stretch,* and as a value investor, you need to be aware of it. Sensitive stretch points occur in both revenue and expense portions of the earnings statement, as the following sections explain.

Revenue stretch

Revenue recognition problems stem from two major sources. The first involves timing, where revenues for long-term deals and contracts may be recognized prematurely. The second involves customer financing or price adjustments, where a customer receives an incentive or is otherwise enabled to buy a product but revenue is overstated by not recognizing the downside of such incentives.

Following are some of the ways companies can manipulate revenue and revenue timing:

- **Contractual revenues, forward sales, service fees:** Accounting principles state that revenue can be recognized for substantial performance of delivering a good or a service. Yet cases abound where companies, perhaps selling a three-year forward service agreement with a product, or perhaps an insurance policy, bundle downstream revenue into the original sale.

- **Channel stuffing:** Manufacturers who distribute through retail or other channels often sell as much as they can downstream into the next channel "tier," only to turn around and reverse the sale with a return or a credit for a price drop somewhere down the line.

Today, some companies don't recognize revenue until the product is *sold through* — that is, sold to an end customer. Others recognize the revenue but with an appropriate reserve for returns. Look for companies that specifically state this practice in their financial statement notes. And avoid companies with large fiscal year-end revenue jumps matched by weak subsequent quarter performance — unless seasonal factors suggest the pattern is normal.

- **Related party revenue:** Some companies mishandle revenue from closely aligned third parties — or even from sales to subsidiaries or other "controlled" entities. Related party revenue is common in the tech industry or other businesses with strong partner relationships or lots of subsidiaries. Accounting and SEC rules are pretty clear about recognizing revenue only when a transaction is done at arms' length — that is, without being controlled in any way by the company recognizing the revenue.

✔ **Creating sales with financing:** An increasing number of companies have resorted to financing their customers as a way to win deals, win customers, and bolster revenues. Although this has been common in department store retailing for years through store credit cards, it takes on new meaning when, for example, billions are lent to single customers to buy telecommunications equipment. These sales may turn out not to be real, and in some cases, the sales may be real but are artificially brought forward, creating gaps in subsequent periods.

To detect these issues, pay attention to revenue recognition policies (usually Note 1 of the statements) and unusual increases or bumps in sales, receivables, or allowances against receivables.

✔ **Warranty costs:** Typically, a reserve for warranty should be set aside for every product shipped or service completed. But companies can change the amount set aside. This item is often invisible because most companies don't break out warranty costs in detail.

Inventory valuation

How inventory is managed — whether LIFO (last in, first out) or FIFO (first in, first out) — impacts inventory valuation. LIFO typically represents the more conservative valuation, particularly in an inflationary environment, because recognized costs are relatively higher. However, LIFO also results in relatively *lower* inventory valuations. Value investors should understand inventory valuation policy, normally disclosed in Note 1, particularly where an accounting policy is changing or has been changed. If a company switches from LIFO to FIFO, watch out.

Book VII

Value Investing

Expense stretch

Expenses, or indirect costs, are easier to stretch because there are more different kinds of them, and typically little detail is given on the consolidated statements. Fortunately, this area has received considerable scrutiny, especially options and amortization expenses, so it's less of an arena for abuse than in the past.

Options

Compensating employees with stock options became much more in vogue toward the end of the 20th century. Investors got very upset about this practice because not only were companies inflating earnings by not recognizing option expenses, but many corporate staffers were getting fantastically wealthy on the resulting awards.

For a long time, accounting rules required only disclosure — not incorporation into actual statements. So option grants and their theoretical expense were noted somewhere deep in the statements, but not in the results themselves. Finally in 2004, that changed: The Financial Accounting Standards Board (FASB) implemented a revised Statement 123, requiring expensing and prescribing a formula for valuing the options. So now, options can still be abused by greedy or irresponsible management teams, but at least investors will see the results more clearly.

R&D and marketing costs

A few companies have been caught deferring certain R&D and marketing costs into the future by *capitalizing* them: recording them as an asset when incurred, rather than an expense, and then depreciating or amortizing the asset over future years. Accounting rules are fairly firm, but not rock solid, around the notion that most R&D expenses should be incurred as they arise due to the uncertain nature of their outcome. There's no way to tell upfront whether an R&D effort will turn into a marketable product. However, where R&D is significant as a proportion of total product expense, as with software, portions are allowed to be capitalized.

Depreciation and amortization

Choice of depreciation and amortization methods — and time periods — can influence earnings and balance sheet statements. More aggressive depreciation results in lower earnings and conservative asset valuations, but the pressure to "meet the numbers" on earnings may lead to less aggressive depreciation. Firms have the choice of method (straight line versus accelerated) and time frame (number of years) to manage their financial reporting.

Depreciation and amortization methods are among the most clearly disclosed of financial statement "levers." Note 1 disclosures are complete with both method and time period, although frequently a mix of different methods and time periods is used for different assets. Look for how hard assets are depreciated and how goodwill is amortized.

The value investor should look for conservatism, consistency (as opposed to frequent changes), and common sense. If a company suddenly switches to longer depreciation schedules without adequate explanation, look out.

Pension costs and assets

Pension fund accounting can be another source of stretch earnings in a pinch. Suppose that a plan is targeted to reach a certain funding level in ten years. Management has diligently set money aside with an assumption of a 7 percent return in order to achieve that long-term goal. Now suppose that management decides that an 8 percent return is more likely. Because the existing balance is bigger than it needs to be to meet the obligation, the plan is said to be overfunded. Some or all of that overfunding can be recognized as income, inflating reported earnings. Large old-line companies — the IBMs and AT&Ts of the world — are more susceptible to pension stretch than newer companies, which use the 401(k) approach, where the company directly carries few or no pension assets.

Pension information is usually deep in the Notes section. Check the fair value of pension assets, the projected benefit obligation, and the difference between the two. Look at the assumptions, and look for changes in accounting policy, especially those not mandated by accounting standards bulletins.

Write-offs: Big baths

Bundling large costs into extraordinary write-offs clears the books of bad assets and bad decisions in order to increase earnings in the immediate future. Generally accepted accounting principles (GAAP) are fairly specific in indicating that write-offs must be unusual and nonrecurring, but these terms are subject to interpretation. Are layoffs, plant closings, and restructurings unusual and nonrecurring? Depends on the company. They're almost annual events for automakers and other smokestack industries.

Be aware of the reasons for and any regularities in such write-offs. Have they gotten to be a habit? Are they actually a cost of doing business in disguise?

Chapter 3

Using Ratios as a Valuation Tool

As you gaze through the myriad numbers in financial statements, pretty soon eye and brain fatigue set in. After all, what do the numbers *tell* you? How do you take away any meaning from them — and quickly, because you don't have all day to address every number for every business you look at?

Are accounts receivable in line or not? Is the company's inventory scaled properly to the size of the business? What about fixed assets, debt, and profitability? Is the company using capital efficiently? And does its stock price make sense? How do you know? This chapter explains how to glean useful information from all the data. The secret: using ratios as a handy tool to make more sense of the numbers.

The Basics of Using Ratios

Applying ratios to numbers is like using a lens to bring them into clearer focus. Ratios explain the relationship between two or more numbers, thus providing you with scale and context.

For example, one major U.S. construction products manufacturer reported $204.1 million in inventory in 2012. That means little until measured against its $687.2 million in sales the same year. The inventory-to-sales ratio of 0.297 puts company raw data into perspective, tells a story, and provides a standard for comparison with other companies and the industry. And it tells the trends — favorable or unfavorable. The company in question had a 2011 ratio of 0.299, suggesting that the amount of inventory required to support sales was roughly unchanged from 2011 to 2012. If the ratio had risen substantially, that would have indicated relatively poor business performance.

Inventory-to-sales is one of dozens of standard ratios. Each ratio by itself provides a clue into some facet of business performance. Taken together as a collection, ratios provide a clearer total picture of a company for the investor to interpret. The following sections list ratio resources and explain what value investors look for when they use ratios in their analyses.

Identifying ratio resources

A great deal of comparative industry ratio data is available to professional financial and credit analysts, but they pay hefty subscription fees to get it. The challenge is finding that information for free (or nearly so). Here are some sources of ratio data and comparison:

- ✔ **Free:** Yahoo!Finance (`finance.yahoo.com`) and similar investing portals provide some ratios and limited comparison tools.

- ✔ **For a modest fee:** At the time of this writing, little is available for the ratio-hungry investor to buy. One source is VentureLine (`www.ventureline.com`), where, for $5.95 to $8.95 (depending on the number purchased), you can purchase an analysis of chosen companies, or for $13.95 to $17.95, you can purchase a fairly complete rundown for a particular industry, such as auto manufacturing. This product provides five years' worth of data, making trend analysis practical. Although the purchases can add up if you invest in a lot of companies or industries, this tool is worth considering if you're doing a lot of ratio analysis.

- ✔ **More expensive:** Value Line Investment Survey (`www.valueline.com`) offers a window to many key ratios. Value Line doesn't present a lot of ratios but does give a lot of history, which can be better. The standard Value Line Investment Survey subscription costs $598 per year but offers a lot beyond ratio analysis.

If you have access to Dun & Bradstreet (`business.dnb.com`) or Standard & Poor's (`www.standardandpoors.com`) industry financial comparisons, don't hesitate to use these rich, complete, and up-to-date resources. They may be out of reach of the average investor due to cost. If you work with a broker or financial advisor, you may get access to some of these services for free.

Using ratios in your analysis

What does a value investor look for when analyzing ratios?

- ✔ **Intrinsic meaning:** What does the ratio tell you? If the debt-to-equity ratio is 3 to 1, the company has a lot of debt. If the inventory-to-sales ratio is greater than 1, the company turns its inventory less than once per year. A price-to-earnings (P/E) ratio of 50 implies a 2 percent return on invested capital ($1 returned per $50 invested). These numbers tell you something without looking at any comparisons or trends.

✔ **Comparisons:** For many analysts (especially credit analysts) trying to get a picture of a company's health, comparative analysis is the most important use of ratios. A ratio acquires more meaning when it's compared to direct competitors, the company's industry, or much broader standards, like the S&P 500. A profitability measure, such as gross profit margin, reported at 25 percent tells more when direct competitors are at 35 percent plus. Analysts make similar comparisons with asset utilization, financial strength, and valuation ratios.

✔ **Consistency:** The hallmark of good management, as well as of an attractive long-term investment, is the consistency of results delivered. If profit margins are consistent and changing at a consistent rate, the company is predictable — and most likely in control of its markets. Inconsistent ratios reflect on inconsistent management, competitive struggles, and cyclical industries, all of which diminish a company's intrinsic value.

✔ **Trends:** Better than consistency alone is consistency with a favorable trend. Growing profit margins, return on equity, asset utilization, and financial strength are all very desirable, particularly if valuation ratios (P/E and so on) haven't kept pace. Value investors who study trends carefully have information that most investors don't have.

Book VII

Value Investing

Key Ratios, Classified and Identified

The following sections explore the different kinds of ratios and their use in value investing. Ratios can be divided into four classifications: asset productivity ratios, financial strength ratios, profitability ratios, and valuation ratios. The following sections identify the most important ratios within each classification.

Asset productivity ratios

Asset productivity ratios describe how effectively business assets are deployed. They typically look at sales dollars generated per unit of resource. Resources can include accounts receivable, inventory, fixed assets, and occasionally other tangible assets. Similar analysis may also be done not just for financial assets but also for operational assets like square footage, employees, number of facilities, and airplane seat miles.

Receivables turnover

Receivables turnover measures the size of unpaid customer commitments to a company. Specifically, it measures how many times a year this asset *turns over* — that is, is cleared out and replaced by similar obligations from other customers. Rapid turnover, not lingering old debts, is what you want to see. Here's the formula:

Receivables turnover = sales ÷ accounts receivable

Accounts receivable is a resource at a company's disposal like anything else and must be paid for, essentially, by sacrificing cash that otherwise would be available to fund some other part of the business. A company selling direct to consumers with cash sales or bank credit card sales will have lower receivables turnover than an industrial supplier. Watch for consistency and compliance with normal billing policy for the industry.

Average collection period

A slightly different way of looking at receivables is to show the average number of days that a given receivable dollar lives on the books. To calculate this ratio, which is also sometimes called *days' sales in receivables*, you use this formula:

Average collection period = 365 ÷ receivables turnover

If, based on industry comparisons or stated billing cycles, the collection period is higher than it should be (or growing), watch out. The company may be losing control of its collections or selling to customers with questionable credit.

Inventory turnover

Inventory turnover works like receivables turnover, only you plug in balance sheet inventory in place of receivables. Here's the formula:

Inventory turnover = sales ÷ inventory

As with receivables turnover, the higher the number, the better. High numbers indicate that raw materials, work in progress, and finished goods are flying onto and off of shelves rapidly. Less dust collects on less stuff in fewer warehouses, and less cash is tied up in inventory. Also, the risk of obsolescence and write-offs is less, as is, in many businesses, the risk of markdowns to clear inventory.

Fixed asset turnover

The fixed asset turnover ratio is straightforward:

Fixed asset turnover = sales ÷ fixed assets

All else being equal, the company that produces the most sales or revenue per dollar of fixed assets wins.

Total asset turnover

Like the fixed asset turnover ratio, the total asset turnover ratio is straightforward:

Total asset turnover = sales ÷ total assets

Here you get a bigger picture of asset productivity as measured by the generation of sales. For the first time, intangible assets are included. Again, industry norms form the benchmark. Comparing a railroad to a software company doesn't make sense.

Nonfinancial productivity ratios

Operational or capacity utilization ratios can be quite interesting yet sometimes hard to find or apply. The raw data often isn't available in company statements or published reports. Calculated ratios are even harder to find, although Value Line and other analysis services make a point of presenting certain nonfinancial operating data. These measures vary by industry, but here are some examples:

- **Sales per employee:** This ratio tells you how productive a company is in regard to investments in human resources. It's worth a look in almost all industries, particularly those that are labor intensive such as retail, transportation, and other service industries.

- **Sales per square foot:** This ratio is especially important for retail and similar businesses where occupancy investments are large and sales can be tied directly to them.

- **Average selling price (ASP):** Many financial reports don't present the number of units sold because they don't have to — and they want to keep selling prices secret. But sometimes this data is available (for example, from Boeing and other very-large-ticket manufacturers), and it can be quite revealing as to the direction of a business.

- **Industry specials:** Airlines and airline investors pay close attention to seat miles and revenues per seat mile flown. Railroads may look at revenue per track mile or car mile. Other service businesses, such as banks and mail-order retail, may look at sales or revenue per *customer*.

Financial strength ratios

The following set of ratios goes by many names (liquidity, solvency, financial leverage), but all the ratios point to the same thing: What is a business's financial strength and position? What is its capital structure? Value investors first look at financial strength ratios for obvious danger; then they base intrinsic value analysis on business-strength and market-strength measures like productivity and profitability.

Current and quick ratios

These commonly used liquidity ratios help evaluate a company's ability to pay its short-term obligations. Here's the formula:

Current ratio = current assets ÷ current liabilities

The current ratio includes all current assets, but because inventory is often difficult to turn into cash, at least for a reasonable price, many analysts remove it from the equation to arrive at a *quick* ratio. The quick ratio emphasizes coverage assets that can be quickly converted to cash:

Quick ratio = (current assets − inventory) ÷ current liabilities

Another ratio, *cash-to-debt,* is often used. It takes a still more conservative view of coverage assets (cash only) and a clearer view of what needs to be covered (total debt, including current and long-term portions).

The traditional thinking is that the higher the ratio, the better off the company. Greater than 2:1 for the current ratio or 1:1 for the quick ratio is good and safe; less than 2:1 or 1:1 is a sign of impending problems meeting obligations.

Debt-to-equity and debt-to-total-assets

Sometimes called *solvency* or *leverage* ratios, this set measures what portion of a firm's resources, or assets, are provided by the owners versus provided by others. The two most common ratios used to assess solvency and leverage are *debt-to-equity* and *debt-to-total-assets.* Here's the formula for debt-to-equity; note that current liabilities, such as accounts payable, typically are not included:

Debt-to-equity = total debt ÷ owners' equity

Here's the formula for debt-to-assets:

Debt-to-total-assets = total debt ÷ total assets

Making a sweeping statement about what these ratios should be for a given company is difficult. When a company has more debt than equity (debt-to-equity > 1 or debt-to-total-assets > 0.5), yellow flags fly. But again, industry comparisons are important. Economic value achieved should exceed the cost and risk incurred with the debt. Sounds good in theory, but precise appraisal can be complex. As with liquidity measures, solvency measures probably deliver a stronger signal for what *not* to buy than what to buy.

Cash flow ratios

Because cash is really the lifeblood of a business, financial strength assessments typically look at these ratios:

✔ **Overall cash flow ratio:** This powerful ratio tells you whether a business is generating enough cash from its business to sustain itself, grow, and return capital to its owners. Here's the formula:

Overall cash flow ratio = cash inflow from operations ÷ (investing cash outflows + financing cash outflows)

If the overall cash flow ratio is greater than 1, the company is generating enough cash internally to cover its business needs. If it's less than 1, the company is going to capital markets or is selling assets to keep afloat.

✔ **Cash-flow-to-earnings ratio:** You can use a comparison of cash flow to earnings as a quick quality test to see how noncash accounting transactions and "stretch" may have gone into a set of statements. It's best when cash flows either march in step with or exceed earnings. If earnings increase without a corresponding increase in cash flow, earnings quality comes into question. The following is a base measure:

Cash-flow-to-earnings = cash flow from operations ÷ net earnings

✔ Because depreciation and other noncash amortizations vary by industry, it's hard to hang a specific goal on this measure. Consistency over time is good. Favorable industry comparisons also are good. Further, it's good when period-to-period earnings increases are accompanied by corresponding cash flow increases.

Profitability ratios

Profitability ratios form a core set of bottom-line ratios crucial to all investment analysis. This section examines four profitability ratios. Each is typically based on net earnings, but occasionally you see variations using cash flow or operating earnings.

Typically, items related to extraordinary charges or discontinued operations should be excluded when calculating these ratios. If you're using figures from a financial portal or calculations from a screener or other financial information package, check to make sure figures exclude extraordinary items. You may have to dig into the company's own issued financial statements.

Return on sales

Return on sales (ROS) tells you how much profit a firm generated per dollar of sales. This figure is much better known as the *net profit margin*. This ratio is just as it sounds:

Return on sales = net earnings ÷ sales

Closely related to ROS is gross margin:

Gross margin = (sales − cost of goods sold) ÷ sales

Obviously, gross margin is a key driver of return on sales and is the most strongly connected to the organization's business strength and operational effectiveness. Some analysts also look at operating margin, where SG&A (selling, general, and administrative) expenses, marketing, asset recovery (depreciation), and special amortizations are factored in:

Operating margin = (sales − cost of goods sold − operating expenses) ÷ sales

Return on assets

How much profit is generated per resource dollar invested? Return on assets (ROA) provides the answer:

Return on assets = net earnings ÷ total assets

This measure is especially important in asset-intensive industries, such as retail, semiconductor manufacturing, and basic manufacturing. Chapter 4 in Book VII takes a closer look at ROA.

Return on equity

Return on equity (ROE) is one of the more important bottom-line ratios in the value investor's repertoire:

Return on equity = net earnings ÷ owners' equity

ROE is the true measure of how much a company returns to its owners, the shareholders. It is the bottom line result of other factors, including asset productivity, financial structure, and top-line profitability. ROE is important as an opportunity benchmark. What else could an investor invest in to get a better return? Again, consistency, trends, and comparisons are critical.

Return on invested capital

Debt, while raising ROE in good times, also can lead to financial disaster. As a result, many investors instead look at return on total capital (ROTC), measuring profit as a percentage of combined owners' equity and debt investments. This measure is sometimes called *return on invested capital,* or ROIC. Here's the formula:

Return on total capital = net earnings ÷ (owners' equity + long-term debt)

Frequently, you see ROE and ROTC side by side in ratio charts and discussions. Sustained ROE of 20 percent or more is considered very good, and ROTC should be higher, because debt increases the size of the business on the same equity base. See Chapter 4 in Book VII for more on ROE and ROTC.

When in doubt, should you average?

Occasionally, you see a variation in ROE and sometimes ROA formulas. Because these ratios use recent snapshot balance sheet items in the denominator, some analysts feel that you get the most accurate financial picture by adding year-end and year-beginning equity or asset values and dividing by 2. Thus, ROE would be

ROE = net earnings ÷ [(beginning equity + ending equity) ÷ 2]

Many information sources and services use the averaged formula. If you use a data source or service to acquire these figures, it's best to understand how your source calculates the figures. Most important, be consistent when evaluating different investments.

Valuation ratios

The ratios presented so far are aimed at appraising a company's performance to get a better understanding of its intrinsic value. If a business were an orchestra, productivity, financial structure, and profitability would be sections, like brass, woodwinds, and strings. The total sound produced depends not just on individual sounds made by individual instruments (ratios) but also how they work together to produce music.

Book VII

Value Investing

Now here's the critical question: As a music buff, how much would you pay to listen to the music? That's the question that valuation ratios try to answer: How much would you pay (and how much are others paying) for tickets to this concert? Here, finally, the stock price enters the stage.

Price-to-earnings

Price-to-earnings (P/E) is just what it sounds like: the ratio of a price at a point in time to net earnings in a period, usually the trailing 12 months (TTM). Here's the formula:

Price-to-earnings (P/E) = stock price ÷ net earnings per share

A high P/E — say, 20 or higher — indicates a relatively high valuation. A low P/E — say, 15 or less — indicates a relatively low or more conservative one. Chapter 4 in Book VII explores P/E in greater detail.

Earnings-to-price

Earnings-to-price is simply the reciprocal of P/E, or 1 divided by the P/E. Why is this important? Earnings-to-price is the functional equivalent of a stock's *yield,* comparable to an interest rate on a fixed income investment. Because we're talking earnings and not dividends, this yield doesn't usually come your way in the form of a check, but it's useful just the same to determine how much return each dollar you paid for a share is generating. Many people call this figure *earnings yield.*

Say a construction products manufacturer has a P/E ratio of 37.9, based on a share price of $33 and TTM earnings of 0.87. Earnings yield would be 1 ÷ 37.9, or 2.6 percent. What's the significance? This investment could be compared to a long-term Treasury security (today yielding about 2.0 percent) as a prospective investment. Which investment is better? An investment in that business returns more and, although riskier, affords the opportunity for gain through growth. The difference in earnings yield illustrates the basic risk/return tradeoff between investing in corporate equities versus safe, fixed-income Treasuries.

Price-earnings-to-growth

Investors pay more for companies with greater growth prospects. Greater growth prospects mean greater earnings and greater earnings yields *sooner.* So when comparing businesses, one popular way to normalize P/Es is to compare them to their respective companies' growth rates. From this comparison, you get a ratio known as *price-earnings-to-growth* (PEG):

Price-earnings-to-growth = P/E ÷ earnings growth rate

If network gear provider Cisco Systems has a P/E of 14.5 and an earnings growth rate of 10 percent, while the construction products manufacturer from the example in the preceding section has a P/E ratio of almost 38 with an earnings growth rate of 5 percent, which — on paper — is the better investment? Which stock has a more justified price?

The PEG rate for Cisco is the P/E (14.5) divided by the earnings growth rate (10), or 1.45, while the construction products maker has a P/E of 37.9 divided by the growth rate of 5 percent, implying a PEG rate of 7.58 — clearly a high and unsustainable number. In this case you'd probably examine the construction products maker more closely to see whether earnings were artificially weighed down by a one-time adjustment — and they were in this case. But suppose the P/E had been a more modest 6, and the growth rate had still been 5 percent — the PEG would have been 1.2, making the construction products maker a less risky investment because the P/E ratio would have been more in line with the growth rate. As a footnote: Any PEG greater than 3 is considered very risky; safer investments usually run in the 0.5 to 1.5 range.

Price-to-sales

Per dollar of shareholder value, how much business does a company generate? Price-to-sales (P/S) is a straightforward way to answer this question. Here's the formula:

Price-to-sales = stock price (total market cap) ÷ total sales (revenues)

P/S is a common-sense ratio. The lower the better, although there's no specific rule or normalizing factor like growth. Somewhere around 1.0 usually is considered good. A value of 2.0 isn't out of hand, but the business had better grow consistently into its valuation. P/S can be a way to filter out unworthy candidates.

Price-to-book

The price-to-book ratio (P/B) is getting varying amounts of attention from investors in different sectors. Here's the formula:

Price-to-book = stock price (total market cap) ÷ book value

Book value consists of the accounting value of assets minus (real) liabilities — sort of an accounting net worth or owners' equity of a corporation. This figure has greater meaning in financial services industries, where most assets are actual dollars, than with respect to factories, inventories, goodwill, and other hard-to-value items. Some book value measures include intangible assets, and others exclude them.

Book VII

Value Investing

Value investors use price-to-book a bit like price-to-sales: as a test for obvious lack of value. A P/B ratio of 1.0 is very good — unless the asset base is a bunch of rusty, unused railroad tracks. A P/B of less than 1.0 signifies a buying opportunity if the book assets are quality assets. A price way out of line with book had better be justified by conservative asset valuation or by the nature of the industry. In the software industry, for example, if R&D (research and development) is properly expensed and intellectual capital intangibles are aggressively amortized, book value and P/B will be low. Again, trends and apples-to-apples comparisons are important.

Chapter 4

Valuing a Business

. . . .

In This Chapter

▶ Calculating intrinsic value and dealing with worksheet models

▶ Evaluating return on equity

▶ Figuring out when the price is right

▶ Using a practical value investing approach

. . . .

To be consistent with the value investing approach, you must understand what a company is worth before you make an investment decision. If only it were so simple. Valuation has been the subject of vast theoretical study and debate — as well as experience and learning — in the investing community. Business valuation is at best an inexact science that no two people do exactly the same way. The goal of this chapter is to expose you to some of the techniques and underlying principles. Whether you apply them rigorously to every investment decision or just keep them in the back of your mind is up to you.

Evaluating Intrinsic Value

Intrinsic value is a present dollar value placed on the expected net returns generated by a business over time. Profits and growth drive intrinsic value. For any fairly priced asset to increase in value over time, the value of the returns must grow. The value you get out of owning a business or a security is the amount you receive in return for your investment. That return may come as a single payment at the end of the ownership period for selling the stock or business, or as payments at regular intervals during ownership (dividends), or as a combination of the two.

As you find out in the following sections, growth and time value of money have a major impact on the final valuation of equity investment returns. In fact, intrinsic valuation is a lot about assessing the effects of future growth on future returns and then assigning a present value to those returns.

Asking key questions

The following questions can guide your assessment of business returns:

- **How much?** How many dollars of return will the business produce, either to distribute to shareholders or to invest productively in the business? Key drivers are profitability and growth rates — and the collection of business factors that drive the profitability and growth.

- **How soon?** If two companies produce the same return but one does it sooner, that company has more value, because those dollars can be reinvested elsewhere sooner for more return.

- **How long?** Although future returns have less value than current returns, they do have substantial value, and 20, 30, or 50 years of those returns can't be ignored, particularly in a profitable, growing business.

- **How consistently?** A company producing slow, steady growth and return is usually more valuable than one that's all over the map. A greater variability, or uncertainty, around projected returns calls for more conservative growth and/or discounting assumptions.

After you assess potential returns (how much, how soon, how long, how consistently), you must assign a current value to those returns. That value is driven by the value of the investment capital as it might be used elsewhere. A return may look attractive until you realize you can achieve the same return with a bond or a less risky investment. Valuing the returns involves *discounting* (using a discount rate) to bring future returns back to fair current value. The discount rate is your personal cost of capital — in this case, the rate of return you expect to deploy capital here versus elsewhere.

Sooner isn't *always* better. A business producing quick, short-term bucks may not be more valuable than one that produces slow, steady growth. Even though the quick-bucker produces a lot of value in the first few years, that may not be better than sustained growth and value produced later on by the slower, steadier company.

Finding out more about returns

When you look at a business, you seek consistent, growing returns on a quality asset base — achieving reasonable returns without taking on unreasonable risk. So what does "returns" refer to? Direct returns to shareholders? Returns to the business? Net income? Cash flow? EBITDA? What's the best "base" for intrinsic value?

Net income to the business is the starting point, but many investors look further:

✔ **Dividends:** As part of intrinsic value, dividends are counted as part of yearly investment returns and grown and discounted in the same way as earnings retained in the business. But deducting dividends reduces the growth base of retained earnings and book value kept in the business. Companies with a high growth rate and return on equity often yield greater intrinsic value if all earnings are retained and reinvested, which is why you often see just that — no dividends in high-growth companies.

✔ **Cash-flow streams:** Any one of the following cash-flow streams can be used as an input to an intrinsic value model:

 • **Cash flow (CF) or discounted cash flow (DCF):** Cash flows (covered in Chapter 2 of Book VII) are yearly cash returns into a business, without accounting adjustments for asset write-downs, amortizations, and the like. Many sophisticated security analysis models operate on cash flow and are sometimes referred to as *discounted cash flow* (DCF) models.

 • **EBITDA (earnings before interest, taxes, depreciation, and amortization):** This is an approximation of cash generated by business operating activities. (***Note:*** Interest and taxes are real, and depreciation comes into play when depreciated fixed assets need to be replaced. Because intrinsic value calculations are long term in view, don't leave out the cost of fixed assets, especially in a business that has a lot of them — so be careful about relying too much on EBITDA.)

 • **Free cash flow (FCF):** This is cash flow generated from operations *beyond* interest, taxes, and capital investments. As a business owner, it's what you'd really be able to put into your pocket.

 • **Net free cash flow (owner earnings):** The most realistic version of free cash flow starts with plain old free cash flow and then makes an additional adjustment for working capital changes.

✔ **Earnings:** Understanding earnings quality and the differences between earnings and cash flow goes a long way toward producing valid results.

When using earnings streams to project future returns, make sure to understand quality and one-time extraordinary gains or losses, because extraordinary earnings items can mess up the intrinsic value calculation. Be especially careful when using a "canned" package, as it picks up whatever is on a company's source earnings database, ordinary or otherwise. To their credit, analysts and Value Line (www.valueline.com) usually filter out these abnormalities when making projections.

Projecting future growth

Beyond the net assets owned by a business today, intrinsic value is driven by current and especially future earnings. For that reason, projecting future earnings growth is vital to determining intrinsic value. True intrinsic value is the total of *all* expected future returns: this year, next year, 5, 10, 20, 40, 80 years from now. How can you possibly project a company's return when part of it includes something that will happen 77 years from now? Answer: by taking it in stages:

✔ **First stage:** Typically the first stage is ten years, although it may be more or less. Near-term growth is by nature easier to model, and as a result of the discounting process, it contributes more toward the final result anyway. For these reasons, intrinsic value models are set up to specifically value a first stage in detail, year-by-year. The first stage is generally assumed to have a higher growth rate and a lower discount rate than the second stage.

✔ **Second stage:** Second-stage returns are harder than first-stage to project with any degree of accuracy, so intrinsic value models use one of two assumptions to estimate what is known as *continuing value:*

- **Indefinite life:** This model assumes ongoing returns and uses a mathematical formula to project returns over an indefinite period of time.

- **Acquisition:** This model bypasses mathematical approximations and assumes that someone will come along and buy the business after the first stage at a reasonable valuation. Returns include all future payouts, including lump sums, so this method works too, so long as resale value is projected reasonably.

Each stage of a business life has a growth rate and discount rate applicable to that stage. To run a model, you need a base, first- and second-stage growth rates, and first- and second-stage discount rates. You calculate net future earnings by first compounding growth over the first stage and then discounting that value back to the present. A generalized formula, either indefinite life or acquisition-based, is applied to the second stage. The value attributed to the second stage is called *continuing value.*

Comparing Intrinsic Value Worksheet Models

With an Excel spreadsheet and a few initial assumptions, you can build your own intrinsic value worksheet for either continuing value assumption: the indefinite life model or the acquisition assumption model. This worksheet model is fairly easy to construct; formulas are shown along with sample results. The following sections have the details.

With intrinsic value models, you get a single-figure result: the estimated per-share value of the company. If you're satisfied with this number and the assumptions supporting it, you can compare this intrinsic value with current market price and make a buying (or selling) decision. More likely, you'll want to model a *range* of intrinsic values based on different assumptions. Then to complete the value appraisal, you'll want to consider strategic financials and intangibles before hitting the buy (or sell) button.

Other ways to determine intrinsic value exist. For example, you can use a pre-packaged web-based analyzer. At this writing, the data and analysis package offered by iStockResearch (`www.istockresearch.com`) is the best available for free. You can also use the intrinsic value formula developed by Ben Graham. Graham's formula is easy to apply and gives surprisingly robust results; for information, head to the nearby sidebar "The Ben Graham model."

The indefinite life model

The mainstream intrinsic value model makes a mathematical assumption about so-called "continuing value." Figure 4-1 shows an example of the indefinite life continuing value model, with formulas to help you build your own. Note that dollar figures, except per-share amounts, are in millions. The worksheet has nine parts.

Book VII

Value Investing

The Ben Graham model

It's worth checking out intrinsic value through the eyes of Ben Graham, based on his 1930s formula:

Intrinsic value = Earnings × [(2 × growth rate) + 8.5] × [4.4 ÷ bond yield]

A simple straight-line formula, no exponents, no first- and second-stage stuff, no discount rate? Could it work? In a word, yes.

The Graham model, derived from the more complex model but philosophically aligned to it, can be used as computational shorthand. It doesn't allow for stages and uses a more simplistic discounting assumption. And it can produce the same wide range of results as the other models. It's a good shortcut — one you may be able to do in your head when looking at a number of investment choices.

INTRINSIC VALUE WORKSHEET

Indefinite Life Model

			Variable	Source
① Growth and discount assumptions				
First-stage growth		10%	*g1*	Assumption
Second-stage growth		5%	*g2*	Assumption
First-stage discount rate		12%	*d1*	Assumption
Second-stage discount rate		15%	*d2*	Assumption
② Earnings, shares outstanding, EPS				
Beginning earnings	$	102.50	*E*	Statements
Number of shares (fully diluted, M)		48.9		Statements
Beginning EPS	$	2.10		Calculation

			Calculations
③ Discounted 10-year earnings stream			
Year 1	$	100.67	
Year 2	$	98.87	Start with beginning earnings
Year 3	$	97.11	
Year 4	$	95.37	
Year 5	$	93.67	First, compound for growth:
Year 6	$	92.00	*multiply E by*
Year 7	$	90.35	$(1 + g1)^n$
Year 8	$	88.74	
Year 9	$	87.16	...then discount:
Year 10	$	85.60	*divide by* $(1 + d1)^n$
④ Total discounted return, first 10 years			
Discounted 10-year value	$	929.54	Sum years 1–10
⑤ Continuing value beyond 10 years			
Continuing value (> 10 years, n=10)	$	941.59	$$\frac{[E * (1 + g1)^{n+1}] / (d2 - g2)}{(1 + d1)^n}$$
⑥ Total future returns value, discounted			
	$	1,871.13	10 year + terminal value
⑦ Long-term debt adjustment			
	$	-	From statements
⑧ Net future returns value			
	$	1,871.13	Subtract LT debt
⑨ Per-share intrinsic value	$	38.26	Net future value / # shares

Implied P/E	18.3
Implied PEG	1.8

Figure 4-1: The intrinsic value worksheet for an indefinite life model.

Step 1: Growth and discount assumptions

Not surprisingly, here at the very top of the worksheet is where you can do the most damage — or the most good — to your analysis because of the potential effects of these assumptions carried over 10, 15, or 20 years, due to the power of compounding.

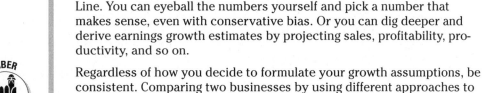

✔ **Choosing a growth assumption:** To choose a growth assumption, you can rely on outside sources, including professional analysts or Value Line. You can eyeball the numbers yourself and pick a number that makes sense, even with conservative bias. Or you can dig deeper and derive earnings growth estimates by projecting sales, profitability, productivity, and so on.

Regardless of how you decide to formulate your growth assumptions, be consistent. Comparing two businesses by using different approaches to growth and discounting assumptions can lead to trouble.

✔ **Projecting second-stage growth:** To project second-stage growth, you can't use the same tools and techniques you use to project first-stage growth. These growth rates should be less than first-stage growth rates and less than 10 percent, probably no more than 5 or 6 percent. Conservative is always better.

Excessive second-stage growth rates distort results because so much time is involved. And no matter what the company is, sooner or later it will exhaust market growth and penetration opportunities.

If you're uncomfortable with second-stage growth rates and their effect on valuation (and many investors are), you can use the acquisition model presented later in this chapter. Although this model implies that an acquisition will take place, it can also be used to reduce sensitivity to input assumptions even if acquisition is unlikely.

✔ **Choosing a discount assumption:** In theory, the discount rate should be your own personal cost of capital for this kind of investment plus *equity premium* that's added to the risk-free cost of capital rate. Here's the reasoning: If you can invest your money with no risk in a Treasury bond at 2 percent, your cost of capital is the risk-free 2 percent you would forego by not investing in the bond. But because Company XYZ common stock is riskier than the bond investment, an equity premium is added as compensation for assuming extra risk.

Most value investors, however, prefer a simpler approach: Just discount at a relatively high rate, usually higher than the growth rate. Conservative value investors usually use discount rates in the 10 to 15 percent range. Here are a few points to remember about discount rates:

- The higher the discount rate, the lower the intrinsic value — and vice versa.

- The second-stage discount rate should always be higher than the first-stage rate. Risk increases the farther out you go.

- If you choose an aggressive growth rate, it makes sense to choose a higher discount rate. Risk of failure is higher with high growth rates.

Book VII

Value Investing

- If the discount rate exceeds the growth rate, intrinsic value will be low, and will implode quickly, the larger the gap. Aggressive growth assumptions with low discount rates yield very high intrinsic values.

Following is the set of growth and discount assumptions used for this example. Consistency is important, but growth rates will vary for each company, and discount rates may also change with differing risk assessments.

First-stage growth	10%
Second-stage growth	5%
First-stage discount rate	12%
Second-stage discount rate	15%

Step 2: Earnings, shares outstanding, EPS

Earnings, number of shares, and earnings per share (EPS) come straight from the statements. This model projects total, rather than per-share, earnings streams, to make it easier to subtract out (not per-share) long-term debt (which happens to be zero in the Figure 4-1 example). When loading beginning earnings, be sure to adjust for one-time or extraordinary gains or charges.

Step 3: Discounted ten-year earnings stream

This section projects growth during each year of the first stage and then discounts the resulting value back to the present. The spreadsheet formulas are straightforward. For each year, you do the following:

1. **Multiply beginning earnings by $[(1 + g1)^n]$, where $g1$ is the first-stage growth rate and n is the sequential future year.**

2. **Divide that figure by $[(1 + d1)^n]$, where $d1$ is the first-stage discount rate.**

The resulting figures represent projected earnings for each year, discounted to the present.

Step 4: Total discounted return, first ten years

To arrive at the sum of the first ten years' discounted earnings stream, simply add the figures for each year. The total represents the total discounted value of the first stage.

Step 5: Continuing value beyond ten years

Higher math enters the picture in calculating a continuing value for all future returns. Here's the formula, where E is beginning earnings; $g1$ and $d1$ are first-stage growth and discount rates, respectively; $g2$ and $d2$ are second-stage growth and discount rates, respectively; and n is the number of years in the first stage, in this case, 10:

$$[E \times (1 + g1)^n + 1] \div (d2 - g2) \text{ all divided by } (1 + d1)^n$$

After you enter this formula into your worksheet, the computation is simple. The resulting single value approximates the discounted value of *all* future returns for the business beyond the first stage.

Step 6: Total future returns value, discounted

In this step you add first-stage and second-stage *continuing* discounted value to find the value of the total discounted future returns.

Step 7: Long-term debt adjustment

To arrive at true value, you take long-term debt away from earnings.

Step 8: Net future returns value

Net of long-term debt, the net future returns value is the total intrinsic value, based on future returns, of the business.

Book VII

Value Investing

Step 9: Per-share intrinsic value

Now, finally, the bottom line. Divide net future returns value by the number of shares outstanding to get a per-share intrinsic value. This is the magic number to compare with market price and with other companies. You're done!

The acquisition assumption model

If the continuing value formula of the preceding section and the idea of trying to project to eternity make you nervous, you may want to try an alternative approach. The approach, known as the acquisition assumption model, is to assume that someone else will buy the business at a fair value at the end of the first stage. In essence, you get continuing value in a lump-sum payment, which of course must also be discounted for time value of money.

The acquisition assumption worksheet model is fairly straightforward:

✔ Growth and discount assumptions are the same as for the indefinite life model. Base values are share price and per-share book value, which are used to calculate an initial price-to-book (P/B) ratio. A per-share earnings figure is then used as a base for growth and discounting. (The formula for growing earnings and discounting to the present is the same, except here you apply it to per-share earnings instead of total earnings.)

✔ The price paid by the acquirer is the key assumption that makes or breaks this model. That price is calculated as a ratio of price-to-book (P/B) value. Earnings during the first stage grow the base book value. You then supply an assumption of what price-to-book value is appropriate ten years down the road and use that to determine the cash-out price. (The book value is assumed to increase by each year's growth and discounted earnings.)

Earnings paid out as dividends don't accrue to long-term book value. So back dividends out of the earnings stream used to grow book value. Do the same with share buybacks. (You may want to value them as a separate discounted income stream, however.)

✔ Because book value already nets out debt, long-term debt doesn't need to be factored in.

Figure 4-2 shows a ten-year acquisition version of the intrinsic value worksheet.

To model the value in Year 10, when the supposed acquisition takes place (you can set it up for a different year), here is a short tour through the steps:

1. **Make your growth and discounting assumptions, just as you would in the indefinite life model, and look up key figures on the financial statements.**

2. **Estimate the annual accretion of earnings to book value, but subtract dividends and other shareholder payments.**

3. **Model the incremental book value per share per year by growing, then discounting, the per-share net earnings over the ten years, much like the indefinite life model.**

4. **Take current book value and assume that it remains intact ten years from now; then discount the value back to the present to get an apples-to-apples view of all components of Year 10 book value.**

One benefit of this version of the model is that some value is explicitly placed on productive *assets* already owned by the business.

INTRINSIC VALUE WORKSHEET
10-Year Acquisition Model

		Variable	Source

(1) Growth and discount assumptions

Earnings growth	8%	*g1*	Assumption
Discount rate	12%	*d1*	Assumption

(2) Beginning share price, book value, and earnings

Current share price	$ 33.00	Quote
Per-share book value	$ 13.50	Statements
Price-to-book (P/B)	2.4	Calculation
EPS (fully diluted)	$ 2.10	Statements
Per-share dividend/net buyback	$ 0.40	Statements
Net per-share earnings to book value	$ 1.70	Calculation

(3) Book value increase per share

Year 1	$ 1.64
Year 2	$ 1.58
Year 3	$ 1.52
Year 4	$ 1.47
Year 5	$ 1.42
Year 6	$ 1.37
Year 7	$ 1.32
Year 8	$ 1.27
Year 9	$ 1.23
Year 10	$ 1.18

Calculations

Beginning net EPS

First, compound for growth
multiply by
$(1 + g1)^n$

... then discount
divide by
$(1 + d1)^n$

(4) Beginning share price, book value, and earnings

$ 13.99 — Sum years 1–10

(5) Initial book value, discounted

$ 3.88 — Initial book / $(1 + d1)^{10}$

(6) Total book value, year 10

$ 17.88 — Initial + incremental book value

(7) Acquisition price-to-book ratio

2.0 — Assumption

(8) Per-share intrinsic value assuming acquisition

$ 35.75 — Total Year 10 book value * P/B ratio

Figure 4-2: The intrinsic value worksheet for a ten-year acquisition.

Illustration by Wiley, Composition Services Graphics

5. **Total the estimated ten-year book value.**

6. **Determine what price-to-book you should use.**

Which one you use depends on the type of business, what other comparable acquisitions show, and your own intuition. In a manufacturing business, a P/B of 2.0 is probably reasonable because book values of productive physical assets tend to be low. If you're valuing a financial institution, with assets mainly in cash and receivables, the model P/B would likely be lower. If you're valuing a technology company, the P/B may perhaps be higher.

Using today's P/B ratio is a place to start, although if it's much higher than 1.0, the ratio has a tendency to decline over time as growth patterns settle and the company matures. Any P/B ratio exceeding 3 is probably excessive.

7. **Multiply the total ten-year book value by acquisition P/B and, voilà, you get intrinsic value.**

Depending on how you set the assumptions, the indefinite life model and ten-year acquisition models yield similar results. That isn't a big surprise, because acquiring firms are (or should be) looking for the same kinds of intrinsic value characteristics that you are.

Examining Return on Equity

Return on equity (ROE), at the end of the day, is one of the most important business growth drivers. Sustained ROE implies sustained growth and shouts out "well-managed company!" Strategic financials represent the factors management can shape and control to achieve growth, ROE, and, hence, intrinsic value. The following sections explain ROE in more detail.

Unlike intrinsic value, ROE doesn't estimate the value of a company. You can't go through a series of calculations culminating in a per-share value estimate. But ROE — and its components — can tell whether things are healthy and moving in the right direction. Another way to look at the difference: Intrinsic value explicitly looks forward into the income-producing capability of the firm in the long run, while strategic valuation is primarily a snapshot of the present, albeit with many components that can predict future performance.

Paying attention to the basics of ROE

ROE, defined as net earnings divided by owners' equity, is a capitalist's bottom line. It represents the return on owners' equity invested in the business and is a good barometer of whether the company is on the right track and whether management is doing a good job. Other things to know about ROE:

✔ Over time, ROE trends toward the earnings growth rate of the company. A company with a 5 percent earnings growth rate and a 20 percent ROE today will see ROE gradually diminish toward 5 percent. A company with a 20 percent earnings growth rate and a 10 percent ROE will see ROE move toward 20 percent.

✔ ROE doesn't just happen all by itself. A series of business fundamentals, all linked together and controlled or influenced by management, leads to respectable, sustained, and growing ROE. When profitability, productivity, and capital structure are all strong and tight, ROE outcome is destined for success. If a business fundamental is poor or failing, it can weaken the entire chain and hamper ROE indefinitely.

✔ Pay attention to ROTC, *return on total capital.* ROTC is owners' equity plus long-term debt. If a company is growing ROE but not ROTC, chances are the company is borrowing to fund growth-producing assets, thus leveraging the company. (In moderation, this *can* be a good thing.) So look at ROTC and ROE together. They should march side by side and change in unison. Many information services such as Value Line provide both figures simultaneously.

Bottom line: Maintaining a constant ROE percentage requires steady earnings growth. For that reason, a company with increasing ROE, without undue exposure to debt or leverage, is especially attractive.

Book VII

Value Investing

Seeing the links in the strategic profit formula

ROE may appear to be a single number, but in fact a complex chain of events or set of factors underlies the figure. A series of business fundamentals, all linked together, leads to respectable, sustained, and growing ROE. That strategic value chain becomes clearer in the strategic profit formula.

In this formula (sometimes called the *DuPont formula* because it originated in DuPont's finance department, it's easy to see the links in the chain: profitability, productivity, and capital structure, in sequence:

$$ROE = [profits/sales] \times [sales/assets] \times [assets/equity]$$

The intermediate terms in this formula tell a great deal about the health of the business. For each intermediate term in the formula, you want to know its value, in what direction it's going (trend), and how it compares to others in the industry.

Checking out ROE value chain components

Each link in the ROE chain has its own component drivers. For instance, *strategic financials* such as gross margins and expenses drive profitability. Asset levels, quality, and turnover drive productivity, while debt and new capital requirements drive capital structure. In turn, *strategic intangibles* such as market position, customer share and loyalty, brand strength, and supply chain strength drive those margins and expenses.

Figure 4-3 illustrates the strategic value chain. ROE, the result, is shown as a result or outcome at the right-hand side of the figure. Working backwards toward the left, the figure lists a few examples of value chain components that drive ROE components and thus ROE. They're grouped into strategic financials (measurable financial factors) and strategic intangibles (mostly immeasurable market and business characteristics that drive them).

The value investor works backward through the ROE value chain to find good or bad in ROE drivers and the things that influence those drivers.

 For the first-tier components of ROE, perform a quality test. Look for characteristics that are off course. For example, low debt doesn't necessarily indicate high value, but frequent trips to the capital markets for debt or stock sales may indicate capital starvation and "un-value."

ROE Strategic Value Chain

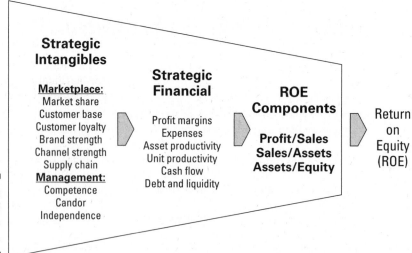

Figure 4-3: The strategic value chain.

Illustration by Wiley, Composition Services Graphics

Measuring profitability

To measure profitability, you want to first consider the financial drivers that lead to the net profit percent. Then you want to test the major ROE components for any signs of trouble. Finally, you need to look at the intangibles.

Financial drivers

Profit/sales, or *net profit percent,* is the primary profitability measure. No surprise here. But when looking at profitability, look at the dynamics behind net profit percent. Specifically, you want to look at gross margin, SG&A, and operating profit percentages:

- ✔ **Gross margin:** Gross margin tells a lot about a business's success in managing its sales and the direct costs of producing products and services. A company on top of its marketing and production game usually produces improving margins.

  Market characteristics and selling aggressiveness can work against margins. Intuitively, you may guess that increased volumes lead to increased margins, as fixed costs are absorbed and economies of scale work in their favor. However, this isn't always the case. A company often must make price concessions to achieve sales goals. And aggressive volume-building also takes its toll on operating costs (not part of gross margin) in the form of marketing expenses and sometimes interest expense to expand the level of business. The key is to understand the industry in which you want to invest.

- ✔ **Selling, general, and administrative (SG&A):** Although not directly tied to net profit percent, SG&A tells a lot about how management controls expenses and how expenses are tied to business production. SG&A percentage is the total SG&A cost divided by sales or revenues (you have to calculate this one yourself; be aware that different companies define SG&A differently, so look to annual reports for clarification). When SG&A increases faster than sales, that's a bad sign, especially in a maturing industry. Chronic SG&A percentage increases are a red flag.

- ✔ **Operating profit:** Depreciation, amortization, and certain facility and employee costs can all influence operating expenses. A company in control of gross margin *and* operating expenses will show increased operating profit.

Even though some companies may go through periods of deteriorating gross margins, a focus on *total* profitability and tight control of SG&A and other operating expenses may keep operating profit percentages relatively flat — a good sign that management is managing total shareholder return.

Book VII

Value Investing

Quality checks

As you do your evaluation of the major ROE components, test each one for signs of trouble or inherent weakness. Here are key quality checks for profitability:

- **Overdependence on acquisitions for growth:** Profitability usually suffers when companies get so caught up in building the top line that they resort to painful and expensive acquisitions to do it.

- **Excessive goodwill:** Often working hand-in-hand with acquisitions, growth in goodwill or a growing gap between total stockholder equity and net tangible assets can signal trouble in the form of future write-offs.

- **Overdependence on expansion:** Growth is good, but if the core business isn't growing or is declining, that's a bad sign. Try to sniff out *organic growth* — that is, growth not sourced from new outlets or acquisitions. If sales are expanding but profits aren't, it's a sign that the most recent expansions aren't working. (However, it depends on the industry: A Starbucks outlet will produce returns more quickly than an aircraft plant.)

- **Cash flow and changes in book value don't march with changes in earnings:** If, over time, earnings rise but cash flow and book value don't, you must question the quality of earnings.

Intangible drivers

Obviously, the intangibles you want to pay attention to are those that are relevant to gross margins. They include things like market position (market leadership, brand dominance, public image, pricing power, and so on), resource acquisition or supply chain power, reporting quality (do a quick spot-check of cash flows and changes in book value as they relate to earnings), and how this business fares in comparison to other businesses in the industry. Basically, you want to look for improving profitability measures and be able to explain those that aren't improving.

Measuring productivity

Productivity measures tell you how well companies deploy and use assets. All things considered, a dollar of sales produced on 50 cents' worth of assets is better than the same company producing a dollar of sales on a dollar of assets (keeping in mind that asset productivity figures vary by industry).

Financial drivers

Sales/assets is the primary measure of asset productivity and is simply the amount of sales generated per asset dollar deployed. As you look at sales/assets, avoid these two traps:

✔ **Misinterpreting changes due to write-offs:** Be careful to distill out major changes in asset deployment that create no change in the business.

✔ **Reading too much into the absolute numbers:** Be careful about comparing across industries; good comparisons — and trends — are most important.

Here are some other points to take into account:

✔ **Deconstructing return on assets (ROA):** Many popular information services show ROA. If ROA and profit margin figures are supplied by an information portal such as Yahoo! Finance (`finance.yahoo.com`) or Value Line (`www.valueline.com`), you can deduce asset productivity. Bad ROA and good margins equal bad productivity.

ROA is net profit divided by total assets, which are the first two links in the ROE chain combined. (Profit/assets = profit/sales × sales/assets, for you math types.) Although ROA has validity and value, looking at the two links separately is preferable. The first measure, profit/sales, has more to do with market power and cost structures, while the second, sales/assets, has more to do with resource requirements and deployment. Deconstructing ROA provides a more bottoms-up, inside-out view of the business.

✔ **Deconstructing sales/assets:** Accounts receivable, inventory, and fixed assets are the major food groups in this value chain.

 • **Accounts receivable turnover:** How many dollars in sales does the business generate per dollar of accounts receivable investment? When examining statements for accounts receivable, use *trade* accounts receivable — those that arise from and support the normal course of business.

 • **Inventory turnover:** A business in control of finished goods, raw material, and production inventories shows greater sales per dollar invested in inventory.

 • **Fixed asset turnover:** This is another turnover measure, this time for fixed assets or PP&E (property, plant, and equipment).

Occasionally you'll see a modest sales/asset gain when accounts receivable, inventory, and fixed assets showed larger improvements, up to 50 percent. In many cases, this is due to cash accumulation — sometimes because of other assets. Scrupulous value investors check to make sure what those other assets represent.

✔ **Unit productivity measures:** If the figures are available, go into sales per facility, sales per store, revenue per mile of track or passenger seat flown, and so on, depending on the industry. You can also track sales per employee, a handy metric for overall efficiency and management competence. Such unit productivity metrics are good for comparing with other firms in the same industry once you understand them.

Book VII

Value Investing

For a possible clue that problems are present, look at asset write-downs. If write-downs are excessive and persistent, asset quality — and really, asset acquisition — problems are evident. On the flip side, a company not taking sufficient write-downs may also be suspect.

Quality checks

Asset productivity measures themselves are pretty good at sniffing out quality problems: If a company has the wrong assets or poor-quality assets, it generally won't generate as much sales or income. Value investors should look at write-offs and write-off history: If a company seems to always be writing off some inventory or writing down accounts receivable with impairment charges and reserves, asset quality may be called into question.

Sometimes a more subjective assessment comes into play: Do company facilities look modern and efficient? Does a company keep up with trends in information technology and supply chain management? These questions can be hard to answer and are more intangible than measurable, but closely following a business usually yields some clues.

Intangible drivers

Looking at trends within individual metrics makes sense — improving values at all tiers is a healthy thing. Give special credit to consistent improvement through business cycles. Depending on the industry, you may balance emphasis on inventory, accounts receivable, and fixed assets differently. And it never hurts to compare companies to other companies, as long as you're comparing apples to apples.

Looking at capital structure

When looking at capital structure, you're trying to determine two things:

✔ Is the business a consumer or producer of capital? Does it constantly require capital infusions to build growth or replace assets?

✔ Is the business properly leveraged? Overleveraged businesses are at risk and additionally burden earnings with interest payments. Conversely, underleveraged businesses may not be maximizing potential returns to shareholders.

Pay attention to the following:

✔ **Assets/equity:** The first-tier measure for capital structure is assets/equity. Per dollar of owners' equity invested, how many dollars of productive assets are deployed in the business? For the second-tier evaluation, the key questions are "Is more capital needed?" and "Is the company properly leveraged?"

✓ **Capital sufficiency:** Capital-hungry companies are sometimes hard to detect, but following are a few obvious signs:

- **Share buybacks:** A company using cash to retire shares — if acting sensibly — is telling you that it generates more capital than it needs.

  When evaluating share buybacks, make sure to look at actual shares outstanding. Relying on company news releases alone can be misleading. Companies also buy back shares to support employee incentive programs or to accumulate shares for an acquisition. Such repurchases may be okay but aren't the kind of repurchases that increase return on equity for remaining owners.

- **Cash flow ratio:** If the cash flow ratio (refer to Chapter 3 in Book VII) shows that cash flow from operations is not enough to meet investing and financing requirements (in this case, the repayment of debt), it's back to the capital markets.

- **Lengthening asset cycles:** Lengthening accounts receivable collection and inventory holding periods forewarn the need for more capital.

- **Working capital:** A company requiring steady increases in working capital to support sales needs capital.

✓ **Leverage:** Some debt is usually regarded as a good thing because it expands the size of the business and hence the return on owner capital. But debt stops being okay when it's too large to cover during a downturn or business strategy change. Here are a couple of supporting metrics:

- **Debt-to-equity (D/E):** A deteriorating D/E over time is a bad sign unless you understand the context. A worsening D/E without a reduction in shares is even less healthy.

- **Interest coverage:** Interest coverage is the ratio of earnings to annual interest, a rough indication of how solvent or burdened a company is by debt.

✓ **Quality checks:** These measures of productivity can let you know whether the company has an insatiable demand for capital: current assets (besides cash) rising faster than business, debt growing faster than business, and repeated financings.

✓ **Intangibles:** Several intangibles enter into play here:

- **Credit ratings and changes in credit ratings:** Declining credit ratings mean that someone somewhere is less secure with the capital structure as currently deployed.

- **Capital intensity, particularly changes in capital intensity:** The semiconductor business happily churning out DRAM chips becomes less happy when equipment must be replaced with more expensive equipment more often. Shortening product cycles can similarly stoke the capital requirement fires for software companies and the like.

- **Quality:** A company that faces its finances head-on is in better shape than one that plays games, delays write-downs, uses good debt to finance bad assets, and the like. Indicators may be either specific or more general in nature, such as the thickness of 10-K reports (refer to Chapter 2 in Book VII), the tone of press coverage, the departure of CFOs, and so forth.

Evaluating strategic intangibles

Warren Buffett once famously said: "If you gave me $100 billion and said 'take away the soft drink leadership of Coca-Cola in the world,' I'd give it back to you and say it can't be done." This quote underlies the essence of strategic intangibles: the difference between a *business* and a mere set of assets and liabilities.

Intangibles come in all shapes and sizes. Every company has different intangibles. This section discusses marketing and management tenets that separate great from good, focusing on those that are clearly strategic in the creation of value in the business and return for the shareholders. So much of what makes excellent businesses excellent transcends the arcane world of factories, storefronts, products, and packages. And most of it can be controlled or influenced by good management.

Market power

Market power is all about advantage. Market power is strength in franchise, brand, customer base, supply chain power, or other competencies that gives the company an advantage in the marketplace. Advantage drives and protects the first component of ROE: profitability.

- **The franchise factor:** A *franchise* is an established, sustainable, powerful position in a market (not to be confused with the term's other meaning: the one you can buy from a restaurant or convenience-store chain allowing you to sell merchandise or services under someone else's logo). Franchise is probably the most valuable asset a business can have.

Coca-Cola is the classic case of the franchise, a situation in which the power of the brand and the reputation of the company have created a near-unassailable fortress around the production and sale of flavored sugar water.

Franchises also create barriers to entry (called *creating a moat*). If you can grill burgers, you can set up a hamburger stand, but can you set up a McDonald's? Would anyone come? "Creating a moat" describes franchise power that keeps competitors away — and keeps the business and its fundamentals moving in the right direction.

✔ **The brand centerpiece:** Strong brands are built over time through a combination of good products and good presentation of those products to the marketplace. Brand can tell a lot about a company's value. It's up to you to decide how valuable the brand is in the marketplace both today and in the future. Key factors that define a brand include:

   • **Image:** How the public perceives the brand in the marketplace, regarding not only product quality but also the ideas and images that people associate with the company.

   • **Familiarity:** Familiarity creates mindshare, drives repeat or habitual purchase, and creates barriers for entry. Most value investors place a high value on habitual repeat purchase.

   • **Reputation:** Reputation builds slowly over time, provides a powerful umbrella giving shelter when things go wrong, and must be nurtured and handled with care. When considering companies to invest in, look for businesses that manage their mistakes well.

✔ **Market share and leadership:** Market leadership means that a company defines the market, sets the pace in price and product, and (usually) is tied to a strong brand. Market leadership often leads to cost advantages through buying power and economies of scale.

✔ **Customer base:** A company with a loyal customer base can depend on repeat sales and spend less money acquiring new customers. Profitability increases through lower marketing costs and repeat sales driven other than by price. A business treating a customer base as an asset is more successful than one that treats it as a liability.

✔ **Special competencies:** Does the company have some kind of infrastructure, business model, or technology that's difficult to duplicate? Does it have special knowledge, experience, or intellectual capital that others don't have? Score a plus if this is the case.

✔ **The supply chain:** Look at the degree of control a company exerts over its suppliers as well as its distribution channels. Also pay attention to how much influence a company has on stability, sustainable and growable sales, and stable costs. A company that can economically sell directly to its customers may have an advantage.

Book VII

Value Investing

All about management

Just as important as market power, company management is another intangible pillar. Four attributes indicate management excellence:

- ✔ **Competence:** Does management have the right vision, make the right decisions, and offer good reasons for those decisions? Does it make sound investments in existing businesses? In new businesses? Does it understand — and control — expenses? Does it make changes when changes should be made, being neither too eager nor too reluctant to make them? Does it make reasonable projections about growth and earnings? I could go on and on, but suffice it to say that good management understands the business, has a realistic view of it, has a solid rationale behind strategies and decisions, and employs resources wisely within it.

- ✔ **Candor:** Value investors like managers who communicate quickly and honestly about business issues and problems — and without undue spin, jargon, or buzzwords.

- ✔ **Independence:** Good management teams think and act independently and for the long-term health of the business, and they resist the temptation to pour energy and resources into achieving this quarter's results. They have a vision, a mission, and a plan and follow them, avoiding distractions.

- ✔ **Customer focus:** A management team focused on customers is more likely to succeed than one focused on its internal issues and on competitors.

Solid information about a company's management is usually hard to find. Yet, a sensitive antenna can pick up a lot over a period of time. Yahoo! Finance provides links to the bios and executive compensation of management. Read the paper and watch corporate communications and press releases to catch the buzz about a company's management.

Ownership

By looking at a company's ownership, particularly those who own the largest pieces of the business, you can discover something about the attractiveness of the business to others — and to its own management.

- ✔ **Management as owners:** Management ownership reflects management commitment.

- ✔ **Institutions as owners:** Institutional owners include large banks, pension funds, and trusts. The larger the holdings, and the more blue-chip names you see, the better.

- ✔ **Mutual funds as owners:** Look at who manages the fund, how much the fund invests, and what kind of fund it is. If the top ten funds all are value funds, that may be a good sign.

Go to Yahoo! Finance (`finance.yahoo.com`) to find information on each of these items. You can also refer to company publications, including annual reports, but these may be a little less current.

Deciding When the Price Is Right

Sooner or later, price enters the value equation. By far, the most popular valuation tool is the price-to-earnings (P/E) ratio, which is one of the major ways that investors make sense of the price tag. This section explores how you can use P/E to price a business.

No formula exists for applying P/E. "If it's 17 you buy, and if it's 25 you sell" doesn't work. A deeper understanding of the P/E and underlying fundamentals is required. The following sections provide some of that depth.

Earnings yield

P/E is the ratio of share price to earnings. But there's more information than meets the eye. P/E tells how many years it would take to recoup an investment with earnings staying the same. A P/E of 17 means that, with flat earnings, it would take 17 years to recover your investment. A P/E of 40 equals 40 years. But a greater revelation occurs when you turn the ratio upside down. The inverse ratio *(earnings yield)* tells the annual percentage return implied by the P/E. It's simply 1/(P/E).

If P/E is 10, then 1/(P/E) is 0.1, or 10 percent. If P/E is 40, then 1/(P/E) is 0.025, or 2.5 percent. An investor can use this figure to compare this earnings stream to, suppose, a bond. A bond returning $5 on a face value of $100 yields 5 percent. A stock returning $5 in earnings on $100 invested (the stock price) could also be said to yield 5 percent and has a P/E ratio of 20 ($100 × $5). Table 4-1 illustrates the wide range of investment yields implied by different P/E ratios.

Book VII

Value
Investing

Table 4-1	Converting P/E to Earnings Yield
P/E	*Earnings Yield*
1	100.0 percent
5	20.0 percent
8	12.5 percent

(continued)

Table 4-1 *(continued)*

P/E	*Earnings Yield*
10	10.0 percent
12	8.3 percent
15	6.7 percent
20	5.0 percent
30	3.3 percent
40	2.5 percent
50	2.0 percent
60	1.7 percent
75	1.3 percent
100	1.0 percent

P/E and growth

Assessing growth is a major factor in analyzing a stock price through P/E. What is the earnings yield today, what will it be in the future, and how does it get into the equation? Table 4-2 shows future earnings yields realized in the case of a bond with no growth versus a stock with a 10 percent earnings growth.

Table 4-2	**Earnings Yield: Bond versus Growth Stock**	
	Bond	*Stock*
Coupon/earnings yield	5 percent	5 percent
Investment	$100	$100
Year 1 return	$5	$5
Earnings growth	0 percent	10 percent
Year 10 return	$5	$12.97
Earnings Yield (EY) Year 1	5 percent	5 percent
Earnings Yield (EY) Year 10	5 percent	13 percent

A PEG in a poke

Determining whether a P/E by itself is good or bad is difficult. A stock with a P/E of 30, for example, may be a better deal than another stock with a P/E of 15 because of growth. Enter the *price-earnings-to-growth* (PEG) ratio, which is introduced in Chapter *3* of Book VII. In the PEG ratio, you divide all P/Es by the company's growth rate. *G* is the growth rate, expressed as a whole number (that is, the percentage times 100). So a company with a P/E of 30 and a growth rate of 20 percent has a PEG of 1.5.

PEG *normalizes* the P/E to the growth rate, making it a better tool to compare stocks with different P/Es and different underlying growth assumptions. Company A with a P/E of 18 and a growth rate of 12 percent has the same PEG as Company B with a P/E of 30 and a growth rate of 20 percent. Although the two P/Es aren't the same (30 versus 18), the PEG ratio reveals that they are indeed priced equally.

Table 4-3 shows the relationship between future earnings yield, P/E, and PEG. Watch what happens to PEG and future earnings yields as growth assumptions rise. Low PEG ratios (less than 2) correspond to high future earnings yields.

Table 4-3	Earnings Growth, Earnings Yield, and PEG				
	Bond	*Stock 1*	*Stock 2*	*Stock 3*	*Stock 4*
Coupon/ Earnings Yield	5 %	5 %	5 %	5 %	5 %
Investment	$100	$100	$100	$100	$100
Year 1 return	$5	$5	$5	$5	$5
Earnings growth	0 %	5 %	10 %	15 %	20 %
Year 10 return	$5	$8.14	$12.97	$20.23	$30.96
EY (Year 1)	5 %	5 %	5 %	5 %	5 %
EY (Year 10)	5 %	8.1 %	13 %	20.2 %	31 %
Year 1 P/E	N/A	20	20	20	20
Year 1 PEG	N/A	4	2	1.3	1

So what is a "good" PEG ratio? It all depends on the implied future rate of return you're looking for, which depends on investment objectives, risk tolerance, and current risk-free (bond) interest rates.

Hurdle rates and the 15 percent rule

Warren Buffett looks at P/E and growth in a slightly different way, using so-called *hurdle rates*. A hurdle rate is what the name implies: a minimum level of compounded annual returns, or a "bar" over which a business — and thus a stock price — must be able to appreciate to be deemed a good investment. Part of Buffett's thought process is this: If an investment cannot clear a given hurdle, the capital is probably better deployed elsewhere.

Taking a Practical Approach

Throughout the four chapters presented in Book VII, you're exposed to many of the tools — and, more importantly, the thought processes — of today's value investor. At the end of the day, value investors develop their own customized approach to analyzing a business and an investment, derived from these tools and thought processes — an approach that works for them. It works because it makes sense, and as it gets fine-tuned over time, it works from experience.

Many value investors, especially in the beginning, make checklists to help evaluate financial and intangible features of business. They evaluate each business opportunity as if they were attempting to buy the business, looking at assets, profits, growth, customer base, market presence, and management quality as if they were going to have to live with it for a while.

It's not unlike the approach a rational, numbers-oriented buyer may use to buy a car: Look at features and performance data, and then test-drive it to see whether it all works well together, to see whether the whole is at least equal to (preferably better than) the sum of the parts. And yes, the tires are kicked and the doors are opened and closed to check for obvious problems and complete the impression. And the car is carefully compared to other cars in the same category — all before talking to the dealer or owner about price.

Over time, you'll get better at and more comfortable with the value investing approach. You'll learn what to look for so you don't have to get down to every detail of horsepower and gear ratios. Experienced value investors do the diligence, but they discover what's most important to look at in a business as they find out about the industry and other similar businesses. Buffett is famous for doing most of his analysis in his head; like most business owners, you'll get to the point where you can do a lot in your head, too. At the end of the day, the thought process is just as important as the mechanics, if not more so.

Book VIII

Socially Responsible Investing

Five Styles of Social Investing

- ✔ **Corporate governance:** Not all companies are run by managers who are committed to responsible, ethical behavior. Investors following this style seek out well-run companies and press the less-than-the-best to change.

- ✔ **Environmental issues:** Are your concerns centered on the use of natural resources, carbon emissions, and sustainability of the world around us? Many companies share your concern and make good investments.

- ✔ **International affairs:** Maybe you don't want to support corrupt governments or finance wars. That's fair. And your money doesn't have to do that, either. You can use your investments to influence global issues.

- ✔ **Religious beliefs:** Your faith may guide many aspects of your life, and maybe you'd like to include it in your financial planning. By carefully choosing the companies you invest in, you can keep the peace between your religious beliefs and investment strategies.

- ✔ **Social change:** Want to invest in companies that make good products, treat workers well, and contribute to the betterment of society while avoiding those that don't have great reputations? This is the style for you.

Socially responsible investors expect the companies they invest in to act ethically. See the characteristics that responsible corporations possess in a free article at www. dummies.com/extras/highpoweredinvestingaio.

Chapter 1

Making Your Investments Match Your Values

In This Chapter

▶ Checking out reasons for investing responsibly

▶ Keeping an eye on your responsible investments

A lot of people want to do good through investing. Of course, "doing good" is defined differently by different people. Some people want to change the world; they want to be part of new technologies and new ideas that could make society better in the years to come. Some want to avoid businesses that produce products that they disapprove of or to align their investment style with their religious beliefs. And some want to make sure that they aren't undermining their charitable activities with their investments.

This investment style, called *socially responsible investing,* can help you put your money to work financing activities that you support. It can also help you avoid businesses that you'd rather not deal with. Done right, your performance should be no different than if you invested without regard to social responsibility. As the number of social investors grows, maybe even more companies will change how they operate.

If you can figure out whether an investment is responsible, you can be a responsible investor all your life, no matter how your finances and social priorities change. In this chapter, find out who invests responsibly and why, and get pointers on how to monitor and affect your responsible investments.

Discovering Who Invests Responsibly and Why

Social investing is big business. Geoffrey Heal, professor of public policy and business economics at Columbia University, estimates that 10 to 12 percent of all professionally managed investments in the United States come with social restrictions of some sort. That's a lot of money! These restrictions can be anything from a refusal to invest in the so-called "sin" industries (alcohol, gambling, pornography, and tobacco companies) to a comprehensive style looking at the environment, society, and corporate governance.

Investors who like this style look at how employees are paid and whether they can become owners in the company. They look at the company's mission statement, and then evaluate how well it's put into practice. They want to know: Does this company understand its business, and is its business making friends rather than enemies?

Who are these investors? Some are religiously observant and want to avoid anything that may interfere with their spiritual journey. Some simply think it's about time that company managers listened to the people who own the joint. And some would just like a mutual fund option in their 401(k) plan that doesn't make them nervous.

The leaders in social investing are the leading institutional investors: pension funds, charitable foundations, and institutional endowments. The role of institutions is important for two reasons:

✔ These investors care deeply about performance. Most pension funds are required by federal law to consider investment performance first. They can consider other factors, such as social criteria, only as long as performance criteria are met. Pension funds for religious orders and labor unions often want to consider social criteria, so money managers have figured out how to accommodate the performance must-have and the values nice-to-have factors. Foundation and endowment managers have a fiduciary responsibility to the philanthropists who donated the money in the first place. Because these investors have to worry about performance, all investors can benefit from their experience with social investing.

✔ In a changing world, investing can be a tool for making a difference. The simple reason to invest socially is to maintain a clear conscience, but many social investors believe they can also get better performance through responsible investments:

- If investors look for companies that are trying to reduce their effect on the environment, they may find companies that are saving money and generating more profits.

- If they search out businesses that pay workers well, they may find some that create more consumers to grow the overall economy.

- If they avoid companies with bloated executive pay packages and cronies on the board of directors, they may avoid scandals and a string of bad financial results.

Addressing common myths about socially responsible investing

A couple of persistent myths linger about socially responsible investing; no doubt you've heard them and may have been put off by them. The following points help clear up a couple of common myths:

✔ **Myth: Social investing is nice if you don't care about return.** Those who buy into this myth suggest that you instead follow a standard, nonjudgmental investment strategy, and then give the extra profits to charity.

Fact: Contrary to popular belief, socially responsible investing *does* pay off. A social portfolio is likely to be no better nor any worse than any other. The keys to success are to carefully select asset classes and use activist techniques to boost returns.

✔ **Myth: Social investing is some sort of pinko plot to undermine capitalism.**

Fact: The vast majority of social and activist investors come to their practice in hopes of making more money. They are the owners, so they're in charge. That means their investments work for them. He who has the gold should be able to make the rules, as the cliché says. Activist investing is pure capitalism. It uses the power of capital ownership to make change.

The fact is that companies can do well by doing good.

The following sections go into more detail on different reasons people have for investing responsibly.

Contributing to the community

Not all social investors want to change the world. They don't care about sin stocks or business practices in far-off lands. They just want their corner of the globe to be in better shape. They'd like to see new employers creating jobs and paying taxes in their hometown. They'd like to see nicer, safer neighborhoods for people to live in. Maybe they just want to keep their money with a bank that isn't likely to be taken over by some major, mega-global financial institution.

If this describes your investing outlook, you can find many different opportunities. If you have substantial assets and an appetite for risk, you can provide start-up funds to small businesses in the area. If you're looking for a safe, conservative investment, you may want to purchase a certificate of deposit with a federally insured *Community Development Financial Institution,* which is a bank that provides services to local residents. In between those extremes are stock, bond, and real estate investments that may make your town a better place to live, work, and play.

Book VIII

Socially Responsible Investing

Monitoring a company's managers

Many investors don't care so much what business a company is in; they're more concerned that the business is truly run for the shareholders (this is called *corporate governance*). That means management has to be paid for performance, no more and no less. The members of the board of directors should concentrate on providing management oversight and accurate reports to shareholders rather than enhancing their social status. Shareholders should be able to vote democratically and present proposals for management to consider.

Some governance investors look for companies that have great internal practices and a demonstrated history of service to shareholders. Others seek out companies where the management and board have terrible conflicts of interest, performance is lousy, and governance is a mere afterthought. They use their power as owners to force the company to change its ways, improving investment results.

And some governance investors combine tactics. They may be interested in companies that are located in their own community, but if the company doesn't perform well, the investors are in there with all of their activist tools to press the company managers to do better. Someone may have inherited shares in a company that can't be sold under the terms of a trust agreement, but that doesn't mean she has to accept the firm's environmental practices. She can use her power as an owner to push for a board and management that are more responsive to her needs.

Not all governance activists care about the public good. Some are more notorious than noble. However, they're doing nothing more than exercising their rights as owners of the company.

Hugging those trees

The way that companies make goods, ship them, sell them, and then handle the waste has a huge effect on the planet — and on the bottom line. The buzzword is *sustainability,* which is a company's ability to maintain its profits over the very long haul. If a company relies on petroleum, for example, its ability to sustain the business is entirely dependent on the supply and the price of oil. If the company figures out ways to reduce total fuel consumption and use more alternative fuels, it will have an easier time staying in business and generating long-term profits for shareholders.

Maybe you're an investor who is excited about environmental investing because of the potential for revolutionary new technologies. Maybe alternative fuels could be the next television, plastics recycling the next instant photography, or greenhouse gas reduction the next Internet. When you're on the ground floor of new technologies, you take a lot of risk, but you have the opportunity for big profits. Where there's a chance of good growth from major change, there will be investors ready to support it.

Not only do investors want to make money, but so do entrepreneurs. People with great ideas are likely to come forward if they see that they can get financing for them.

Investing internationally and socially

The modern corporation operates all over the world. Its managers don't pay too much attention to borders unless taxes are required to get across them. Investors do pay attention to the countries where companies operate, though. Companies that operate in many countries can choose how much they pay workers and how they operate their facilities. (Wages too high in one country? Move the work somewhere with a lower standard of living.) They also have to deal with governments everywhere they operate, and some national leaders are downright unsavory people.

An international social investor wants to support businesses that do the right thing, even if there aren't laws forcing proper behavior. The "right thing" can range from paying better-than-market wages to refusing to pay bribes to government officials. In many countries, corporations have the money and the power to improve conditions, and social investors want to be a part of that.

Getting reminders from religion

Some investors have religious practices that set forth stringent restrictions. These people must avoid certain investments if they want to live according to their faith. Others aren't necessarily risking their salvation, but they'd prefer that their investments line up with their beliefs. If they don't smoke, for example, they may not want to be involved with companies that grow, distribute, or sell tobacco. If they're opposed to war, they may not want to invest in defense contractors. If they aren't allowed to receive interest, they won't be buying bonds.

New mutual funds and financial services have been cropping up to meet the needs of religious investors. These range from index funds that exclude offending companies to new ways to finance home purchases — new ways from an American perspective, at least.

Finally, some of the most active investors are affiliated with religious schools, charities, and other institutions. They are quick to use the power of their material resources to push for positive change. If you're interested in activist investing, check out groups such as the Interfaith Center on Corporate Responsibility (www.iccr.org), which works to get company managers to pay attention to its interests. It's the owner's prerogative, after all.

Book VIII

Socially Responsible Investing

If your religion has strict rules about money and finance, you should talk to your clergy to make sure your investing program follows them.

Taking the Long View: Monitoring and Influencing Your Investments

After social investors identify their investment criteria — what they look for in terms of risk, returns, and value-alignment — they can start looking for the investment vehicle that aligns with those criteria. Your criteria may exclude certain investments, whether they're industries, such as alcohol, or investment classes, such as bonds. Other social strategies may actually expand your investment universe.

Then social investors have to invest the same way that any other investor would: by reading financial statements, looking up news reports, and maybe even visiting the company.

Easier said than done, right? After all, companies and situations change. Investing socially requires more than simply picking things that meet your investment needs now and then forgetting about it. Not to worry. The following sections tell you how to ensure that the investment opportunities you pursue remain on your "companies I want to do business with" list and what to do if they don't. For specifics on researching companies to evaluate whether they align with your goals, head to Chapter 2 in Book VIII.

Social investors tend to fall in love with a company's mission and then assume it will be a great investment. It doesn't work that way. You have to combine social criteria with information about the investment's financial condition and outlook. No investment will do well just because you want it to.

Keeping abreast of changes

The beauty of social investing is that it forces companies to make changes. But the marketplace is so dynamic that companies change all the time anyway. To be a successful social investor, you have to stay on top of the news. You want to know whether your investment is making financial progress and whether it still fits your style.

Some companies that fit when you first put money into them won't always stay aligned with your goals: Maybe you don't invest in companies involved in gambling, and the company just acquired a hotel and casino operation. Some companies that didn't fit your criteria initially may be a good match for you now because the management has responded to shareholder pressure. You may want to reward the positive change with your investment.

The specific issues that matter to social investors change all the time. International investors have to change their lists of companies and tactics as new world hot spots develop. Thirty years ago, many people wouldn't invest in companies that did business in South Africa. Today, the concern for many investors is companies that do business in Sudan. What will the concern be in 30 years? Who knows, but an investor clinging to old notions of good and bad will miss opportunities that an up-to-date investor will seize.

Making a careful selection of assets

To be successful as a social investor, you have to do more than just find good companies to invest in. You need to find a mixture of investments that reflects your risk and return parameters. If you only invest in stocks, you may take too much risk and lose too much money in those years when the stock market is down. If you put your money in a federally insured bank CD, even if the bank specializes in community lending, you'll have a responsible investment that barely beats inflation and probably won't help you meet your goals.

Fortunately, with the huge range of investments available, you can diversify your risk and improve your returns without compromising your investment goals. Your options range from very secure life insurance to very risky hedge funds. You can invest in real estate, venture capital, and exchange-traded funds without compromising your social beliefs. And that diversification across assets can help you get a better return at the same time.

Using shareholder activism

Shareholders are part owners of a company. *Bondholders* are lenders. In either case, money gives them power. Even if you're a relatively small investor, you can still be an activist. Even smaller investors can research issues, find out who the big investors are, and put the power of their purses to work.

As a stockholder, you have the right to vote on some corporate issues, including the members of the board of directors and certain compensation packages. Although no one shareholder usually has enough votes to count, many shareholders together can combine their votes and put pressure on a

Book VIII

Socially Responsible Investing

company's management to make changes or else face dealing with new directors who may not be as accommodating.

Companies also accept proposals for shareholders to vote on. You can ask for a report on environmental policies or for the closing of operations in a world trouble spot or for more equitable pay for workers. Even if these resolutions don't pass (and, in truth, they rarely do), the mere fact that they're proposed can sometimes get a management group to think about addressing the issue later.

Andrew Carnegie and "The Gospel of Wealth"

Andrew Carnegie was on the scene long before Bill Gates and Warren Buffett. Adjusted for inflation, Carnegie was worth about $300 billion, which made him far richer than either of his early 21st-century counterparts. He was a Scottish immigrant who arrived in Western Pennsylvania in 1848 at the age of 13. He went to work almost immediately, and at a series of successively better jobs, he proved himself to be clever and hardworking. He saved as much money as he could and invested it in railroad, oil, and steel companies, which were the high-tech industries of their day. Carnegie developed a reputation for being tight with money and ruthless in business. He didn't pay his workers well because he believed that they'd squander their money. His deputy, Henry Clay Frick, hired security guards who shot and killed striking workers at Carnegie's Homestead Steel Works.

And yet, although he may not have been a model employer, Carnegie believed he had an obligation to give his money back to society. He became one of the greatest philanthropists in history, funding libraries around the United States, sponsoring paleontological expeditions, establishing a university in Pittsburgh (now Carnegie-Mellon University), and creating many other institutions all over the world that still thrive today, including Carnegie Hall in New York City and the Carnegie Corporation, a $3 billion charitable foundation.

In 1889, Carnegie wrote an essay about his views of philanthropy, entitled "The Gospel of Wealth." In it, he says that capitalism makes society better for everyone, but that it also creates disproportionate wealth for a few. Those few have an obligation to spend it on philanthropy while they're alive rather than spend it on themselves, give it to their children, or leave it to charity only after they die.

Carnegie's practices have influenced those who have come after him, even if they choose to pay their workers well and negotiate rather than open fire. You can read "The Gospel of Wealth" online at www.swarthmore.edu/SocSci/rbannis1/AIH19th/Carnegie.html.

Chapter 2

The Socially Responsible Enterprise: Evaluating Companies

*O*rganizations need financing to grow, and they often have to rely on outside investors to help them. That means they need to operate in ways that make investors comfortable and ensure a good return on the investment. A business that plays fair and respects all of its stakeholders (employees, customers, vendors, and the community), not just its shareholders, is likely to do well in the long run. And that's the point of social investing.

This chapter gives you the tools you need to evaluate whether a business is worthy of your investment dollars. Here you discover how a business model impacts a company's willingness to embrace socially responsible business practices, how businesses balance making money for their shareholders with being responsible corporate citizens, what's required to head off problems between investors and managers, and what a business's financial reports reveal. And then, because all the preceding documents are generated by the businesses themselves, you find out how to go outside the bubble to see how others view the business's practices.

Seeing How a Company Makes Its Money

The hardest thing for any company to do is to come up with a product or service that people are willing to pay for. Companies have to do that (and, hopefully, do that responsibly) to stay in business.

In academic theory, a firm has no purpose other than to maximize shareholder value. In practice, many companies can maximize shareholder value while also behaving responsibly.

Businesspeople like to talk about their *business models,* which simply explain how a company makes its money. A company whose model is to be the lowest-cost provider approaches business differently than one offering luxury goods. A company's business model influences the social choices that a company can make because it affects how it can spend money while keeping shareholders happy. If customers demand the absolute lowest prices, then management may have less leeway to spend money on responsible initiatives and still keep their customers — and shareholders — happy.

But this isn't always the case. For example, Wal-Mart (NYSE: WMT), which uses a low-price business model, found that it could keep prices low by reducing energy costs in its stores and throughout its supply chain, enabling the company to deliver on its business model while improving the environment.

In the following sections, I explain how business models work, as well as how a company's product may influence your decision to invest in the company. Then I take a look at how a company gets its products and services into customers' hands.

Searching for clues in the company's mission, strategy, and tactics

A business model is set out in three parts: the mission statement, strategy, and tactics. An organization that really wants to be socially responsible needs to behave well in all three areas. Ultimately, though, the tactics are most important because they are responsibility in practice. Tactics are where the rubber meets the road.

Although a few companies set these out in a nice brochure, most make you figure out what's what. Also, some mission statements are marketing tactics rather than true guidelines for corporate behavior. More than one company has written a highfalutin mission statement and used a business model that could be socially responsible. Day to day, though, the managers used tactics that generated immediate results with no thought to long-term effects or social missions. Why? Because they were paid for those immediate results, with no questions asked about how they got them. So don't invest based on a mission statement. Do your research to see whether the management walks the talk in its strategy and tactics.

Mission statements

Many companies have *mission statements* to describe what they hope to do. The statements are usually just two or three lines long and describe the company's business and operating philosophy at the very highest level: "We will be the premier widget company, exceeding customer expectations. We recognize that employees are our number-one asset and that everyone in the organization is responsible for our sterling reputation."

Even though many mission statements rely on clichés to telegraph complex ideas, they still give an indication of what the company's priorities are: Does the company give top priority to the product or the service? Does it emphasize low prices or high quality? Does it make an explicit statement of responsibility toward customers, the community, or employees? Is the mission high-minded (creating a healthy world, for example), or is it practical (being the market leader)? The mission statement is the starting point for all decisions down the line.

Not all companies have an explicit mission statement, but you can get a sense of a company's mission from its different shareholder reports and marketing materials. Head to the later section "Paying Attention to Company Reports" for details.

Strategy

The *strategy* is the plan for putting the mission statement into action. It looks into the future. It isn't updated frequently, but it does change as needed to reflect changes in the company's operating environment. If the company's mission is to offer low prices to customers, then the strategy may be to buy in volume, sell direct rather than through retail stores, or operate with very low overhead.

Tactics

Tactics are the methods the company uses to meet its strategy. If the strategy is to do intensive research, then the tactics may include such matters as recruiting scientists, choosing promising areas for further study, and applying for patents whenever appropriate. Because the tactics are the specific steps used to run the business, managers may change them frequently to meet the needs of the ever-changing marketplace.

Evaluating the company's goods and services

Many social investors look at the revenue line first. Does the company make alcohol? Pork sausage? Pornography? Weapons? If so, then the investment

Book VIII

Socially
Responsible
Investing

may not be acceptable under their investment guidelines, and no other factor can change that — not the company's governance, its treatment of employees, nor its environmental practices.

If the company passes that top-line cut, though, you have some more work to do if you care about what a company produces. Here are some things to consider:

- ✔ **Are the products good ones that add value to or profoundly change society?** Are the fastest growing markets ones that you want to support as a shareholder? Many businesses come about because a visionary entrepreneur sees the opportunity to make a lot of money by developing a product that changes the way the world works. Some are good; some are bad. A bottled water company simply takes something that's more or less free from the tap, puts it into plastic packaging, hauls it to stores in trucks that burn fossil fuels, and charges more money per gallon for it than gasoline costs. It's a sweet business model — it takes a lot of vision to realize that there's a way to charge people $1.49 for something that used to be free. It's not exactly socially or environmentally responsible, but it's a product people are happy to buy.

   Others see that huge profits can be made from designing a car that runs on something other than fossil fuels, growing food without pesticides, and developing low-cost computers for people in developing countries.

- ✔ **How is the product used, how is it disposed of, and does the company's management oversee the product portfolio responsibly?** For example, toymaker Mattel (NASDAQ: MAT) had a serious problem on its hands in 2007, when many of its toys tested with higher lead levels than were allowed. Consumers were upset, needless to say, and the stock price fell. Investors wanted to be confident that the company was going to make good products that didn't harm the children who played with them.

Investigating how the company gets products to market

Selling a product involves a combination of packaging, advertising, promotion, and distribution; like all things socially responsible, getting the product from the factory to the shop and into the customers' hands can be done in responsible, neutral, or irresponsible ways.

Packaging and distribution are closely related matters of sustainability and cost control. Is the packaging designed with reused and recycled materials that can be easily reused or recycled again, or is it made from all new materials? Likewise, how efficient is the supply chain? Can the company get goods from place to place using a minimum of resources?

You also should think about who buys those packaged goods after they end up on the shelf. Are you comfortable with the customers being targeted by the advertising and promotion campaigns? Some investors aren't comfortable investing in companies that market to teenagers with R-rated catalogs, that sell expensive products to people who can't afford them, or that push goods too aggressively toward children.

Finding out about a company's marketing practices is probably easier than investigating almost any other aspect of its business, because the goal of marketing is to grab attention.

Noting How a Company Balances Shareholder and Stakeholder Needs

A business can't be socially responsible unless it can make the business case that being socially responsible is good for the bottom line. Legally, corporations are managed for the benefit of their shareholders, who own the company. In the United States, corporate managers have a fiduciary responsibility to maximize shareholder value while complying with other laws. Some managers interpret that to mean that even the teensiest bit of philanthropy is wrong because it hurts shareholders. Others argue that behaving responsibly benefits shareholders.

The following sections cover the differing interests of shareholders and others and introduce a philosophy — the so-called *triple bottom line* — that can bridge the gap between the shareholders and everyone else.

Maximizing shareholder value

The key responsibility of a company is to maximize wealth for its owners, the shareholders. This mandate isn't as mercenary as it may seem. Usually, what makes shareholders happy makes everyone else happy, too: good products or services that customers gladly pay for, employees who run the company efficiently, and so on. Also, a well-run business can generate profits for shareholders long into the future. But some potential pitfalls in maximizing shareholder value exist:

- ✔ **Cutting corners:** Sometimes management's desire to get paid well while keeping pesky shareholders off its back leads to cut corners and even outright fraud. This short-term thinking can destroy a business.

> ✔ **Neglecting customer service:** Customer service is an ongoing expense that creates long-term value. A company with a short-term perspective can boost its profits in the short run by cutting back on customer service, which may make the short-term shareholders happy, but all the annoyed customers will go elsewhere, harming long-term shareholders.

The key debate about socially responsible behavior by corporations is whether it's good or bad for shareholder wealth. Is socially responsible behavior a big expense that detracts from the ongoing mission of making money, or is it an investment that may take a little from profits now but make the company stronger for years to come? Investments in good governance, clean technology, or sustainable economic development may take years to pay off, even if the payoff will be spectacular. Not all shareholders are patient enough to wait, and some may push the company to give up the project.

Remembering stakeholder value

Stakeholders are not shareholders. They're all the other people who contribute to the success or failure of the corporation: employees, vendors, customers, members of the community where the company has facilities, regulators, and so on.

In the short run, corporations can maximize shareholder value without even thinking about the other stakeholders, but it can't do so in the long run. A company that wants to maximize shareholder value for years to come needs to think about its stakeholders — how it recruits workers, retains employees, and works with the community at large.

Although companies have a fiduciary obligation to maximize shareholder value, they use more than just shareholder capital to make the business possible. They need other inputs to operate: roads, communities, an educated work force, and so on, as well as key inputs that belong to no one but affect everyone, such as air, water, and soil.

Externality is the term economists use to describe the effects that a business has on things that are outside the price of the goods or services it sells. For example, if a business pollutes the water, there's a cost to the world, but this cost isn't included in the price of the product. That's a negative externality. Externalities can be positive, too. For example, maybe the company sponsors the local symphony as a way of marketing to its target customers, but all music lovers benefit from the donation.

Uniting shareholders and stakeholders with the triple bottom line

Because a company's management team has the responsibility to maximize shareholder value, it can't pursue any projects that benefit stakeholders unless it can show that these will ultimately pay off for the shareholders. Still, a company that plans to stay in business for a long time needs to keep other stakeholders happy.

The *triple bottom line,* popularized by a book of the same name (written by Andrew Savitz and Karl Weber), asks companies to account for how their operations and strategies affect people, the planet, and — of course — profits. The goal is to get companies thinking about how they will generate profits over the long haul by protecting important inputs.

✔ **The people:** Companies are accountable to the people they touch: employees, customers, contractors, and residents in the communities surrounding their facilities. Although what people need may vary from place to place and time to time, paying attention to — and keeping track of — how they are treated leads the company to do the right thing for its stakeholders and shareholders alike.

An organization's reputation is built on how it treats the people it deals with, no matter who they are or what they do.

✔ **The planet:** This component of the triple bottom line looks at how a company's activities affect the environment. A company's environmental responsibility derives from how a product is sourced, manufactured, and moved to market, but it's also affected by what the company does at headquarters and how it works with its contractors. (No fair claiming to be clean while outsourcing your manufacturing to a contractor in a country with no environmental laws, and then flying in a big, old, carbon-spewing airplane to check up on things!)

✔ **The profit:** Without profits, the business will close, an event that harms the employees who need jobs, the customers who need what the company provides, the government that relies on it for taxes, and the shareholders who need a rate of return to meet their goals. Ideally, the short-term profits will allow the company to afford its investments in people and planet, while those sustainability investments will pay off in long-term profits for the smart, socially responsible shareholders.

A U.K. organization, AccountAbility (www.accountability.org), has drawn up standards similar to Generally Accepted Accounting Principles (GAAP; the rules that govern accounting in the United States) to help companies report their social and sustainable activities. Many global companies use them now, and the hope is that more will soon adopt the standards to help investors and others understand the effects of business activities.

Heading Off Principal-Agent Problems

Socially responsible investors want to invest in companies that reflect their values. As owners, they want the managers who work for them to behave in responsible ways. But managers, being human beings, may want to do what's best for themselves, not necessarily for the people they work for. Then throw into the mix that investors themselves have different opinions about how best to increase their returns: Some investors have a short-term perspective, while others want the company to be around for the ages.

The term denoting the conflicts of interest between managers and different types of investors is *principal-agent problem.* The investors (or owners) are the *principals,* and the managers are the *agents.*

Principal-agent conflicts are hardly insurmountable, but they require the following:

✔ **That management be transparent about what it's doing so the shareholders have enough information to make decisions:** As a shareholder, you don't have the right to information about the tiniest details of the business, because the business can't compete without keeping some information confidential. However, you have the absolute right to basic information about the company's finances. Find out more about that in the later section "Paying Attention to Company Reports."

In a perfect world, the managers tell you everything you need to know. But most managers report only what they have to, usually as mandated by such government regulators as the U.S. Securities and Exchange Commission (SEC), and not always in a format that's easy for regular folks to read. Because the managers don't perfectly represent the interests of all the shareholders, you have to do your own research to see how management is doing.

✔ **That shareholders pay attention so they can influence what the management team is doing before problems develop:** In addition to doing all the work that regular investors do (figuring out your risk parameters and your desired return, setting appropriate financial goals, finding suitable investments, and tracking your returns to see whether you need to make changes), as a social investor, you also need to track how an investment is meeting your personal goals. As an owner, you take on the task of making sure that the business you invest in meets your priorities.

Turning managers into owners

Owners and managers don't have to be locked in bitter combat. Just as a business can do well for shareholders while still respecting the interests of other stakeholders, it can make shareholders wealthy while still rewarding managers for their hard work. The way to do that is by making owners out of the managers. When employees have ownership stakes in the company, they benefit when the shareholders do. Companies can do this several ways: by giving stock as compensation, offering retirement plan matching, granting employee stock options, and so on.

Keep in mind, however, that although stock options can make managers rich, they don't always benefit shareholders. Companies have been known to give too many options away, to set the price so low that holders will always make money, or even to reset the price so employees can exercise the option at a profit even if the stock price went down on their watch. Although stock options can ally managers with owners, giving employees actual shares is more effective if reducing conflicts of interest is the goal.

Paying Attention to Company Reports

Social investing means different things to different people; for example, a Muslim has a different investment universe than a tree hugger. Furthermore, companies change over time, so a definitive list of acceptable investments would be out of date in a matter of months.

For these reasons, a socially responsible investor must also be a *fundamental analyst,* a person who does careful research into the financials and the business to figure out how a company makes its money, whether that source of profits will continue, and how the company fits into an investment portfolio. Social investors need to figure out what to look for, and then find it, before making an investment. That's what the following sections are all about.

Book VIII

Socially Responsible Investing

Reading and understanding an annual report (10K)

The *annual report* is the key to understanding what a public company does to earn money. In most cases, it's the first place to look for information to help you determine whether to make an investment.

Every year, publicly traded corporations have to file an annual report with the SEC. The required form is called *10K,* and it's a veritable treasure trove of information about a company. Chapter 2 of Book VII provides all sorts of details about an annual report. The following sections provide a brief overview and indicate particular things to pay attention to as a social investor.

Every quarter, the SEC requires companies to file an update on their progress on form *10Q.* These reports are similar to the annual report, although without as much detail; they're important for tracking changes in the business over the year. See the section "Reviewing quarterly reports (10Q)," later in this chapter, for more info.

Want to find a 10K report to help you follow along as you read the next sections? Go to the SEC's EDGAR database (`www.sec.gov/edgar.shtml`), which includes all filings of all public companies in the United States. You can search for a company that interests you and find its 10K report. Any company will work because the basic format is standard.

Management's discussion and analysis

Management's discussion and analysis (MD&A) is the executive spin on what happened. It's not a marketing document, though, so you can expect to see bad news. What it tells you is where the company made its money and what the outlook is for its different business lines. It may break revenues down into different business lines and geographic areas, describe such extraordinary circumstances as natural disasters or lawsuits that affected operations, and discuss areas where the management plans to invest and expand.

Signatures and certifications

Financial reports are prepared by company management, but publicly traded companies have to have their financial reports audited by an outside firm. The audit firm issues two statements:

- ✔ **Certification of financial results:** This certificate is a letter from the accounting firm describing what it did in the audit and what it found. In addition to text establishing that the company's management is responsible for the numbers and asserting that it followed the guidance of the Public Company Accounting Oversight Board (PCAOB) in preparing the report, it also indicates whether the financial statements are a fair representation of the firm's financial position (an *unqualified opinion,* meaning there are no exceptions or catches to the statement) or, occasionally, that the financial results are fair representations except for whatever issues the auditors uncovered (a *qualified opinion*). Investing in a company with a qualified auditor opinion is riskier than investing in a company without one, but an unqualified opinion doesn't necessarily signify an unsafe investment.

The report also discusses the *financial controls* of the company, things like whether people lose access to the computer system when they quit, who approves any adjustments to sales figures, and so on.

✔ **Certification of financial controls:** Here, the auditing firm describes a bit of what it did to determine whether the company's accounting process comes up with accurate numbers. Having good internal controls means that the company has some assurance that the numbers being tracked are accurate. Keep in mind, however, that the standards for internal controls are complex, and it's not unheard of for a good company to miss a few. You may see a qualified statement that explains that the company has good controls except for a new acquisition, except for one or two international operations, or except for a new accounting system that's been installed but not yet tested.

Income statements

The *income statement* tells how much money the company brought in from sales of its goods and services, and how much money it had to spend to get those sales. Here's what you should note while examining the income statement:

✔ **Sales:** The money that came in from selling the company's goods and services (also called *revenue* or *turnover*). In most cases, you want to see sales go up each year.

✔ **Cost of goods sold (COGS):** Any expenses that can be directly tied to a particular sale. This amount should stay more or less constant, or go down, as a percentage of sales.

✔ **Gross profit:** The difference between sales and the cost of goods (sometimes called *gross margin*). You calculate it as a percentage by dividing gross profit by sales. The result is a useful number for tracking how the profits from sales change over time.

✔ **Selling, general, and administrative costs (SG&A):** The costs of running the business that can't be directly tied to any particular sales (sometimes called *operating expenses*). These costs should grow more slowly than sales.

✔ **Operating income:** Gross profit minus SG&A. It shows how much money the company has to cover its financing, both debt and equity. It's sometimes called *EBIT,* for *earnings before interest and taxes* (yes, people really say *ee*-bit).

✔ **Interest expense:** The money that the company has to pay to anyone to whom it owes money. It should be a small percentage of operating income; if the company misses payments to anyone who has loaned it money, it may be forced into bankruptcy.

- ✔ **Interest and other income:** The money that a company makes on its cash balances. Companies often provide financing to customers, and that generates interest income, too.

- ✔ **Income tax:** The liability that the company is expected to have, given current tax rates. The taxes actually paid are reported in the footnotes to the financial statements.

- ✔ **Net income:** How much of the profit is left over for shareholders after interest and taxes are considered.

After you look at the annual report and financial statements for a company that you're interested in investing in, check out the annual report of its largest competitor, even if you would never consider buying shares in that company. The comparison will give you a sense of what your company is doing right, where it has room to improve, and where it's vulnerable.

Balance sheets

The *balance sheet* tells you what a company owns *(assets)* and what it owes *(liabilities)*. It has to balance, by definition, because every transaction has to have an offsetting transaction somewhere else. That's a useful check for the company's bookkeepers when they're looking for errors. By the time the balance sheet gets published for your perusal, everything adds up nicely. The only question for you is, how strong is it? In other words, what are the company's assets, and how are they financed?

The difference between assets and liabilities is the *shareholders' equity.* It's what the shareholders get to keep after all the bills are paid, at least according to the values recorded on the balance sheet. The total value matters more to you than any of the line items.

Statement of cash flows

The *statement of cash flows* is one of the most mysterious of the financial statements, but it's also really important. It tells you how much of a company's sales brings in cash and how much of a company's expenditures sends out cash. The statement of cash flows is broken down into three sections:

- ✔ **Cash from operating activities,** which shows how much money was generated from the company's basic business. In addition to other information, pay particular attention to the bottom line for this section, which is *net cash from operations.* This line tells you whether the company's business is bringing in cash or using it up. Over the long run, this number has to be positive or the company can't stay in business. When a company is expanding, it may have negative cash from operations as it spends on inventory and extends credit to more customers. When a company is running into trouble, it may also have negative cash from operations, so check to see where your business is.

✔ **Cash from investing activities,** which shows spending on property, plants, and equipment. In order to grow, businesses have to invest. They have to spend money on the equipment that employees need to get their jobs done. They may need to add more office space or larger manufacturing facilities. The company may even want to acquire another business. This section of the statement of cash flows will usually be negative, and that's okay. Smart investments can help a company stay around for the long haul. In fact, a company that's not spending enough on investments won't be able to sustain its business.

✔ **Cash from financing activities,** which explains how the company raises money or returns it to shareholders. This section shows how the company is getting the money it needs, other than the money that it generates from operations.

Following these three sections, the company reports its net change in cash for the year. Over several years, it should be slightly positive. If a company has too much cash, it should be paying dividends, buying back stock, or investing in the business. If it's short of cash, it won't be in business much longer.

Footnotes

The footnotes to the financial statements are like a treasure map. Following the footnotes can be tedious, but that's how you get to where all the good stuff is hidden: how much money the company actually paid in taxes, how much money it owes its employee pension plan, whether it has pending lawsuits that could hurt it, when its debts come due, what kinds of debts — like leases — it has that aren't reported on the balance sheet, and so on.

It's worth the slog through the bog of legalese. Many times, good news or bad news is leaked in the footnotes to those who bother to read them.

Perusing the precious proxy

Book VIII

Socially Responsible Investing

Each year, companies send their shareholders statements of issues for them to vote on. *Proxies* are important sources of information to consult before you invest. Just like annual reports (described earlier in this chapter), proxies are public information that must be filed with the SEC. You can often get them from the company, even if you aren't a shareholder, or you can go to the SEC's website, www.sec.gov.

Proxies contain three key tidbits of interest to prospective investors: who the members of the board of directors are, what potential conflicts of interest exist that may cloud the executives' or the board members' judgments, and how much money the executives make.

Reading the board of directors' information

Legally, companies are owned by shareholders who elect a board of directors that oversees the work of management. The proxy is the medium for electing the board, so the proxy statement includes biographical information about the people in the running. Look it over. Here are some things you definitely want to know if you're a social investor:

- **Do these seem like people who understand business, finance, and the company's industry?** You want to see that the board has members who understand their responsibilities and who have the time to do the work. Some boards nominate glamorous people, maybe because the other board members want to hobnob. Now, a celebrity may well be able to do the job, but do your research to make sure.

- **How often do the board members attend meetings?** Most governance experts believe that a board member needs to attend at least 75 percent of all meetings to provide good guidance.

- **Do the board members have any conflicts of interest?** You'll find this info in the section titled something like "Committee Interlocks and Related Transactions." A common issue is compensation, because the CEO may well be on a board determining compensation for a board member who is an officer at another company. In that situation, both have incentives to push for big raises and little oversight. You may also see board members arranging jobs for their children, receiving significant discounts on products that the company sells, or working for customers. Then decide: Are these conflicts great enough that the board member may not be making good decisions for me?

Checking out the execs' compensation and conflicts of interest

The fun part of the proxy is the section on executive compensation. It usually starts with a description of the company's philosophy, or mission statement: Is it to be an industry leader in all aspects, including executive pay? Is the goal to reward top performers? Share gains with all employees? Maintain equity? Promote loyalty? Provide incentives? These different attitudes affect the way that people at all levels are paid. No system is right or wrong, but the choice affects the organization's culture. It may also affect the company's performance, depending on what market conditions it faces.

Following the discussion of how the firm approaches pay, the proxy includes a description of employee stock option programs and other incentive compensation that involves stock. Shareholders care because new stock issued reduces the percentage of the firm that other shareholders have. They want to know whether the performance incentives offset that dilution.

The proxy then lists the compensation of the five most highly paid officers in the firm, as well as the compensation for members of the board of directors and the chairman of the board, if the chairman isn't also an executive.

There's nothing wrong with executives making a lot of money as long as they're generating results for shareholders and as long as all employees are compensated for their work, too. There's a problem if the executives get fat raises while everyone else sees their returns go down.

The best part of the proxy statement's discussion of compensation is usually found near the end under the heading "Certain Relationships and Related Transactions." Here, the executives disclose any conflicts of interest they may have, which can range from owning the office building that the company leases for its headquarters to giving their children summer jobs. Most of these conflicts at most companies are minor, but on occasion, you'll see conflicts so large that they smack of management contempt for the shareholders.

Reviewing quarterly reports (10Q)

Every three months, publicly traded companies have to update shareholders on their progress. They usually issue a news release and hold a conference call, but the minimum requirement is to file a quarterly report on form 10Q with the SEC. You can get the 10Q from the company or from the SEC's website, www.sec.gov/edgar.shtml.

The 10Q is similar in format to the 10K report but much less detailed. It includes a discussion of what has changed over the quarter and then includes quarterly financial statements with footnotes. The presentation may have fewer lines than the annual report, and it isn't audited by any accounting firms, but it should give you enough information to determine how your company is doing relative to the same time period last year.

Most companies have seasonal businesses. Most retailers, for example, post almost all of their sales in December. Hospitals show more admissions in winter months, because of flu and pneumonia, than they do in the summer. That's why you need to compare quarterly results to the same quarter a year ago rather than to the quarter that just passed.

Checking up on current report filings (8K)

If a company has significant news to announce between the due dates for its 10K and 10Q filings, the SEC has it issue an *8K report,* also called a *current report of material events or corporate changes.* An 8K may contain information about a management change, a disaster at an operating facility, the announcement of a major new product, or the outcome of a pending lawsuit.

In most cases, the company also issues a press release that you can find online. The 8K filing ensures that the news announcement becomes part of a company's permanent record, available to everyone through the SEC, no matter what happens to the press release or other news archives.

Poring over the prospectuses

Whenever a company issues a significant amount of new securities, it has to issue a *prospectus.* A prospectus looks a lot like a 10K report, but has even more information about the history of the business and the qualifications of the management team. Some companies issue only one prospectus at the time of the initial public offering and never issue another. Other companies may do another public offering of stock, issue public bonds, and make large acquisitions by using enough stock that a prospectus has to be printed.

The company that you're researching may not have any prospectuses. But if it does, be sure to read the most recent one to help you decide whether the investment will help you meet your financial and social objectives.

Following is some key information about the various types of prospectuses:

- **Stock prospectuses:** When a company issues stock for the first time in an *initial public offering (IPO),* it has to issue a prospectus on SEC form S1. This sets out the company's history, gives detailed biographical information on the senior managers and board members, and describes its industry in depth.

  Some companies make other large offerings of stock after the IPO, referred to as a *follow-on offering* if new shares are issued or as a *secondary offering* if current owners are selling large blocks of stock. For these, a new prospectus has to be filed on form S3.

  If a company makes a major acquisition and has to issue stock to do it, it will issue an S3 prospectus, possibly in combination with a proxy if current shareholders have to vote on the deal. This prospectus describes the combined business, including *pro forma* financial statements that show what the financial results would look like if the companies were already combined. It's usually the best source of information about how a merger will work.

- **Debt prospectuses:** Many companies issue publicly traded bonds. They usually do this through a *shelf registration,* which means they can file a bond offering with the SEC and then sell the bonds as they need to in order to raise the money. If the company's stock is already public, it can usually make the offering under form *FWP* (for *free-writing prospectus*), a supplementary statement that explains what the offering is and how the securities will work. It doesn't go into details about the company and its history. If a company doesn't have public stock but wants to issue public bonds, it has to issue a prospectus with information similar to that of a stock offering.

- **Mutual fund prospectuses:** Open-end mutual funds issue new shares every day to people who want to invest in them. They are sold through prospectuses that are updated at least once a year.

> A mutual fund prospectus is a little different from a company prospectus. Instead of giving an extensive history of the fund, it explains what the fund is like right now, gives an overview of the fund's investment objectives and the strategy, and usually describes the amount of risk the fund is expected to have so investors can determine whether it matches their desires. The fund also has information about historic performance, as well as a detailed discussion of the types and amounts of fees that are charged.

Staying Up-to-Date in Other Ways

The annual report and the proxy tell you the general state of the company at the end of the last fiscal year. But a lot can happen in the intervening days between annual reports. If you're considering investing in a company, you should check out the latest facts. You can get some of the information from the company in conference calls and investor presentations, and the rest you can find from reading the news.

Listening in on conference calls

Many companies hold a conference call for analysts and investors after they report their earnings each quarter. One or two of the senior executives go through the results and explain what happened (with a hefty dose of positive spin, natch), and then take questions. In most cases, only analysts and institutional investors invited by the company can ask questions, but anyone can listen. Companies usually announce these calls on their websites. Most companies also post a recording or a transcript of the conference call on their websites. (Companies don't have to have conference calls, but if they do, they are required to make the information available to all investors.)

These calls are great sources of information about where the business is headed. The questions — and the answers — give you a good sense of what concerns experienced analysts have about the financial results and the prospects for the future. The managers answering the questions may be cheery, candid, evasive, or even a combination of the three. The information helps you track the progress of the business, or find out where it's been and where it's going if you're a prospective shareholder.

Viewing investor presentations

When you're checking out the investor section of the company's website, you may see some presentations that company executives have given to groups of investors, usually at brokerage firm conferences. The SEC requires presenting

Book VIII

Socially Responsible Investing

companies to share their presentations with all investors through transcripts, Webcasts, or slide shows that you can find on their websites.

As with the conference calls (see the preceding section), there will be a lot of happy talk about how the company is the best at everything. You'll also get some data and news updates that can give you a sense of how the company is progressing toward its targets.

Doing a news search

The SEC filings contain a ridiculous amount of information about a company, but it's all from the company's perspective. You also want to get information from people outside the company, who have different perspectives on the business.

Besides the major newspapers (the *New York Times,* the *Wall Street Journal,* the *Financial Times*), many companies are covered in great depth by the media of the town where the headquarters is. Some companies are followed by bloggers who are obsessed with the good, the bad, and everything in between. And sometimes, interesting tidbits about the company come up when you least expect them.

As an investor, you need to be comfortable with online research so that you can take advantage of all this information! Several financial sites let you monitor stock prices during the day, and many of these sites carry press releases announcing corporate news. A simple query through any of the popular search sites can turn up information that you may not have considered.

Google offers a service called Google Alerts (www.google.com/alerts) that lets you place your search terms on file. You'll then receive an e-mail whenever a site with those terms comes up on Google. But that may not be enough for you. You may also want to consider searching blogs through a service like Technorati (technorati.com); you may even uncover a few related to your investments or to your social activism style that you want to monitor regularly.

Major news databases, such as LexisNexis (www.lexisnexis.com) or ABI/INFORM (go to www.proquest.com and enter ABI/INFORM in the search box in the top right corner of the page), can help you find articles in smaller newspapers, trade magazines, and other publications that may not offer online access to their archives. Subscriptions to these services are pricey, but most public libraries have subscriptions. Your library may allow you to get access to these databases through its website by using your library card. Your friendly local librarian may direct you to other investment databases the library subscribes to that you can use to help you find out more about companies before you invest in them.

Chapter 3

Introducing the Islamic Capital Market

*W*hen the global financial crises started doing serious damage in 2007, nearly everyone felt the pinch. Interestingly, the Islamic finance industry survived these crises with less stress and better performance than many nations' conventional industries. In addition, assets sold in the Islamic market must comply with Islamic religious principles that result in certain industries and certain conventional trading practices being prohibited. As a result, many non-Muslims now invest in Islamic financial markets.

This chapter explains what Islamic finance is, examines how it differs from its conventional counterpart, and explains its fundamental principles.

Defining the Concepts and Principles of Islamic Finance

Islamic finance is a financial system that operates according to Islamic law (which is called *sharia*) and is, therefore, sharia-compliant. Just like conventional financial systems, Islamic finance features banks, capital markets, fund managers, investment firms, and insurance companies. However, these entities are governed both by Islamic law and the finance industry rules and regulations that apply to their conventional counterparts.

Islam is more than a religion; it's also a code of life that deals with social, economic, and political matters. A person who follows Islam is a Muslim, and every Muslim is expected to live according to the Islamic code, which is sharia (Islamic law). Each issue addressed by sharia is entwined with all other issues;

therefore, economic matters are related to religion, culture, ethics, politics, and so on. This section introduces the concepts that support the Islamic finance system and the principles that every institution within it must apply.

Searching for balance

Islamic economics is based on core concepts of balance, which help ensure that the motives and objectives driving the Islamic finance industry are beneficial to society. Here are these core concepts:

- ✔ **Balancing material pursuits and spiritual needs:** In Islam, economic activity conducted according to sharia is, itself, an act of worship. That is, Muslims believe they will be granted rewards or merits for sharia-compliant economic activities just as they're rewarded for worshipping Allah (God). The key to achieving such rewards is to find balance between economic activities and spirituality. In other words, a follower of the faith shouldn't focus on business success so much that he neglects worship, for example.

- ✔ **Balancing individual and social needs:** A Muslim is expected to consider society in general when enjoying the bounties granted to her by Allah. These considerations include promoting justice in all economic activities, remembering that all people have mutual responsibility for all others, and using the earth's resources wisely.

Islam promotes moderate consumption and prohibits extravagant spending. That word *extravagant* applies both to spending too much on acceptable products and activities and to spending any money at all on prohibited ones. In addition, even though the supply of resources in this world is limited, Muslims believe that Allah has provided everything that humans need (and in an appropriate quantity). Islam ensures that humans use resources wisely by placing limits on demand through the directive to be moderate in consumption.

Managing wealth in a way that promotes justice

A core concept of Islam is that the owner of all wealth in the world is Allah and that humans are merely its trustees. Therefore, humans must manage wealth in a way that promotes justice and prohibits certain activities. At the same time, Muslims have the right to enjoy whatever wealth they acquire and spend in sharia-compliant ways; they don't need to feel shame about being wealthy as long as their behavior aligns with Islam.

Islam allows for a free-market economy where supply and demand are decided in the market, but at the same time, Islam directs the function of the market mechanism by imposing specific laws and ethics that promote social justice. Therefore, social justice is a key concept of the Islamic finance industry.

Islam doesn't allow for a society in which a small number of people enjoy most of the wealth while many people have very little. Economically speaking, *social justice* is the distribution of wealth in a way that helps correct such an imbalance. Islam tries to achieve social justice in the economy in many ways, among them

- ✔ **Requiring zakat:** To promote justice related to the distribution of wealth, Islam imposes a property tax called *zakat*. Every Muslim who meets certain criteria regarding the accumulation of wealth must pay zakat, which is distributed to people in need. By taxing the property of people who acquire wealth and distributing that tax to people in need, Islam promotes the socially responsible distribution of wealth.

- ✔ **Prohibiting riba (interest):** Islam prohibits interest-based transactions. No individual or business entity should hoard money in order to earn interest; instead, people and businesses should use money (keep it in circulation) to support productive economic activities — those that create investment, trading, and jobs. The returns of successful economic activities are then distributed to the different parties involved; wealth is shared.

- ✔ **Encouraging shared risk:** Islamic finance encourages risk-sharing in economic transactions. When a risk is shared among two or more parties involved in an economic activity, the burden of the risk faced by each party is reduced.

Citing key principles that Islamic firms follow

Based on the core concepts of Islamic economics, Islamic finance institutions adhere to certain principles that distinguish them from conventional finance. Following are four major principles that every Islamic financial firm must follow. (*Note:* If a company doesn't adhere to these principles, it can't call itself *Islamic.*)

Prohibiting interest (riba)

In a riba-based transaction, the owner of the wealth gets return without making any effort and bears no risk. The person receiving the loan, on the other hand, assumes all the risk and bears the responsibility of returning to the lender both the capital and the riba no matter what the outcome of the economic activity. From the Islamic point of view, in a riba-based transaction, the lender uses the misfortune of the borrower in order to acquire wealth, which is unjust.

Book VIII

Socially Responsible Investing

The prohibition against riba-based transactions means that Muslims should not take out loans from conventional banks, invest in interest-based products (such as conventional certificates of deposit, savings accounts, and bonds), or invest in funds that purchase the equity of firms that promote interest-based products (such as conventional banks).

Steering clear of uncertainty-based transactions (gharar)

Islam requires Muslims to avoid transactions that are uncertain or ambiguous; not everyone involved knows what to expect and can make an informed decision. Gharar can exist in these situations:

- ✔ **When two parties enter a contract and one party lacks complete information:** For example, a party purposely withholds some information in order to wield greater control over the transaction.

- ✔ **When both parties lack control over the underlying transaction:** For example, two parties enter a contract related to the sale of fish that haven't yet been caught. Both parties lack control over that transaction because outside forces (such as weather or overfishing) may prevent the delivery of all the fish expected per the contract.

Avoiding gambling

In Islam, both the acquisition of wealth by chance (not by effort) and games of chance are prohibited because they're based on uncertainty.

The Islamic prohibition against transactions that involve gambling prevents Muslims from purchasing conventional insurance products because conventional insurance is a gamble, and the outcome, whether the buyer ends up using the policy or not, is unjust: If a policyholder makes small payments and then receives a large sum because a misfortune occurs, that's unjust. If she makes small payments but never receives anything in exchange for them (because no misfortune occurs), that's unjust, too. Instead, Islamic insurance, called *takaful,* is based on a very different model of risk management that involves shared risk and mutual responsibility.

Avoiding investment in prohibited industries

Islam prohibits industries that it considers harmful to society and a threat to social responsibility. These industries include alcohol, prostitution, pornography, weapons of mass destruction, pork, tobacco, and illegal drugs. By prohibiting certain industries, Islam also prohibits profiting from them in any way. Therefore, an Islamic financial institution can't finance a project or asset that is prohibited, and a Muslim investor cannot put money into a mutual fund or other equity product that funnels money to a company that participates in a prohibited industry.

Adhering to Criteria for Islamic Investments

To qualify as a sharia-compliant investment, an activity or a financial asset must be allowed per Islamic law. Islamic scholars determine which investment activities are prohibited and which are permitted. The following sections outline activities and businesses that don't make the cut. (If you're interested in what, exactly, these scholars look at, head to the later sidebar "Screening stocks for Islamic investments.")

Fleeing from forbidden industries

Most of the industry investments that Islam prohibits seem pretty obvious; you probably aren't shocked to find that prostitution isn't sharia-compliant. Here's an overview of the industries Islamic investments must steer clear of:

✔ **Gambling:** Muslims can't invest in companies or activities that support gambling. In addition to prohibiting investments that would themselves involve too much risk, this criterion also means that an investor can't support the construction of a casino; the operation of a lottery; or the promotion of horse and dog racing, Internet gambling, and so on. Leasing an investment property to a company that conducts a gambling-related business is also banned.

✔ **Pornography, prostitution, and the adult-entertainment industry:** Islam considers the pornography, prostitution, and adult-entertainment industries to be harmful to society. Therefore, an investor can't put money into a venture that involves products or businesses in these fields.

✔ **Specific food and beverage products:** Some products in the food and beverage industry are prohibited because Islam prohibits their consumption. Foods and beverages that Muslims can consume are called *halal.* Forbidden items include

  • **Pork:** The Quran (the holy scripture of Islam) prohibits consuming pork and pork-based products (as well as any other meat that isn't slaughtered according to Islamic principles), so investing in companies dealing with pork-based products isn't acceptable.

  • **Alcoholic beverages:** Investing in companies involved in alcoholic products is also banned because the Quran specifically bans "intoxicants."

✔ **Tobacco:** Islamic scholars hold the opinion that tobacco isn't good for personal health and therefore believe that Islamic standards prohibit investments in tobacco-related business.

✔ **Illegal drugs:** Investing in any company or activity that supports the sale, distribution, or use of illegal drugs is also prohibited. (In fact, investing in a way that promotes any illegal activity goes against Islamic law.)

Forgetting about financial market trading

Some types of financial market activity, such as margin trading, day trading, options, and futures, are considered gray areas in Islamic law. The majority of Islamic scholars believe that sharia law prohibits these transactions because the activities involve interest, speculation, and excessive risk without market knowledge. Here's a quick refresher about each type of activity and how it fails to follow sharia law:

✔ **Margin trading:** In *margin trading,* you buy stocks by getting a loan from your broker. (The broker charges you interest on the loan.) In addition to the interest itself being problematic, the risk involved with this type of activity is extremely high. If you invest the loaned money in a stock that loses value, you may find yourself unable to pay back the money you've borrowed and the interest you owe your broker for providing the loan.

✔ **Day trading:** From the Islamic perspective, day trading in the stock market isn't actually an investment activity because the person doing it isn't concerned about the underlying product or economic activity being supported. Instead, *day trading* is just a transaction based on observing the market price fluctuations on a given day. Of course, it involves a substantial amount of risk because the day trader is essentially gambling that the price of a certain stock is going to rise or fall on a given day. This makes day trading a no-no from a sharia perspective.

✔ **Options:** A financial contract is sold by the option writer to another party, giving the second party the right to buy or sell a specific financial asset at a fixed price on or before a certain date. In other words, the second party is given the chance to buy or sell without an obligation to buy or sell.

In theory, options are used to reduce investment risk. However, they themselves are highly risky and speculative in nature. The majority of Islamic scholars agree that options have features of speculation and gambling. In addition, the investor (second party) doesn't intend to hold the asset (which is generally considered crucial for an investment to be sharia-compliant). Based on these characteristics, most Islamic scholars believe that options are prohibited investments.

✔ **Futures:** A financial contract to buy or sell financial assets or commodities on a future date is traded on *futures exchanges.* The basic difference between futures and options is this: In a futures contract, both the buyer and seller are obliged to perform the contract; an options contract is optional and can be allowed to simply expire, unused.

Identifying Types of Islamic Financial Products

Islamic financial companies have developed many different products to meet customer needs and provide sharia-compliant alternatives to widely available conventional options. In this section, you discover some common categories of Islamic financial products. Head to Chapter 4 in Book VIII for a list of products that fit into these categories.

In practice, a product can be developed to serve many purposes — not only to satisfy social justice demands. However, no matter the motivation for creating a product (such as to meet market demand), every Islamic financial product must exist under the framework of sharia law.

Products based on profit and loss sharing

To establish social justice, Islam requires that both investors and entrepreneurs share involvement in economic activities that result in profit and loss. Here are two broad categories of well-known, widely used equity products that support the sharing of profit and loss:

- **Mudaraba products:** In a *mudaraba* contract, a financier provides capital to an entrepreneur who manages an economic activity such as property construction, a business, or a joint venture. When this economic activity returns a profit, both parties share the proceeds; when a loss occurs, only the financier bears the financial loss. (The entrepreneur loses his effort and time.) However, if the loss is due to the misconduct of the entrepreneur, then he must suffer the financial loss as well.

- **Musharaka products:** In a *musharaka* contract, both parties become involved in a joint venture project or property by investing capital and entrepreneurship. Both parties share any profit or bear any loss generated by the activity.

Products based on investment financing (sale and lease contracts)

In Islamic economics, debt-based transactions (interest-based lending and borrowing) are prohibited. If you've grown up in a society where every home, car, and other major purchase is financed by debt, you may wonder how people and businesses can function without it. But doing so is, indeed, possible! As part of the Islamic finance system, contract products are available to facilitate the sale or lease of a property (a home or car, for example).

Islamic law is clear: Only real assets can be transacted with Islamic sale and lease contracts, and such assets must be owned by the lessee or seller — not by a third party. These conditions make it impossible to sell debt in a capital market and create imaginary assets, which enable transactions of a speculative nature.

For example, if an Islamic bank purchases a home and sells it on an installment basis to a buyer, the bank is the owner of the home until the final payment is made. The bank earns a fee from the buyer but may also be responsible for repairs on the home for the duration of its ownership period if stated in the agreement.

Islamic funds

Islamic funds are investment products (such as mutual funds and unit trusts) that are based on equities that are screened, or filtered, to ensure sharia compliance. (You can read about the various types of Islamic investment products available in the capital markets in Chapter 4 of Book VIII.)

Screening refers to the process of checking the sharia compliance of every entity included in an equity fund. The first step in the screening process is to filter out any company whose business involves industries or types of transactions that are prohibited by Islamic law. The second step in the process involves looking closely at each company's financial ratios; a company must meet certain financial benchmarks to assure Islamic investors that it isn't engaged in prohibited speculative transactions (involving uncertainty or gambling), which are likely leveraged with debt. For more information, see the sidebar "Screening stocks for Islamic investments."

Products for social development

The Islamic finance industry has developed a product based purely on the goal of lifting up society in general: *Qard hasan* are interest-free loans given by Islamic financial institutions to people who need them. This loan is the only type of loan that Islamic banks offer. No interest or fee is assigned to the loan; banks require only the principal to be repaid.

An alternative to bonds: Asset-based securities (sukuk)

Sukuk are often referred to as "Islamic bonds," but they're very different from conventional bonds, which benefit one party more than another and, therefore, can't promote social justice.

Sukuk are asset-based securities; they're certificates (sold to investors) that represent ownership in a tangible asset, service, project, business, or joint venture. Every asset that supports a sukuk must be sharia-compliant. Check out Chapter 4 in Book VIII to find out what types of sukuk are available in the Islamic capital market.

Screening stocks for Islamic investments

Islamic fund management companies must invest in the stocks of companies that are sharia-compliant. A fund management company must use a screening (or filtering) process to determine (with the guidance of sharia scholars) whether a company qualifies as sharia-compliant.

Few companies can truly comply 100 percent with sharia law, however. Therefore, a company doesn't need to get a grade of 100 in order to pass the sharia test. Instead, scholars and fund managers allow for a certain percentage of non-sharia-compliant activity (which is almost impossible to avoid) without booting the company from the approved list of possible investments.

Because a business doesn't remain static year after year, this screening process must be ongoing. If an investment is determined to be non-sharia-compliant, action must be taken to purify the fund's holdings. If, after giving the noncompliant corporation time to resolve the noncompliance issue(s), it still remains in non-compliance, its stocks are removed from the fund. Depending on the situation, any capital gains from the liquidation are either distributed to investors or given to charity.

The first step of the screening process is looking to ensure the companies don't engage in prohibited industries. The first test a sharia scholar or fund manager applies when considering whether a company is sharia-compliant focuses on the company's core business. If the company's business centers on prohibited activities, the company is out — period; it doesn't even make it to the financial round. Groups of companies with subsidiaries that engage in activities prohibited by sharia — a hotel (owned by a large corporation) that derives a substantial amount of its income from a nightclub or casino that's prohibited per sharia, for example — also are excluded from Islamic investment funds.

The second step of the screening process is passing the financial test. The objective of the financial test is to ensure that the company's non-sharia-compliant financial facts don't have a significant influence on the company's stock price and the company's overall performance. For example, the Islamic investment fund wants to avoid investing in companies that carry too much debt. The financial ratios are prepared based on financial statements such as the income statement and the company's balance

Book VIII

Socially Responsible Investing

sheet. Evaluators then compare the results of these ratios with certain benchmarks.

The benchmarks used for financial screening can vary from fund to fund. The sharia boards of Islamic financial institutions or Islamic indexes are the ones who establish the benchmarks, and different boards (adhering to different schools of thought) may establish different thresholds. The following three separate financial tests are commonly applied during this screening step.

✔ **Debt-to-equity ratio:** The company's *debt-to-equity ratio* is determined by dividing its total debt by its total market capitalization. For sharia compliance, the accepted debt level is generally between 30 and 33 percent. This test is important because, although investing in companies that pay interest on debt isn't allowed in theory, in reality, finding a company that is 100 percent free from interest-bearing debt is difficult. A debt-to-equity ratio of 30 to 33 percent is a benchmark representing an acceptable level of debt.

✔ **Interest income ratio:** This ratio is interest income divided by total revenues.

Generally, the benchmark is less than 5 percent. Although sharia interest income is prohibited because sharia doesn't allow interest-based transactions, if the interest income is negligible, investing in the company is still acceptable. However, stockholders are encouraged to donate the interest income portion of their dividends to charity.

✔ **Liquidity:** A company should achieve a certain balance between liquid and illiquid assets. After all, it needs to have enough liquid assets on hand to cover its short-term expenses, but it also needs to invest in illiquid assets to sustain and grow its operations. From the perspective of sharia compliance, current (liquid) assets are considered to be the same as cash. Sharia forbids the trading of cash for cash and restricts how much profit a company can earn from cash-based (rather than asset-, product-, or service-based) activities. So a company that has too many liquid assets is considered noncompliant, and its assets can't be part of a sharia investment fund.

Introducing Islamic Financial Institutions

Although Islamic financial institutions may have very different structures, types of customers, and goals, they all share one key element: They must comply with Islamic law. The following types of Islamic financial institutions serve Muslim and non-Muslim populations throughout the world:

✔ **Islamic banks:** Islamic banks have many functions that mirror those of their conventional counterparts, but they must fulfill those functions in sharia-compliant ways. Therefore, the products available at an Islamic bank look very different from those available at a conventional commercial bank. And the ways in which an Islamic bank invests its funds differ significantly as well.

✔ **Islamic capital market participants:** The Islamic capital market, explained in Chapter 4 of Book VIII, is where sharia-compliant financial assets are transacted. The individuals and institutions involved in the Islamic capital market work parallel to those in the conventional capital market, and they help investors find sharia-compliant investment opportunities. The Islamic capital market is open to any investors, including non-Muslim customers.

Products that are bought and sold in the Islamic capital market include Islamic funds; sukuk, or Islamic bonds; and Islamic interbank money market funds (which are quite new and just now developing). Therefore, capital market participants include Islamic investment fund managers, sukuk issuers (including governments and major corporations), high-net-worth individuals who need sharia-compliant products in which to invest their money, and any other individual or entity that seeks sharia-compliant and/or socially responsible investment vehicles. Because this capital market is very young, it's likely to grow and include more types of investment products as the Islamic finance industry matures.

✔ **Islamic index providers:** When Islamic investment funds were first being developed, their investment performance was benchmarked against well-known conventional indexes (such as the S&P 500). But that comparison was flawed because Islamic funds can't invest in so many of the industries represented by those indexes. As a result, Islamic indexes emerged that now serve as more appropriate benchmarks for examining the performance of Islamic investment funds. Key index providers who offer Islamic indexes include Dow Jones Indexes, S&P, FTSE, and MSCI. I cover the importance of these indexes in Chapter 4 of Book VIII.

Book VIII

Socially Responsible Investing

Chapter 4

Managing Assets in Islamic Investments

C hapter 3 in Book VIII familiarizes you with Islamic finance, explaining its key principles and general categories of products. In this chapter, you delve into the Islamic capital market and the investment products you can purchase there: Islamic mutual funds, bonds, exchange-traded funds, and more. You discover how fund management companies are monitoring fund performance with Islamic market indexes, and you find out about the products available for managing risk in the Islamic market.

The word *Islamic* in this context means that a product is sharia-compliant: It adheres to the principles of Islamic law and avoids all industries and activities that this law prohibits.

Shopping at the Islamic Capital Market

The term *capital market* refers to any financial market where debt and equity are demanded and supplied. A capital market helps investors find a platform for making their investments and helps both borrowers and investors by channeling funds from those with excess funds to those in need of such funds. Businesses and governments raise funds in the capital market.

Simply put, the Islamic capital market is where sharia-compliant financial assets are transacted. It works parallel to the conventional market and helps investors find sharia-compliant investment opportunities. The following sections list exchanges and liquidity issues in the Islamic capital market.

The increase of wealth among Muslim investors (especially from nations that are part of the Gulf Cooperation Council — Bahrain, Kuwait, Oman, Qatar, Saudi Arabia, and United Arab Emirates) is spurring growth in the Islamic capital market. The market's current growth is between 12 and 15 percent annually. In total, Islamic assets are worth an estimated $1 trillion at the time of this writing, and about 25 percent of that amount is tied to the Islamic capital market.

Identifying exchanges on the Islamic capital market

Where, exactly, is the Islamic capital market located? In many of the same places you'd find the conventional capital market. Islamic capital market instruments are traded on many of the world's leading exchanges (where conventional market instruments are traded as well).

Table 4-1 lists six of the many exchanges that currently trade Islamic capital market instruments. Right now, no Islamic-only exchanges exist.

Table 4-1	Exchanges Trading Islamic Capital Market Instruments	
Market	**Description**	**Securities Traded**
Bursa Malaysia (MYX)	An exchange holding company that lists almost 1,000 companies	Sukuk, sharia-compliant equities, IETFs, IREITs, as well as conventional capital market products such as equities, derivatives, and bonds
Labuan International Financial Exchange (LFX)	A Malaysian-based offshore exchange, launched in 2000 and operating 24/7	Sukuk, Islamic funds
London Stock Exchange (LSE)	One of the largest stock exchanges in the world; also owner of the Alternative Investment Market (AIM), which includes on its list sharia-compliant companies	Sukuk, equity funds, and IETFs

Market	Description	Securities Traded
Luxembourg Stock Exchange	The first European exchange to issue sukuk (the Islamic version of bonds — certificates sold to investors that represent ownership in a tangible asset, service, project, business, or joint venture)	Sukuk, sharia-compliant funds
NASDAQ Dubai	A capital market exchange serving the West, Middle East, Europe, and East Asia; considered the largest exchange for sukuk in the Middle East	Sharia-compliant equities (stocks), Islamic funds (mutual funds and unit trusts), Islamic exchange-traded funds (IETFs), Islamic real estate investment trusts (IREITs)
Tadawul (the Saudi Arabian stock exchange)	The only stock exchange in Saudi Arabia; lists companies operating in various industries, including oil and gas, agriculture, food, technology, banking, and other financial sectors	Equities, IETFs, sukuk, and mutual funds

Capital markets must be supervised and controlled by regulatory bodies. Because the Islamic capital market is in its infant stage, no organized regulatory authority exists for it. Generally, the conventional capital market authority in any given country or region supervises the Islamic capital market as well. In Malaysia, where the Islamic capital market first got its legs, the Securities Commission of Malaysia has a *sharia council* that is specifically responsible for sharia-related matters of Islamic capital market activities (*sharia councils* are religious boards steeped in the knowledge of Islam and responsible for determining whether an institution's practices and products comply with Islamic principles). In time, regulatory agencies in other nations where the Islamic capital markets are thriving may follow suit.

Recognizing liquidity issues in the Islamic capital market

Like all investors, people investing in Islamic assets need to manage liquidity so they can feel confident about meeting their current and future financial obligations. However, investors in the Islamic capital market face two issues that investors in conventional assets don't face:

✔ **Islamic product development is slow compared to conventional product development.** As a result, Islamic investors don't have as many highly liquid investment options as conventional investors do. This delay exists for two reasons:

- The market share for Islamic investments is still small compared to the conventional capital markets.

- Islamic investments must comply with sharia, which requires screening processes and debate among scholars that can be quite time-consuming.

✔ **Investors sometimes lack access to the Islamic capital market.** For example, because of a lack of financial infrastructure, a customer in Canada may not be able to access the U.S. Islamic asset market as easily as she can access the conventional market. If she lacks market access, she lacks the ability to turn her investments into cash as quickly as she can in the conventional markets.

Stocks, Bonds, Mutual Funds, and More: Investigating Your Options

Just as conventional financial assets are sold in the conventional market, Islamic assets are sold in the Islamic capital market, as the following sections outline. Many non-Muslim investors are interested in the Islamic capital market for two basic reasons: Islamic investments are ethical and invested with social responsibility, and compared to the conventional market during financial crises, the Islamic market is stable.

Because of increasing global awareness about sharia-compliant investing, more and more investors are turning to the Islamic capital market. This point is crucial: The Islamic capital market is open to *any* investor who wants to achieve the objectives involved in the capital market. Non-Muslim customers are active participants in the Islamic capital market. Participants include high-net-worth investors, corporations, and governments.

Tapping into the pros and cons of the Islamic equity market

Equity markets (where stocks are traded) are crucial to any economy because they provide capital to companies. The Islamic equity market is where sharia-compliant stocks are traded.

Spotlighting some high-performing funds

To date, no standardized criteria exist for assessing the performance of various Islamic equity funds, but individual researchers express their own ideas about which funds excel. Here is information from two sources to offer a sense of which funds are considered among the best in the Islamic equity market: FE Trustnet Middle East, a sister site of FE Trustnet UK (www.trustnetmiddleeast.com), and Invest Direct Online (www.invest-direct-online.com).

Top-performing funds, identified by FE Trustnet Middle East:

✔ Kenanga Syariah Growth (KUTEQIS)

✔ Eastspring Inv Dana Al Ilham (PRUALIL)

✔ Public Islamic Select Enterprises (PUBIENT)

✔ MAAKL Al-Fauzan (MAAFAUZ)

✔ Public Islamic Dividend (PUBPIDF)

Top-performing funds, identified by Invest Direct Online:

✔ Allianz RCM Islamic Global Equity Opportunities AT USD

✔ Amundi Capital Islamic BRIC Quant (CAISBQI)

✔ Amundi Capital Islamic Global Resources (CAISGRS)

✔ BNP Paribas Islamic Equity Optimiser Classic (BNPIEOC)

✔ Emirates Islamic Global Balanced (EMISGBB)

✔ Emirates Islamic MENA Opportunities A USD (EMIRAED)

✔ HSBC Amanah Global Equity Index (AMAGAEF)

✔ Reliance Global Shariah Growth (WLRGSIU)

✔ Asian Pacific Shariah Growth (WSAPSUA)

High-performing, Western-based Islamic equity funds:

✔ AlAhli Islamic US Equitybuilder Certificates, managed by the National Commercial Bank of Germany

✔ Lyxor Index S&P Europe 350 Shariah, managed by Lyxor Asset Management in Luxembourg

✔ iShares MSCI USA Islamic (ISUS), managed by BlackRock of the United Kingdom

✔ Dow Jones Islamic Fund (IMNAX), managed by Allied Asset Advisors in the United States

✔ Azzad Ethical Mid-Cap Fund (ADJEX), managed by Azzad Asset Management in the United States

Book VIII

Socially Responsible Investing

Obviously, for a Muslim, the primary benefit of investing in Islamic equities is assurance that the funds are purchasing only sharia-compliant assets. But non-Muslim investors are also attracted to Islamic equities, so the benefits go beyond the religious. Here are some other advantages of investing in Islamic equity funds:

> ✔ **Transparency:** Investors in Islamic equity funds expect a high level of transparency. After all, if one of a fund's key objectives is to comply with sharia, the fund managers must be quite open about which industries and companies they invest in.

✔ **Financial screening:** Part of the screening process for determining whether an equity asset is sharia-compliant involves considering a company's financials, including how much debt the company carries. Islamic equity funds avoid investing in firms that carry very high levels of debt. Therefore, Islamic funds may be considered more conservative and slightly less risky than some conventional equity funds.

✔ **Diversification:** Investing in any fund (Islamic or conventional) that purchases assets from multiple companies reduces the risk of losing capital when disaster strikes and a company declares bankruptcy or closes its doors.

✔ **Liquidity:** For the Islamic investor, a benefit of investing in a fund versus putting money into a fixed-term investment is liquidity. When situations change and the investor wants or needs to cash out, doing so is much easier when the investment is in a fund. Keep in mind, however, that overall, Islamic investments, including Islamic funds, tend to be less liquid than their conventional counterparts. To understand why, head to the earlier section "Recognizing liquidity issues in the Islamic capital market."

The main drawback to investing in Islamic equities is the limited options. Whereas investors in conventional equities have so many choices that they can tailor a portfolio to meet any investment objective, investors in Islamic funds have significantly fewer funds to choose from.

Comparing commodity and equity funds

If you're looking to build a sharia-compliant investment portfolio with the potential for significant growth (as opposed to a portfolio focused mostly on safeguarding your funds), chances are good you want to include funds that invest in commodities and/or those that invest in equities. As with conventional funds of this type, the Islamic variety of commodity and equity funds present some risk to the investor because you can't know with certainty that the price of a certain commodity or a company stock is going to increase. No way around it: You can't hope for returns without facing some associated risks. That's just the nature of investing, Islamic and otherwise!

Commodity funds

Commodity funds may invest in purchases or projects based either on the cost plus murabaha contract or, in the case of construction projects (or other projects to be completed in the future), the leasing (ijara) contract.

In the conventional market, many types of commodity funds are available that allow you to invest in oil, wheat, pork bellies, orange juice, and so on. Conventional investors (who don't necessarily want to see and touch the commodities in question) look to fund management companies to make savvy trades — often using derivative products — to garner profits from the commodity's price changes.

Islamic commodity funds also invest in physical commodities but must avoid short selling as well as investment products of a speculative nature, such as commodity futures. In an Islamic commodity fund, the commodities are actually purchased for resale. (The fund management company doesn't try to short sell a commodity security, for example.) The profit from the sale is distributed among the investors according to the investment contract.

In order to be accepted as sharia-compliant, the commodity fund must meet the following basic criteria:

- ✔ **The commodities involved can't be prohibited in Islam.** In other words, no pork, alcohol, or other forbidden items.

- ✔ **Short selling isn't allowed.** The seller must actually have possession of the commodities in question.

- ✔ **All parties involved must know the price of the commodities to be traded.**

- ✔ **Forward sales aren't allowed, except under salam and istisna contracts.**

Here are just two examples of existing Islamic commodity funds:

- ✔ Riyad Capital Bank (`www.riyadcapital.com/index.php`) in Saudi Arabia has two Commodity Trading Funds available to investors. One fund deals in U.S. dollars, and the other deals in Saudi Riyals; both are sharia-compliant.

- ✔ Al Rajhi Capital (`www.alrajhi-capital.com/en`), also in Saudi Arabia, offers three commodity fund products: a U.S. dollar commodity fund, a Saudi Riyal commodity fund, and a Euro commodity fund.

You say "unit trust"; I say "mutual fund"

Many Islamic fund management companies use the terms *unit trust* and *mutual fund* interchangeably (or use just one term to refer to all fund products). For example, in Malaysia, all Islamic funds are called *unit trusts*. In the United States, they're all called *mutual funds*. However, in theory, a difference exists between the two terms:

- ✔ **Unit trusts** generally have a fixed term of one, two, or three years. Also, they generally manage a *fixed* portfolio of stocks,

bonds, and other investments, which means that the trust doesn't buy and sell assets in the market.

- ✔ **Mutual fund** investments include stocks, bonds, and money market instruments. Mutual funds do *not* hold a portfolio in fixed instruments; instead, the mutual fund managers take an active role in diversifying investments and trading assets on the exchanges. Also, mutual funds don't tend to have a fixed term.

Equity funds

An equity fund gains profit by buying and selling stocks to achieve capital gains and by receiving corporate dividends. The capital gains and dividends are distributed among investors proportionally according to the size of each person's investment. The key difference between an Islamic and conventional equity fund is the requirement for an Islamic equity fund to invest in sharia-compliant assets.

Islamic equity funds really opened the door to investing for people seeking to purchase sharia-compliant stocks and to make socially responsible investments. And because these funds avoid investing in companies that are highly leveraged with debt, Islamic equity funds may have a performance advantage over some of their conventional counterparts. The drawback is that the investment criteria for inclusion in an Islamic fund are strict enough to eliminate certain industries altogether, which can negatively affect such funds during economic downturns. (As with all things in the investment world, Islamic equity funds have their pros and cons!)

Here are just three examples of the hundreds of Islamic equity funds currently available:

- ✔ Malaysia's AmIslamic Funds Management launched the AmASEAN Equity Fund (AMASEQY) in 2011. The fund's investments focus on the nations of Brunei, Cambodia, Indonesia, Laos, Malaysia, Myanmar, the Philippines, Singapore, Thailand, and Vietnam. For more information, go to invest.com.my/personal/funds/profile/one?fund_id=875.

- ✔ HSBC Amanah GCC Equity Fund (SAMGCCE), launched in 2006 and managed by HSBC Saudia Arabia, strives for medium- and long-term capital growth by making investments in sharia-compliant products and services in Malaysia and Saudi Arabia, and by offering wholesale banking (Islamic financing/Sukuk) globally through those countries. For more information, visit www.hsbcamanah.com.

- ✔ Launched in 2003, the Meezan Islamic Fund (MEZISLM) is a product of Al Meezan Investment Management Limited (www.almeezangroup.com). The management company's website states that this fund is "not only Pakistan's largest Shariah compliant equity fund but also Pakistan's largest equity fund in the private sector."

Understanding the Islamic unit trust and mutual funds market

An Islamic *unit trust* or a *mutual fund* is a type of equity fund that collects funds from investors and pools them for investment in stocks, bonds, or other investment products. The return from the investment is paid back to the investors proportionately after deducting the cost related to the fund and the administration fee, or the fund's portion of the profit (depending on the contract used). These funds are similar to their conventional counterparts but differ in their mode of financing and in the nature of their investments (which must, of course, be sharia-compliant).

Islamic unit trusts and mutual funds are managed per one of the following three Islamic contracts:

- **Mudaraba:** Most of the funds work on a partnership basis. The fund manager is the *working partner,* and the investor is the *silent partner.* The fund profits are distributed among the partners, but only the investor loses the initial capital if the venture is unsuccessful. (The working partner loses any time and effort invested.)

- **Ijara:** The fund management company purchases assets (such as real estate and vehicles) and leases them out to users. The company collects rent for each asset, pools it, and distributes it among the investors.

- **Murabaha:** The fund management company uses investments to purchase assets. It then sells the assets on a cost-plus-profit basis, and the profits that it collects are pooled and distributed among the fund investors.

Currently, estimates indicate that more than 350 sharia-compliant investment funds — both unit trusts and mutual funds — are established globally.

Investing in Islamic exchange-traded funds (IETFs)

Exchange-traded funds are open-ended fund pools that may be composed of stocks, bonds, and/or commodities. Initially, only institutional or authorized investors bought and sold ETFs; these days, individual investors have easy access to these funds and make up a good chunk of the market. (For more information on conventional ETFs, head to Chapter 3, Book I.)

Islamic ETFs (or IETFs) bear all the features of conventional ETFs but are sharia-compliant. IETFs are very attractive investment instruments because they offer instant diversity (much like mutual funds). Because they're based on indexes (discussed later in this chapter), they also boast a great deal of transparency; at any given moment, an investor knows which companies the IETF has invested his money in.

Book VIII

Socially Responsible Investing

IETFs are still very young but are poised for great growth. They serve a purpose not only for the Muslim investor, whose primary objective is sharia-compliant investment, but also for non-Muslim investors who want to support socially responsible investing and tap into low-debt securities. Though the

Middle East region has enormous wealth that should support a thriving IETF market, the relative lack of stock exchanges makes this product (which trades much like shares of stock) less accessible than Islamic mutual funds and unit trusts.

Diversifying with the sukuk (Islamic bond) market

As Chapter 3 in Book VIII explains, sukuk are one of the major sectors in the Islamic capital market and are an alternative to conventional, debt-based bonds. Sukuk are asset-based and thus the preferred mode of investment for many high-net-worth investors and governments. Sukuk are issued by governments (Japan, South Korea, Germany, and the United Kingdom, for example), by international financial bodies (such as the International Financial Corporation), and by global corporations (such as GE Capital).

International, conventional bond-rating agencies such as Standard & Poor's (S&P) and Fitch have recently started to issue ratings for sukuk. The ratings system used for conventional and Islamic bonds is the same, and the ratings offer an assessment of the issuers' ability to make repayments. (Check out Chapter 2 in Book I for an introduction to conventional bonds.)

Developing the Islamic derivative market

A *derivative* is any financial asset based on the value of one or more underlying financial assets. Derivatives are used to hedge the risk of the assets. Many derivatives are available on the market, but the most commonly used are swaps, options, futures, and forward contracts. (Note that many financial regulators have blamed derivatives for the global financial crises that emerged starting in late 2007.) Here's what these terms mean:

- ✔ **Swap market:** This instrument is used to transfer risk. The Islamic swap market has two components:

  - *Profit rate swap:* This option is based on exchanging fixed-rate for floating-rate profits.

  - *Cross-currency swap:* Investors use this swap to transfer currency fluctuation risk among themselves.

- ✔ **Options:** In this financial contract, the option writer offers a second party the right to buy or sell a financial asset at a fixed price on or before a certain date — without obligation to do so.

✔ **Futures:** This type of financial contract solidifies an agreement to buy or sell financial assets or commodities on a future date. In a futures contract, both the buyer and seller are obliged to perform the contract.

✔ **Forward contracts:** These contracts, which are used to hedge risk, let two partners agree today on the price of a future asset sale/purchase. Forward contracts and futures have some things in common but are different in certain ways; for instance, forward contracts aren't traded on the exchanges.

The Islamic investment industry is divided regarding its outlook on Islamic derivatives because of varying sharia interpretations. Many scholars don't agree with Islamic derivatives, arguing that such products inherently involve speculation. The relationship between recent financial crises and derivatives for hedging risk supports this argument. On the other hand, some Islamic bankers point out that in the midst of recent financial turmoil, conventional banks have options that help them manage their risks, while Islamic banks don't. As a result, the Islamic finance industry is looking for solutions to manage the risk — which could include derivatives. (See the later section "Developing New Methods for Managing Market Risk.")

Standard Chartered Saadiq Malaysia is already offering some Islamic derivative products, such as the Islamic Profit Rate Swap, Islamic Cross Currency Swap, and Islamic Forward Rate Agreement. If you want to find out more about Islamic derivative products, check out www.standardchartered.com.my/saadiq/wholesale-treasury-products.html.

Benchmarking the Performance of Islamic Funds: Islamic Indexes

To manage any investment fund effectively, you need to understand your fund's performance. The best way to examine performance is to compare it to industry benchmarks and performance indicators. In the financial industry, indexes serve as such benchmarks and indicators. Everyone knows what a fund means when it claims to have "beaten the S&P every year for the past decade." Investors cheer.

When Islamic investment funds were first being developed, the funds were benchmarked against the well-known conventional indexes. But that yardstick was flawed because Islamic funds can't invest in so many of the industries represented by those indexes.

Book VIII

Socially Responsible Investing

As a result, Islamic indexes were created and now serve as more-appropriate benchmarks for examining an Islamic investment fund's performance. The Dow Jones Islamic Market (DJIM) indexes, created in 1999, were the first successful Islamic indexes developed, and they have been joined by many others, such as

- ✔ The FTSE Shariah Global Equity indexes
- ✔ Global GCC Islamic Index (by Global Investment House Kuwait)
- ✔ Global Islamic Index (by MSCI Indices Company)
- ✔ The Kuala Lumpur Sharia Index (KLSI)
- ✔ MSCI Global Islamic Indices
- ✔ The S&P Shariah indexes

Most of these indexes use a similar set of criteria to screen companies for inclusion.

Islamic indexes provide invaluable services to investment fund managers. The process of selecting companies for inclusion in a sharia-compliant equity fund is technical and time-consuming (refer to Chapter 3 in Book VIII). Because Islamic indexes conduct their own initial compliance screening research under the guidance of a sharia board or committee, Islamic fund managers can trust that any stock included in such an index is fair game for investment. Thus, Islamic indexes reduce the costs associated with an Islamic fund's screening process and help funds tap into a wider diversity of stocks.

Just as individual funds must strive to maintain sharia compliance by conducting ongoing screening and purifying when necessary, indexes must do the same.

The following sections profile four Islamic indexes to point out the benchmarks and screening processes they use.

Dow Jones Islamic Market (DJIM) indexes

The Dow Jones Islamic Market (DJIM) is a whole family of broad-market, blue-chip, fixed income, and other indexes. According to its website (www. djindexes.com/islamicmarket), the DJIM screens companies to remove those that engage in the prohibited industries (alcohol, pork-related products, conventional financial services, and tobacco). The website also lists the broad terms "entertainment" and "weapons and defense" as industry screens. The DJIM conducts financial tests to ensure that each of the following financial ratios is less than 33 percent:

✔ A company's total debt divided by its "trailing 24-month average market capitalization"

✔ "The sum of a company's cash and interest-bearing securities divided by [its] trailing 24-month average market capitalization"

✔ The company's "Accounts receivables divided by [its] trailing 24-month average market capitalization"

A supervisory board of five sharia scholars guides the DJIM. This board currently has members from Bahrain, Malaysia, Saudi Arabia, Syria, and the United States. Per the Dow Jones Indexes website, "The geographic diversity of the scholars helps to ensure that diverse interpretations of Shari'ah law are represented."

S&P Shariah indexes

Standard & Poor's introduced its first sharia indexes in 2006. Initially, three indexes were screened for sharia compliance, creating the S&P 500 Shariah, the S&P Europe 350 Shariah, and the S&P Japan 500 Shariah. Since that time, S&P has developed significantly in this market. It now has three index series — the S&P Global Benchmark Shariah Index Series, the S&P Global Investable Shariah Index Series, and the S&P Global Strategy Shariah Index Series — with a total of 27 indexes as of this writing.

In conducting its industry screening, the S&P excludes companies in the traditional list of prohibited industries: alcohol, gambling, pornography, tobacco, pork products, conventional finance, and cloning. It also excludes advertising and media companies, with some exceptions: Newspapers, news channels, and sports channels, as well as advertising and media companies that derive more than 65 percent of their total income from Gulf Cooperation Council (GCC) countries, are accepted. The S&P also screens out any companies that deal in the "Trading of gold and silver as cash on [a] deferred basis" (according to the Standard & Poor's website: www. standardandpoors.com).

FTSE Bursa Malaysia Hijrah Shariah Index

The website for the FTSE Bursa Malaysia Hijrah Shariah Index (which you can access from www.ftse.com/Indices; click on Global Equity Indices → FTSE Shariah Global Equity Index Series) indicates that the index operates with direction from the Malaysia Securities Commission's Shariah Advisory Council. Launched in 2007, the index screens to exclude companies whose core business activities relate to conventional banking and other interest-related activities, life insurance, alcohol, tobacco, arms manufacturing, gaming, and pork and other prohibited food products.

The index also excludes the following:

✔ Companies carrying a level of debt that indicates "an inappropriate use of leverage relative to their assets"

✔ "Companies that have income from cash or near cash equivalents or inappropriate levels of receivables to assets"

✔ Companies with an unacceptably high percentage of "liquid assets to illiquid assets"

✔ "Companies whose cash and cash equivalent to total assets exceeds the percentage permitted under Shariah principles and commonly accepted philosophies"

MSCI Global Islamic Indices

Per its website (accessed at www.msci.com; click on Indices → Faith-Based), this family of indexes excludes businesses that derive more than 5 percent of their revenue (cumulatively) from alcohol, tobacco, pork-related products, conventional financial services, defense and weapons, gambling, music, hotels, cinema, and adult entertainment.

The MSCI indexes publicly provide more detail than most other indexes regarding what, exactly, they look for during the industry screening process. Visit the website for details on each prohibited industry.

As well, the MSCI indexes examine three financial ratios for each company when determining sharia compliance:

✔ Total debt divided by total assets

✔ The sum of the company's cash and interest-bearing securities divided by its total assets

✔ The sum of the company's accounts receivable and cash divided by its total assets

Each of these ratios should be less than 33.33 percent.

Developing New Methods for Managing Market Risk

Managing risk is a crucial aspect of investment management. The Islamic capital market is developing rapidly. As its exposure to *market risk* (the very real possibility that the value of a security or group of securities can drop on any given day) increases, the market's inability to tap into certain conventional risk management instruments becomes more problematic. This section offers a quick overview of the concerns related to Islamic market risk and some products being developed to try to curb it.

Identifying the issues

Conventional investment funds have quite a few options for managing market risk, including futures, forward contracts, options, and swap markets. (Refer to the earlier section "Developing the Islamic derivative market" for a rundown of these derivative products.) But the Islamic derivatives market is very small and very young. And in many cases, it faces restrictions from sharia boards that are wary of the speculation involved in derivative products as a whole.

Adding to the concern is that Islamic funds can't diversify as much as conventional funds. Their screening processes remove entire industries from investment consideration, narrowing the field of equity selection. Although diversification can't, by itself, eliminate market risk, it certainly can soften the blow when one large company — or even one entire industry — faces a sudden decline in equity value.

Creating products that mitigate market risk

Two groups of products are currently being developed to help hedge risk in the Islamic market: derivatives (specifically futures and forward contracts) and capital protected equity funds. Both types of products are familiar to conventional investors.

Futures and forward contracts

Futures and forward contracts are familiar derivatives in conventional finance. Both products are used to hedge risk, and both allow a buyer and a seller to agree today on the price of a future asset sale/purchase. (That asset may be a financial asset or commodity, for example.) A difference is that futures are traded on exchanges but forward contracts aren't.

Many sharia scholars have concerns about the compliance of derivatives in general. In fact, some scholars don't permit futures under any circumstances because these contracts involve goods that don't yet exist and therefore involve too much uncertainty. However, some scholars accept futures and forward contracts as sharia-compliant if the following conditions are met:

- ✔ The delivery of the underlying asset is compulsory.
- ✔ The delivery date of the asset can't be adjusted.

In Islamic finance, a *salam* (purchase with deferred delivery) contract is used to support futures and forward contracts. In a salam contract, the price of the goods to be received in the future is paid in full at the time of purchase. Therefore, this type of contract can be used to protect the value of assets in Islamic funds and Islamic bonds. This product differs from conventional futures and forward contracts, in which both the payment and the asset exchange take place in the future.

Capital protected equity funds

Capital protected equity funds require that the majority of assets in the funds be allocated to fixed-term cost plus murabaha contracts that are supported by third-party guarantees issued by A1/P1-rated financial institutions. (The financial institutions providing the guarantees have the highest short-term ratings from S&P and Moody's.) This product was introduced to help investors feel safer about their investments.

In the murabaha contract, the cost plus profit is deferred. When a fund is invested with such a contract, the investor receives profit plus capital in installments. Therefore, the fund is better able to return all the capital it invested.

Book IX
Crowdfund Investing

Five Inspiring Crowdfund Stories

- **Fighting homophobia:** In response to the suicide of an adolescent who was bullied, screenwriter and director Gregor Schmidinger launched a crowdfunding campaign with the goal of raising $6,000 to film a story about a young boy coming to terms with his sexuality and having to deal with the social pressures as well. He raised well more than that and made a 23-minute film that received over 100,000 views.

- **Building a family:** After trying unsuccessfully for three years to conceive a child, Jessica and Sean Haley turned to in vitro fertilization (IVF), a procedure their insurance would not pay for. They launched a campaign on Indiegogo. They asked for $5,000, and they ultimately raised $8,050. Their son Landon was born in 2012.

- **Sharing a personal tragedy:** When Jennifer Merendino's breast cancer recurred, she and her husband, Angelo, decided to create a photo exhibit to share with others what they were going through and to give people a better understanding of what people battling cancer go though. Seeking to raise $8,500 to cover the costs of prints and to travel to show exhibits, Angelo and Jennifer raised over $15,000 on Indiegogo.

- **Crowdfunding hope:** Dustin Dorough, a Superman fan, planned on going to children's hospitals in each of the lower 48 states as well as several provinces in Canada to bring comfort and hope to sick children. He launched a crowdfunding project on Indiegogo to raise money to pay for his trip. On September 6, 2012, his campaign successfully reached its goal of $6,500, enough for the journey.

- **Producing a play:** For New York writer Louise Rozett, volunteering at Ground Zero after the 9/11 attacks was the most profound experience of her life. She wrote a play depicting her experiences and turned to Kickstarter to raise the money (over $25,000) needed for its production at the New York Fringe Festival.

Find free information on the importance of making a crowdfund investment in cash at www.dummies.com/extras/highpoweredinvestingaio.

Chapter 1

Getting the Lowdown on Crowdfund Investing

. . . .

In This Chapter

▶ Understanding the crowd's collective power

▶ Joining the crowd

. . . .

*O*nly in very few instances in history has the start date for an entire industry disrupted the way the world looks at business. This chapter is about one of them. For the first time in 80 years, the average Jane and Joe have the ability to start a business with the help of the crowd or own a part of a friend's American dream.

How? Through crowdfund investing, where the social network meets seed/early-stage financing — and where you become an active participant instead of a passive investor. This chapter introduces this new industry and explains what it's capable of accomplishing.

Seeing the Power of the Online Crowd

Although the world is operating more and more as one global community, people everywhere still rely on their local communities for the bare necessities. The goal here is to show you how to rally your online crowd to conquer your own part of the world by connecting people at a local level to create businesses that benefit communities. Instead of doing it at city hall, you do it online, where most people spend their days.

Crowdfunding has many applications: from raising funding for disaster relief and philanthropic causes to supporting creative endeavors by musicians, artists, and others; to supporting research and scientific breakthroughs; and more. The area of crowdfunding that this book focuses on is *crowdfund investing,* in which early-stage or start-up businesses raise capital by selling small amounts of equity or debt to many investors.

Prior to the 2012 JOBS Act, businesses were forbidden by law to solicit capital through advertisements. The fear was that, due to the nature of these investments, only accredited (read "rich") investors could safely assume the risk. In addition, people who raised the money could not legally give back any financial return, including even giving back the original investment. What they could give, however, were perks. If an artist wanted to raise money to make a new music album, he might give people a sticker for a $5 contribution, a digital copy of the completed album for a $10 contribution, and so on. The JOBS Act, however, changed these rules. All the great benefits of crowdfunding still exist, but the perks that investors stand to receive now also include financial gain.

Here's why this change is so important:

- ✔ The legalization of equity- and debt-based crowdfund investing has broken down the barriers for the small investor, who can now invest in start-up companies. You now have the choice to be an active participant in the growth of a business, to reap rewards for doing so, or to see your returns tied in with those of entrepreneurs over the long term.

- ✔ As an investor, you can find businesses that people in your social networks are launching and can support them with your dollars and your expertise. We all like being part of something that's bigger than ourselves, and crowdfund investing allows you to do exactly that. From the comfort of your own living room, you can help your nephew or former roommate or coworker get a new company off the ground.

Crowdfunding through the ages

Going to the crowd for funding is nothing new; in fact, people have been doing this for decades:

- ✔ The first large-scale endeavor to put a spotlight on the power of small donations to achieve a gargantuan goal was the March of Dimes campaign in the mid-20th century, which relied on small (10 cent) donations to fund the fight against polio.

- ✔ The American Cancer Society (ACS) has been crowdfunding for decades, hosting events like Making Strides Against Breast Cancer, in which teams form to raise money to fight cancer.

- ✔ Politicians crowdfund their reelection campaigns all the time. In fact, one reason for President Obama's 2008 success was his ability to harness the power of crowd donations. Instead of relying on individual large contributors, the campaign went to hundreds of thousands of Americans and asked them for small contributions.

In practical ways, crowdfunding has been around for a long time and has always illustrated the power of pooling small-dollar contributions together. The difference is that today, with access made possible through the Internet and social media, regular people — people like you — have the ability to harness the power of the crowd.

Investing in a start-up company is very risky. Your risky investments should occupy only a small portion of your overall portfolio, and your crowdfunded investments should be considered some of your riskiest investments. The chances of your investing in the next Facebook are very slim, but at least you now have the opportunity to make investments that were previously reserved for only the wealthiest Americans. With that opportunity comes a great deal of responsibility to be a well-informed investor.

The following sections note the businesses that can benefit from crowdfund investing and how to find specific businesses to invest in.

Book IX

Crowdfund Investing

Spotting the business beneficiaries

The types of businesses most likely to benefit from crowdfund investing include start-ups, small businesses (including technology companies, bricks-and-mortar retail shops, and service companies), and anyone else who doesn't easily qualify for traditional financing. The term used in the JOBS Act for such entities is *emerging growth companies*.

These businesses benefit from more than just the capital they can raise through crowdfunding. Entrepreneurs and small business owners also need the support of as many people as possible to be successful. Whereas large, publicly traded companies have the support of many successful people (they have vast resources to pay experienced people to help guide them), start-up businesses, especially those that are actively seeking capital, generally lack the resources to spend on top-notch talent. But crowdfund investors offer growing companies and entrepreneurs both financial support and expertise.

Crowdfund investing should be an active investment. If you buy stock in Apple or General Motors, all you give is your money. But when you engage in a crowdfund investing campaign, you can also support a company with your knowledge and skills. The collective knowledge of the crowd is much greater than the knowledge of any group of experts.

Finding businesses to invest in

Prior to the passage of the JOBS Act in 2012, it was difficult or even impossible for businesses needing funding to find willing investors. The laws governing how private businesses could seek capital from individual investors, written in the height of the Great Depression, were set up to protect people from scams and rip-off schemes. The JOBS Act permits private companies to *generally solicit* for equity and debt offerings, meaning they can publically advertise and discuss such offerings (subject to certain restrictions). Also, it makes crowdfund investing possible by enabling business owners to communicate with anyone via their social networks (such as LinkedIn, Facebook, and Twitter) to find potential investors for their business or start-up ideas.

Companies can position themselves to find crowdfund investors by crafting excellent business plans and by posting their offerings on SEC-registered online funding portals. As a potential investor, you should shop for campaigns only via SEC-approved funding portals. (For an introduction on how to evaluate crowdfund investing campaigns, head to Chapter 2 of Book IX.)

Becoming Part of the Crowd

Make no mistake: Investing in start-ups and small enterprises is risky business. No matter how well you may know the person seeking funds or how rock solid the business proposal seems, you must proceed with caution and prepare for worst-case scenarios (all of which can lighten your wallet).

This section helps you begin to figure out whether crowdfund investing is right for you and how much you can invest. For detailed information on how to investigate a campaign to see whether it would be a good one to add to your portfolio, head to Chapter 2 of Book IX.

By the way, becoming part of an investment crowd doesn't mean following the actions of the crowd. Successful investing of any kind requires that you make your own decisions. The wisdom of the crowd can emerge only if each investor uses her best judgment to decide whether an investment opportunity is a good one. Sharing these thoughts in an open dialogue guides the crowd toward reasonable decisions. Pooling these thoughts together is what creates crowd wisdom.

Diversifying your portfolio

If you've ever taken an investment course, the first thing you probably learned is that you don't protect yourself from loss by picking winning companies; you do it by diversifying your portfolio. If you invest in the public markets, you diversify by investing in a combination of stocks (large and small, both domestic and international) and bonds. The goal is to spread out your risk among all your investments. That way, if one goes belly up, it won't wipe out your entire savings.

You need to approach your crowdfund investments with the intention of using them to diversify your portfolio. Making a decision to invest in a crowdfund offering should take into account your investment psychology: If you're completely risk averse, you have no business investing in small, private companies. If, however, you can tolerate volatility and risk in a small portion of your portfolio for the sake of potentially receiving some significant financial returns, a crowdfund investment may make sense.

In any case, a crowdfund investment should be a small part of your portfolio. (Less than 10 percent of your portfolio should be in high-risk investments, and crowdfunding may be a portion of that 10 percent if you have other high-risk investments.) Whether you're investing in a campaign that offers you equity in the company or that's selling debt (which will be repaid to you in steady increments over a set period of time), you should treat a crowdfund investment as the riskiest part of your portfolio. That's because statistics show that, on average, 50 percent of new companies fail within their first year.

You have to be very smart when considering your crowdfund investment options (for example, investing only in products or services you'd buy yourself, revenue models you understand, and entrepreneurs you know and trust). But no matter how smart you think your decision may be, you also have to be prepared for failure (see the upcoming section "Preparing for the worst-case scenario"). Therefore, if you choose to put money into a crowdfund investment, you likely want to scale back on the funds you put into other high-risk investments, such as emerging market stocks, so that you don't exceed 10 percent of your portfolio in high-risk investments.

Doing your homework and offering expertise

Here are some key concepts that all potential investors must keep in mind when considering investing in crowdfund campaigns:

- ✔ **You should plan to make small investments in at least ten crowdfund investing campaigns.** Most professional investors (angel investors and venture capitalists) expect that out of ten investments in private companies and start-ups, seven will lose money, two will break even or have a small return, and one will have a significant return. Are these numbers guaranteed? Absolutely not! You must do research on each potential investment, talk with people you trust, consider carefully, and then make small investments in people you know, products you use, businesses you trust, or entrepreneurs you believe in.

- ✔ **Crowdfund investing is an active form of investing.** As an investor, you get to know these businesses much more personally than you know any public company you invest in. As you find out in Chapter 3 of Book IX, you can help the businesses with your expertise, but you must make sure you don't become a nuisance to the business owner.

Weighing the risks and potential rewards

This statistic bears repeating: On average, 50 percent of investments in early-stage companies fail within the first year. Among the failures, 50 percent of early-stage companies run out of cash before they can succeed. The other 50 percent of failures suffer from poor management decisions, poor hiring decisions, poor use of funds, and so on. Therefore, as a potential crowdfund investor, you have to make the effort to figure out a couple key things about the business you're considering:

- ✔ If its campaign is successful, will it have enough cash to meet its stated milestones?

- ✔ Have the owners and managers thought through crucial decisions such as who to hire and how to use the money being raised?

Luckily, you don't have to be a super sleuth to find answers. The business or entrepreneur seeking funds is required to provide a lot of information in its campaign pitch. Your job is to read (and watch and listen to) all that information and to participate in online crowd conversations when you find certain answers to be lacking. You can't be a passive investor; you must commit to taking an active role in finding out as much information as possible.

Calculating your maximum investment

If you're a non-accredited investor (meaning your net worth is less than $1 million excluding your primary residence, and you haven't earned more than $200,000 for each of the past two years), you can't invest every dime you have in crowdfund investment campaigns. Doing so would be a nightmare for your portfolio (you'd be doing the opposite of diversifying), and it also wouldn't be legal. That's because, per the JOBS Act, the SEC sets specific limits on how much any individual can invest. The limits are based on how much you make (your annual income) or have in your savings (your net worth).

Table 1-1 offers the breakdown of how much the SEC allows you to risk on crowdfund investments based on your annual income (specifically, your adjusted gross income) or net worth (the value of all your stocks, bonds, and savings outside the equity that you have in your house). Note that the SEC allows you to use the greater of these two figures when calculating your limit.

Table 1-1	SEC Investment Limits Based on Annual Income or Net Worth	
If Your Annual Income or Net Worth Is . . .	*You Can Invest Up to . . .*	*Which Caps Out at . . .*
Less than $40,000	$2,000	$2,000
$40,000 to $99,999.99	5% of your annual income or net worth	$5,000
$100,000 or more	10% of your annual income or net worth up to $100,000	$100,000

Earlier, this chapter encourages diversity in crowdfund investing (because the failure rate for these types of ventures is so high). Therefore, if your annual cap is $2,000, you shouldn't invest most of that amount in a single campaign. Doing so impedes your ability to invest in other crowdfund investment projects for the rest of the calendar year. It also breaks the rules that venture capitalists use for their investments, which is to make small investments in several companies to diversify risk.

What are the rules for accredited investors? The SEC has determined that accredited investors are individuals with income above $200,000 per year if single ($300,000 per year if married) for each of the past two years or with a net worth over $1 million (excluding the value of your home). If your income/net worth qualifies you as an accredited investor, with the proper legal disclosures, the SEC allows you to make investments of any amount you choose in any private company. Although having this flexibility to make investments at any level may sound like a great thing, it also means no guardrails are in place to help limit your potential losses from investments in companies that fail.

If you're an accredited investor, you should use the same principles of portfolio investing that a non-accredited investor uses. High-risk investments (including crowdfund investments) should not comprise more than 10 percent of your investment portfolio. No matter how much of a sure thing the investment may seem to you, don't put all your eggs in one, high-risk basket. Venture capitalists make ten investments in start-ups to try to get one large winner. Following their example, aim to make a larger number of small-dollar investments in crowdfund investing.

If you're an accredited investor, you have two options when it comes to funneling dollars into crowdfund-investing campaigns:

- ✔ If you're investing through an online crowdfunding portal (see Chapter 3 in Book IX), you're limited to caps that are provided by the legislation.

- ✔ If you're investing directly into a company (outside of a funding portal or broker-dealer) that is running a crowdfunding offering online, you can invest as much as you want, provided that the *company* doesn't exceed its yearly cap of $1 million of crowdfunded investments per the legislation.

Preparing for the worst-case scenario

Although you certainly hope for the best-case scenario when making an investment decision, you must plan for the worst. The worst-case scenario in crowdfund investing:

YOU COULD LOSE YOUR ENTIRE INVESTMENT.

Is that clear enough?

The vast majority of the time, when a business fails, a variety of legitimate, above-board factors contribute to the failure, including having unreasonable market expectations and failing to execute the business plan.

As an investor, you have to set your expectations low when you think about what your returns may be from a crowdfund investment. You can't invest money that you need to tap into within the next year (because you're tied to the initial investment for at least that length of time; see Chapter 3 in Book IX for details on making and managing your investment). And you can't invest money assuming that you'll earn a certain percentage of return within a certain amount of time; new and small businesses simply aren't that predictable. As noted earlier in this chapter, risk only a very small percentage of your total investment portfolio on crowdfund investments. That way, if you make a good investment, you can be excited, and if you make a poor investment, it doesn't prevent your retirement or otherwise devastate your long-term financial situation.

Chapter 2

Evaluating Crowdfund Investing Opportunities

*I*f you've never invested in start-ups and small businesses before, crowdfund investing may seem really exciting. After all, you have the chance — perhaps for the first time — to put your money directly behind an entrepreneur's concept or into a small business that seems poised for great things.

A word of caution: Take your time, become very educated about the opportunities themselves and the risks involved, and stay on a strict budget if you decide to invest. Before you jump into any investment, stop and repeat the following:

✔ I will invest only in people I know and trust.

✔ I will invest only in products or services I will use myself or believe will have real value for others.

✔ I will invest only in businesses for which I am willing to be a marketing engine or help out in some way.

✔ I understand that this is a long-term investment, I may never see my investment, and if I do, it may be a long time off and may not be the amount I put in.

✔ I am investing only as much as I can afford to walk away from or lose today.

Now wash, rinse, and repeat. And keep reading to find out what to look for when deciding which businesses to invest in.

Protecting Yourself through Due Diligence

When you invest in a more traditional financial vehicle, such as a mutual fund, you depend pretty heavily on other people to tell you what to expect. The fund company creates a hefty prospectus (which, thankfully, is available in electronic format these days — let the trees rejoice!). This document outlines past performance, fund components, and management experience so you can get a decent sense of what you're in for when you part with your dollars. (Of course, you must actually *read* the prospectus in order for it to be of benefit; you can't let the sheer size of the document scare you off.)

If the people running a crowdfund investment campaign are doing their jobs well, you should be able to pretty easily put your hands on information that can help you anticipate what to expect from your investment. But seeking out that information is your job; no 72-page prospectus is going to magically appear in your mailbox or inbox when you express interest in a certain campaign. This section walks you through the fundamentals of familiarizing yourself with a crowdfund investment opportunity.

Studying the candidates

If you decide that you want to put a small portion of your investment portfolio into one or several small businesses and start-ups, a number of crowdfund investing platforms (websites) are available to help you make the best decisions possible.

To pave the way for a possible positive outcome, you have to do your homework. Nothing replaces a thorough review of all information available on the investment in question. One of the biggest benefits of crowdfund investing is that lots of individuals are doing the same research at the same time, and you can use online forums to discuss tactics and information. That said, collaborative efforts should never take the place of your own primary research so that you fully understand what you're investing in and what the risks are. The following sections explain what steps to take as you study the companies attempting to raise capital via crowdfund investing.

Take a lesson from angel investors and venture capitalists (professional or experienced investors in start-up businesses) and invest small amounts in a number of companies. If you were to invest in ten companies, for example, you could assume that, over time, some of them would lose money, some would break even, and a few would make money. If you were lucky, one might generate a very positive outcome.

Knowing how your money will be used

A company wants to grow, so it runs a campaign to raise the necessary capital via crowdfund investing. What exactly will it do with the money being raised? The question is obvious, but you have to make sure you get a concrete answer.

Look at the campaign proposal and how much the company wants to raise. Carefully review its plans for using the funding. Ask yourself these questions:

- ✔ **Do you think the amount of money being raised is enough to enact the company's plans, or is the company asking for too much?** For example, say the business plan is to start a cable television channel and the company is attempting to raise $200,000. If the plan states that the company can be operational with that money alone, that's a red flag. The legal bill alone for working with cable companies and the Federal Communications Commission (FCC) is likely to cost more than $200,000.

   On the flip side, if a business plan suggests that it will cost $200,000 to start a small landscaping business, you should find out a great deal more information before deciding to invest because that number seems high. (Maybe it isn't, but you need to study the plan to find out.)

- ✔ **Do the company's assumptions and timelines feel credible?** Does the plan suggest that the company can open a restaurant in three weeks? On the other hand, does it suggest that three years of research are required before the company can decide on a restaurant location? Both timelines seem unreasonable and should raise red flags.

- ✔ **Has this company used investor money wisely in the past?** If this isn't the first time this company has raised money from debt or equity, ask questions about its financial history. If the business has used debt in the past, did it repay the debt on time? If the company offered equity in the past, does it still have good relationships with those earlier investors, and did the company use the money to grow?

If you can't glean these answers from the information the company itself has provided, use the online crowdfund investing forums to ask very specific questions. If you don't get satisfactory answers from the company in a timely manner, don't invest.

Reading online opinions and questions about a proposal

All pitches on crowdfund investing websites (called *funding portals*) offer potential investors the ability to post questions and read comments and answers from other potential and current investors and company representatives. Keep a few things in mind when you enter these conversations:

✔ **Perform due diligence before asking.** These are small companies working under intense time constraints. Review what has already been asked and answered. That way, if your question has already been answered, you save time for yourself, as well as for the business owner or representative.

✔ **Be a constructive part of the dialogue.** Posting random or unrelated comments or making inflammatory statements is not appropriate. Be respectful of everyone in the conversation.

✔ **Leverage other investors' experience.** Let others in the online community help you build your investment skills. Try to find a few trusted individuals you can chat with online about the merits and weaknesses of investments you're considering.

Pinpointing your connection to the entrepreneur or small business owner

The premise of crowdfund investing is that you put your money into ventures run by people you know and trust — or by people who have a secondary connection to you. What does a secondary connection look like? If people you know and trust have a connection with — and faith in — the people running the investment campaign, you have a secondary connection. You're just two degrees away from the entrepreneur or company owner.

Why the desire for such a close connection between business owner and investor? Because it takes a lot more than a good idea to make a business profitable. It takes hard work, determination, and focus. (Not to mention luck!) Lots of people can come up with good ideas, and salesmen can make it sound like these ideas are going to be profitable for investors. When you invest your dollars in people you know, you can make choices based on an individual's ability and tendency to follow through. You need to know enough about this person to understand his work ethic and be familiar with his past business endeavors.

Be cautious about investing in someone you may have met once but know very little about. (Laughing over drinks at a cocktail party doesn't give you the insight you need to figure out this person's business acumen.) And be cautious when friends forward information to you via social media about investment opportunities you should check out. If your friends have some financial sense, then be prepared to consider what they're sharing. But always follow up by finding out as much as possible about the entrepreneur or business owner. Here are some great questions to ask yourself as you do:

✔ Is this person trustworthy?

✔ Is she a hard worker?

✔ Does she have entrepreneurial or other business experience?

✔ Does she generally follow through on what she wants to do?

✔ Would I recommend her for a job to another friend or family member?

You are *not* evaluating people for friendships here. You're evaluating them for their ability to handle your money wisely. You can like someone a lot and not trust him with your money. Therefore, if the answer to any of these questions is "no," walk away.

Watching the pitch video

The pitch video that the entrepreneur or small business owner creates is your window into his business concept and plan. You can find this video by visiting the particular online funding platform that is hosting this person's investment campaign. Watching this video is your opportunity to hear this person's passion and drive. It also gives you an idea how the business owner's mind is organized.

View funding pitch videos *only* on SEC-approved crowdfund investing sites. The SEC wants to insure that you have access not only to the video but also to the complete information about the company's offering, which is available on the same website.

If the pitch video is scattered or wishy-washy and doesn't really say much of importance, chances are the business itself is going to be disorganized and lack focus. After all, the entrepreneur or business owner should be well aware that the pitch video is his opportunity to sell everyone on the business. If he hasn't put a lot of time and energy into organizing it, this dearth of effort should be a major red flag.

On the other hand, a pitch video that is well thought out should give you a good sense of who the entrepreneur is, what kind of team he has created, and what his business model looks like. It doesn't have to be an Oscar-quality video to achieve these ends. The content is what really matters, and that content should include how investors' money is going to be used and why this entrepreneur is the right person for the job.

Pitch videos shouldn't be longer than five minutes, so don't expect a video to contain every bit of information you need to make an investment decision. Instead, consider it an advertisement that either piques your interest in the entrepreneur and the business or turns you off completely. The detailed pitch and financial information, which are explained in the next two sections, allow you to really dig into the business plan.

Reading the pitch information on the company page (and asking questions)

You should be able to locate the meat of the business model on the same funding portal where you find the pitch video. The entrepreneur or business owner should provide the equivalent of a business plan's executive summary, which contains about three pages of information on the entrepreneur, her team, her competitors, and the business model. As you read this information, take notes and consider what questions you have.

If, after reviewing all the available information, you still have unanswered questions, you need to reach out to the entrepreneur or business owner directly. The online funding portal provides discussion forums that allow you to do just that. Don't be shy about asking questions, especially when the answers will help you determine whether to spend your money. Instead, assume that you're doing a community service here; if you couldn't find all the answers you were looking for, chances are other potential investors are in the same boat.

Watching how an entrepreneur answers your questions gives you a very good glimpse into how she will relate to her investors after the investment campaign reaches a successful completion and she is growing her business. If questions are left unanswered in this phase, you may assume that you'll have a hard time getting information from the entrepreneur down the road. (If the entrepreneur is busy now, just wait until she has launched her business!) This person needs to demonstrate that she can manage her time effectively, and this question-and-answer interaction is a good window into her time management and communication abilities.

If the campaign is for an existing business and the business owner is looking for growth capital, the executive summary information should feel quite solid. After all, this person isn't just speculating about what the business will look like; he's in the midst of it and should know the company's strengths and weaknesses and its competitors. The pitch information section should address why this company is better than its competitors and how it's going to overcome any existing weaknesses.

Reviewing financial information

The financial information connected to the investment campaign is one of the most important elements for you to review and understand. That's because no matter how sound the idea for the business is, if the financials don't make sense, you're never going to see a return on your investment.

The financials should include clear explanations that walk you through what you're seeing. If that's not the case, don't get embarrassed and assume you should just trust that everything's fine. That's how people lose money! Instead, reach out to someone with an accounting or other financial background (*surely* there's an accountant somewhere in your family) and ask for help analyzing the data.

If you're looking at a campaign for an existing business, it should provide a good history of past performance. Consider whether its future goals mesh with that past performance; if a big leap is planned and the owner hasn't explained how the leap is going to occur, be very wary. For example, say the company is a $100,000-revenue, bricks-and-mortar store, and it wants to raise $50,000 for a new location. If the owner is saying that the combined revenue is going to be $500,000, send up a big red flag. Make sure you can locate a good explanation for every assumption the entrepreneur has made.

When you make investments in the public stock markets, you can review quarterly and annual reports to see a company's revenues, expenses, profits, and losses, as well as the typical ratios that investors review prior to making investment decisions. But companies seeking crowdfund investments will likely be newly formed or very young and may be creating externally visible financial reports for the first time. This fact doesn't mean that you should expect any less accuracy or completeness from them, however.

To promote transparency of financial information, the SEC requires companies using crowdfund investments to supply certain information to potential investors. Take full advantage of any financial information supplied by the company during your decision-making process, and if you don't see the kind of detail that allows you to make a decision you feel confident in, walk away.

Applying Some Common-Sense Tactics

When you're looking at lots of numbers, ratios, facts, and charts all whizzing by at 100 miles per hour, you may think, "Wow! This company can't lose! I gotta buy this now!" You experience the infomercial effect; you get so caught up in how amazing this business/product/spray-on hair is that your common sense flies out the window. You don't stop to consider how you would incorporate this business/product/spray-on hair into your daily life.

When you run across a great pitch video and clear, concise online documents, you may immediately jump to the "Invest!" mindset. You begin, naturally, to look for reaffirming information and data for that investment or person. As you look at all the financials, for example, you may find yourself focusing on all the strong sales numbers and not asking as many questions about the unrealistic marketing plans to get to those sales numbers.

In this section, you're encouraged to apply some common-sense tactics to avoid being swept up in your enthusiasm. You need to protect yourself from making bad decisions, and you have the means to do so if you just slow down, employ your gray matter, and take some additional steps.

Making sure you actually understand the business or project

Okay, this step is *really* fundamental. After watching and reading the pitch materials, answer these questions:

- ✔ **Do you understand exactly what the product or service is?** If someone asked you to describe it, could you give a 30- to 60-second description of what the product or service is and how it works?

- ✔ **Can you easily describe what problem this product or service solves for a person or a business?** Most purchases are made either to stop current pain or to keep pain/discomfort from happening in the future. (Pain is not always physical pain, of course; it's often emotional or psychological pain.) No matter how cool a product may sound, until it solves a problem for a person or business, it's simply something that you pick up at a store, look at, and put back on the shelf.

- ✔ **Who is the customer for this business?** When talking with entrepreneurs, a common answer is "Women will love this product!" or "Every dog owner is our customer." But a start-up business *never* has the capital to sell to every woman or every dog owner. And even if it did, not everyone in those groups would buy the product.

Make sure the entrepreneur has a *very* clear picture of the target customer. For example, "My customers are women within 6 miles of my store who work, have children, and want nutritious organic meals delivered to their homes twice a week so they don't have to cook. The age range for our product is women between 30 and 45." That type of answer indicates that the business has a good idea of its customer demographics, as well as what a reasonable geography is for targeting customers.

Asking a simple question: Would you buy it?

Be sure to ask yourself these simple questions:

- ✔ Would you really buy this product or service?

- ✔ Would you really use this product or service? (Be honest! Buying is one thing; fitting this item or service into your daily life is quite another.)

✔ Would you really tell your friends about how great this product or service is and that they should buy or use it?

These may seem like obvious questions, but many times in the rush of excitement potential investors don't ask them. Of course, the answers depend on who the customer for this product or service is and whether the product or service actually provides a solution to a problem. (See how you're circling back to the fundamentals here?)

Discussing the opportunity with people you trust

Rushing to buy anything — especially stock in a company — is never a good idea. You don't necessarily want to wait for weeks or months to buy a stock; after all, crowdfund investment campaigns don't last very long (30 to 90 days, generally). However, you should take enough time to talk with trusted friends or colleagues. Ask for feedback from people you know whose investment judgment and knowledge you respect. These people may be able to give you outside validation or ask helpful questions so that you have a second opinion about the quality of the investment and whether it's right for you.

In addition to having one-on-one conversations with people, you may consider starting a crowdfund investing club. Maybe some of your friends are interested in this small-business investing space. If so, you each spend an hour or two of your own time researching companies every week or two weeks or month. Then you meet to discuss and debate whether companies that you like stand up to other members' scrutiny. At the end of the discussion, everyone makes her own individual investment decision. But you've had the opportunity to spend some time with friends and talk about interesting topics, and maybe you leave the meeting with some good input that helps you make better investment decisions.

Reading the crowd feedback online

Crowdfund investing is an online activity; the business owner or entrepreneur must use an online funding portal, and he reaches out to potential investors almost entirely online via social media. Therefore, you can find potential investors online discussing the owner, the business model, the product, the financials, and anything else related to this opportunity. And that's a good thing; crowdfund investing as a whole can only benefit from vibrant, active crowds that parse these opportunities and determine which are worthwhile and which aren't.

Is it important to read online feedback about the product and the entrepreneur? Yes! Doing so can certainly move you closer to understanding the strengths and weaknesses of the campaign. Should you believe every single comment as fact? Probably not. Treat the feedback much like you'd treat a restaurant or movie review. After all, these are opinions, and you need to judge for yourself just how closely you think they track to the facts.

Avoiding impulse buys

Do not buy stock or invest in crowdfunded debt on impulse. Period. You're not buying an ice cream cone here, or even an exercise system you see on late-night TV. You're making an investment, and you should take it seriously. Making an impulse buy will almost certainly lead to regret.

Keep in mind that buying into a crowdfund investment campaign is *not* the same as buying into a publicly traded stock, a bond, a mutual fund, or another traditional financial vehicle. These other vehicles are *liquid,* meaning that markets exist for their trade, and you aren't locked into holding them for any length of time. As a crowdfund investor, however, you're locked into your investment for a minimum of 12 months. And even after that time, you may find it somewhat challenging to find a buyer for your equity or debt. (Secondary markets for these securities will emerge, undoubtedly, but the industry is brand new as of this writing so they don't yet exist.) Therefore, you must do your research, talk with trusted friends, and carefully consider what to do. Then, and only then, should you make your decision of whether to invest.

Sniffing Out Fraud

The minute you start thinking about investing in a company through crowdfund investing, you assume responsibility to help watch for fraud. The power of the crowd — which includes you! — is precisely what makes crowdfund investing so great.

Historically, fraud has taken place one-on-one. In other words, one person (such as a crooked financial advisor) dupes one other person (such as a single investor). In crowdfund investing, for fraud to exist, one person has to fool many, many people in a very public forum (the online funding portals and social media). Good luck, fraudsters!

As you're studying campaigns, asking questions, and monitoring crowd feedback on various business models, you may find that something raises a red flag. If that's the case, you have a responsibility to take action. This section explains first why and then how.

Trusting that the crowd can spot signs of trouble

Before Bernie Madoff's name became permanently associated with a mind-boggling investment scandal, many people had major doubts about his claims. Some of them refused to invest because they knew what he was doing was a scam. But the primary outlet they had was to raise questions to Madoff's team, which meant (of course) that no other potential investors ever got to hear them.

Crowdfund investing changes the playing field. When one person has a doubt, it can quickly and powerfully become everyone's doubt. Mind you, this fact makes life tough for an honest entrepreneur who may have a paranoid potential investor in his crowd. One person can potentially raise lots of doubts about a legitimately good business plan being promoted by someone with the skills to make it a success. Is that fair? Maybe not. But it's not entirely a bad thing. Raising money from investors is not and should not be an easy thing to do.

Crowds are likely to be able to spot signs of trouble shortly after they arise. The collective knowledge of the crowd is greater than the knowledge of any single person or small group of people. If 2,000 people have decided to invest in a business through crowdfunding investing and none of them has raised any serious concerns in the online discussion forums, let this be a good sign to you. However, if *you* see a problem — even if you're the only one to do so — you can't be scared to call it to the crowd's attention. If your concerns are unwarranted, the crowd will help you figure that out. If you've spotted something truly troubling, the crowd will thank you for stepping up to your responsibility.

Reporting your suspicions to the funding portal

If you see something in a crowdfund investing campaign that raises your suspicions, you should first ask about it in the dialogue section of the campaign itself. But then you need to go a step further and report your suspicions to the online funding portal.

Funding portals should take every complaint and suspicion extremely seriously; they have a legal responsibility to do so. Funding portals are monitored by the SEC, and the SEC is always looking for any signs of fraud. If the SEC finds a problem and the funding portal knew about it (and failed to report it), that portal will suffer for its poor choices.

Plus, there's no worse press for a funding portal than allowing fraud to happen on its website. Everyone in the crowdfund investing community will hear about it, and potential investors will think twice before investing in a company listed on that website.

Chapter 3

Committing Your Capital and Adding Value

*Y*ou've considered the risks spelled out in Chapter 1 of Book IX, and you're prepared for the worst-case scenario (which is losing every dime you invest), and you can still clearly see the value of committing your capital. Now you've decided you're ready to take the plunge and become a crowd-fund investor. In this chapter, you find out how to make the actual invest-ment, what your responsibilities as an investor are, and how (and when) you can end your investment, including explaining the kinds of exits (IPO and merger or acquisition) you're probably hoping for.

Making Your First Crowdfund Investment

After you've done your research into potential investments (with the help of Book IX, Chapter 2) and reached out to someone you trust for a second opin-ion, you may feel ready to commit to an investment. But you have to be aware that committing your money to a crowdfund investing campaign doesn't lead to instant equity that immediately starts increasing or decreasing in value.

If you want to buy stock in a public company, you can go to your online bro-kerage account (with Fidelity or Vanguard, for example) and purchase that stock in real time. You can also purchase *exchange-traded funds* (ETFs), which are bundles of stocks or other securities, in real time. You simply log in, do your research, and purchase the stock or ETF. When you buy stock or an ETF on the New York Stock Exchange or the NASDAQ, you're purchasing on the public stock markets: places where buyers and sellers know they can meet and trade stocks at publicly available prices. If you decide tomorrow that you no longer want that stock or ETF (it now reminds you of a certain pair of eggplant-colored pants hanging in your closet), you can sell it just as easily, although the price likely will have fluctuated even in the single day since your purchase.

When you decide to purchase equity shares or debt through a crowdfund investing campaign, the entire process is different. You aren't sending your money into a public stock market. You're not interacting in a place where lots of buyers and sellers congregate, ready to do business. Instead, you're sending your money to one start-up or small business. (As you find out, you're actually sending the money to a middleman called an *escrow agent* who holds the cash until the crowdfund investing campaign is complete, but that's getting ahead of the game here.)

In addition, you take this step knowing that you're making a commitment of at least 12 months (per the JOBS Act legislation). You're making an *illiquid investment,* which means you're putting your money into something that can't be turned back into cash quickly or easily. When you're completely comfortable with the level of commitment required here — you have the engagement ring in hand and are ready to bend your knee — it's time to invest.

The following sections walk you through what happens and what to expect when you make a crowdfund investment.

Make your first crowdfund investment a fairly small one. Even if the campaign is being run by your best friend or your brother, don't max out your annual investment limit on the first campaign. After all, you don't yet know what being a crowdfund investor will actually feel like. Give yourself this first opportunity to warm up to the whole process — to find out how much you like (or dislike) being on the business owner's marketing team and playing other supportive roles.

Pledging your amount on the funding portal

When you're ready to pledge your funds to a crowdfund investing campaign, you log onto the online funding portal that supports this particular campaign. Here are the steps you'll most likely take next:

1. **Register with the portal.**

    You provide your name and preferred contact information.

2. **Take the investor quiz.**

   This quiz determines whether you're an educationally accredited investor (translation: you understand what you're risking by pursuing a crowdfund investment). Don't stress: The quiz really isn't very difficult as long as you have realistic expectations about crowdfund investments.

3. **Accept the crowdfund investing portal's disclosure statements.**

   Doing so verifies that you understand the risks of investing in start-ups and small businesses.

4. **Input your checking account, savings account, or debit account number.**

   A credit card won't fly when you're making this type of investment. You can't use a credit card to buy public stock on an online brokerage account, and you aren't allowed to use a credit card to make crowdfund investments either.

   Why the restriction? Because a credit card purchase can be disputed, which can interrupt the business funding process. Using a credit card creates the possibility of a phantom transaction. You must buy stock and make crowdfund investments with real money that you actually have in an account.

5. **Specify how much you intend to invest.**

   The amount you choose must be above the minimum established by the campaign and below your maximum allowed by the JOBS Act. Where you fall in the middle of those two numbers is up to you, your financial portfolio, and your investment advisor (if you have one).

6. **Start signing.**

   Buying crowdfund investments isn't as easy as simply hitting the purchase button. There are also documents like a subscription agreement, which summarize and standardize the offering. In other words, you're buying a certain number of shares at a certain price and those shares come with specific rights. You need to review and sign these documents.

Going into escrow until the campaign is complete

After you follow the steps outlined in the preceding section, your money is transferred to what is known as an *escrow agent.* If you've ever bought a house, you're likely well versed in the concept of escrow. If not, escrow is fairly easy to understand.

In crowdfund investing, the escrow agent is a neutral third party — a company that holds investors' cash, as well as the shares of the company, in trust. When the conditions of the sale are met — in this case, the crowd-fund investing campaign reaches 100 percent of its funding target — the escrow agent releases the cash to the seller of the stock and releases the stock to the buyers (the investors). If the conditions of the sale aren't met — the campaign fails to reach 100 percent of its funding target — the escrow agent returns the money to the investors.

The escrow process is a safety check: It eliminates the risk of paying for stock and not receiving what you pay for. The JOBS Act legislation states that a funding portal cannot be an escrow agent; it can't hold investors' cash. Funding portals don't carry insurance to guard themselves against potential fraud or failure with investor money; escrow agents do.

Assuming that the crowdfund investing campaign is a success, the last step of the process is for the escrow agent to transfer stock certificates or debt notes to the investors and wire the funds to the company's account. (These certificates or notes are electronic; don't expect to receive hard copies in the mail.) At that point, you are officially a private equity or debt investor!

Knowing Your Rights as an Investor

You need to do a bit of independent research and reading to find out what your rights are as an investor in a specific company's campaign. For starters, your rights depend on whether you invest in equity or debt.

If you're an equity investor, your rights largely depend on the type of stock you purchase, such as common stock or preferred stock. You may have certain voting rights as a stockholder, for example. The online funding portal for the campaign is the best resource for this information; your rights and responsibilities as an investor should be spelled out in documentation associated with the campaign offering.

The same is true if you buy into the company on the debt side: There are many ways to structure a debt deal, and you need to know the specifics for your individual case. Here are some things you should make sure you know before you purchase private company debt:

✔ What is the payoff schedule?

✔ When will the company start paying down the loan: right away, or only after it starts producing revenue?

✔ Is there a time limit for how long the company has to pay you back?

✔ Are any contingencies built into the deal that would allow the company to postpone debt payments?

✔ Is the company allowed to pay off the balance early without interest (prepayment)?

✔ Is the payoff revenue-based financing (RBF)? RBF terms allow the company to pay off the loan based upon a certain percentage of revenue.

Although you should definitely do your homework to understand your specific rights, this section covers two fundamental rights that apply to every crowdfund investor.

The right to be informed

Whether you own debt or equity, and no matter what type of debt or equity you own, you have the right to receive regular updates on the progress of the company. The entrepreneur or small business owner should send out reports to investors at least on a quarterly basis, if not more often. (The entrepreneur or owner should be very clear from day one about how often such reports will be released.) These reports should include the following types of updates:

✔ Problems encountered since the last report

✔ Successes achieved

✔ Revenue generated

✔ Major expenses incurred, including any major *unplanned* expenses (along with explanations of why they were necessary)

In addition, you should also receive an annual report that is more detailed and includes thorough financial statements that reflect the company's cash position, revenues and expenses for the entire year, and more.

The right to sell

The biggest right you have as an investor is the right to sell your shares in the company after the 12-month holding period is complete. (If you're holding debt in the company, a similar holding period may apply.)

If things aren't going too well for the business, the entrepreneur or business owner will probably try to discourage you from selling your stock or debt. That's smart for him to do; the business needs all the financial stability it can get, especially when times are tough. But you must realize that no one can stop you from selling.

Anticipating Rewards for Your Investment

Your crowdfund investment can be structured in a variety of ways. If you're a debt investor, you invest a certain amount of principal and, in exchange, you receive a certain amount of interest each month or quarter. If you're an equity owner, you receive dividends quarterly or yearly, or you receive no payment for your investment until you sell your shares.

Before you make the decision to invest in a specific campaign, know exactly how and when you can expect to have your capital returned. Researching that information is a key part of the due diligence described in Chapter 2 of Book IX, and the information should be readily accessible on the campaign's funding portal. You may very well find that your compensation comes only if the company meets and exceeds financial expectations; a lag in company performance could spell zero payoff for you.

In this section, you get the scoop on two types of rewards that you may encounter as a crowdfund investor: dividends and other perks.

Dividing up profits: Dividends

A common perk for owning stock in a company (whether a public or private one) is having the right to dividends. Dividends don't (usually) diminish the amount of stock that you own. Instead, they're a reward based on the amount of equity you own; you're given a certain percentage of the money in the dividend pool.

A start-up or small business should pay you dividends only if it's making a significant profit. In the early stages of a business, its success depends on its ability to reinvest as much money as possible. Therefore, you likely won't see dividends in the first months or even the first years of a start-up.

How dividends are paid varies widely; they may be issued monthly, quarterly, yearly, or not at all. For a small start-up company, paying dividends can be very time consuming, so chances are, your dividends (if you get any) will be issued quarterly or — more likely — yearly.

As with all investments, there are major tax implications to money you receive from dividends. Be very careful not to spend every dime that you reap from your investments, because you need a portion of it to cover your tax bill come April. Speak to an accounting professional, and don't get caught with your pants down (and pockets inside out).

(Possibly) benefitting from other perks

Before the JOBS Act legalized equity- and debt-based crowdfund investing, crowdfunded investments offered investors specific perks. Now that equity- and debt-based crowdfund investing exists, some companies may still choose to reward investors with specific perks.

The perks can vary widely depending on the company. If you invest in a restaurant or another bricks-and-mortar establishment, you may be given discounts each time you visit or on certain dates. In exchange for investing in technology-based companies, you may be given reduced fees for using their services.

If a company decides to give you perks, be grateful, but don't feel compelled to take advantage of them. Keep in mind that every discount you receive means that the company will have that much less revenue. In turn, this means your stock, as an owner of the company, will be worth less money. You want to support the business as much as possible without taking advantage of it and undermining your own investment. Remind yourself that you aren't *entitled* to discounts; the company that offers them is being generous.

If the entrepreneur or small-business owner offers you and other investors very deep discounts, consider this action a red flag. Significant discounts for all investors and supporters will seriously affect the company's financial projections. If you sense that the perk is too good, don't be shy about letting the entrepreneur or business owner know what you're thinking.

The best reward systems are tied to current investors and customers bringing new customers to the business. That way, rewards are based on the company's existing supporters helping to increase its revenue and expand its customer base.

Playing the Right Role as an Investor

As a crowdfund investor, you may have opportunities to help the company beyond providing your financial capital. You may be asked to participate in product research and testing, in marketing the product or service being offered, or in advising the business owner on a specific area of your expertise.

Keep in mind that not every company that you invest in will make such requests, but if you do get a chance to add value to the company, you have to strike the right balance with your participation. You don't want to act like an overprotective parent and risk smothering the business owner with your advice. Instead, strive to be the smart, yet cool, aunt or uncle who can offer help and then stand back and watch what happens. This section helps you understand how to achieve this balance, whether you're sharing your network, serving on a board of advisors, evaluating product or service quality, or playing a marketing role. In addition, you find out how to handle a situation that hopefully you'll never have to deal with: discovering that the company you invested in is breaking the law.

When investing in people you know, you need to enforce boundaries to separate your personal and financial relationships. You invest in someone because you believe in that person's vision, capabilities, and skills. Don't become so enmeshed in the day-to-day workings of the business that you hamstring the entrepreneur with second-guessing, too much advice, or too much communication. If you do, you may risk hurting not only the business but also your relationship with its owner.

Sharing what and who you know

Part of the reason that you've invested in a small private company may be your desire to feel more connected to your investments. One way to do that is to help connect the business owner with information, resources, and people who can help the company succeed. Providing knowledge and introductions can be very helpful if done in the right way, and when the entrepreneur asks.

Tapping into your professional experience

What professional experiences do you have in your background? Do they relate to the crowdfund investment you've made? How can you structure this information and deliver it in a way that's helpful and not distracting to the entrepreneur?

Don't underestimate what you may have to offer. What may seem like common sense and very basic information to you as an experienced person in your field may be new and valuable information to someone who needs to gain that skill set.

If you're willing to help, let the companies that you invest in know (in the manner by which they prefer to receive communication) that you have skills in certain areas. When the business owner needs help in those areas, she'll very likely contact you.

How advice is received by others has a lot to do with how you deliver it. Carefully follow the entrepreneur's requests for how she would like to interact with investors. Regardless of how amazing the information you have may be, you're an investor, not a majority owner in the business. You need to respect the decisions of the entrepreneur, including decisions related to investor communication.

Connecting people who can benefit each other

The most powerful connections are two-way streets: They engage both parties in delivering and receiving value. When you become a crowdfund investor, try to identify relationships for the entrepreneurs or small-business owners that can have bi-directional benefits.

Don't bombard the companies you've invested in with lots of communication about all the people you know. Instead, make this step a highly targeted exercise. No matter how great your connections, they need to match what the business needs at that time.

For example, say that you're investing in a small bakery that just started a year ago. It's located about 5 miles from the world headquarters of a multibillion-dollar corporation. You know the head chef at this corporation, who just happens to be looking for a new bakery to supply his breakfast and lunchtime bread and pastry needs. Introducing the chef to the owner of the small bakery at this moment in time would be a recipe for failure because the corporation needs many times more bread than a small, new bakery can provide. When the bakery is a bit older, larger, and more experienced, this type of introduction could be truly valuable, but right now, the connection wouldn't help either party.

When you do identify connections that can be helpful, make the introduction and step back. Don't try to micromanage the conversation. Let the two parties take it from there because your job — playing matchmaker — is done.

Serving on a board of advisors

On occasion, you may be asked to serve on a board of advisors for a new enterprise. This entity is different from a board of directors, which must represent the rights and interests of the stockholders and can take actions on their behalf as prescribed by the bylaws of the company. A board of advisors has no formal authority over the company or the CEO. Its function is to provide advice, know-how, connections, and (in some cases) additional financial support to the business owner. An advisory position is typically unpaid but is also very important to a new or small business.

Essentially, as an advisor you agree to be a mentor to the entrepreneur or business owner. You bring experience and a fresh perspective to whatever issues this person is dealing with. Your primary job is to offer honest, direct opinions in a respectful way.

A board of advisors also demonstrates to the outside world that the company is connected to people in the industry who are experts or powerful or successful. Affiliating with a board of advisors helps a company provide social proof to its customers or other investors that it's on target for success.

If you're asked to join the board, make sure you have the time to commit to it. The time commitment usually isn't too intense, but during certain periods of time you may need to help in more active ways — when the business owner needs an introduction, for example, or is seeking access to angel or private equity investments. Being asked to serve on a board of advisors is an honor but also a significant responsibility. You're attaching your name and reputation to this company publicly, and you want to make sure that you want the public affiliation with the company, the owners, and the mission or brand.

Evaluating the quality of what's being produced

These days, anyone who buys a product goes online to find out what other buyers say about it. It doesn't matter whether you're talking about a big-ticket item like a refrigerator, television, or car, or a smaller purchase such as a book or a pair of shoes. Online reviews (like online photos from a drunken weekend) seem to live forever, so a company wants to make sure that even its very first reviews out of the gate are glowing.

To get positive reviews, the company needs to offer good quality at a good price. Sounds simple, but achieving those two things from day one isn't always easy. That's why companies test their products or services prior to launching them to the public, and it's why you may find yourself called on to test a company's wares and offer your opinions. If that happens, keep these suggestions in mind:

✔ **If the business owner doesn't offer the opportunity to sample its product or service, you should probably ask.** Elsewhere in this chapter, you're encouraged to take a step back and let the entrepreneur or business owner determine when and if he needs your input, but when it comes to testing a new product or service, it's fine to be more proactive. Based on the communication you receive from the business owner, you should be able to determine when a product or service is getting close to public release. If you've invested your money but you haven't actually seen or experienced the product or service being created, you likely want to request the opportunity to do so before it's made public. After all, you have a huge incentive for wanting to make sure this product or service is polished and ready to go before the public launch date.

If the business can't offer you the chance to sample the product or service (you invest in a company that offers its services to a narrow market niche that you don't belong to, for example, or the company is developing software for the biotech industry and you know nothing about biotechnology and therefore can't offer helpful feedback), you just have to keep reading the company's communication, including its descriptions of trials it has run to test the product's or service's effectiveness. If you aren't satisfied with the type or extent of testing being done, you can certainly say so. But at a certain point, you have to accept your limitations as a participant in this phase and let the business owner be the business owner and make the final decisions.

✔ **Offer feedback that is constructive and will enhance the company's reputation and chances for success.** You can and should do so in a way that is kind and helpful. The entrepreneur or business owner is emotionally invested in this product or service and likely is scared that the crowd will tear it apart. Even if your interaction with the product or service is problematic, try to think about why it was developed in this specific way and what the entrepreneur or owner is trying to accomplish. Then consider how you might ask questions or offer comments that can elicit improvements without bruising egos.

Avoid using the word *you* when offering your feedback. *You* statements or questions can feel like personal attacks. Often, questions that start with *who, what, where, when, why,* or *how* can take some of the sting away from negative criticism. Another great tactic is to offer feedback from your first-person perspective, grounded in your own similar experiences (if you have any). For example, "I had similar trouble when I was working with XYZ Company a few years ago. We debated whether to hire a local programmer or to outsource the job. When we made the decision, we considered these factors. . . ."

✔ **Allow the business owner to make the decisions he thinks are best for his business.** Don't expect that every piece of advice you offer will be followed exactly as you wish. You invested in the management team, and you have to allow them to do their jobs as managers and business owners.

Becoming an ambassador for the company

When you become a member of a company's investment crowd, you also become a marketing engine for that business. You can do so by asking the entrepreneur how she specifically needs help getting the message out, or you can make marketing this company your own personal mission. This section explains how you can promote what the company is creating, as well as the company itself (as a great investment).

Conducting grassroots marketing

Grassroots marketing involves organizing and motivating volunteers to engage in personal or local outreach. It requires that you develop relationships with other stakeholders or representatives to make them enthusiastic about the entrepreneur's product or service so that they become advocates, spreading the word about it and becoming an additional sales force. And it means that you do all this without being paid (because entrepreneurs are cash poor).

Why grassroots? Because this is the earliest stage of marketing and, if planted correctly, it has the ability to grow wild like grass. The planting can take place via blogs, Twitter, Facebook, Google+, LinkedIn, or any other social networks, as well as face to face when you talk about this new product or service with your friends, business associates, and people you meet at a bar.

A specific kind of grassroots marketing is called *buzz marketing*. It's word-of-mouth marketing among potential consumers and users of a product or service. Buzz marketing works because individuals are easier to trust than organizations that may have a vested interest in promoting the product or service.

This word-of-mouth marketing among peers amplifies the original marketing message, creating a vague but positive association, excitement, or anticipation about a product or service. Positive buzz is often the goal of viral marketing, public relations, and social media. The term refers both to the execution of the marketing technique and the resulting goodwill that is created.

Encouraging other investors to follow your lead

In addition to promoting the specific product or service being created, you may find that you want to promote the company itself to other potential investors. Can you do so without breaking the law? Yes, if you read this section.

If the business is still raising capital, the entrepreneur or owner is very restricted regarding how he can market the investment opportunity. He can market it only through the online funding platform he's using. He can't send out an e-mail telling people what they'll get by investing a certain sum of money, and he can't make phone calls describing the specific investment opportunity. If he breaks these rules, his entire crowdfund investment pitch can be shut down by the SEC, whose regulations govern this new type of investment.

An entrepreneur will have trouble hitting his funding target if he has to rely solely on his first-degree connections for investments. Based on what the SEC allows, he needs you — and other investors like you — to spread the word about why investing in him is worth considering. You may want to use your own Facebook, LinkedIn, Twitter, or other social networks to direct your contacts to the crowdfund investing portal where the offering is being made; there, they can learn more about what the company is doing and why you wanted to invest. You can share the URL of the online funding portal and encourage your networks to check it out.

If you're an ambassador for a business in which you have an equity investment, unless you're a broker-dealer, you *can't* receive a commission for bringing investments to the entrepreneur. You can't say to the entrepreneur, "Hey, if you give me 5 percent of the money I bring in, I'll go out to my network and get as many of them to invest in your business as possible." *That's illegal!* The percentage in question is called a *finder's fee,* and it's absolutely not allowed per the JOBS Act. The only way you can promote an offering is to do so out of your true desire to help the entrepreneur and the business to succeed.

Serving as a role model for other investors

As an educated investor and a true ambassador for the company, you have the opportunity to set a very good example for other people to follow. Doing so may provide the best help possible to the entrepreneur. When you're on the funding portal, be vocal in the dialogue or chat rooms. Explain that you're there to support the entrepreneur and that you understand the decisions are his to make. Direct your comments to the entrepreneur in this way:

- ✔ "I know you must be getting a lot of advice from a lot of different people. If you'd like some help performing market research, I've done market studies in the past and I'd be more than willing to lend some hours."

- ✔ "I'm here to support you. I know sometimes dealing with investors can be a big headache. If you need any help communicating with people, feel free to post your needs, and I'll be here to help where I can. I'm sure you're extremely busy, so if I don't hear back from you I understand you're busy building the business."

When you post comments like this that other investors can read, they may think twice before pestering the entrepreneur. Some investors undoubtedly will never before have invested in a company where their voice can be heard. This experience is completely new to them, and they won't be sure how to act. If you present yourself confidently and professionally in your comments, some people are very likely to follow suit.

If you read comments written by another investor who's setting a bad example by being demanding and disrespectful of the business owner's time, try your best to share with that person what you know about how to be the best possible investor. Encourage patience, but try not to offend. Let the investor know you understand the desire for immediate answers, but the entire crowd needs to trust the entrepreneur or owner and respect the communication timeline he has established.

Walking a fine line: Participating without becoming a nuisance

As noted elsewhere, the best thing you can do is let the entrepreneur or business owner know what your strengths are and where you can provide value. Be a resource for this person to tap into when and how she sees fit. By participating in this manner, you're walking that tightrope between providing value and becoming a nuisance.

 Try to limit your communication to the entrepreneur or business owner. Before you write a post in a dialogue room or send an e-mail to the entrepreneur or owner, make sure that you gather your thoughts. Include everything about the topic in one communication, and write as clearly and concisely as you can. If possible, use bullet points to separate your ideas.

Taking these steps is even more important if you have a personal relationship with the entrepreneur or business owner. Avoid the assumption that because this person is your friend or part of your family, you have carte blanche to reach out whenever you have a thought about the business.

 A good rule to follow is to write an e-mail or conversation post and then leave it for the night. Come back to it in the morning and ask yourself three questions:

✔ Do I really need to send it?

✔ If I do need to send it, is there anything else I should add?

✔ If I do need to send it, is there anything I can remove?

If you do send a communication, be patient. The entrepreneur is extremely busy. If you don't hear back immediately, it's because either she decided not to take your advice or she's so busy taking your advice that she doesn't have time to write back. Either way, you've had your say, and it's best to let the business owner move forward as she sees fit.

Taking action if you believe the company is breaking the law

In an ideal world, this section wouldn't need to be written, but unfortunately, people do break laws. In the case of a start-up or growing business, you may find out that the entrepreneur or business owner is doing one of these things:

✔ Soliciting investments on the phone or by e-mail instead of via the online funding portal

✔ Paying an employee under the table

✔ *Cooking the books* (fudging the company's financial reports) in some other way, whether big or small

When an entrepreneur or business owner breaks the law, he puts not only himself but also your investment at risk. Therefore, you need to take action right away if you believe something illegal is happening.

Weighing the appropriate action

Depending on what exactly is happening, you may want to start off by contacting the entrepreneur or business owner directly to explain what you know. (Presumably, if you know about something illegal going on, other investors may know as well, so the sooner you act the better.) This course of action may be best if you suspect the entrepreneur or owner is simply making a mistake or misunderstanding the law. (Maybe you overheard him explaining the investment opportunity to someone in person, for example, and you suspect he just doesn't realize the ramifications of what he did.)

If you have bigger concerns about what's going on, and you suspect the entrepreneur or owner knows exactly what he's doing and chooses to do it anyway, you may need to notify the SEC, which polices the rules governing crowdfund investing. The best way to do so likely is to contact the online funding portal, which should have a system in place for handling this type of complaint. Send an e-mail to the portal first, and then follow up within a day or two with a phone call. The funding portal is on your side, so don't be shy about bringing a problem to light.

Of course, you have options in the middle of these two courses of action, so seeking advice from an attorney is always a good idea. Maybe *you* are the one misunderstanding the law; you need to rule out that possibility before blowing the whistle publicly. But if the attorney confirms your suspicion, you have to take action of some kind; you accept that responsibility as a member of the crowd.

Making sure the crowd is informed

If you have completely confirmed that illegal activity is occurring, the funding portal should notify all investors of what's happening. If you've reached out to the funding portal with a complaint, you have the right to ask how and when the portal will send this notification. As long as the funding portal does its job correctly, your work is done.

But if the funding portal drags its feet about notifying investors of the problem, you have a responsibility to inform the rest of the crowd of what you know. Of course, you want to exercise extreme caution when posting a message that alleges illegal activity; you don't want to put the company in a

terrible position based on unconfirmed suspicions. Only if and when you are 100 percent certain of the facts of the situation should you take this step and share your concerns with fellow investors.

Debating Whether You Should Exit a Crowdfund Investment

The way to exit a crowdfund investment is similar to the ways you can exit any other investment in the private capital markets. Until 2012, only a very small number of people were allowed to make these kinds of investments. Now, with crowdfund investing, most people have this opportunity. With this opportunity come rules — rules that make good sense and that protect investors and small-business people.

A very good year?

Why does the SEC demand that investors in companies that raise capital through crowdfunding hold their investment for a minimum of one year? For these reasons:

✔ **The SEC doesn't want you (or anyone else) buying a stock in a company and then immediately trying to inflate its worth.** If you and other crowdfund investors acted in this way, the whole crowdfund investment opportunity would sink. Potential investors would be looking to get rich quick instead of investing in companies they really believe in. The entire process would get a bad reputation, and entrepreneurs and small-business owners with solid business plans in plain-Jane industries would watch their funding opportunities dry up.

✔ **Requiring crowdfund investors to hold on to their stocks for a year creates more** transparency in the marketplace, and transparency is a great thing. After the year period is up, if an initial investor decides to sell her stock, other potential investors will be able to evaluate whether the company in question is really worth the price she paid for the stock — or more, or less. Twelve months' worth of information about the company (including an annual report that the company files with the Securities and Exchange Commission [SEC] and sends out to its investors) will be available for review, and anyone willing to do his homework should be able to avoid getting duped.

✔ **Holding on to a stock for a minimum of a year decreases the stock's volatility.** Decreased volatility allows entrepreneurs and business owners to focus on what they should be doing: running a business.

Deciding to stay for more than your mandatory year

As a crowdfund investor, you must hold your company stock for a minimum of one year. (If you hold a company's debt instead, you may or may not be subject to the same holding period.) But you should consider holding on to your stock for longer than the required year. That's because entrepreneurs and small-business owners are committed to crowdfund investing for the long haul. Their return is tied to the long-term productivity of the company, and that productivity can increase if the company's funding base is stable. (To understand the one-year holding requirement, head to the nearby sidebar "A very good year?")

If you're doing your part as an investor — using the product or service that's sold by this company, acting as a marketing engine for the company, and driving sales — your investment should be increasing over time, which should keep you committed. After all, exiting a company that's on a growth trajectory eliminates your future returns.

New businesses take a long time to scale and almost always take longer to reach their goals than originally planned. You need to understand these facts about start-ups so you aren't disappointed when your $1,000 investment doesn't turn into $50,000 in a couple years. Even early investors in Facebook waited years to cash in. The company was launched in 2004, but it didn't go public until 2012. Manage your expectations, be patient, and be realistic about the results you're hoping for.

Want to look like a smart investor? Consider going into a crowdfund investment the same way venture capitalists go into an investment. When venture capitalists look at an investment opportunity, they don't look at it from a short-term point of view; they look at it from a five-year point of view. They understand that investing in a business requires a combination of money and experience. Money may come from a quick injection, but experience comes only with time. Entrepreneurs will only benefit as the business grows.

Knowing your exit options

If you want to exit your investment after the first year, you can. No chain tethers you to the entrepreneur or business owner after this point. The following sections cover your options.

Of all the ways you can exit your investment, the only option that offers you a degree of control is selling on the secondary market. All the other options, including mergers and acquisitions, are decided by the majority stockholders. This fact could frustrate you, so you should think about it upfront. Consider this example and how you would've reacted as an investor: Groupon, the well-known group-buying website, was offered $6 billion to sell the company. Amazingly, the majority shareholders turned down this offer. Undoubtedly, many minority shareholders were furious with this decision, but they had zero control over it. As with all things related to crowdfund investing, you have to manage your expectations and understand the lack of control you may have over how you exit your crowdfunded investment.

Selling on the secondary market

A *secondary market* is akin to one of the public exchanges, like NASDAQ, that exists for buying and selling public company stocks. Of course, a secondary market for a crowdfund investment needs to allow for the sale of private shares. It operates under the same principles of supply and demand that a public exchange does. In other words, you have to wait until the demand exists (a buyer is available) before you can sell your shares.

To be clear, secondary markets for crowdfund investments are *not* the same as NASDAQ. Instead, they are private exchanges that act *similar* to the public exchanges. You need to understand that it's much harder to sell your crowdfund investment stock on the secondary market than it is to sell the stock of a public company on a public exchange. There simply aren't enough buyers available to make shares on the private secondary market very liquid. This fact is especially true if you own shares in a local business (think about a bakery or a dry cleaner, for example).

Being bought out by a professional investor

This option could arise at any time, or it may never happen (depending on the specific company you're invested in). The majority owners in the company may vote on allowing a buyout, and you then have the opportunity to sell your shares. If this scenario happens, you may experience a gain on your investment because companies that attract professional investors have probably significantly increased their value.

Holding out hope for an IPO

An initial public offering (IPO) occurs when a company goes public — it lists its shares with a stock exchange for the general public to be able to purchase. IPOs can be the exit of all exits. They're what some investors dream of when they invest in start-up companies. Many entrepreneurs and start-up companies talk about getting an IPO, and they try to hype up their team and investors with talk of an IPO as the goal. No doubt, an IPO is a great goal to have, but achieving it is very unlikely.

The chances of your crowdfund-invested company getting an IPO are extremely small — minuscule, in fact. To give you an idea of how small the chances are, in 2012, there were a total of 128 IPOs. That's right, 128. Compare this to the nearly half a million businesses that incorporate each year. (Granted, a company can't go from zero to public in one year, but these numbers illustrate the fact that an IPO is rare.)

Furthermore, your chances of investing in a company at the start-up stage via crowdfund investing and being able to keep your investment to the IPO stage are even smaller. The company will likely need much more growth capital along the way to get ready for an IPO. If the company raises professional capital, the chances of these investors buying out your stock are very large.

If you have an opportunity to exit with a gain on your investment, that's a great exit — even if it isn't an IPO.

Waiting for a merger or acquisition

A merger or acquisition is another common way for an investor to have an exit. It occurs when a company combines forces with another company (merger) or when a company gets bought out by a larger company (acquisition). These deals can be structured in many ways, and the details are beyond the scope of this book.

However, it's possible to offer some generalities. Usually, when a company is bought out, investors are given cash or stock — or a combination of both — as compensation. The value of the company buying out your shares will dictate which one (cash or stock) is better for you. For instance, if your crowdfund investment company is a specialty food shop selling pasta and cheese with one location, and a larger company that has six locations buys you out, you'll likely be better off if you get cash for your shares and not stock. On the other end of the spectrum, if your company makes high-tech widgets and Apple buys you out, getting stock may very well be much better.

Book X
Technical Analysis

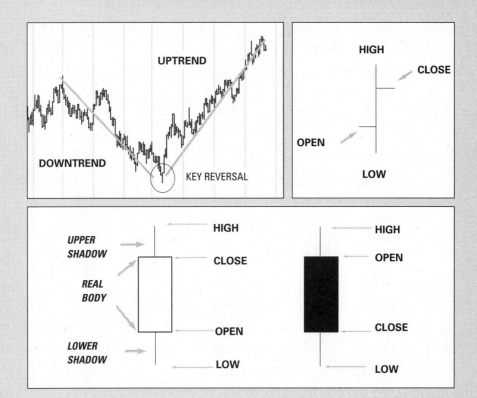

Chapter 1

Wrapping Your Brain around Technical Analysis

In This Chapter

▶ Understanding the basic principles of technical analysis

▶ Recognizing how crowd extremes and market sentiment influence trading action

▶ Examining and choosing indicators that match your trading style

▶ Starting your journey as a technical trader

*T*echnical analysis is a set of forecasting methods that focus on the price and volume of a security rather than the fundamentals (supply and demand for commodities, earnings per share for companies, and so on). In technical analysis, you observe how prices move without regard for what analysts are saying about the price (such as whether it's above or below "fair value"). You use past regularities in price movements to predict future regularities. This chapter gives you basic information about technical analysis. Consider it the foundation on which to understand and use the topics in the rest of Book X.

Realizing That the Trend Is Your Friend

Technical analysis is the study of how securities prices behave and how to exploit that information to make money while avoiding losses. With technical analysis, you work to identify price trends (a *trend* is a discernible directional bias in the price — upward, downward, or sideways). These basic observations underlie technical analysis:

✔ Securities prices move in trends much of the time, and trends remain in place until some major event comes along to stop them.

✔ Trends can be identified with patterns and indicators, including the core concept of *support and resistance* (covered in Chapter 4 of Book X).

✔ Primary trends (lasting months or years) are punctuated by secondary movements (lasting weeks or months) in the opposite direction of the primary trend. Secondary trends, or *retracements,* are the very devil to deal with as a trader. See the later section "Retracements" for details.

Your goal is to forecast the price of the security over some future time horizon in order to buy and sell the security to make a cash profit. The emphasis in technical analysis is to make profits from trading, not from owning a security as some kind of savings vehicle. You may *also* do that — own securities with no intention of selling in order to get a dividend or long-term gain — but technical trading by definition entails selling in order to realize gains in cold, hard cash. The purpose of technical trading is to build capital. In conventional investment management, the purpose is to preserve capital. In the technical mindset, the security you're trading is only a vehicle for making profits. If you find it hard to sell a security because you're emotionally attached to it, that security belongs in your "buy-and-hold" portfolio, not your "technical trading" portfolio.

Technical trading entails selling at a gain or a loss according to specific rules that you devise yourself. Many indicators have embedded buy/sell rules, but those rules may entail losses beyond what you can tolerate. Even after you pare down and refine your indicators to suit your risk preferences — that is, your tolerance for losses — you will still take losses. Taking losses is part of the technical trader's modus operandi; your goal is to design a trading regime that produces more gains than losses. Learn to take losses without emotion and move on to the next trade.

The following sections discuss having reasonable expectations about technical analysis and charting trends.

Using reasonable expectation

Critics say technical analysis–based trading is speculation. *Speculation* is a semantically-loaded word and sometimes confused with gambling. But technical analysis–based trading offers a reasonable and measurable expectation of gain, while gambling does not. The probability of heads coming up more than 50 percent of the time in a fair coin toss is zero. The gambler has no realistic expectation of a gain on any single play, whereas the probability of a gain in each trade by a skillful technical trader should be well over 50 percent. A good technical trader never takes a trade unless he has a reasonable expectation of a gain. Just about every technical trader can recite his gain-loss ratio, such as 3 to 1 (meaning he makes $3 for every $1 lost). While the gambler has no edge in the face of randomness in coins, cards, or roulette wheels, the technical trader does have an edge — the technical tools.

Technical traders observe that while some price changes in securities markets are indeed random, much of the time prices move in regular patterns that can be identified and exploited. To the technical trader, securities prices are not random. If prices were random, you couldn't identify trends — and you can identify trends. You can't do it all the time, but trendedness is visible on every chart of every security in some timeframe.

Charting course

The technical analysis toolkit contains techniques for winnowing out useful forecasting ideas (the *signal* or *trading trigger*) from the noise of massive amounts of price data. Technical indicators may be expressed as statistics, tables of numbers, and other formats, but the central workspace is the chart, like the one shown in Figure 1-1, which illustrates a classic uptrend following a downtrend.

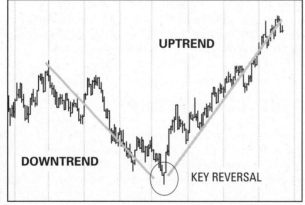

Figure 1-1:
Uptrend and downtrend.

Illustration by Wiley, Composition Services Graphics

At the most basic level, your goal is to buy a security whose price is moving upward and to shun or go short a security that is visibly on a downward trajectory. It's up to you whether to buy a security that's a real dog just because its price is going up and offers a profit opportunity. You may choose to trade only securities that meet some criteria of worthiness. But technical analysis would have you sell even your gold-plated favorite security if indicators were to point to a price drop. You can always buy it back later.

Knowing What to Do about Crowd Extremes

Technical analysis is the art of identifying crowd behavior in order to join the crowd and take advantage of its momentum. This is called the *bandwagon effect.* Here's how it works: A fresh piece of news comes out, a majority of traders interpret it as favorable to the security, and buying overwhelms selling so that the price rises. You profit by going with the flow, without necessarily knowing the news that triggered the rally. Then when everyone is jumping off the bandwagon and preferably just before, you jump, too.

As market participants get excited about a security, they become increasingly bullish and either buy for the first time or add to positions, a phase named *accumulation.* When traders become disillusioned about the prospect of their security price continuing to rise, they sell, in a phase named *distribution.*

After traders have been accumulating the security on rising prices, eventually the price goes too far. *Too far* is a relative term and can be defined in any number of equally valid ways, but basically it means any price extreme that specific indicators identify as showing traders' positions are extended and overdone. For example, say a security has rallied 40 percent in ten days, and such a big rally in so short a time is wildly abnormal behavior for this security. You suspect it's time to take profit, but you use indicators to confirm the judgment and to refine the timing of your exit. The following sections describe a few terms that are used when prices go too far.

Overbought and oversold

When a price has reached or surpassed a normal limit, it's at an extreme. In an *upmove,* everyone who wanted to buy has already bought. The market is called *overbought,* a term specific to securities trading. In a *downmove,* everyone who wanted to sell has already sold. The security is called *oversold.* The concept of overbought/oversold is applied to market indices as well as individual securities. It's usually measured by the momentum indicators described in the later section "Examining how indicators work."

Retracements

When a price has gone too far and traders deem the security overbought or oversold, the price stops rising or falling. Instead of hovering at a particular level, however, the price moves in the *opposite* direction for a while. A move in the opposite direction of the main trend is named a *retracement.* (Other names for it are *correction,* which explicitly recognizes that the security has gone too far and is now correcting course; *pullback;* and *throwback.*) The following sections explain how to recognize a retracement and estimate when it will end.

Recognizing a retracement

Prices seldom move in one direction for long. Even a major trend exhibits retracements. When the market runs out of cash, traders have to close positions to get their cash back so they can put on new trades. If they've been buyers, they need to sell. If they've been sellers (shorting the security), they need to buy. Position squaring always causes a price move in the opposite direction of the trend. Therefore, at the extreme outside limit of a price move, you should expect a temporary, minor reversal of the previous price move. In an uptrend, a retracement is always a drop in price. In a downtrend, a retracement is always a rise in price.

Figure 1-2 shows a primary trend with several retracements, each outlined by an ellipse. In this instance, the retracements last only a day or two — but retracements can last a lot longer, several weeks on a daily chart, for example. They can also retrace over more ground.

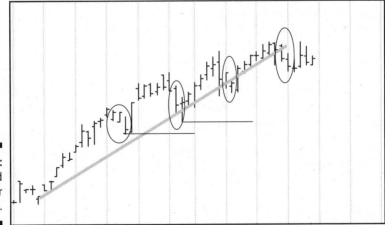

Figure 1-2:
A trend with four retracements.

Illustration by Wiley, Composition Services Graphics

When a retracement starts, you don't know for sure that it *is* a retracement. Maybe it's a full reversal, with the price switching direction. This is one of the occasions when it may pay to check the *fundamentals* (the news and events pertaining to the security). An ordinary retracement caused by normal position squaring can suddenly turn into a full-fledged rout in the opposite direction if fresh news comes out that supports a reversal.

Catching a falling knife: Estimating when a retracement will end

Trying to estimate where a retracement will stop is called *catching a falling knife*. Unfortunately, no reliable rules exist to tell you where a trend correction will end or when the primary trend will resume. One of the chief uses of indicators and combined indicators is to get guidance on where and when a retracement will stop.

Your tolerance for retracements is the key to deciding what time frame you want to trade in. If the specific security you want to trade has the bad habit of regularly retracing 50 percent, but the prospect of losing 51 percent turns you into a nervous wreck, you need to trade it in a shorter time frame — or find another security.

Acknowledging that no one can forecast a retracement hasn't stopped technical traders from trying to establish forecast rules. The following rules are generally helpful:

- **Assuming a retracement won't exceed a significant prior high or low:** In Figure 1-2, for example, the second retracement doesn't challenge the lowest low of the first dip, and the third retracement doesn't challenge the second.

- **Looking for round numbers:** Research shows that support and resistance levels (see Chapter 4 in Book X) occur more often at round numbers than chance would allow.

- **Observing the 30 percent rule:** Measure the percentage change and assume that a majority of traders will place stops to avoid losing more than *x* percent, such as 30 percent. The problem with this idea, and it's a chilling one, is that you're measuring from a peak and you don't know the price level where the majority of traders entered.

Logically, if any or all of these guidelines are violated — the price does exceed the previous high or low, it does surpass a round number, or it moves over 30 percent — you don't have an ordinary retracement and may have an outright reversal.

Looking at Market Sentiment

In technical analysis, sentiment comes in two flavors: *bullish* (the price is going up) or *bearish* (the price is going down). Sometimes the bulls and bears are slugging it out so strenuously that the net price move by the end of the day is zero. After several days of little or no closing price change, the market is described as *congestive* or *consolidative,* meaning the two sides are equally matched.

In that situation, you have to wait for one side or the other to win. Sometimes you get lucky and the price chart exhibits a particular bar configuration or pattern that you know from past experience means one side is winning. In order to get into the trade in the right (profitable) direction, you work extra hard to identify these reversal indicators. Unfortunately, the best ones, like the key reversal bar or island reversal pattern, are fairly rare. Most reversals are messy, and price patterns can be ambiguous for long periods. The following sections highlight factors to look at as you try to understand market sentiment.

Book X

Technical Analysis

Tracking volume

Volume — the number of shares or contracts of a security traded in a period — is the most powerful confirming indicator of a price move, and *confirmation* is a key concept in technical analysis.

You can feel more confident that a price move has staying power if you know that many traders — not just one or two — are involved. In technical trading, therefore, you use volume to measure the extent of trader participation. When a price rise is accompanied by rising volume, you have confirmation that the direction is associated with participation. Similarly, if you see a price fall by a large amount unaccompanied by a change in volume, you can deduce that the price change was an aberration.

Volume often leads price. The most obvious situations are when volume spikes. A *spike* is a volume number that is double or more the size of volume on the preceding days. Say volume has been running at 100,000 shares per day for several days or weeks, and suddenly it explodes to 500,000 shares. If the price has been in a downtrend, this wild increase in volume means that the crowd is throwing in the towel and exiting en masse. You need to wrap your mind around the initially counterintuitive idea that a wild increase in selling is an indicator of an imminent buying opportunity.

A volume spike is one of the occasions when fundamental information is complementary to a technical observation. If volume spikes higher but price fails to rise proportionately and you can't find fresh news that should inspire new buyers, for example, be wary. Chances are the top is in. If the security has new, legitimately exciting news, you can reasonably deduce that it has attracted new buyers.

You have several indicators to measure volume in conjunction with price. One is *on-balance volume* (OBV), an accumulation of volume data that can be charted as a single line on the chart. You add volume to a cumulative total for each day that the close is higher than the day before and subtract volume for days that the close is lower than the day before. The OBV doesn't work all the time, but a change in the indicator often precedes a change in the price. Several OBV variations and refinements have been developed over the years.

The divergence of price and an indicator that normally rises and falls in tandem is a wake-up call. For example, if prices are consistently putting in new highs but *closing* a bit lower, you may think the security is still on an uptrend and your position is safe. But even if volume is steady at more or less the same levels, when OBV starts to fall, it's showing you something you can't see with the naked eye — the exhaustion of the buyers.

Understanding market effects

An old saw in trading lore has it that a rising tide lifts all boats. Some percentage of any security's price move is attributable to changes in the market environment. You may have the inside scoop on the best stock ever, but if the entire market has a case of the collywobbles, your best-ever stock is likely to fall, too. Conversely, when the market is in a manic phase, even the worst of stocks gets a boost.

To get a handle on possible market effects on a specific security, technical traders measure overall market sentiment by looking at market statistics. Strictly speaking, market statistics are not technical analysis, which is the study of how specific prices behave. Nevertheless, sentiment measures (see the next section) can be very helpful as a supplement and complement to work on your individual charts.

Sampling information about sentiment

Most sentiment indicators look outside the price dynamics of a particular security or index of securities for information about whether the trading crowd is humming along normally or is forming a plan to jump ship. In technical trading, the key principle is to study what people *do* (price and volume), not what they *say*. Following are a few suggestions:

- **The bull/bear ratio** is an indicator published by vendors such as Investors Intelligence. The metric measures when a majority (60 percent or more) of investors are bullish or bearish. When a high percentage are bullish, it's getting to be time to exit — the market is getting overbought.

✔ **Breadth indicators** measure the degree of participation by traders in the overall market represented by an index, such as the Dow or NASDAQ. Breadth indicators include the ratio of advancing to declining issues, which measures the mood of the market, and the difference between issues making new highs and those making new lows. If more stocks in an index are closing at higher prices than the period before, bullishness is on the rise. When a higher number of stocks are putting in new lows, supply is overwhelming demand and the mood is bearish.

✔ **The put/call ratio** published by the Chicago Board Options Exchange (CBOE) is an indicator of whether sentiment is bearish or bullish. A high put/call ratio means bears are winning. The same line of thinking holds true for a low put/call ratio: When emotions are strongly optimistic, watch out for an opportunity to take advantage of a change. (Chapter 4 in Book II has more information on put/call ratios.)

✔ **The volatility index (VIX)** is a contrary indicator. When the crowd is feeling an extreme emotion, like anxiety, it's usually wrong. Therefore, a high VIX value means exactly the opposite of what it seems to mean — the bottom isn't coming, it's already in! When VIX is low, traders are complacent; they're projecting the same price levels, or nearly the same levels, into the immediate future with little variation and therefore little risk. When VIX is either abnormally high or abnormally low, you know it's the right time to trade against the crowd.

✔ **Seasonality** (also known as *calendar effects*) refers to the natural rise and fall of prices according to the time of year. Heating oil futures go up as winter heads for Chicago, for example, and prices of agricultural commodities rise when the crop is poor and fall when farmers get a bumper crop. Equities and financial futures exhibit a similar effect. The changes are regular and consistent enough to warrant your attention. Here are a few:

- **January barometer:** When the S&P 500 closes higher in January, it'll close the year higher than it opened.

- **"Sell in May and go away":** For decades, it has been observed that selling all equities at the end of April and buying them back on November 1 increases total gains by a very large amount. Recent research indicates this is true in non-U.S. equity markets as well.

- **President's third year:** Since 1939, the third year of a presidential term is always an up year for the Dow.

- **Presidential election cycle:** Wars, recessions, and bear markets tend to start in the first two years, while prosperity and bull markets tend to happen in the second two years.

Book X

Technical Analysis

Using Chart Indicators

Technical traders go to great lengths to remove emotion and impulsiveness from decision-making. The chief tool for squelching emotion is the *indicator,* a calculation that you put on a chart to identify chart events, chiefly whether the price is trending, the degree of trendedness, and whether a trend turning point is being reached. The purpose of indicators is to clarify and enhance your perception of the price move. These indicators come in two varieties:

- ✔ **Judgment-based indicators,** including visual pattern-recognition methods such as bar, line, and pattern analysis, as well as candlesticks (see Chapters 2 through 4 in Book X for details)

- ✔ **Math-based indicators,** including moving averages, regression, momentum, and other types of calculations (see Chapter 5 in Book X)

Because some randomness exists in every market, plus imperfect information or at least imperfectly distributed information, no indicator works all the time. Each indicator works best in one situation and not as well in others. Technical traders argue the merits and drawbacks of indicators in each situation, and the indicator you choose for each task depends, to a certain extent, on the security and also on your choice of analytical time frame.

Examining how indicators work

An indicator is usually an arithmetic rearrangement of the four basic components of the price bar: the open, high, low, and close (OHLC). Indicators aren't inherently tied to a particular time frame; you could be looking at the OHLC of 15-minute price bars rather than the more usual daily bars. The sections that follow describe the general way indicators work, but be aware that technical traders are inventive and use indicators in an infinite variety of ways.

Finding relevant time frames

Most indicators measure price and volume changes relative to previous prices and volume over a specific *look-back* period, such as 12 days or 21 days. For example, you can divide the closing price today by the closing price 12 days ago to create a momentum indicator and graph it on a chart. When this indicator is rising, you have a different and more context-rich way of looking at an uptrend than just looking at prices alone. Now say the momentum indicator stops rising, even though closes are still higher. The point of the momentum indicator in this case is that closes are not *relatively* higher. This is a valuable indication that the upmove is losing momentum. You may not want to sell just yet, but you have an alert.

With the exception of historic highs and lows, most indicators have a range of time in which research shows they work best. This is why charting software has preformatted indicators with default parameters specifying a particular time range, such as 12 days for a simple momentum indicator. However, adopting the default parameter doesn't mean that you must trade according to that time range. Consider it a starting point; if the default doesn't work for you, use a different number of periods.

Most indicators work equally well on any time frame. Intraday bars (such as hourly bars) are like microcosms of daily bars, and daily bars are like microcosms of weekly or monthly bars. Traders respond to price changes in regular, consistent, and repetitive ways whatever the time frame. This is called the *fractal* nature of securities prices; therefore, you can't tell whether an unlabeled chart represents hourly bars or daily bars.

Book X

Technical Analysis

Heeding indicator signals

Indicators are designed to give buy and sell signals, although in many instances, like the momentum indicator, the signal is more like a warning and doesn't have a black-and-white embedded decision rule. The following list introduces signals to pay attention to:

- **Crossovers:** Crossovers — when one line crosses another line — include the price crossing a fixed historic benchmark, the indicator crossing the price or the price crossing the indicator (called a *breakout*), or one line of a two-line indicator crossing the other.

- **Breakouts:** The breakout concept is one of the most important concepts in technical analysis. A breakout occurs when the price or an indicator exceeds some kind of benchmark, such as support or resistance, a moving average, a statistical measure of the normal move, or lines devised to signify important levels, such as pivot points.

- **Range limits:** A variety of indicators fall into this category:

    - **Darvas box:** The most simple range limit indicator, the Darvas box (named after its inventor) draws a horizontal line off the last two lows into the so-far uncharted future and, when the price is rising, assumes the maximum drop will be at the last low (support), and the maximum rise will be the same number of points as the distance in points between the first two lines.

    - **Oscillators:** Fancier than Darvas boxes, oscillators describe where today's price stands relative to its recent trading range. They're usually based on 100, so they range from 0 to 100, –100 to +100, or some other variation using the number 100. In practice, the scope of the price range usually falls under the outer limits and doesn't vary by more than 20 to 80 percent of the total possible range.

Traders draw maximum likely range lines at 20 percent and 80 percent. When the indicator approaches one of the lines, you know that the price is nearing an extreme of its recent range and is likely overbought or oversold.

- **Channels, bands, and envelopes:** *Channels* are generally straight lines drawn on either side of a central line like a linear regression line, while *bands* and *envelopes* are terms used to describe dynamic or wavy lines formed by adding space on both sides of a wavy line like a moving average. The outer limits of the channel or band are determined arithmetically by applying a standard deviation of the prices to a moving average of prices, or the standard error to a linear regression, or by devising pivot lines based on past price performance.

✔ **Convergence:** *Convergence* refers to two indicator lines coming closer to one another, indicating less difference between their numerical values. Convergence generally means that the price action is starting to go sideways or has a narrower high-low range, or both. A sideways move, in turn, generally leads to a breakout.

✔ **Divergence:** *Divergence* refers to two indicator lines moving farther apart, as when the spread between two moving averages widens, or when an indicator and the price go in different directions. Advanced momentum indicators, in particular, reshuffle the components of the price bar to come up with the rate of change of a price, so that the slope of the indicator is a sophisticated measure of the strength of a trend. When the price is still rising (making new highs) as the momentum indicator starts to fall (making progressively lower highs), the price and indicator are diverging, which is an important leading indicator that the price rise is probably ending. (See Chapter 5 in Book X for more on momentum.)

Choosing indicators

Indicators only *indicate;* they don't *dictate* the next price move. In other words, you may buy a security because your indicator tells you to, only to find out that the indicator's wrong. After you buy, the price falls. What you do next is a function of your risk appetite plus your confidence in the indicator. If you find losses hard to stomach, you exit the trade upon losing a certain dollar amount and chalk the loss up to experience. You may also decide to change the parameters of your indicator or start looking at additional indicators that would have kept you from the losing trade, a process called the *confirmation approach.* Or, if you're stubborn and have faith in the indicator, you may keep holding the losing position until it turns around into a winning position — or the loss becomes catastrophic.

Make the exit decision before you place the trade. You should know in advance how much you can expect to gain from a specific trade and how much you're willing to lose. If you back-test an indicator, such as the price crossing the 20-period moving average, you'll get an estimate of how this indicator worked in the past — the win-loss ratio. But you always need to acknowledge that the indicator won't perform in the future exactly the same way it did in the past.

Indicators are useful only in the context of your appetite for risk, which is another way of saying your tolerance for losses. Your indicator may be perfectly good in the long run and may deliver the expected gain, but not before retracement losses force you to exit early, either because the losses scare you or because you've run out of money. Tolerance for loss is deeply personal, but it's also a function of how much starting capital you have.

The following sections provide some important guidelines for choosing indicators.

Looking at your starting capital

Starting capital is the starting point for choosing indicators and trading style (covered in the next section). You don't want to select the price crossing the 20-day moving average as your sole indicator to buy or sell if you have so little starting capital that you'd be wiped out at the first normal retracement, based on the history of the indicator. But the 20-period moving average may be just the ticket when applied to a 4-hour moving average, depending on the amount of your starting capital.

You don't have to be a rich trader with a high capital stake in order to trade on daily or weekly indicators. But how much capital you have does impact your holding period. If you have less capital, your holding period shouldn't be weeks and months because of those pesky retracements (discussed earlier in this chapter). A skilled trader can identify and evade retracements using daily indicators, but it does mean more frequent trading. This situation may take some getting used to.

Choosing an analysis style

Your choice of indicators and indicator parameters should also be a function of your analysis, or trading, style. Picking a trading style before getting a good grip on indicators may seem to be putting the cart before the horse, but as long as you're reprogramming your mind to accept the usefulness of indicators, you may as well begin to imagine trading on shorter time frames.

Trading more frequently than you previously did doesn't mean you'll become a minute-by-minute fiend handcuffed to the computer screen every hour of every day. It does mean, however, that whatever your capital stake, you need to have an exit plan that minimizes losses and preserves the stake. You want to pick indicators and indicator parameters that, based on past experience, would have done just that (even though traders know, from sad experience, that indicators don't work the same way all the time).

In general, trading styles are a function of the holding period, or how much time elapses between buying and selling the security.

- ✓ **Position traders** identify big-picture trends lasting weeks and months, and are willing to sit out retracements and sideways range-trading situations until they resolve back into a trend. Position traders hold securities for weeks, months, and years.

- ✓ **Swing traders** buy at relative lows and sell at relative highs, with *trend* defined as any move that indicators show is likely to persist for some additional time. Swing traders have a holding period of 3–10 days, although analysts argue over the "right" holding period.

- ✓ **Day traders** are a subset of swing traders who prefer to get in and out in a single day, sometimes more than once. Day traders apply indicators to short-term charts, such as the 15-minute and one-hour charts, in order to identify micro-trends that may last only two or three hours. The micro-trend could even be a counter-trend to the big-picture trend on the daily chart.

- ✓ **Scalpers** have a holding period of seconds and minutes. The term *scalping* originally referred to taking advantage of the big-offer spread available by different parties or parties in different places, but with the advent of super-fast computer programs, scalping now includes algorithmic trading that automatically places rule-based buy and sell orders based on a few seconds' advantage in obtaining information or identifying a technical pattern.

Getting Started

You can get started as a technical trader in one of two ways:

- ✓ **Taking a systematic, security-centric approach:** You find indicators that would have worked on your favorite securities to generate more gains than losses and apply them going forward. It's always wise to pretend-trade for a while before committing actual money.

Say the indicators you're comfortable with would have generated a gain/loss ratio of $2.50 for every $1 in losses over the past five years using daily data and a holding period averaging five days. Now you know: You're a swing trader, and applying indicators on daily data works for you. Now imagine that applying your indicators on 4-hour bars of the same security would have generated $4.50 for every $1 in losses. This is a better gain/loss ratio but involves more trades, say, triple the number of trades. You decide the extra gain is worth the extra time and commission expense. Now you're a day trader. In both cases, you're applying the same indicators to the same security and taking every trade the indicators tell you to take. This is a systematic, security-centric approach.

✔ **Taking an opportunistic, indicator-centric approach:** You scan the universe of securities for candidates that are displaying a pattern or bar configuration that your review of historical prices tells you resulted in big gains in the past. These are sometimes called *setups*. You may know nothing about the security, only that it has just put in a historic low, a volume spike on a downtrend, an island reversal, or some other indication of an impending price change. Your goal is to get in early on the breakout or reversal for a fast profit. Whether this style makes you a swing trader or a day trader depends on the time frame to which you apply the indicator. The opportunistic approach requires more knowledge of indicator behavior and the ability to troll for the opportunities.

Book X

Technical Analysis

The systematic, security-focused approach has the advantage of helping you develop real skill in a small set of indicators and deep familiarity with a small set of securities. The drawback is that when using a trading system, you must take every trade the indicators tell you to take, because you never know in advance which signal will deliver the abnormally big gain.

In contrast, the opportunistic, indicator-based approach has the advantage of letting you choose where and when to trade — you don't have to take every trade, just the most promising setups. This approach makes you a guerilla rather than a foot-soldier. The drawbacks are that the scanning or screening process may be badly programmed or biased to certain types of securities, or the scanner may misrepresent the track record of the indicators.

Whichever approach appeals to you, you can literally begin applying it immediately. It takes about an hour to plot an indicator on a chart of a specific security and see how it would have worked in the past. It takes about an hour to apply screening software to a universe of available securities (usually equities) and see what opportunities the indicators identify. You may want to check out both approaches to see what suits your personality and capital stake.

Chapter 2

Bars and Bar Reading

· ·

In This Chapter

▶ Mining information from basic bars

▶ Identifying trends by reading bars

▶ Becoming familiar with special bars

▶ Getting the lowdown on spikes and gaps

· ·

*A*ll indicators (except volume) use the components of the price bar in one way or another to give evidence of the next move. The bar and its components are the raw material of indicators, so to speak. Traders devise indicators by choosing one or more bar components and crunching them arithmetically to chip away noise and find the signal. They apply a slew of techniques — averaging, statistical measures, relative ranges evaluation, pattern identification, and so on.

With four bar components and multiple manipulations, the number of indicators that can be devised is enormous, and if you consider varying the number of bars covered, literally without limit. That's a chilling statement but don't be intimidated. After you really understand the bar, you'll be able to readily dissect and evaluate any new indicator you run into.

And, on their own, the price bar and its placement on the chart deliver a ton of information about market sentiment. You don't need much practice to start reading the mind of the market by bar-reading; you just have to be patient, imaginative, and thoughtful. And if you're a day-trader, you can trade on bar-reading alone for steady and reliable profits. Even if you're a longer-term position trader, you should watch daily bars for any special configurations (such as a breakaway gap) that could modify your judgment. This chapter explains what to look for in both basic and special bars.

Building Basic Bars

The *price bar* describes and defines the trading action in a security for a given period. Price bars consist of four components — open, high, low, and close, abbreviated OHLC (see Figure 2-1):

- ✔ **Open:** The horizontal line on the left is the opening price.
- ✔ **High:** The top of the vertical line defines the high of the day.
- ✔ **Low:** The bottom of the vertical line defines the low of the day.
- ✔ **Close:** The horizontal line on the right is the closing price.

Price bars can encompass different periods, anything from a minute to a month. This discussion refers to a daily price bar, but the scope of the period doesn't change the price bar dynamics.

The two horizontal lines on the price bar are called *tick marks*. The opening tick is on the left and the closing tick is on the right. A *tick* represents a single trade at a single price, so the tick mark representing the open or close refers to a single transaction or batch of transactions at the same price.

The price bar tells you the outcome of the battle between the buyers (bulls) and the sellers (bears). Hidden in every price bar are a winning group and a losing group. If the price opened at the low and closed at the high, the winners were the buyers. If the price opened at the high and closed at the low, the winners were the sellers. If the bar is very tall, encompassing a $10 range when the normal bar for this security is only $3, the trading was a titanic battle. If the bar is very short, say $1, it was a mere pillow fight.

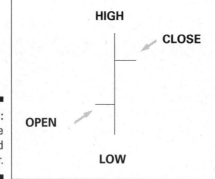

Figure 2-1:
The standard price bar.

Illustration by Wiley, Composition Services Graphics

Setting the tone: The opening price

The *opening price* is the very first trade between a buyer and a seller. The meaning of the open, like all the price bar components, comes from its relationship to the other components of the bar as they develop and to the components of the bars the day before. The most important relationship is to the close of the day before.

When the open is up

If the open is up from the close the day before, the first trader of the day expects favorable news. The open sets the tone, in this case a hopeful one. A higher open than the close the day before implies *demand* for the security.

Book X

Technical Analysis

 You shouldn't automatically attribute optimism to an opening bounce beyond yesterday's close, however, because sometimes a good opening is due to traders *buying on open.* When fresh money comes in to mutual funds, the managers must allocate a certain percentage of it to all the securities in the fund. Buying on open is how they top off a fund; it's not necessarily a judgment on that specific security that day.

When the open is down

If the opening price is below the close of the day before, the tone is negative. Maybe bad news came out after the close last night, or the entire market is down. The open may also be down if some traders have executed a *sell on open,* but don't count on it — selling on open isn't a common practice.

 Exploiting the difference between yesterday's close and today's open is a tried-and-true trading technique, especially when there's a gap (see the later section "Grasping Gaps" for details). Some market players use nothing except the close yesterday-open today relationship as a setup pattern to determine trades.

Summarizing sentiment: The closing price

The *closing price* is the last price at which a buyer bought and a seller sold before the closing bell. The close is the most important part of the price bar because it summarizes trader sentiment.

 Factor in *selling on close.* Many traders sell at the close to avoid overnight event risk; therefore, you should expect falling prices near the close and discount their sentiment value. The close is hardly ever at the high of the day, and when it is, it means people who do hold overnight positions are buying right up to the last minute, offsetting the usual end-of-day sales.

Hope springs: The high

The *high* of the price bar is the highest price at which a buyer and seller exchanged cash for the security. The meaning of the high depends on where it stands relative to the other bar components on the same day and the day before. A high well over the open means rising demand. A high at the open and a lower close means traders are bearish and offering *supply* of the security.

Hitting bottom: The low

The *low* of the day is the cheapest price at which a buyer and seller struck a deal. As with all bar components, consider context. When the low is lower than the open, it may mean fresh news has come out after the opening bell that offsets any buy-on-open orders or initial sentiment. When the close is at the low, it means that bad news or negative sentiment ruled for the day. Whatever the cause, the available supply of the security is rising.

Using Bars to Identify Trends

The preceding section explains how to interpret price bar components to one another *within* a single bar. When you look at the components *across* a series of bars, you get even more information.

The price bar embodies all the supply/demand dynamics of the day, and a series of bars on a chart shows the evolution of the supply/demand dynamics over time. The evolution is often visible in the form of a trend. This section describes how to use combinations of bars to identify trends.

Identifying an uptrend

The textbook-perfect *uptrend* is a series of bars that has some or all of these features:

- ✔ The close is higher than the open.
- ✔ The close is higher than the day before.
- ✔ The high is higher than the day before.
- ✔ The low is higher than the day before.
- ✔ The median price (high + low ÷ 2) is higher than the day before.

The most important combination is higher highs and higher closes, but that's not a hard-and-fast rule. You can have lower highs if you have higher closes and higher lows, and still believe an uptrend is in place.

You may get some, but not all, of these features and still have a trend. Prices don't move in straight lines. You seldom see an unbroken series of higher highs on every single day, for example.

Identifying a downtrend

Book X

Technical Analysis

The textbook definition of a *downtrend* is the mirror image of the uptrend criteria — you want the close lower than the close the day before, the low lower than the low the day before, and so on. The most important is the combination of lower lows and lower closes, but in parallel with the warning about uptrends, you can have lower closes without lower lows and still have faith that what you're looking at is a downtrend.

But wait. . . nothing is that simple

To identify an uptrend, you want higher highs and higher closes, and it would be nice if the close is over the open, too. Alas, technical analysis doesn't offer a hard-and-fast rule on which identifier is more important. Traditional technical analysis emphasizes that you need higher lows to confirm the higher highs in an uptrend, but candlestick analysis, covered in Chapter 3 of Book X, says that the position of the close trumps every other factor, including a new high or low.

The following sections describe a few situations in which identifying trends may be tricky.

Bar components influence the next bar

When a security puts in a new high or low, market players start wondering why. A new high or low can arouse greed or fear.

- New highs imply "Better buy now so you don't miss an opportunity," even if you don't have a reason for new highs to be occurring. The result is a higher close as buyers pile in.

- New lows scare just enough traders that they sell their positions, even in the absence of any fresh news that justifies the sale. Sellers are unwilling to hold a falling asset and create the very thing they fear, a lower close.

Trends can be relative

Markets are not neat and tidy, and not every bar is going to qualify on all the criteria traditionally needed to indicate an uptrend or downtrend. The chart in Figure 2-2 depicts an uptrend — even though not every bar qualifies as belonging to an uptrend. You see lower lows as well as several days on which the close is lower than the open. Trends can be relative in the following ways:

- ✔ **Significance:** In Figure 2-2, not every high is higher than the day before, but every significant high is higher than the highs that came before. You can judge significance by eyeing the chart, or you can specify rules, such as "A significant high is one that is x percent higher than the average of the past y highs." In Figure 2-2, two significant higher highs stand out — each is 50 percent higher than the previous high.

- ✔ **Preponderance:** Figure 2-2 illustrates that not every high in an uptrend has to be higher than the one before. You just need to identify a preponderance of higher highs and a preponderance of higher lows. What constitutes a preponderance? You decide; you can eyeball it or use software.

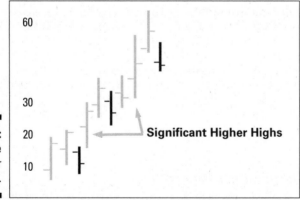

Figure 2-2:
Relative
higher
highs.

Illustration by Wiley, Composition Services Graphics

Your eyes can deceive you

Sometimes you need to be careful not to misinterpret what you're seeing. You may see a series of higher highs but forget to make sure that most bars have a higher low and that the close is over the open. Take a look at Figure 2-3 for a chart that can easily be misread. This figure shows a price series where every day brings a new high, but every day also brings a close lower than the day before, and many days bring a low that's lower than the lows on preceding days.

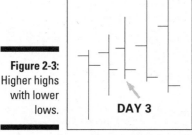

Your eye may want to see an uptrend, but when you look more closely and analyze the bars for all three conditions, you have only one uptrend condition (higher highs) that is more than offset by the two downtrend conditions (close under open and lower lows). It's hard to swallow, but this figure displays a downtrend emerging at the third bar.

Bar reading doesn't always work

Sometimes you can't figure out what the market is thinking, because it's changing its mind just about every other day. Figure 2-4 is such a chart. The series of higher highs and closes forms a minor uptrend, and the following series of lower lows and closes is a minor downtrend — but then things fall apart. You see higher highs followed by lower lows and no consistency in the placement of the close.

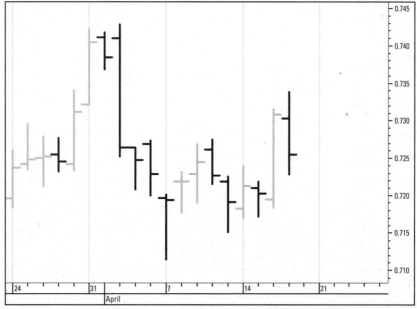

Figure 2-4:
Nontrending
bars.

What do you do in a case like this? Nothing, at least not anything based on interpretation of the bars. When bars are in a chaotic mess like this, the probability of picking the right direction is low. You'd just be guessing.

Reading Special Bar Configurations

Some bars are just a little out of line, but once in a while you see bars that really stand out. It takes almost no practice at all to differentiate ordinary out-of-line bars from special configurations that technical traders consider associated with specific interpretations. In these special cases, you know you've got a valuable clue to upcoming price behavior.

Closing on a high note

A series of *closes at the high* — and the downtrending counterpart, *closes at the low* — indicate that a new trend may be starting or the existing trend is likely to continue. In Figure 2-5, Configuration A illustrates closes at the high. The price has closed at the high for three days running, and the third bar is much longer than the others, which means the high-low range is wider than the previous two days. So, what's happening?

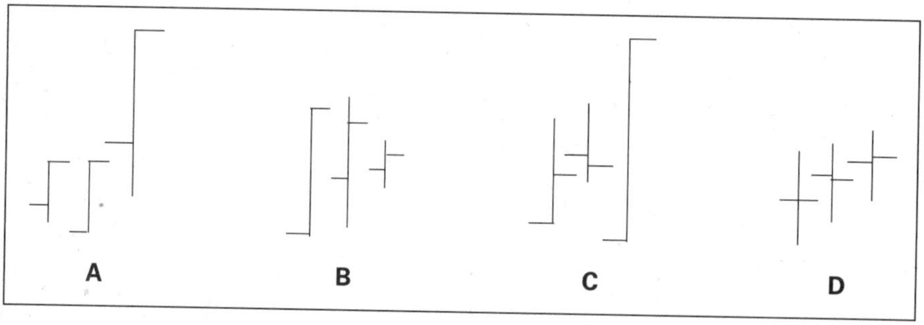

Figure 2-5: Common special bars.

A B C D

Illustration by Wiley, Composition Services Graphics

The first two bars show the close at the high at about the same level. On the second bar, the low of the day was lower than the low the day before, meaning that sellers came out of the woodwork. But the bulls fought back, buying more and more, so that the close was at a fresh high on that second day. The close at the high for a second day trumps the lower low, and Day 3 delivers a third close at the high and a whopping gain.

A big gain is often followed by *profit-taking* by active traders who got in early. Profit-taking doesn't change a trend, but it can put a dent in the performance of the bar the next day. You may see a lower high or a lower close, which can be very discouraging when you're trying to identify a new trend. Putting on a new position in a promising move only to take a paper loss on your first day is also annoying. If you're using bar-reading alone to make trading decisions, stick with the trade (while cursing short-term traders), but also reconsider where you placed your stop-loss order.

Spending the day inside

Configuration B in Figure 2-5 shows the inside day. An *inside day* refers to a price bar that has both a lower high than the day before and a higher low than the day before.

An inside day is a bar inside the previous day's high-low range. It reflects indecision. Buyers didn't feel strongly enough about this security to buy more. Sellers weren't particularly inspired to sell, either. The inside day doesn't suggest the next day's movement but does warn that the market is starting to reconsider its judgment about this security. Sometimes the next day brings a false move higher or lower that lasts only one day. Market lore has it that the market will resume the pre-existing trend after an inside day, but this is not necessarily the case. Inside days can point to reversals, too.

Getting outside for the day

Configuration C in Figure 2-5 is the outside day. On an *outside day,* the high-low range of the bar is outside the range of the preceding bar. The open and close ticks can appear anywhere on the outside day bar, but two variations stand out:

- ✔ **The open is at the low and the close is at the high.** This configuration suggests that something new has happened to inspire bullish buying right up to the end of the day.

- ✔ **The open is at the high and the close is at the low.** Sentiment turned bearish and sellers overwhelmed buyers, right to the end of the day.

After considering where the open and close are located on the bar, take a look at what else is going on in the market, especially the configuration of the preceding bars. If you didn't have a trend when the outside day appears, the outside day may mean one is starting. If you did have a trend when the outside day appears, look to the close. In an uptrend, the close at or near the high means a trend continuation. If you had an uptrend and the outside day bar closes at or near the low, it's probably a sign of a pending reversal.

Finding the close at the open

Configuration D in Figure 2-5 shows a series of bars where the close is at or near the open. *Close-at-open* most often occurs near the center of the daily price range, not at the high or the low, and reflects indecision among market participants. Trader opinion is divided as to whether this bar generally signifies a continuation or reversal pattern. Consider it a clue to look at what else is going on, such as trading volume.

When the open and close are at (or almost at) the same price, *and* they're at the high or low of the day, you have a greater chance of determining whether the trend will continue or reverse. Which way the cookie crumbles depends on what was happening before:

✔ **In an uptrend:** If the open and close are near the high, look for the uptrend to accelerate. If they're near the low, look for a reversal.

✔ **In a downtrend:** If the open and close are near the low, expect more of the same. If they're near the high, think about a reversal.

Understanding Spikes

Sometimes the market delivers a price bar that looks like the market went nuts. The high or the low is very far away from the general trend of things and the bar itself is abnormally large (displaying a wide high-low range). Figure 2-6 shows two of these uncommon price bars, called *spikes*. A spike is a bar that encompasses a much bigger high-low range than the bars that came before.

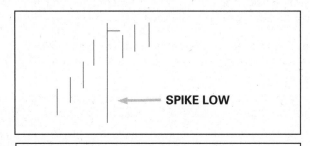

SPIKE LOW

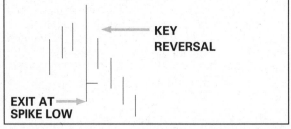

KEY REVERSAL

EXIT AT SPIKE LOW

Figure 2-6: Uncommon special bars called spikes.

Illustration by Wiley, Composition Services Graphics

In some cases, like the top example in Figure 2-6, a spike turns out to be an anomaly. The spike low suggests that some people panicked and were selling at such a high quantity and at such a frantic pace that the few buyers still around were able to buy at abnormally low prices. On this chart, the panic was unwarranted. The next day, the price resumed its uptrend and its same, normal high/low range. The spike was just a random move.

Even though price spikes *can* be an anomaly, you can't afford to ignore them. The spike may be a reaction to fresh news or perspective that has the potential to create a new trend.

The bottom spike example in Figure 2-6 is a key reversal because on the next few days, the price proceeded to make lower highs and lower lows. This spike in the size of the daily high-low range was a warning of a reversal. *Key reversals* can be ordinary bars and aren't always spikes, but when you see a spike, always ask yourself whether it may mark a reversal. Key reversal bars are actually quite rare. The characteristics of a key reversal bar are

Book X

Technical Analysis

- ✔ The price opens in the direction of the prevailing trend but closes far below the previous close (in an uptrend).
- ✔ The trading range is very wide relative to the preceding bars.

You seldom know whether a spike is random or meaningful on the day that it happens. Only hindsight can tell you that. A spike is a warning to investigate the environment — what else is happening? As a general rule, you should trust the close as the final arbiter of sentiment. When the close is wildly lower in an uptrend, the spike probably means a reversal.

Grasping Gaps

A gap is one of the most important of the special bar configurations. A *gap* is a major, visible discontinuity between two price bars on a chart (see Figure 2-7). Because every bar encompasses all the transactions made during a specific period, a gap marks the absence of any transactions at the prices in the gap space.

The gap is a void, meaning no demand if there was supply and no supply if there was demand, at least not at those prices. Prices had to shift considerably in order for supply and demand to meet again and for both buyers and sellers to be satisfied. On daily charts, a gap is initially seen when today's opening price diverges dramatically from yesterday's high or low, although you can also see gaps between bars on intraday charts.

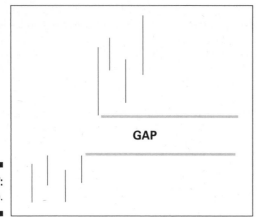

Illustration by Wiley, Composition Services Graphics

Figure 2-7:
A price gap.

You can *identify* a gap at the open, but you can't *measure* a gap until the day's trading is over. Then you measure it from yesterday's high to today's low (for an upside gap) or from yesterday's low to today's high (for a downside gap). The gap is between the bars, not between the opens and closes. If the security opens on a gap but the gap is filled during the day, the gap doesn't show up on a daily chart. The same thing is true if a security gaps during the day on an hourly chart — the daily bar doesn't show it.

Gaps are often the result of positive or negative news, like earnings or some other event, whether true or invented (from rumors). Events are the source of most key price moves, including trends, whether starting or stopping. Prices don't, on the whole, move randomly. Traders usually have reasons — right or wrong — to buy and sell. Even the strongest trend can be broken by a piece of fresh news contrary to the trend direction. Authentically big news trumps the pre-existing trend (nearly) every time.

Gaps are a wonderful trading opportunity if you can differentiate between common and uncommon gaps. The following sections give you the lowdown on various types of gaps and their significance.

Showing up out of nowhere: Common gaps

A *common gap* is one that appears out of nowhere for no particular reason that you can find. Common gaps can occur in trending and nontrending prices. If the price is trending, the gap fails to change the trend. If the price isn't trending, it fails to initiate a trend. Common gaps are generally insignificant.

A common gap tends to have low volume on the gap day. If you see an opening gap, one way to evaluate whether to take it seriously is to consult volume. If volume is low or normal, traders aren't jumping on the bandwagon, and it's probably a common gap. If volume is abnormally high, traders are jumping on the bandwagon, and the gap will probably lead to a big rise or fall in the coming days.

A security that normally has low volume tends to have more gaps than heavily traded securities. A low-volume security is described as *thinly traded,* meaning few market participants. Don't try to interpret gaps in thinly traded securities. These gaps are usually just common gaps and mean nothing at all.

Book X

Technical Analysis

Kicking things off: Breakaway gaps

A *breakaway gap,* shown in Figure 2-8, is an important event because it almost always marks the start of a new trend. Not only do you get the gap and a new trend, but you also get a major change in the appearance of the chart, such as a widening of the normal high-low daily trading range, an increase in day-to-day volatility, and much higher volume. All these changes occur because breakaway gaps draw in new traders. A breakaway gap is event-driven, usually on some news about the security itself.

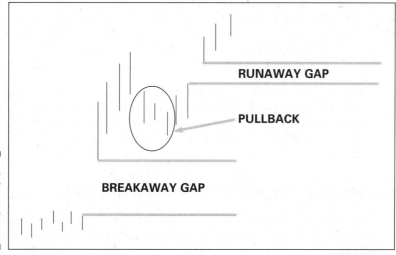

Figure 2-8: A breakaway gap and a runaway gap.

Illustration by Wiley, Composition Services Graphics

To qualify as a breakaway gap, the gap has to

- **Be proportionately big to the usual trading range:** If the security normally trades in a $3 range between the daily high and low, and the gap is $15 between the preceding day's high and the gap-day open, you can instantly recognize that something big happened.

- **Occur when a price is either slightly trending or moving sideways:** Nothing much is going on in the chart, and then bam! Fresh news creates new supply and demand conditions and ignites a trend.

You interpret a breakaway gap depending on whether it's upward or downward:

- **Upside breakaway gap:** Good news creates demand. New buyers want to own the security and are willing to pay ever-higher prices to get it. Volume is noticeably higher than usual.

- **Downside breakaway gap:** Traders can't wait to get rid of their holdings and accept ever-lower prices to achieve that goal. Volume is usually abnormally high (although not always).

Continuing the push: Runaway gaps

A *runaway gap* (refer to Figure 2-8) occurs after a security is already moving in a trended way and fresh news comes out that promotes the existing trend. Whereas a breakaway gap starts a trend, a runaway gap continues a trend. In both cases, buyers become exuberant and offer increasingly higher prices. Sometimes fresh good news or rumors are spreading, and sometimes the buying frenzy is just feeding on itself in the absence of any news at all.

A *pullback* (a retreat after a dramatic move) represents profit-taking by the early birds and is very common. In fact, professionals count on the pullback to *buy on the dip.* If they get really enthusiastic, traders getting back in often supply the energy for a runaway gap that follows a breakaway gap.

Calling it quits: Exhaustion gaps

Exhaustion gaps occur at the end of a trend, signaling the party's over. Volume is usually low. What's exhausted is the news that propelled the security up in the first place and the energy of the early buyers. An exhaustion gap is often followed by a reversal.

You can distinguish an exhaustion gap from a runaway gap by looking at volume, which is usually low at an exhaustion gap. Anytime you see wild new highs (or lows) that aren't accompanied by wild new high volume, be suspicious of the staying power of the move.

Scoring big: Island reversals

Sometimes an exhaustion gap is followed immediately by a breakaway gap going in the opposite direction. This is how an island reversal forms. An *island reversal* is a single isolated price bar with a gap up on one side and a gap down on the other. It looks like an island in a sea of price bars and is almost always an unusually long bar with a wide high-low range.

In Figure 2-9, you see a series of higher highs, including a minor gap up, but then the last buyers realize they are all alone on the mountaintop. They start to sell in a panic and are willing to accept a much lower price. Now the price takes off in the opposite direction on a breakaway gap, which tends to have high volume. The island reversal bar has a higher high but is accompanied by low volume. This combination is the warning. The next day, as the breakaway gap develops, it has unusually high volume. You need live data to evaluate the new breakaway gap as it emerges at the open. High volume in combination with the downward gap is an indication that early selling is strong, and prices later in the day aren't going to go back and fill that gap.

Book X

Technical Analysis

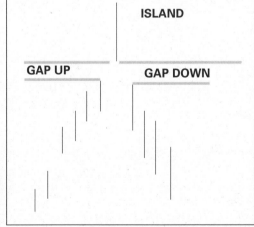

Figure 2-9:
An island reversal.

Illustration by Wiley, Composition Services Graphics

You see lots of gaps, but you seldom see an island reversal. When you do see one, you know what to do:

- ✔ An island reversal at the bottom: Buy.
- ✔ An island reversal at the top: Sell.

Back to the beginning: Filling the gap

Filling the gap means that prices are returning to the level they occupied before the gap, as shown in Figure 2-10.

With a runaway gap or a common gap, demand for the security is more a function of buyers egging each other on than changing conditions, so the gap may be filled quickly. Sometimes a gap gets filled just because all the chatter about filling the gap makes it a self-fulfilling prophecy.

A breakaway gap is another matter. If a security takes off on a breakaway gap, sometimes the price doesn't return to fill the gap for many months or even years, if ever. When the fundamentals of a security change dramatically, market participants perceive that conditions have changed permanently, and so has the price of the security.

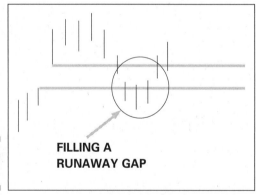

**FILLING A
RUNAWAY GAP**

Figure 2-10:
Filling a gap.

Illustration by Wiley, Composition Services Graphics

Chapter 3

Charting the Market with Candlesticks

Candlestick charting displays the price bar in a graphically different way from the standard bars described in Chapter 2 of Book X:

✔ They're easy to use and simple to interpret. You can use candlesticks on any chart, with any other indicators, just like standard bars.

✔ Candlestick names are widely known and suggest other traders will see stand-out candlesticks and react in specific ways.

✔ Candlesticks are used mostly to identify market turning points, such as a reversal from up to down.

This chapter breaks down the components of a candlestick and covers those candlesticks and combinations that stand out the most from the dozens that exist.

Anatomy of a Candlestick

The candlestick form emphasizes the open and the close (see Figure 3-1). The open and the close mark the top and bottom of a box, named the *real body*. A thin vertical line at the top and bottom of the real body, named the *shadow*, shows the high and the low.

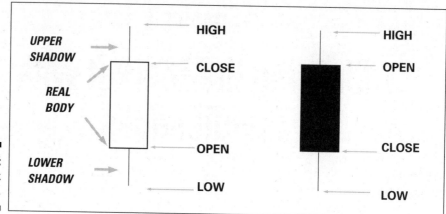

Figure 3-1:
Candlestick
bar notation.

Drawing the real body

The real body encompasses the range between the open and the close. The color of the real body defines who won the daily struggle between the bulls and the bears:

- ✔ **White real body:** The close is higher than the open. A white body is bullish, and the longer the body, the more bullish it is. A long candlestick implies aggressive buying.

- ✔ **Black real body:** The close is lower than the open. A black body is bearish, and the longer the body, the more bearish it is. A long black candlestick indicates a preponderance of sellers.

The two candlestick bars in Figure 3-1 show the identical open and close, but coloring one of them black creates the optical illusion that it's bigger. That black bar demands your attention.

The color of the candlestick bar is determined only by today's open and today's close. As in all bar analysis, *context* is crucial. Although you may sometimes use a single candlestick bar as an indicator in its own right, most of the time you use it in relation to the bars that precede it. One small white-body bar in a sea of black bars, for example, may mean the bulls won that day and may signal that the bears are losing power, but you wouldn't use it all by itself to call the end of a black-bar downtrend.

Defining doji: No real body

A candlestick that has no real body or only a very small one is named a *doji*. In a doji, the open and the close are at or nearly at the same level. Figure 3-2 displays three doji bars. When the close is at or near the open, market participants are indecisive. Bulls and bears are at a standoff. One of the two sides is going to blink and a trend reversal is possible.

Figure 3-2: Doji candlestick patterns.

PLAIN DOJI   **DRAGONFLY DOJI**   **GRAVESTONE DOJI**

Illustration by Wiley, Composition Services Graphics

Book X

Technical Analysis

A doji is a neutral bar, neither bullish nor bearish, that gains meaning from its placement within a set of bars. If the price series has been in an uptrend, for example, the doji may reflect that the buyers are coming to the end of their bullish enthusiasm. A doji coming immediately after a very long white bar shows that the market is tired.

Studying the shadows

The high and the low are shown in the *shadows*. Although the shadow is secondary to the real body in importance, shadows contribute useful information about market psychology and modify your interpretation of the body. Shadows offer special clues, especially when the real body is a doji or when the shadow is missing.

Shadows in the doji

In many instances, a doji is just a plain one, but the dragonfly and gravestone dojis are more useful (refer to Figure 3-2):

   ✔ **Dragonfly doji:** Features a long lower shadow. A very long lower shadow tells you that the open, high, and close were all the same or nearly the same, meaning sellers were trying to push the price down and succeeded in making a low — but they didn't succeed in getting it to close there. Because the close was at or near the open, buyers must have emerged before the end of trading and fought back, getting the price to close at or near what was both the open and the high. How you interpret the dragonfly depends on what bar patterns precede it:

- If the price move is a downtrend, the dragonfly may mean that buyers are emerging and the downtrend may be ending.

- If the dragonfly appears after a series of uptrending bars, buyers failed to push the price over the open to a new high while sellers succeeded in getting a low, so the uptrend may be in trouble. (Flip to Chapter 2 of Book X for more about uptrends and downtrends.)

✔ **Gravestone doji:** Features a long upper shadow. This bar is formed when the open, low, and close are the same or nearly the same, but a high creates a long upper shadow. Although buyers succeeded in pushing the price to a high over the open, by the end of the day the bears were fighting back and pushed the price back to close near the open and the low. This is a failed effort at a rally, but you can interpret the bar only in the context of the bars that precede it:

- If the gravestone bar appears after a series of uptrending bars, buyers failed to get the close at the high. Sellers dominated and the uptrend is at risk of ending.

- If the price move is a downtrend, the gravestone doji may mean that buyers are emerging and the downtrend may be ending.

Missing shadows

The absence of a shadow at one end is called a *shaven top* or a *shaven bottom.* To get a shaven top or bottom, the open or close must be exactly at the high or the low (see Figure 3-3).

Illustration by Wiley, Composition Services Graphics

Figure 3-3: Missing shadows.

SHAVEN TOP **SHAVEN BOTTOM**

✔ **Shaven top:** No upper shadow exists when the open or close is at the high. A shaven top can be black or white, and it comes about in two ways:

- If the open is at the high, the day's trading was all downhill from there. Not only is the candlestick black, or bearish to begin with, but it's doubly bearish that no net new buying occurred after the open.

- • If the close is at the high, the net of the day's trading was at higher prices, which is bullish. The candlestick is also (by definition) white, a bullish sign.

✔ **Shaven bottom:** No lower shadow exists when the open or the close is at the low of the day. A shaven bottom can come about in two ways:

- • If the open is at the low, all the day's trading was euphoric. This is bullish, adding to the bullishness of the white candlestick.

- • If the close is at the low, all the day's trading points to developing negative sentiment (depending on what bars precede it, of course). This is a black bar, with bells on.

Book X

Technical
Analysis

Identifying Emotional Extremes

Identifying when traders are reaching the end of their emotional tether is one of the primary goals of candlestick charting. A change in bar-size is one of the best indicators of this situation. If you're looking at a series of medium-sized bars and suddenly see one relatively long bar (as shown in Figure 3-4), it may be telling you that support or resistance has been reached.

✔ **Support** marks an extreme level where buyers perceive that the price is relatively cheap.

✔ **Resistance** marks an extreme level where sellers perceive the price is relatively high, inspiring profit-taking or at least an end to accumulation.

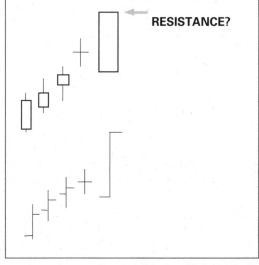

Figure 3-4:
Bar
placement.

Illustration by Wiley, Composition Services Graphics

In the top illustration in Figure 3-4 is a series of three white bars making higher opens and higher closes, followed by a doji and an exceptionally long white bar. If you were looking at this in standard bar notation, as seen in the bottom illustration, you might say to yourself, "Higher highs, higher lows, higher closes, trend okay." But the unusually tall bar stands out more prominently in candlestick mode, especially following the doji, and alerts you to the possibility that buyers just exhausted themselves and the price may have formed a resistance level at the top of the bar (the close, in this case).

If the long bar were a black bar, denoting that the close was lower than the open, deducing that the upmove might be ending would be easy. A long black bar implies panic selling. But the *white* bar as an ending burst in an uptrend is more subtle. Dozens of possible bar placement combinations and permutations are possible. The following sections cover several of the most popular patterns.

Two similar candlesticks or candlestick patterns often have the exact opposite interpretation, depending on where they fall in a series. You have to memorize the exact patterns to avoid getting confused.

Hammer and hanging man

Both the hammer and the hanging man have a small real body and only one shadow, a long lower shadow. The long shadow of the hammer extends to the downside off a white body, while the long shadow of the hanging man extends to the downside off a black body (see Figure 3-5).

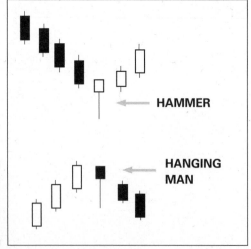

HAMMER

HANGING MAN

Figure 3-5: Hammer and hanging man.

Illustration by Wiley, Composition Services Graphics

You'd think that the white-body version would automatically be a bullish indicator and the black-body version a bearish one, but interpreting this candlestick depends on its placement on the chart, regardless of the real-body color. If the pattern appears in a downtrend, for example, it marks the likely end of the trend even if the real body is white.

You may see a hammer in many other contexts, but when it has a white body and it comes after a series of black downtrending bars, as in Figure 3-5, it implies reversal. Note that the close is higher than the previous close, too. In this context, the long lower shadow means the sellers were able to achieve a new low, but buyers emerged at some point during the day and the close was higher than the open, indicating last-minute buying.

The hanging man looks the same except it has a black body coming after a series of white uptrending bars. The long lower shadow marks the bulls' failure to prevent the bears making a new low. You may see this bar in other places within a series of bars, but when you see it at the top of an uptrending series (as in Figure 3-5), you should consider that the trend is probably over.

Book X

Technical
Analysis

Harami

A small real-body candlestick that comes after a bigger one, as shown in Figure 3-6, is called a *harami*. The harami pattern requires both bars. A harami implies that a change in sentiment is impending. This chart shows the shadows of the harami bar as also inside the scope of the first big bar, which is common although not essential to identifying the pattern.

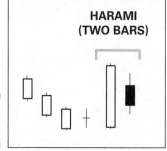

**HARAMI
(TWO BARS)**

Figure 3-6:
Harami.

*Illustration by Wiley, Composition Services
Graphics*

A harami can be white or black, and, in fact, it can even be a doji. The smaller the real body is, the more powerful the implication that a reversal is impending. In Figure 3-6, white bars, seemingly downtrending, are followed by a large white bar, reflecting a high level of emotion. Seeing just the big white bar after a series of smaller ones that are downtrending, you may think that the bulls finally got the upper hand, and this is the start of an uptrend, especially because you have an indecisive doji just ahead of it. The black harami follow-ing the big white bar should disillusion you. If an uptrend was forming, the harami just put the kibosh on it.

Turning to Reversal Patterns

Identifying reversals is the main application of candlesticks. The engulfing candlestick and the shooting star, shown in Figure 3-7, are two of the most popular and easily identified candlesticks showing reversal patterns:

- **Engulfing candlestick:** An *engulfing pattern* signals the reversal of a trend. The word *engulfing* refers to the open and close of the bar encom-passing a wider range than the open and close of the day before. In Figure 3-7, which shows a bearish engulfing candlestick, the engulfing nature is the dominant characteristic, so that the lower close pops out at you even though the bar also has a higher open. When a bar starts out at a higher open but then closes at a lower level, the bears won that day. Not shown is a *bullish engulfing candlestick,* which is white. The higher close is visually compelling because the real body is so big.

- **Shooting star:** The *shooting star* is characterized by a small real body and a long upper shadow, as you can see in Figure 3-7. The long upper shadow implies the failure of the bulls; they could get a higher high but couldn't hold it against the bears. Notice the indecisive doji bar just before the shooting star.

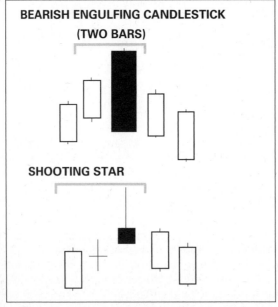

BEARISH ENGULFING CANDLESTICK
(TWO BARS)

SHOOTING STAR

Figure 3-7:
Reversal
patterns.

Illustration by Wiley, Composition Services Graphics

Recognizing Continuation Patterns

Candlestick patterns are most often used to identify reversals, but continuation patterns do exist. As the name suggests, a continuation pattern gives you confirmation that the trend in place will likely continue. Two such patterns are the rising (or falling) window and the three white soldiers:

✔ **Rising/falling window:** *Rising window* is the term for a gap, in this case, an upward gap. A downward gap is a *falling window.* (Go to Chapter 2 in Book X for more on gaps.) In Figure 3-8, the gap separates two white candlesticks, which are themselves bullish. The next bar doesn't fill the gap. The gap between the two price bars is confirmation of the existing trend, and the market's refusal the following day to go back and fill the gap is further confirmation that the trend is okay.

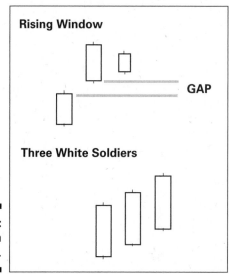

Figure 3-8:
Continuation
patterns.

Illustration by Wiley, Composition Services Graphics

✔ **Three white soldiers:** The bottom bars in Figure 3-8 show three white soldiers. In this pattern, what's important are three large white candlesticks in a row. Seeing the close consistently over the open for three days confirms that the price series is in an uptrend, and the size of the bars indicates its robustness.

Interpreting a Series of Patterns

To do a good job interpreting candlesticks, you need to understand the dynamic and complex relationships of many patterns all at once, like juggling six oranges instead of three. Figure 3-9 shows a series of candlesticks that reveal several patterns. (***Note:*** This figure also shows a set of parallel support and resistance lines called a *channel,* which is used to outline the probable limit of future price moves, either up or down. You can read more about support and resistance in Chapter 4 of Book X.)

The harami is followed by a rising window (upward gap) and a big white candle. These three candlesticks together are bullish and alert you to go back and start the channel at the lowest low, the bar before the harami.

In reading this chart, notice that the real bodies push against the top of the channel resistance line, but the doji, which suggests that traders are having second thoughts, is followed by two higher white candles. The two white candles indicate that the reconsideration of the move on the doji day culminated in the traders' decision to keep taking the price up. This was an occasion when the doji wasn't a reversal indicator, at least not for the next day. After the two white candles comes a bearish engulfing candle, a reversal warning that this upmove may be ending. The engulfing candle alerts you to watch the next day's activity, especially the open, with an eagle eye.

No matter how compelling a particular bar may seem, you still need confirmation of the interpretation, which comes only after you see the next day's bar. Sometimes you get a strong reversal pattern that is invalidated the very next day. Candlestick analysis may offer a forecast of the general direction of the price move over the next day or few days, but it doesn't suggest the extent of the move (such as a price target).

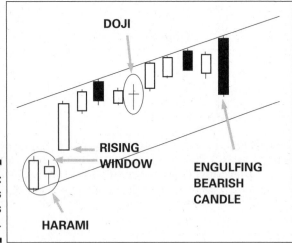

Figure 3-9:
Candlesticks
as
confirmation.

DOJI

RISING WINDOW

ENGULFING BEARISH CANDLE

HARAMI

Illustration by Wiley, Composition Services Graphics

Chapter 4

Seeing Patterns and Drawing Trendlines

. . . .

In This Chapter

▶ Getting the basics on patterns

▶ Recognizing continuation and classic reversal patterns

▶ Drawing support, resistance, and linear regression lines

. . . .

Securities prices move in regular ways that professional traders expect and respond to. Chart patterns are powerful indicators, and having some basic knowledge of patterns and pattern jargon is a good idea for all traders.

We use patterns and trendlines to identify support and resistance and break-outs of support and resistance. Even a rough application of these two concepts can save you a bundle or help you make profits, because they're among the top technical ruling concepts in the market and you can expect others to heed the meaning of the patterns in consistent ways. This chapter illustrates a few of the many common patterns and tells you how to use them.

Introducing Patterns

Chart patterns are indicators consisting of shapes, such as triangles, drawn on the chart. Although most patterns employ straight lines (such as triangles), a few use semi-circles or semi-ellipses (such as head-and-shoulders). Pattern lines generally follow either the highs or the lows rather than the close.

Not everyone can see patterns right away. Pattern identification takes practice until you get the hang of it. For example, consider Figure 4-1. Do you see the pattern?

Illustration by Wiley, Composition Services Graphics

Figure 4-1:
Find the
pattern.

The pattern in Figure 4-1 is a symmetrical triangle, as you can see in Figure 4-2, characterized by a series of lower highs along which you can draw one trendline and a series of higher lows along which you can draw another trendline. The two lines eventually come together at an apex. Before then, we expect the price to pierce one of the trendlines. Which one? Because most of the bars are trending downward, you imagine the odds favor a break to the downside. But it could also be to the upside.

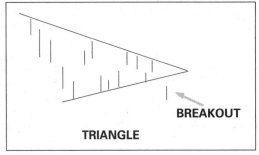

BREAKOUT

TRIANGLE

Illustration by Wiley, Composition Services Graphics

Figure 4-2:
Pattern
revealed.

Here are a few points to keep in mind as you identify and interpret patterns:

✔ Pattern types are usually organized according to whether they forecast a continuation or a reversal of the current price move, although many patterns can be applied either way. As with most indicators, a price forecast is embedded in the pattern identification.

✔ You usually see a burst of higher volume when a pattern reaches completion. This makes sense, because other chartists in the crowd are seeing the same pattern. For triangles, low volume often *precedes* the breakout and serves as a bonus warning of an impending move.

✔ Pattern identification doesn't require that each single price in a series line up perfectly. Not every price high hits an overhead resistance line, for example. Seeing that several hit the line suffices.

✔ Triangles come in several forms (symmetrical, ascending and descending, flags and pennants, and so on) but they all incorporate *support* (bottom) and *resistance* (top) lines. Find out more about these lines later in this chapter.

As with most aspects of technical analysis, a pattern is a work in progress, and pattern identification can be frustrating and time-consuming. You may think you see a pattern developing, only to have the price action change course and fail to complete the expected formation. You may have to erase your work and start over a number of times on any single set of bars. Resign yourself to making a lot of mistakes. The reason to tolerate the pattern recognition process is that when you get it right, you have a powerful forecasting tool that can deliver 20 to 40 percent returns in a short period.

Book X

Technical Analysis

Identifying Continuation Patterns

A *continuation pattern* tells you that buying or selling pressure is pausing. If a big-picture trend is well-established, the pattern suggests it will accelerate after the pause. A continuation pattern is a good place to add more to a position, because you expect an additional move in the same direction. Because continuation patterns like the ones in the following sections tend to be fairly short-term, sometimes only a few days, they're often neglected.

Ascending and descending triangles

To draw ascending and descending triangles, you draw a line along the highs of a price series and another one along the lows (see Figure 4-3), as with symmetrical triangles.

In the ascending triangle, the price isn't making new highs, and the topmost (resistance) line is horizontal. You may worry that the failure to make new highs means the upmove is over. But the price isn't making new lows, either. You expect a breakout of the top line to the upside.

When you can draw a horizontal line along a series of highs, be sure to look for a rising line along the lows at the same time. Not only does the ascending line confirm the trend continuation, but it also provides you with a ready-made stop-loss level at the ascending support line. The ascending triangle pattern delivers the expected rise about two-thirds of the time, but it fails about 32 percent of the time. If you wait for prices to close above the top trendline, then the failure rate drops to a mere 2 percent. The *expected rise,* by the way, is equal to the height of the triangle pattern.

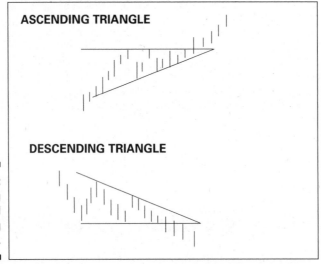

Figure 4-3:
Ascending and descending triangles.

Illustration by Wiley, Composition Services Graphics

A descending triangle is the mirror image of the ascending triangle. The important point is that the price is failing to make new lows in the prevailing downtrend. You wonder if the trend is failing. But if you can still draw a line along the series of lower highs, it would be a mistake to buy at this point. The probability is high that the downtrend is going to continue.

Pennants and flags

A *pennant* is shaped like a triangle but the price swing between the top and bottom lines is smaller (see Figure 4-4). Usually a pennant lasts only a few days and hardly ever longer than three weeks. A pennant is a form of retracement often accompanied by a drop in volume. (Flip to Chapter 1 in Book X for details on retracements.) A *flag,* also shown in Figure 4-4, is another retracement, but its support and resistance lines are parallel.

A trend is usually punctuated by minor retracement moves in the opposite direction when traders take profit and set off a small cascade of profit-taking by others. With pennants and flags, the pattern lasts about ten days on average and is accompanied by falling volume. In Figure 4-4, note the upward-sloping line that roughly describes the overall uptrend. The flag is a retracement in the context of that overall upmove.

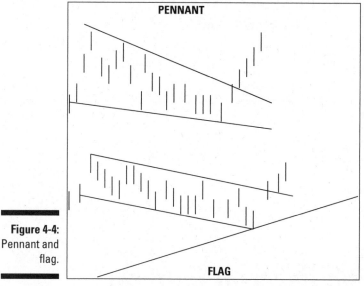

Book X

Technical
Analysis

Figure 4-4:
Pennant and
flag.

Illustration by Wiley, Composition Services Graphics

If you have confidence in the trend, you can tolerate a minor and short-lived break when it's a pennant or flag doing the breaking. In fact, pennants and flags are what pattern chartists call *half-mast patterns.* That is, they form midway in a trend, and you can use the pattern to estimate the end of the trend by projecting the distance already traveled from the start of the trend.

Dead-cat bounces

A dead-cat bounce, shown in Figure 4-5, is a peculiar continuation pattern that looks like a reversal at the beginning, with a sizeable upward retracement of a downmove, but then fades back to the same downward direction. Note that a dead-cat bounce occurs only in downmoves, and no equivalent named pattern exists for a parallel sequence of events in an upmove.

The dead-cat pattern starts off with a negative fundamental event that triggers a massive downmove. The *bounce* is an upward retracement that may make you think the drop is over. The pattern includes a breakaway downside gap about 80 percent of the time, and sometimes the bounce upward fills part of the gap. (See Chapter 2 in Book X for a discussion of gaps.) Many traders mistakenly think that if a gap is filled, even partly, the preceding move has ended. The dead-cat bounce is one of the patterns that disproves that idea.

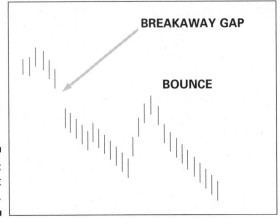

Figure 4-5:
Dead-cat
bounce.

Illustration by Wiley, Composition Services Graphics

Noting Classic Reversal Patterns

Patterns come into their own when used to identify a trend reversal. No matter how a trend ends, chances are good that a pattern exists to identify it.

Double bottoms

A double bottom looks like a W (see Figure 4-6) and predicts a price breakout to the upside and substantial gains. A valid double bottom includes these characteristics:

- A minimum of ten days between the two lows and sometimes as long as two or three months
- A 4 percent or less price variation between the two lows
- A center upmove of at least 10 percent from the lower of the two bottoms
- A price that rises above the confirmation line (which confirms that the pattern is indeed a double bottom and the forecast of a continued rise is correct)

The *confirmation line* is a horizontal line drawn from the highest high in the middle of the W. The point where the price rises above the line is called the *confirmation point*. Reaching the confirmation line drawn horizontally from the confirmation point is the most important identification key of the double bottom. This is where you buy.

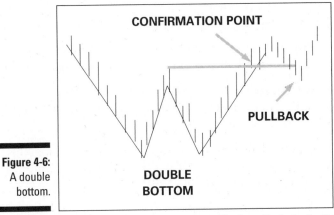

CONFIRMATION POINT

PULLBACK

DOUBLE BOTTOM

Figure 4-6:
A double
bottom.

Illustration by Wiley, Composition Services Graphics

Book X

Technical
Analysis

Notice that some of the price bars break the lines you draw to form the double-bottom pattern. Breaking some of the bars is allowed in a formation where the line is not a support or resistance line.

Not every twin bottom is a true double bottom. Only about one-third of all the patterns that look like a double bottom end up meeting the confirmation criterion. In other words, the pattern fails about two-thirds of the time. This statistic sounds terrible, but on the occasions when you do get confirmation, the double bottom is tremendously reliable. If you wait for the price to break above the confirmation line, the pattern delivers a profit an astonishing 97 percent of the time — and the average gain is 40 percent.

Other characteristics of a double bottom are

- A large increase in volume on the price crossing above the confirmation line, demonstrating increased interest by the crowd and implying widespread recognition of the pattern.

- Frequent retracements to the downside right after the price breaks the confirmation line. A retracement occurs 68 percent of the time in confirmed double bottoms, making it hard, psychologically, to hang on to the trade that you just put on only a few days before when the price crossed the confirmation line.

Not every double-bottom pattern is as easy to detect as the one in Figure 4-6. One or both of the two lows of the double bottom could be rounded instead of pointed, for example. Often the two lows of a double bottom are separated by many months, even a year, and it's easy to miss the pattern altogether. Also, minor retracements and other wobbles within the W can obscure the pattern.

Double tops

A double top is the mirror image of the double bottom in Figure 4-6 — it looks like the letter M. The price makes a high, pulls back on profit-taking (as usual), and then bullish traders try but fail to surpass the first high. The failure to rally a second time through the first high means the bulls were beaten and the bears are now in charge. A true double top is usually accompanied by falling volume as the second top is being formed.

As with the double bottom, you need to see the price surpass the confirmation level (the lowest point in the center bar of the M) for the pattern to be valid. When that condition is not met, twin tops fail to deliver a sustained downmove 65 percent of the time. When the condition is met, however, the pattern delivers a downmove 83 percent of the time, which is less reliable than the double bottom (97 percent), but still impressive. The average drop after a confirmed double top is 20 percent and lasts three months.

Again, as with double bottoms, the price pulls back after the confirmation 69 percent of the time, leaving you to doubt the pattern. Fortunately, the pullback period averages only ten days before the downtrend resumes.

The triple top: Head-and-shoulders

The head-and-shoulders pattern is a triple top that's easy to see; one bump forms the left shoulder, a higher bump forms a head, and a third bump forms the right shoulder. A triple top or bottom is somewhat rarer than the double version, but the meaning is the same — the price fails to surpass the previous low or high, signaling a trend reversal.

The head-and-shoulders patterns shown in Figure 4-7 are easy enough to see, but many head-and-shoulders patterns are more complex and contain other patterns within them. The second head-and-shoulders pattern in Figure 4-7, for example, contains a little double top and a gap (see Chapter 2 in Book X for more about gaps). You may also see what appears to be two heads or two shoulders, although one is always higher, which makes it the head.

In a head-and-shoulders pattern, the confirmation line connects the low point of each shoulder and is named the *neckline*. The price breaking the neckline predicts a price decline, whether the neckline is sloping upward or downward. Seldom do you see the neckline perfectly horizontal. A downward-sloping neckline tends to deliver the biggest price move.

A head-and-shoulders pattern usually forms after a long uptrend. The dip from the first shoulder represents the normal retracement after a new high. The head then represents the triumph of bullish sentiment and sets a new, higher high. The dip after the higher-high head represents more profit-taking, whereupon the bulls buy again. When the bulls are making their third try at a rally, their price target is the last highest high, which is the top of the head. The failure of the second shoulder to surpass the head is the end of the rally. Buying demand diminishes and selling pressure takes hold, forcing prices down and completing the pattern.

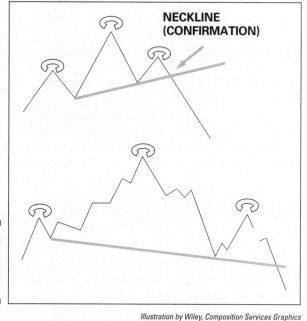

Figure 4-7:
Head-and-
shoulders
patterns.

Illustration by Wiley, Composition Services Graphics

Book X

Technical Analysis

As with double tops and bottoms, some traders refuse to accept the pattern, and they cause a pullback to the confirmation line 45 percent of the time. Pullbacks average only 11 days before the security resumes its decline. This is your last chance to jump off before the price hits the wall.

As with every trend that's losing steam, volume falls after the head, although about half the time the highest volume is at the left shoulder and about half the time at the head. Volume is low at the second shoulder. Volume on the breakout day and the next few days after the breakout day, however, tends to be very large, because by that point a great number of chart-oriented traders have identified the pattern and its neckline.

Drawing Trendlines

A *trendline* is a straight line that starts at the beginning of the trend and stops at the end of the trend. Often you can see a trend with the naked eye, but to impose order on your visual impression, you can connect the dots by actually drawing a line along the price bars. When you look at a chart, sometimes the trendline pops out at you. Other times, a line isn't obvious, in which case you study the chart for a few minutes and may even draw a few experimental lines. Figuring out where trends start and stop can be complicated, but this section explains how to spot them, plot them, and figure out what they're telling you.

Here are a few things to keep in mind about drawing trendlines:

- ✔ The time frame of the chart you're looking at influences what you see. A trader with a long-term time frame sees one trend on a chart, whereas a swing trader with a shorter time frame sees two or three. There is no single "correct" answer.

- ✔ You have to accept that charting is a dynamic process. Your work is never done. Every day (or hour, or week) provides new data. You need to be willing to discard a trendline when it stops representing the trend — or to restore an old trendline if your original line turns out to be right.

- ✔ In the transition from a downtrend to an uptrend, you can't draw a single line that captures the trend, because no single trend exists that captures both moves. In other instances, all you can see is a meandering line that's practically horizontal. This may be a pause while the same trend resumes, or it may mark the transition period from up to down or down to up.

- ✔ No security is in a trending mode all the time. Be realistic about whether a trendline is drawable. Often, you can't draw a trendline on the chart you have in front of you, but if you generate another chart with a longer time frame (such as a weekly chart), a trendline jumps out at you.

Creating rule-based trendlines

A rule-based trendline is one that starts and stops according to well-defined conditions, such as a line starting at the lowest low of the last three days and ending at the highest high of the last three days. A rule-based trendline is better than an impressionistic trendline (one you eyeball) for three reasons:

- ✔ It doesn't let you impose your personal view of what the trend should be.

- ✔ It improves your ability (and self-confidence) to buy a security when its price is rising or sell it when the price is falling.

- ✔ It helps prevent loss by showing you the exit at the right time.

To draw a rule-based trendline for an uptrend, follow these steps:

1. **Start at the lowest low and connect the line to the next low that precedes a new high.**

2. **As long as new highs are being made, redraw the line to connect to the lowest low before the last high.**

3. **When prices stop making new highs, stop drawing. Extend the line out into the future at the same slope.**

To draw a rule-based trendline for a downtrend, follow these steps:

1. **Start at the highest high and connect the line to the next high that precedes a new low.**

2. **As long as new lows are being made, redraw the line to connect to the highest high before the last low.**

3. **When prices stop making new lows, stop drawing. Extend the line out into the future at the same slope.**

Notice that this is a dynamic process. You often have to erase one line and draw another one as conditions change.

Drawing support lines

The trendline in Figure 4-8 illustrates the rule-based trendline called a *support line,* so named because you expect the line to support the price — traders won't let the price fall below it. To draw a support line, you start at the lowest low and draw a line to the next low. This generates a line that can be extended at the same slope, but it becomes a trendline only when another daily price low touches the line.

The following sections explain when to enter and exit with the guidance of a support line.

Knowing when to enter

The support-line entry rule says "Buy on the third touch of the support line by the low of a price bar." The third touch is confirmation that the line is more than just a line and is a true trendline.

You use the support line to identify an uptrend. The price is rising, and rising consistently. This provides comfort that the purchase of this security is returning a profit and may continue to return a profit. Notice in Figure 4-8 that on many days, the low price touched the line but didn't cross it.

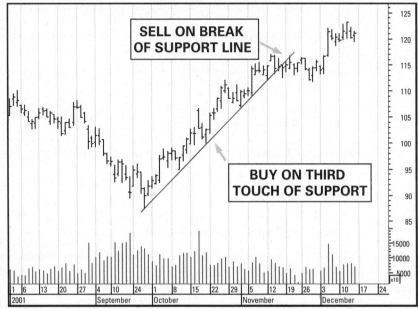

Illustration by Wiley, Composition Services Graphics

Figure 4-8:
Drawing a
support line.

The more times that a low-of-the-day touches the support line without cross-ing it, the more confidence you should have that it is a valid description of the trend. This is called a *test of support* and encourages buyers of the security to buy more after the price passes the test. Fresh buying constitutes demand for the security and is called *accumulation*.

Sometimes traders engineer a test of support by selling the security down to the support line to see whether support will hold. If you put on a new long position above the support line, you're sweating bullets when other traders test support. Will holders of the security rush in to buy more of the security to defend their position? When the support line does hold, the traders who were selling become big buyers. They've just been given proof that the bulls put their money where their mouths are.

Some technical traders say that to require a third touch is to be overly cau-tious and to miss out on some perfectly good trends that fail to meet the third-touch qualification. This is true. Many valid trends do have only two touches before they end. If you're waiting for the third touch, you may miss the entire move. But experience shows that your trust is better placed in a trendline with three or more touches.

Knowing when to exit: The breakout

The support-line exit rule says "Sell when the low of the price bar falls below the support line."

When any part of the price bar penetrates the line on the downside, support has been broken, and you may think that the trend is over. This may or may not be true. In Figure 4-8, the move continues after the line was broken, but never mind — experience teaches that the trendline is no longer reliable. A break of support is literally just that— some holders of the security were willing to break ranks with the other holders and to sell at progressively lower prices.

A *breakout* is any part of the price bar penetrating a line you drew on the chart. The word *breakout* is used in a dozen contexts in technical analysis, but it always refers to a significant violation of a trendline. Sometimes the offending breakout is quickly roped back into the herd, but usually a breakout means that the trend is changing direction.

A one-day break of the line is called a *false breakout*. To estimate whether a breakout may be false, master trader Larry Williams recommends you consider the position of the close on the day before the breakout. In an uptrend, if the close is at or near the high, chances are good that it's a false breakout. The breakout was due to profit-taking that got carried away, it was triggered by a false rumor, or it was a random move. If the close on the day before is at or near the low, though, chances are the breakout is real.

Even though you should discard the support line as a trading tool after it's been broken, you may want to leave it on the chart for a while. Sometimes old support becomes new resistance (and vice versa; see the next section).

Book X

Technical
Analysis

Drawing resistance lines

Resistance is the mirror image of support: A line drawn along a series of highs marks where buyers resist buying more — because they judge the price too high. Traders expect sellers taking profit to emerge at the resistance line. You should care about a downtrend using the resistance line for two reasons:

- ✔ When a downtrend ends, the next move may be an uptrend. Because you want to get in on the action as early as possible, you care when a downtrend is broken to the upside. The breakout is an important clue that an uptrend may be starting and you should start paying attention.

- ✔ Someday, you may sell short.

The more times the high-of-the-day touches the resistance line and doesn't cross it, the more confidence you have that it's a valid description of the trend. This is called a *test of resistance* and encourages sellers of the security to sell more after the price passes the test. Fresh selling constitutes supply of the security and is called *distribution*. Those who own the security are reluctant to hold it after resistance has proven to resist an effort to break above it. They're willing to sell their inventory at increasingly lower prices.

In trend-following trading, you never enter at the absolute high and never exit at the absolute low. The goal is to capture most of the trend. You hardly ever capture all the trend.

Fine-tuning support and resistance

You need patience and persistence to work with trendlines because you need to adjust the lines often, sometimes daily.

- ✔ **Trend reversal:** The uptrend that you identified by drawing the support line (refer to Figure 4-8) turned into a downtrend a few weeks later. This is often the case. But you can't count on black-and-white trend reversals.

- ✔ **Sideways movements:** In both support and resistance trendline cases, the price often enters a period of sideways price movements just before the breakout of the line that triggers the exit rule. Such sideways periods, named *congestion,* are common during trends as well as when a trend is ending. Another term for a sideways price movement is *consolidation,* which refers to market participants consolidating their ideas about the security being traded. Consolidation (which by definition incorporates less high-low volatility) often precedes a breakout.

- ✔ **Retracement:** A trendline breakout doesn't necessarily lead to formation of a trend in the opposite direction. Sometimes you get a temporary retracement called a *correction* or *pullback.* At the time it's occurring, you don't know whether it's a full reversal or just a retracement. Drawing trendlines is especially frustrating and difficult during retracement periods.

Every single trend contains retracements. If you heed every one, you are at risk of overtrading (and running up commission costs). Some analysts have a near-religious belief that retracements occur according to some magic amount of the previous move, such as 25 to 50 percent, or according to special number sequences. In practice, retracements range all over the place. A 50 percent retracement is a special one, because if you're absolutely certain that the pullback has ended, you can count on a return to the previous high (or low). Expect to spend a high proportion of your chart-reading time trying to figure out retracements. This is when consulting the fundamentals is especially useful, as well as redrawing the chart on a wider time frame (weekly or monthly).

Drawing internal trendlines: Linear regression

Wouldn't it be nice to know the *true* trendline — a line that would reveal the true price trendedness? Such a line *does* exist. It's a line that goes through the center of the price series rather than along its edges.

How do you draw a straight line through the center of each price bar? Technically, you can't, at least not on charts of securities prices. But scientists have a solution to price jumpiness: to "fit" a line that minimizes the distance from itself to each price along the line. The best-fit line is named the *linear regression line, linear* referring to *line* and *regression* referring to the mathematical calculation.

You don't need to know how the line is calculated to be able to use it. Spreadsheet software and all charting packages come with the linear regression already built in.

In Figure 4-9, the linear regression line doesn't actually go through the center of each price bar. But if you look closely, you'll see that no other line gets you as close to Point A *and* to Point B at the same time. Only one linear regression exists for any set of prices on the chart.

Book X

Technical Analysis

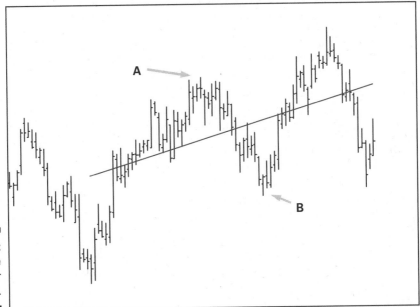

Figure 4-9:
Simple
linear
regression.

A linear regression is the true, pure trendline. If you accept the core concept of technical analysis, that a trend will continue in the same direction, at least for a while, you can extend the true trendline to obtain a *forecast.* In some software packages, a linear regression extension is called exactly that — a *time-series forecast.* This is tremendously useful. You now have a high-probability forecast for the upcoming period.

If you select a good starting point, the linear regression delivers pure trend. Unlike support and resistance lines, the linear regression line doesn't have any trading rules associated directly with it, but visually, it's the most informative line. If you use linear regression lines, keep these things in mind:

✔ Figuring out where to start and where to end a linear regression line is the first big obstacle in using the line in a practical way. The simple answer is to start at an obvious high or low. This means you need to look backward at the historical data to see where the current move began. This can be trickier than it sounds. You can get very different slopes, depending on how tightly you want the data to fit to the line. Seeing a welter of slopes cluttering your chart can get frustrating. But stick to it. The linear regression could save your bacon someday.

✔ The linear regression line can slope this way or that way or no way (horizontal), depending on where you start drawing. If you take a V-shaped price series like the one in Figure 4-10 and draw a single linear regression line, you get. . . garbage. Obviously two trends on a chart require two linear regressions. In other words, you can draw linear regression lines that are totally useless.

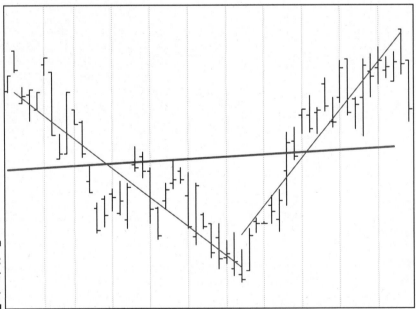

Figure 4-10:
Invalid linear
regression.

Illustration by Wiley, Composition Services Graphics

✔ You can do some really dumb things using the linear regression line, too. If you extend a line out into the indefinite future, you get a fantasy, not a forecast. The market is a collection of human beings, not a science project. Prices simply don't move in a straight line indefinitely.

Chapter 5

Transforming Techniques into Trades

Chapter 4 in Book X reviews patterns and lines, emphasizing the key concepts of support, resistance, and breakouts of support and resistance. This chapter takes a look at the math-based indicators that make up the bulk of technical indicators and help you fine-tune your trading. Don't panic at the word "math." Although some chartists do use advanced math, you have plenty of choices among indicators that use simple arithmetic — addition, subtraction, division, and multiplication.

Math-based indicators fall roughly into three categories:

✔ **Trend:** Direction of the trend

✔ **Volatility:** Reliability of the trend

✔ **Momentum:** Strength of the trend

Volume may be added as a confirming indicator to all of the price-based indicators. Whether it can stand alone as the sole criterion for buy/sell trading decisions is debatable.

This chapter also covers ways in which you can combine simple patterns and lines with indicators to improve your trading decisions.

Capturing Trendedness with Channels

When you draw a support line under a set of rising prices, you capture trendedness in one form. But although the support line may deliver a good exit if it's broken to the downside, it doesn't tell you how far the trend may go. It doesn't tell you how strong the trend may be either, although the slope of the support line gives you a clue. A somewhat flat slope, near the horizontal, means a weak trend. A very sharp slope, such as 45 degrees, is a strong trend that offers profit opportunities. A nearly vertical slope is explosive and hardly ever sustained for long.

Drawing straight-line channels

A *channel* is a pair of straight-line trendlines encasing a price series. It consists of one line drawn along the top of a price series and another line, parallel to the first, drawn along the bottom of the price series. This is named a *Donchian channel* after its inventor, Richard Donchian.

The purpose of a channel is to train your eye to accept prices within its borders as *on the trend* and to detect prices outside its borders as *off the trend* (which can mean a different phase of the same trend or the end of it). In other words, the channel is a more complete measure of trending behavior than a single line. As long as prices remain within the channel, you deduce that the trend is still in place. When prices break out of the channel boundaries in either direction, you're alerted to make a decision — hold, buy more, or sell.

Two types of straight-line channels are available: those you draw by hand and those that depend on software providing you with a statistical tool.

- ✔ **A straight-line channel drawn by hand:** Start with a top line connecting at least two highs, and draw the bottom line parallel to it. Alternatively, start with the bottom line connecting at least two lows, and draw the top line parallel to that.

   Figure 5-1 shows a line that starts on the bottom of the price series after the lowest low. You connect it to another low, disregarding the next few days. The two key lows are marked with circles. The upper resistance line is parallel.

   If you draw a support line farther out, encompassing all the lows, it's never touched again and delays the exit by one day after the downside breakout. Also notice that, at the place the price series ends, the lowest low is nearly at the earlier lowest low where you started drawing the channel. A test of a previous high or low is very common.

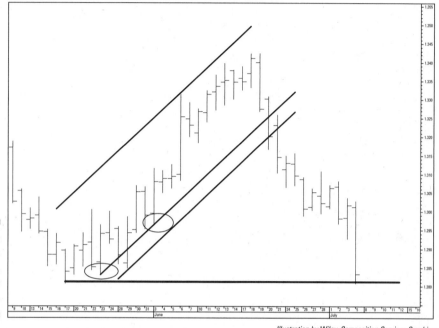

Figure 5-1:
Hand-
drawn,
straight-line
channel.

Illustration by Wiley, Composition Services Graphics

✓ **A straight-line channel created using software:** Draw a linear regression line (see Chapter 4 in Book X for details) and draw the top and bottom of the channel at an equal distance on each side of it (you can do this by hand or by using software). You can make the equal distances a function of the standard error provided by the software, as in Figure 5-2. In this instance, although not always, the linear regression channel is narrower than the hand-drawn version in Figure 5-1, and therefore the exit on the downside breakout is a day earlier.

You don't need to calculate the standard error yourself — let software do it. Note that the *standard error* measures how closely the prices cluster around your linear regression line.

Most chartists use two standard errors, which results in a channel top and channel bottom that enclose a high percentage (95 percent) of the highs and lows. An extreme high or low constitutes a bigger error away from the trendline than 95 percent of the highs and lows. If you add an additional fudge factor to enclose *all* the prices, it's named a *Raff channel* after its inventor, Gilbert Raff. This ensures that an opposite direction breakout is the real deal.

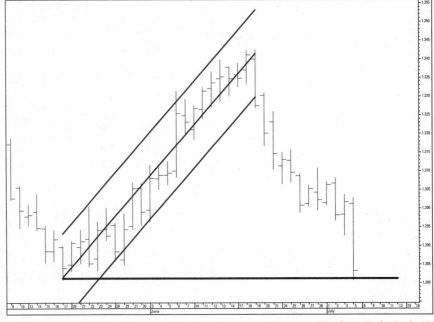

Figure 5-2:
Linear
regression
channel
using two
standard
deviations.

Illustration by Wiley, Composition Services Graphics

Interpreting straight-line channels

As a practical matter, every time a price breaks a channel line, you face a higher risk. The channel defines what is normal, and any foray outside the channel is not normal. You know instantly that, when the price breaks a rising trend to the downside, it's a sell signal. But what does it mean if the breakout is to the upside in a rising trend?

- ✔ These latest high prices can mark a third shift to a new, more steeply sloping channel yet to be drawn.

- ✔ A blowout breakout may be forming that will be followed by a crash — one last gasp.

- ✔ The price series may subside back into the channel, rendering the upside breakout meaningless.

You have no way to know which of these three outcomes is the most likely from the information on the chart. You may choose to exit on every channel-line breakout, or you can add another indicator to guide your decision.

Channels tell you the maximum probable future price range. Note that word *probable.* Channels are visually compelling and can seduce you into thinking that the forecast range *must* occur. It's all too easy to start drawing channels and forget that they're only a forecast. A zillion factors can come out of the blue and knock your trend off the rails.

To some extent, a channel is valid because many others can see the same thing. One of the top reasons that a technical analysis method works is because it creates a self-fulfilling prophecy. When everyone can see the same lines, a consensus builds as to what constitutes breaking the lines. When you draw a channel so wide or so narrow that only you can see it, you can't expect other traders to respond to it. To forecast a price range is really to forecast the probable collective behavior of the people who trade the security.

Using Channels to Trade

Channels are a tremendous tool to guide your trading. What can you do with channels?

- ✔ **You can buy near the channel bottom and sell near the channel top repeatedly for as long as the channel lasts.**

- ✔ **You can estimate your future gain.** If the width of the channel is $5 and you bought near a support line, your maximum probable gain over the next few days is about $5 as long as the channel remains in place and you're able to sell near the resistance line. This is more useful than you may think at first:

    - **It's a sanity check:** You can't reasonably expect a gain that would call for a price far outside the channel.

    - **It's a reality check:** You can use the channel to evaluate a forecast made by someone else. If the forecaster is calling for a price far outside the channel, you have grounds to question the forecast.

    - **It's an options trader trick:** You can buy a put option (to sell) at a price far outside the channel, collecting the premium with low risk of having to deliver the security. (Flip to Chapter 1 in Book II for more about put options.)

- ✔ **You can calculate your maximum loss.** Regardless of where you bought the security, you know that when a price bar breaks the bottom support line of the channel, the channel is no longer valid. The trend is likely over. You don't have to wait for the actual breakout. You can place a stop-loss order with your broker at the breakout level.

Dealing with Breakouts

The *breakout* is one of the most important concepts in technical analysis. It's a direct, graphic representation that something happened to change the market's sentiment toward the security. In the simplest terms, a breakout implies that a trend is over, at least in its present form. After a breakout, the price can go up, down, or sideways, but it seldom resumes at exactly the same level and rate of change you had before the breakout.

A breakout must always be respected, but you want to be sure it's authentic. Because so many traders draw support and resistance lines, there's always some wise guy in the market who tries to push the price through the lines. In an uptrend that's retracing downward, he tries to break the support line and panic holders into selling. He may believe in the uptrend; he's just trying to get a lower price for himself. In a downtrend, he's the joker who buys so much that the price puts in a new high and a close higher than on previous days, which scares the pants off sellers, who then cover their shorts and propel the price higher. In addition, a breakout can be just a random aberration.

Distinguishing between real and phony breakouts

You often see a tiny breakout and don't know how to evaluate it. Say your support line is at precisely $10 and the low of the price bar is $9.85. Is that a legitimate breakout or just an accident? A lot depends on how other traders see it. Do they allow a small breakout or do they panic and set off a selling cascade? Consider the price nearing the last lowest low in Figures 5-1 and 5-2. It's a coin toss whether the historical low forms horizontal support or will be broken. To judge which it will be at this critical moment usually entails looking to the fundamentals to figure out why the uptrend reversed so sharply in the first place.

Sometimes you get a minor break of a channel line that lasts one or two days, but then the price returns back inside its channel and performs just as before. The breakout was a *false breakout,* which is a breach of a trendline that then fails to deliver the expected additional moves in the same direction. To call it false is misleading, because the price bar unmistakably breaks the trendline. What's false is the conclusion you draw from it.

False breakouts are especially damaging because you may automatically assume that the breakout means a reversal. This isn't necessarily so, but it's tempting to jump on a breakout because the first few periods (usually days) after a breakout are often the best time to get in on the action. As much as one-quarter to one-third of a post-breakout move occurs in the first few days. It takes courage to jump on a security that just had a breakout, especially if you can't discover why it broke out. If you look for fresh news to justify the price pop but can't find any, you need to be suspicious. It may be false.

Pressuring the channel

Sometimes you see prices pressing against the top or bottom of the channel line, which can lead to a breakout in the same direction as the trend. In other words, higher volatility can mean an acceleration of an existing trend. A breakout can be to the upside in an uptrend as well as to the downside in a downtrend.

How can such a pattern come about? Easy. The crowd becomes overheated with greed to buy a security that is rising with tremendous force, or over-whelmed by fear to dump a security that is declining with great momentum. At some point, everyone who was going to buy has bought. Because these are traders who bought only to get a fast profit, when the rise slows down and a lower high or a lower low appears, these buyers exit in a horde. By selling a lot of the security in a very short period of time, the market has an oversup-ply, and buyers can command a low price.

Book X

Technical Analysis

The same thing happens when a downmove exhausts itself. Everybody who was going to sell has sold. Supply is now limited. Anyone who wants to buy has to start bidding the price up until he induces a longer-term holder of the security to part with it.

Why are the lines parallel?

When you draw a support line connecting a series of lows, you often see a parallel resis-tance line that mysteriously connects the highest highs. This is so common that most charting software programs have a standard command, "create parallel line." No one knows for certain why support and resistance lines are so often parallel. Here are a few pos-sible explanations:

✔ This kind of orderliness appears when the high/low trading range is stable. Volume is steady, too. An orderly crowd is trad-ing the security, so the channel is orderly. Market participants know where the price is relatively high, near the top of the chan-nel. They expect no more gains at this point and are prepared to sell at the top. Die-hard buyers, in turn, see when the price is rela-tively cheap, near the support line. They add to their position, propelling the price upward.

✔ Many technical analysts perceive a cyclical quality to the ebb and flow of prices within a channel. They rely on the security alternat-ing between support and resistance, and the perceived cycle is the basis of their trading plan. This often works, at least for short periods, as long as you don't project the price bouncing off the support or resistance line several cycles into the future. In other words, don't get cocky. You never know when fresh news is going to come along and cause prices to break the channel.

✔ Humans have an innate need to impose order on a chaotic universe — or market. Parallel lines don't always appear, of course, but they appear often enough that observers speak of trading ranges with a certain air of authority. When you hear of a *trading range,* this kind of parallel support and resistance channel is usually what the commentator has in mind.

Picking Apart Pivot-Point (Horizontal) Channels

What do you do when you stop getting higher highs (in an uptrend) or lower lows (in a downtrend)? In other words, the price is still within its channel but moving sideways.

The pause in movement may be temporary, but the sideways action can also be a warning that forward momentum is gone. From this you may deduce that if you're going to take profit, now is the time. The sideways action may also imply that a breakout in the opposite direction is impending.

One technique for dealing with sideways moves within a channel is to draw horizontal support and resistance lines off pivot points. The term *pivot point* is used in many different ways. One standard definition is that the pivot point is the center bar of three where the center bar is the highest high or lowest low. Another definition of pivot is the median price (the numerical average of the high, low, and close). Other traders cook up yet more definitions. Today, the median price version is probably the most accepted.

The following sections explain how to calculate zones of support and resistance and use pivot-point channels in trading.

Calculating the first zone of support and resistance

The logic of the pivot point is that after a trend pauses, you need a breakout that's a significant distance from the median price to decide whether the old trend will resume or a reversal is really at hand. So you start with the median price and to that you add a factor to get upside resistance and you subtract a factor to get downside support.

On the chart in Figure 5-3, the lightest horizontal line extends off the pivot point calculated on the day of the highest high in the series. You're worried about this bar because it had a close lower than the open, despite the higher high. It's a weak higher high. The next day is an inside day (see Chapter 2 in Book X), which may imply a reversal. You're starting to get suspicious that the uptrend is stalling.

To calculate the first (inner) line of resistance, multiply the pivot- point value by two and, from that number, subtract the low of the pivot day. To calculate the first (inner) line of support, multiply the pivot value by two and, from that number, subtract the high of the pivot day. This sounds like a lot of arithmetic, but it's easy enough to do in a spreadsheet or by hand. It's also a sensible

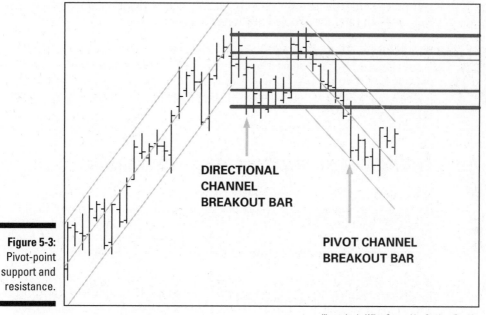

Figure 5-3:
Pivot-point
support and
resistance.

Illustration by Wiley, Composition Services Graphics

procedure — you're using a multiple of the median price to estimate a range going forward that subtracts the high and the low to yield a *norm*. Any price higher or lower would be an *extreme*. If the upcoming price breaks the horizontal support and resistance lines calculated this way, the direction of the breakout is your clue that the trend is truly over.

And that's exactly what happens in Figure 5-3. The day after the inside day, the price makes a new low below the first support line. It closes within the zone and also closes a hair under the linear regression channel, but the low is well below both the directional channel and the horizontal channel. This is a double breakout — it's a break of your linear regression channel and of the first pivot channel as well. Note that analysts who work with pivot-based support and resistance don't call it a *channel*, a word I am using for consistency and convenience. If it looks like a duck. . . .

Calculating the second zone of support and resistance

The first inner zone is fairly narrow. In fact, it contains only about half of the breakout bar. To get a wider horizontal support and resistance channel, you can add the first zone to the pivot level to get a second resistance level and subtract the first zone from the pivot level to get a second support level. You can see both the first and second zones in Figure 5-3.

When you see R1, R2, R3 and S1, S2, S3 noted on a chart or in a table, these abbreviations refer to the first resistance level, second resistance level, and so on, calculated from a pivot point. The pivot point may or may not be the median price; many technical analysts take the liberty of choosing their own pivot-point definition.

Using pivot support and resistance

You can use pivot support and resistance all by itself, and many day-traders do. In the case presented in Figure 5-3, upon seeing the inside day, you would set your stop-loss order at the first pivot support level. Anticipating a bounce, you can also place a buy order at the second support level with an accompanying sell order at either of the two resistance levels.

If you're using the standard error channel for directional guidance, the breakout of the channel means you're at a loose end. You can't construct a new channel based on the linear regression because you simply don't have enough data. The pivot-based support and resistance channel suffices to define the likely trading range until it is, in turn, broken.

You leave the pivot-based horizontal support and resistance zones in place until you get a new swing bar that is substantially higher or lower than your pivot support and resistance zones. Notice that on the chart in Figure 5-3, you do get a matching high to the pivot bar. In fact, it's a few pennies higher. But it doesn't set your hair on fire, and right afterwards, the price subsides back into the support and resistance zone. What's important about the pivot-based support and resistance lines is that they effectively outline a period of activity where traders don't know the trend. Bulls try to make a new high and get only a few pennies' worth. Bears try to make a new low but fail to get a close under the second support line (S2).

Then the price convincingly breaks below the second support line. Almost the whole bar is below the line. This is a breakout of the pivot channel and usually a sign that you can now go back and start a new directional channel, either hand-drawn support and resistance or a standard error channel. In Figure 5-3, a new standard error channel is started; notice that it's drawn from the highest high, not from the breakout point. At this time, you can discard the pivot channel — or you can leave the support line on the chart. Note that old support often becomes new resistance.

Digging into Dynamic Lines and Channels

Straight-line channels are widely used, but the real workhorse of technical analysis is the moving average and the bands and envelopes built off the moving average. Here's the rule: When a channel is based on straight lines, it's called a channel. When its raw material is a moving average, it's named a band or envelope.

Everyone in securities analysis and trading uses the moving average, whether they consider themselves technical analysts or not. One of the most often used indicators, the Bollinger band, is based on a moving average. A high proportion of other indicators build on or employ moving averages in some way, including some very fancy ones.

You know what a moving average is: You add up ten daily closing prices. The next day, you drop off the first day's price and add today's to keep the total number of prices at ten. A moving average cuts out the "noise" of the occasional aberrant number. Traders like specific numbers of days in their moving averages because they represent units of time — 5 days is a trading week, 20 days is a trading month, and so on. You've probably heard of the 100-day and 200-day moving averages as benchmarks meaning long-term.

The following sections describe three types of moving averages: single, double, and weighted.

Book X

Technical Analysis

Single moving average

A standard trading rule says: Buy when the price today breaks out above the *x*-day moving average and sell when it falls (breaks out) below the *x*-day moving average. What is *x*? It may be one of the standards (5, 10, 20, 50 days) or it may be a number that you figure out for yourself by performing back-tests on historical data of your security to see what would have worked the best over a long period of time.

Securities prices can go through strong rallies when a short-term moving average like 10 days would work the best and then periods of sideways congestion when a longer moving average would be more appropriate — or wouldn't work at all to generate gains. Instead you'd be told to get in and get out for a series of *whipsaw losses*. The problem is that you don't know ahead of time whether your security will perform according to its historic norm.

In addition, one size does not fit all. The best number of days to use for Apple stock is not the same as the best number of days for IBM, or the Swiss franc, or soybeans.

Double moving average

If a single moving average gives you a trading edge, how about two? Sure enough, if you combine a shorter moving average with a longer one and trade when the shorter one crosses the longer one, you get more reliable trades than using a single moving average alone. "Reliable" means you avoid jittery whipsaw losses during a sideways congestive market. A standard trading rule is to buy when the 10-day moving average breaks out above the 20-day and to sell when it falls below the 20-day.

All moving averages lag the price action. In fact, all indicators lag the price action because they're based on past data. But moving averages are the most lagging of the top indicators, and the more days you put in them, the more lagging they will be. If you're hot to trot, moving averages can be annoying. If you're ultra-conservative and hate false signals that reverse quickly for whipsaw losses, moving averages are for you.

Weighted moving average

You can alter a moving average by the method of calculation. A simple moving average gives equal weight to each day's price. But you can weight more recent prices more heavily using something called a *weighted moving average,* or weight more recent prices even more by using an *exponential moving average.* Most technical traders prefer the exponential moving average.

See Figure 5-4, which shows the 10-day and 20-day moving average superimposed on the linear regression channel. The arrow marks the crossover point where this system would have you sell. Clearly, the straight-line channel did a better job in this case of warning you to exit. But if you're ultra-conservative and want to be certain the breakout is authentic, the moving average crossover is confirmation.

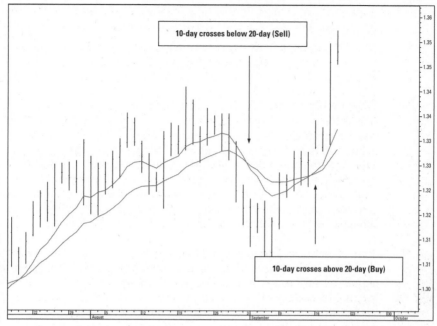

Figure 5-4:
Moving
average
crossover.

Illustration by Wiley, Composition Services Graphics

Understanding Volatility

Volatility is a tricky subject. In the context of measuring security prices for trendedness, volatility refers to the degree of variability away from some central norm, like a moving average. To illustrate: Say you follow a stock that is on a rising trend and it has tended to move up by an average of 50 cents per day over the past 100 days, even including the days on which it lost. The average high-low range is $3.00. Now fresh news about the market or the company has emerged, and the price change from day to day tends to be triple the usual number, or $1.50. In addition, the average high-low range is widening to $6.00. This is an increase in variability, or *volatility*. The opposite is true, too — if the average daily change sinks to 10 cents and the average high-low range contracts to $1.00, volatility is much lower.

Higher volatility offers profit opportunities (as well as opportunities to suffer a loss) and low volatility reduces opportunities — but low volatility often precedes a breakout, too.

Here are three other possibilities for forming a band:

✔ You could make a moving average of the highs and of the lows and form a band.

✔ You could calculate the daily high-low range, average that, and add a fudge factor to the central number to form a band.

✔ You could use the average true range band, based on the work of J. Welles Wilder, that adds a fraction or a multiple of the average true range to a central moving average to get the outer limits of what is likely to happen in the price series.

The *Bollinger band,* named after its inventor, John Bollinger, is probably the most widely used of the dynamic line bands. The Bollinger band starts out with a simple 20-day moving average, and the bands are formed on either side of it by adding and subtracting double the standard deviation from the moving average. The standard deviation measures the variability or volatility of the prices in the 20-day sample, so a wide band means lots of volatility, and a narrow one means little volatility. Notice in Figure 5-5 that as the price rise accelerates, the bands widen, meaning volatility is high.

You expect prices to remain within the band and to rise and fall from the top band to the bottom and back again. You don't expect a breakout because that would be seriously abnormal behavior. You do expect that, after pressuring the top or bottom of a channel, the price will cycle to the midpoint (named *reversion to the mean*) or to the other side.

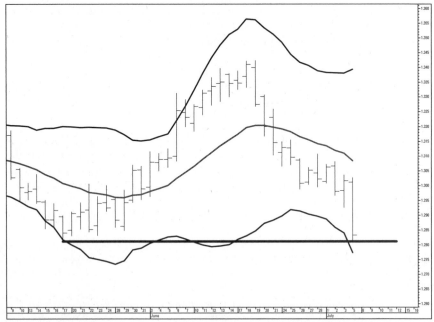

Figure 5-5:
Bollinger
bands.

Illustration by Wiley, Composition Services Graphics

A Bollinger band doesn't give you a specific buy/sell signal (except in the case of the rare breakout), but the widening of the bands mean higher volatility and higher volatility means higher risk of loss. Conversely, contracting bands (lower volatility) implies a pending breakout. The bands don't tell you which way, and for that you need to consult other indicators or the fundamentals.

Notice that the price on Figure 5-5 is at the historic low, but the Bollinger band crosses the horizontal line. Does this mean the price will break it, too? Probably.

Many other bands and envelopes have been developed over the years, including a fancy Japanese version named *ichimoku kinko hyo,* which looks like a cloud and also offers estimates of support and resistance.

You don't need to understand standard deviation or standard error beyond grasping that they are measures of variability away from a norm. You certainly don't need to calculate them yourself — let software do it for you, either your own or that which is offered on the many websites that show charts and indicators.

Book X

Technical Analysis

Gauging Momentum

Momentum refers to the speed at which prices are changing, or the rate of change. Simple momentum tends to be somewhat underrated because it offers nuance about a move rather than a black-and-white buy/sell signal. Complex momentum uses more arithmetical manipulation and can be used to generate buy/sell signals.

Simple momentum

To understand simple momentum, consider that in a rally, the average price change each day is more than the day before. You can measure this bullish sentiment by taking today's closing price and dividing it by the closing price (say) ten days ago to get a simple momentum indicator. There are several different ways of calculating momentum, but they all compare today's price to a price several periods back.

✔ **When the simple momentum indicator is rising, it means prices in recent days are higher than before — accelerating.** The trend has strong momentum, and it's therefore safe to consider your trend identification to be correct.

✔ **When the simple momentum indicator is falling, today's prices are decelerating.** If the momentum indicator is a negative, it means prices must be lower than before. The move has lost momentum, and the trend is weaker, possibly signaling a trend reversal.

Figure 5-6 shows the addition of a simple momentum line. Notice that it lags the straight-line breakout by a few days but it signals you to sell earlier than the moving average crossover.

Momentum is useful for confirming or modifying your trend identification rather than as a stand-alone indicator on which to base trading decisions. The rate of change of prices reflects market sentiment toward the security, and thus momentum can be a handy early warning system.

Complex momentum indicators

Following are some complex indicators to be familiar with:

- **Relative strength indicator (RSI):** You can find several variations of the RSI, but the core concept is to take prices from the days on which the price moves up from the open and compare them to the prices on the days the price moved down, over a fixed period, like 21 days. The original concept comes from J. Welles Wilder. The RSI indicator gets rid of the problem of the simple momentum indicator of comparing today's price to a single price *x* number of days ago when that particular day may have been wild and aberrant. The RSI is, therefore, a smoother-looking indicator on a chart. RSI is converted into an index so that it fluctuates between 0 and 100. Prices hardly ever go as far as 0 or 100, so when the RSI indicator is nearing those extremes, you may deduce that the security is becoming overbought or oversold (see Chapter 1 in Book X for details on the terms *overbought* and *oversold*).

- **Moving average convergence-divergence (MACD):** Devised by Gerald Appel, MACD is a refinement of the moving average crossover decision tool mentioned in the earlier section "Double moving average" and contains a big dose of momentum. It takes a little thought to wrap your mind around how it's calculated:

  1. **Take the difference between a longer-term moving average (26 days is recommended) and a shorter-term one (such as 12 days). Plot that difference on the chart.**

     Think about it — if prices were lower 26 days ago, and you subtract them from prices 12 days ago, you'll get a rising line.

  2. **Take a 9-day moving average of the difference and plot that, too.**

     This becomes your signal line. When the 9-day signal line converges to the 26-12 difference line and crosses it, you have rising momentum and a buy signal. Similarly, when the 9-day diverges from the difference line, momentum is being lost.

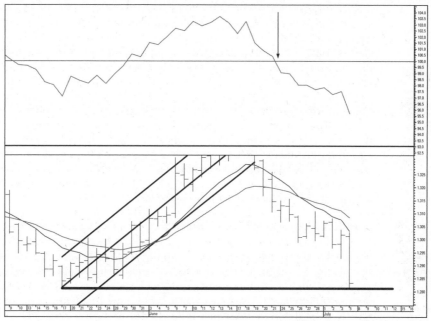

Figure 5-6:
Adding
momentum.

Illustration by Wiley, Composition Services Graphics

MACD is one of the most consistent and reliable of indicators, but only when prices are trending. When prices are consolidative and moving sideways, momentum is lacking. MACD will generate false buy/sell signals just like any indicator based on moving averages.

Putting Lines and Indicators Together

Every trader has his own favorite indicators. Many invent their own indicators. What indicators you prefer is a direct function of how much risk you're willing to take that your trend analysis is correct. If you're convinced your security is on a long-lasting uptrend, you are unwilling to heed indicators that are giving warnings of a pause or a reversal. After all, the reversal could be a false breakout or a temporary pullback.

If you're a more active trader and not averse to exiting to book gains only to reenter in the same direction after a pause or a pullback, you'll like the zippier indicators, like RSI or MACD (see the preceding section). They give buy/sell signals tighter to the price action.

Grasping how MACD melds direction and momentum takes a little practice, but persistence pays off. Take a look at Figure 5-7. On this chart, you see that

MACD comes the closest to the support line breakout in generating the sell signal. It's closer than simple momentum, which is closer than the moving average crossover. This is tremendously valuable because even a linear regression channel entails some subjective judgment (specifically, your starting point), whereas the MACD and other math-based indicators are calculated by their own internal formulas and objective.

You use technical indicators to fight back against preconceived ideas about the value of a security and against your own emotions. In the case presented here, no matter how much you believe or wish that this security will continue rising, it becomes increasingly clear as you add indicators that you really, truly need to exit in order to avoid losing your entire stake, assuming you entered at the low on the left-hand side of the chart. Even the Bollinger band in Figure 5-5 screams a warning as it widens out.

In the end, avoiding losses is just as important as selecting high-value securities in the first place. If the technical mind-set confers one gift, it's that selling is a good thing when the chart dictates it. If you love your security, you can always buy it back later at a lower price. Prices fall back for many reasons, including overall market conditions and temporary corrections, that are not a disgrace of your security's reputation. In a way, using technicals to add systematically to your portfolio is a form of price-averaging — smart price-averaging.

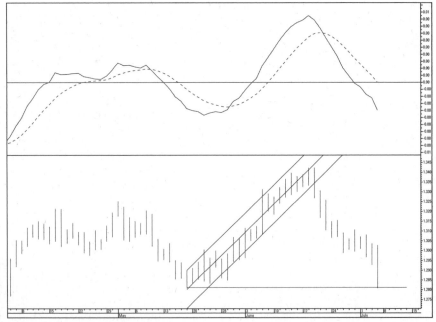

Figure 5-7:
MACD.

Illustration by Wiley, Composition Services Graphics

Index

• *N* •

About the Authors

Jason W. Best, co-founder and principal of Crowdfund Capital Advisors (CCA), co-authored the crowdfund investing framework used in the JOBS Act and was a leader in the U.S. fight to legalize debt- and equity-based crowdfunding. CCA is an advisory firm to investors, governments, and development organizations on early-stage finance issues. His prior experience has been in leadership roles in successful web-based healthcare businesses. Jason is an Entrepreneur in Residence at the Center for Entrepreneurship and Technology at UC Berkeley, and is an author of *Crowdfund Investing For Dummies*.

Amine Bouchentouf is a partner at Commodities Investors, LLC (CI), an international financial advisory firm headquartered in New York City. A world-renowned market commentator, Amine has appeared in media in the United States, Great Britain, France, the United Arab Emirates, and Brazil. He is a member of the National Association of Securities Dealers and the Authors Guild and is also involved with the Council on Foreign Relations. He's the author of *Commodities For Dummies,* 2nd Edition.

Zak Cassady-Dorion is currently the CEO and co-founder of Pure Mountain Olive Oil, LLC, a chain of olive oil and balsamic vinegar tasting shops in the Northeast United States. He is also a co-founder of Startup Exemption, where he led the effort to legalize debt- and equity-based crowdfunding. He co-authored the crowdfund investing framework that was used in the JOBS Act to legalize equity- and debt-based crowdfunding in the United States and is a partner of Crowdfund Capital Advisors (CCA). Zak speaks regularly across North America about crowdfunding to entrepreneurial groups and universities; he's an author of *Crowdfund Investing For Dummies*.

Brian Dolan is the author of *Currency Trading For Dummies,* 2nd Edition, and a career veteran of the foreign exchange market. He has more than 20 years of experience as both a trader and a strategist at leading global banks, including Dai-Ichi Kangyo, Credit Suisse, and Julius Baer. Most recently, Brian was the Chief Currency Strategist at Gain Capital/FOREX.com from 2003–2012, where he was a frequent commentator on CNBC, Bloomberg TV, and BNN (Canada), as well as a regular source for Reuters, DJ/WSJ, MarketWatch, and numerous other financial media. Brian is currently the head of global market education at Market Trader Academy.

Joe Duarte, MD, is a widely read market analyst, writer, and active trader. He is the author of *Successful Energy Sector Investing, Successful Biotech Investing,* and *Trading Futures For Dummies,* and is a coauthor of *After-Hours Trading Made Easy.* His daily "Market IQ" columns appear at www.joe-duarte.com and are syndicated worldwide by FinancialWire.

Janet Haley is a securities industry professional and has a bachelor's degree in international business and political science from Marymount College. She's the coauthor of *Value Investing For Dummies,* 2nd Edition.

Faleel Jamaldeen, DBA, is the founder and editor of the Islamic Finance Expert website (ifinanceexpert.wordpress.com/) and an assistant professor of Islamic finance and conventional finance at the College of Business, Effat University, Jeddah, Saudi Arabia. He has published multiple journal and newspaper articles on the subject of Islamic finance and has presented papers at international forums. Dr. Jamaldeen has a Doctor of Business Administration degree from the California University of Business and Technology. His research interests include Islamic finance, Islamic accounting, and Islamic financial engineering. He's the author of *Islamic Finance For Dummies.*

Ann C. Logue, MBA, has more than a dozen years of experience working in financial services and has taught business administration at the University of Illinois. She is a finance writer who has written numerous articles on investment and has edited publications on equity trading and risk management. She is the author of *Day Trading For Dummies,* 2nd Edition; *Hedge Funds For Dummies; Socially Responsible Investing For Dummies* (2010 Green Book Festival Award Winner); and *Emerging Markets For Dummies.*

Paul Mladjenovic is a national seminar leader and author of *Stock Investing For Dummies,* 4th Edition; *Micro-Entrepreneurship For Dummies; Precious Metals Investing For Dummies;* and *Zero-Cost Marketing.* His educational programs on investing and home business start-up and his free newsletter, the *Prosperity Alert,* can be found at www.RavingCapitalist.com.

Sherwood Neiss is a successful entrepreneur who returned 37.8 times what his investors put into the company he co-founded by focusing on cash and customers. He co-wrote the framework for Title III, the crowdfunding portion of the JOBS Act; speaks about crowdfunding globally; and consults with the World Bank. He's an author of *Crowdfund Investing For Dummies.*

Optionetics has provided investment education services and trading tools to customers from more than 50 countries, helping traders navigate the markets and chart paths to financial security. The company provides a practical, balanced approach to trading profitability and has a diverse range of educational offerings including seminars, publications, workshops, and study materials.

Kerry Pechter, the author of *Annuities For Dummies,* is the editor and publisher of *Retirement Income Journal* and *RIJAdvisor,* two online magazines for and about the retirement industry. He is a graduate of Kenyon College in Gambier, Ohio.

Barbara Rockefeller is the author of *How to Invest Internationally,* published in Japanese in 1999, *CNBC 24/7, Trading Around the Clock, Around the World,* and *The Global Trader*. She also writes a monthly column for *Currency Trader Magazine*. She's the publisher of *The Strategic Currency Briefing*, a daily newsletter on the foreign exchange market that combines technical and fundamental observations. Barbara has a B.A. in economics from Reed College in Portland, Oregon, and an M.A. in international affairs from Columbia University. She's the author of *Technical Analysis For Dummies*, 2nd Edition.

Peter J. Sander, MBA, is a professional author, researcher, and investor whose 15 personal finance and location reference book titles include *The 250 Personal Finance Questions Everybody Should Ask, Everything Personal Finance,* and the Frommer's *Cities Ranked & Rated* series. He has developed more than 150 columns for MarketWatch and TheStreet.com. His education includes an MBA from Indiana University, he has completed Certified Financial Planner (CFP) education and testing requirements, and his experience includes 20 years as a marketing program manager for a Fortune 50 technology firm and more than 40 years of active investing. He's the coauthor of *Value Investing For Dummies*, 2nd Edition.

Russell Wild, MBA, is the author or coauthor of nearly two dozen nonfiction books, including *Bond Investing For Dummies*, 2nd Edition; *Exchange-Traded Funds For Dummies*, 2nd Edition; and *Index Investing For Dummies*. He has contributed to many national magazines and currently writes a regular column on personal finance for *The Saturday Evening Post*. Wild is also a NAPFA-registered, fee-only investment advisor based in Allentown, Pennsylvania.

Publisher's Acknowledgments

Senior Acquisitions Editor: Tracy Boggier

Compilation Editor: Tracy L. Barr

Senior Project Editor: Georgette Beatty

Copy Editor: Christine Pingleton

Technical Editor: Juli Erhart-Graves

Senior Project Coordinator: Kristie Rees

Cover Image: ©iStockphoto.com/Danil Melekhin